ESSAYS IN THE HISTORY OF CANADIAN LAW
VOLUME VII
INSIDE THE LAW: CANADIAN LAW FIRMS IN
HISTORICAL PERSPECTIVE

EDITED BY CAROL WILTON

PATRONS OF THE OSGOODE SOCIETY

Aird & Berlis

Blake, Cassels & Graydon

Davies, Ward & Beck

McCarthy Tétrault

Osler, Hoskin & Harcourt

The Harweg Foundation

Tory Tory DesLauriers & Binnington

Weir & Foulds

The Society also thanks the Law Foundation of Ontario
and the Law Society of Upper Canada for their continuing support.

Essays
in the History of
Canadian Law

INSIDE THE LAW:
CANADIAN LAW FIRMS IN
HISTORICAL PERSPECTIVE

Edited by
CAROL WILTON

VOLUME VII

Published for The Osgoode Society for
Canadian Legal History by
University of Toronto Press
Toronto Buffalo London

Printed in Canada

ISBN 0-8020-0935-2

Printed on acid-free paper

Canadian Cataloguing in Publication Data

Main entry under title:

Essays in the history of Canadian law

Includes bibliographical references and index.
Partial contents: v. 7. Inside the law : Canadian law
firms in historical perspective / edited by Carol Wilton.
Vols. 5–7 published for the Osgoode Society for Canadian
Legal History by University of Toronto Press.
ISBN 0-8020-0935-2 (v. 7)

1. Law – Canada – History and criticism. I. Flaherty,
David H. II. Osgoode Society. III. Osgoode Society
for Canadian Legal History.

KE394.Z85E87 1981   349.71   c81-095131-2
KF345.E87 1981

University of Toronto Press acknowledges the financial assistance to its
publishing program of the Canada Council and the Ontario Arts Council.

To Margaret Wilton-Siegel

Contents

viii   Contents

Contents   ix

Foreword

THE OSGOODE SOCIETY FOR CANADIAN LEGAL HISTORY

The purpose of The Osgoode Society for Canadian Legal History is to encourage research and writing in the history of Canadian law. The Society, which was incorporated in 1979 and is registered as a charity, was founded at the initiative of the Honourable R. Roy McMurtry, former attorney general for Ontario, and officials of the Law Society of Upper Canada. Its efforts to stimulate the study of legal history in Canada include a research support program, a graduate student research assistance program, and work in the fields of oral history and legal archives. The Society publishes volumes that are of interest to the Society's members and that contribute to legal-historical scholarship in Canada, including studies of the courts, the judiciary, and the legal profession; biographies; collections of documents; studies in criminology and penology; accounts of significant trials; and work in the social and economic history of the law.

Current directors of The Osgoode Society for Canadian Legal History are Jane Banfield, Tom Bastedo, John Brown, Brian Bucknall, Archie Campbell, Susan Elliott, J. Douglas Ewart, Martin Friedland, Charles Harnick, John Honsberger, Kenneth Jarvis, Allen Linden, Colin McKinnon, Virginia MacLean, Roy McMurtry, Wendy Matheson, Brendan O'Brien, Peter Oliver, Paul Reinhardt, James Spence, and Richard Tinsley.

The annual report and information about membership may be obtained by writing to The Osgoode Society for Canadian Legal History, Osgoode Hall, 130 Queen Street West, Toronto, Ontario, Canada M5H 2N6. Members receive the annual volume published by the Society.

A pioneering study of an important but neglected Canadian institution, *Inside the Law* offers numerous case-studies of Canadian law firms as well as more general analyses. Law firms are important legal and business institutions in this country, but their nature remains obscure. Most previous publications in this field have been sponsored by law firms themselves, and such accounts have generally reflected the self-image which the current partners wished to project. Carol Wilton and her contributors here offer a fresh and independent perspective, one which sheds new and often unanticipated light on law-firm development in every Canadian region in both the nineteenth and the twentieth centuries. The introduction by Carol Wilton, an outstanding overview of the subject since 1820, emphasizes the distinctiveness of the Canadian pattern of law-firm development.

R. Roy McMurtry
President

Peter N. Oliver
Editor-in-Chief

Acknowledgments

This book originated with the board of directors of The Osgoode Society. In the summer of 1992 the Society sponsored a meeting of lawyers, judges, and scholars to consider the possibility of developing a volume of historical essays on the subject of law firms in Canada. A year later, The Osgoode Society committee on the history of Canadian law firms approached me to act as volume editor.

The committee, chaired by Brian Bucknall, also included John Honsberger, C. Ian Kyer, and Mr Justice James Spence. Their contribution to this volume has been invaluable. Closely involved in the planning stages, they have also offered every possible assistance and encouragement since that time. I am particularly thankful to Brian Bucknall for his insights into the profession, and more generally for his unfailing moral support and wise advice. John Honsberger's unflagging enthusiasm and sage counsel have also been much appreciated.

It has been a delight to work with the contributors to this volume, who have been consistently courteous, cooperative, and efficient. The heroic efforts they made to complete their manuscripts over the Christmas holidays of 1995 are but one example of the team spirit which has carried this project through to completion.

Numerous others have offered assistance with this book. Professor Brian Young and Christopher Moore offered helpful suggestions in their assessments of the manuscript. Susan Binnie, Ann-Marie Langlois, and Gabrielle Earnshaw at the Archives of the Law Society of Upper Canada pooled their expertise to help find the cover photo. The staff of the Law Society of British Columbia cheerfully photocopied the oral-history interviews held by that institution. Peter Oliver, editor-in-chief of The Osgoode Society, reviewed the manuscript. Also at The Osgoode Society, Marilyn MacFarlane handled many administrative details. The index was prepared by Michael Power under the direction of Peter Oliver. The University of Toronto Press supplied the able services of Beverley Beetham Endersby as copy-editor. It has been a pleasure to work with Anne Forte of the Press, who has supervised the production process.

The book's title, *Inside the Law*, was the suggestion of my nephew Andrew Morgan.

CAROL WILTON

Contributors

JAMIE BENIDICKSON teaches legal history and environmental law in the Faculty of Law, University of Ottawa.

DALE BRAWN practised law in rural Manitoba for a number of years before obtaining master's degrees in both history and law. He is in the doctoral program at Osgoode Hall Law School.

BARRY CAHILL is an archivist in the Government Archives Division of the Public Archives of Nova Scotia and editor of the *Nova Scotia Historical Review*.

CURTIS COLE teaches history at the University of Western Ontario and Canadian studies at Wilfrid Laurier University. He is also the author of *Osler, Hoskin & Harcourt: Portrait of a Partnership* (1995).

PHILIP GIRARD is Professor of Law at Dalhousie Law School, where he is working on a biography of Nova Scotian jurist Beamish Murdoch.

JOHN HAGAN is Professor of Sociology and Law at the University of Toronto. He is the author (with Fiona Kay) of *Gender in Practice: A Study of Lawyers' Lives* (1995), co-editor (with Ruth Peterson) of *Crime and Inequality,* and editor of the *Annual Review of Sociology*.

DECLAN BRENDAN HAMILL has a master's degree in history and is a graduate of the McGill University Faculty of Law. He is a student-at-law at the Ottawa firm of Johnston & Buchan.

JOHN D. HONSBERGER is a director of the Osgoode Society for Canadian Legal History and the senior partner of Raymond & Honsberger, Toronto.

FIONA KAY is an assistant professor in the Department of Anthropology/Sociology at the University of British Columbia. She is the author (with John Hagan) of *Gender in Practice: A Study of Lawyers' Lives* (1995), and was the principal investigator in the preparation of the 1990 Law Society of Upper Canada report entitled *Transitions in the Ontario Legal Profession*.

HENRY C. KLASSEN is Associate Professor of History at the University of Calgary. His most recent publications include 'The Hudson's Bay Company in Southwestern Alberta, 1874–1905,' in *The Fur Trade Revisited* (1994), and 'Transfer of Power in the Scots Canadian Family Business,' *British Journal of Canadian Studies* (1994).

LOUIS A. KNAFLA is Professor of History at the University of Calgary, president of the Canadian Law and Society Association, and editor of *Criminal Justice History*. His Canadian publications include *Law & Justice in a New Land* (1986); 'Richard "Bonfire" Bennett: The Legal Practice of a Prairie Corporate Lawyer, 1898 to 1913,' in Carol Wilton, ed., *Beyond the Law* (1990); and (as editor with Susan W.S. Binnie) *Law, Society, and the State: Essays in Modern Legal History* (1995).

C. IAN KYER has a doctorate in history from the University of Toronto and practises corporate-commercial law (with an emphasis on computer-related transactions) as a partner in the law firm of Fasken Campbell Godfrey.

GREGORY P. MARCHILDON holds degrees in law, economics, and history. He taught for five years at Johns Hopkins University and is currently Deputy Minister of Intergovernmental Affairs and Deputy Provincial Secretary of Saskatchewan. His most recent publication is *Profits and Politics: Beaverbrook and the Gilded Age of Canadian Finance* (1996).

T.D. REGEHR is Professor Emeritus of History at the University of Saskatchewan and has published many books and articles on Canadian business history.

REGINALD H. ROY, PhD, FRHistS, Professor Emeritus of History at the University of Victoria, is the author of a dozen books and more than forty articles on Canadian history.

PHILIP J. SWORDEN is a Burlington lawyer who articled with Millar, Alexander. He is also a historian with a doctorate from McMaster University. He has published several articles on Sir John Beverley Robinson.

CAROL WILTON has written extensively about political and legal history. She is the editor of *Beyond the Law* (1990) and *Change and Continu-*

ity: A Reader in Pre-Confederation History (1992). Her '"A Firebrand amongst the People": The Durham Meetings and Popular Politics in Upper Canada,' published in the *Canadian Historical Review* (1994), won the Riddell Award of the Ontario Historical Society for the best article on Ontario history in 1994.

Law office of Frank A. Anglin (right) and John W. Mallon (left), Victoria Street, Toronto, c. 1897. A typical law-office interior of the turn-of-the-century period. (Courtesy of The Law Society of Upper Canada Archives, 87-555-2)

Essays in the History of Canadian Law

1

Introduction: Inside the Law – Canadian Law Firms in Historical Perspective

CAROL WILTON

The legal profession in Canada today is dominated by two dozen or so very large law firms, located in the country's major cities. These firms are important economic institutions, collecting hundreds of millions of dollars in fees annually. They order the affairs of businesses and of many government agencies. Their offices operate around the clock, maintaining links with affiliates in Europe and Asia. Many of these mega-firms employ hundreds of partners and associates, along with vast numbers of office staff. Their members include some of the country's most influential former politicians. Their alumni run major Canadian corporations, staff the judiciary, and head royal commissions; one is currently Prime Minister of Canada.[1]

It was not always so. In fact, these legal behemoths have emerged only in the past generation. Yet through the 1990s, in spite of intense, if sporadic, public and academic interest, the history that precedes them – for some firms as long as a hundred years or more – remains shrouded in mystery. One reason for this neglect of law-firm histories is obvious – the need to protect client confidentiality makes lawyers reluctant subjects for investigation. The primary reason, however, may be one of focus. Sociologists who study the profession have been preoccupied with more general questions about law and the economy, or about the social origins of lawyers. More conventional studies of the bench and bar have concentrated on the criminal branch of the law and have celebrated the wit and wisdom of leading barristers and judges. Most of the few histories of corporate and commercial firms that are available were prepared 'in-house'; they are anecdotal, uncritical, and somewhat ahistorical. Most make only limited efforts to relate changes in professional practice to social and economic changes on a larger scale.[2]

This volume enlarges our understanding of the subject by offering the first focused study of a variety of Canadian law firms, both large and small. Twelve of the fourteen essays here trace the development of an individual firm in a large Canadian city. Each captures a discrete period in a particular firm's history and, together, they provide a kind of picture album of Canada's law firms. Two of the essays depart from a narrative approach, addressing important specific issues in the history of Canadian law firms: Dale Brawn provides a path-breaking study of the role of large-firm lawyers in late-nineteenth- and twentieth-century Manitoba; and John Hagan and Fiona Kay offer a perceptive analysis of gender in the modern law firm.

Though their subject-matter is diverse, the essays tackle one or more common themes: first, law-firm development in the context of economic and, to a lesser extent, social change; second, law-firm organization; and, third, law-firm culture. This introduction provides a historical overview of these topics for the period from 1820 to 1995, with the intention of setting these essays in a larger historical context, and relating the history of Canadian law firms to economic and, to a lesser extent, political and social change.

As the essays in this volume indicate, law firms are not islands unto themselves. On the contrary, their work, organization, and culture are intimately tied to the economies and societies of which they are a part. The character of legal work, for example, changed significantly as Canada's economy moved from the era of staple production in the early nineteenth century to the age of industrial and finance capitalism at the turn of the century, and to our present post-industrial era. At another level, changes in the level of economic activity – booms and busts in the economic cycle – have powerfully affected the amount and types of legal work available.

Another important determinant of legal work has been the role of the state. The scope and nature of lawyers' work have been altered by governments responding to changing public attitudes towards a variety of social questions. Among these have been marriage and divorce, labour, imprisonment for debt, and discrimination on the basis of race and gender. Moreover, increasing state intervention, particularly after 1940, has created or greatly expanded many areas of legal practice.

Although not all alterations in the character of legal work have resulted in modifications to the organization of law firms, historically there has been a significant relationship between the two. Broadly speaking, changing economic and social circumstances have given rise to five types of law-firm organization. During the golden age of the sole practitioner (1820–80), the profession was dominated by the classic small firms comprising one to three lawyers involved in general practice. The age of industrial and finance capitalism (1880–1919) produced larger firms of five or more lawyers doing at least some corporate work. The interwar years (1919–39) saw the emergence of the corporate firm with ten to twenty lawyers focusing primarily on corporate office practice. Prosperity and the expanded role of government during the two generations after the start of the Second World War (1939–73) contributed to the rise of 'giant' corporate firms employing fifty or more lawyers. Developments since the early 1970s have given rise to the advent of corporate 'mega-firms' of one hundred or more lawyers.

As new types of law firms emerged, the shift from one form of organization to another was not industry-wide; the classic small firm endures to this day, as do firms of twelve, and fifty. In effect, what happened was that each new form of organization was superimposed on existing types at the top of the profession. Thus, changes over time have had the effect of increasing the variety of types of firm structures.

Like law-firm organization, law-firm culture has responded to economic and social imperatives.[3] The pace of change in this area, however, has often been notably slow. Perhaps this tendency reflects a strong attachment among many lawyers to traditional professional norms. Whatever the explanation, lawyers have historically mounted a stubborn resistance to such innovations as democratic methods of firm governance, aggressive programs of client development, meritocratic hiring practices, and the adoption of new technology. Even in these areas, however, time-honoured practices have generally been modified in the years since the Second World War, and law firms are still undergoing a process of adjustment.

The themes of the changing demand for legal services, law-firm organization, and legal culture during the five periods mentioned above are explained in this introduction. Each section sets law-firm organization and culture in the context of the political and social, as well as the economic, changes of the period.

THE EARLY YEARS, 1820–1880[4]

The years from 1820 to 1880 were ones of profound change for British North America. Politically, the union of Upper and Lower Canada in 1841 proved to be prelude to Confederation in 1867. Shortly thereafter, Canada acquired the prairie West and other territories from the Hudson's Bay Company, though not without turmoil; the resistance of the Métis under Louis Riel in 1869–70 resulted in the creation of the province of Manitoba in 1870. Within three years, British Columbia and Prince Edward Island had also joined Confederation. The tiny, scattered population of British North America in 1820 had by then mushroomed into 3.5 million people.

From the viewpoint of lawyers, perhaps the most significant political change of these years was the coming of responsible government to the British North American colonies in the 1840s and 1850s. Responsible government was essentially a devolution of political power from appointed officials to elected representatives, along with a reduction of the involvement of the British government in colonial affairs. Lawyers like Robert Baldwin and Louis Hippolyte LaFontaine in the province of Canada were among the leading proponents of responsible government. Moreover, in the succeeding decades, lawyers both in central Canada and in the Maritimes played a prominent role in designing changes in legislation, the courts, and the scope of state intervention.[5] While these alterations had a significant impact on the practice of law, they produced no known modifications to the structure of law firms.

Political transformation in the period 1820–80 was accompanied by economic changes. In the 1820s, the economies of all the British North American colonies were pre-industrial, dependent on a variety of staple products, including wheat in central Canada, timber in central Canada and New Brunswick, and mining and fishing in Nova Scotia. Commerce was the principal business activity; banking and other financial institutions such as insurance companies emerged in the 1820s and 1830s. In the 1820s, waterways remained the principal arteries of transportation.[6]

A new form of transportation – railways – began to transform the colonial economy in the 1850s, at least in central Canada, where almost two thousand miles of track were completed in this decade. A rail link between the Maritimes and central Canada had to await the completion of the government-funded Intercolonial Railway in 1876. By this time, visionaries were confidently predicting the creation of a transcontinental rail network. This dream became a reality with the completion of the Canadian Pacific Railway in 1885. Railways not only provided year-round transportation and communication, but also constituted a major form of manufacturing. Other types of industry had taken root in British North America by the 1850s, including food-processing, furniture-making, and leather-working. The industrial age, however, did not truly arrive in Canada until the late nineteenth century.[7]

The nature of legal practice during this period closely reflected economic development. In Ontario during 1841–67, for example, property, the market, and enforcement of claims against debtors were among the most frequently litigated matters.[8] The solicitor's side of practice was also closely tied to the economy. As R.D. Gidney and W.P.J. Millar indicated, solicitors' work in nineteenth-century Ontario involved 'proffering advice and drafting the pertinent documents for a large number of transactions relating to the business of everyday life, including wills; deeds; the sale, lease, and purchase of land; affidavits; assignments and bonds of various kinds; contracts; mortgages; powers of attorney; and many other routine documents.'[9] A similar economy produced comparable work in Quebec, where civil rather than common law governed commercial matters. Pre-Confederation lawyers in firms such as the Torrance–Morris partnership of Montreal supervised the commercial, financial, transportation, and real estate portfolios of their relatives and clients.[10] The dominance of land, debtors, and commercial contracts was typical in pre-industrial common-law countries like Britain before 1800, and in the United States before about 1820.

Law firms did not entirely monopolize the legal work offered by the developing economy of these years. In Quebec, of course, notaries had been providing their specialized legal services since the seventeenth century, largely in real estate and family law (and continue to do so). Elsewhere, the prevalence of legal services offered by lay figures was attributable in part, no doubt, to the inability of the relatively small number of lawyers to service a widely scattered population. In Upper Canada and in the Maritimes, non-lawyers were often appointed to the minor judicial position of justice of the peace. Moreover, Gidney and Millar have pointed out that, at least in the early nineteenth century, lay figures performed much of the conveyancing work that would later require the services of a qualified lawyer.[11] More significant for the future was the emergence of the first in-house lawyers, such as Aemilius Irving, whose career with the Great Western Railway is chronicled in the essay by Jamie Benidickson in this volume. Though few other lawyers likely pursued their careers in this fashion in the mid-nineteenth century, the position of in-house lawyer would become increasingly attractive in the period after the Second World War, and especially in the 1980s.[12]

The character of a law firm's business might well change over time. This was certainly the experience of Halifax's Beamish Murdoch, as

Philip Girard's essay in this volume shows. In his early years of practice, Murdoch did a great deal of debt-collection work, largely on behalf of clients who were smaller merchants and mechanics. By the 1830s, however, he began to provide 'a wider range of services to a more affluent and more regular clientele.' This shift was doubtless a result not only of increasing expertise, but also of the contacts Murdoch established through his many interests beyond the law, including journalism, politics, and a host of voluntary societies.

The type of work in which Murdoch and his fellow lawyers were engaged was typically handled, from the early nineteenth century through to the 1880s, by sole practitioners or by two lawyers acting in partnership. This was true not only for rural lawyers, but for their urban counterparts as well, who might perform a good deal of agency work for out-of-town colleagues. As late as 1870, in Toronto, where there were 199 lawyers, only twenty firms had three or more partners. Outside Toronto, in the entire province of Ontario, only sixteen firms had as many as three members, and none was any larger.[13] Vast client lists might be handled by sole practitioners or two-person partnerships. The Torrance–Morris firm in mid-nineteenth-century Montreal, for example, specialized in commercial law, with a significant wills-and-estates practice. Their clients included many pillars of the Montreal business community, including wholesalers, printers, importers, insurance companies, and industrial concerns. They serviced this large clientele with a tiny staff of two or three lawyers, a law student, a clerk, and 'an apparently incompetent bookkeeper.'[14]

The state of the law and of law-office technology helps account for the small size of law firms during this period. Clearly, not many transactions of the period required the attention of more than one lawyer at a time, as the mergers-and-acquisitions work of today does. Moreover, since most of the legal writing was done with quill pens by law students and clerks, there were no economies of scale to be effected through pooling resources in order to obtain expensive equipment.

The emergence of law firms with an identity distinct from that of their leading members is a relatively recent development. In the pre–1880 period, the golden age of the sole practitioner, the lawyer in most cases *was* the law firm. A lawyer's practice, moreover, served him in a number of different ways which have changed dramatically since. First, it was the outward and visible sign of a lawyer's status in colonial society. Lawyers – at least those who had qualified as barristers – were, above all, 'gentlemen,' part of a self-conscious professional élite aspiring to leadership roles in their societies. It was for this reason that the Law Society of Upper Canada exhibited so much concern about the character rather than the academic achievement of those who presented themselves for admission to the bar. Lawyers and aspiring lawyers in the Maritimes were similarly concerned to acquire or extend their claims to genteel status.[15]

Gidney and Millar have described the gentlemanly code of conduct which complemented such pretensions: 'Professional men ... showed courtesy by not poaching each other's clients ..., by not underbidding fees or defaming the reputation of a fellow practitioner. They did not advertise or hire themselves out to others.' They did not receive wages.[16] As Jamie Benidickson's essay on Aemilius Irving indicates, many in the profession in the mid-nineteenth century deplored their in-house competitors in part because their activities violated some of these rules. In spite of apparent renegades like Irving, however, the chief tenets of this code were to prove remarkably long-lived among Canadian lawyers.

Interestingly, the gentlemanly code of conduct did not include effective sanctions against involvement in business and politics. Today prominent lawyers move from law to judicial office, business, and/or politics in sequence, and sometimes back again. In the early nineteenth century, however, the practice of law was commonly combined simultaneously with the holding of government offices like judgeships and collectorships of customs. As Philip Girard's essay in this volume indicates, Beamish Murdoch in Halifax combined his law practice with minor judicial office by the late 1830s. Until the advent of responsible government, the lucky few obtained such offices largely through personal connections with members of the appointed governing élite. By the mid-nineteenth century, however, the importance of such connections declined in favour of evidence of partisan political activity.[17]

Law firms frequently provided a base for such activity, as the careers of Beamish Murdoch and a host of Upper Canadians such as the Baldwins demonstrate.[18] Moreover, as Philip Girard shows here, Beamish Murdoch's political fortunes were intimately tied to the character of his practice; his representation of Nova Scotia's underdogs in the courts stood him in good stead on the hustings in 1826; no doubt his political activity also raised his profile as a lawyer. Law and politics were complementary in other respects as well. The income from practice helped finance many a political career at a time when legislators were not paid for their services. Beyond this, lawyers might well enter politics to further the business interests of their clients, as lawyer William Badgley of Montreal did in the 1840s.[19]

Law firms additionally served as the *de facto* headquarters of their members' often diverse business concerns. In the early nineteenth century, their work naturally brought lawyers into contact with merchants and landowners. They were thus well positioned to exploit advantageous openings in commerce and in real estate. Real estate investments had the added advantage of requiring little direct time away from practice. The advent of the railway age, moreover, allowed lawyer–entrepreneurs like Sir Allan MacNab to embark on lucrative careers as railway promoters, directors, and company presidents.[20] Nor did lawyers, at least in the early years, necessarily confine themselves to one profession. Two well-known Upper Canadian lawyers, John Rolph and W.W. Baldwin, also practised as doctors. Rolph in fact rounded out his knowledge of the professions by undertaking 'studies leading to a divinity degree' as well![21]

However diverse their interests outside the law, novice lawyers had reason to be grateful if they had chosen their relatives well. At this period in Canadian legal history, and well into the twentieth century, legal opportunity was in large measure a function of who you were. As Blaine Baker has noted, the classes at McGill Law School, after its founding in the late 1840s, received 'heavy representation from Montreal's intermarried commercial dynasties.'[22] Members of the mercantile and commercial élite evidently liked to keep the business in the family, and encouraged sons and nephews to enter the law. The client base of the Torrance–Morris firm, for example, consisted of concerns controlled by relatives of those two powerful Montreal and Upper Canadian families.[23] Family connections were not the only route to success in the law, but they were of inestimable value in assisting the novice practitioner.

Beamish Murdoch's career, which began in Halifax in the 1820s, illustrates some of the hazards of entering practice without the plethora of highly placed connections that contributed to the foundation of so many nineteenth-century legal careers. Murdoch did make good use of the lesser advantages at his command. He employed an inheritance, for example, to finance his entry into the profession. Moreover, he was able to attract favourable attention from within Halifax's Anglo-Irish legal establishment. In spite of such good fortune, however, Murdoch's early years in practice were neither easy nor financially very rewarding.

If law-firm histories are replete with tales of hardships in the formative years of various firms, the drudgery entailed in the articling process is legendary. During the nineteenth century, certainly, many students occupied an inordinate amount of time performing routine chores. Larratt

Smith, articled to Attorney General W.H. Draper in Toronto, spent his first year 'making up accounts, copying letters and documents with a quill pen, running errands, and serving subpoenas, six days a week.'[24] Though some found ways both inside and outside the office to enliven their years of legal apprenticeship, Gidney and Millar note the persistence of student complaints that 'business was often slack and covered a narrow range of problems.'[25]

If the unappealing character of the articling period proved to be a constant in the history of law firms, so did the continuing existence of a few of the firms with which the students served their apprenticeships. Among the well-known Canadian law firms which trace their origins to these early years are McInnes Cooper & Robertson in Halifax and McMaster Meighen in Montreal, along with Blakes and Fraser & Beatty in Toronto. The secret of the longevity of these firms appears to have been their ability to attract a corporate clientele. Some of these clients were remarkably faithful to their lawyers. The firm history of Fraser & Beatty, for example, recorded in 1989 that the Bank of Montreal had been a client for almost a century and a half![26] Such relationships, however, are highly exceptional. Most law firms of the pre–1880 period, like that of Beamish Murdoch, followed a far more common pattern and disappeared when their founders ceased to practise.

THE PROFESSION TRANSFORMED, 1880–1920

The years between 1880 and 1920 featured political upheaval, explosive economic growth, and considerable social unrest. Ongoing tensions between French and English found expression in controversy over the Riel Rebellion of 1885, the Manitoba Schools Question, and conscription during the First World War. The war also brought to a head the long-simmering discontents of labour, which erupted in the Winnipeg General Strike of 1919.

Though many workers had good reason to be dissatisfied with their economic circumstances, the same was not true of most lawyers. A generally prosperous economy, particularly during the 'Laurier boom' of 1896–1913, meant a host of new legal opportunities. The two new transcontinental railways that materialized to service the West's developing wheat economy were among them. Moreover, the exploitation of 'the new generation of staples' – hydro-electric power, mining, and pulp and paper – offered further promise of new business for lawyers in central Canada and the West. Rapid industrial development in all regions, along with significant corporate restructuring, greatly expanded the scope of the practice of corporate and commercial law. So did the emergence of new types of financial institutions, including mortgage and loan companies, trust companies, and the Montreal and Toronto stock exchanges.[27]

Developments in transportation provided lawyers with a host of opportunities to hone their litigation skills and to develop their aptitude for office practice. The railways, for example, continued to require the assistance of courtroom lawyers to defend them against 'local business-men, passengers, and employees.'[28] The Canadian Pacific additionally provided considerable work for real estate lawyers.[29] Other forms of railway diversification, such as shipping and mining, generated both litigation and office practice.[30]

One of the most celebrated railway lawyers of the age was Zebulon A. Lash of Toronto, the prime example of the newly emerging corporate lawyer whose strength was drawing up agreements and conducting negotiations.[31] Lash serviced the many business interests of William Mackenzie and Donald Mann, including the Canadian Northern Railway.[32] When Mackenzie expanded from railways into utilities in Canada and abroad, notably with the establishment of Brazilian Traction in Brazil in 1912, Lash and the Blake law firm were an integral part of the movement. Moreover, the firm contributed the services of lawyer Alexander Mackenzie (no relation to William), who eventually became president of Brazilian Traction.[33]

Blakes' role in William Mackenzie's foreign enterprises was mirrored by that of the Halifax firm of Harris, Henry and Cahan. The Harris firm acted on behalf of Halifax interests centred on promoter John F. Stairs and the Nova Scotia Steel and Coal Company. Robert Harris concentrated on the Canadian work for domestic and foreign utilities. His partner C.H. Cahan took a leading role before the First World War in establishing utilities in the West Indies, before becoming chief executive officer of the Mexican Light and Power Company. The utilities industry brought not only solicitor's work to law firms, but litigation as well. Among the most common types of courtroom actions were those involving rates, services, and personal injury.[34]

These glamorous undertakings did not exhaust the scope of law-firm involvement in the utilities field, as C. Ian Kyer's essay in this volume demonstrates. At the turn of the century, lawyer David Fasken in Toronto was instrumental in developing hydro-electric power to service mines at the northern Ontario sites of Cobalt, Porcupine, and Kirkland Lake. These ventures ultimately led him to organize two power companies, and to

become president of one of them. It was not hydro-electric power, however, but mining, which most occupied David Fasken and his brother,
Alex. Early participants in the turn-of-the-century rush to exploit the mineral finds at Cobalt, the brothers acted as executive officers, directors, and
fund-raisers for a number of mines. The Faskens directed the legal business of these concerns to their law firm, Beatty Blackstock, thereby providing the foundation of a sound reputation for the firm in the area of
mining law. On the west coast, too, lawyers Joe and Finley Russell of the
future Russell & DuMoulin firm held interests in gold and copper mines.
Other developing primary industries such as lumber and salmon fishing
also brought work to their firm.[35]

As Canadian businesses enlarged beyond the boundaries of the family
firm, they required the services of lawyers for a variety of purposes. Lawyers were needed to incorporate limited-liability companies, to draw up
more complex contracts with employees and business associates, and to
devise the legal infrastructure for an increasingly complex array of securities instruments. Lawyers were also required to defend businesses
against government regulation and to provide them with the capacity to
function in multiple jurisdictions. Moreover, as business activity
increased, there was more occasion than ever before for legal representation in the courts. The needs of industry, no less than of railways and utilities, continued to demand effective litigators.

The merger movement of 1909–13 saw 275 firms collapsed into a mere
58, providing considerable business for a few lawyers at big-city firms. In
Montreal, for example, C.H. Cahan did the legal work for Max Aitken
and Royal Securities in the days after 1907–8, when all three relocated
from Halifax. Also in Montreal, the Campbell, Meredith firm acted for the
largest companies in the cotton industry, the Dominion Textile Company
and Canadian Cottons.[36]

Lawyers had a role to play, too, in the expansion of the financial-services sector of the economy. Major law firms, including Albert J. Brown's
Montreal concern (later Ogilvy Renault), typically numbered several
financial institutions among their clients. Clients of the Brown firm
included the Royal Bank, Montreal Trust, the Imperial Bank of Canada,
the Montreal City and District Savings Bank, Wood Gundy, and Royal
Securities.[37] A predecessor of the Raymond and Honsberger firm in Toronto acted for a bank and a trust company; McCarthy, Osler, Hoskin, and
Creelman serviced banks and insurance companies, including the
Dominion Bank and the Osler Brokerage; and Colin Campbell's clients in
late-nineteenth-century Winnipeg included loan companies, banks, and

insurance companies. The predecessors of the Vancouver firms Bull, Housser and Russell & DuMoulin attracted similar clients. Significantly, some financial institutions challenged the structure of legal work by offering lawyers positions as in-house counsel. Toronto lawyer Home Smith, for example, began his career in the Estates Department at National Trust.[38]

A unique view of the relationship between law firms and the financial services industry is provided by Declan Brendan Hamill's essay in this volume. It shows that the Campbell, Meredith firm of Montreal offered far more than technical legal services to the Montreal Stock Exchange (MSE), the client that is the subject of the study. In the late nineteenth century, the MSE stood at the centre of the developing securities market in Canada. It called upon its lawyers for advice on a wide range of matters, including securities law, negotiable instruments, real estate transactions, and relations with governments. Throughout, the exchange's lawyers played a crucial role in implementing the MSE's key objective of maintaining the autonomous and self-regulatory character of the institution. In this endeavour the Campbell, Meredith lawyers were not unique; instead, as Hamill shows, they were part of a more general North Atlantic movement of commercial interests during the late nineteenth century 'away from state law and towards alternative and specialized forms of regulation and dispute resolution.'

Campbell, Meredith was one of a small group of large law firms of five or more lawyers which developed in the larger Canadian cities at the turn of the century as a result of urbanization and industrialization.[39] In 1912, more than fifty firms in the country, most of them in Winnipeg, Toronto, or Montreal, had reached this size.[40]

Although their clients included major corporations and financial institutions, these large law firms evidently did not limit their activities to office practice on behalf of corporations; their clients required a wider range of legal services. Like their American counterparts, they provided work in the areas of 'collections, personal injury, and probate, in addition to strictly corporation law business.'[41] Lawyers at such firms might well specialize, but they could hardly confine their activities strictly to the practice of corporate law.

These firms were distinct from the 'law factories'[42] which developed in large American cities during the same era. The 'law factories,' according to legal historian Wayne Hobson, were like the large law firms in that they comprised at least eight to ten lawyers. Unlike the large law firms, however, they confined their practice to corporate law, and their new recruits to the top graduates of the élite law schools. Moreover, the 'law factories' developed a formalized system of progression through the legal ranks, from clerk to associate, to partner.[43] The Campbell, Meredith firm resembled the law factories in occasionally recruiting beyond the relatives of partners and clients. Yet, while hiring gold-medallists from McGill Law School represented an enlargement of this pool, this was surely a modest step towards fully meritocratic hiring practices. Moreover, the firm continued to accept new lawyers on the basis of their connections rather than of their academic credentials.

Although many lawyers prided themselves on their skills as generalists well into the twentieth century, by 1900 some were already eager to specialize. Individual lawyers had their preferences for certain areas of practice, their particular skills, and no doubt valuable contacts in various fields. For example, in the 1880s, Colin Campbell of Winnipeg intended to divide the firm's work with his two partners on the basis that he would do civil and commercial law, and the other two chancery and insolvency. About two decades later, the death of one of these partners prompted the Campbell firm to recruit Isaac Pitblado, an expert in the grain trade and freight rates, a highly specialized field. In Toronto, meanwhile, when E.E.A. DuVernet expanded his business activities in 1906, he added a corporate lawyer, W.E.B. Raymond, to his firm.[44]

Instead of creating ever-larger law firms, lawyers in the late nineteenth and early twentieth centuries were engaged in expanding the geographic scope of the profession. In central Canada, they contributed to the intensification of the provision of legal services. Here, the ever-more-numerous individuals who qualified to practise law pushed into new communities at the end of the nineteenth century. Elizabeth Bloomfield found that in Ontario, for example, more than a hundred communities attracted their first lawyers between 1870 and 1900. No doubt this was in part a reflection of the growing number of lawyers relative to the population. Concurrent with this process of diffusion, however, was a contrary trend of concentration, with increasing numbers of lawyers locating in Toronto, significantly depleting the number of lawyers in the county towns.[45] This phenomenon was not confined to Toronto, as Dale Brawn's essay in this collection shows. As early as 1909, two-thirds of Manitoba's lawyers were practising in Winnipeg.

The geographic scope of the profession also expanded as lawyers from longer-settled areas of the country migrated to newly opening areas of the prairie West and British Columbia. In Manitoba, the original contingent of lawyers trained in Quebec was overwhelmed in the 1870s by an influx of Protestant Ontarians.[46] Lawyers from the Maritimes also increasingly migrated to central and western Canada. While it was primarily junior lawyers who began the emigration from the Maritimes in the 1880s, by the early twentieth century increasing numbers of senior members of the bar joined them.[47]

Law firms in central Canada did not necessarily recruit from so wide a field. For example, the relationships of brothers, cousins, and uncles at the Beatty Blackstock firm in Toronto, as described in C. Ian Kyer's essay, would have been a fit subject for the talents of Gilbert and Sullivan. There is also evidence, in Kyer's essay and elsewhere, that firms tended to exhibit a degree of religious homogeneity.[48] Yet religious diversity flourished in some unexpected locations. For example, Arthur Anglin, who became a partner at the Anglican-dominated Blake firm in Toronto in 1897, was not only a Roman Catholic, but a well-known activist on behalf of his co-religionists.[49] Similarly, in late-nineteenth-century Halifax, there were a number of instances of Protestants in partnership with Roman Catholics.[50] Moreover, there are a few examples of prestigious Toronto firms at the turn of the century taking on members of the Jewish faith as articling students and as junior lawyers.[51]

Significantly, lawyers at large firms did not generally include the sisters and the aunts. Conventional wisdom had it that women did not belong in the professions. The biggest hurdle for women was not admission to law firms, but the call to the bar. Clara Brett Martin's battle with the Law Society of Upper Canada is well known. Similarly, when Mabel Penery French sought to join the bar in New Brunswick in 1906, the Supreme Court of that province decided that she could not be considered 'a person' under the Legal Professions Act. The Court of Appeal of British Columbia reached the same verdict a few years later. In both provinces, legislative action was required before women could practise. Women were admitted to the bar in all provinces except Quebec before 1920, but in very small numbers; John Hagan has found that in 1911 there were only seven women practising law in the entire country.[52]

While large law firms occasionally took on women and members of ethnic minorities, most members of these groups who qualified as lawyers during these years had little alternative but to practise alone.[53] Such exclusion certainly had its drawbacks. One of the advantages, however, was a certain freedom of action. Unlike today's minority lawyers in large firms, they did not have to conform to the conventions of a culture that was in many ways unfamiliar to them.[54]

However they found their niche in the profession, lawyers continued the pre-Confederation practice of combining law with other activities. Not all of these were of immediate pecuniary benefit to their firms. The rise of voluntarism at the turn of the century provided a host of charitable and religious causes to which lawyers could offer their time and energies. Some, like Jimmy Jones at Toronto's DuVernet firm, found such interests incompatible with the increasingly demanding pace of law firms on the cutting edge of practice.[55] Others, like David Fasken, kept their enthusiasm for such activities within closer bounds. Fasken himself combined the law with an important role on behalf of Toronto Western Hospital. This association was not, however, without benefit to the firm, as C. Ian Kyer indicates. The law firm provided advice to the hospital, and even to its patients! For lawyers like Fasken, high-level community involvement served as an effective means of increasing legal business.

As we have seen, Fasken also pursued a great many business ventures outside the law. These included the presidency of a life insurance company as well as interests in Ontario's booming natural-resources sector. Many of Fasken's contemporaries learned the same lesson as he did: involvement in business brought clients to the firm. Such episodes, of course, occasionally ended in disaster for the law firm, as the career of E.E.A. DuVernet indicates.[56] Notwithstanding such catastrophes, lawyers continued to flock to business, attracted by the proliferation of economic opportunities, the nature of their contacts, and the potential to enhance their income.[57] Moreover, many lawyers combined practice with a political career; a seat in the legislature was an excellent place from which to advance both personal interests and those of clients. Some firms, however, decided to forgo the marketing advantages of political involvement; the partnership agreement at Beatty Blackstock, for example, prohibited partners from seeking public office.[58]

The period 1880–1920 had a most unhappy ending. The 'Laurier boom' of 1896–1913 ended in a depression. The First World War followed shortly thereafter. Though war brought dramatic production increases to both agriculture and industry, it also resulted in severe dislocations, notably the deaths of more than 60,000 young Canadians. Law firms willingly endured the departure of young lawyers for the armed services, and sincerely mourned those who failed to return.[59] For some firms, the manpower shortage was a blessing in disguise; business dried up because all available capital was channelled into the war effort.[60] The war, however, brought few lasting changes to the structure of law practice or to the character of legal business.

THE INTERWAR YEARS, 1919–1939

Both beginning lawyers and their more established fellow practitioners might well have faced the future of their profession with some trepidation in the post-First World War period. The 1920s are generally remembered as 'roaring,' but, from a business point of view, they have been more accurately characterized by Michael Bliss as 'stuttering.'[61] For business, this was a decade of great instability, beginning with a postwar recession and ending with the celebrated stock-market crash of 1929. In between, there were profits to be made in a variety of businesses, including distilling, lumber, oil, and the auto industry. The difficulties experienced by some businesses in the 1920s foreshadowed the far more severe dislocations of the Depression. The 1930s brought legendary hardship to Canada in the wake of the stock-market crash, the evaporation of overseas markets for primary products, and soaring unemployment rates. For prairie farmers, the drying up of their foreign markets was secondary to the almost biblical series of disasters that engulfed them. Winters were exceptionally cold, and summers unusually hot. Drought dried up their soil, and the wind carried it away. Plant diseases attacked the crops, along with a plague of grasshoppers. The country's economy generally began to rebound in 1934, but that recovery was interrupted by the recession of 1938.[62]

During the 1920s, while some smaller law firms scrambled in the wake of many financially precarious commercial clients, larger firms across the country were anchored by institutional clients like banks and underwriters, and even expanded their business. In Halifax, the McInnes firm attracted a host of new clients, among them oil and wood-products companies, while continuing to act for the Bank of Nova Scotia.[63] The real success story in Halifax during this era, however, was the rise of James McGregor Stewart. The leading position of Stewart's firm, then known as Henry, Rogers, Harris and Stewart,[64] was established in the late nineteenth century under the direction of R.E. Harris, the pre-eminent Halifax corporate lawyer of his day. After Harris joined the Supreme Court of Nova Scotia in 1915, J. McG. Stewart, newly made a partner, took his place.

As the essay by Gregory P. Marchildon and Barry Cahill in this book shows, the foundation of Stewart's reputation was the masterminding of the restructuring and reflotation of the Acadia Sugar Refining Company in 1926. Two years later, Stewart assumed the presidency of the company, in addition to his responsibilities at the law firm. In the meantime, he had acquired no less a client than Izaak Walton Killam, soon to become one of

Canada's financial giants. The Nova Scotia Light & Power Company, Royal Securities, and the Mersey Paper Company – all Killam concerns – became important clients of the firm. Killam was attracted not only to Stewart's consummate legal skills, but also to his business acumen. Stewart's business contacts and judgment were also highly valued at the Royal Bank, a long-time client of the firm; his usefulness as a director after 1931 was rewarded with a vice-presidency twenty years later.[65]

For Toronto's Osler, Hoskin firm, the 1920s was a period of readjustment after the departure of three McCarthys in 1916 ended their family's thirty-four-year association with the firm. In general, the McCarthys kept the litigation files, while the corporate clients remained with Osler, Hoskin. The province's growing automobile business provided a new client in the form of General Motors. The expansion of American corporations into Canada provided other additions to the firm's client list, including Canadian Kodak Company. Osler, Hoskin was also a beneficiary of Ontario's thriving mining industry, cherishing International Nickel as its largest client at the beginning of the decade.[66]

Like some other Toronto law firms, Osler, Hoskin was touched by public scandal in the 1920s. The firm received a good deal of unwelcome publicity when its senior partner, H.S. Osler, refused to testify before American authorities in matters related to the Teapot Dome Scandal in 1924. Luckily for the firm, this episode did no lasting damage to its revenues.[67] Meanwhile at the Rowell firm (later McMillan Binch), Casey Wood was a director of the Home Bank, whose senior officials were trying to disguise its financial instability by making false monthly returns to Ottawa. Wood, inexperienced in banking law and practice, seems to have signed whatever documents were set in front of him. This unwise and unlawyerly practice resulted in his being charged with making false returns. The verdict of guilty at the county-court level was reversed on appeal, but the reputation of the firm had suffered some damage in the meantime.[68]

The vicissitudes of the economy of the prairie West in the 1920s had a negative impact on many law firms. This was true of sole practitioner George F. Downes, of Edmonton, whose career is detailed in Henry Klassen's essay in this volume. Downes, who had been in practice in Alberta since 1903, wrote in 1927: 'I have never found it so hard to make a living as in the past four years. This is to a large extent owing to the fact that times have been so bad that I can not keep a stenographer to do my typewriting.' Downes nevertheless eked out a living from estates, land transfers, and work for a hospital. Others seem to have had better luck than

Downes. In Regina, Saskatchewan, the McKenzie, Thom firm was thriving, housing a group of ten or twelve lawyers working on commercial law, collections, and mortgages, and doing agency work.[69]

On the west coast, the postwar economic decline hit hard, prompting some creative rain-making at the Vancouver firm of Russell, Hancox & Anderson. The founder of the firm, Finley Russell, had connections to the Liberal party that led to his appointment to a commission to consolidate the Revised Statutes of Canada in 1923. They also brought him work assisting in the suppression of Native potlatches, and business in Vancouver involving the city's sewers and water supply.[70]

Another response to the financial difficulties on the west coast was the merger of two Vancouver firms, Tupper and Bull, and Walsh, McKim, Housser and Molson. The new firm, known as Walsh Bull Housser, was created in 1927, in part to effect economies in office staff, rent, and equipment. The death or departure of some senior lawyers from the Tupper firm, and the compatability of firm cultures, were additional spurs to the merger. In addition to general corporate and commercial work, the firm prospered on the basis of work in real property and the relatively new field of automobile insurance.[71]

The 1930s was a far more perilous decade for law firms. Though lawyers perhaps fared better than members of most occupational groups, it was not unheard of for members of the profession to be on the welfare rolls. More commonly, firm revenues plunged dramatically. Senator John Godfrey recalled that his father's income, once $25,000 annually, fell 90 per cent during the early 1930s; Godfrey senior was delighted in 1934 to become chair of the Ontario Securities Commission, at $7,500 a year.[72] Similarly, at the Vancouver firm of Robertson, Douglas & Symes, according to A.B. Robertson, 'my Dad's earnings in one year at the beginning of the depression were just one-third of what they had been in the year before the depression hit.' This was notwithstanding the fact that the firm enjoyed the patronage of some major corporate clients, including the Bank of Montreal and the Royal Trust Company.[73]

At smaller law firms, too, business was often hard to come by. Nathan Strauss, of Toronto, who made more in his first year of practice in 1929 than he did in his fifth year, remembered the hardships of the Depression well: 'You would sit in an office and just sit and wait, like a frog waiting for a fly to fly by, it was really tough.'[74] Lawyers who did have some business, like Raymond and Honsberger in Toronto, sometimes found it necessary to accept payment in kind, with chickens and a new suit of clothes among the 'fees'! The worst year of the Depression for the firm was 1936, when the two lawyers together 'took home less than one half of what their only secretary received.' George Johnston, also in a two-person Toronto firm, recalled his experience succinctly: 'We nearly starved in the 30's.' The Dales, Johnston practice was sustained by foreclosure law and selling under Powers of Sale.[75] Emmett Hall's Saskatoon practice was another which accepted chickens in payment of legal fees, along with much-used cars and an old cottage.[76]

Among those who remained employed, pay reductions were common. At the McInnes firm in Halifax, everyone, including partners, took a 10 per cent pay cut. At the Russell firm in Vancouver, 'the firm cut costs by engaging a law student who could also type, take dictation, act as a receptionist and complete dockets' – all for $30 a month.[77] Other firms were more fortunate. A leading member of Blakes in Toronto commented that the Depression 'did not affect the earnings of Blakes appreciably although it made it more difficult to obtain the increase in remuneration that otherwise would have been given.'[78] At the Osler firm, also in Toronto, no one among the support staff was laid off or suffered a salary reduction, even in the depths of the Depression; partners, however, took less and less.[79] Firms like Oslers, with their stable of corporate clients, were thus able to weather the Depression relatively painlessly, no doubt also doing their share of bankruptcy work, foreclosures, and debt-collections, like other firms.

One of the groups that suffered most in the Depression was the young, and law students, relative to lawyers, were no exception. The economic downturn had hit the Maritimes earlier than other regions of Canada, and Donald McInnes found himself working without pay for a year at the McInnes firm in the late 1920s. This may not have been a great hardship for the son of the firm's leader, but his embarrassment made him very secretive about the conditions of his employment.[80] During the 1930s, at McMaster Meighen the students found that their pay had been reduced from $10 a month to nothing. In Toronto, a student at Holden, Murdoch found it impossible to survive on $35 a month, but his pleas for a raise fell on deaf ears.[81]

In those hard times, lawyers sometimes resorted to desperate measures. In Ontario, the Law Society struck no fewer than forty-nine lawyers off the rolls for various forms of theft between 1929 and 1934. This was more than three times the number disbarred for similar offences in the five years before the onset of the Depression, and almost double the number in the five years after 1934.[82] These presumed victims of economic calamity were not without their sympathizers in the profession.

Among their supporters was Shirley Dennison, who chaired the discipline committee of the Law Society in the 1930s and early 1940s before becoming treasurer from 1944 to 1947. Dennison's will, as John Honsberger records, 'left the bulk of his estate to the Law Society to establish a benevolent fund for members of the Society and their dependents, including those who had been disbarred.'[83]

Fortunately, better days lay ahead. By the mid-1930s, the economy was beginning its recovery, with the result that firms like McMaster Meighen began hiring new lawyers again.[84] In Toronto, moreover, litigator B.V. Elliot was optimistic enough about future prospects to enter into partnership with tax lawyer Henry Borden in 1936. This was the first step in the development of the future legal giant Borden & Elliot. Elliot, a man without connections in Toronto, had begun practice in the city in the mid-1920s, running an insurance business on the side. By 1935, he was making $10,000 a year, a result of his aggressiveness in seeking business and in pursuing his clients' interests in court.[85] Elliot's hard-driving attitude, though common among successful litigators, was out of the ordinary for a corporate lawyer.[86] Borden & Elliot was likely the first of the large corporate firms in Toronto to break out of the gentlemanly and patrician mode that characterized big-city law in Toronto and elsewhere in Canada, at least until the middle decades of this century. In later years, J.S.D. Tory would build his Toronto firm in much the same way.

Even on the prairies, the story of the late 1930s was not entirely bleak for lawyers, as Louis A. Knafla's essay on the Goodall and Cairns law firm of Calgary illustrates. This two-person partnership flourished after 1935 on the basis of business from oil and gas interests and a variety of other industries. In British Columbia, too, the late 1930s brought a resurgence of business to law firms. When Oscar F. Lundell joined the firm of Lawson & Clark in Vancouver in 1935, he was 'immediately swamped with work.' Among the firm's clients were the Standard Oil Company of British Columbia, Standard Stations, Powell River Company, Pacific Mills, and other large newsprint and pulp-mill concerns.[87] The economic recovery of the late 1930s, however, was generally a modest one, certainly by comparison with the boom that followed the Second World War.

In spite of the economic upheavals of the interwar years, many of the firms that then counted as 'large' saw significant increases in their numbers in the 1920s. Between the end of the First World War and 1930, for example, Blakes in Toronto grew from twelve to nineteen, and McCarthys from six to nine; Winnipeg's Aikins, Loftus, Aikins expanded from seven to nine; and, in Montreal, Meredith, Holden grew from seven to ten, and Brown, Montgomery & McMichael from ten to twenty. Other large firms, including Rowell Reid Wright, and Oslers (Toronto), Campbell, McMaster (Montreal), and the McInnes firm of Halifax, experienced stable numbers. In Halifax, on the other hand, numbers at the Stewart firm (formerly Henry, Rogers, Harris and Stewart) fluctuated widely, and were smaller at the end of the decade than at the beginning.

The prosperity of the 1920s, then, did not produce the kind of exponential growth that large corporate law firms experienced sixty years later – probably because the boom was smaller in scale, and unevenly distributed. Nor were there any great national economic projects, like the pipelines of the 1950s, which provided so much work for postwar lawyers. Moreover, in most fields, government regulation was still in its infancy.[88] The relatively moderate expansion of the 1920s meant that many larger firms were able to weather the Depression without losing significant numbers of lawyers. During the 1930s, most of the firms mentioned above, with the exception of the still-growing Oslers and McCarthys in Toronto, saw their numbers remain stable, or experienced incremental growth.[89]

The growth that took place in some of the larger firms during the interwar years was, however, the sign of a notable alteration in the character of law practice at the top of the profession. Numbers at the very biggest law firms were approaching twenty lawyers – a qualitative as well as a quantitative change from the large firms of the previous era. Moreover, some major big-city firms had begun to specialize in corporate law. The Osler, Hoskin firm in Toronto, for example, concentrated almost exclusively on corporate work after the departure of the McCarthys in 1916. By the 1930s, however, even the McCarthy firm was shifting away from litigation in favour of corporate work. The declining importance of litigation to large firms more generally is highlighted in Dale Brawn's contribution to this volume, which focuses on the large-firm lawyers of Manitoba. On the basis of extensive statistical materials, Brawn concluded that, by 1939, the large firms of Manitoba had for the most part moved their activities away from the courtroom – in part because their corporate clients preferred to avoid the courts. It was the lawyers from small firms who increasingly conducted litigation in the courts of Manitoba.

In spite of significant developments affecting corporate law firms during the interwar years, there was a remarkable degree of continuity in the culture of the larger firms. This was true in relation to firm governance, hiring practices, and the use of technology. Dictatorial governance, along with secrecy, and insensitivity to productivity and market concerns, were characteristic of large American law firms during these years. These qualities were also prevalent in their Canadian counterparts. Autocracy was the rule in the running of most firms. Thomas Reid, a leader of the Toronto bar in the 1920s and 1930s, ensured that there were no firm meetings during the time he ran the Rowell firm. Nor did he attempt to create a coherent firm culture, or weld its members into a harmonious unit. 'What we want,' he is recorded as saying, 'is cheap labour,' presumably from juniors in the firm.[90] At Blakes, young Allan Graydon was confounded in his arguments for a greater share of the profits on the basis that his contribution to the firm was as valuable as senior partner Glyn Osler's. Osler stated his position succinctly: 'Allan, you are *more* valuable, but I am older.'[91]

Hiring practices also exhibited a high degree of continuity, as T.D. Regehr's essay on the Blake firm for this volume convincingly documents. Personal contacts remained the basis of recruitment, and the vast majority of those hired were White males.[92] The few women practising in these years generally assumed very limited roles in the law. Joan Brockman's study of women lawyers in British Columbia revealed that most 'simply accepted that women lawyers played a different role in the profession than men. Most were prepared to play supportive roles, work in the office, and limit their practice to that [to] which "women [were] particularly fitted."' Those who stepped outside this role found the public wary.[93]

A major restriction for women was that they were generally denied the chance to practise in the courtroom. John Arnup recorded that the prevailing view in the 1930s was that women's 'emotional background and make-up didn't permit them to be as cold blooded as you had to be to make those hard decisions.'[94] Lawyers at one firm may have typified attitudes among their peers to the appropriate role for women in the law: Their wives were personally responsible for cleaning the offices![95] For the very few women in the profession, opportunities for meaningful employment began to improve only when the Second World War created a shortage of young male lawyers.

The lawyers who saw no need for changes in firm governance and hiring practices were similarly conservative in their adoption of new technology. When Allan Graydon first joined Blakes in 1921, copies of letters were made on an antique letter press, and 'it was only after a most protracted argument that it was agreed that the letter book could consist of carbon copies.'[96] The practice of entering all searches of title in specially prepared leather-bound volumes was discontinued in the mid-1920s, at least by Graydon. Typewriters had become standard equipment in law offices by the 1920s, though many lawyers had stoutly resisted sending typewritten letters for years.[97] Dictation machines were a major innovation, but they remained fragile and inefficient.[98] Further technological innovation would have to await the introduction of electric typewriters in the 1950s. Until the advent of accounting machines and computers, moreover, billing practices everywhere remained haphazard. At Blakes, for example, the financial statements of the firm were prepared only twice a year, and included accounts receivable.[99]

The offices of many of the country's largest firms remained unimpressive. Clients cooled their heels, not in a comfortably appointed waiting-room, but on hard benches in the hall. At Blakes in Toronto, for example, the floors were linoleum, and the offices featured an open stairwell and elevator shaft. When the windows were open, the wind sometimes swept clients' files onto the roofs of adjoining buildings. In Halifax, the McInnes firm still occupied premises first acquired in 1909 and affectionately known as the 'rabbit warren.' On the other side of the country, at Walsh Bull Housser, accounts in the late 1920s were compiled by 'a former tugboat master who chain-smoked matches in his pipe ... at the end of the day the floor was *covered* with matches.' At Blakes, too, Glyn Osler's careless disposal of matches made fire a constant possibility. A reform which began in Toronto in the 1930s was spearheaded by Borden & Elliot; the offices were closed on Saturday for the first time.[100]

The pace of practice in the larger firms remained slow during the interwar years, and lawyers indulged in some luxuries which have since vanished. Allan Graydon considered Sam Crowell an early bird, arriving at the office 'never later than 8.30 [A.M.].'[101] It was common for lawyers to be chauffeured to work in their limousines, a sign of affluence that largely disappeared with wartime gas rationing. At many firms, all available lawyers took a break for afternoon tea, a custom which survived on both coasts into the 1940s.[102] Their counterparts in New York lamented the 'grinding hard work, long hours, and the lack of any aim higher than money and prestige.' In Canada, however, even at the corporate firms, lawyers found that life was easier, and they still made major time commitments to community service.[103]

During the interwar years, lawyers continued to be active in other fields of endeavour. As Dale Brawn's study of Manitoba shows, politics continued to attract lawyers, not only from the large firms, but from small and medium-sized firms as well. There was a particular importance, however, to the participation of large-firm lawyers in politics, according to Brawn; it provided them with another arena in which to advance the interests of the corporations who dominated their client lists. Similarly, as Brawn also demonstrates, corporate interests were well protected when large-firm alumni assumed judicial positions.

In times of economic upheaval, and even hardship, then, lawyers appear to have clung to traditional methods of doing business. The degree of apparent continuity, however, masked significant developments that were occurring at the top of the profession. Among the most notable were the emergence of the corporate law firm, and the shift in the relative importance of litigation to some large firms. Traditional methods of firm organization, governance, and culture, moreover, were soon to be effectively challenged as a result of changes induced by the Second World War and its aftermath.

THE SECOND WORLD WAR AND ITS AFTERMATH, 1939–1973

The Second World War claimed fewer Canadian lives than had the First World War, but its impact on the economy was far more profound. Propelled first by war and then by the necessity of planning for reconstruction, the federal government embarked on a far-reaching program of economic development and regulation. In the process, it laid the foundations for a dramatic new level of state intervention in the postwar years.[104]

One example of the effects on legal practice is the area of labour law. Wartime changes to labour regulation instantly made labour law an important new specialty in the postwar period. Under this sheltering legislation, unionization sky-rocketed from 17 per cent of non-agricultural paid workers in 1939 to 36 per cent in 1973.[105] Accordingly, companies required enhanced legal assistance in labour relations, and lawyers in this field found themselves much in demand. They soon discovered, however, that their practices required what the historian of Borden & Elliot has called a more 'conciliatory style' than was common in litigation in that period. Lawyers who persisted in pre-war attitudes that identified labour as the enemy might well find themselves deserted by their clients.[106]

While some types of regulation have altered the character of work for lawyers in private practice, the broadening scope of government regulation has brought increasing numbers of lawyers directly into government service at all levels. It is likely that the expansion of government during the Second World War provided a significant push in this direction;

between 1931 and 1951, the number of lawyers in government service more than doubled, from 3 per cent to more than 6 per cent of all practising lawyers.[107] Government employment, then, has become an ever more significant alternative to private practice. The choice between public and private employment for lawyers need not, however, establish a lifetime employment pattern. As Jamie Benidickson has observed, 'lots of lawyers in private practice today learned their fields as government lawyers working with regulatory agencies and departments.'[108] Law firms have indeed reaped substantial benefits from expertise acquired by their members while working for government.

In the aftermath of the the Second World War, Canadians experienced the boom period of 1945–73, which has been called 'one of the most prosperous in Canada's economic history.'[109] Though broken by a recession during Diefenbaker's prime-ministership (1957–63), the good times rolled on into the 1970s. Part of the explanation was that the baby boom and the return of prosperity had unleashed consumer demand, previously dormant because of the Depression and the Second World War. The resulting clamour for new houses, highways, schools, and hospitals transformed the landscape just as surely as televisions, freezers, and jet travel changed the lives of Canadians. The voracious appetites of industries – both Canadian and American – for Canada's primary resources also fuelled economic growth. Their targets included those staple products which had helped produce the boom of 1896–1914 – pulp and paper, hydro-electric power, and mining. Canada, however, had new riches to offer in the postwar years, notably large prairie contributions of oil, natural gas, and potash. Uranium was another addition to Canada's list of offerings. Technological advances were among the factors which made exploitation of these resources possible and profitable, but more sophisticated methods of financing new mega-projects like pipelines and hydro-electric power projects also deserved a share of the credit.

During the 1950s, it was the pipelines that particularly captured the imaginations, and the attentions, of corporate lawyers, many of them in central Canada. The most famous was TransCanada PipeLines Limited, designed to bring natural gas from Alberta to Ontario.[110] The project gained notoriety after its financing became the subject of a bitter parliamentary debate in the Canadian House of Commons in May 1956, a debate that prefigured the defeat of the twenty-two-year-old Liberal government in the 1957 general election.[111] TransCanada PipeLines was a bigger political football than most such undertakings, but, like other pipeline projects, it provided work for lawyers at virtually every stage. The original contracts establishing the companies, the financing arrangements, the process of construction, the distribution of the product – all required legal assistance on behalf of a variety of agencies.

Much of the financing work for the TransCanada and other pipelines was done in Toronto, which was on its way to replacing Montreal as the financial centre of the country. It was Borden & Elliot's proud boast that they were the first legal firm involved in financing a pipeline, in this case TransMountain Pipeline. The pipelines might require not only mortgage bond financing, but also the services of underwriters, and law firms like Borden & Elliot found new business in advising both institutional lenders and securities firms.[112] The McCarthy firm in Toronto acted in 1962 for TransCanada PipeLines in another capacity, doing the legal work for the company which arose out of the purchase of the government-built part of the line from the Manitoba–Ontario border to Kapuskasing. In later years, TransCanada PipeLines would occupy the firm's lawyers with constitutional issues and work related to rate-making. This mega-project, however, spread its work around, and the Arnoldi, Parry & Campbell firm did its Ontario real estate work. At the distribution end, firms like McCarthys acted for companies which sought to obtain franchises for supplying natural gas carried by the pipelines to communities in far-flung regions of the country.[113]

Companies involved in the forestry industry also kept lawyers across the country occupied during the 1950s. In British Columbia, H.R. MacMillan, returned from government service in wartime Ottawa, pursued the process of vertical integration begun during the 1930s, merging in 1951 with timber giant Bloedel, Stewart & Welch. During the 1950s, MacMillan and Bloedel Limited, as this multifaceted empire was christened, used not only lawyers in its home province, but Toronto experts on financings and takeovers as well.[114] Meanwhile, McMaster Meighen in Montreal serviced some of the legal needs of the Bowater organization, a British concern which became involved in the wood-products industry in Nova Scotia in the mid–1950s. During the same period, the McInnes firm of Halifax acted for Nova Scotia Pulp, a subsidiary of Stora Kopparberg, a Swedish mining and forestry giant.[115] The forestry industry also contributed to litigation business, most notoriously in British Columbia's 'Sommers Affair' of the mid–1950s, which involved allegations that a minister of the Crown had taken bribes from lumber companies in return for the granting of forest-management licences.[116]

During the 1960s, issues relating to hydro-electric power assumed a new importance with nationalization in British Columbia and Quebec, and the development of the Churchill Falls project in Labrador. In Vancouver, the Russell & DuMoulin firm acted for B.C. Electric Company after the Bennett government expropriated it, presumably because its president had refused to agree to buy large blocks of power from Bennett's pet project, the Peace River Power Development Company. The B.C. Power Corporation, the holding company of B.C. Electric, hired Russell & DuMoulin lawyer Doug Brown, who had offered an opinion that Bennett's actions were unconstitutional and compensable in damages. After the courts upheld Brown's position, the parties reached a settlement which provided the company with an additional $86 million over the government's original offer. This victory proved to be 'a major landmark in the firm's history,' bringing both Brown and Russell & DuMoulin recognition throughout the country.[117]

While corporate activity preoccupied many of the larger law firms, their smaller counterparts flourished as a result of the growing prosperity of ordinary people. The end of the war unleashed an unprecedented demand for houses, and the postwar boom made housing more affordable than ever before. Smaller firms such as Raymond and Honsberger in Toronto, and Millar, Alexander in Hamilton, prospered largely on the basis of conveyancing work, as the essays in this volume by John D. Honsberger and Philip J. Sworden indicate. Significantly, many clients of such firms were drawn from members of immigrant communities in the process of establishing themselves in this country.

Another development of the postwar years would have a considerable impact on smaller firms. This was the introduction in most provinces, by the early 1970s, of a publicly funded legal-aid plan. Such schemes soon greatly overshadowed the traditional *pro bono* work undertaken by lawyers on an *ad hoc* basis. They were intended to provide greater access to justice for those who could not afford legal services, but they also had consequences for law firms. By underwriting fees in the fast-developing areas of matrimonial, immigration, and especially criminal law, legal aid greatly expanded the scope for practice in these fields over the following generation.[118]

The sheer volume of business activity, the increasing size and complexity of transactions, and the development of new areas of specialization were among the factors which encouraged law-firm expansion. The historian of McCarthys in Toronto has observed that the period after 1950 saw 'a great growth in the scope and diversity and complexity of the practice' – in part as a result of growth of the firm, and in part owing to the 'growth of the Canadian economy, new technology, much more sophistication in public financing and massive capital projects.'[119] The activities of the government were important as well, not just in relation to labour law, but because of the new Companies Act of 1964 and the Income Tax Act of 1971. The latter, in particular, appears to have been a turning-point, marking the end of the all-rounder – the lawyer who was able to handle essentially any kind of case. As John Godfrey commented: 'The final nail in the coffin of generalization came with the Income Tax Act in 1971. There was no way a corporation lawyer could continue as such and be as familiar with the new Act as he had been with the old.' [120]

By comparison with recent rates of law-firm growth, expansion in the size of law firms during the postwar period was slow but apparently sure. In 1952, only two law firms in the country (McMichael, Common in Montreal, and Blakes in Toronto) had more than twenty lawyers. By 1962, all of the top ten firms in the country had more than twenty lawyers, though none had more than forty. A decade later, the Blake firm in Toronto and the Ogilvy firm in Montreal had more than sixty lawyers, and the top ten firms in the country all had more than thirty-five lawyers. The pace of this post-war growth of corporate law firms was different in Canada than in the United States. South of the border, the golden age of the 'giant' firm occurred in the 1950s and 1960s. As a result of legal opportunities offered by the New Deal and the postwar boom south of the border, by the late 1950s the Americans could boast thirty-eight firms with more than fifty lawyers. These developments were not duplicated in Canada, where, as late as the early 1970s, only a handful of firms had reached this size.[121]

Toronto and Montreal had a diminishing share of spots among the largest firms in Canada. In 1932 all but two of the top fifteen firms in the country had been located in one of these two cities. By 1962, however, four of the top ten were located in the West, three of them in Vancouver.[122] During the generation after 1945, then, the country's largest firms expanded both their corporate business and the numbers required to service such clients.

Increasing the amount of business done was a goal at many law firms, but the legal culture of the time demanded that this be achieved in a genteel fashion. John Godfrey, for example, complained that Peter Campbell, his firm's senior partner, 'was reluctant, where a client had obtained control of another company, to ask the client to switch the legal business of that company to our firm.' It was also considered bad form to 'steal' clients from a law firm which had introduced you to the client in the first place.[123]

In fact, many lawyers at the big central Canadian firms demonstrated a rather limited grasp of marketing strategies during these years. Stanley Edwards has said of Toronto's Fraser & Beatty at this time that 'there was no conscious effort to develop new business or obtain new clients ... We were very busy and wouldn't have been able to handle much more business in any event.'[124] J.S.D. Tory, who formed his own firm in 1941, was rather frowned-upon by the established firms in Toronto because of the determination with which he went after clients.

A more subtle way of attracting clients was to increase the range of services the firm provided. At McCarthys, in Toronto, the decision to become a 'full-service' law firm was arrived at early – in the late 1940s. In that case, it was symbolized by the decision to ask the country's outstanding litigator, J.J. Robinette, to join the firm. Until the 1930s, McCarthys' strength had been in litigation, though it had been developing a corporate practice since the late nineteenth century.[125] During the 1930s, the firm had moved increasingly away from litigation as Leighton McCarthy and Salter Haydon had responded to client demand by shifting to the solicitor's side of practice. Robinette's accession to the firm, then, represented a recognition of the necessity for specialization in the postwar world.

Other aspiring giants of corporate law followed a similar pattern, if not always with the same degree of deliberation as McCarthys. In Halifax, the McInnes firm acquired two litigators in the early 1950s. The Borden & Elliot firm in Toronto diversified by the 1970s into a whole host of speciality areas, including administrative and communications law, trademark and patent law, insolvency, municipal law, and real estate. In Vancouver, Russell & DuMoulin was, by the early 1970s, divided into five departments: litigation, corporate, estates, mortgages, and labour.[126]

Departmentalization was an important step on the way to formalization (including the holding of formal partnership meetings and the signing of partnership agreements) and bureaucratization (the elaboration of mechanisms of firm governance). The pace and scope of these changes varied widely from firm to firm, but by the early 1970s certain trends were clearly visible at large firms in central Canada and the West. Some firms appear to have drifted rather painlessly into more formalized and bureaucratized practices. At Bull, Housser, as Reginald H. Roy's essay in this volume shows, the autocratic and paternalistic rule of Reginald Tupper was gradually replaced by a management system which emphasized wider participation in decision making. Curtis Cole's essay shows a similar pattern of transition in management practices at Oslers in the late 1950s and early 1960s.

At the other extreme was Borden & Elliot, where in 1961 dissatisfaction with the unwritten partnership agreement of 1956, along with an explosive growth in numbers, helped precipitate a split described by the firm historian as 'cataclysmic and bitter.' Eleven members, all but one of them from the corporate department, left to form the firm which became Smith, Lyons. In the aftermath of this exodus, more democratic methods of governance were introduced in 1963.[127] The firm thus appears to have vaulted from autocracy to democracy in a few traumatic years. Painful as the split at Borden & Elliot had been, however, it may have proven a healthy development; firms whose leaders were unshakably wedded to autocratic methods of governance suffered the 'death of a thousand cuts,' experiencing severe attrition over these years.

Bureaucratization was characteristic of the more forward-looking firms, which were small by today's standards but whose size doubled or trebled between 1945 and 1970. At many firms, those in the vanguard of the shift from an autocratic to a more democratic management style tended to be war veterans.[128] Experience in the armed forces seems to have had the effect, not of accustoming them to taking orders, but of habituating them to thinking in terms of a more bureaucratized workplace organization.

Bureaucratization typically took the form of establishing a management committee, which would gradually assume the functions formerly undertaken by a single firm leader. The management committee in turn would establish various subcommittees, including planning committees for particular purposes, and student committees. In some firms, this form of organization proved too decentralized, a situation that was rectified by the appointment of a managing partner who spent a majority of his or her working life on running the firm.

The bureaucratization of a firm was often accompanied by more efficient billing practices. Well into the 1950s, and perhaps afterwards, lawyers at some firms were slow to send out their accounts, and cash shortages periodically embarrassed even the most well-established firms.[129] It was not unheard of in the 1950s for a lawyer to fail to keep time records altogether, with the result that clients might be presented with an entirely unitemized bill for 'Counsel's Brief.'[130] An improved billing system was instituted by Bull, Housser in 1957, providing for an hourly fee scale for each lawyer. Before that time, 'the charge for service rendered depended largely on the individual lawyer who would fix the amount of the fee and send it out.'[131] At many firms, moreover, accounting machines contributed significantly to improved billing practices. Other machines which greatly enhanced office efficiency were electric typewriters and the early versions of copying machines.[132]

Hiring practices as well as firm governance and billing procedures were in a state of transition during these postwar decades. Established Canadian firms continued to recruit their lawyers from relatives of partners and clients well into the 1950s and beyond. In Toronto, it was John Godfrey who took credit for introducing in 1949 the practice of hiring on the basis of academic standing in the law schools. 'It's a wonder,' he said later, 'that it was some years (with the notable exception of the Tory firm) before other firms adopted the same policy.' By the 1960s, Torys was relying on their 'self-appointed talent scout' – future Chief Justice of the Supreme Court of Canada Bora Laskin – to recruit top students from the University of Toronto Law School, where he taught.[133] Curtis Cole's essay in this volume reveals that, at Oslers, the late 1950s was a watershed in terms of hiring. Until that date, traditional connections were key elements in the hiring process; afterwards, academic achievement became much more important.

Women generally remained shut out of corporate legal practice until the Second World War, which also brought opportunities for employment in other traditionally male-dominated workplaces.[134] In Quebec, the war brought important changes relating to women's rights, including their securing of the provincial suffrage and of the right to practise law. Constance Short joined the McMaster firm in Montreal in the 1940s and practised with them until her death in 1959.[135] Curtis Cole's essay in this volume details the early career of a woman who began practising in Ontario after the Second World War – future Supreme Court Justice Bertha Wilson. As a woman lawyer at an established Toronto firm, Wilson was a path-breaker in the late 1950s. Significantly, however, her role was limited to advising the firm's lawyers rather than dealing directly with clients. Many firms, however, continued to reject women, even in limited roles such as this; as recently as the late 1960s, Borden & Elliot in Toronto refused to consider hiring a highly qualified candidate because 'the firm did not hire women.'[136]

Members of ethnic minorities also found large firms generally reluctant to take them on. John Godfrey broke with current practices when, in 1952, his firm hired Jack Gellner, who was Jewish, and then ensured that Gellner became the first Jewish member of the prestigious National Club. The Osler firm in Toronto was more typical, hiring its first Roman Catholic in 1954, and its first Jewish lawyer nine years later.[137] Ultimately, many lawyers would come to believe that gender and ethnic barriers to élite law-firm practice must be removed in the interests of academic excellence.

In the meantime, members of visible minorities made their own opportunities, sometimes assisted by more senior lawyers. Philip Sworden's essay in this volume, on the Millar, Alexander firm, offers an excellent illustration of how minority lawyers could establish a niche for themselves in the profession. In the 1960s, John Millar founded a firm in Hamilton which eventually included a Japanese, a Black, and an aboriginal Canadian lawyer. The multiracial character of the firm proved a positive attraction to post-Second World War immigrants. As Sworden observes, an examination of Millar, Alexander shows how small firms could offer leadership to the profession more generally.

The lot of articling students during these years was often not a happy one; after many years of post-secondary education, they too often found themselves acting in menial capacities for their law firms. At the Arnoldi, Parry & Campbell firm in the 1950s, for example, students were used as messengers because they cost less; Godfrey tried put a stop to the practice after one articling student announced his intention to quit because he spent so much time on these errands. At Bull, Housser, it was the duty of articling students to shelve the books and clean the library. This lasted until one student appeared at work dressed as a cleaner, explaining that if his job was a housekeeping one he wanted to dress appropriately.[138]

Postwar affluence was reflected in a new look for law offices across the country. As firms expanded, they found their old quarters too small for comfort, and virtually every major firm in the country changed locations between 1950 and 1970. Once again, McCarthys was in the vanguard when it moved to the new Toronto-Dominion Centre in 1967 and decorated its offices in a high style, to which clients eventually became accustomed.[139] The days of heavy oak furniture, globe light fixtures hanging from the ceiling, and the omnipresent linoleum were gone forever, to be replaced by modern furniture, tasteful lighting, and plush carpeting, whose colours were a source of light-hearted contention at many firms.[140]

Such luxuries were but one sign of the effect of the postwar boom on the fortunes of law firms. Large and small, they almost all flourished. Small firms and sole practitioners prospered on real estate and other consumer-oriented transactions. Their large colleagues became giants, developing in the process the foundations of a management structure which paved the way for future expansion.

THE TURBULENT YEARS, 1973–THE PRESENT

Since 1973, Canadian law firms have found their ability to cope with change tested as never before. On the demand side, a volatile economy, economic globalization, the enhanced role of government, political uncertainty, and changes in the legal framework have helped transform the profession. On the supply side, corporate firms have expanded geometrically in response to perceived benefits of bigness (economies of scale and scope), and the logic of hiring practices. Results include the rise of the mega-firm, interprovincial and international expansion, and the bifurcation of the profession. The practice of law has been radically transformed, and the profession is still considering the nature and consequences of these changes.

The Canadian economy has been on a roller-coaster ride for the past generation. In the mid-1970s the country experienced 'stagflation,' the combination of high inflation and high unemployment which hit many industrialized nations in this period. In the recession of the early 1980s, inflation hit a high of 12 per cent (in 1981); efforts to control it produced chartered-bank interest rates usually associated with loan sharks and organized crime (over 20 per cent). By the mid-1980s, inflation was back down to a liveable 4 per cent, and the economy of central Canada made a brilliant recovery. In fact, the gross domestic product of the country during 1984–9 rose from $400 billion to nearly $700 billion.[141] Prosperity, however, was evanescent, and the 1990s brought a recession that hit central Canada severely, inviting comparisons with the Depression of the 1930s.

The resources which had historically contributed so much to Canada's economic booms encountered serious troubles in these years. In the Maritimes, the steel and coal industries of Nova Scotia essentially collapsed after 1973, and by 1982 the federal government was forced to bail out the Atlantic fisheries. Central Canada and British Columbia were hard-hit when the bottom dropped out of the market for forest products and minerals in the late 1970s.[142] The most dramatic events, however, took place in Alberta's oil patch, where the energy crisis of 1973–4 was followed by a boom which saw prices double in 1979–80 in the wake of the outbreak of war between Iran and Iraq. High prices encouraged extravagant expenditures on oil exploration, a significant factor, along with an acquisitions spree, in the collapse of Dome Petroleum in 1982. In the meantime, the federal government's National Energy Program (1980), which assumed that energy prices would spiral upward, was introduced at the precise moment when world prices began to plummet, with serious consequences for the oil producers of Alberta.[143]

The financial-services sector was in a state of seemingly constant flux. The 1967 Bank Act forced the separation of banks and trust companies, and in its aftermath a host of entrepreneurs scrambled to secure control of the trusts. One of the most celebrated episodes was Robert Campeau's abortive effort to take over Royal Trust, which ultimately fell to the Toronto Bronfmans' Edper organization.[144] Through the 1970s, the banks aggressively pursued business by offering new deposit instruments, providing innovative kinds of loans, expanding their credit-card networks, and elaborating their merchant banking and international activities. In the 1980s, changes to banking legislation dismantled the barriers between the 'four pillars' of the Canadian financial system – banks, trust companies, investment houses, and insurance companies. The large chartered banks swiftly seized control of trust companies and securities dealers, and began selling insurance. In the meantime, two banks based in western Canada, the Canadian Commercial Bank and the Northland Bank, had collapsed in 1985 and had to be bailed out by the federal government.[145] The recession of the 1990s spelled disaster for many of the country's trust companies, which had overextended themselves in real estate, and went down with the crash in that market.

These years also saw the emergence of a series of massive business empires, including that of Ken Thomson, son of newspaper baron Roy Thomson. In a celebrated business epic of the late 1970s, dubbed 'Store Wars' by the press, the Hudson's Bay department stores took over Simpson's, only to be swallowed in turn by the Thomson organization. Another newspaper baron, Conrad Black, had seized control of Argus in the late 1970s, and presided over the collapse of Massey–Harris in the early 1980s; Black found his true calling managing his newspaper empire and pursuing his social ambitions in London, England. Robert Campeau, who had risen from humble beginnings as a Franco-Ontarian contractor, made his grab for fame when he took over the Allied Department Stores and then used Allied to take over the Federated Department Stores in 1988 in one of the most celebrated junk-bond financings of the decade. The Reichmanns, Jewish immigrants from Hungary by way of Morocco, built a real estate conglomerate in three countries and diversified into oil, distilleries, and forest products before falling victim to the recession of the early 1990s. The Toronto Bronfmans' Edper group seized control of Brascan (the old Brazilian Traction) in 1979, and went on a binge of accumulation which included forest products, breweries, insurance, a trust company, and more than one hundred other businesses. In the West, these years are associated with the empires of Dr Charles Allard, the Ghermezian brothers, Peter Pocklington (Edmonton), Nelson Skalbania (Vancouver), and the Belzburgs (Calgary and Vancouver).[146]

'Globalization' was the buzz-word of the early 1990s, but in fact the process of integrating national markets into larger trading areas was well under way before Canada and the United States ratified their free-trade agreement in 1988.[147] Falls in international trade barriers since the 1940s, and increases in international capital flows since the early 1970s, were signposts on the way to globalization. Among its effects have been the restructuring of North American industry, most evident in the wave of mergers and acquisitions which swept the continent in the 1980s. In Canada, the number of these transactions occurring annually went from a low of about four hundred in the 1981 recession to more than a thousand at its peak in 1989. Lawyers have benefited from increased economic activity, the complications of conducting business across jurisdictional boundaries, and the volume and complexity of merger-and-acquisition activity.[148]

Governmental intervention in the economy has also been productive of much legal work, directly and indirectly. The establishment in 1973 of the Foreign Investment Review Board to monitor foreign investment in Canada brought lawyers to Ottawa in droves. The Wage and Price Controls of 1975–8 provoked constitutional challenges and labour disputes. Government bail-outs of private-sector concerns such as Massey-Harris, Dome Petroleum, and the aircraft industry required legal advice of byzantine complexity.[149] Privatization of Crown corporations in the 1980s had the same effect. Businesses may lament the effects of the Canadian Charter of Rights and Freedoms of 1982, but no one denies that it has been a bonanza for lawyers, in part because of the amount of litigation generated. Free trade with the United States, which went into effect in 1989, created numerous opportunities for business expansion guided by legal advice. Even the less hopeful consequences of free trade, including sell-offs of vacated plants, brought business to lawyers. Prime Minister Mulroney's other major economic legacy to Canada, the wildly unpopular Goods and Services Tax (1991), opened a new chapter in tax regulation. For lawyers outside the corporate and commercial fields, changes in family law in the 1980s contributed to an upsurge in business.

Political uncertainty had the effect, not so much of creating new business, but of helping to shift its location. The most obvious source of political disquiet was the nationalist movement in Quebec, whose growing strength during the 1960s culminated in the election of a separatist government there in 1976. This development accelerated business departures from Montreal, once the financial capital of the country, in favour of Toronto, which now became Canada's undisputed business centre. Though the separatist Parti Québécois suffered electoral defeat in the mid-1980s, uncertainty continued because of a series of unsuccessful efforts to achieve accommodation between French and English. These included the Constitution Act of 1982, the Meech Lake Accord of 1987, and the Charlottetown Accord of 1991. Together with the Quebec referendum battle of October 1995, these developments had continuing negative side-effects on the economy of Quebec.[150]

Ronald J. Daniels has identified 'the legalization of corporate activity' as a key factor on the demand side of law-firm growth in the years since 1970. One dimension of this was the increase in private-sector litigiousness, which went beyond a new consumer willingness to take on corporate giants; it involved a significant increase in litigation in commercial and contract law undertaken by businesses themselves. The second aspect of legalization of corporate activity is a consequence of the dramatic rise of in-house counsel in Canada, particularly since 1980; the numbers of corporate counsel employed by fifty-six corporations rose by more than 86 per cent during the 1980s. In-house lawyers have increased the amount of legal work by sensitizing senior management to legal issues. The increase of in-house counsel means not only that more legal work can be done within a corporation's own legal department, but also that the market for legal services has become more volatile.[151]

Economic, business, and political factors together with perceived client demand for 'full-service' law, then, were among the factors which fundamentally transformed the practice of law in Canada during the 1970s, and especially the 1980s.[152] One result was the ballooning of corporate law firms across the country. In fact, the age of the 'giant' law firm and that of the mega-firm essentially arrived in Canada simultaneously. Between 1971 and 1981, five firms (four of them in Toronto) expanded from approximately fifty to about a hundred lawyers. During the same period, at least ten firms, most of them in the prosperous provinces of Alberta and British Columbia, reached giant-firm status with approximately fifty lawyers. During the 1980s, moreover, there was a kind of explosion in size in Toronto firms, the five largest ones reaching totals of between 154 and 225 lawyers. The Osler, Hoskin firm in Toronto, for example, expanded by 235 per cent between 1981 and 1989. Outside of Toronto, the largest firm became Ogilvy Renault in Montreal, which went from from 95 to 142 lawyers between 1981 and 1989. Indeed, by the end of the 1980s, more than nineteen law firms each employed more than one hundred lawyers.[153] The rise of these legal behemoths has contributed to an increasing bifurcation of the profession, as the mega-firms increasingly monopolize corporate and commercial law, leaving individual clients largely to the smaller firms and sole practitioners.[154]

The expansion of law firms in the United States during the 1970s and

1980s drew attention to what Marc Galanter and Thomas Palay called 'the promotion-to-partnership tournament' – essentially the hiring practices of American corporate law firms.[155] Simply put, Galanter and Palay argue that law firms essentially make their money by charging significantly more for the labour of employed lawyers than they pay out in salaries to these associates. From the viewpoint of the associates, it is the possibility of promotion to partnership which makes this genteel form of exploitation endurable, the prospect of the bonanza of a partner's income preventing them from jumping ship to seek employment elsewhere. In order to keep their associates, therefore, law firms must, over time, elevate a constant percentage to partnership, as recurrent proof that the associates' loyalty and hard work have a good chance of winning the ultimate reward. The result has been geometric, not linear, growth in law-firm numbers.[156] Other internal factors behind the emergence of the mega-firm include economies of scale (sharing the costs of expensive equipment); economies of scope (reduction in costs to clients provided by full-service firm); the sharing of risks (by diversification in complementary areas); and the provision of better-quality legal services because of an extraordinarily high degree of specialization. [157]

This supply-side analysis of law-firm growth is of limited value in illuminating the development of law firms in Canada for a number of reasons. First, it is particularly directed towards explaining a phenomenon which is relatively recent in this country.[158] Second, indications are that Canadian mega-firms do not achieve the level of associate-to-partner ratios which are characteristic of this method of law-firm expansion.[159] John Hagan and Fiona Kay's essay in this volume explores a number of other reasons why the promotion-to-partnership theory is an inadequate explanation of law-firm growth in Canada.

A second notable feature of the 1980s was geographic expansion, as manifested in affiliations among firms in different Canadian cities and jurisdictions, and in the opening of foreign offices. Between 1981 and October 1990, there were thirty regional and national mergers and affiliations across the country. To some degree, these arrangements were useful in financing foreign offices, which were both expensive to open and unproven as profit centres. Between 1985 and 1990, fourteen Canadian firms opened eighteen foreign offices, more than double the number opened in the previous twenty years.[160] While many lawyers have expressed serious doubts about these foreign ventures, recent reports indicate that 'years of hard work in centres like Moscow, Paris and Hong Kong are beginning to pay dividends.'[161]

The effect of these developments, along with technological change (the fax machine, personal computers, and centralized computerized billings) has been to further transform the legal workplace, promoting bureaucratic growth and disrupting traditional hiring practices. These changes have provoked anxieties among lawyers and their critics. Concerns centre on commercialization, professionalism, and accountability in this brave new legal world.

The Vancouver firm of Russell & DuMoulin provides what is probably a typical example of the enhanced bureaucratization of the 1980s, when the firm more than trebled in size, from 51 to 161 lawyers. In 1982 the firm first took the step of formally appointing a managing partner, Leopold Amighetti. Amighetti in turn brought in an American management consultant to reorganize the firm. The result was the establishment in 1984 of a strategic-planning committee and the preparation of a 'firm "mission statement" intended to replace the perception that the firm operated as a collection of single practitioners.' In the mid-1980s, 'a host of new committees [were] established in an attempt to both streamline management decisions and involve more partners in the process.' Further changes in management structure followed in the late 1980s, producing a 'quasi-corporate management structure,' and an elaborate division of management functions within the firm's various departments.[162]

The impact of law-firm growth in the 1980s was nowhere more obvious than in the hiring of new lawyers. As firms expanded and bureaucratized, many instituted 'anti-nepotism' rules, barring the children of partners from joining the firms. As law schools admitted increasing numbers of women and members of ethnic minorities, corporate law firms found themselves hiring more of both, particularly the former.[163] This was in part a result of the search for academic excellence. The new hiring practices also reflected, somewhat belatedly, the growing disapproval in society more generally of discrimination on the basis of race and gender. Ironically, as John Hagan and Fiona Kay's essay on the legal profession in Ontario indicates, changes in law-firm structure appear to be narrowing opportunities for women's advancement in the law at the very time when traditional barriers to entry have fallen. Customary methods of hiring from within, meanwhile, have in recent years been supplemented by lateral hiring ('cherry-picking') and mergers.[164] All of these developments, taken together, have radically altered the traditional bases of law-firm culture which have proven such a useful cement in the profession.[165]

Bureaucratization and more meritocratic hiring practices may produce greater efficiency within law firms, but the growth of the mega-firm has

given rise to a series of other problems, including conflicts, incompatibility of firm cultures, a breakdown of communication with the firm, and
alienation among articling students and secretaries.[166] The press has
recently reported several instances of senior corporate lawyers leaving
the mega-firms to practise in new 'boutique' firms, which they themselves control.[167] (Historically, of course, many lawyers at the outset of
their careers determined that they preferred the independence of the
small firm to the constraints of big corporate practices.)

Concerns about the commercialization of law practice have been
voiced since the turn of the century, but as the number of hours billed
annually came to exceed 2,000 in Toronto in the 1980s, corporate lawyers
saw opportunities to assume community leadership roles, or indeed a life
outside practice, fading.[168] Outsiders wondered what incentives could
keep legal noses to the grindstone to this extent: the excitement of the
work, the opportunity to be creative, and the chance to make a great deal
of money are among the most common explanations.

Those who accept these challenges, however, pay a price in reduced
economic opportunities outside the law. In recent years, the more
demanding character of legal work, together with concerns about politicians' conflicts of interest, mean that the days when a lawyer in corporate
practice can simultaneously undertake a political career and a host of
entrepreneurial activities are long since over, certainly in the big firms.[169]
Law practice, however, can still serve as a springboard for a full-time
career in business or politics, as the examples of Purdy Crawford
(Imasco), Trevor Eyton (Brascan), and Jean Chrétien (prime minister)
indicate. Moreover, practising lawyers continue to be active in the back-
rooms of politics as fund-raisers and party organizers, and in business as
advisers and counsellors. In effect, links between law firms, on the one
hand, and politics or business, on the other, continue to exist, though in a
somewhat different form than in previous eras.

Closely related to concerns about commercialism were fears that, in the
new and ferociously competitive legal climate of the 1980s and 1990s, the
independence of lawyers from their clients was fast eroding. The Ontario
Securities Commission raised legal hackles when its chair, Robert J.
Wright, suggested in 1991 that clients seemed less responsive than in the
past to lawyers' reservations about a proposed course of action. 'The
more usual approach now,' Wright argued, 'is for the client to see the
lawyer as technician who is to carry out instructions.'[170] The tendency of
clients to provide work on a transaction-by-transaction basis is certainly
said by American authorities to have had the effect of making lawyers

more zealous advocates than ever before on behalf of clients from whom they hope for future business.[171]

It is far from clear, however, that professional autonomy was ever a notable feature of the practice of corporate law.[172] The major evidence for it appears to be a frequently cited statement by turn-of-the-century American lawyer Elihu Root: 'about half the practice of a decent lawyer consists in telling would-be clients that they are damned fools and should stop.'[173] Anecdotal evidence from Canadian law-firm histories, however, fails to demonstrate a similar insouciance towards client schemes.[174] Trevor Eyton, formerly a lawyer at Toronto's Tory law firm, is on record as saying: 'If I don't like a client, I'll send him to someone else in the firm – or more likely out of the firm.'[175] This is a very limited form of professional autonomy: Clients are not deterred, just referred. A lawyer who says no too often, however, will soon find that he or she has no clients.

The rise of the mega-firm has also raised new concerns about professional discipline. John Hagan has noted that American studies have shown that only about 2 per cent of lawyers known to have committed breaches of professional discipline have ever been punished with professional sanctions; he suggests that there is no reason to believe that this figure is any different for Canada.[176] Recently, concern in Ontario has centred on effective means of policing the big firms, not just the small-firm lawyers who have historically been the target of Law Society scrutiny; this issue assumed immediate salience in the early 1990s in the wake of the so-called Pilzmaker Affair involving members of the blue-chip firm Lang Michener.[177]

CONCLUSION

This examination of the history of Canadian law firms reveals evidence of both change and continuity. The most obvious change has been the extraordinary development since the turn of the century of law firms specializing in corporate and commercial law. In 1900, business interests took their legal problems to 'large' firms of five or more lawyers. By the interwar years, corporate firms of twenty or more lawyers had emerged. These, in turn, were succeeded by the 'giant' firms and the 'mega-firms' of the 1970s and 1980s.

The pattern of Canadian law-firm development has been distinctive in North America. Law firms in Canada have altered in size and function largely because of changes in the Canadian economy, which developed at its own pace and in ways different from the American economy. As a result, the timing of the appearance of new law-firm structures in Canada has been different from that south of the border. For example, whereas the Americans produced giant firms by the 1950s, their Canadian counterparts appeared only shortly before the mega-firms of the 1980s. Because major changes in size have profound consequences for the character of law-firm organization and culture, these aspects of Canadian corporate law firms contributed to their distinctive character. It is clear, for example, that the pace of change among corporate law firms in Canada has been much swifter during the past generation in Canada than in the United States. If the timing of organizational evolution has been different, however, the patterns of development over the past twenty years reveal a similarity between the Canadian and the American forms of law-firm organization among the largest firms. To some extent, this is a product of deliberate imitation on the part of Canadians.

The most evident aspect of continuity in Canadian law-firm history is the survival of the small firm of one or two lawyers. Like their nineteenth-century predecessors, lawyers at such firms today spend much of their time servicing the legal requirements of ordinary life, including real estate transactions, wills, personal-injury cases, and minor commercial matters. A major change for small firms is that their lawyers no longer, as they did in the nineteenth century, handle the work of major business concerns.

Law-firm culture has also exhibited a high degree of continuity, at least until the post-Second World War period. For more than a century after 1820s, lawyers clung to customary ways of doing business. Law-firm culture remained largely autocratic, patriarchal, somewhat ethnically exclusive, and resistant to the introduction of new technology. In the past two generations, economic and social changes have seriously undermined the bases of this culture, though elements of it survive to this day. The era of autocracy in firm governance may be over, and law-firm operations may be fully computerized; debate continues, however, within law firms and in the profession, on issues relating to gender, race, and class representation.

NOTES

For their helpful comments on this introduction. I would like to thank Brian Young, Christopher Moore, Philip Girard, Brian Bucknall, T.D. Regehr, Philip Sworden, Barry Cahill, Jamie Benidickson, Curtis Cole, Jim Phillips, and C. Ian Kyer.

1 The connection between top Canadian politicians and the country's larger law firms has been strong indeed. Eight of the nine Canadian prime ministers since the Second World War (Louis St Laurent, John Diefenbaker, Pierre Elliott Trudeau, Joe Clark, John Turner, Brian Mulroney, Kim Campbell, and Jean Chrétien) have been lawyers. The sole exception was Lester Pearson. Of the eight, all but Diefenbaker, Clark, and Campbell have at some time been members of leading Canadian law firms.

2 There are few firm histories in general circulation in Canada. An exception is Curtis Cole, *Osler, Hoskin & Harcourt: Portrait of a Partnership* (Toronto: McGraw-Hill Ryerson 1995). In addition, Carol Wilton, ed., *Essays in the History of Canadian Law*, vol. 4: *Beyond the Law: Lawyers and Business in Canada, 1830 to 1930* (Toronto: The Osgoode Society 1990) contains several very useful essays. Among the very best firm histories are two American ones, Kenneth J. Lipartito and Joseph A. Pratt, *Baker & Botts in the Development of Modern Houston* (Austin: University of Texas Press 1991), and Robert T. Swaine, *The Cravath Firm and Its Predecessors*, 2 vols. (New York: Ad Press 1946 and 1948).

3 Scholars have recently turned their attention to the importance of this phenomenon to the success of contemporary law firms: See Ronald J. Daniels, 'The Law Firm as an Efficient Community,' *McGill Law Journal* 37 (1992), 801–34.

4 The sources on pre-Confederation lawyers in British North America are extensive. A good place to start is the publications of the Osgoode Society, listed at the end of this volume.

5 With regard to state intervention, Philip Girard rightly observes an expansion of activity in the mid-nineteenth century in areas including 'education, railway-building, [and] resource development.' While this activity represented a considerable increase over previous state involvement, it pales by comparison with the interventionist state of the post-Second World War era. See Philip Girard, 'The Maritime Provinces, 1850–1939: Lawyers and Legal Institutions,' *Manitoba Law Journal/Journal de Droit Manitobain* 23 (1995), 379–405; R.C.B. Risk, 'The Law and the Economy in Mid-Nineteenth-Century Ontario: A Perspective,' in David H. Flaherty, ed., *Essays in the History of Canadian Law*, vol. 1 (Toronto: The Osgoode Society 1981), 102; John D. Blackwell, 'William Hume Blake and the Judicature Acts of 1849: The Process of Legal Reform at Mid-Century in Upper Canada,' in ibid., 132–74; G. Blaine Baker, 'Law Practice and Statecraft in Mid-Nineteenth-Century Montreal: The Torrance–Morris Firm, 1848 to 1868,' in Wilton, ed., *Beyond the Law*, 45–91.

6 See generally John McCallum, *Unequal Beginnings: Agriculture and Economic Development in Quebec and Ontario until 1870* (Toronto: University of Toronto Press 1980); Robert Armstrong, *Structure and Change: An Economic History of*

Quebec (Toronto: Gage 1984), 110–71; Douglas McCalla, *Planting the Province: The Economic History of Upper Canada, 1784–1870* (Toronto: University of Toronto Press 1993), 45–141; E.P. Neufeld, *The Financial System of Canada: Its Growth and Development* (Toronto: Macmillan of Canada 1972), 75–81; Michael Bliss, *Northern Enterprise: Five Centuries of Canadian Business* (Toronto: McClelland and Stewart 1987), 129–60; Graeme Wynn, *Timber Colony: A Historical Geography of Early Nineteenth-Century New Brunswick* (Toronto: University of Toronto Press 1981); E.R. Forbes and D.A. Muise, eds., *The Atlantic Provinces in Confederation* (Toronto: University of Toronto Press 1993); P.A. Buckner and J.G. Reid, eds., *The Atlantic Region in Confederation* (Toronto: University of Toronto Press 1994).

7 W.T. Easterbrook and Hugh G.J. Aitken, *Canadian Economic History* (Toronto: Macmillan of Canada 1956; rpt 1975), 293–319; Douglas McCalla, 'Railways and the Development of Canada West, 1850–1870,' in Allan Greer and Ian Radforth, eds., *Colonial Leviathan: State Formation in Mid-Nineteenth-Century Canada* (Toronto: University of Toronto Press 1992), 192–229; Paul Craven and Tom Traves, 'Canadian Railways as Manufacturers, 1850–1880,' Canadian Historical Association, *Historical Papers* (1983), 254–81; Armstrong, *Structure and Change*, 189–203

8 Risk, 'The Law and the Economy,' 92

9 R.D. Gidney and W.P.J. Millar, *Professional Gentlemen: The Professions in Nineteenth-Century Ontario* (Toronto: University of Toronto Press 1994), 37

10 Baker, 'The Torrance–Morris Firm'

11 Earl Kimmel, 'The Notarial System and Its Impact in Canadian Law,' in Raymond A. Landry and Ernest Caparros, eds., *Essays on the Civil Codes of Quebec and St. Lucia* (Ottawa: University of Ottawa Press 1984), 110–15; Gidney and Millar, *Professional Gentlemen*, 37

12 Ronald J. Daniels, 'Growing Pains: The Why and How of Law Firm Expansion,' *University of Toronto Law Journal* 43 (1993), 170–2; for developments in the role of corporate counsel in the 1990s see Michael Fitz-James, 'Corporate Lawyers Becoming Rare,' *Financial Post*, 24 October 1995.

13 Elizabeth Bloomfield, 'Lawyers as Members of Urban Business Elites in Southern Ontario, 1860 to 1920,' in Wilton, ed., *Beyond the Law*, 121

14 Baker, 'The Torrance–Morris Firm,' 57–8

15 Gidney and Millar, *Professional Gentlemen*, 73–84; D.G. Bell, 'Paths to the Law in the Maritimes, 1810–1825: The Bliss Brothers and Their Circle,' *Nova Scotia Historical Review* 8 (1988), 6–39. See also G. Blaine Baker, 'Legal Education in Upper Canada, 1785–1889: The Law Society as Educator,' in David H. Flaherty, ed., *Essays in the History of Canadian Law*, vol. 2 (Toronto: The Osgoode Society 1983), 49–142.

16 Gidney and Millar, *Professional Gentlemen*, 11. Adherence to this code did not necessarily preclude the occasional resort to political violence. Most of the rioters in the celebrated Types Riot case of 1826 involving the destruction of William Lyon Mackenzie's press in York (Toronto), for example, were lawyers or law students. They were neither prosecuted in the criminal courts nor reprimanded by the attorney general. See Carol Wilton, '"Lawless Law": Conservative Political Violence in Upper Canada, 1818–41,' *Law and History Review* 13 (Spring 1995), 111–36, for a fuller discussion of this question.

17 See, for example, Robert L. Fraser, ed., *Provincial Justice: Upper Canadian Legal Portraits* (Toronto: The Osgoode Society 1992), 108; and Patrick Brode, *Sir John Beverley Robinson: Bone and Sinew of the Compact* (Toronto: The Osgoode Society 1984), 27. See also Bell, 'Paths to the Law,' 39; D.G. Bell, 'Judicial Crisis in Post-Confederation New Brunswick,' in Dale Gibson and W. Wesley Pue, eds., *Glimpses of Canadian Legal History* (Winnipeg: Legal Research Institute of the University of Manitoba 1991), 191; Gidney and Millar, *Professional Gentlemen*, 139.

18 For biographies of W.W. and Robert Baldwin, along with many other Upper Canadian lawyers, see Fraser, ed., *Provincial Justice*.

19 Doug Mitchell and Judy Slinn, *The History of McMaster Meighen* (Montreal: McMaster Meighen 1989), 13

20 On MacNab, see Peter Baskerville, 'Sir Allan Napier MacNab,' *Dictionary of Canadian Biography*, vol. 9 (Toronto: University of Toronto Press 1976), 519–27; and Donald R. Beer, *Sir Allan Napier MacNab* (Hamilton: Dictionary of Hamilton Biography 1984).

21 Fraser, ed., *Provincial Justice*, 256

22 Baker, 'The Torrance–Morris Firm,' 53.

23 Ibid., 47ff. For a discussion of opportunities for social mobility in the law in Upper Canada see Baker, 'Legal Education in Upper Canada,' 78, and Gidney and Millar, *Professional Gentlemen*, 73–5, 82–4.

24 Mary Larratt Smith, *Young Mr Smith in Upper Canada* (Toronto: University of Toronto Press 1980), 17

25 As a student, Larratt Smith seems to have found ample time to go shooting, sing in the church choir, and attend the theatre: ibid., 17–40. See also Brian D. Bucknall, Thomas C.H. Baldwin, and J. David Lakin, 'Pedants, Practitioners and Prophets: Legal Education at Osgoode Hall to 1957,' *Osgoode Hall Law Journal* 6 (1968), 147–8; Gidney and Millar, *Professional Gentlemen*, 167.

26 Stanley E. Edwards, *Fraser & Beatty: The First 150 Years* (Toronto: Fraser & Beatty Desktop Publishing 1989), 4

27 For a general introduction to these years see P.B. Waite, *Canada, 1874–1896: Arduous Destiny* (Toronto: McClelland and Stewart 1971), and Robert Craig

Brown and Ramsay Cook, *Canada, 1896–1921: A Nation Transformed* (Toronto: McClelland and Stewart 1974).

28 Louis A. Knafla, 'Richard 'Bonfire' Bennett: The Legal Practice of a Prairie Corporate Lawyer, 1898 to 1913,' in Wilton, ed., *Beyond the Law*, 331

29 Curtis Cole, 'McCarthy, Osler, Hoskin, and Creelman, 1882 to 1902: Establishing a Reputation, Building a Practice,' in Wilton, ed., *Beyond the Law*, 155

30 Mitchell and Slinn, *McMaster Meighen*, 51–2

31 Duncan McDowall, *The Light: Brazilian Traction, Light and Power Company Limited, 1899–1945* (Toronto: University of Toronto Press 1988), 182–3 indicates that Lash was also involved in incorporating land companies for Mackenzie and Mann.

32 See T.D. Regehr, *The Canadian Northern Railway: Pioneer Road of the Northern Prairies, 1895–1918* (Toronto: Macmillan of Canada 1976).

33 McDowall, *The Light*, 117

34 Wilton, 'Introduction,' in Wilton, ed., *Beyond the Law*, 17–18; Gregory P. Marchildon, 'International Corporate Law from a Maritime Base: The Halifax Firm of Harris, Henry, and Cahan,' in ibid., 201–34

35 Christine Mullins and Arthur E. Harvey, *Russell & DuMoulin: The First Century, 1889–1989* (n.p., *circa* 1989), 24–7

36 Bliss, *Northern Enterprise*, 338; Marchildon, 'International Corporate Law,' 211–25; Mitchell and Slinn, *McMaster Meighen*, 55

37 D.H. Tees, *Chronicles of Ogilvy, Renault, 1879–1979* (Montreal: Ogilvy Renault 1979), 56–7

38 John D. Honsberger, 'E.E.A. DuVernet, KC: Lawyer, Capitalist, 1866 to 1915,' in Wilton, ed., *Beyond the Law*, 181–2; Cole, 'McCarthy, Osler, Hoskin, and Creelman,' 158; Richard A. Willie, '"It Is Every Man for Himself": Winnipeg Lawyers and the Law Business, 1870 to 1903,' in ibid., 278–83; James H. Gunn, 'The Lawyer as Entrepreneur: Robert Home Smith in Early-Twentieth-Century Toronto,' in ibid., 239; Reginald H. Roy, 'Bull, Housser and Tupper: A Century of Service' (typescript *circa* 1990), 12; Mullins and Harvey, *Russell & DuMoulin*, 27, 40

39 Philip Girard has noted that the corporate lawyer assumed a key ideological role in the profession during the period 1890–1910: See Girard, 'The Maritime Provinces.'

40 *Canadian Law List*, 1912

41 Wayne K. Hobson, 'Symbol of the New Profession: Emergence of the Large Law Firm, 1870–1915,' in Gerard W. Gawalt, ed., *The New High Priests: Lawyers in Post–Civil War America* (Westport, CT: Greenwood Press 1984), 6

42 This use of the term 'law factory' differs from current use in Ontario, where it refers to a small firm doing a lot of routine and similar files, such as

conveyances, at a cut rate. (I am grateful to Brian Bucknall for this information.)

43 Hobson, 'Symbol of the New Profession.' Philip Girard reports (in a private communication) an important organizational development in Halifax law firms of more than two lawyers in the 1880s: the emergence of the distinction between partners and salaried associates.

44 Willie, 'Every Man for Himself,' 276, 285; Honsberger, 'E.E.A. DuVernet,' 182

45 Bloomfield, 'Lawyers as Members of Urban Business Elites in Southern Ontario, 1860 to 1920,' 119–20

46 Willie, 'Every Man for Himself,' 267, 271

47 Girard, 'The Maritime Provinces'

48 John Honsberger, 'Raymond and Honsberger: A History of It and Its Predecessor Firms' (manuscript 1989), 34. Even Beatty Blackstock, however, contained lawyers of diverse religious backgrounds; see note 51.

49 I am grateful to Ted Regehr for the information about Blakes.

50 The most prominent was the pairing of Roman Catholic John Thompson with Baptist Wallace Graham: P.B. Waite, *The Man from Halifax: Sir John Thompson, Prime Minister* (Toronto: University of Toronto Press 1985), 88. One's religious affiliation might affect one's client base. When Thompson was considering converting from Protestantism to Roman Catholicism in his twenties, he was concerned that his Protestant clients would desert him: ibid., 28

51 One of these firms was Beatty Blackstock, where Lionel Davis, an early Jewish lawyer, practised. Admittedly, the few Jewish lawyers in Toronto at this time were both Canadian-born and highly educated. I am grateful to Christopher Moore, author of the *History of the Law Society of Upper Canada* (forthcoming 1997), for sharing this result of his research.

52 Constance Backhouse, '"To Open the Way for Others of My Sex": Clara Brett Martin's Career as Canada's First Woman Lawyer,' *Canadian Journal of Women and the Law* 1 (1985), 1–41; Constance Backhouse, *Petticoats & Prejudice: Women and Law in Nineteenth-Century Canada* (Toronto: The Osgoode Society 1991), 294, 300–9; Mullins and Harvey, *Russell & DuMoulin*, 34–6; Lois K. Yorke, 'Mabel Penery French (1881–1955): A Life Re-Created,' *University of New Brunswick Law Journal* 42 (1993), 2–49; Joan Brockman, 'Exclusionary Tactics: The History of Women and Visible Minorities in the Legal Profession in British Columbia,' in Hamar Foster and John McLaren, eds., *Essays in the History of Canadian Law*, vol. 6: *British Columbia and the Yukon* (Toronto: The Osgoode Society 1995), 508–19; John Hagan, 'Transitions in the Legal Profession,' *Law Society of Upper Canada Gazette* 27 (June 1993), 94

53 See, for example, Barry Cahill, 'The "Colored Barrister": The Short Life and

Tragic Death of James Robinson Johnston, 1876–1915,' *Dalhousie Law Journal* 15 (Fall 1992), 336–79.

54 I am grateful to Philip Girard for pointing this out.

55 Honsberger, 'E.E.A. DuVernet,' 182–3

56 Ibid., 195

57 See Wilton, 'Introduction,' in Wilton, ed., *Beyond the Law*, 21–2, for an elaboration of these themes.

58 See also Cole, 'McCarthy, Osler, Hoskin and Creelman,' 157

59 Mitchell and Slinn, *McMaster Meighen*, 61–2; Franklin O. Leger, QC, *Palmer O'Connell Leger Roderick Glennie Barristers & Solicitors: One Hundred Years in the Practice of Law, 1888–1988: Being a Brief History of a Saint John, N.B. Law Firm* (Saint John 1988), 40, 55. Many lawyers who remained at home took an active part in the domestic war effort. See, for example, Lee Gibson, *A Proud Heritage: The First Hundred Years of Aikins, MacAulay and Thorvaldson* (privately printed 1993), 79–80. For the war record of one firm, see T.D. Regehr's essay in this volume.

60 Honsberger, 'Raymond and Honsberger,' 190

61 Bliss, *Northern Enterprise*, 381

62 Ibid., 414–24; James H. Gray, *The Winter Years: The Depression on the Prairies* (Toronto: Macmillan of Canada 1966), 105–18. The Maritimes suffered as intensely during the 1920s as in the following decade. For a more extended discussion of Canadian law firms during the 1920s and 1930s see Carol Wilton, 'Canadian Law Firms in Troubled Times: The Interwar Years 1919–39,' *Law Society of Upper Canada Gazette* 29 (December 1995), 232–51.

63 Harry Fleming, *McInnes Cooper & Robertson – A Century Plus* (1989), 43, 48–9

64 This firm, now known Stewart McKelvey Stirling Scales, is currently the largest law firm east of Montreal.

65 For the early history of the firm see Marchildon, 'International Corporate Law.'

66 Cole, *Osler, Hoskin*, 65–9

67 Ibid., 71–88. The following decade also produced notable legal scandals, including the conviction of prominent Winnipeg lawyer John A. Machray for fraud, and the 'Beauharnois Affair.' On Machray see Gibson, *Proud Heritage* 113, and David Williams, *Just Lawyers: Seven Portraits* (Toronto: The Osgoode Society 1995), 144–6. On Beauharnois and lawyers see T.D. Regehr, '"High-Powered Lawyers, Veteran Lobbyists, Cunning Propagandists": Canadian Lawyers and the Beauharnois Scandal,' in Wilton, ed., *Beyond the Law*, 403–24.

68 Gordon McMillan, 'McMillan, Binch: A History, 1903–1976' (typescript n.d.), 7–8

69 Osgoode Society, Oral History Interviews (hereinafter OSOHI): Stuart Douglas Thom, 1981–2, 81–2

70 Mullins and Harvey, *Russell & DuMoulin*, 55–6

71 Roy, 'Bull, Housser and Tupper,' 50–3

72 OSOHI: Senator John Godfrey, 1988, 68

73 Law Society of British Columbia, British Columbia Legal History Collection Project, Aural History Program (hereinafter BCAHP): A.B. Robertson, 1980, 33–9

74 OSOHI: Nathan Strauss, 1986, 15

75 OSOHI: George Johnston, 1982–3, 49, 58

76 Dennis Gruending, *Emmett Hall: Establishment Radical* (Toronto: Macmillan of Canada 1985), 22

77 Fleming, *McInnes Cooper*, 50; Mullins and Harvey, *Russell & DuMoulin*, 62

78 Allan Graydon, 'Some Reminiscences of Blakes' (typescript *circa* 1970), 52

79 Cole, *Osler, Hoskin*, 89–90

80 Fleming, *McInnes Cooper*, 50

81 Mitchell and Slinn, *McMaster Meighen*, 72; 'Diary of an Articling Student, 1930–1,' in possession of author

82 Law Society of Upper Canada, 'Struck off the Rolls Since 1st January, 1920.' I would like to thank Susan Binnie, Research Coordinator at the Law Society of Upper Canada, for these figures.

83 John D. Honsberger, *The County of York Law Association: A History of the First Hundred Years, 1885–1985* (Toronto: The County of York Law Association 1989), 80

84 Mitchell and Slinn, *McMaster Meighen*, 73

85 Valerie Schatzker, *Borden & Elliot: The First Fifty Years, 1936–1986* (Toronto: Borden & Elliot 1986), 11

86 A certain feistiness was common to successful litigators of the 1930s and 1940s, including W.N. Tilley, B.B. Shapiro, David Edson Haines, Isidore Levinter, and Donald Bell. For Tilley's style as a litigator see OSOHI: John Arnup, 1982–3, 94, and John J. Robinette, 1987, 143–4. See also Dave Walker, *Fun Along the Way: Memoirs of Dave Walker* (Toronto: Robertson Press 1989).

87 BCAHP: Oscar F. Lundell, 1980, 24–5

88 T.D. Regehr has observed, however, that railway regulation was well developed by this period. (Private communication).

89 *Canadian Law List*, 1918–20, 1930, 1940

90 McMillan 'McMillan, Binch,' 14

91 Graydon, 'Blakes,' 36

92 It has been suggested that aspiring Jewish lawyers in Ontario during the interwar years faced increasing difficulties in establishing themselves in the law.

Unlike the Jewish candidates for entry into the profession at the turn of the century, the new cohort encountered obstacles related to their working-class and Yiddish-speaking backgrounds. I am grateful to Christopher Moore for pointing this out.

93 Brockman, 'Exclusionary Tactics,' 533. A good example is Caroline (Carol) McInnes, the daughter of the leading lawyer at the McInnes firm in Halifax. After graduation from Dalhousie Law School in 1919, she joined the family firm. Significantly, though she practised as a solicitor with the firm for twenty years, she was 'never paid by the firm or included on the letterhead': Fleming, *McInnes Cooper*, 44.

94 OSOHI: John Arnup, 129. See also the comments of the Honourable Walter Stewart Owen in the essay in this volume by John Hagan and Fiona Kay.

95 Schatzker, *Borden & Elliot*, 15

96 Graydon, 'Blakes,' 24. A letter press was a device for copying correspondence that used sheets of damp tissue which were pressed down on the original letter, leaving an impression in ink: See Michael Birks, *Gentlemen of the Law* (London: Stevens & Sons 1960), 247.

97 Brian D. Bucknall, '"My Dear Osler", "My Dear Boland": Chronicles of an Early Real Estate Flip,' *Law Society of Upper Canada Gazette* 24 (1990), 331–5, shows Toronto lawyers in 1909 using a combination of handwritten letters and typewritten ones.

98 Mullins and Harvey, *Russell & DuMoulin*, 69

99 Graydon, 'Blakes,' 36

100 Ibid., 21, 37; Fleming, *McInnes Cooper*, 15. By way of contrast with the McInnes firm, the Stewart firm in Halifax 'occupied the Roy Building, the most prestigious office centre in downtown Halifax,' from 1920 to 1960: private communication from Barry Cahill. Roy, 'Bull, Housser and Tupper,' 54; Schatzker, *Borden & Elliot*, 15

101 Graydon, 'Blakes,' 43

102 Fleming, *McInnes Cooper*, 61; Roy, 'Bull, Housser and Tupper,' 86. Canadians may be surprised to learn that afternoon tea was also customary at some American firms, including some Wall Street concerns: See Sol M. Linowitz, with Martin Mayer, *The Betrayed Profession: Lawyering at the End of the Twentieth Century* (New York: Charles Scribner's Sons 1994), 27, 49.

103 Hobson, 'Symbol of the New Profession,' 21. For lawyers' community service see for example Gibson, *Proud Heritage*, 119–20.

104 Robert Bothwell, Ian Drummond, and John English, *Canada since 1945: Power, Politics, and Provincialism* (Toronto: University of Toronto Press 1981), 78–101

105 Desmond Morton, with Terry Copp, *Working People: An Illustrated History of Canadian Labour* (Ottawa: Deneau & Greenberg 1980), 184; Gary N. Chaison,

'Unions: Growth, Structure, and Internal Dynamics,' in John C. Anderson and Morley Gunderson, eds., *Union–Management Relations in Canada* (Don Mills, ON: Addison-Wesley 1982), 149. Absolute numbers rose from 359,000 to 2.5 million in the same period.

106 Schatzker, *Borden & Elliot*, 28; Cole, *Osler, Hoskin*, 148–51

107 David A.A. Stager, with Harry Arthurs, *Lawyers in Canada* (Toronto: University of Toronto Press 1990), 287. By 1986, almost 11 per cent of all practising lawyers worked in public administration.

108 Private communication

109 Kenneth Norrie and Douglas Owram, *A History of the Canadian Economy* (Toronto: Harcourt Brace Jovanovich 1991), 559. On the economy for these years, see also the relevant sections of Bliss, *Northern Enterprise*, and Graham D. Taylor and Peter A. Baskerville, *A Concise History of Business in Canada* (Toronto: Oxford University Press 1994).

110 See William Kilbourn, *PipeLine: TransCanada and the Great Debate: A History of Business and Politics* (Toronto: Clarke, Irwin 1970).

111 See Robert Bothwell and William Kilbourn, *C.D. Howe: A Biography* (Toronto: McClelland and Stewart 1979), 283–316.

112 Schatzker, *Borden & Elliot*, 25, 27

113 Anon, 'McCarthy & McCarthy' (typescript 1978), 65–7; John M. Godfrey, 'Personal Reminiscences and a History of the Law Firm of Campbell, Godfrey & Lewtas, 1870–1975' (typescript 1983), 50

114 Donald MacKay, *Empire of Wood: The MacMillan Bloedel Story* (Vancouver: Douglas and McIntyre 1982), 164–74; Godfrey, 'Reminiscences,' 44

115 Mitchell and Slinn, *McMaster Meighen*, 86–7; Fleming, *McInnes Cooper*, 64

116 This case is covered at length in David J. Mitchell, *WAC Bennett and the Rise of British Columbia* (Vancouver: Douglas and McIntyre 1983), 211–54

117 Mullins and Harvey, *Russell & DuMoulin*, 87–90

118 For the foundations of legal aid in Ontario see Mary P. Reilly, 'The Origins and Development of Legal Aid in Ontario,' *Windsor Yearbook of Access to Justice* 8 (1988), 81–104. See also Dieter Hoehne, *Legal Aid in Canada* (Queenston, ON: Mellen Press 1989), and Justice Information Report, *Legal Aid Services in Canada 1979/80* (Ottawa 1981).

119 Anon, 'McCarthys,' 64

120 Godfrey, 'Reminiscences,' 62; Mitchell and Slinn, *McMaster Meighen*, 92

121 See Marc Galanter and Thomas Palay, *Tournament of Lawyers: The Transformation of the Big Law Firm* (Chicago: University of Chicago Press 1991), 46; Stager and Arthurs, *Lawyers in Canada*, 176. As late as 1971, Stager and Arthurs found only four firms in Canada had more than fifty lawyers; these were Ogilvy Renault, in Montreal, and Blakes, McCarthys, and Oslers, in Toronto.

122 Cole, *Osler, Hoskin*, Appendix II
123 Godfrey, 'Reminiscences,' 18; Cole, *Osler, Hoskin*, 149. See also Curtis Cole's essay in this volume.
124 Edwards, *Fraser & Beatty*, 31
125 On Robinette see Jack Batten, *Robinette: The Dean of Canadian Lawyers* (Toronto: Macmillan of Canada 1984). Cole, 'McCarthy, Osler, Hoskin, and Creelman,' in Wilton, ed., *Beyond the Law*, 155; Anon, 'McCarthys,' 61
126 Fleming, *McInnes Cooper*, 61–2; Schatzker, *Borden & Elliot*, 43ff.; Mullins and Harvey, *Russell & DuMoulin*, 99
127 Schatzker, *Borden & Elliot*, 34–6
128 In Toronto, John Godfrey and Beverley Matthews (who had achieved the rank of brigadier-general) were leaders of their firms. Another forceful personality in Toronto law was Swatty Wotherspoon, a leader of Oslers and another brigadier-general.
129 Edwards, *Fraser & Beatty*, 32
130 Mullins and Harvey, *Russell & DuMoulin*, 86. One senior lawyer of the post-war generation in Toronto is reported to have held the view that the only form of billing which was acceptable professionally was 'To Services Rendered – $——.' For a client to question such a bill was to impugn the professional integrity of the lawyer: private communication from Brian Bucknall.
131 Roy, 'Bull, Housser and Tupper,' 123
132 Russell & DuMoulin began using electric typewriters in 1957: Mullins and Harvey, *Russell & DuMoulin*, 121. On the occasion of a major transaction in 1962 involving American as well as Canadian counsel, McMaster Meighen benefited from the services of advanced copying machines flown in by the New York firm of Cravath, Swaine, Moore: Mitchell and Slinn, *McMaster Meighen*, 92. Failure to keep up with the new technology could have serious consequences for a firm. Barry Pepper, an outstanding Toronto litigator, has recorded that this matter was a major factor in his decision to leave McMillan Binch in 1961. OSOHI: Barry Pepper, 1987, 127–8.
133 Godfrey, 'Reminiscences,' 50–1; Jack Batten, *Lawyers*, (Markham, ON: Penguin Books 1985) 62
134 At the Russell firm in Vancouver, which had a history of sponsoring women's opportunities at the bar, two female secretaries were taken on as articling students during the war because there was no one available to file court documents. Both were called to the bar in 1946, and one, Katherine I. McArthur, eventually became a partner. A member of the Russell family, Jean McD. Russell, articled to her brother during the war and received her call in 1949; she effectively became the office manager thereafter: Mullins and Harvey, *Russell & DuMoulin*, 71–4. See also T.D. Regehr's essay in this volume.

135 Mitchell and Slinn, *McMaster Meighen*, 80
136 Schatzker, *Borden & Elliot*, 49
137 Godfrey, 'Reminiscences,' 58–9; Cole, *Osler, Hoskin*, 118
138 Godfrey, 'Reminiscences,' 53; Roy, 'Bull, Housser and Tupper,' 87
139 Cole, *Osler, Hoskin*, 141–2
140 For example, the Russell & DuMoulin firm in Vancouver, after the 1968 move to the MacMillan Bloedel Building, found itself factionalized on the subject of carpet colours, the 'anything-but-grey' contingent in conflict with the 'anti-checkerboard' crew: Mullins and Harvey, *Russell & DuMoulin*, 97.
141 Taylor and Baskerville, *Concise History of Business in Canada*, 467
142 MacMillan Bloedel had special problems; in the 1970s it went into the general shipping business as a way of diversifying, a venture that proved disastrous: See McKay, *Empire of Wood*, 296–315.
143 For a general account of business developments during this period see Bliss, *Northern Enterprise*, chaps. 18 and 19.
144 See John Rothchild, *Going for Broke: How Robert Campeau Bankrupted the Retail Industry, Jolted the Junk Bond Market, and Brought the Booming Eighties to a Crashing Halt* (New York: Simon & Schuster 1991), 22–4, 97–8.
145 See Arthur Johnson, *Breaking the Banks* (Toronto: Lester & Orpen Dennys 1986).
146 See Susan Goldenberg, *The Thomson Empire: A Multi-Billion Dollar Canadian Dynasty* (Toronto: Bantam Books 1985), 233–42; Conrad Black, *A Life in Progress* (Toronto: Key Porter Books 1993); Rothchild, *Going for Broke*; Peter Foster, *Towers of Debt: The Rise and Fall of the Reichmanns* (Toronto: Key Porter Books 1993); Patricia Best and Ann Shortell, *The Brass Ring: Power, Influence and the Brascan Empire* (Toronto: Random House 1988), 2; and Diane Francis, *Controlling Interest: Who Owns Canada?* (Toronto: Macmillan of Canada 1986; rpt. Seal Books 1987).
147 See Daniel Drache and Meric S. Gertler, *The New Era of Global Competition: State Policy and Market Power* (Montreal and Kingston: McGill–Queen's University Press 1991), and Linda McQuaig, *The Quick and the Dead: Brian Mulroney, Big Business and the Seduction of Canada* (Toronto: Viking 1991).
148 Daniels, 'Growing Pains,' 164–6
149 See Peter Cook, *Massey at the Brink: The Story of Canada's Greatest Multinational and Its Struggle to Survive* (Don Mills, ON: Collins 1981), and Peter Foster, *Other People's Money: The Banks, the Government and Dome* (Don Mills, ON: Collins 1983).
150 On the other side, Quebec could boast the rise of its own financial giants, including Paul Demarais of Power Corp., the Caisses de Dépôt, and the magnificent (if ecologically dubious) accomplishments of Hydro-Québec.

151 Daniels, 'Growing Pains,' 167–72, and Linowitz and Mayer, *Betrayed Profession*, chap. 4

152 In the 1990s, corporate firms have been moving away from full-service law, preferring to concentrate on the most lucrative work.

153 *Canadian Law List*, 1971, 1981; Cole, *Osler, Hoskin*, Appendix II; Daniels, 'Growing Pains,' 155

154 Hagan, 'Transitions in the Legal Profession,' 96

155 Galanter and Palay, *Tournament of Lawyers*

156 Galanter and Palay's model has been criticized as too simplistic in its analysis of hiring practices and law-firm structures: See Frederick W. Lambert, 'An Academic Visit to the Modern Law Firm: Considering a Theory of Promotion-Driven Growth,' *Michigan Law Review* 90 (May 1992), 1719–38.

157 Richard H. Sander and E. Douglass Williams, 'A Little Theorizing about the Big Law Firm: Galanter, Palay, and the Economics of Growth,' *Law and Social Inquiry* 17 (1992), 391–414; Daniels, 'Growing Pains'; Robert L. Nelson, 'Of Tournaments and Transformations: Explaining the Growth of Large Law Firms,' *Wisconsin Law Review* (1992), 732–50

158 Galanter and Palay date the geometric growth of law firms to the 1920s, whereas Daniels can trace the same phenomenon in Canada only back to the 1960s.

159 Author's conversations with a number of mega-firm lawyers. In at least one case, a Canadian law firm, on the advice of an American consultant, experimented with higher associate-to-partner ratios. Junior lawyers responded by abandoning the firm, and the project was discontinued.

160 Daniels, 'Growing Pains,' 157–9, 187–8

161 Randy Ray, 'Lawyers Go Global,' *National* 3 (May 1994), 32ff.

162 Mullins and Harvey, *Russell & DuMoulin*, 108–15

163 By 1991 there were more than 15,000 woman lawyers in Canada: See John Hagan and Fiona Kay's essay in this volume. It has been suggested that the hiring of female lawyers at corporate firms has served to preserve the class and race exclusivity of these firms at the expense of lawyers of more varied socio-economic and ethnic backgrounds.

164 Lawrence J. Fox, 'Professionalism: Misplaced Nostalgia or Meaningful Loss?,' paper presented at American Bar Association 17th National Conference on Professional Responsibility, May 1991

165 Galanter and Palay, *Tournament of Lawyers*; Daniels, 'The Law Firm as an Efficient Community,' 801–34

166 The question of the changing role of legal secretaries in Canada is finally receiving some preliminary attention. Early indications are that, since the 1960s, secretaries at larger firms have been undergoing a process of proletarianization. Technological change, the devaluation of their skills, and a change in working

relationships are among the explanations: Tracy Shannon, 'Legal Secretaries: Proletarianization in Process' (research paper in possession of author).

167 Ellen Roseman, 'Legal Eagles Fly Alone,' *Globe and Mail* 23 May 1994, B4. For an American perspective, see Anthony T. Kronman, *The Lost Lawyer: Failing Ideals of the Legal Profession* (Cambridge, MA: The Belknap Press of Harvard University Press 1993), 271–314

168 Morris Gross, quoted in 'Law Firm Mergers: A Case of Greed or Survival,' *Globe and Mail*, 5 May 1990, D1. In the 1980s, Paul Moore of the Tory firm in Toronto made heroic efforts to attend his Scout meetings: Batten, *Lawyers*, 70.

169 Evidence from the United States suggests that legal entrepreneurialism is thriving among rural lawyers: Jon T. Johnsen, 'Rural Justice: Country Lawyers and Legal Services in the United States and Britain,' *Law and Social Inquiry* 17 (1992), 415–36

170 James Spence, Luncheon Address to the Canadian Institute Conference on Legal Opinions, 15 June 1992

171 This argument is offered in Robert L. Nelson, *Partners with Power: The Social Transformation of the Large Law Firm* (Berkeley: University of California Press 1988), chap. 7

172 The subject of professional autonomy is naturally linked to the major question posed about the legal profession by sociologists: What is the nature of the power of the profession? American sociologists who have studied this question have concluded that lawyers have little independence in relation to their clients. As representatives of those clients, however, and because of their access to an increasing share of the financial resources allocated to the law, they have a great deal of power indeed. For a discussion of these questions in the American context see Nelson, *Partners with Power*, and John P. Heinz and Edward O. Laumann, *Chicago Lawyers: The Social Structure of the Bar* (New York: Russell Sage Foundation and American Bar Foundation 1982). There is insufficient Canadian material available to offer independent observations on the profession here.

173 Quoted in Hobson, 'Symbol of the New Profession,' 4

174 Many of the firm histories contain anecdotes featuring a senior partner instructing a junior one on the importance of determining just how a client's wishes can be carried out. I have found no material suggesting that junior lawyers are instructed to give careful scrutiny to client plans with a view to determining whether or not they are ethical, though of course that may happen.

175 Batten, *Lawyers*, 64

176 Hagan, 'Transitions in the Legal Profession,' 97

177 Michael Crawford, 'The Lang Michener Affair,' *Canadian Lawyer* 14 (April 1990), 27–41. See also Brian Martin, *Never Enough: The Remarkable Frauds of Julius Melnitzer* (Toronto: Stoddart 1993).

2

The Making of a Colonial Lawyer: Beamish Murdoch of Halifax, 1822–1842

PHILIP GIRARD

A study of the Halifax law practice of Beamish Murdoch (1800–1876), who began articling in 1814 and retired in the 1860s, may almost be said to be an examination of the prehistory of the Canadian law 'firm.' With one exception, the only form of law-firm organization aside from the sole practitioner in pre-1850 Nova Scotia was the familial firm, based on fraternal or paternal relationships.[1] This pattern is unsurprising in a society where kinship was of such fundamental importance, but it is probably misleading to identify such 'firms' with the modern partnership. Such associations were transitional and functioned principally to set up younger members in practices of their own, rather than to establish multi-person firms of indefinite duration. This trend can be seen in the most prominent of such familial groupings, the Uniackes, comprising Attorney General Richard John Uniacke and his five lawyer sons: James Boyle; Crofton; Richard John, Jr; Norman Fitzgerald; and Andrew Mitchell. Calling this group a 'firm' suggests a greater degree of cohesion than actually existed. A whole generation separated the eldest and youngest brothers, and Crofton and Norman Fitzgerald made their careers largely outside Nova Scotia. The Uniackes were essentially sole practitioners, as was their pupil, Beamish Murdoch.

Murdoch began practice at a time when a few other young men from non-gentry backgrounds in the Maritimes were beginning to make their way into the world of the law, and retired just as the (non-familial) two- or three-man partnership began to appear more frequently in Nova Scotia.

Beamish Murdoch (1800–1876), *c.* 1865 (courtesy Public Archives of Nova Scotia)

His career thus spans the heyday of the sole practitioner in North America, which may be said to end with the assassination of its best-known icon, Abraham Lincoln. A study of the career of a sole practitioner is essentially a study of what lawyers did, a subject which has to date attracted little interest. As Richard Scott Eckert recently observed in the New England context, there has been no 'detailed treatment of the legal career of a representative member of the legal profession in either colonial Massachusetts or one of the other colonies.'[2] This lacuna exists as well for pre-Confederation British North America and for the ante-bellum United States.

There are a number of reasons, both material and ideological, for this gap in the literature. First and most obvious is the problem of documentation. There is nothing in the common law equivalent to the notarial registers of the civil-law tradition, which have survived in considerable quantities. Lawyers' papers have tended not to survive, and without them the reconstruction of an individual law practice is rendered extremely difficult. Where the ravages of fire and moth have spared such papers, lawyers themselves have often destroyed them out of a concern over possible violations of client confidentiality. At a time when most lawyers practised law alone, there was nothing to impede this action.

A lawyer's own records are not indispensable to the reconstruction of a law practice, however. Court records and newspapers contain a wealth of information, although naturally oriented to the forensic rather than the solicitorial side of law practice. The failure to exploit such records as do exist makes it clear that the lack of interest in colonial lawyers' work is not based simply on the absence of adequate primary sources. Historians have not believed that the task was a particularly important one. This belief is based on a somewhat outdated conception of power as comprising only its official political forms. Since one of the major historical questions of the colonial period, whether in pre-revolutionary America or colonial British North America, is the nature of power and authority, historians have been most interested in those lawyers who have been closest to the centres of power. Thus historians of colonial America have been most interested in lawyer-officeholders and in lawyers who were active in the revolutionary movement,[3] while historians of the nineteenth-century United States have been fixated on the question of how lawyers became the 'American aristocracy.'[4] Historians of British North America have been particularly interested in the role of Loyalist lawyers as architects of the new society which was being established in Upper Canada and New Brunswick.[5]

Certainly this political role was important, but lawyers were often leaders of colonial society, even when they did not wield direct political power. In part this was the case because law was ubiquitous in colonial society. Citizens high and low regularly came into contact with the law, mainly in the form of civil rather than criminal justice. They depended on it in a much more direct way – principally, but certainly not exclusively, to enforce debt obligations – than citizens do in the twentieth century. The administration of criminal law was important as spectacle and morality tale, but it unfolded almost entirely with lay rather than professional participation, except for the most serious offences. It was for ordinary matters of civil law – debt, conveyancing, succession, marriage, business transactions – that people sought out lawyers, and it was their constant reliance on lawyers that allowed the latter to assume their unique role in colonial society.

This essay examines the law practice of Halifax lawyer Beamish Murdoch during its first twenty years. By analysing the nature of his clientele in terms of its social class, gender, ethnicity, its growth over time, the variety of services performed for these clients, and his professional income, it will be possible to understand better the role that lawyers played in the lives of their clients and in the broader community. It may also allow some reflections on change within the legal profession and on social change within the community that Murdoch served.

A few words about the documentary base for this study are in order. Exploration of Murdoch's law practice is possible because a good collection of his letter-books, account-books and daybooks has survived. His 'non-Halifax' letter-book for the years 1823–9 contains copies of (most of?) the letters which he wrote on behalf of clients, whether from Halifax or not, to parties who lived outside Halifax County. It also contains a number of letters written to parties in the United States and the United Kingdom who had sought advice.[6] Several account-books have also survived, covering the periods 1827–30, 1825–51, 1831–7, and 1846–56, along with a daybook for January 1834 to August 1836 (which appears to contain a complete listing of his clients over this period), a ledger-book covering the period 1845–57, and a small booklet entitled 'Halifax Conveyancing' which covers the years 1850–5.[7] When supplemented by newspaper accounts and cross-checked against surviving court records, this material permits the reconstruction of an early-nineteenth-century law practice in often surprising detail.

GETTING ESTABLISHED: THE EARLY YEARS, 1822–1827

The early life of Beamish Murdoch was filled with tragedy. He was born in Halifax in August 1800, but his mother, Elizabeth (Beamish) Murdoch, died before he was three years old. At the same time, his father, Andrew, partner in a Halifax mercantile establishment, was imprisoned for debt and young Beamish was raised by his grandmother Amelia Beamish and a maiden aunt, Harriette Ott Beamish. A broken man when finally released from prison about 1808, Andrew Murdoch spent the rest of his life eking out an existence as a schoolteacher in rural settlements. Though father and son seem to have been emotionally estranged, Beamish contributed greatly to his father's support once he came into his own income. Fortunately, an inheritance from the maternal side of the family allowed Beamish to prepare himself for the legal profession. Ethnicity also helped. Scots-Irish on his father's side, Anglo-Irish on his mother's, Murdoch came to the attention of the dean of Nova Scotia's Anglo-Irish community, Richard John Uniacke, Sr. Murdoch commenced his articles with the elder Uniacke's son Crofton in 1814, but had his articles assigned to Uniacke *père* in October 1817 when Crofton was named judge of Vice-Admiralty Court at Halifax.

Murdoch's five years of apprenticeship to the Uniackes ended on 23 November 1819. He still had to wait eighteen months, until reaching the age of majority, before being admitted an attorney of the Supreme Court of Nova Scotia on 14 July 1821. He then spent the mandatory year 'attend[ing] the Supreme Court at its regular sittings at Halifax, for at least three terms after his admission as an Attorney' before his call to the bar.[8] Murdoch would also have spent much of his time reading at the Barristers' Library. About this time he set up his own office-cum-household with his aunt Harriette, in rented premises at 32 Barrington Street, just across from St Paul's Church in the heart of Halifax. He also acquired additional domestic responsibilities during this year. Already supervising the education of his twelve year-old cousin Thomas Beamish Akins, he invited their cousin Charles Ott Beamish, also aged twelve, to live with him in Halifax after the death in January 1821 of the boy's father, Murdoch's uncle Frederick Ott Beamish, of Blandford.[9] The long-awaited day finally arrived on 14 July 1822, when Murdoch was called to the bar of the Supreme Court and signed the barristers' roll.[10] Mere admission did not guarantee a clientele, and it was nearly a year before Murdoch was able to exercise his professional skills. In itself this was not surprising: William Johnstone Ritchie related in later life that it took six months after he opened his office in Saint John, New Brunswick, in 1837 before he welcomed his first client, and his second year of practice netted him only £5.[11] Murdoch was well aware of the effort which would be required to create a niche for himself, as he later warned prospective law students in his *Epitome of the Laws of Nova-Scotia*, in terms which would warm the heart of any Victorian: 'In the race of competition the lover of his own ease must be left far behind – among the number who press eagerly forward, he who loiters on the way and wastes the precious moments he should devote to self improvement, cannot expect to bear away a prize.'[12]

Increasing numbers were indeed pressing 'eagerly forward' just as Murdoch began his career. Halifax was supplied with twenty-five lawyers for a population of some 12,000 in 1821. A further three were called to the bar in that year, Murdoch was part of a 'class' of an unprecedented nine young men in 1822, and a further six were called to the bar in 1823. The capital thus offered a competitive market which had no parallel elsewhere in the province. Seven county towns counted no more than one lawyer each in 1821, though Pictou boasted three, and Annapolis two.[13] Given that 1822 represented the nadir of the postwar slump in Halifax's fortunes, the town simply could not absorb eighteen newly minted barristers.[14] Only five of this group remained in Halifax, while the rest spread out across the province.

Most Halifax lawyers were well established and connected by kinship or marriage to the political, legal, ecclesiastical, military, or mercantile élites. Murdoch began his career without such advantages. His apprenticeship with Uniacke provided him with some cachet, but Murdoch lacked the kind of assistance which Uniacke lavished on his own sons. Backing from family or patron was crucial in the early years after admission to the bar precisely because of the time it took to build up a clientele.[15] A government post with some income, even if modest, could greatly assist a man in those lean years. Murdoch's friend James Scott Tremain, called to the bar in 1823, was the son of powerful merchant Richard Tremain. In 1825 this fledgling lawyer became deputy registrar to the Court of Vice-Admiralty, an office which carried with it handsome fees. His brother John Lewis Tremain married the daughter of the former Chief Justice of Cape Breton in 1822, and was promptly named judge of probate, registrar of deeds, and prothonotary of the Supreme Court for the County of Inverness – and he was not even a lawyer. Such rewards eluded unconnected men such as Beamish Murdoch.

Fortunately Murdoch began his practice when the demand for legal services from the non-élite section of the population was reasonably strong. Artisans, proprietors of small businesses, shopkeepers, small landowners, mariners, that group of urban society between the wage labourers and the small professional, mercantile, and officeholding élite, depended on the law for a whole host of services, but particularly on the law of creditor and debtor.[16] Since debt-collection was such an important part of all lawyers' work in this period, some brief account of legal representation in debt matters in the various courts is required.

Lawyers were not necessary for the recovery of small sums, since debts of less than £5 could be brought before a justice of the peace, and lawyers were not usually involved at this level.[17] Debts between £5 and £10 could be sued for in either the Inferior Court of Common Pleas or the Supreme Court, the latter court being authorized to try such cases in summary fashion (i.e., without a jury), in an effort to reduce costs. Legal representation for plaintiffs was almost invariable in the Supreme Court, but for defendants much less so; the only study, which covers the years 1830 and 1831, shows only 4 per cent of plaintiffs unrepresented, whereas 40 per cent of defendants had no lawyer.[18] In the Inferior Court of Common Pleas, plaintiffs were invariably represented by lawyers from at least the 1770s, while defendants seldom appeared by counsel until about 1820, when lawyers began to represent them more frequently.[19] Once the Commissioners' Court was created at Halifax in 1817, it rapidly became the forum of choice for the recovery of medium-sized debts (those between £5 and £10), favoured because of its summary procedure and low costs.[20] Its records have not survived, but the pattern of legal representation there is likely to have been broadly similar to that in the Inferior Court of Common Pleas, although the proportion of plaintiffs with lawyers was probably lower.

Murdoch's account-books show a sprinkling of entries for appearances in both these inferior courts in the 1820s and 1830s, with no more than a half-dozen for the Commissioners' Court. The bulk of debt-collection which Murdoch carried out took place in the Supreme Court. Already in 1823, Murdoch filed eleven claims in the Supreme Court, for sums ranging from just over £10 to £174.[21] In several of these his clients were merchants or suppliers, but he also represented Daniel Grant, Jr, tailor, in his claim against George Creelman, yeoman, for £12. By 1824 Murdoch filed thirty-three claims in the Supreme Court, almost all for debt, then twenty-three in 1825 and thirty-two in 1826, falling to fourteen in 1827. A Supreme Court practice, comprising mainly debt-collection, was an essential part of Murdoch's professional activities in the early years. Some of his contemporaries featured even more prominently in debt litigation: William Young and James Stewart Clarke, both called to the bar in 1826, filed fifty-four and fifty-seven claims, respectively, in the Supreme Court in 1827. Young had extensive mercantile connections, however, and Clarke's father, David Shaw Clarke, was clerk of the peace, Halifax's senior judicial administrator.

A unique overview of the development of a young lawyer's practice in the 1820s can be found in Murdoch's first letter-book, covering the period 1823–9,[22] supplemented by his account-books and court records for the same period. The letter-book contains eighty-four documents, of which eighty are letters, three are petitions, and one is a draft partnership indenture. Of the letters, seventy-six relate to debt-collection or to the drafting of mortgages as security for loans, although a few of these also contain advice on matters of property management. The most common addressee of these letters (thirty-four) is the sheriff of a particular county, who had the responsibilty for serving summonses, seizing property under writs of execution and attachment, and imprisoning debtors under writs of *capias*. Since this letter-book contains only correspondence relating either to clients resident outside Halifax or to Halifax clients with claims outside Halifax County, it overstates the proportion of Murdoch's practice devoted to debt matters, but not dramatically. There is very little in it regarding conveyancing or the settlement of decedents' estates, for example, services which Murdoch performed for his Halifax clientele, albeit infrequently, in the 1820s.

Long-distance debt-collection was somewhat tedious and required considerable persistence. On 12 May 1824, Murdoch wrote to the sheriff of Cumberland County, enclosing a writ against a carpenter 'named Turpel,' with the unhelpful observation that he was 'settled somewhere in Cumberland.' Unsurprisingly, the sheriff could not find Mr Turpel, and three months later Murdoch wrote to the sheriff of Kings County, with the slightly more helpful advice that Turpel was now believed to be living somewhere near Parrsboro.[23] He eluded detection for another year, until finally run to ground in Halifax. On 15 September 1825, Murdoch obtained a writ of *capias* against William Turpel on behalf of his client William Wells, for a debt of £10.[24] Murdoch also sought to obtain redress for William Hesson, a Halifax tailor, who had a claim of £8 against one John MacDonald of Antigonish. Hesson had hired lawyer J.T. Hill to sue for the debt in the Commissioners' Court, but somehow the wrong MacDonald was sued. This MacDonald in turn sued Hesson, who became liable for the costs of the suit (nearly £3). On 8 March 1824, Murdoch wrote to his friend and 'classmate' W.F. DesBarres, of Guysborough, who had been called to the bar in the same year, asking him if he could investigate. DesBarres ignored this request, and Murdoch wrote again over three years later, asking DesBarres to 'endeavor to put it in a train for settlement.' Hesson had 'been very hardly used,' said Murdoch, and he implored DesBarres to write him on the subject. The slowness of travel and communication, and difficulties involved in securing accurate information about personal names and residences, meant that the expenses involved in debt-collection could easily mount.

Once the right debtor had been impleaded in the right court, the law afforded a whole arsenal of weapons to the creditor. In particular, imprisonment for debt, or the threat of it, was a highly visible feature of the debt-collection process. Murdoch's familial history of imprisonment for debt made him an uneasy participant in this process, as he revealed in his *Essay on the Mischievous Tendency of Imprisoning for Debt and in other civil cases*.[25] His letters show that he sought imprisonment only as a last resort, and usually with an expression of regret. Murdoch felt sorry that a debtor at Annapolis should be detained for a small sum, 'but as he has not made any offer of arrangement it is the only course I have to pursue.'[26] The sheriff played a key role in negotiating with debtors in this regard, especially out-of-town debtors whom neither Murdoch nor his client could meet face to face. When Murdoch obtained a writ of *capias* for his clients Halifax merchants John Starr & Son against one James Johnson, he asked the sheriff of Sydney County to enforce it immediately, but then gave further instructions. The object of the plaintiffs, he said, 'is to obtain security for their debt, not to distress the defendant, but as they think themselves unfairly dealt with by him they wish his arrest, to bring him to terms.' Starr was prepared to give Johnson up to a year to pay, provided he would sign a promissory note for the debt. Murdoch simply asked Sheriff McDonald to use his discretion in this regard.[27]

Imprisonment for debt was not used just by wealthy merchants. In fact, they could probably afford to forgo it if they thought that there was any prospect of repayment. Poorer creditors could not always afford to be so generous. In 1828 Murdoch wrote to lawyer Henry Blackadar at Pictou for some assistance in enforcing three writs of execution, for three different creditors, against one Lowden. Two of them, Murdoch's uncle Thomas Ott Beamish, and tailor William Hesson, did not insist on Lowden's imprisonment and were resigned to him taking the benefit of the Insolvent Debtors' Act.[28] Under this act a debtor whose total debts amounted to less than £100 could escape imprisonment by assigning all his assets (saving some personal items) to his creditors and swearing that he had not concealed any other assets. However, the third creditor, Thomas Marvin, whose claim was for a small sum of wages, would 'not agree to his being discharged and in the event of his taking the oath wishes him to be supplied with bread according to the act of the Province.'[29] Until an 1832 amendment to the act abolished the privilege, a creditor possessed a veto over the release of any otherwise eligible debtor, provided he supplied 'the full quantity of eight pounds of good and wholesome biscuit bread per week unto the said prisoner.' If the debt were small, however, presumably the creditor would not wish it to be literally eaten up by feeding the prisoner over an extended period.

Debtors employed legal counsel much less frequently than creditors, either out of poverty or because in many cases they knew they had no valid legal defence. Murdoch did occasionally represent a debtor, in which case he would deploy his best persuasive efforts to secure a delay in the collection of the creditor's due. He put the claims of the Rev. Archibald McQueen, who had just confessed a judgment for £12, to the creditor's lawyer Alexander Stewart in the following terms:

If you could delay adding expence or trouble to it for some time he is striving very hard to maintain a wife and large family. The Rev. Mr. Uniacke has just appointed him teacher of the school in Dutch town to which £50 was given last session but of course he cannot receive his salary till he has earned it by the quarter of year's services. I know him to be a worthy man though unfortunate and if without deviating from what you should do for your client you could extend some indulgence to him in the collection of the demand I should take it as a personal favor. He is willing to give up 300 acres of land in Cumberland if he could liquidate the demand in that way.

Murdoch certainly knew that Stewart's own father had been a penurious Church of Scotland clergyman, and no doubt hoped that a plea on this theme would find a sympathetic ear.[30]

Murdoch's account-books and the Supreme Court records supplement the picture derived from the letter-book. While debt-collection retained its predominant role in his law practice throughout the 1820s, it is impossible to quantify that role any more precisely. The most common entry in the account-books is for a 'letter' written for a named client to a named party. The contents of the letters are not specified, and although most of them no doubt contained demands for the payment of debts, letters would sometimes have been written for other purposes. The account-books provide some 120 entries for the years 1823 through 1826 inclusive, but there are more than 120 entries for the year 1827 alone, covering a range of services for some 75 clients. Aside from debt-collection and drafting letters, these services fall into five broad categories: drafting documents for private parties; drafting petitions to the lieutenant-governor or the Assembly on behalf of individuals; providing 'advice'; arranging property matters, including *inter vivos* conveyancing and the transmission of assets on death; and attending at court on matters other than routine debt-enforcement. Each of these is examined in turn.

The documents which parties were most likely to ask the young Murdoch to draft between 1823 and 1827 related to partnerships, powers of attorney, and arbitration bonds, with the last appearing most frequently. Very few other documents such as contracts or leases are apparent. In 1823 Murdoch drafted a partnership indenture between two Halifax tailors, Daniel Grant, Jr, and John Fraser, containing detailed provisions about the respective contributions of each party, the location of the business, and so on.[31] In 1827 he drafted a deed of dissolution of partnership between Alexander Gordon and Hector McLennan, but was compelled to threaten a suit in Chancery when the latter refused either to settle the accounts with his erstwhile partner or to refer the matter to arbitration.[32] The numerous entries for 'arbitration bonds' provide no further details. Such bonds commonly specified that the parties should each name an 'indifferent person' resident in Halifax, with these two naming a third who would act as umpire in case they could not agree.[33] The parties obliged themselves to observe the terms of the award and not to commence suits at law or equity on pain of forfeiting a stated sum of money. In this way the parties tried to preserve some control over the dispute-resolution process. Partners had a special incentive to do so since the Court of Chancery, with its higher fee structure, was the normal forum for litigating partnership disputes.[34]

The nineteenth century has been called the 'heroic age of the petition,' and Nova Scotians certainly participated avidly in this mode of addressing authority.[35] In part as a result of relatively low literacy rates, and in part because the petition was conceived of as a legal document, lawyers were often retained to draft them. Murdoch's records show that he drafted at least five petitions on a variety of subjects during his first five years of practice. One of his very first acts as a lawyer was to draft a petition on behalf of two Halifax mariners who alleged that they had been unjustly excluded by the Newfoundland authorities from the Labrador fishery, and had suffered losses, for which they claimed compensation from the Assembly.[36] In 1824 he petitioned the Secretary of War of the United States of America for a pension on behalf of one Anthony Beecham, who alleged that he had been seized with blindness while on duty after serving two and one-half years in the United States Artillery.[37] More usual were two petitions for roads which he addressed to the lieutenant-governor, and one to the magistrates of Halifax regarding ferry service to Dartmouth.[38]

Murdoch's entries regarding 'advice' do not always indicate the subject of the client's problem. He seems to have reserved the label for those cases where some reflection was required beyond a simple letter, such as one demanding the payment of a debt. For example, he charged Mrs Mary McPherson 11s 8d for a 'letter to Mr. Clarke & advice re overholding tenant' on 11 November 1826.[39] His normal fee for a letter was 6s 8d, suggesting that Murdoch had done more than just send a notice to quit to the tenant. He also provided advice regarding a promissory note and another troublesome tenant in 1827, but one can only speculate what the 'advice re Brig Feronia' involved, which he supplied to merchant James Forman, Jr, in the same year. Fees of 5s for advice on relatively simple matters and 10s for more complex opinions may seem high in comparison with the wages of skilled craftsmen (4s per day until at least mid-century), but they seem to have been remarkably stable over time. Such sums were identical to those charged by Boston lawyer Richard Dana during the early years of his practice nearly a century earlier, in the 1730s and 1740s.[40] They were also identical to those charged by Murdoch's contemporary William Young.[41]

These early years saw Murdoch involved in some conveyancing and estate work, but in modest quantities. Occasional entries for 'searches at Registry' indicate title searches for either prospective purchasers or mortgagees, but in the period 1822–7 he would appear to have drafted only one mortgage, one assignment of mortgage, and one memorandum of lease. He petitioned the lieutenant-governor in council for letters of administration in four cases of intestacy, but did not draft his first will until 1829. The simple and routine nature of most of the work carried out by Murdoch at this early stage was directly related to the class background of his client base, as will be seen.

The courts in which Murdoch did not appear are as significant as those in which he did. With the exception of his first Chancery case in 1827, the more lucrative pay scales of the Courts of Chancery, Marriage and Divorce, and particularly Vice-Admiralty, would elude him until the 1830s. He none the less appeared in several significant Supreme Court cases during this period. The earliest was *Robertson* v. *Phillips*, which Murdoch argued in fall 1824. Mrs Robertson was a widow who had cohabited with Halifax grocer Samuel Phillips for some years, and borne him three children. They parted, and he bound himself by a separation agreement to pay a weekly sum for maintenance of the children. When he defaulted, Murdoch succeeded in obtaining a substantial jury award on her behalf.[42] The press coverage which this case received no doubt assisted Murdoch in the early days of his career, and it is examined more closely in that light below. A case of less general interest but more legal significance was *Knodel et al.* v. *Little*, which Murdoch argued and won in 1826. This was an action in partition where all but one of several tenants in common agreed that the land in question should be divided. There were no provincial precedents relevant to a contested partition action, and the application of English precedents was unclear. Murdoch argued that the defendant's technical objection was invalid, and successfully moved for confirmation of the writ of partition.[43]

In the mid-1820s Murdoch was admitted as a proctor and advocate (the equivalents of solicitor and barrister) to the Court of Chancery, which was put on a more professional footing with the appointment of the prominent lawyer Simon Bradstreet Robie as Master of the Rolls in 1826.[44] Murdoch's first case was a simple uncontested foreclosure action. He represented carpenter James Dechman, Jr, who had lent £130 at 6 per cent interest to Robert Knox, a ministerial assistant at St Matthew's Church. The amount was secured by a mortgage dated 17 May 1823, on which the full principal was due in two years. In June 1825, Knox died intestate, leaving as his only heir his mother, the impugnant (defendant) Jane Knox. She maintained the interest payments, but could not pay the principal, and agreed to a foreclosure in November 1827; the final order for sale of the property was issued in January 1829.[45]

The ethnic, gender, and class identity of Murdoch's clientele during these early years is of some interest, as a way of judging the extent of access to legal services, and ultimately to justice. Names are the only indication of ethnic identity, making it the hardest to quantify. All that can usefully be said is that only 11 of his approximately 153 clients (1823–7 both inclusive), or about 13 per cent, have names which can be identified with some confidence as being Irish, when the Irish made up close to one-quarter of the city's population. Murdoch certainly publicized his Irish ties, joining the Charitable Irish Society in 1823 and already serving as its vice-president in 1824. On St Patrick's Day 1825, he and five other men patronized the Irish community to the tune of some £50, which they spent on a lavish meal for a large number of guests.[46] If the proportion of his Irish clients is significantly lower than that of the town's population, the simple explanation is that the Irish occupied the second-lowest rung in Halifax society, just above the Blacks. Their marginal economic power was reflected in reduced access to lawyers' services. They retained some access to courts, however, as the 'humorous' newspaper coverage of their presence in the Commissioners' Court demonstrates;[47] the quality of the justice they received is less certain.

No other ethnic or racial groups appear prominently in Murdoch's records for this period. It is unlikely that he had any Black clients, but this possibility cannot be eliminated on the basis of names alone. One Acadian shows up: Christian Tybo appears from newspaper evidence to have been a landlord in Halifax, but he consulted Murdoch about a claim against a Cape Breton justice of the peace, William Watts.[48]

At least 12 per cent of Murdoch's clientele (18 of 153) were women,[49] virtually all of whom were widows. Widows needed the same assistance collecting debts and dealing with tenants and other property matters as men did, and were not afraid to pursue their remedies at law, though they seldom resorted to imprisonment for debt. It is not possible to tell if Murdoch's female clients carried on businesses, as some women did in Halifax at this time. A number of them consulted him with regard to property matters, suggesting the traditional roles of landlady or provider of lodging. Their claims were not necessarily small. Margaret Hogg claimed £248 from 'gentlemen' James, Peter, and William Donaldson in October 1824,[50] while Mrs Ann Hinshelwood, widow of a Halifax military officer and a resident of New York City, owned a substantial property on fashionable Argyle Street about which she sought advice from Murdoch on numerous occasions. Ellen Moore, a widow resident in Twickenham, Middlesex, appointed Murdoch her attorney in October 1826 with power to dispose of a property held by her on Duke Street.[51]

The vast majority of Murdoch's clientele during this early period came from a modest class background. He was usually careful to note those of his clients who warranted the appellation 'Esquire' (four), three more can be identified as 'gentlemen' from court records, and another client was his own physician. Another three clients, all non-residents, might be thought to possess high social status – Mrs Hinshelwood, as an officer's widow; an army captain from Wales; and a London clergyman. No more than 7 per cent (11 of 153) of his clientele came from the élite. A further group comprised a few reasonably prominent merchants, although none of the city's most prominent. About 90 per cent of his business thus came from smaller merchants and 'mechanics,' leavened by a few farmers and mariners, and their widows. Occupations have been identified for eighty of his non-élite clients,[52] and of these twenty-seven were traders of some sort, ranging from small grocers to large wholesale merchants. Artisans and skilled craftsmen were the next most numerous group, at nineteen, including a tinsmith, a portrait painter, two confectioners, brewer Alexander Keith, several tailors and carpenters, two cabinet-makers, a brass founder, a saddler, a baker, a butcher, and a shoemaker. A few fell into a miscellaneous category: schoolteacher William Barry, auctioneer Richard Bulger, veteran Anthony Beecham, truckman Edward Warren, and pedlar Patrick Brown. It is probable that more of those with unidentified occupations were artisans than merchants, since merchants can usually be traced through newspaper advertisements whereas artisans often cannot. Merchants and 'mechanics' and their respective widows probably made up similar proportions of Murdoch's client base, about 40 per cent each. Their legal needs were relatively simple, relating to debtor–creditor matters rather than the more lucrative property and estates work which would occupy Murdoch in later years.

What income did Murdoch's law practice generate? It is clear from his account-books that he handled a lot of money, but not always clear how much of it he retained. When a client lost a suit and paid Murdoch a sum for 'costs,' it is often not possible to distinguish how much of this sum was profit over and above the court fees which he had already paid on the client's behalf. Fortunately, Murdoch tried to calculate his earnings for 1827 and the first five months of 1828. He showed his gross income for the calendar year 1827 as £101 12s 9d, from which he deducted 'charges of business' in the amount of £4 12s 1d, for a total of £97 0s 8d net income.[53] The rent on his combined residence/office at 32 Barrington Street was £90 per annum, so Murdoch had to depend on his private means to cover anything more than his basic expenses.[54] Yet an annual income of £100 was respectable for a young man of his profession. It was much less than the £600 salary accorded the assistant judges of the Supreme Court in 1822, but twice the wages of a labourer, who typically earned £1 per week or less.

If Murdoch's professional income was satisfactory in 1827, it became even more so in 1828. His tally for the first five months of 1828 showed a gross income of nearly £150, almost three times the £56 he had grossed in the same period in 1827. The 'charges of business' are not listed for 1828, but if they represented the same proportion of total income as in 1827, Murdoch would still have substantially augmented his income over the previous year. The 'unusual brisk trade' which Murdoch referred to in a letter to a client in 1828, as well as his own growing reputation, obviously had a rebarbative effect on his professional business.[55]

It seems that, in these early years at least, Murdoch was prepared to do almost all of his business on credit. He seldom asked for retainers or for court costs to be paid 'up front,' and indeed advanced money to his clients on the anticipated success of their lawsuits. In a society chronically short of specie and without savings banks, most suppliers of goods and services were obliged to provide them on credit. Generous credit arrangements might also have been a way of attracting business in the early years of his practice. Predictably, Murdoch suffered his share of bad debts. An estimate of their quantity can be gleaned from the 'Accounts Current, made up Nov. 1830' found in one of his account-books. These show an outstanding balance of £291 owed him, of which he notes £34 were 'very doubtful balances.' If we assume these to be uncollectable, they would represent a default rate of 11 per cent, which is probably optimistic. Clients often took years to pay, and were seldom charged interest. From a few entries which show Murdoch himself as the debtor, it is apparent that he too sometimes took years to settle his accounts with others.

One example of this delay also demonstrates Murdoch's willingness to accept payment in kind. His medical bills with Dr Joseph Prescott for services provided to himself and his aunt Harriette amounted to some £9 over the period 1826–30. He had provided legal services to Prescott over the same period, and finally deducted the physician's fees from the bill he prepared in 1830. In later years he would deduct from his account with West India merchants Saltus & Wainwright the cost of '1 barrel of Canada flour' and 'one Bermuda plait for H. Beamish.' William Donaldson of Sherwood was given credit for 'lodging etc. last summer' (a summer cottage?) in 1830, while Robert Geddes acquitted part of his bill by supplying 25 pounds of butter. Such entries were unusual, however: the vast bulk of Murdoch's accounts were ultimately settled in cash.

The organization of Murdoch's law practice remained very simple. His cousin Thomas Beamish Akins began assisting him in 1823, at the age of fourteen and would complete his articles with Murdoch in 1830.[56] There is only one indication that Murdoch contemplated taking on another lawyer in some form of association. Two letters, dated August and October 1827, are recorded in Murdoch's letter-book as signed by himself and lawyer Thomas Forman, who had been called to the bar on 10 October 1827. Perhaps the extra time required for his political duties after his election to the House of Assembly in September 1826 suggested to Murdoch the need for additional help in his law practice. If so, the experiment seems not to have continued. Little is known of Forman's later career except that he was reported to have died at Sydney, Australia, in October 1831.[57]

By 1827 Beamish Murdoch had already established himself in the eyes of both the public and his peers as a well-known member of the profession. He drew his clientele mostly from the middling and humbler classes of Halifax society, who had shown their trust by electing him to the House of Assembly in fall 1826, but he was also beginning to serve a few of the more substantial merchants and rentiers.[58] He had managed to carve out a more satisfactory niche for himself than had some of his peers.[59] How, precisely, had he done this? Talent, persistence, and a fondness for hard work he had in ample measure, but presumably others did too. What, then, went into the 'making' of this colonial lawyer?

Two factors were key: the rise of journalism, and the changing nature of the market that Murdoch served. Murdoch's entry into practice coincided with the efflorescence of journalism in his native Halifax. Newspaper accounts assisted him in becoming better known among the city's growing numbers of artisans, shopkeepers, and minor merchants, who were gaining in affluence as trade recovered after the initial postwar slump of 1815–22. His activities in court, in municipal affairs, provincial politics, church controversies, and literary, philanthropic, and cultural endeavours were avidly chronicled by the numerous weekly newspapers circulating in Halifax in the second quarter of the nineteenth century. Murdoch himself participated in this journalistic frenzy, as has been noted; through his editorial work for the *Acadian Recorder* during 1824–6, to which he would return a decade later. It is almost impossible to find a period of more than a few months in the second half of the 1820s in which some reference to Murdoch is not made in the newspapers.

In the press Murdoch was portrayed as independent, in the eighteenth-century sense of that word. In the political, legal, and ecclesiastical spheres, he appeared to act on his own beliefs, without fear of reprisal or hope of reward from the powerful. A few examples of his appearances will be analysed to show the kind of image which grew up around Murdoch, and why it might have been attractive to his nascent clientele. His role as counsel for the plaintiff in the case of *Robertson* v. *Phillips* in fall 1824 has already been mentioned.[60] The case did not look particularly bright for Murdoch. His client was a 'fallen woman,' a widow who had had three children out of wedlock with Mr Phillips. He had orally agreed to support them at a rate of 7s 6d per week, plus clothes and schooling, while she retained custody. She had brought one of the children back to him at one point, then changed her mind and clandestinely removed the child from his home. The law allowed an agreement for the support of illegitimate children to be rescinded at any time, which meant Mrs Robertson's position was rather tenuous.

Phillips was represented by J.W. Johnston, a decade senior to Murdoch and already possessed of a large practice. Johnston tried to argue that Robertson was jealous of 'a new, and a laudable connexion' that Phillips had formed with another, 'virtuous female,' and was thus motivated by simple malice in pursuing her claim. Yet Murdoch neatly turned the tables by painting a tragic picture of Robertson as a wronged woman 'struggling in widowhood and poverty with that energy of mind which could only inspire a mother,' who had managed to support her children alone for sixty-eight weeks. He urged the jury not to judge her too harshly for taking back her child, as 'it would be sinning against the best feelings of human nature to condemn her for this – it might be a misfortune, but certainly it was not a crime.' Judge Wilkins recommended £19 compensation, but the jury awarded £22.

The *Novascotian* gave full rein to Murdoch's panegyric to wounded maternity. It gave equal coverage to Johnston, but his arguments sounded stiff and technical in contrast with Murdoch's heartfelt appeal. At a time when the parties to an action were disabled from giving evidence on the ground of their interest in the outcome, there was no chance for the jury to judge their credibility.[61] Everything depended on the lawyer's skill in painting a positive portrait of his client. Murdoch's ability to show Mrs Robertson in a favourable light not only swayed the jury, but was conveyed to a wide public through detailed newspaper coverage. Of course, Murdoch was in the process of creating an image for himself as well: as the man who speaks truth to power, who is not afraid to champion the claims of a poor woman against a more respectable male antagonist with a clever lawyer. The image of power being constrained by law was as old as the common law itself, but in the Halifax of the 1820s, there was a new, political edge to it. As the shopkeepers and mechanics of the capital began to question the established political order, Murdoch's upset victory over the more seasoned Johnston could be read as a portent of things to come.

Two much more public disputes loomed large in Halifax in the mid-1820s, in both of which Murdoch's important roles were duly chronicled in the press. In both he again appeared as the champion of the common man and woman. One was the dispute over the nomination of the new rector of St Paul's, Halifax's Anglican cathedral, in 1824–5. When the incumbent rector of St Paul's, John Inglis, was promoted to the bishopric in fall 1824, the Crown named as his successor the Archdeacon of New Brunswick, the Rev. Robert Willis. A large body of the congregation preferred the more evangelical curate, the Rev. John Thomas Twining.[62] The dispute was rapidly framed in legal and constitutional terms. Letters to the editor discussed whether Crown prerogative could prevail over the 1759 provincial statute, which expressly gave the right of presentation to the congregation, and whether the Crown's claim rested on provisions of ecclesiastical law, which arguably had not been received into the colony.[63] The matter was also framed in terms of freedom of conscience, with the choice put starkly: the dissenters 'must either submit and sit down contented under the ministry of a gentleman who is forced upon them contrary to their sentiments; or they must nobly assert their independence ... [out of] a just regard for their political and spiritual welfare.'[64]

The secretary of state would not turn back, but neither would the dissenters. A day-long public meeting, which Murdoch and others addressed, resulted in a vote of fifty-seven in favour of the right of the parish, and seventeen against.[65] One group of seceders ultimately founded the Granville Street Baptist Church, while another took refuge at St George's Anglican, the 'round church' which had been erected in the year of Murdoch's birth. Along with Thomas Chandler Haliburton and Richard John Uniacke, Jr, Murdoch joined the St George's group, abandoning the prestige that accompanied attendance at Halifax's 'first church' in the name of freedom of conscience. Haliburton's and Uniacke's connections were such that their stand did not harm them – within a few years each would be promoted to the bench, as would William Blowers Bliss, who conspicuously supported Bishop Inglis during the controversy. Just as Twining was consigned to the margins of Halifax Anglicanism, Murdoch too was vulnerable, perhaps more so than he realized. His outspoken opposition to the bishop gave another reason to the Halifax élite to distrust him.[66] His public opposition to what was widely considered as an arbitrary act of royal prerogative was, however, more favourably regarded in those groups from whom he drew his clientele, who continued to vote for him in the 1830 election (which he lost). It rested squarely within the traditions of the Glorious Revolution of 1688, which Greg Marquis has shown to be a staple of Maritime political discourse in the nineteenth century.[67]

Murdoch also played a prominent role in the controversy which surrounded the Poor Man's Friend Society. This philanthropic society had commenced activity in 1820 with the aim of relieving distress among the Halifax poor in the winter season. With the reduction in wages and general decline in trade which followed the end of the war in 1815, the plight of the poor in Halifax had become more acute and more evident, especially in winter. The society claimed to help 1,380 persons each year (over 10 per cent of Haligonians), mainly by providing wood and operating a soup kitchen. Its budget of some £400 was raised entirely by subscription. A series of letters in the *Novascotian* by 'Malthus', beginning in January 1825, attacked the society for dispensing charity indiscriminately and encouraging profligacy and immorality. The society was thrown on the defensive and compelled to articulate its mission, which it had assumed to be universally accepted.

Rising to the challenge, Murdoch accused 'Malthus' of being 'led astray by the cries of a cold calculating spirit.' He had once acted as a visitor for the society, and had 'found greater poverty than he could imagine, even in a respectable ward.'[68] As secretary to the society (jointly with fellow lawyer E.A. Crawley), Murdoch probably authored the report on the society's history and current activities which he read at the society's general meeting in February 1825.[69] As a defender of traditional forms of charity, Murdoch's position could not have been seen as upsetting the status quo. Yet it must have been some comfort to the humbler classes of Halifax society that Murdoch could articulate the basic needs of the poor in a convincing manner, and fend off attacks based on fashionable new theories of political economy. Charity on the part of the better-off was seen as an important part of the moral economy by all classes, and Murdoch's affirmation of its role could only have been seen as reassuring.

The key role played by craftsmen and small merchants in sustaining Murdoch's practice in the early years could probably have occurred only in the 1820s. By this point Halifax had a population sufficiently large, prosperous, and economically diversified to support the services of a lawyer like Murdoch, who could not depend on government appointments or the legal business of the mercantile élite. In the 1826 election, which resulted in his upset victory over the well-known merchant John Albro, Murdoch received his principal support from smallholders, shopkeepers, and artisans precisely because of his independence from both the official party and the influence of the major merchants. This election may be seen as the first in Nova Scotia in which a recognizable middle-class interest sought to achieve political expression, with Beamish Murdoch as its exemplar.

THE MIDDLE YEARS: GROWTH AND MATURITY, 1827–1840

The busy pace which Murdoch had set for himself in his law practice and his community, political, and cultural involvements did not slacken in the years after 1827. His law practice continued to grow, not only in terms of client volume, which probably doubled by the mid-1830s,[70] but in the variety and complexity of work which he performed and the amount of remuneration per client. The proportion of his practice devoted to debt-collection remained important but declined overall, as Murdoch spent more time on some types of work he had done little of before, such as conveyancing and the settlement of deceaseds' estates. Some tasks developed naturally from transactions he had engaged in during the 1820s: from drafting arbitration bonds, he went on to appear before arbitrators fairly frequently, and to sit as an arbitrator himself by the 1840s. He also began to engage in new professional endeavours, some of which had not existed before, such as work related to insurance, patents, and business corporations. Other horizons opened for him when he was admitted to practice before the Court of Marriage and Divorce and the Court of Vice-Admiralty in the 1830s, and his Chancery practice grew considerably. By the early 1840s Murdoch had achieved official recognition by his appointments as deputy judge in Vice-Admiralty (1838) and master in Chancery (1840). These achievements form an appropriate point of closure for the 'middle age' of his legal career.

The year 1840 also represented closure in another sense. After offering himself as a candidate in the elections of 1836 and 1840, Murdoch finally gave up his ambitions to regain the seat in the Assembly which he had lost in 1830. The changing political landscape of the 1830s had been very stressful for Murdoch. One of reformer Joseph Howe's most prominent supporters at his famous libel trial in 1835, Murdoch the next year opposed him on the hustings. Labelled a Tory and turncoat, he threw himself into the municipal politics which emerged after the incorporation of the city of Halifax in 1841. Here he achieved some success, serving as recorder for the city for the entire decade of the 1850s. This is not the place to examine in detail Murdoch's post-1835 political views, but some awareness of the shifting political landscape is a necessary backdrop to any examination of his legal career during these years.

In addition to his political activity, Murdoch remained in the public eye in the 1830s through literary and community involvements. His four-volume *Epitome of the Laws of Nova-Scotia*, modelled on Blackstone and on James Kent's *Commentaries on American Law* (1826), appeared in 1832–3. Although it did not provide him with the recognition he sought in the legal world, it was a substantial cultural achievement, fitting squarely within the parameters of the province's 'intellectual awakening' in the 1815–50 period.[71] Murdoch retained membership in a number of fraternal societies, but devoted his efforts principally to the Halifax Temperance Society, founded in 1831. He became its president in 1837, and when he retired from that office nine years later his colleagues noted that he had 'been oftener before the public than any other man resident among us (clergymen excepted). His unaffected kindness and gentleness of manners ... and the language and temper with which he generally addressed himself to the very numerous audiences that he has frequently spoke [sic] to, have made him well and acceptably known to almost every inhabitant of the City.'[72] With his evangelicalism, his relentless voluntarism, and his eminent respectability, Murdoch was a veritable icon of the early Victorian middle class.

The organization of Murdoch's law practice remained unchanged during this period, and indeed until his retirement. One might have expected him to go into partnership with his cousin Thomas Beamish Akins. Such an association would have fit comfortably within the parameters of familial law practices discussed earlier. In addition, Akins and Murdoch followed very similar life courses, both ending their days as bachelor lawyers devoted to historical research and scholarship. Yet when Akins was called to the bar in 1831, he soon established his own practice in an office on Granville Street. One might read into this action a rebellious assertion of independence by Akins, resistant to playing perpetual helpmeet to his dominant cousin. The continuing good relations between the two men, however, cast doubt on any such interpretation. More likely Akins's separate establishment reflects the widespread assumption that a sole practice was the 'natural' way for a lawyer to offer his services. In the absence of large corporate concerns, there was no particular incentive for lawyers to organize their practices any differently, and the non-specialist nature of both lawyers' services and their clientele was seen as the guarantee of the lawyer's independence.

Akins's departure would certainly have posed a labour problem for Murdoch. Virtually all legal papers, whether pleadings for litigation or private documents such as mortgages, wills, and deeds, were drawn up individually for each occasion, standard printed forms not being in use until some time after mid-century. The labour required for all this copying was supplied by articling students, possibly supplemented by scriveners who worked by the piece. Upon Akins's departure, it was likely Murdoch's young cousin Charles Ott Beamish who helped out in the office, although he did not ultimately become a lawyer. Francis Stephen Beamish (b. 1821), the son of Murdoch's uncle Thomas Ott Beamish, articled with Murdoch from about 1842 until his call to the bar in 1847, and his brother Thomas (b. 1829) also assisted in the office in the 1840s, but ultimately became a bookkeeper.

The principal records for this part of the analysis are Murdoch's day-book for the period January 1834–August 1836 and an account-book covering the period 1825–51. The daybook provides an apparently complete list of his clients, which permits an analysis of their class, gender, and ethnicity similar to that undertaken for the earlier period. The daybook can also be used in conjunction with the account-book and original court files to provide a window on the variety of legal work in which Murdoch engaged, and on his professional income.

After the early 1830s it became increasingly rare for Murdoch to write a letter or two for a client whom he would not see again. His practice slowly shifted from one in which he provided a few relatively simple services to a large number of 'small' clients, to one in which he provided a wider range of services to a more affluent and more regular clientele, although the 'small' clients never entirely disappeared. Murdoch's practice focused almost exclusively on private law: he continued to provide almost no legal services to government, the military, or the churches, and he very seldom represented clients in criminal proceedings.[73] The range and sophistication of legal services performed by Murdoch provides evidence of both his widening reputation and his enhanced experience, skills, and knowledge. More prominent clients came to him partly because they perceived that he was capable of doing more for them.

Over the years 1828–42, Murdoch represented Halifax merchant Benjamin Wier, a scion of the pre-Loyalist élite and future Canadian senator. He appeared for him in fourteen lawsuits, including two actions by Wier for defamation; advised him on his interest under a will; searched the title for properties on which Wier wished to take a mortgage; prepared mortgages, including one on Nova Scotian land owned by Wier's Upper Canadian brother to a lender in New Brunswick; prepared a variety of bonds; and provided advice on customs fees regarding the import of seal skins. In the early 1830s Wier's bill usually amounted to £20 per annum. For West India merchants Saltus & Wainwright, Murdoch drafted agreements; protested bills of exchange regarding shipments from Trinidad, Puerto Rico, and St Vincent; and provided advice on bottomry with regard to a schooner out of Antigua; he also drafted a deed and will for Wainwright. For rentier Dunbar Douglass Stewart, a Loyalist descendant who married into the Wier family, he provided constant conveyancing services and advice connected to money-lending through the 1830s. In 1839 Murdoch represented capitalist Enos Collins in an ejectment action at Windsor, and in 1842 he appeared before the new Halifax City Council to object to the assessments levied on Collins's properties for municipal-tax purposes.

This shift in the nature of Murdoch's practice is reflected in the class composition of his clientele as of 1834–6, although not noticeably in the gender or ethnicity of his clients, which remained steady at about 10 per cent female and 10 per cent Irish. It should be noted that some of the Irish population were quite upwardly mobile during this period, with the result that Irish ethnicity was not as reliable a proxy for disadvantage in the 1830s as it had been a decade earlier. The legal acculturation of Irish Catholics in Halifax would also have been facilitated by the appearance of Roman Catholic lawyers such as Laurence O'Connor Doyle, who was called to the bar in 1829.[74]

Murdoch's clientele underwent an almost complete turnover between the 1823–7 period and 1834–6. Only eleven clients from the earlier period, or about 7 per cent of the total, appear again in Murdoch's daybook of 1834–6. This change coincides with a decline in the number of artisans in Murdoch's clientele. Only five artisans or their wives can be positively identified in the daybook: carpenter James Dechman, Jr, who had been Murdoch's client from an early date; cabinet-maker James Scott, also an old client; Mrs Catherine Laffin, for whom Murdoch successfully obtained a judicial separation from her 'brushmaker' husband, Edward; John Robinson, hatter; and Samuel Cowan, furrier, who sought help regarding a troublesome apprentice, among other matters. Undoubtedly there were more who cannot now be identified, but the nature of the services performed by Murdoch for a large majority of the clients in the daybook makes it clear that they can only be merchants or persons of substantial property. Small merchants and widows still made up a significant proportion of Murdoch's clientele in 1834–6, but the artisans showed a substantial decline.

It is unclear whether they sought out other counsel, whether Murdoch actively discouraged them from continuing as clients, or whether legal services were becoming too expensive for them. Two facts taken together suggest a subtle but visible reorientation of Murdoch's public profile. He was not active in the Mechanics' Institute, founded in 1832, a notable absence, given his numerous community commitments. As well, the temperance cause, with which Murdoch was so actively engaged, was regarded with some suspicion by many artisans. Whatever the reasons, Murdoch's client base had a decidedly more middle-class cast in the mid-1830s than in the mid-1820s.

This change in clientele provided Murdoch with a higher professional income. He recorded his net income for the fifteen-month period May 1835–July 1836 as £349, or £280 for the year May 1835–April 1836.[75] The near tripling of his income since 1827 was a direct result of a more afflu-ent clientele, requiring more complex services, for which Murdoch could charge higher fees. Murdoch did not charge more for the same services because of his greater experience; his standard fee for a letter, for exam-ple, remained at 6s 8d from 1823 until the end of his practice in the 1860s. The calculation of fees remained transaction-based throughout his profes-sional life, although the idea of fees as remuneration for professional time appeared here and there in his records. Occasionally Murdoch charged a higher-than-usual fee for a particular service for 'extra trouble,' which must reflect some sense that he had to spend additional time on the matter.

There is no convenient source from which to calculate Murdoch's pro-fessional income after the mid–1830s. All that can be said is that it proba-bly continued to rise throughout the 1840s, especially after Murdoch began an active practice in Vice-Admiralty in 1836. His fees for eight cases in which he appeared in that court in the years 1836–9 amounted to an estimated £90, almost his entire annual income of a decade earlier. As well, Murdoch probably had more time to devote to his practice after the mid–1830s. His career in the House of Assembly had taken up a fair amount of his time in the years 1826–30, after which he plunged into the writing of his four-volume *Epitome of the Laws of Nova-Scotia* during the years 1830–3. Although he remained very active in voluntary societies and public affairs, Murdoch would still have had more time to devote to clients' business after the publication of the *Epitome*. The 1850s were prob-ably Murdoch's most prosperous decade, since he was able to cumulate his £200 salary as recorder with a still active practice.

The variety of legal services undertaken by Murdoch as his career matured poses a striking contrast with his earlier letter-book, so preoccu-pied with routine matters of debt. Some of these services were the result of new economic activities being carried on in the province. In early 1836 Murdoch was involved in a flurry of activity regarding a proposed 'Marine Slip or Railway, ... as will enable Owners of Ships or Vessels to obtain the repair thereof with dispatch and convenience.'[76] His mandate included drafting a petition to the legislature; agreements between the promoters, on the one hand, and the patent-holder and the builders, on the other; a partnership indenture between the promoters; and a long lease for the opinion of the attorney general. Twelve years later he advised John Ross in his negotiations with the Londonderry Mining Co. and on several points relating to its act of incorporation. He also began to do insurance work, both for and against the American insurance companies which began to offer their services in the province in the 1830s; the Aetna Insurance Co. was his only real corporate client during his entire career.

The vast bulk of his billings, however, related to kinds of transactions and litigation which had been familiar in the province for almost a century. The advertisement which Halifax lawyer Charles E.W. Schmidt inserted in the *Novascotian* in 1836 could just as well have been Murdoch's; Schmidt promised to 'bestow prompt attention to the Collection of Debts, Agencies, and Searches of Titles to Real Estate; and [to] draw ... Deeds, Mortgages, Bonds, Wills, Powers of Attorney, Indentures Agreements and Instruments of all descriptions.'[77] Most of these would be based on the precedents which students-at-law copied out so laboriously during the early years of their apprenticeship.[78] Drafting such documents and advising parties about their consequences formed the backbone of Murdoch's law practice. Such arrangements depend on 'facilitative law,' principally the law of contract, agency, partnership, trust, and property, which allows parties to order their affairs as seems best to them. As Halifax's middle class grew in numbers, self-consciousness, and prosperity, it created more of a demand for such mechanisms to assist both business planning and the transmission of familial assets to the next generation.

Dispute resolution, principally but not exclusively in the courts, formed the second major part of Murdoch's practice. Much of his litigation practice involved debt-collection, but a growing part of it did not. This development can be traced through the dizzying variety of courts and other bodies before which Murdoch appeared in the years between 1827 and 1842. In addition to the Supreme Court and the Court of Chancery, he appeared in the Court of Marriage and Divorce, Vice-Admiralty Court, Probate Court, Commissioners' Court, Inferior Court of Common Pleas, Quarter Sessions, the new Mayor's Court created after Halifax's incorporation in 1841, and, on one occasion, a court martial. He also represented clients before City Council, the House of Assembly, the lieutenant-governor in council, and private arbitrators. Once he carried on a long negotiation with the Commissioners of Sable Island with regard to the fate of a ship stranded on that unlucky shore. An examination of Murdoch's activity in the courts of Chancery, Vice-Admiralty, and Marriage and Divorce provides a good overview of both the shifts in his practice over this period, and the social and economic context in which this practice was carried on.

Murdoch's practice in Chancery and the two civil-law courts (Vice-Admiralty and the Court of Marriage and Divorce) did not get under way until the 1830s. Admission to the bar of the Supreme Court did not automatically entitle a barrister to plead in these courts. Lawyers had to apply for admission to each separately, but it is not clear whether the judges had any discretion to refuse an application from a duly qualified barrister. While the British North American colonies did not in general recognize a 'split' profession, the distinction between 'proctors' (solicitors) and 'advocates' (barristers) was retained to some extent in these three courts. Most cases tended to have two counsel on each side, one playing each role, something like the English system of senior and junior barristers.[79] In Vice-Admiralty especially, particular pairs of lawyers worked together on a number of cases over a period of years, forming a kind of specialized litigation partnership, while leaving their individual practices intact.

These three courts were united by a procedural system derived from canon law and Continental civil law, which was at sharp variance with the common-law procedure followed in the Supreme Court and (as a rule) the inferior courts. Common-law procedure essentially relied on oral testimony before a jury. The written pleadings which launched a case were largely formulaic and derived from precedents. Once a case got to court, neither the evidence nor the lawyers' arguments were written down, and often the judge's decision was oral as well, or written down very briefly.

The courts of Chancery, Vice-Admiralty, and Marriage and Divorce, by contrast, relied on written testimony heard by a judge[80] with no jury. Pleadings were not formulaic, but recounted the plaintiff's tale of woe in lengthy narrative. The defendant replied in kind, and commissioners were then appointed to take the evidence. The witnesses were called to respond to questions which had been written down by counsel and submitted to the commissioners, who conducted the interrogation. The answers were taken down in writing and 'published,' i.e., collated in the form of a (frequently sizeable) pamphlet for the perusal of the court. Oral argument was then allowed on points of law. Given this manner of proceeding, it was not surprising that court costs were much higher than in the common-law courts, leaving aside entirely the more liberal fee scale which the lawyers were entitled to charge.

Of the three courts, Chancery was the one which would most likely touch an ordinary citizen. The principal subject of its jurisdiction was the foreclosure of mortgages, which featured in four of the six cases in which Murdoch appeared between 1830 and 1834. Certain remedies such as injunctions and orders for an accounting could only be sought in Chancery, and were sought in the remaining two cases.[81]

The four foreclosure actions were all undefended, with final sale of the property occurring four to six months after the filing of the initial bill of complaint. The time did not vary significantly as between lands inside and outside of Halifax: In one case the lands were in Truro, and in another in Hants County, with the remaining two in the capital. In two cases one of the mortgagors was absent from the province, but the standard procedure was simply to order one month's notice in the *Royal Gazette* to the absentee. Failing an answer, the proceedings resumed.[82] Other complicating factors could arise. In *Hugh McDade et ux.* v. *Mary Hay et al.*, there were interventions by two other parties. First, claimants under an earlier mortgage appeared, seeking to ensure that their claims were not ignored (they were not). Second, the widow of Michael Leonard, the deceased mortgagee, had taken Mr McDade as her second husband, causing the guardians of Leonard's minor children to intervene. Laurence O'Connor Doyle and John Schrage wished to ensure that a portion of the proceeds of sale would be paid into court for the children's benefit (which they were). Despite these complications, Murdoch succeeded in getting the property sold and all claims settled in just over four months after the filing of the bill of complaint in November 1833.

The speed of the Chancery in these cases belies the constant criticism about its delay and inefficiency. Chancery could be quick in uncontested cases because there was no need to take written evidence; contested actions would unfold much more slowly. Whether speed was a good thing in foreclosure actions depended on one's point of view. What seemed expeditious to the mortgagee might have seemed unduly hasty to mortgagors in the process of losing their land. The actions of the mortgagees in these cases do not seem particularly oppressive when viewed in context. The mortgage in *McDade*, for example, dated from 1817, with the principal stated to be payable in one year. The original mortgagor, Peter Hay, a Halifax mason, had still not paid back the principal by the time of his death in February 1832. The mortgagee Leonard, and subsequently his estate, must have been content to operate on oral renewals as long as Hay could keep up the interest payments. It seems to have been Hay's death that precipitated the action for foreclosure, as his heirs proved less creditworthy than their father. In *John Crowe* v. *Isaiah Smith*, the mortgagors were found not to have paid a cent of interest during the four-year term, leaving the mortgagee little choice but to foreclose. And in *Dunbar Douglass Stewart* v. *Halliburton Grant et ux.*, the mortgagee absconded about the time that the mortgage term expired, again leaving the mortgagor little choice.

Complaints about the oppressive costs of Chancery were closer to the mark. The total bill of costs (lawyers' fees plus court costs) did not necessarily vary according to the size of the mortgage debt in question, with the result that the costs of foreclosure for small mortgage debts could be disproportionately high. For example, Murdoch acted for Newport gentleman Dunbar Douglass Stewart in foreclosing two mortgages in 1834. In one the mortgage debt was for about £150, in the other over £300, yet the costs in the first were £13 (8.6 per cent of the debt), in the second £14 (4.6 per cent). Both were much higher than Murdoch's charges for ordinary debt collection, which were 5 per cent on sums less than £100 and 2.5 per cent on larger sums.[83] Aside from the actual costs, Chancery seemed oppressive in another way, in that only cash auction sales of foreclosed property were allowed.[84] In a cash-poor society, this practice not only depressed the sale price but ensured that the mortgagee was likely to acquire it, as happened in *McDade*.

The real reason that many thought of Chancery as oppressive was simply that its proceedings laid bare the deep economic inequalities of Nova Scotian society. All the mortgagees for whom Murdoch acted were described as 'Esquire' (Stewart) or 'gentleman' (Crowe, Leonard). D.D. Stewart was the son of an assistant judge of the Supreme Court, James Stewart, and the nephew of another, Brenton Halliburton, who became Chief Justice in 1833. Called to the bar in 1816, Stewart appears to have been a dilettante lawyer who preferred the life of a county squire at Newport. In the *Rhalves* proceeding, it was recounted that Frederick Rhalves had taken out mortgages on various properties with not only Simon Bradstreet Robie, but prominent Halifax merchants James and Michael Tobin, Samuel Cunard, and Henry Yeomans. Those being foreclosed against were such people as Isaiah Smith, yeoman, and his wife, Lydia; grocer Halliburton Grant and his wife, Mary Ann;[85] the family of mason Peter Hay, and farmers Robert and Anna Kent of Truro. Murdoch's developing Chancery practice assisted his professional bottom line, but it also represented a significant shift in his clientele, towards the holders of wealth and status in provincial society.

Murdoch was admitted as a proctor and advocate before the Court of Vice-Admiralty sometime in the mid-1830s. The first reference in his own records to an 'appearance in V-A Court' is in August 1835, in proceedings taken by the attorney general to declare forfeit the cargo of the American schooner *Caleb* for violation of the Navigation Acts.[86] The earliest trace of

Murdoch in the minute-book of the court is in the October 1836 case of *Enoch Sears* v. *Nicholas Moran*.[87]

Proceedings in the Vice-Admiralty Court did not reveal the inequalities of Nova Scotian society in the same stark way that those in Chancery did. In some ways, the former allowed the tables to be turned, as sailors and disgruntled passengers used the court's pre-trial procedures to arrest captains and shipowners in order to answer claims over unpaid wages and breach of contract. In *Sears*, for example, Murdoch defended Captain Moran against an action by the ship's cook for £6 15s in wages alleged to be due. Moran was arrested on 8 October to prevent him from leaving port until the action could be heard, which was the usual procedure in Vice-Admiralty. When judgment went against him five weeks later, he became liable for the cook's costs in the amount of £36 15s 10d, not to mention the sums he would have had to pay his own lawyers. Two years later Murdoch unsuccessfully defended the captain of the brig *Ann* against a claim for unjust dismissal. This time the sailor was entitled to £55 damages plus costs, being seven months' wages and return-travel expenses to Halifax from Pernambuco, where he had been put off the ship.[88] These vignettes accord with Judith Fingard's interpretation of pre-1845 sailors' wage litigation in Vice-Admiralty, 'where residual mercantilist notions made the judge the special protector of the transient, vulnerable seafarer.'[89]

Murdoch had more success in defending the four actions brought against George Barker, captain of the ship *Panther*, in 1837.[90] In these, as in the two wage cases, he acted as advocate, with lawyer William Sutherland appearing as proctor. The *Panther* litigation involved an American ship which had accepted £5 each from a group of passengers for a passage from County Sligo to New York in summer 1837. The ship was damaged in a storm during the crossing, and put into Halifax for repairs and provisions, at which time the passengers instituted their claims for breach of contract. Barker was arrested at the end of August and remained in jail until Murdoch and Sutherland secured his release by a writ of *habeas corpus* from the Supreme Court in October. The court decided that Vice-Admiralty possessed no jurisdiction over the contracts of passage since they were made on land in Ireland, and not only released Barker but issued a writ of prohibition to Vice-Admiralty judge Charles Rufus Fairbanks.

The case escalated into a *cause célèbre* when Fairbanks refused to recognize the writ and proceeded with the case, upon which Sutherland wrote him a private letter indicating his client's intention to pursue legal action against the judge. Fairbanks chose to treat this act as a contempt of court, fined Sutherland £20, and prohibited him from practice.[91] When Sutherland refused to pay, Fairbanks had him committed to jail on 19 December. The same day Murdoch sought his release by a writ of *habeas corpus* from the Supreme Court, which was granted two days later on the basis that the Vice-Admiralty Court had, at most, power to fine or imprison for contempt in open court, which was not the case here.[92] The contretemps illustrates once again Murdoch's refusal to tolerate abuse of authority, even at a time in his life when he was coming to be identified more closely with the very 'establishment' he had so often challenged in the past.

The late 1830s saw Murdoch involved in two other Admiralty cases, both involving salvage. His work for the salvors in the salvage of the ship *Ajax* netted him an estimated £20.[93] In the case of the ship *Scio*, he worked as proctor for Captain John K. Lane, master of the fishing schooner *Franklin* out of Gloucester, Massachusetts. His application for salvage compensation illustrated the drama, danger, and courage which accompanied the seagoing life in the age of sail. The crew of the *Scio* had abandoned ship on 16 May 1838, when the vessel was totally surrounded by ice and fog off the east coast of Nova Scotia. Adrift in a small boat, they were rescued thirteen hours later and brought to Halifax. Lane found the unoccupied ship drifting off Liscomb Harbour three days later, and had it brought to port. His crew of ten unloaded its cargo of lumber and repaired the ship over the next two weeks, with the intention of sailing it back to the United States. On the return voyage a storm blew up off Halifax, and the vessel had to be abandoned after it began to leak badly. It drifted to shore and was eventually sold under authority of the court. Its sale price of £194 was awarded half to the owners of the *Franklin* and the salvage crew, and half to the owners of the *Scio* and her cargo, but the latter share of £97 had to bear the full legal costs of £64, which included Murdoch's fee for £22.[94]

Murdoch's practice in the Court of Marriage and Divorce was not large in absolute numbers, but in view of the court's very small case-load, he was its most experienced lawyer in the 1830s and 1840s. A lifelong bachelor, Murdoch may seem an unlikely champion of women's rights. Yet he represented women in four of the five cases which he pleaded before the court between 1831 and 1850, and in three of these he put the application on the ground of cruelty. He was successful only on the first of these, probably because he advised Catherine Laffin to seek only a judicial separation rather than a full divorce.[95] Terminating a marriage for anything less than adultery met with much reluctance, not just on the part of the judges and executive councillors, but among Nova Scotians in general.

Cruelty had been a cause of divorce in the province since at least the statute of 1761, which formally constituted the court, and had been pleaded on occasion. Unfortunately, the sketchiness of the records before the 1830s makes it impossible to know whether the plea succeeded.[96]

The first recorded instances of divorces being granted on the ground of cruelty occurred in 1834 and 1835, while Murdoch had obtained Catherine Laffin's separation from bed and board in 1832 or 1833.[97] The 1830s would remain the high-water mark of indulgence to the plea of cruelty for decades: not until 1879 was it again successfully invoked. Murdoch's efforts on behalf of Eliza Parker in 1841–2 were unsuccessful, in spite of the fact that her husband, Joseph, did not appear.[98] His efforts on behalf of Patricia Carey, who also sought a divorce on the basis of cruelty, came to nought when her 1842 petition was not pursued.

The libel which Murdoch composed on behalf of Patricia Carey in 1842 was particularly eloquent and moving. It recounted in agonizing detail her life with Captain Lamarchand Carey of the 76th Regiment of Foot after their marriage at Gretna Green in the early 1830s. Captain Carey was stationed at Quebec for some years, where their three children were born, and where Mrs Carey alleged he had two children by their servant Mary Dodd. She also alleged that he began to beat her after their first child was born. In 1839 they entered into a separation agreement, when he returned to England with their son and she went to live at Peterborough, Upper Canada, with the other children. Contrary to her wishes, he allowed their son to become part of his household with Dodd. When he proposed a reconciliation in 1841, she went to New York to meet him, whence they sailed to his new posting in Bermuda. There, she said, he abused her, refused to send for a doctor when she suffered a miscarriage, and habitually went to brothels. When he returned to Halifax with his regiment in November 1841, she saw her chance and consulted Murdoch.

Only the declaration exists in the court file, but it provides a useful guide to Murdoch's views on the law of marital cruelty. He put the emphasis, not on the physical brutality, but on Carey's disrespect and the psychological indignities he inflicted on Patricia Carey. The document reflects an underlying philosophy of a companionate marriage between equals, rather than the Old Testament view of marriage which continued to hold sway in the Court of Marriage and Divorce until well into the twentieth century.[99] The other two cases in which Murdoch appeared involved a schoolteacher from Blandford, who succeeded in obtaining a divorce from his adulterous wife, and a farm wife from the Antigonish area, for whom he was appointed defence counsel by the court.[100] Even as his client base shifted towards the propertied, Murdoch remained sympathetic to the claims of women in distress.

CONCLUSION

The entire legal career of Beamish Murdoch was carried on before the formal trappings of modern legal professionalism existed. University legal education, autonomous statutory bodies of professional governance, codes of ethics, the law firm, specialization – all postdated Murdoch's death. Yet considering the contours of his legal practice over time, one is struck by the continuity between his life and that of the modern lawyer. There is the same struggle to acquire a clientele and a reputation in the early years, resulting in the same devotion to voluntary organizations as a means of meeting and understanding one's market and obtaining leadership experience. There is also the same need for many years of hard work while one acquires the necessary skills and experience to attract more clients, with the attainment of a superior level of remuneration achieved fairly late in one's career. The main differences at the level of daily practice are simply technological: the quill pen, the post, and personal attendance versus the typewriter, telephone, and computer.

In some respects, however, Murdoch does look back to the old idea of the profession as a personal calling rather than forward to the time when a law (or other professional) practice might be considered as a business enterprise whose 'goodwill' could be sold or evaluated. Early Victorian lawyers did not believe that their law practices were marketable. Inheritable, yes – as noted at the outset, fathers often hoped to be able to pass on their clientele to their lawyer sons. But transferable to a stranger – no. If a lawyer left no sons, he might well practise law until he died, or, as Murdoch did, simply fold up his tent and retire. This unwillingness to consider a law practice as 'property' was congruent with the commitment to sole-practitionership as the ideal form for the practice of law. It would take a much deeper penetration of capitalist ideals into Maritime society before lawyers would come to think of their practices as constituting a kind of capital, or come to model their organization on business enterprises.

NOTES

1 The exception was the firm of James W. Johnston, William Blowers Bliss, and Alexander Stewart, which was established at Halifax *circa* 1830; its existence is

known only from correspondence in the DesBarres family fonds at the Public Archives of Nova Scotia, and I am grateful to archivist Barry Cahill for sharing this information with me.

2 Richard John Eckert, 'The Gentlemen of the Profession': The Emergence of Lawyers in Massachusetts, 1630–1810 (New York: Garland Publishing 1991), p. 2 of unpaginated preface. Works such as A.G. Roeber's Faithful Magistrates and Republican Lawyers: Creators of Virginia Legal Culture, 1680–1810 (Chapel Hill: University of North Carolina Press 1981) tell us little about the actual work of lawyers, and even Eckert's book contains only a few pages on the subject (203–8). See, though, Carol Berkin, Jonathan Sewall: Odyssey of an American Loyalist (New York: Columbia University Press 1974), chap. 2; Milton M. Klein, 'The Rise of the New York Bar: The Legal Career of William Livingston,' in David H. Flaherty, ed., Essays in the History of Early American Law (Chapel Hill: University of North Carolina Press 1969), 392–417.

3 Stephen Botein, 'The Legal Profession in Colonial North America,' in Wilfrid Prest, ed., Lawyers in Early Modern Europe and America (New York: Holmes & Meier 1981), 129–46

4 Gerald W. Gawalt, The Promise of Power: The Emergence of the Legal Profession in Massachusetts, 1760–1840 (Westport, CT: Greenwood Press 1979)

5 G. Blaine Baker, 'The Juvenile Advocate Society, 1821–1826: Self-Proclaimed Schoolroom for Upper Canada's Governing Class,' Canadian Historical Association, Historical Papers (1985), 74–101; G. Blaine Baker, 'Legal Education in Upper Canada, 1785–1889: The Law Society as Educator,' in David H. Flaherty, ed., Essays in the History of Canadian Law, vol. 2 (Toronto: The Osgoode Society 1983), 49–142; G. Blaine Baker, "So Elegant a Web": Providential Order and the Rule of Secular Law in Early Nineteenth-Century Upper Canada,' University of Toronto Law Journal 38 (1988), 184–205; Paul Romney, 'From the Types Riot to the Rebellion: Elite Ideology, Anti-legal Sentiment, Political Violence, and the Rule of Law in Upper Canada,' Ontario History 79/2 (1987), 113–44; D.G. Bell, 'Paths to the Law in the Maritimes, 1810–1825: The Bliss Brothers and Their Circle,' Nova Scotia Historical Review 8/2 (1988), 6–39

6 Murdoch's letter-books devoted to clients with business in Halifax County have not survived.

7 These can be found in Public Archives of Nova Scotia (hereinafter PANS) as, respectively, MG 3, vols. 1838B, 1836B, 1836A, 1836C, 1835B, 1838A, 1837, and 1835A. All future MG or RG references are to PANS materials, unless otherwise noted.

8 An Act for the better regulation of Attornies, Solicitors and Proctors, practising in the Courts of Law and Equity in this Province, Statutes of Nova Scotia (hereinafter, SNS) 1811, c. 3, s. 16

9 When Beamish Murdoch's will was contested by Charles Beamish, the latter testified that he had come to Halifax to live with Murdoch after his (Charles's) father's death for a year and a half. From this I deduce that Murdoch had his own establishment by 1821.

10 RG 39, ser. M

11 Gordon Bale, *Chief Justice William Johnstone Ritchie: Responsible Government and Judicial Review* (Ottawa: Carleton University Press 1991), 15

12 Beamish Murdoch, *Epitome of the Laws of Nova-Scotia*, 4 vols. (Halifax: Joseph Howe 1832–3), vol. 1, 12

13 The towns were Shelburne, Digby, Cornwallis (Kentville), Windsor, Yarmouth, Amherst, and Truro: 'Pythagoras,' *The Nova Scotia Almanack for Town and Country for the Year of our Lord 1821* (Halifax: Edmund Ward 1821).

14 For an overview of the provincial and urban economy during this period see David Sutherland, 'Halifax Merchants and the Pursuit of Development, 1783–1850,' *Canadian Historical Review* 59/1 (1978), 1–17.

15 Daniel Duman, *The English and Colonial Bars in the Nineteenth Century* (London: Croom Helm 1983), 202

16 One study of access to justice in early modern England found that 70 to 80 per cent of litigants appearing in the courts of King's Bench and Common Pleas between 1560 and 1640 came from the ranks of yeoman farmers, merchants, artisans, labourers, professional men, and their widows: Christopher W. Brooks 'Litigants and Attorneys in the King's Bench and Common Pleas, 1560–1640,' in J.H. Baker, ed., *Legal Records and the Historian* (London: Royal Historical Society 1978), 41–59.

17 Neither Murdoch's account-books nor his letter-book give any hint that he ever appeared before a justice of the peace in a debt (or any other) matter.

18 Dale Darling, 'Nova Scotia Supreme Court Records, Halifax County, 1830–1832' (unpublished ms. on file with the author 1993). These figures include all claims, not just debt claims, but the debt cases constituted between 80 and 90 per cent of all Supreme Court litigation during these years. The Supreme Court case files are virtually complete for these years, but become much less so in the later 1830s.

19 Inferior Court of Common Pleas, Halifax County, RG 37 HX, vol. 25

20 At least, this can be deduced from the rapid decline in the number of judgments rendered in the Inferior Court of Common Pleas for Halifax County after 1818. From an average of fifty cases per year in the years 1815–18, the number of judgments declined to three or four annually for the next five years, to zero in 1824–6, and to one or two annually until 1831. A study of the caseload of the Commissioners' Court for the period 1827–37 requested by the House of Assembly revealed that the court rendered 435 judgments in 1828

alone. Nova Scotia, *Journals and Proceedings of the House of Assembly* (1837), App. 81.

21 Supreme Court Book of Original Entries, 1815–30, RG 39, ser. J, vol. 105

22 MG 3, vol. 1838B. There are eighty-five documents in the letter-book, but I have excluded the last one from consideration since it relates to Murdoch's personal business. The top right-hand corner of the volume is shorn off, and consequently there is no pagination, but the documents follow in chronological sequence and are thus referred to here by date only.

23 Parrsboro was part of Kings County at this time; it would not become part of Cumberland County until 1840.

24 RG 39, ser. J., vol. 105, 15 September 1825. A similar train of events occurred when Murdoch tried to collect a debt from merchant Israel Harding on behalf of Halifax merchants William and Francis Letson. A summons sent to the sheriff of Cumberland in January 1826 could not be served on Harding, but by the end of the year Murdoch had found that Harding was living in Yarmouth. He wrote Harding there on 16 November, informing him that he was now responsible for the expenses of the Cumberland writ (£1 3s 8d) as well as the original debt of £4 12s 7d, and urged him to settle as soon as possible, 'as I have directions to sue for the same and do not wish to put you to greater expense.'

25 Halifax: Cunnabell 1827

26 MG 3, vol. 1838B, Murdoch to E.H. Chandler [*sic*: error for Cutler], Sheriff of Annapolis County, 17 November 1826

27 Ibid., Murdoch to Kenneth McDonald, Sheriff of Sydney County, 10 August 1825

28 SNS 1819, c. 22 (first passed in 1763). See generally Philip Girard, 'Married Women's Property, Chancery Abolition, and Insolvency Law: Law Reform in Nova Scotia 1820–1867,' in Philip Girard and Jim Phillips, eds., *Essays in the History of Canadian Law, Vol. 3: Nova Scotia* (Toronto: The Osgoode Society 1990) [hereinafter *Essays 3*], 92–100.

29 MG 3, vol. 1838B, Murdoch to Henry Blackadar, 8 June [*sic* – 8 July] 1828

30 Ibid., Murdoch to Alexander Stewart, 27 May 1828

31 Ibid., 10 April 1823

32 Ibid., Murdoch to Ross and William Murray, 23 June 1828. The Murrays had agreed to act as sureties to McLennan.

33 The partnership agreement drafted in 1823 contained such a clause. For a fuller precedent, see the one at p. 39 of 'Charles E.W. Schmidt's Precedent Book 1827,' a manuscript held in the Rare Books collection of the Dalhousie Law Library (hereinafter 'Schmidt Precedent Book').

34 On arbitration generally, see Murdoch, *Epitome*, vol. 4, 36–41. In cases where no more than two partners disputed over less than £500, the legislature pro-

vided in 1829 that they had to choose arbitration on the model described rather than go to Chancery. If the parties refused to choose arbitrators, the Supreme Court would do so for them: SNS 1829, c. 28. Murdoch supported the bill in the Assembly: *Novascotian*, 12 March 1829.

35 J.M. Bourne, *Patronage and Society in Nineteenth-Century England* (London: E. Arnold 1986), 9. The consideration of petitions took up a good deal of time at each sitting of the House of Assembly.

36 MG 3, vol. 1838B, undated petition of William Long and Thomas Phelan. The petition was presented to the House of Assembly on 3 March 1823: *Journals and Proceedings of the House of Assembly 1820–1826* (Halifax 1826), 243.

37 MG 3, vol. 1838B, Murdoch to Hon. J.C. Calhoun, 30 November 1824

38 MG 3, vol. 1836B

39 Ibid.

40 Eckert, *'Gentlemen of the Profession,'* 205

41 William Young Papers, MG 2, vol. 760 (Young's daybook for period 1825–34)

42 *Novascotian*, 13 April 1825, 124–5. The original case file is extant in RG 39, ser. C (Halifax), box 169, but it is framed as a formulaic demand for debt and gives no hint of the context.

43 The case file is no longer extant, but Murdoch gives a brief account of the case in his *Epitome*, vol. 3, 82–3.

44 Unlike Upper Canada, Nova Scotia had had a separate Court of Chancery since at least 1751, provided for in the Governor's Commission. See generally C.J. Townshend, *History of the Court of Chancery in Nova Scotia* (Toronto: Carswell 1900); Barry Cahill, *'Bleak House* Revisited: The Records and Papers of the Court of Chancery of Nova Scotia,' *Archivaria* 29 (1989–90), 149–67; Barry Cahill, 'From Imperium to Colony: Reinventing a Metropolitan Legal Institution in Late Eighteenth-Century Nova Scotia,' in D.W. Nichol, Iona Bulgin, Sandra Hannaford, and David Wilson, eds., *Transatlantic Crossings: Eighteenth-Century Vistas* (St John's, NF: Memorial University of Newfoundland 1995), 11–24; Jim Cruikshank, 'The Chancery Court of Nova Scotia, Jurisdiction and Procedure 1751–1855,' *Dalhousie Journal of Legal Studies* 1 (1992), 27–48. The contributions by Girard and by Clara Greco, 'The Superior Court Judiciary of Nova Scotia, 1754–1900: A Collective Biography' to Girard and Phillips, *Essays* 3, also contain relevant material.

  Admission to the Chancery bar after the statute of 1811 was *pro forma* for those already admitted to the bar of the Supreme Court, but the exact date of Murdoch's admission is unknown.

45 RG 36, ser. A, box 163, file 773

46 *William Sutherland* v. *Thomas J. Keegan, Beamish Murdoch, Michael Burnet, Bartholomew Hackett, David Fletcher, and John Albro*, RG 39, ser. J, vol. 105, 20 Septem-

ber 1826. Sutherland catered the meal and sued for the agreed price in this
action, which he said had not been paid.

47 George Renny Young's *Novascotian* contains satirical coverage, reported in
dialect, of disputes between Irishmen in the Commissioners' Court in many
issues in early 1825.

48 Tybo is mentioned as a landlord in the account of a court case reported in the
Acadian Recorder, 21 January 1826. For the letter to Watts, see MG 3, 1838B, 13
August 1827. Tybo alleged that Watts had purchased a horse belonging to
Tybo from Tybo's vendor, with whom Tybo had left the horse, knowing that
the vendor had already sold the horse.

49 This calculation is not as straightforward as it might seem, given the presence of 'collective' clients such as the families of deceased persons. If it was
clear that a deceased man had left a widow, the estate was counted as two
clients, one male and one female. While somewhat arbitrary, this method
allows some generalizations to be made without having to trace the families of each deceased client, and without overestimating the number of
women.

50 RG 39, ser. J, vol. 105, 13 October 1825

51 MG 3, vol. 1838B, Murdoch to Hinshelwood, 14 August, 23 December, and 30
December 1823, and 10 September 1824. RG 47, vol. 49, 444 (Halifax County
Registry of Deeds)

52 This includes the eighteen women identified as widows.

53 MG 3, vol. 1836B, 61–2

54 Ibid. The account with James Scott at the end of the volume shows that Murdoch was paying £90 p.a. rent for the house at 32 Barrington St before he purchased it for £1,102 on 27 November 1832, after which he paid annual interest
of £66.

Murdoch's total income from other sources is not known. He received £40
p.a. from Philip J. Holland for editorial assistance on the *Acadian Recorder* over
the period May 1824–September 1826. Murdoch had begun to invest in mortgages by at least 1827: MG 10, vol. 23, no. 47b, is the release of the equity of
redemption in a Cape Breton property from Thomas Nowlan to Murdoch and
J. Scott Tremain, which recites that they had taken a mortgage for £37 on the
property in 1827.

55 MG 3, vol. 1838B, Murdoch to Capt. Thomas Hurlow, 7 June 1828

56 Curiously, there is extant a draft of an indenture of apprenticeship between
Murdoch and George Renny Young, the brother of future premier and chief
justice William Young: William Young Papers, MG 2, vol. 731, no. 42. Dated 1
November 1821, the document suggests that Murdoch contemplated taking on
Young as an articling student. Young postponed his decision to study law

until the 1830s, however, and occupied himself with the editorship of the *Novascotian* in the interim.

57 *Novascotian*, 31 May 1832

58 Brian Cuthbertson, *Johnny Bluenose at the Polls: Epic Nova Scotian Election Battles, 1758–1848* (Halifax: Formac 1994), 58, has analysed voting patterns in the 1830 election (which Murdoch lost) and concluded that 'almost all Murdoch's votes were 'independent' ones, ... and came from the middle and humble classes.'

59 It is difficult to assess what 'success' means for an individual lawyer, much less to determine the relative success of a number of lawyers. As a rough index of size of client base, I counted the number of Supreme Court cases for the year 1827 in which Murdoch and thirteen other near contemporaries appeared. The top group comprises David Shaw Clarke, William Young, Charles Twining, and J. Scott Tremain with fifty-seven, fifty-four, twenty-five, and twenty-two cases, respectively. Murdoch came next, with fourteen; Wentworth Flieger, with six; and all the rest had between one and four appearances. This was a low year for Murdoch, as he had thirty-three, twenty-three, and thirty-two appearances in the previous three years, respectively, putting him far ahead of most of his contemporaries.

60 Note 42, above, and accompanying text

61 It is possible, of course, in a small community such as Halifax in the 1820s, that some at least of the jurors would have known the litigants personally or by repute and been able to form opinions about their credibility based on out-of-court experiences.

62 Judith Fingard, 'John Thomas Twining,' *Dictionary of Canadian Biography*, vol. 8 (Toronto: University of Toronto Press 1985), 901–2

63 Letter by 'Martin Luther,' *Acadian Recorder*, 4 December 1824. Under English ecclesiastical law, the Crown could appoint a new rector to an English parish only in the unusual case where the incumbent rector was promoted to a bishopric, as Inglis was.

64 See the letter by 'Juridicus,' *Novascotian*, 27 April 1825, 140–1. The tone and style of the letter are very much that of Murdoch, but there is no clear evidence proving his authorship.

65 *Novascotian*, 4 May 1825

66 Norah Story, 'The Church and State "Party" in Nova Scotia, 1749–1851,' Nova Scotia Historical Society, *Collections* 27 (1947), 46

67 Greg Marquis, 'In Defense of Liberty: 17th-Century England and 19th-Century Maritime Political Culture,' *University of New Brunswick Law Journal* 42 (1993), 69–94

68 *Novascotian*, 2 February 1825

69 Ibid., 18 February 1825. The annual reports for the society for the years 1820–

25 survive at PANS as part of the Akins Collection. See generally George E. Hart, 'The Halifax Poor Man's Friend Society, 1820–27: An Early Social Experiment,' *Canadian Historical Review* 34/2 (1953), 109–23.

70 This is only a rough estimate derived from comparing Murdoch's known client base during his first five years of practice (1823–7 inclusive, ignoring the second half of 1822, when he had no known clients) with his client base as revealed in his daybook for the period January 1834–August 1836, found at MG 3, vol. 1838A. Murdoch's known client base during the first five years of practice (153) equals almost exactly the number of clients recorded in his daybook in the later period (143), which is only half as long. Thus one can say that his practice increased in volume by no more than 100 per cent, and the increase might well have been less than that.

71 See generally Philip Girard, 'Themes and Variations in Early Canadian Legal Culture: Beamish Murdoch and his *Epitome of the Laws of Nova-Scotia*,' *Law and History Review* 11 (1993), 101–44.

72 Quoted in Sandra Lynn Barry, 'Shades of Vice and Moral Glory: The Temperance Movement in Nova Scotia, 1828–48,' MA thesis, University of New Brunswick, 1986, 64

73 In 1834 Murdoch was retained by the District of Halifax to assist Clerk of the Peace David Shaw Clarke in drafting eight bills for the consideration of the legislature, but this is the only such entry in his account-books. There are very occasional references to representing clients at trials at Quarter Sessions, and in 1841 Murdoch was paid £36 to prosecute Lieut. A.B. Parker of the 64th Regiment before a court martial at Halifax.

74 See generally Terrence M. Punch, *Irish Halifax: The Immigrant Generation* (Halifax: International Education Centre, St. Mary's University, 1981).

75 While this was a very respectable income, it does not mean Murdoch was necessarily in easy circumstances. Two judgments were obtained against him in the Supreme Court in 1835, the first on a promissory note for £90 given to Joey H. Metzler by Murdoch in February 1834, the second on an 1833 note for £50 given jointly by Murdoch and his uncle Thomas Ott Beamish to Simon Crabbs: RG 39 C (Halifax), box 179. These judgments suggest a liquidity problem, perhaps brought on by the debts incurred by Murdoch in the publication of his *Epitome*.

76 An Act for securing to John Story, and his Assigns, the exclusive Right in a certain Slip or Railway, for the use of Vessels, SNS 1834–5, c. 23. The act allowed Story the exclusive use of this device for ten years, provided it should be erected within a year. It was not, and Murdoch successfully lobbied the legislature to give him an extension to 1 August 1836: SNS 1836, c. 77.

77 *Novascotian*, 17 August 1836

78 A specimen of this kind from Murdoch's own apprenticeship survives in the Rare Books collection of the Dalhousie Law Library, under the title 'Forms of the Supreme Court' (*c.* 1816–21).

79 This was true in Vice-Admiralty and the Court of Marriage and Divorce, but was less common in Chancery. I would like to thank Barry Cahill for pointing out the parallel with the English bar.

80 The Court of Marriage and Divorce sat with several judges. Before 1841, the governor-in-council possessed this jurisdiction, which was held to require the presence of a majority of the members of the council, in addition to the governor's personal presence. In 1841 the court was reconstituted, and the governor was authorized to appoint a judge of the Supreme Court to preside as vice-president, assisted by two members of the council. The chief justice was given this commission in 1841, and was usually but not invariably assisted by the master of the rolls and the attorney general. See generally Kimberley Smith Maynard, 'Divorce in Nova Scotia, 1750–1890,' in Girard and Phillips, eds., *Essays 3*, 241, and 'Divorce Book May 1840–February 1902,' held at the Prothonotary's Office, Law Courts, Halifax, NS.

81 The cases files are all found in RG 36: *James Black* v. *James and Andrew Muir* (1830), box 190, no. 917 (injunction); *John H. Flohr and Sarah Rahlves* v. *Simon B. Robie et al.* (1830), box 192, no. 924 (accounting); *John Crowe* v. *Isaiah Smith* (1830), box 197, no. 951; *Dunbar Douglass Stewart* v. *Robert Kent et ux.* (1833), box 213, no. 1038; *Hugh McDade et ux.* v. *Mary Hay et al.* (1833), box 213, no. 1039; *Dunbar Douglass Stewart* v. *Halliburton Grant et ux.* (1834), box 215, no. 1056. For the period to 1836, a list prepared by the registrar in Chancery provides the name of counsel beside each case. The post-1836 list has disappeared, making it difficult to trace a particular lawyer's profile in the court after that date.

82 They could be reopened within three years upon the return of the debtor, and the foreclosing mortgagee had to provide security to cover the eventuality that the foreclosure might be successfully defended within that time.

83 MG 3, vol. 1838B, Murdoch to Rev. Alexander Waugh, 20 June 1826

84 Ibid., Murdoch to Mrs Ann Hinshelwood, 10 September 1824

85 Grant's 'absence' in the foreclosure suit brought by Dunbar Douglass Stewart might well have been a polite fiction, or a way of saving the expense of a contested suit, since he soon afterwards appears in Murdoch's daybook filing for protection under the Insolvent Debtors Act.

86 MG 3, vol. 1838A. The case file for *Caleb* is RG 40, vol. 9, no. 7. Murdoch recorded that he appeared for Joseph Bryant, a merchant from Castine, Maine, who owned the cargo.

87 RG 40, vol. 9, no. 15. For an excellent overview of the development of the

Court of Vice-Admiralty in Nova Scotia, see Arthur J. Stone, 'The Admiralty Court in Colonial Nova Scotia,' 17 *Dalhousie Law Journal* 2 (1994), 363–429.

88 RG 40, vol. 12, no. 2

89 Judith Fingard, *Jack in Port: Sailortowns of Eastern Canada* (Toronto: University of Toronto Press 1982), 187. Fingard asserts that Vice-Admiralty's jurisdiction over seamen's wages was limited to claims over £20 at this time. In fact the House of Assembly passed such a measure in 1837, ostensibly to assist seamen (but probably in response to the *Sears* case of the previous year), but London disallowed it because Vice-Admiralty was an imperial court over which the provincial legislature had no authority: Stone, 'Admiralty Court,' 406. A similar proposal in 1841 met with the same response, but the Colonial Office suggested that the province take advantage of the imperial act 5 & 6 William IV, c. 19, s. 15, which gave the magistrates a summary jurisdiction for seamen's wage claims under £20. This act did not actually deprive the Vice-Admiralty Court of jurisdiction over such claims, but provided that a plaintiff who succeeded in that court when he could have brought the claim before the magistrates, would not be entitled to costs: RG 40, vol. 13, no. 12, J. Dodson and T. Wilde to Russell, 13 August 1841. It is not clear to what extent this suggestion was taken up in Halifax.

90 RG 40, vol. 11, nos. 1–4. See also Stone, 'Admiralty Court,' 407–9, for a treatment of what follows.

91 Such techniques remained in use thirty years later, when Chief Justice William Young chose to treat an allegation of bias against him in a private letter from Halifax lawyer T.J. Wallace as a contempt of court, and struck Wallace from the barristers' roll. This time it took the Judicial Committee of the Privy Council to undo the precipitous act of an outraged judge: See Sandra Oxner, 'A Fractious Fraternity: The Nova Scotia Supreme Court under Sir William Young, 1860–1881,' paper delivered at the Atlantic Law and History Workshop II, Dalhousie Law School, Halifax, NS, 4 March 1995; *In re T.J. Wallace* (1865), 5 *Nova Scotia Law Reports*, 654. Such abuses ultimately resulted in the removal of much of the judges' disciplinary power over the bar during the professional reform campaign of the 1880s. There is a delicious irony in Young's role in *Wallace*: He had been prominent in the bar's investigation of the Sutherland suspension, which in effect censured Fairbanks for the same action for which Young was taken to task by the Privy Council – the report is found in Sir William Young Fonds, MG 2, vol. 732, no. 210.

92 *In re William Sutherland's application for habeas corpus* (1837), RG 39, ser. C (Halifax), box 180. *Novascotian*, 6 December, 20 December, 27 December 1837

93 RG 40, vol. 13, no. 1. The file does not show the costs which were awarded to Murdoch. The estimate is based on his fees in the *Scio*, which amounted to £25

in all. The court file in the *Ajax* is even more voluminous, so the £20 estimate is a conservative one.

94 RG 40, vol. 12, no. 12. The file is voluminous, and must have involved a good deal of work on Murdoch's part. He charged Lane £3 for 'extra work' above the costs he received from the court.

95 This case is known only through oblique references; no case file has survived. On 17 October 1831, Murdoch wrote to Sir Rupert George to set a date for the hearing of the case: RG 1, vol. 238, no. 72 1/2. His account-books show Catherine Laffin as a client, and in 1838 he was obliged to sue the surviving executor of her husband to recover his fees in the action, which Mr Laffin had failed to pay during his lifetime: *Murdoch* v. *Cassedy*, RG 39 C (Halifax), box 181. Murdoch alleges that he successfully obtained a decree of judicial separation and an order for alimony on Mrs Laffin's behalf. This case is also the first known in which Murdoch appeared before the Court of Marriage and Divorce; he was presumably admitted as a proctor and advocate by mid-1831 at the latest.

96 See, generally, Maynard, 'Divorce in Nova Scotia.'

97 The 1835 divorce of Charlotte Hynes was obtained in the usual way through the Court of Marriage and Divorce. The 1834 divorce of Anne Kidston was obtained via a private act of the House of Assembly, the only such divorce in Nova Scotia history. She remarried shortly after, her new husband being Mr Justice William Hill of the Supreme Court of Nova Scotia. Hill had been acting solicitor general prior to his appointment to the bench in 1833, and may have assisted in drawing up the legislation in his capacity as deputy provincial secretary.

98 All the evidence was taken, but the last document in the file is the petition for its publication. It is not known whether a final decree was issued.

99 J.G. Snell, 'Marital Cruelty: Women and the Nova Scotia Divorce Court, 1900–1939,' *Acadiensis* 18/1 (1988), 3–32

100 This practice was adopted to ensure that there was no collusion between the parties.

3

Aemilius Irving: Solicitor to the Great Western Railway, 1855–1872

JAMIE BENIDICKSON

Although the private law firm – whether the conventional partnership or the sole practitioner's office – was, and remains, the predominant mechanism for the delivery of legal services, other options have appeared. Through a review of the work of Aemilius Irving at the Great Western Railway, this essay explores the early Canadian development of one of these alternatives, the in-house counsel.

In the course of a legal career that extended from his call to the bar in 1849 to the time of his death in 1913 as Canada's oldest practitioner, Aemilius Irving retained the respect of colleagues for his skills as a legal adviser and for a number of much-admired professional qualities. Eulogies credited him with having made a vital contribution to the province of Ontario as a long-serving treasurer of the Law Society and as one closely associated with many formative constitutional conflicts between the federal and provincial governments. As the *Globe* explained, Irving undertook vast quantities of laborious but unostentatious work in complex situations involving constitutional law or technical questions concerning easements, franchises, and the like. 'Only those on the inside of the Provincial Administration,' the newspaper account continued, 'knew how much Ontario owes to him for extensive research that no other available member of the profession had the ability and the lore to carry as he did.'[1] To appreciate the significance of such praise, one need only recall a few of Irving's contemporaries – Edward Blake, B.B. Osler, Christopher Robinson, Leighton McCarthy, and Zebulon Lash – many of whom left their names to enduring law firms.[2]

The *Globe* referred to Irving as 'in an important sense a professional partner of Sir Oliver Mowat' in the latter's capacity as premier and attorney general. Formidable as it might have been, no partnership was ever actually established between Irving and Mowat, at least not in the sense that the two men were ever associated as professionals in a firm created for the delivery of legal services. Indeed, with the exception of very short periods of time, Irving had no professional partners. Although he collaborated in various ways with other lawyers, he was neither a sole practitioner nor a partner in a firm. Aemilius Irving honed his skills and developed his reputation as a salaried corporate solicitor. He practised law from his Hamilton office in the Canadian headquarters building of his employer, the Great Western Railway (GWR). In the pre-Confederation era, when his employment with the GWR began, the nature and structure of his practice were distinctive, and in some respects controversial.

It is the purpose of this essay, in describing one part of Irving's legal career, to highlight not only the unique features of the practice of one of the country's first in-house counsel, but to suggest ways in which his experience as a railway lawyer fitted him for a number of the tasks he subsequently undertook as assistant and confidant of Premier Mowat.

IRVING'S APPOINTMENT TO THE GREAT WESTERN RAILWAY

When Irving joined the Great Western in the mid-1850s, the railway was one of Upper Canada's most active rail carriers, transporting freight and passengers along a prosperous and expanding corridor through the southwestern section of the province. A significant proportion of the eventual traffic originated in the United States, travelling through Upper Canada to rejoin American lines for the completion of its journey.[3]

The great range and volume of legal transactions inherent in its operations made the Great Western a very attractive client. Thus, John Ogilvie Hatt enjoyed an active practice in the service of the railway, so long, at least, as its business affairs were under the close control of his law-office partner and brother-in-law, Allan Napier MacNab.[4] Land acquisition for the route and the process of construction required constant efforts to reconcile railway interests with those of landowners, municipalities, contractors, and financial institutions. Given the distinctive nature of its requirements for rail, cars, and equipment, the railway, almost from the outset of its operations, could also be regarded as one of the country's major manufacturing enterprises.[5] Once in operation, the Great Western's ongoing interaction with passengers, shippers, and other lines with which it was in competition or in alliance produced commercial irritants and disputes requiring resolution. A good number of accident compensation claims involving both employees and ticketholders linked the railway with the personal fate of provincial residents and non-resident travellers.

In late October 1854, a Great Western train had collided with a train of ballast cars involved in continuing work on a railway line that had been opened to traffic before the completion of roadbed construction. The deaths of some fifty passengers and crew, and injury to a like number, immediately triggered a coroner's investigation, a commission of inquiry, numerous pieces of private litigation, and, in due course, legislation.[6]

Railways in the United Kingdom, where the GWR's corporate headquarters were located, had begun, as Rande Kostal has described in an innovative account, *Law and English Railway Capitalism, 1825–1875*, a process of corporate reorganization that would involve a close integration of counsel in operations. Kostal argues, in relation to escalating damage claims from railway accidents in the 1860s, that the companies set out 'to minimize these costs by creating private industry's first corporate legal departments staffed by salaried solicitors kept under the close supervision of management.'[7] And he documents the creation of England's first corporate legal department in 1861.[8]

At the time of Irving's appointment at mid-century, the GWR was still in the midst of the aftershock arising from the calamitous Baptiste Creek accident, and the development of an in-house legal department might be viewed as one element of the railway's response to the legal entanglements that had placed onerous demands on senior railway officials and had exposed them to criminal charges in the matter. On the other hand, the railway's records contain little to suggest a specific linkage between personal-injury claims and the creation of salaried legal positions at corporate headquarters. Other factors – those frequently recognized as motivations for the creation of legal departments inside larger enterprises – were equally relevant.[9] Yet, in the specific context of the Great Western, the decline of MacNab's authority and the rise of managing director C.J. Brydges – appointed by the railway's English owners to safeguard their investment – helped to precipitate the termination of the GWR's arrangements with John O. Hatt.

In July 1854, the Great Western's Canadian directors undertook an assessment of the existing relationship with the company's independent legal adviser.[10] Citing the grounds of convenience and cost, they reported that the GWR's legal business should be placed on a different footing, and resolved 'to appoint a solicitor at a paid salary, who shall occupy himself exclusively with the business of the company, and have rooms at the General Offices.'[11] Miles O'Reilly signed on as of 1 October 1854, one month before the Baptiste Creek tragedy, accepting for his 'undivided services' an annual salary of £1,000, out of which he was expected to provide personally for a clerk or clerks, as required.[12] Although his salary was increased to £1,250 as of the first anniversary of his appointment, O'Reilly resigned within a month of the raise. The Great Western advertised for a replacement.

The advertisement, inviting application for the position of a solicitor to be paid an annual salary, provoked the *Upper Canada Law Journal* to express its doubts 'as to the propriety or practicality of the proceeding.' Putting the invitation on a par with that of 'a tradesman who advertises for "a hand,"' the *Law Journal* was later surprised to learn that the in-house position had been filled.[13] This would not be the last occasion on which those who were comfortable with the established pattern of practice would scorn an innovation that challenged the authority of existing firms as exclusive suppliers of legal services and advice.

Aemilius Irving, together with his more senior associate John Wellington Gwynne, QC, reached an agreement with the Great Western late in 1855. The date of the appointment is some five or six years ahead of the establishment of the first in-house railway legal department in England, but is quite in keeping with the experience of the United States, where a small number of legal departments had been established by railways in the 1850s.[14]

Given a general effort at mid-century to reaffirm strong professional norms within the legal community,[15] and in particular the measure of hostility towards salaried counsel suggested by the *Law Journal*'s outburst against the GWR's advertisement for a solicitor, one might wonder why Irving and Gwynne were attracted to positions with the Great Western. The question may be more easily answered in Gwynne's case than in Irving's, for the former, at least, was already thoroughly familiar with railway matters: Gwynne had actively promoted railway schemes for many years, and had provided solicitor's services, parliamentary lobbying, and public-relations help to the Toronto and Guelph Railway in the early 1850s.[16] Perhaps Irving, a much younger man, was perceived merely as an assistant to Gwynne, although, when the senior lawyer left the Great

Western after not much more than a year or so, Irving seemed fully able to satisfy all the railway's requirements.

Irving was born in England in 1823, and studied there and in France before emigrating to Canada in 1834 with his father, Jacob Aemilius, a justice of the peace who was soon prominent in Reform ranks as a member of the Legislative Council. Young Irving continued his studies at Upper Canada College and was called to the bar in 1849. He practised law briefly in Toronto before moving to Galt (Cambridge) in 1851 to become Waterloo County's first clerk of the peace. How he came to be associated with Gwynne in the practice of law is unknown, but, as a fellow Reformer, Gwynne had likely become familiar with his young colleague's family.

Charles J. Brydges, managing director of the GWR for at least the first half of the period of Irving's service, later had occasion to describe elements of the financial relationship between the railway and its in-house legal advisers. According to Brydges, whenever counsel recovered costs in litigation in which they were employed on behalf of the GWR, the funds received neither were payable to the railway nor served to reduce the amount owed by the railway for the services of its full-time legal staff. The only exception involved the recovery of expenditures for disbursements where such funds had in fact been advanced by the railway. Irving and Gwynne, who moved on after a year or so, offered the railway no indemnity against costs that could be recovered by parties who succeeded in litigation against the railway.

These arrangements were the subject of detailed judicial consideration when an unsuccessful litigant, Jarvis, urged that certain items claimed in a bill of costs following Irving's successful defence of the Great Western's interests were not properly taxable.[17] Costs (particularly on an attorney-and-client basis), the argument ran, are awarded to the client as reimbursement for the expense of litigation. Counsel's only claim for payment would be against his own client, and not against the opposing party. Since counsel for the railway was presumed to practise as the 'salaried servant' of the railway, Jarvis protested that Irving had no entitlement to a personal claim for costs, and that in seeking to recover attorney-and-client fees following successful litigation, the railway would profit unlawfully from Irving's professional services. While the argument is framed from the perspective of Jarvis, the client, it may readily be imagined on the basis of the *Law Journal*'s outspoken condemnation of the attorney as 'tradesman' that some members of the profession welcomed the opportunity to attack Irving's deviant approach to the delivery of legal services.

Perhaps any general inclination to question the financial arrangements the GWR had with its in-house legal adviser was even strengthened by the railway's decision in 1857 to discontinue an established practice of giving retainers to firms whose services it occasionally required.[18]

Chief Justice William Henry Draper found the terms of Irving's arrangements unique in his experience, an observation tending to confirm the innovative nature of this lawyer–client relationship. Draper considered the terms of the agreement 'well calculated to stimulate the exertions of the attorney, whose income must increase with every cause in which he succeeds for his clients, if the opposite parties are solvent, while he has the certainty of his salary to remunerate him for his time and labour if unsuccessful.'[19] It was impossible, Draper concluded, to attribute elements of the salary to individual suits, nor could anything other than an arbitrary division be made between legal work associated with litigation and general advice, conveyancing, and like services. Draper's analysis led him to reject any suggestion of champerty or maintenance, but in the circumstances he restricted the railway's claim for costs to actual disbursements.

The case of the railway lawyer's fees did not pass without public comment, nor was it without significance for Irving's relations with the GWR. The *Law Journal* took the opportunity to restate its highly opinionated objections to the arrangements:

The hire of a solicitor, body and bones, at an annual salary, appeared to us to be not only something new in the practice of the law, but something which savored of a studied insult to the profession ... every man who has at heart the dignity of his profession must see throughout a meretricious union between a trading corporation and a solicitor of the courts, which appears to be as dishonourable in the one as it is degrading in the other.[20]

The GWR's response to the *Jarvis* decision was stimulated in part by a desire to reconcile the terms of its original agreement with Irving and the prohibitive implications of Draper's judgment. Equally significant, however, were the anticipated consequences of the court ruling. The *Law Journal* remarked in the immediate aftermath of the *Jarvis* decision that unsuccessful parties in proceedings against the GWR would doubtless thank the railway for imposing on them costs of about £2 when £12 or more might otherwise have been payable. The railway's finance committee, in a discussion that law and economics theorists of a later age would instinctively appreciate, noted that 'the knowledge of this freedom from the payment of the Company's costs, even though the verdict should be obtained by the Company, would probably operate to induce parties to commence doubtful actions against the Company, and in which they would not have ventured had they been liable for costs in the event of losing the verdict.'[21] Relations between Irving and the railway were therefore re-configured, with a base salary to remain at its then current level of $3,200 per annum for all his legal services with the exception of 'his costs as taxable between party and party in suits for and against this Company in which the Company shall be successful.'[22] This agreement eliminated any need to consider a legislative response to Draper's ruling.

THE SOLICITOR'S CASE-LOAD

Notwithstanding the contribution of railways to the provincial economy and acceptance of the idea that this new form of transportation represented progress,[23] the GWR was engaged in an extraordinary amount of litigation.[24] The case-load involved numerous claims with competitors, with suppliers and business associates, with those whose lands had been occupied or injured in some way as a result of the construction, with dissatisfied shippers, and particularly with injured travellers, or with the estates of patrons whose journeys had ended in fatal accidents – a tragically frequent occurrence in the early years of the GWR's operation.

Shippers' Losses

The claims of shippers whose cargoes were damaged, lost, stolen, or delayed while in the hands of Upper Canada's railways, or the complaints of passengers who had experienced loss or damage to goods accompanying them on their travels, did not fare well in the courts. Where the railways defended, they did so vigorously, relying heavily upon contractual terms designed to exclude liability. R.C.B. Risk, citing several of Irving's cases, notes that the railways were successful, 'regardless of the unfairness, the lack of power of the shippers, and the lack of any alternative.'[25] In practice, however, an alternative did exist in the form of a direct application to the railways. The GWR records indicate that, following investigation of the original complaint, many such claims received formal consideration from company officials, and that 'compensations' were regularly awarded. Messrs Hurd and Roberts, for example, were paid sixty dollars for twenty-nine bags of timothy seed that had been 'missent' from Hamilton to Rome rather than Oneida, where, regrettably, 'they remained until the season for their use had passed.'[26] Although claims such as this were small, the availability of in-house counsel had at least two attractions over reliance on outside firms. First, conflicts were eliminated; that is, the Great Western would never have to hear that independent counsel also represented the shipper and felt unable to act in the circumstances. More significant, the incentive that potentially large payments for legal services might create to settle generously for a payment above an otherwise achievable level of agreement on damages was also removed: The cost of the in-house legal department would not rise just because one, or even a few shippers' claims might require an unusual effort to resolve.

Municipal Assessments

The coming of the railways to rural England presented parish officials with an irresistible opportunity to impose some of their expenditures on enterprises that had little direct influence over local affairs. As Rande Kostal explains, 'uncertainty regarding the correct application of the law of local rates assessment to railways, and the not unnoticed fact that railway companies only rarely were locally owned, combined to create an exceptional opportunity for rural elites to realize a windfall of tax revenues.'[27] Kostal ultimately concludes that, in the United Kingdom, railway companies were 'singularly ineffective' in litigation designed to check the tax-gouging of rural officials, and that, by the 1870s, many of the largest operations instructed their parliamentary lobbyists to pursue the cause that the trial lawyers had lost.[28]

When municipal-assessment officers across southern Ontario engaged in their own local efforts to maximize the tax burden facing the new transportation network, they were met with determined resistance from the railways. Irving was regularly engaged in litigation against aggressive municipal assessments, generally involving attempts to tax 'superstructure' rather than land value alone.[29] Quite apart from his appearances in court on precisely formulated questions of legal principle, Irving was responsible for the systematic scrutiny of municipal assessments of railway property. At the end of 1858, he reported the results of a four-year analysis of each municipal assessment, providing detailed annotations on the nature of each local claim and identifying any remaining opportunities for reductions. In many cases, Irving's negotiations had already resulted in significant savings to the railway.[30] Municipalities, more than any other of his employer's antagonists, seem to have raised the solicitor's ire, for in connection with one dispute he lamented a 'senseless' verdict in a case involving 'injustice and tyrannical conduct' on the part of local officials.[31] Again, the continuity provided by knowledgeable counsel operating within the overall structure of the enterprise probably reduced demands on the time of senior officials, and certainly facilitated a systematic and ongoing effort to lessen the Great Western's tax expenditures.

Railway Legislation and the Regulatory State

The introduction of general railway legislation to supplement and alter the terms of incorporating statutes or charters was accompanied by the appearance of public officials intent on exercising newly created regulatory powers. When government inspectors requested documentation and information from the Great Western, or when – still more intrusively – they instructed the railway to undertake certain repairs, clearing operations, or tree removals along the main line or branches, the managing committee regularly sought the advice of its solicitor.[32] Irving also took charge of the formulation of by-laws prepared for submission to the Board of Railway Commissioners and was similarly involved in compiling the internal rules and regulations applicable to all employees. Indeed, management required that 'every person in the service ... keep a copy of these Regulations on his person while on duty, under a penalty of five shillings currency for neglect of the same.'[33]

On an ongoing basis, Irving assumed responsibility for monitoring legislative developments with a view to protecting the company's interests in forthcoming enactments. In this regard, he was occasionally dispatched to Quebec City to make representations to legislative committees, as occurred in 1860, for example, when he intervened in connection with a proposal by the Hamilton Water Works Commissioners to obtain authority to assess water rates on all real and personal property adjacent to the water pipes.[34] At another point Irving personally prepared the original draft of legislation conferring on railway constables a jurisdiction that was independent of the localized county-based legal structure and more in keeping with the requirements of an enterprise whose operations extended across the province.[35]

Perhaps not surprisingly, Irving was soon in attendance – on behalf of the Great Western – at the Quebec Conference of 1864 leading to the Canadian Confederation arrangements three years later. As W.L. Morton explains, the railways could not go unrepresented at a forum where so much depended on the extension of their lines: 'The railway chieftains had to know what was going on, and they had to be available to tell any politician under pressure what was possible and what might be dared.'[36] The GWR solicitor's performance at the Quebec Conference and on other occasions was such that George Brown – among others – urged him to consider running for a seat in the House of Commons in 1867. Irving, though flattered by the invitation, replied from Hamilton that he was 'too closely engaged here to think of it,' yet he expressed a willingness to consider the provincial legislature as an alternative, for a seat in Toronto 'would not interfere with my arrangements.'[37]

He was apparently quite content to live on James Street in Hamilton, with his office in the Great Western Railway building. With four trains running daily between Hamilton and Toronto, the two cities were only ninety minutes apart. It was thus entirely possible to put in a full working day and return home in the evening.[38] Such convenient arrangements allowed Irving to maintain and develop professional relationships with Toronto-based practitioners. Yet it is also clear from the correspondence that, like so many of his contemporaries at the bar, he harboured political aspirations. The right circumstances might well induce a change of career, or at least the addition of political commitments alongside his ongoing legal responsibilities.

Personal Injury and Accident Compensation

The Baptiste Creek incident a year or so before Irving's appointment was far from the last major accident on the GWR line. Accordingly, as corporate solicitor, Irving had occasion to serve the Great Western in connection with the legal aftermath of several other major disasters, and numerous lesser accidents involving personal injury or the loss of life of passengers and company employees.

When a passenger train proceeding slowly along the GWR's Hamilton branch (also known as the Hamilton and Toronto Railroad), approached the swing bridge over the Desjardins Canal connecting Dundas with Burlington Bay, a second calamity on a par with Baptiste Creek entered the railway's tragic history. Shortly before 6:00 P.M. on 12 March 1857, an engine car – the *Oxford* – the tender, the baggage car, and two first-class passenger coaches crashed through the bridge timbers and plummeted forty feet to the icy waters of the canal. Of ninety-five or ninety-six passengers and crew, only twenty escaped the wreckage and a dozen or so were rescued from the canal.

The dead included professionals, men of commerce and industry, as well as a number of women and children. The Great Western's managing director, C.J. Brydges, lost a brother-in-law; Samuel Zimmerman, a very prosperous builder from Niagara Falls who had constructed over 120 miles of the railway and had been contracted to build still more, also perished.[39] Irving's household was not untouched by the disaster, as Diana McFiggan, a domestic servant of the railway's solicitor, was either killed in the crash or drowned in the immediate aftermath.[40]

The coroner's investigation, under the direction of Dr H.B. Bull and Dr J.W. Roseburgh, began almost immediately with an examination of the bodies. Seventeen jurors were sworn on Friday, 13 March, with the investigation itself under way by Saturday in the context of funeral preparations and memorial services. Hamilton, it was reported, was a city 'shrouded in sackcloth,' with immense crowds estimated at ten thousand and processions observing 'the mournful requiem.' 'It seemed,' ran one account, 'as if the entire city had turned out to express their sorrow for the dead and their sympathy for the bereaved.' Dignitaries from various parts of the province and the United States were joined by the families of victims in mourning. 'All seemed deeply affected by the loss which has been sustained and desirous of paying the last tribute of respect to the departed.'[41]

At the inquest, Stephen Richards appeared for the Crown, while the Great Western, many of whose employees and officials would give evidence over an intense two weeks, was represented by John Wellington Gwynne. Gwynne's most important interventions were directed towards the task of discrediting F.P. Rubidge, Assistant Engineer of Public Works, and undermining his claim that the Desjardins Canal Swing Bridge had been 'in an unsound, impaired and dangerous condition on or before the 12th of March last.'[42] Irving, it would appear, was engaged in the preparation of documentation and, perhaps even in early settlement discussions.

Following more than fourteen days of evidence, the jury's verdict, dated 8 April 1857, attributed the immediate cause of the accident to the breakage of a forward axle on the engine, an incident that occurred barely six days after the *Oxford* had been 'turned out of the repair shop in a good and satisfactory condition.' As for the bridge itself, the inquest found it sufficiently sound to ensure safe conveyance, 'provided that the locomotive and cars remained on the railway track, but that the said bridge was not built of sufficient strength to sustain an engine and train in case they should run off the track while passing over the said bridge.'[43]

It is not entirely clear how many claims, with what overall damages, were brought against the GWR. English accidents giving rise to claims running from £80,000 to £150,000 in the mid to late 1860s were considered noteworthy;[44] so, judging from the nature of the known claims, the Desjardins Canal accident would clearly have been remarkable for its time. The number of claims was such that Irving and Gwynne could not have taken on all the proceedings, even if they had been so inclined. Indeed, the Desjardins litigation illustrates another important feature of in-house counsel's practice: the selection and instruction of other practitioners to represent the Great Western in individual cases forming part of a larger legal controversy. George Skeffington Connor, QC, and J. Hillyard Cameron, QC, were among those with assignments in 1857, but over the years Irving had occasion to hire a good many other lawyers on the railway's behalf. Law firms' unease about the adverse consequences of in-house counsel was no doubt tempered, therefore, by the realization that valuable and important work would still be available to them.

The Great Western frequently allowed default judgment to go against it in claims brought on behalf of family members of the Desjardins accident victims.[45] There were exceptions, however, the Samuel Zimmerman litigation being one example; in that case, the railway mounted a determined defence based on its claim that Zimmerman, a director of the Niagara Falls Suspension Bridge Company, was travelling on a free pass, under the terms of which he assumed all risks of accident and damages.[46] Where supported by the facts, such a defence precluded compensation, as Irving, perhaps with mixed emotions, reported to railway officials in connection with a Berlin court's rejection of a claim advanced by the father of his household servant, Diana McFiggan. The girl had been travelling on a free pass – quite possibly obtained for her by her employer – 'with the usual conditions.'[47]

Non-resident claimants such as the family of a seller of Indian curiosities from Niagara Falls, New York, might also find their claims opposed.[48] The GWR was more likely, though, to resist damages where it considered the jury's award excessively generous to the plaintiffs,[49] and, on occasion, succeeded in having the question of compensation submitted to a new jury.[50] Large claims, such as the £15,000 in damages sought on behalf of the widow and unborn child of the barrister and attorney Adam Ferrie, might require particular care. Here, Irving personally pursued an application for interrogatories concerning the terms of the deceased lawyer's will, hoping perhaps to identify assets or insurance arrangements that might moderate the level of recoverable damages.[51] Given that damages of

£9,000 in an English railway-accident claim several years after the *Ferrie* case was considered a record, it is not surprising that the Canadian case merited close scrutiny.[52] In related litigation, the GWR pursued the Desjardins Canal Company for certain comfort concerning the condition of the rerouted canal and the now-destroyed bridge.[53]

Another accident, the collapse of a stretch of an embankment near Flamboro, outside Hamilton, in March 1859, again called for most careful attention: Four claims alone involved damages totalling $130,000. The trials of these four cases – claims by Braid, Fawcett, Cook, and McAleese – resulted in damage awards of $19,000 and presented Irving with a delicate situation. The most detailed of Irving's memoranda recorded formally in the minutes of the GWR concern these cases.[54] They reveal a highly refined mastery of the technical considerations combined with an astute sensitivity to the railway's overall interests. Ultimately, on Irving's advice, these cases proceeded to the Judicial Committee of the Privy Council, where the legal principle was lost, much to the regret of the wider railway community.[55] Yet the Great Western's immediate exposure to higher damage awards had never been increased as a result of Irving's strategy.

Despite their notoriety, major accident claims reaching the courts represented only a modest number of the total compensation awards to injury victims and their families. Personal-injury claims were customarily settled through negotiations. Injured employees, or the families of employees who died through work-related accidents, were also eligible for compensation through an informal process of application and, later, insurance. Records suggest a clear distinction in the minds of management between deserving and undeserving applicants, with limited consideration going to any employee 'killed by his own imprudence.' On the other hand, the survivors of the 'very old and faithful servant' or of those who 'bore a good character for sobriety and attention to ... duties' could anticipate at least modest payments, described as 'donations' or 'gratuities.'[56] By the early 1870s, with Irving then in regular attendance at the meetings of the Canadian directors of the GWR, the company's arrangements with Citizens Insurance provided coverage for railway employees both in Canada and the United States.[57]

Intercorporate Relations

Relations between the Great Western and the Grand Trunk produced further requirements for Irving's legal services. The two rival lines, for the purpose of avoiding injurious competition between them, agreed in 1860 to standardize 'through rates' for passengers and freight over certain routes which shippers or travellers might view as equivalent means of reaching their destinations. The arrangement between the railways provided for revenue-sharing as well as mutual access to accounting records for the ten-year life of the agreement.[58] Yet, in the early 1860s, when the Great Western calculated that some $50,000 was owed to it, the GTR challenged the validity of the agreement as lacking the consent of two-thirds of the stockholders. This formal requirement, clearly embodied in railway legislation, had not actually been satisfied by either company, even though the shareholders of both enterprises were well aware of the agreement and received regular reports about its operational results.

In the initial proceedings, the court fully accepted the Grand Trunk's *ultra vires* argument that, where the statute authorized interchange and rate-setting agreements 'subject to the consent of two thirds of the stockholders,' then it clearly 'requires the expression of such consent as a condition precedent to the validity of the agreement.'[59] Following this setback, Irving and M.C. Cameron astutely reformulated the Great Western's claim on equitable grounds, seeking an injunction to prevent the Grand Trunk from invoking the *ultra vires* defence. Hagarty, J, viewed the new challenge as raising 'a very grave question.' As he explained the circumstances: 'The alleged equity is, that the existence of the agreement, after it had been in actual operation, was made known to the shareholders in written reports, and announced at a regular meeting, and that they had full notice of it, and neither then nor afterwards dissented, but knowingly permitted it to be continued and acted on, and approved of sums found due as balances.'[60] Though ultimately unsuccessful, the attempt was typical of Irving's ability to reconceptualize a dispute for the purpose of obtaining a thorough judicial airing of important matters. Similar ingenuity was also required in connection with some of the Great Western's ongoing clashes with financial institutions over interest levels, rates of exchange, and so on. In one such case, the English directors awarded Irving a substantial financial bonus for his contribution.[61]

Expansions and Acquisitions

Irving's responsibilities extended well beyond the remedial or defensive work that so often took him before the courts of Upper Canada. Property-management issues, such as fencing, minor compensation for flooding, easements, insurance, and the recording of deeds, required detailed attention on an ongoing basis. Irving was there to oblige. Having applied himself diligently to mastering the intricacies of the existing operation, Irving was occasionally overwhelmed by new strategic developments. Expansion through acquisition strained even Irving's capacity for work. In submissions to the Canadian board and to officials at the Great Western's London office, Irving argued that his efforts in connection with the right of way on the new Canada line fell outside the parameters of his ordinary responsibilities. The examination of numerous deeds, often leading to 'long and difficult' negotiations, encouraged him to re-examine his professional arrangements and to compare his situation with that of colleagues in private firms. He proposed remuneration on the basis of an average fee of $5 per deed executed, an amount he considered to be moderate and to fall well below the level 'I should expect if any other relations subsisted between me and the Company than those which exist.'[62]

OUTSIDE INTERESTS

The railway had intended its solicitor to devote himself exclusively to its concerns, and although there is no reason to imagine that Irving ever failed to put the GWR at the top of his list of obligations, he had other preoccupations. He had inherited responsibility for overseeing the administration of 'Ironshore,' a family estate in Jamaica, and it is clear that both the financial obligations and the time required in connection with the property were sources of concern to him. This direct exposure to the vicissitudes of international markets and property values may have satisfied whatever personal entrepreneurial inclinations Irving ever had. Nevertheless, after attaining a position of considerable prominence within the Great Western organization, Irving appears to have accepted certain external positions of strategic importance to his employer.

Chartered in 1835 and open for business shortly thereafter, the Gore Bank, like the Great Western, enjoyed the close attention of Sir Allan MacNab. The bank directed its operations towards the financing requirements of the western reaches of the province. Although it survived the crisis of 1857–8, it remained crippled by uncollectible debts and gradually succumbed to the subsequent downturn of the mid-1860s.[63] Irving joined the bank's board of directors in this difficult period, and was in fact president in the late 1860s. His abrupt resignation arose from an acrimonious clash with an individual whose bitter resentment over a personal misunderstanding presented difficulties for both the Gore Bank and the Great Western. In explaining his resignation, Irving stated that he had stepped down 'with very great regret,' feeling, however, that his departure would put beyond question any suggestion that in supplanting an aggrieved rival he had acted 'from motives, personal to myself.' 'Perhaps there is no satisfactory reason,' he continued, 'why I should have conceded so much, but I thought the Great Western Directors hoped that by resignation, some of the feelings which animated Mr. Street on parting with them would be removed, and this idea influenced me.'[64]

RESIGNATION AND RETIREMENT

The combination of his long-standing political aspirations and the impact of his labours on details associated with the GWR's acquisition of the 'Canada' line eventually stimulated Irving to reassess his relationship with the railway. Within a year of his petition for further remuneration in connection with the new right-of-way negotiations, Irving tendered his resignation, anticipating a political career and seemingly unable to reconcile the income from his current employment with his personal requirements as the father of eight children and the proprietor of a troublesome Caribbean estate. The financial position of his more successful professional contemporaries in independent practice seems to have become a source of increasing irritation.

Rande Kostal observes that railway officials 'rarely (and grudgingly)' acknowledged the contributions that lawyers and their skills made to achieving the organizational and commercial goals of their enterprises.[65] Yet the GWR, as a gesture of thanks for his invaluable service over seventeen years, offered a retirement gift of £500, and the Canadian directors urged their London superiors 'to make some arrangement by which his knowledge of the affairs of the Company, and advice can be availed of.'[66] Irving expressed his sincere thanks in September 1872, but – presumably in the absence of an ongoing relationship – Irving corresponded with the railway's directors to remind them of the minuted decision dating back to the aftermath of the *Jarvis* case on his eligibility to recover litigation costs. The reminder was accompanied by an account for $4,500, Irving's calculation of the amount outstanding under the agreement.[67]

Irving then pursued his political inclinations with mixed success during the early 1870s, leaving his mark in the House of Commons chiefly for moving a legislative amendment intended to eliminate appeals from Canadian courts to those of Great Britain.[68] Partway through the decade, though, he returned to the practice of law, with the Province of Ontario as his principal client.

THE RAILWAY SOLICITOR AS GOVERNMENT LAWYER

Irving's transition from in-house counsel for the GWR to a status amounting more or less to that of 'government lawyer' does not – on first impression – appear as logical as it may have to Premier Oliver Mowat. The relationship between the premier and Irving may have been a far-sighted one from the outset, but perhaps Mowat simply offered a little work to a qualified political associate and then discovered – as the GWR had learned – that Irving's usefulness had few limits.

The inclination to attribute Irving's eventual stature and reputation to longevity alone must be tempered with the acknowledgment that his involvement in intricate constitutional matters such as the Manitoba Boundary controversy, the executive-powers cases, the fisheries reference, and other high-profile litigation such as the prosecution of George Bennett for the murder of George Brown extended back over several decades. Yet his original appointment by Mowat as Crown counsel in the 1870s came some years after Irving had concluded a distinctive and remarkable legal career with the Great Western Railway.[69]

When he left the Great Western Railway in 1872 after nearly two intense decades as counsel, Irving brought with him a thorough understanding of the intersection of public and private legal interests, a legacy upon which his subsequent four decades of service to public life was solidly founded.[70] Indeed, Irving's service as in-house counsel for the Great Western had provided him with connections and experience that proved to be extremely relevant. He was, of course, thoroughly acquainted with the legislative process, and with the details of discussions leading to Confederation. As a consequence of his work with the railway, he was familiar with complicated financial instruments, with the difficulties of interjurisdictional negotiations, and with the logistical difficulties that might arise in conducting multiparty transactions. He had seen and participated in several public inquiries and commissions, and especially coroner's proceedings and other legal investigations following in the wake of accidents.

Irving's railway practice had also given him close contact with numerous municipalities, and with counsel throughout Ontario who had either opposed him or been engaged by him during the course of the Great Western's litigious beginnings. And he had a range of experience, perhaps second to none, in negotiating compensation settlements and in arbitration proceedings centring on land values. Thus, as Ontario squared off with the new federal government and with its Quebec neighbour over trust funds, interest payments, the common school accounts, obligations under Indian treaties, and any number of additional intergovernmental financial claims and debts, Irving had much to offer. That, however, is another story.

CONCLUSION

Aemilius Irving was not Canada's first corporate or in-house counsel, but he was certainly among the most successful of those who chose to prac- tise law outside the confines of the traditional firm. His decision to prac- tice law exclusively in the interests of the Great Western Railway intrigued his contemporaries, some of whom – if the *Upper Canada Law Journal* is any guide – found his status as 'salaried servant' offensive to their understanding of professional norms. Irving weathered that criti- cism, although he appears to have paid a price for the *Jarvis* decision. He went on to establish an enviable reputation and earned the respect of col- leagues at the bar, despite the unorthodox nature of his practice. No doubt his early ordeal came to mind in 1908, when he penned a note to then attorney general J.J. Foy on the subject of amendments to Ontario's Solicitors Act intended to relax somewhat restrictions on the manner in which solicitors might secure or receive remuneration.[71]

Within the ranks of the Great Western bureaucracy, he advanced sys- tematically from an employee who had been recruited in part for the sim- ple purpose of regularizing the railway's expenditures on legal fees. He was soon participating directly in the affairs of the managing committee, and later personally attended the meetings of the Canadian directors, who seem to have understood the nature of their loss when he retired.

It seems entirely appropriate to view Irving as fully on a par with the group of nineteenth-century English lawyers whose importance has been so forcefully explained by Rande Kostal. Lawyers, according to Kostal, were an essential element of railway capitalism, contributing 'a singu- larly useful combination of legal and commercial skills.' They were accordingly relied upon, not only for expert technical advice, 'but equally for their general knowledge of the English business world.'[72] Remark- ably, in Irving's case, a comparable effort over nearly twenty years consumed less than the first half of his career as a pioneering Canadian in-house counsel.

NOTES

I would like to thank Ellen Kaine for research assistance in connection with a *DCB* article which led to this essay, and to the Osgoode Society for its financial contribution to that project. Barry Ditto recently provided research assistance for which I am also grateful.

1 An indication of the vast scope of Irving's responsibilities in the service of Ontario may be found in the Irving Papers, Public Archives of Ontario.
2 Margaret Prang, with reference to the 1890s, states that 'the legal fraternity of Toronto at the time displayed a brilliance probably unexcelled in any other period of its history': Margaret Prang, *N.W. Rowell: Ontario Nationalist* (Toronto: University of Toronto Press 1975), 18.
3 Douglas McCalla, *Planting the Province: The Economic History of Upper Canada, 1784–1870* (Toronto: University of Toronto Press 1993), 209
4 Information on Hatt and MacNab's personal and professional relations may be found in Donald R. Beer, *Sir Allan Napier MacNab* (Hamilton: Dictionary of Hamilton Biography 1984).
5 McCalla, *Planting the Province*, 213
6 Paul Craven, 'The Meaning of Misadventure: The Baptiste Creek Railway Disaster of 1854 and Its Aftermath' in Roger Hall, William Westfall, and Laurel Sefton MacDowell, eds., *Patterns of the Past: Interpreting Ontario's History* (Toronto: Dundurn Press 1988), 108. The legislation included 'An Act for the Better Prevention of Accidents on Railways,' Province of Canada, 20 Victoria (1857), c. 12. For a broader account of railway accidents, see Paul Craven, 'Law and Railway Accidents, 1850–1880,' in Wes Pue and Barry Wright, eds., *Proceedings of the Canadian Law in History Conference*, June 1987, Vol. 2, 47–70.
7 Rande Kostal, *Law and English Railway Capitalism, 1825–1875* (Oxford: Clarendon Press 1994), 299
8 Ibid., 324
9 H.W. Arthurs and David A.A. Stager, *Lawyers in Canada* (Toronto: University of Toronto Press 1990), 267–78
10 Public Archives of Canada, RG30, vol. 2, 4 July 1854, no. 243. This was John Ogilvie Hatt, a partner of Allan MacNab.
11 RG30, vol. 2, 22 September 1854, no. 373
12 RG30, vol. 2, 26 September 1854, no. 379
13 'The Great Western Railway Company,' 4 *Upper Canada Law Journal* (1858), 223
14 Alfred D. Chandler, *The Visible Hand: The Managerial Revolution in American Business* (Cambridge, MA: Harvard University Press 1977), 105–6

15 R.D. Gidney and W.P.J. Millar, *Professional Gentlemen: The Professions in Nineteenth-Century Ontario* (Toronto: University of Toronto Press 1994), Chap. 4

16 Paul Romney, 'From Railway Construction to Constitutional Construction: John Wellington Gwynne's National Dream,' in Dale Gibson and W. Wesley Pue, eds., *Glimpses of Canadian Legal History* (Winnipeg: Legal Research Institute of the University of Manitoba 1991), 95–102

17 I have not been able to identify the litigant further.

18 GWR Minutes, 2 January 1857, no. 1137

19 *Jarvis* v. *Great Western Railway* (1859) 8 UCCP 280 at 287

20 'The Great Western Railway Company,' 4 *Upper Canada Law Journal* (1859), 223. See also 'Right of an Attorney to Costs,' 4 *Upper Canada Law Journal* (1859), 244.

21 GWR Papers, Managing Committee Minute no. 1327, RG30, vol. 7

22 GWR Papers, Managing Committee Minutes, 27 January 1859, no. 1327

23 T.C. Keefer, 'Philosophy of Railroads,' in H.V. Nelles, ed., *Philosophy of Railroads and Other Essays by T.C. Keefer* (Toronto: University of Toronto Press 1972)

24 Corporate records provide evidence of many other cases that went to trial, and countless matters resolved outside the courts on the basis of minuted instructions to the solicitor 'to settle on the best terms he can manage.'

25 R.C.B. Risk, 'The Golden Age: The Law about the Market in Nineteenth-Century Ontario,' 26 *University of Toronto Law Journal* (1976), 311. Irving appeared for the railway in *Gamble* v. *Great Western Railway* (1864) 24 UCQB 407, and *Spettigue* v. *Great Western Railway* (1865) 15 UCCP 315.

26 GWR Managing Committee Minutes, 18 June 1862, no. 684

27 Kostal, *English Railway Capitalism*, 223

28 Ibid., 253

29 *Great Western Railway* v. *Rouse* (1856) 15 UCQB 168; *London* v. *Great Western Railway*, 1858 (17) UCQB 262; *Toronto* v. *Great Western Railway* (1866) 25 UCQB 570.

30 GWR Papers, Managing Committee Minutes, 17 December 1858, no. 1302. The task of moderating municipal assessments may have been easier to undertake in Upper Canada than in England as a consequence of favourable legislation, 16 Victoria, c. 182.

31 GWR Managing Committee Minutes, 18 October 1861, no. 1615

32 RG30, vol. 7, Managing Committee Minutes of 17 December 1858, no. 1293

33 GWR Directors' Minutes, 1 December 1856, no. 1115. For some of the legislative background associated with the internal regulation of railway operations in this era see Craven, 'Law and Railway Accidents.'

34 Managing Committee Minutes, 12 May 1860, no. 1507

35 Managing Committee Minutes, 16 April 1859, no. 1366, and 12 May 1860, no. 1507

36 W.L. Morton, *The Critical Years: The Union of British North America, 1857–1873* (Toronto: McClelland and Stewart 1964), 154

37 Irving Papers, Irving to George Brown, 3 July 1867

38 McCalla, *Planting the Province*, 211

39 On Zimmerman see J.K. Johnson, '"One Bold Operator": Samuel Zimmerman, Niagara Entrepreneur, 1843–1857,' *Ontario History* 74 (1982), 26–44.

40 Descriptions of the accident, including the names of victims and survivors, can be found in Harriett Annie Wilkins, 'The Great Railway Catastrophe of the 12th March 1857 on the Desjardins Canal Bridge, Hamilton on the Line of the Great Western Railway' and in 'Full Details of the Railway Disaster of the 12th March, 1857 at the Desjardins Canal on the Line of the Great Western Railway,' 20 March 1857(?). Canadian Institute of Historical Microreproductions, microfiche 49886.

41 'Full Details.'

42 Ibid., 41–5

43 Ibid., 52

44 Kostal, *English Railway Capitalism*, 298

45 Such claims were authorized under comparatively recent legislation, 'An Act for compensating the Families of Persons killed by Accident' (1847) 10 & 11 Victoria, c. 6.

46 *Woodruff* v. *Great Western Railway* (1859) 18 UCQB 420. Claims by the Zimmerman estate and the deceased contractor's widow were eventually resolved upon payment by the railway of nearly $60,000. See GWR Managing Committee Minutes, 25 July 1860, no. 1529.

47 GWR Managing Committee Minutes, 17 December 1858, no. 1300

48 *Grant* v. *Great Western Railway* (1857) 7 UCCP 438

49 *Secord* v. *Great Western Railway* (1857) 15 UCQB 631; *Ferrie* v. *Great Western Railway* (1857) 15 UCQB 513

50 *Morley* v. *Great Western Railway* (1857) 16 UCQB 504

51 *Ferrie* v. *Great Western Railway* (1857) 15 UCQB 513. Adam Ferrie was presumably the son of Colin Ferrie, a prominent Hamilton merchant and a man long-associated with Sir Allan MacNab in various local ventures.

52 Kostal, *English Railway Capitalism*, 296, discussing *Pym* v. *Great Northern* (1861) 2 B. & S. 761 (QB)

53 *Great Western Railway* v. *Desjardins Canal Company* (1862) 9 *Grant's Chancery Reports* 503

54 GWR Managing Committee Minutes, 18 November 1859

55 (1863) 1 Moore (NS) 101 (JCPC). The decision, amounting to acceptance of the

res ipsa loquitur principle in cases of accidents associated with alleged deficiencies in the engineering of railway works, has been described as a setback for railways generally. See Kostal, *English Railway Capitalism*. See also 'Solicitor's Report on the Flamboro Accident,' GWR Managing Committee Meeting, 16 March 1860, 301.

56 Employee compensation payments appear throughout the GWR Minute-Books.

57 The Directors' Minutes for 14 April, no. 3272, show that, when James Collinson, engine driver, died on duty in a collision, he was covered by $1,500 in insurance. The board decided 'to aid the family by taking the sons into the service as they come of suitable age.'

58 The essential terms of the agreement are set out in *Great Western Railway* v. *Grand Trunk Railway* (1864) 24 UCQB 107 at 108

59 Ibid., 107 at 111

60 *Great Western Railway* v. *Grand Trunk Railway* (1865) 25 UCQB 37 at 44

61 *Commercial Bank of Canada* v. *Great Western Railway* (1866) 25 UCQB 335

62 Irving Papers, Irving to Brackstone Baker, 31 August 1871

63 McCalla, *Planting the Province*, 151, 156, 237

64 Irving Papers, letter 308, Irving to John Treller, 24 August 1868

65 Kostal, *English Railway Capitalism*, 5

66 Directors' Minutes, 26 July 1872, no. 3677

67 Irving Papers, Irving to Brackstone Baker, 20 September 1872; Irving to Joseph Price, 4 December 1872

68 For discussion of Irving's role in the so-called 'Clause 47' debate see David Swinfen, *Imperial Appeal: The Debate on the Appeal to the Privy Council, 1833–1986* (Manchester: Manchester University Press 1987), 38–40.

69 In her discussion of the patronage dimensions of appointments to judicial office in post-Confederation Ontario, A. Margaret Evans acknowledges that Irving was among a list of 'outstanding lawyers, highly suitable appointees': Evans, *Sir Oliver Mowat* (Toronto: University of Toronto Press 1992), 189–90.

70 Any reference to public and private interests threatens to raise more elaborate conceptual debate than I intend to arouse. I use the comparison here in a sense not unlike R.C.B. Risk's observation that 'the creation of these corporations was a delegation of public power to private organizations for the construction and management of public utilities, particularly transportation facilities': Risk, 'Business Corporations,' 271.

71 Irving Papers, Irving to Foy, 28 March 1908

72 Kostal, *English Railway Capitalism*, 322

4

The Campbell, Meredith Firm of Montreal: A Case-Study of the Role of Canadian Business Lawyers, 1895–1913

DECLAN BRENDAN HAMILL

INTRODUCTION: RECONSTRUCTING THE LINK BETWEEN LAW AND BUSINESS

As Gregory Marchildon has observed, while there is an obvious connection between business and corporate-commercial law, 'there has been surprisingly little research on the nature of this relationship and even less on the links between the practitioners of law and business.'[1] Legal historians have generally concentrated their efforts on other areas, and business historians seem reluctant to acknowledge that lawyers had even a minor role in the development of commercial enterprises.[2] In the Canadian context, almost the entire body of published research on the connections between lawyers and business is contained in a single volume of essays.[3] These articles represent an excellent foundation for the reconstruction of the relationship, but the question of what turn-of-the-century lawyers actually did for their corporate clients on a daily basis has yet to be examined. This essay, based on the examination of a rich and possibly unique archival source, is an attempt to reach some tentative conclusions about the role played by the lawyers of one firm in the development of an important Canadian institution. It also demonstrates the immense potential value of legal opinions as historical records.

In the introduction to this volume, Carol Wilton noted that the study of the history of large urban law firms necessarily yields an incomplete picture of the history of Canadian legal practice, since only a relatively small percentage of lawyers were employed by these organizations.[4] However, the information available on such firms provides an obvious point of departure for the reconstruction of the history of the Canadian legal profession. In contrast with the records of smaller practices, the business-client base of these firms occasionally results in the deposition of their opinions with other corporate records in public archives. In addition, the association of prominent lawyers with political parties or large private corporations has resulted in some attention from political, business, and social historians.[5] Furthermore, several major Canadian law firms have commissioned commemorative 'official histories.' While these works are often self-congratulatory in tone and rarely engage in historical analysis, they do provide valuable information for scholars attempting to reconstruct the practice of Canadian lawyers.[6]

This essay is an attempt to examine the work of a thriving commercial law practice between 1895 and 1913 (referred to throughout this essay as the Campbell, Meredith firm) on behalf of an institution that played an important role in the emergence of modern Canadian capitalism, the Montreal Stock Exchange (the MSE). The practice is still a major law firm, and is known today as McMaster Meighen.

The MSE was similar to the firm in that its expansion during the 1895–1913 period reflected the growth and changing character of the central Canadian economy. While regular meetings of Montreal 'brokers' commenced in 1832, and a board of stock and produce brokers was later created, the market for securities remained underdeveloped until the end of the nineteenth century.[7]

The McGill University Archives possesses more than 150 opinions delivered to the Governing Committee of the MSE by the Campbell, Meredith firm between 1895 and 1933. For the purposes of this essay, approximately 80 opinions delivered to the exchange in that period were examined. While only a few letters from the MSE to the firm were included, the lawyers typically initiated their correspondence by reiterating the question posed by the exchange, providing valuable information on the client.[8] In addition, through the examination of legal issues in the context of a series of opinions written by the firm, it is possible in many cases to discern the reaction of the Governing Committee to the legal advice provided.[9] Since the files of many Canadian firms remain confidential for decades and are subsequently destroyed, the Campbell, Meredith opinions provide a rare opportunity to examine the daily work of some prominent turn-of-the-century lawyers on behalf of an important

The Merchant's Bank Building, St James Street, Montreal: headquarters of the Campbell, Meredith firm from 1900 to 1960 (courtesy Notman Photographic Archives)

client.[10] It should be noted from the outset that access to additional sources, such as the MSE's correspondence with the firm and the meeting-books of the Governing Committee, would have been of great assistance. The inferences which may be drawn from the available correspondence, however, provide a new perspective on the role of some Canadian lawyers at the beginning of the twentieth century.

Three factors encouraged selectivity in the examination and analysis of the records. The first was the existence of a homogeneous sample: While the institution obtained advice from several firms after 1914, the pre-war opinions are almost entirely the work of the Campbell, Meredith firm. The second was completeness: While the 1895–1913 files contain correspondence from almost every year within that period, the amount of missing correspondence from subsequent years appears to be more significant. The third relates to the growth of the Canadian securities industry in the period: The rapid pace of pre–First World War economic expansion and corresponding increase in trading necessitated sweeping changes to the structure of the institution. During this period, the MSE was transformed from a purely local organization to an important regional securities centre, albeit a satellite of the major markets in London and New York.

This essay is also intended to be an exploration of the role of lawyers in the development and application of what Gerry Rubin and David Sugarman have defined as 'facilitative' or 'power-conferring' laws. Rubin and Sugarman argue that scholars have been preoccupied with the study of state-made law of a negative or coercive nature. As a result, they often overlook or minimize the positive and empowering role of some legal ordering in society. Instead of imposing duties and restrictions, facilitative legal work assists clients with the realization of their objectives. Formulated by practitioners in response to client needs, such work, Rubin and Sugarman suggest, provides 'individuals with facilities for realising their wishes, by conferring legal powers upon them to create, by certain specified procedures, and subject to certain conditions, structures of rights and duties within the coercive framework of the [state] law.'[11]

Rubin and Sugarman note that facilitative laws are linked to the larger development of the utilization of the law for the 'legitimization of semi-autonomous realms – a role which has yet to be fully chronicled.'[12] The evidence presented here indicates that the MSE was one such realm: The exchange provides an example of how the employment of facilitative law by the Campbell, Meredith lawyers enabled the leadership of the exchange to create a self-governing institution based on the powers delegated to it by the Act of Incorporation.[13] The lawyers also advanced the interests of the client by providing opinions on securities, banking and negotiable instruments, and real-property law. Even when engaged in the provision of technical legal services, the firm promoted the larger strategic interests of the exchange. In addition, they assisted the MSE with civil actions and occasionally acted as advocates of the institution's interests to the federal and provincial governments. Moreover, the correspondence between the firm and the client suggests that, because of their specialized corporate-law expertise, the lawyers were an integral part of the management and development of the MSE.

THE FIRM: THE EARLY HISTORY OF CAMPBELL, MEREDITH

The firm that provided the opinions to the MSE in the 1895–1913 period was founded by William Badgley in 1823. Like the lawyers examined by G. Blaine Baker in his essay on the Torrance-Morris firm, Badgley enjoyed what might be defined as an élite legal practice.[14] Connected by blood or marriage to many of Montreal's Anglo-Scottish business dynasties, Badgley and his partner, Sir John Abbott, both enjoyed illustrious professional careers. After several decades representing railway companies and pre-industrial mercantile interests, Badgley was appointed batonnier of the Montreal bar. He subsequently became the first dean of the McGill University Faculty of Law in 1853, was appointed to the Superior Court in 1855, and was promoted to the Court of Queen's Bench in 1866.[15]

Sir John Abbott carried on Badgley's practice after his partner's judicial appointment, and soon became one of the most successful lawyers in Montreal, making £600 to £700 a year representing prosperous clients such as the Merchants' Bank and Sir Hugh Allan's commercial enterprises.[16] He succeeded Badgley as the dean of the McGill Faculty of Law before commencing a highly successful political career. Sir John Abbott served as attorney general for Canada East in 1862, and was part of the first government of Canada before being forced out of politics by the Pacific Scandal that undermined Sir John A. Macdonald's Conservatives in 1873–4.[17] After his return to practice, the firm expanded into one of the largest commercial law practices in Quebec, adding the Bank of Montreal, Molson's Bank, and the Bank of British North America to its client base.[18] Sir John Abbott became an integral part of Sir Hugh Allan's efforts to build the Canadian Pacific Railway before again returning to politics in 1887. He subsequently served for two terms as mayor of Montreal, was later appointed to the Senate, and became a cabinet minister for a second

TABLE 4.1
The Partnership

1889–98	Abbott, Campbell & Meredith
1898–1903	Campbell, Meredith, Allan & Hague
1903–8	Campbell, Meredith, Macpherson, & Hague
1908–10	Campbell, Meredith, Macpherson, Hague & Holden
1910–12	Meredith, Macpherson, Hague & Holden
1912–16	Meredith, Macpherson, Hague, Holden, Shaughnessy & Heward

time. Abbott ended his political career with a brief tenure as prime minister in 1891, after the death of Sir John A. Macdonald.[19]

As a result of the efforts of its founders, the Campbell, Meredith firm entered the 1895–1913 period with an enviable reputation and an impressive client base. In the years following the departure of Abbott from practice, the firm underwent significant changes in personnel (see table 4.1). While his two sons initially played a prominent role in the practice, its leadership passed out of the family in 1898, when partner Henry Abbott died at the age of forty-one. The older son, John B. Abbott, had apparently always been more interested in painting than law and chose to retire the same year.[20] Leadership of the firm was assumed by Charles Sandwich Campbell and Frederick Edmund Meredith. Although Campbell retired in 1910, he continued to influence the management of the firm, serving as its counsel for several years afterward.[21] It seems clear from the McMaster Meighen official history and the correspondence to the MSE that these two partners were the firm's leading members during the 1895–1913 period.

The background of the new leadership was in keeping with the firm's patrician and Conservative traditions. Originally from Kingston, Charles Sandwich Campbell was a graduate of Bishop's University and Laval University, joining the firm in 1884. He came from a prominent Conservative family: His father, Sir Alexander Campbell, had served as a senator and cabinet minister in the government of his home-town law partner Sir John A. Macdonald, and was later appointed lieutenant-governor of Ontario. Frederick Edmund Meredith, who had joined the firm in 1887, was from a remarkably similar background, having graduated initially from Bishop's and then from Laval, where he was awarded the gold medal. Like the Campbells, the Meredith family was patrician in character: His father, Sir William Meredith, under whom Sir John Abbott had articled, had been Chief Justice of Quebec.[22]

In 1898, James Bryce Allan was made a partner: He was a contemporary of Campbell's and Meredith's at Laval University's law school, and a nephew of Sir Hugh Allan's, former president of the Merchants' Bank and head of the Allan Steamship Line, both clients of the firm.[23] The 'old boy' nature of the firm during this period was perhaps best symbolized by the cable address 'CAMMERALL' that appeared on its stationery, an amalgamation of the surnames of its three senior partners.[24]

The other members of the firm during the 1895–1913 period were either from élite Montreal business families or had distinguished themselves through academic excellence. Henry John Hague, who joined the partnership in 1898, was the son of the general manager of the Merchants' Bank. The close links between this corporate client and the firm were demonstrated by the latter's decision in 1900 to move its offices to the Merchants' Bank Building on St James Street.[25] Similarly, William James Shaughnessy, who joined the firm in 1911, was the son of the first Lord Shaughnessy, president of Canadian Pacific Railway between 1899 and 1923. The younger Shaughnessy had attended McGill University before travelling to England to study law at Cambridge University.[26] Arthur Ramsay Holden and Chilion Graves Heward, who became partners in 1908 and 1911, respectively, had both been gold-medallists at the McGill University Faculty of Law. With the exception of Kenneth Rose Macpherson, who had previously practised with the Dunlop, Lyman and Macpherson firm, all of the lawyers during the 1895–1913 period had articled with the firm.[27]

As a firm of more than five lawyers, Campbell, Meredith was a large organization by contemporary standards. Since the majority of Canadian practitioners at the time worked alone or in smaller partnerships, the firm was unrepresentative of the average legal practice of the time. In spite of the exceptional academic performance of some of its lawyers, the background of the majority of the firm seems to suggest that legal opportunity was in large measure a function of who you were. In common with most prestigious urban Canadian firms of the time, the Campbell, Meredith partners clearly regarded the relatives of partners and important clients as the best source of new members. While no longer dominated by the Abbotts, the firm remained a highly insular organization.

There were already signs, however, that the firm was gradually evolving into an American-style 'law factory' in adapting to its clients' needs and contemporary economic conditions. W.K. Hobson has written that these 'factories' of ten or more lawyers emerged in late-nineteenth-century American cities as a response to the demand for specific legal services created by industrialization. Their ascendancy coincided with the displacement of the trial advocate and the subsequent rise of the corporate lawyer to the pinnacle of the legal profession.[28] The new urban firms were characterized by an ability to provide a range of specialized legal services for clients, and by hiring practices which gave priority to White males who had attained excellent standings at prestigious schools.[29] The variety of legal services provided to the exchange, the gradually increasing number of associates employed in the first decade of the twentieth century, and the hiring of several gold-medallists who were not the relatives of partners or prominent clients seems to suggest that the Campbell, Meredith firm was a legal institution on the verge of a major transformation in the 1895–1913 period. The 'law factory,' however, was a by-product of industrialization and urbanization, both gradual processes which occurred in central Canada long after equivalent developments had taken place in the northeastern United States. Several decades would elapse before some of Canada's established urban law firms completely evolved into this new form of legal institution.

If it was in the vanguard of Canadian law firms in terms of structural development, the Campbell, Meredith firm was utterly conventional in its hiring practices. Indeed, the firm was exclusively composed of Protestant and English-speaking males during the 1895–1913 period. The first appointment of a Francophone to partner was in 1915: Pierre Badeaux, who was subsequently appointed to the Quebec Court of Appeal, remained with the firm for only a few years after his promotion. It would be several decades before the firm appointed its first female lawyer: Constance Garner Short, a member of a prominent Quebec business family, was hired in 1942.[30] In its gender and ethnic exclusivity, the firm mirrored the contemporary prejudices of Canadian society. However, given that these prejudices were societal rather than institutional in origin, it would be presentist to criticize Campbell, Meredith for exhibiting racist or sexist tendencies: The firm was merely a product of its time and culture.

Despite the privileged origins of its lawyers and an enviable client base, it is unlikely that the Campbell, Meredith chambers on Hospital Street, or later at the Merchants' Bank Building, were luxurious. Contemporary law offices were quite spartan, and probably resembled those of the Brown Montgomery firm, described by Douglas Tees in his history of Ogilvy Renault: 'The premises leased by the firm were plain by today's standards. Bare wooden floors greeted the visitor. No colourful paintings or indoor plants broke the monotony of the decor.'[31] The inhospitable surroundings reflected the utilitarian function of turn-of-the-century law offices. None of the correspondence during the 1895–

1913 period mentions MSE representatives visiting or being summoned to the firm's chambers. The Campbell, Meredith lawyers and the exchange typically corresponded by mail. The lawyers were summoned periodically to the exchange for consultation, or requested to participate directly in Governing Committee meetings.[32] The correspondence clearly suggests that the office of the Campbell, Meredith firm was solely a place of work. In stark contrast to most modern urban law offices, the firm's chambers were not a vital component of its public image, and consequently there was no need for ostentation or opulence to impress the corporate clientele.

THE CLIENT: THE INDUSTRIAL REVOLUTION AND THE RISE OF THE MSE

The 1895–1913 period was characterized by unprecedented economic growth and industrialization in central Canada, which proved to be highly lucrative for commercial-law practitioners. Montreal was at the centre of the regional industrial revolution: The combination of economic expansion, migration from the rural areas of Quebec, and immigration from Europe resulted in the doubling of the city's population to almost 500,000 between 1890 and 1910. The economic expansion was characterized by an intense concentration of wealth in the hands of the English-speaking Montreal business community. It is estimated that approximately two-thirds of Canada's wealth at the turn of the century was controlled by fewer than one hundred men domiciled in the palatial mansions of the famous 'Square Mile' area of the city.[33] Based upon information gleaned from the McMaster Meighen official history, table 4.2 demonstrates how the firm's client base expanded with the growth of the central Canadian economy and the resulting corporate concentration in the Montreal area.[34]

The MSE's expansion before the First World War, like that of the Campbell, Meredith firm, was the result of dramatic economic growth in central Canada. The small securities market counted only twenty issues in 1857, and was largely dominated by bank stocks.[35] Despite the prevalence of bank stocks, trading was also conducted on issues by railways and mines, and government debentures.[36] The sluggish volume of trading justified only one meeting of brokers every week at a local coffee-house.[37] In his study of the origins of the Toronto Stock Exchange, John F. Whiteside noted that, until 1885, Toronto brokers were rarely specialists, and the limited trading activity on the mid-nineteenth-century Montreal

TABLE 4.2
The Firm's Changing and Expanding Corporate Client Base

Clients, pre–1890

Banks	*Other*
Merchants' Bank	Canadian Pacific Railway
Molson's Bank	Montreal Overseas Steamship
Bank of Montreal	Lines (later Allan Steamship
Bank of British North America	Line)

New clients, 1890–1913

Textiles	*Brokerage houses*
Canadian Cottons	Dominion Securities
Dominion Textile Co.	A.E. Ames & Co.
Utilities	*Resources/manufacturing*
Royal Electric Co.	Dominion Iron and Steel Co.
McLaren-Quebec Power Corp.	Dominion Coal Co.
Beauharnois Light, Heat and Power Co.	American Tobacco Co.
Montreal Street Railway Co.	

market strongly suggests that the city's brokers were also engaged in other business activities.[38]

The organization of local securities trading appears to have increased in 1863, when a formal board of brokers with eleven members was established.[39] The board collected fees, determined commissions, and created regulations for its membership. The renting of an office by the organization three years later provides a further indication that the local securities market was gradually becoming more sophisticated.[40] In 1874, the board successfully obtained an Act of Incorporation from the Province of Quebec, officially creating the MSE.

At the time of its incorporation, the exchange had 63 issues listed and a volume of 800 shares per day.[41] Poor economic conditions during the 1880s resulted initially in stagnation, and later in a slight decline in the number of listings. Larger corporate interests, however, were gradually listed, while smaller issues disappeared, and the total volume of trading continued to rise slowly until the last decade of the nineteenth century.[42] Nevertheless, in contrast to the frenetic pace of the major American markets, Edgar Andrew Collard recounts that business in Montreal was a leisurely affair. The brokers traded six days a week during the winter months, with a 10:45–12:30 morning session and a 2:15–3:00 afternoon session each day except Saturday. The hours were shorter still during the

TABLE 4.3
The Growth of the MSE

a. Listings and shares traded per day, 1857–1914

Year	Number of listings	Number of shares traded per day
1857	20	
1874	63	800
1884	64	
1892	–	4,500
1894	51	
1901	–	7,000
1904	65	
1914	109	10,000

b. Number and price of seats, 1874–1913

Year	Number	Price
1874	40	$ 800
1876	40	$ 2,500
1877	40	$ 2,900
1882	40	$ 2,820
1883	40	$ 5,750
1900	40	$12,000
1901	45	$12,850
1902	60	$20,000
1908	60	$27,500
1910	65	–
1912	75	–
1913	75	$30,000

summer months, when the Saturday-morning session was cancelled. Even during the short trading sessions, one writer noted, 'there is never any of the exciting scenes on the floor to be seen daily at the New York Exchange and Chicago.'[43]

The character of the MSE was altered by industrialization and urbanization during the 1895–1913 period. While the number of bank stocks declined through the 1870s and 1880s, industrial and utility listings increased dramatically during the last decade of the century.[44] The same concentration of wealth in the Montreal area that provided clients for Campbell, Meredith also ensured the MSE would remain the leading Canadian exchange until the mid-twentieth century.[45] Since only a small percentage of the population at the time invested in securities, the more advanced development of Montreal and the affluence of the 'Square Mile' gave the MSE an advantage over its Toronto rival.[46] Table 4.3 provides an overview of the market's growth during this period.[47]

As a direct consequence of the increasing number of listings and volume of shares being traded, the value of the forty members' seats on the MSE had to be periodically revised upward. In *Northern Enterprise*, Michael Bliss described the members of Montreal and Toronto exchanges during this period as being essentially 'private cartels trying to control stock trading.'[48] The actions of the MSE seem to vindicate his claim: While the Act of Incorporation established no limit on the number of seats, the institution resisted external pressure to create new positions until 1901. An increasing share of the lucrative securities trade motivated this resistance to change. As Collard's account suggests, while the membership was frozen at forty, the existing brokers were the exclusive beneficiaries of the spectacular increase in the market: 'For many years the number of seats had been limited to forty. Anyone wishing to become a member had to wait until a seat came up for sale. Then he would have to outbid many competitors. The more conservative members of the Exchange opposed the creation of any new seats. Those impatient to get in began calling them "The Forty Thieves."'[49]

The burgeoning securities market eventually resulted in the MSE's decision to create new seats, and by 1912 the number of members had nearly doubled, from forty to seventy-five. It is a measure of the lucrative nature of trading during this period that, despite the substantial increase in number, the valuation of individual seats continued to rise.[50]

Perhaps the most tangible indication of the prosperity of the MSE was its decision to erect a new building on St François Xavier Street. In a real estate transaction symbolic of the changing character of the local economy, the land for the new headquarters was purchased from the Seminary of Montreal, an institution that had dominated pre-industrial economic activity in the region throughout the nineteenth century.[51] Completed in June 1904, the new edifice was modelled on the Temple of Vesta at Tivoli, Italy.[52]

Perhaps a more significant influence was suggested by the Governing Committee's choice of George B. Post, the architect who had designed the New York Stock Exchange, for the building project.[53] The rise of the MSE during the 1895–1913 period must be placed in the larger context of the international securities industry. Ranald Michie has asserted that, while the growth of the Montreal and Toronto exchanges was impressive, it was limited by foreign competition for the listing of Canadian securities. Before the First World War, the majority of Canadian government issues and railway stocks were traded on the London Stock Exchange.[54] In addition, a substantial amount of trading in Canadian securities occurred in the United States: The first foreign bonds marketed on the New York Stock Exchange were $3 million in Province of Quebec bonds in 1879, and the exporting of capital from the American market to Canada would increase dramatically in subsequent decades.[55] While the resource stocks traded on the Montreal and Toronto exchanges generated substantial business, the speculative and volatile nature of these listings did not provide the markets with the stable basis required for sustained growth. Furthermore, profitable new Canadian companies often attracted the attention of international investors: Once the 'Canadian content' of a stock decreased as a result of substantial purchases by foreigners, the locus of trading moved offshore.[56]

The net result of these factors was to transform the Montreal and Toronto markets into 'trial exchanges' for foreign investors. Therefore, despite substantial growth, the Canadian markets were in fact 'junior partners' in an increasingly international securities industry centred in London and New York.[57] Significantly, the total volume of shares traded on both the Montreal and Toronto markets in 1910 was equivalent to 2 per cent of contemporaneous activity on the New York Stock Exchange.[58]

THE CAMPBELL, MEREDITH GENERAL OPINIONS

Categorization of the Correspondence

Like the work conducted by modern Canadian 'full-service' law firms for corporate clients, the Campbell, Meredith firm provided the MSE with a wide variety of legal work and advice. The resolution of securities and negotiable-instruments problems, representation to governments, real-property law, and assistance with civil actions were among the tasks executed: These services are canvassed below.

Much of the correspondence, however, concerned either the Act of Incorporation or the by-laws administered by the governing committee to regulate the market and its membership. These opinions, on what might be defined as corporate constitutional law, are examined in the next section. This categorization of the correspondence best illustrates the facilitative character of the firm's work. The opinions could also have been examined by contrasting predominantly technical activities with more facilitative services. However, such a dichotomy would create a somewhat misleading impression of the work conducted by the firm. As will be demonstrated, even the technical tasks undertaken by the lawyers were often components of a larger facilitative design.

Securities Law Problems and the Maintenance of Efficiency

Throughout the 1895–1913 period, the Campbell, Meredith firm was consulted by the Governing Committee on a variety of securities law issues. Most of this correspondence was in the form of short opinions addressing specific problems that had emerged during transactions on the floor of the exchange. Occasional difficulties, such as which shareholders were entitled to a dividend declared by a company, or the resolution of a dispute between two brokers caused by a clearing-house clerical error, were relatively rare, considering the volume of transactions. However, the Governing Committee seems to have been anxious to receive the expert opinion of the firm in order to resolve issues quickly as they arose.[59] In this capacity, the Campbell, Meredith lawyers acted as 'legal technicians,' providing timely advice to ensure that the market continued to function efficiently.

The firm also seems to have acted very occasionally in a purely informational capacity at the request of the Governing Committee. In 1896, for example, the lawyers wrote a lengthy opinion explaining that the relationship between broker and client was analogous to that of agent and principal, and described situations of potential broker liability in exhaustive detail. Since the hypothetical nature of the problems addressed and significant length of this correspondence are at variance with the concise and specific opinions usually delivered, it was probably produced for general distribution to the entire membership of the MSE, presumably in response to a request from the Governing Committee.[60]

Negotiable Instruments and the Influence of the
International Securities Market

On three occasions in the 1895–1913 period, the MSE consulted the firm for legal opinions regarding negotiable instruments. In May 1901, the firm examined and approved of the stock certificates, known as 'scrip,' issued by the Montreal Light, Heat and Power Company.[61] On the two subsequent occasions that the Campbell, Meredith lawyers considered problems of negotiability, the powerful influence of the practices of the New York Stock Exchange was evident. Since the secretary-treasurer of the MSE asserted that the rights of holders of 'scrip' were 'very important ... to the members,' the lawyers considered the negotiability of stock certificates again in early 1910.[62] Campbell, Meredith concluded that the certificates were not really negotiable instruments, despite the market custom to treat them as such.[63] However, it is notable that the MSE did not consider an opinion based on the jurisdiction's law to be sufficient and wanted to ascertain what protection was afforded to holders of stock certificates in the United States. In order to comply with this request, the Campbell, Meredith firm wrote to an associated New York City firm about American practices.[64] Lord, Day and Lord referred the Montreal lawyers to the second volume of *Cook on Corporations*, which they asserted to be 'the most recent work and standard authority in the United States on the subject of Corporations,' and Campbell, Meredith based their analysis of the American law on this source.[65] In a subsequent letter, the Lord, Day and Lord firm advised Campbell, Meredith that they had consulted the counsel of the New York Stock Exchange on the issue, and the Montreal firm subsequently forwarded this opinion to the MSE.[66]

Three years later, the MSE consulted the firm on the negotiability of a $100 bond of the Quebec Railway, Light, Heat and Power Company bearing the revenue stamp of 'one of the provinces of France.'[67] Once again, the opinion given was influenced by the practice of major foreign exchanges: Campbell, Meredith borrowed materials on the London, Boston, and New York stock exchanges from MSE members in order to address the question.[68]

These opinions suggest that the practices of the Montreal market during its emergence as a regional securities trading centre were significantly influenced by those of the major stock exchanges, notably New York. Given the comparative size of the exchanges, and the interconnected and competitive nature of the international securities market, it is not surprising that the MSE was concerned with the legal rights of holders of stock certificates outside the province of Quebec. The Campbell, Meredith firm acted as both a source of expert opinion on the law of the jurisdiction and as a conduit for legal information from important foreign jurisdictions to the MSE. The firm's opinions for the MSE seem to confirm that the exchange was a subsidiary of a larger North American securities market centred in New York.

Given the importance of the New York Stock Exchange to North American capitalism, it is evident that both the Governing Committee and its legal representatives were acutely sensitive to securities law developments emanating from Wall Street. These attitudes may have been indicative of larger developments in Canadian economic history: By the turn of the century, the 'Empire of the St Lawrence' was slowly giving way to a new period of transcontinental capitalism.[69]

Representation of Client Interests to Government

On several occasions in the 1895–1913 period, the Campbell, Meredith firm acted for the MSE in its relations with governments. For example, in February 1899 it sent representatives to Quebec City to comment on the taxation implications for brokers of a proposed 'Montreal City Bill' before a select committee of the provincial government.[70]

A somewhat more important issue requiring representations to government by the Campbell, Meredith firm on behalf of the MSE emerged in 1900. Throughout the late 1890s, the Yukon 'gold rush' had resulted in the proliferation of highly speculative issues of mining securities. Consistent with its approach to negotiable instruments problems, the MSE was careful to consider the practices of the major North American exchanges with regard to the associated problem of 'curb trading,' the expression used for transactions by members conducted outside of the institution. On behalf of the MSE, in February 1900 the lawyers consulted the Boston and New York exchanges to ascertain their approaches to the problem. They reported to the Governing Committee that the Americans had implemented only vague and permissive measures against 'curb trading.' Campbell, Meredith concluded that a more stringent by-law could be drafted, but was inadvisable:

We think upon general principles you will find it undesirable to pass any by-law, however stringent the terms of it may be, if it exacts from the members something which they find at times very much against their interests to comply with. The general tenor of the by-laws we think should not go beyond what is in the common interest and what the Committee feel they will at all times have the support of the majority of the members in enforcing.[71]

The MSE apparently followed the recommendations of the firm in this matter, which clearly went beyond merely 'technical' expertise with regard to a specific legal issue. In a half-hearted attempt to prevent the growth of the 'curb market,' the MSE by-laws stated that members could purchase and sell securities only on the premises and during the exchange's hours of business. For a first infraction of this by-law, a member was subject to a fine of five hundred dollars. A second offence resulted in a three-month suspension from trading, while a third would be punished by deeming the member to be in default of the by-laws and could therefore result in loss of the right to entrance. The prohibition on 'curb trading' extended to the business partners of the membership, but did not apply to transactions with parties outside Montreal. No registration requirement was imposed on the membership during the 1895–1913 period to supplement these provisions.[72]

In Toronto and Montreal, widespread trading in unlisted mining stocks eventually resulted in the formation of rival exchanges for securities that could not meet the listing requirements of the major Canadian markets.[73] While the MSE was apparently willing to ignore 'curb trading' by some of its members, it was unwilling to entertain the creation of rival exchanges. If substantial profits could be made on 'external' stock transactions, membership on the established exchanges would lose value, and there would be no incentive to abide by its rules and regulations.

In order to preserve its monopoly position over the local market, the exchange strictly prohibited members from belonging to or doing business with any other organization dealing in securities within the city of Montreal. Furthermore, a member who became a defaulter by reason of any external speculations on his account was forbidden to reapply for membership in the corporation for a period of one year. All defaulters were required to submit proof of their legal discharge before they could be considered for readmission.[74]

At the instigation of the Governing Committee, the Campbell, Meredith firm intervened with the provincial government to limit any potential interference with the MSE's local monopoly in securities trading. A letter dated February 1900 indicates that they were partially successful: The lawyers reported that a bill to incorporate the 'Montreal Mining Exchange' had been amended, restricting it to trading in mines and related industries.[75] According to E.P. Neufeld, the Montreal Mining Exchange functioned sporadically after its incorporation, and ceased trading completely after the creation in 1926 of the Montreal Curb Market, an exchange closely affiliated with the MSE.[76] Through this institutionalization of unlisted trading, the MSE eventually managed to restore its monopoly over the securities market.

The significance of the firm's contribution should not be underestimated: The 1900 correspondence suggests that Campbell, Meredith was instrumental in limiting the potential challenge through representations to influential members of the legislature. By limiting traders on the Montreal Mining Exchange to a segment of the securities market, the rival market's Act of Incorporation placed it in a position of competitive disadvantage with the more balanced MSE.[77] Given the extensive family, political, and professional connections of the firm, it was ideally positioned to lobby politicians on behalf of an important client such as the exchange. The firm apparently had the Montreal Mining Exchange's

Act of Incorporation amended with the assistance of the provincial treasurer, A.W. Atwater, since the letter suggests that the chairman of the
MSE thank him for 'his good offices in connection with this amendment.'[78]

On the issue of 'curb trading,' the instigation to lobby the provincial
government emanated from the client. However, Campbell, Meredith
played a more proactive and strategic role in a subsequent episode relating to the activities of 'bucket-shops.' In July 1903, the lawyers offered to
make representations on behalf of the MSE to the federal government
regarding an amendment to the Criminal Code. The bill related to the evi-
dentiary burden imposed upon the Crown in relation to various offences,
including the prohibition on gaming in stocks. Many North American
stock and commodities exchanges were acutely concerned about the activities of 'bucket-shops,' where persons gambled against stock-exchange
price fluctuations without actually buying or selling shares.[79] J.W.
Markham described the 'bucket-shop' as 'an establishment where bets can
be placed on current prices ... The bets are not executed as contracts on any
exchange, but rather are placed on the bucket shop's books, just as would
be done by a bookie, who offsets his bets by his own resources. Such
resources were often sadly lacking, as discovered by successful wagerers
when they came to collect their winnings.'[80] Such activities were harmful
to the business of the MSE, since they diverted the funds of potential
shareholders from the market. R.T. Naylor noted that, in the first decade
of the twentieth century, some of the larger Montreal 'bucket-shops' were
trading thousands of imaginary 'shares' every day.[81]

In addition, gaming on stocks was highly deleterious to the public
image of the institution, since the vast majority of Canadians who were
not investors often had difficulty distinguishing 'legitimate' speculation
on markets from the 'gambling' which occurred in bucket-shops. Indeed,
as Michael Bliss has noted, even businessmen were highly suspicious of
the growth in securities trading at the turn of the century. They did not
understand market fluctuations, and were most concerned that 'an excess
of speculative fervour' could result in economic depression. Bliss notes
that publications such as the *Monetary Times* and the *Journal of Commerce*
denounced speculators, and at least one editorial suggested that Canada's
stock markets should be abolished. Contemporary public concern over
speculation was duly noted by politicians, who responded with proposals for legislative intervention.[82] Consequently, while the MSE had a vital
interest in the criminalization and suppression of the 'bucket-shop' trade
by the government, it was equally concerned with maintaining institutional independence.

In light of these conflicting objectives, the by-laws included merely a vague prohibition against bucket-shop trading, asserting that 'fictitious sales or contracts' were not permitted by the exchange.[83] This was supplemented by the requirement that the seller of a security was responsible for the 'genuineness' and 'regularity' of the transaction documents until the purchaser had sufficient time for verification and registration.[84]

The effect of the proposed 'Article 704' was to reduce the burden of proof required by the Crown, which would have to prove only that an agreement existed for the making of a purchase or sale of shares. Previously, the Crown also had to demonstrate that the accused had no *bona fide* intention of actually buying or selling shares. The amendment provided that, once the existence of an agreement had been proven, the accused would have to demonstrate that he had a *bona fide* intention to buy or sell shares in order to exculpate himself from a conviction for gaming in stocks. While such an amendment would seem to coincide with the interests of the institution, the MSE was concerned about the implications of the bill for stockbrokers, suggesting that some members of the exchange were involved in speculation. Alternatively, the Governing Committee may have been concerned with minimizing any potential legislative interference in the securities industry. Campbell, Meredith advised that, provided the broker's client was willing to testify as to the *bona fide* nature of the transaction, it would be difficult to contradict such testimony. In addition, the firm consulted a judge in order to obtain another informed view on the proposed change. The lawyers also offered to make representations to the government, but cautioned: 'It is a matter of policy to be decided by the Board whether it is desirable that they should come forward to resist a contemplated change of the law of evidence which cannot affect legitimate business, nor even business not strictly legitimate, provided the broker is unaware of the intentions of the client.'[85] Since there seems to have been no further correspondence between the firm and the stock exchange on the proposed amendment, it is probable that the Governing Committee elected to follow the advice of its solicitors.

This episode demonstrates the lobbying expertise that an established turn-of-the-century law firm could provide for its clients. While the lawyers anticipated that the Governing Committee might request that some representation be made to the federal government, they advised against it, based on the foreseeable public relations complications that might arise from opposing such a Criminal Code amendment. It should be emphasized that the lawyers were not merely engaged in the provision of technical legal services to the MSE, but were acting in the facilitative capacity of strategic advisers. However, the relative paucity of examples of institutional interest representation by the Campbell, Meredith firm during the 1895–1913 period suggests that the exchange favoured the lobbying of legislators only as a last resort, since such activities could jeopardize its primary objective of retaining institutional independence through the avoidance of government scrutiny or regulation.

Property Law

On several occasions, the Campbell, Meredith firm acted on behalf of the MSE in both routine and exceptional matters relating to property law. The lawyers advised the institution in October 1900 with regard to the appropriate course of action to protect its lease in the event of a judicial sale of the property owned by the Western Trust & Loan Company. The filing of an *opposition afin de charge* would notify others of the MSE's rights, and ensure that, in the event of sale, the purchaser would be bound to respect the lease.[86] In 1902–3, the lawyers negotiated with the Seminary of Montreal to purchase property on St François Xavier Street for the construction of the MSE's first official headquarters. The firm arranged to have a notary translate the deed of sale into English for the benefit of the Governing Committee, and renegotiated several clauses of the agreement as they requested. It is significant that the exchange insisted on the inclusion of an arbitration clause to resolve any disputes arising from the transaction. This was consistent with the general policy of avoiding state law whenever possible: Campbell, Meredith's expertise was often enlisted by the MSE to create facilitative legal arrangements designed to bypass the justice system. This episode also provides an example of the constant interaction between the facilitative and technical roles of the firm.[87]

With the completion of the building, the exchange became a landlord, leasing surplus space to Laidlaw and Company. However, by October 1912, the expansion of the membership and the dramatic increase in trading activity before the First World War resulted in the need to occupy all of the available space. Acting as 'legal technicians,' Campbell, Meredith advised the institution as to the rights of its tenants and when it could take possession of the property. In keeping with its proactive approach to the client's legal service requirements, the firm also drafted the letter to be sent by the institution advising Laidlaw of the need to vacate the premises by May 1915.[88]

Assistance with Civil Actions

An examination of the legal opinions written by the Campbell, Meredith firm for the MSE in the 1895–1913 period reveals that it was hardly a litigious organization. There is no evidence that the exchange initiated a single legal action during the entire eighteen-year period. While this finding is surprising, given the thousands of transactions and financial interests involved in trading, it is consistent with the exchange's policy of avoiding external dispute resolution mechanisms. A complex arbitration scheme was buttressed by the inclusion of severe penalties for members who elected to resort to the courts. In addition, the institution took care to avoid being taken to court by third parties: recall the significance of the deed of sale with the Seminary of Montreal, which was modified by the firm to include an arbitration clause.[89]

On the rare occasions when the MSE was involved with the justice system, the Campbell, Meredith firm attempted to extricate the institution if possible and otherwise took steps to minimize the length and impact of the proceedings. In the unreported 1905 case of *Parry* v. *Clarke* involving one of its employees, the exchange was a garnishee. It is revealing that the lawyers first attempted to settle the matter out of court by offering money to the plaintiff as an alternative to being ordered to garnish the wages of the defendant.[90] Similarly, in the unreported 1909 action of *Drouin* v. *Withell*, the lawyers advised the Governing Committee that each MSE member provide the plaintiff with a statement of property belonging to or owed to the defendant in their possession in order to obtain their release from the seizure imposed by the court for Drouin.[91] In the October 1912 unreported case of *Stackhouse* v. *Rykert*, they advised the subpoenaed secretary-treasurer of the MSE on what elements of the institution's business he was required to divulge to the court.[92] These cases confirm that, in order to preserve institutional independence and avoid publicity, the MSE pursued a policy of avoiding the judicial system whenever possible. This policy was largely successful, owing to the expertise of the Campbell, Meredith firm.

THE CAMPBELL, MEREDITH CORPORATE CONSTITUTIONAL OPINIONS

The MSE By-Laws in the Context of Contemporaneous Anglo-American Developments

In his study of the origins of the securities industry in Ontario, John F. Whiteside stated that the 1878 Act of Incorporation which officially created the Toronto Stock Exchange was 'little more than a confirmation of the organization of the institution.'[93] This is probably correct in the sense that the internal structure of the exchange remained unchanged, but the writer underestimated the significance of such an act. Legislative incorporation had the effect of entrenching the position of the exchange as a self-regulating marketplace, and bestowed the imprimatur of the state on its activities. Even if the members continued to perceive it as a 'self-regulating local trading forum,' the Act of Incorporation altered the perception of the public, since the government had officially endorsed the institution.[94] Moreover, such a legislative sanction had the effect of deterring potential competitors: What had previously been an unofficial monopoly was given legitimacy and prestige through the passage of the Act of Incorporation by the Ontario legislature.

Since the Montreal securities market predated the MSE's 1874 Act of Incorporation, the institution likely possessed a pre-existing set of rules and regulations applicable to the membership. This is supported by section 8 of the act, which states: 'The by-laws and rules of the Montreal stock exchange, now in force, shall be the by-laws and rules of the corporation until amended or repealed.'[95] However, as with the Toronto exchange, the MSE's Act of Incorporation was more than a statutory endorsement of existing practices. Rather, it was a piece of facilitative legislation conveying broad powers of self-government to the institution. In order to understand the activities of the Campbell, Meredith lawyers on behalf of the exchange during the 1895–1913 period, it is informative to canvass several important sections of the aforementioned act.

The MSE was given corporate personality: It could sue and be sued, implead and be impleaded, and defend and be defended in the courts. It could also acquire, alienate, sell, convey, and lease real or personal property. Furthermore, it could borrow money on the hypothecary (mortgage) security of the corporation's property. The Quebec legislature placed two restrictions on the exchange. First, it could only exercise the corporate powers expressly conferred by the act, or powers necessary to give effect to the act. Second, the total value of the real and personal property it possessed could not exceed $500,000.[96]

The Act of Incorporation also concerned the management of the exchange, which was entrusted to the Committee of Management, comprising a chairman, a secretary-treasurer, and three managers. These members were to be elected at the annual meeting, provided for in section 6.[97] Section 7 conveyed complete discretion to the institution with regard to the admission of members, and provided that it might expel members for any reason provided for in the by-laws. This provision was crucial to the viability of institutional self-governance, since it provided the Governing Committee with a powerful method of enforcing institutional regulations.[98] However, stock exchanges were not the only contemporary organizations that derived quasi-legal authority from formal government recognition. For example, Paul Craven has documented how late-nineteenth-century Canadian railway companies engaged in 'lawlike practices' with the sanction of the state.[99]

Perhaps the most important part of the act related to the exchange's power to enact by-laws to govern its activities. The by-laws were 'to promote the observance of such regulations and requirements as may be,' and anything was permissible provided they were 'not contrary to the law.' This section also established that 'ordinary, special or general' meetings would be held in order to propose, ratify, amend, and abolish by-laws, as required.[100]

Working from the broad corporate constitutional framework provided by the Act of Incorporation, the MSE published a series of by-laws to govern the conduct of the members.[101] Given the size of the institution and the nature of its membership, it is reasonable to assume that these complex regulations were drafted with the assistance of counsel. This hypothesis is supported by consultations with the Campbell, Meredith firm during the 1895–1913 period by the Governing Committee with regard to the creation, amendment, and repeal of by-laws. If the committee was willing to remunerate the firm for periodic advice on such changes, it seems rather unlikely that legal advice was not obtained during the initial drafting.

The creation and subsequent development by the Campbell, Meredith firm of a complex system of corporate governance and internal regulation for the MSE must be placed in the wider context of developments in the late-nineteenth-century common-law world. In nineteenth-century England, as Harry Arthurs concluded, despite the eradication of many specialized systems of adjudication by the state, '*de facto*, if not *de jure*, legal pluralism survived, and indeed flourished.'[102] Arthurs noted that certain powerful groups within English society, notably businessmen, concluded that state law was both cumbersome and inadequate, and therefore required circumvention. Jonathan Lurie's conclusions support Arthurs: By the late nineteenth century, English merchants no longer had access to specialized commercial courts, but had created adjudication regimes through the use of delegated state power and facilitative law.[103] Robert J. Ferguson's conclusions concur with those of Arthurs and Lurie. Ferguson found that late-nineteenth-century English businessmen were highly dissatisfied with the public legal system's treatment of commercial disputes.[104] The courts were perceived to be slow and expensive, and judges often lacked the specialized expertise needed to adjudicate such actions.[105] Ferguson identified three facets of a commercial movement towards alternative methods of dispute resolution: arbitration mechanisms, the use of standard forms based on trade customs, and the development of methods of coercion to enforce the decisions of non-judicial systems of adjudication.

An examination of the by-laws of the MSE reveals the presence of these trends, demonstrating that the lawyers were influenced by contemporaneous developments in the North Atlantic legal community. The first part of the by-laws, 'Of the Corporation,' outlined the act's requirements to hold meetings and elect officials. The annually elected Governing Committee was composed of the chairman, vice-chairman, secretary-treasurer and two managers. In addition to the annual meeting, the Governing Committee was empowered to call special meetings on its own initiative, or if requested to do so by five members. While the act stated that annual meetings needed a quorum of half of the membership, special meetings required only fifteen members for validity.[106] To counterbalance the special meeting provisions, strict and specific regulations delineated the amount of notice required before all meetings and on proxy voting for the election of Governing Committee members.[107] The committee also required the support of two-thirds of the membership to amend or repeal by-laws.[108]

The first section of the by-laws also supplemented the nebulous membership and management provisions of the Act of Incorporation, giving substantial powers to the Governing Committee. Until the act was amended in 1901, the number of members of the corporation was limited to forty. The administration of the exchange, including the listing of stocks, voting on new issues, and receiving and posting of applications for membership, were to be transacted during the daily meetings of the Governing Committee.[109]

'Of the Governing Committee,' the following section of the by-laws, was concerned with the managerial power of that body over the affairs of the exchange. It established that the chairman and vice-chairman had a duty to enforce the provisions of the act and the by-laws with the assistance of the other committee members.[110] If the Governing Committee suspected that any member was contravening the by-laws, it was given the authority to investigate the matter. Members, their 'attorneys,' and 'clerks' could be compelled to appear before the committee and to divulge information relating to the investigation.

'Of Membership,' the final section of the by-laws, regulated the admission process, discipline, commissions, and trading on the exchange floor. The admission process more closely resembled the entrance requirements of an exclusive club rather than of a securities exchange. The purchase of a seat was a necessary but not a sufficient condition for being granted trading privileges, since existing members also had to approve of the candidate. Prospective members had to be at least twenty-one years old and could initiate the process by writing to the Governing Committee before applying. Upon receipt, two members of the exchange had to sponsor the application, and 80 per cent of the membership present at an ordinary meeting had to approve the candidate. If the application was accepted, the Governing Committee would collect an entrance fee from the new member in addition to the annual subscription of twenty-five dollars required from all participants.[111] If 'blackballed' by more than 20 per cent of the membership present at the meeting, the unsuccessful candidate was required to wait at least six months before applying again. This approval process was mandatory for all members, regardless of whether the candidate had purchased a new or vacant seat from the MSE, or acquired the seat of a retiring member.[112]

Provided that their 'attorneys' were approved by the Governing Committee and an annual fee paid, members could permit others to represent them at meetings. These 'attorneys' had be either the business partners of the members or 'clerks' in their employ. For the determination of legal liability, the 'attorneys' were designated to be agents of the members. These appointees were forbidden from participating in the management of the exchange and could not vote on questions arising during its business.[113]

Bankruptcy, insolvency, or being found in default of certain by-laws resulted in the loss of the member's right of entrance to the MSE. Since this meant that the member could no longer trade, the financial consequences would have been devastating. Upon default, the seat reverted to the MSE, and the committee was empowered to sell vacant positions.[114]

The Governing Committee had the power to issue fines of five hundred dollars, and to suspend or expel members who were guilty of 'dishonourable' or 'disgraceful' conduct, violated any of the by-laws or rules, failed to obey and conform to its decisions, or became 'defaulters' within the meaning of the by-laws. All disciplinary measures required passage at a special meeting of the Governing Committee called for the express purpose of assigning the punishment in question. In addition, the institutional justice system provided members with an avenue of appeal: If the 'sentenced' party protested to the committee in writing within twenty-four hours of the decision, the punishment would have to be confirmed by two-thirds of those present at a special meeting.[115] Members were specifically prohibited from doing business with defaulters, on pain of also being found to be in contravention of the by-laws.[116] Because of the importance of being a member in good standing, the Governing Committee possessed an important disciplinary tool. Unlike many other commercial associations in the North Atlantic legal community, its monopoly over the local securities industry ensured that disgruntled members could not threaten to take their business elsewhere.

Ferguson has written that, throughout the late nineteenth century, British merchants were concerned with having commercial disputes resolved according to customary trade practices, rather than through the mechanical application of abstract legal principles. In an attempt to insulate themselves from the legal system, many trade organizations created elaborate standard-form contracts based on previously implicit mercantile custom and usage. Ferguson has suggested that these 'private codifications of commercial custom' were instrumental in the process of limiting the possibility of internal disputes being decided according to state law.[117] One of the activities of the Campbell, Meredith firm on behalf of the MSE was the drafting of by-law clauses that effectively codified customary practices between brokers, such as the declaration that all offers made by members on the trading floor were to be considered as binding contracts.[118]

In the event that two or more members claimed to have purchased or sold the same stock, the by-laws included an expeditious method of resolving disputes in order to preserve the efficiency of the trading process. After hearing the parties, the chairman resolved the issue: If this decision was challenged, the members present on the floor would vote, with a majority being deemed sufficient to settle the matter.[119]

Nineteenth-century British trade associations favoured arbitration mechanisms because they allowed for the expeditious resolution of disputes. The trade associations appointed adjudicators familiar with business practices, and the entire process was less expensive than the courts. Commercial arbitration was facilitated by the decision of the House of Lords in *Scott* v. *Avery*, in which a contractual clause stating that the parties must resort to arbitration before pursuing legal action was upheld by the majority.[120] In the aftermath of this decision, '*Scott* v. *Avery* clauses' became commonplace in English commercial agreements.[121] The by-laws of the MSE also contained an elaborate arbitration process for the resolution of disputes and compelling reasons to avoid the civil justice system. If one member had a claim against another that was not settled on demand, the former party could appeal to the Governing Committee to resolve the matter to his satisfaction. If the allegation of the claimant was disputed, the matter was then referred to arbitration.[122] The aggrieved party sent a written summary of his position and choice of arbitrator to the secretary-treasurer. The latter conveyed this information to the second party, who was required to prepare a similar document and select a second arbitrator within twenty-four hours. The two representatives then selected a third member of the arbitration board. The three individuals, all of whom had to be members, were empowered to hear the arguments of the parties concerned, collect evidence, and make such enquiries as necessary before delivering their award to the secretary-general. The language of the by-laws with regard to the force of the decision was unequivocal: 'both parties shall conform themselves to such award in all respects' and 'the decision of the majority of such arbitrators ... shall be binding on the parties.'[123]

A problem confronted by many contemporaneous adjudicative processes was enforcement: To be effective, arbitration mechanisms required at least the possibility of some form of punishment for non-compliance. However, Ferguson has noted that enforcement was relatively simple for the management of a centralized, self-contained, and relatively small commercial community such as a stock exchange: 'the rules of the [London] Stock Exchange forbade recourse to the Courts by one member against another, except by special leave of the Committee. At the same time the Committee took it upon itself to adjudicate upon such internal disputes as were not settled by informal arbitration. Conformity to the Committee's decision was a matter of course because it could suspend or expel members.'[124] At the MSE, the Governing Committee was charged with the enforcement of the arbitral decision. Ambiguities in the award could be resolved by the chairman, who was permitted to make 'any further order' which he considered to be 'requisite to do justice between the parties in conformity with the spirit of the award.' However, there was no appeal: Any member who initiated legal proceedings before, during, or after the arbitration process was deemed to be in default of the by-laws. Refusal to abide by either the decision of the arbitrators or any subsequent order made by the chairman also resulted in default and loss of membership.[125]

In light of the remarkably similar British arbitration processes and disciplinary sanctions, it seems likely that the drafters modelled the structure of the MSE on its counterpart in the imperial capital. However, one writer has asserted that the institution's constitution closely resembled that of the New York Stock Exchange. John Steele Johnson asserted that the Montreal and New York institutions possessed similar processes of membership selection, governance, seat transferral, and internal discipline.[126] While the precise model followed is not readily ascertainable, it is clear that the legal structure of the MSE was modelled on pre-existing securities markets. As was the case with the securities law and negotiable instrument problems confronted by the exchange, the drafters who created its system of regulation were knowledgeable about the application of company law to securities markets in the metropolitan centres of the North Atlantic legal community, and may very well have been influenced by the internal regulations of these institutions.

Some General Comments on the Corporate Constitution Opinions
Provided by the Firm

The MSE's by-laws were highly complex and provided for many possible contingencies. However, a variety of pressures resulted in the need for substantial changes between 1895 and 1913. An increase in the volume of listings and number of shares traded, the rise in the price and demand for seats, curb trading, attempts to raise money for a new headquarters, and the statutory limit on the value of exchange property were among the issues which required the repeal, amendment, and creation of by-laws. Yet another problem requiring changes to the rules governing the MSE was the desire of some brokers previously belonging to partnerships to form limited liability companies.[127] Finally, increased trading also necessitated changes in the 1895–1913 period: Several by-laws were modified during this period to permit the creation of subcommittees and an increase in the number of managers.[128]

While the period was undoubtedly characterized by favourable economic conditions that resulted in the need for numerous changes to the institution's governmental structure, it is not unreasonable to suggest that an element of professional self-interest motivated the lawyers who drafted these by-laws. By creating a complex set of regulations, the lawyers had effectively ensured that their advice would be required by the management of the MSE for years to come. This hypothesis is supported by the fact that many of the legal opinions during the 1895–1913 period related to the interpretation of existing rules. Campbell, Meredith was constantly consulted as to whether sufficient notice had been given

before meetings, the propriety of amendments, whether election procedures had been followed correctly, the legal consequences of a variety of
proposed amendments, and the limits of the institution's authority under
the Act of Incorporation.[129] This last function was particularly important for institutional independence, since the lawyers ensured that the
MSE did not overstep the boundaries of the authority granted by the
legislature.

The approach of the lawyers to the modification of the exchange's regulations was characterized by clear and coherent language. Almost all
of the opinions followed a standard format: The question submitted by
the client would be restated and then addressed in a complete manner.
While thorough, the letters were generally economical in style, and
rarely exceeded five typewritten pages in length. The firm also seems to
have been sensitive to the legal knowledge and practical concerns of the
MSE, since the letters contained almost no technical terminology or
Latin maxims, and lengthy opinions were often prefaced with summa-
ries of the conclusions. Furthermore, services were often provided in a
proactive manner: The firm not only answered the questions posed by
the Governing Committee, but took the initiative to draft necessary
forms, propose by-law alterations, and suggest other possible courses of
action. When appropriate, the Campbell, Meredith firm avoided dupli-
cation of effort and presumably saved the client money by referring the
Governing Committee to previously rendered opinions that addressed
their concerns.[130] It is interesting to note that, while allusions were
made to treatises on company law and to the Act of Incorporation, no
reference was ever made to jurisprudence or to the Civil Code of Lower
Canada.[131]

It is apparent that the lawyers were attuned to business realities: The
corporate constitutional opinions on the by-laws were in no sense theoretical exercises, but were intended to assist the Governing Committee in
regulating the membership. In response to the committee's concern about
brokers changing their partnerships into limited liability companies, the
firm advised that the enactment of a by-law prohibiting such reorganizations was probably beyond the power of the exchange, and could result
in litigation. While the lawyers offered to draft a by-law, they tactfully
observed to the Governing Committee:

It has also occurred to us that any rulings or by-laws limiting the manner in which
transactions may be made on the Exchange, or the business connections that the
members make outside, will necessarily limit to a greater or less extent the

amount of business done on the Exchange. This point is of importance also, but you are in a better position to judge its relative importance than ourselves.[132]

Two general conclusions result from an examination of the opinions relating to the Act of Incorporation and the by-laws. It is apparent that the Campbell, Meredith lawyers were intimately involved in the ongoing process of institutional reform. In addition, the correspondence indicates that the exchange constantly consulted the firm on company law issues as it was determined to avoid state law and retain its semi-autonomous and self-regulatory status.

A Case-Study: Opinions Relating to the Statutory Limit on the Value of MSE Property

The importance of the legal services regularly provided to the MSE by the Campbell, Meredith firm was evident from 1912 correspondence on the issue of the $500,000 statutory limit on the value of property owned by the institution.[133] Owing to membership expansion in the 1901–12 period and the erection of the new building in 1903–4, by March 1912 the MSE was close to exceeding the limit established by the Act of Incorporation.[134] In response to a variety of proposals and at the request of the Governing Committee, the lawyers delivered an exhaustive opinion on the issue. The importance of the problem to the MSE was demonstrated by committee's willingness to authorize the exceptional request of F.E. Meredith to consult A.J. Brown, of Brown, Montgomery and McMichael, on the matter. The opinions of the two firms were submitted in April 1912: While they differed somewhat in reasoning, they arrived at similar conclusions. At sixteen pages, the Campbell, Meredith letter was by far the longest opinion composed by the firm for the MSE between 1895 and 1913, and was supplemented by a separate seven-page document from A.J. Brown.[135] The two opinions also likely constituted the largest single expenditure by the exchange on legal services during the same period. F.E. Meredith later wrote to the chairman and requested $425 for Brown's services, in addition to the $400 for his own work. The difference can be attributed to the fact that, since the client was a regular customer of his firm, Meredith chose not to bill the MSE for attendance at a Governing Committee meeting. In the billing letter, Meredith stated: 'This opinion entailed a very considerable amount of time and work and the amount charged by Mr. Brown, I consider very reasonable.' He concluded by stating on his own behalf: 'You will probably appreciate the amount of work that was entailed in answering the different inquiries which were submitted for opinion, some of which entailed a very considerable amount of time and work.' By the standards of the time, $825 was undoubtedly a substantial fee, but the handwritten notice, 'Two cheques sent to Mr. Meredith,' suggests that the prosperous exchange promptly paid for this expensive legal expertise.[136]

The lawyers informed the committee that while the government could not seize the excess assets of the exchange, it or another interested party could take legal action and compel the institution to divest itself of some property. To alleviate the problem, the Governing Committee had considered issuing bonus capital stock to members and paying dividends until the value of assets held was less than the statutory limit. However, the Campbell, Meredith firm advised against this, owing to the limitations contained in the Act of Incorporation. The lawyers instead suggested that the problem could be alleviated either by lobbying the government to modify the act, or through the passage of a by-law authorizing a one-time payment of $1,000 to each member.[137] Consistent with the MSE's preference for internal solutions for avoiding both the courts and the legislature, the Governing Committee opted for the latter solution. Accordingly, the lawyers drafted a receipt for members to sign upon receiving the payment.[138]

A difficulty arose, however, as to who was entitled to payment, since two seats were held in trust at the time. The Governing Committee was divided as to whether future purchasers of these seats were entitled to the money, and requested that F.E. Meredith attend its next meeting. The trust placed by the committee in its legal adviser was evident from the language of the message: He was to hear the divergent views of the committee, and then give them his 'judgement on the question.'[139] The lawyer subsequently advised the committee that, according to the by-law, only members were entitled to receive the money. Since ownership of a seat did not in itself constitute membership, no money should be allocated for seats held in trust.[140]

The correspondence relating to the one-time payment issue in 1912 is illustrative of the role of the Campbell, Meredith firm in assisting with the governance of the MSE during the entire 1895–1913 period. The lawyers acted as drafters, advisers, and occasionally even as adjudicators with regard to the institution's complex system of self-government. Far from being merely 'legal technicians' charged with the maintenance of an organizational system, they played an important part in the MSE's development during a period of change and expansion.

SOME TENTATIVE CONCLUSIONS ON THE ROLE OF LAWYERS IN
THE DEVELOPMENT OF CANADIAN BUSINESS INSTITUTIONS

This survey of the legal work conducted by the Campbell, Meredith firm on behalf of the MSE during the 1895–1913 period is based on the examination of the work of one particular élite practice for an atypical corporate client.[141] Nevertheless, the wide diversity of tasks undertaken is indicative of the multiplicity of roles assumed by some Canadian business lawyers at the turn of the century. Carol Wilton has observed that there is a 'widespread and forcefully argued assumption that lawyers were simply the hired guns of the business élite, who generally determined tactics rather than strategy.'[142] However, a careful examination of the work of the firm for the MSE over an eighteen-year period demonstrates the sophisticated nature of the services provided. Even when acting merely as 'hired guns,' the lawyers had the client's strategic interests in mind.

In the resolution of securities law issues, negotiable instruments problems, real estate transactions, and the provision of legal representation on behalf of the exchange, the Campbell, Meredith lawyers sometimes seemed to act as mere legal technicians. But it is important to examine these activities in a broader context: Minor services were often performed in a fashion which advanced the larger objectives of the institution. Thus, in providing opinions on securities law and negotiable instruments problems, the firm was aware of the increasingly international character of the securities industry and the position of the MSE in relation to the major markets in London and New York. Consequently, it provided expert advice on the law of the jurisdiction, but also acted as a conduit for information on practices in the financial centres of the North Atlantic legal community.

In the negotiation of real estate transactions on behalf of the client and with regard to representation in legal actions, the Campbell, Meredith lawyers were sensitive to the underlying objective of the MSE to preserve the semi-autonomous and self-regulatory prerogatives granted by the Act of Incorporation. The arbitration clause in the agreement with the Seminary of Montreal, the absence of litigation initiated by the MSE, and the attempts to reach out-of-court settlements should be perceived as components of an overall strategy devised to protect institutional independence.

The role of the Campbell, Meredith firm in providing expert representation to governments for the MSE provides yet another example of a non-technical service rendered by the lawyers. The client probably benefited from the firm's prestigious reputation and important political connections, which could be employed to forestall or modify legislative actions deleterious to the objectives of the institution. Significantly, the correspondence demonstrates that the firm did not hesitate to advise its client if it deemed a course of action to be inappropriate. In the context of the MSE's relations with governments, it is clear that the lawyers were trusted advisers rather than mere providers of legal services.

However, it is in the examination of the correspondence relating to company law that the firm is revealed to have been vital for its client's operations. The Campbell, Meredith lawyers were in close and constant collaboration with the Governing Committee, participating in the management and regulation of the MSE. Given the evidence, David Sugarman's observations on nineteenth-century lawyers acting in this capacity seems highly appropriate. He suggests that the role of the nineteenth-century business lawyer was analogous to that of an architect: 'Knowledge is power. Nowhere is this more evident than in the diverse ways that lawyers used their specialist expertise to shape the form and content of company law, and therefore, the organizational structure of the business corporation.'[143]

The creation, amendment, and interpretation of by-laws was not a theoretical exercise conducted to satisfy the legalistic whims of the Governing Committee. Rather, the maintenance of an efficient market and the creation of a comprehensive system of internal regulation was at the heart of an institutional strategy to preserve control and to retain the maximum degree of autonomy. Through advice based on expertise in company law, the firm provided the committee with by-laws designed to promote the interests of the MSE, resolve disputes, and avoid state interference. Nevertheless, it is vital to perceive the activities of the firm in the larger context of the late-nineteenth-century movement of commercial interests away from state law and towards alternative and specialized forms of regulation and dispute resolution. Just as the MSE's spectacular growth in the 1895–1913 period must be interpreted in relation to the international securities market, the work of the Campbell, Meredith lawyers must be understood in light of developments in commercial dispute resolution and adjudication throughout the North Atlantic legal community.

NOTES

The writer wishes to thank Professor G. Blaine Baker and Carol Wilton for their advice and assistance. This essay was awarded the Wainwright Prize by the McGill University Faculty of Law in 1995.

1 G.P. Marchildon, 'International Corporate Law from a Maritime Base: The Halifax Firm of Harris, Henry and Cahan,' in Carol Wilton, ed., *Essays in the History of Canadian Law*, vol. 4: *Beyond the Law: Lawyers and Business in Canada, 1830 to 1930* (Toronto: The Osgoode Society 1990), 201

2 For example, lawyers are mentioned only four times in the index of Michael Bliss, *Northern Enterprise: Five Centuries of Canadian Business* (Toronto: McClelland and Stewart 1987), 631.

3 See generally Wilton, ed., *Beyond the Law.*

4 Carol Wilton, 'Introduction: Inside the Law – Canadian Law Firms in Historical Perspective,' this volume, 3

5 For example, B.J. Young, *George-Etienne Cartier: Montreal Bourgeois* (Kingston and Montreal: McGill–Queen's University Press 1981)

6 For a catalogue of the published histories of Canadian law firms, see Wilton, 'Introduction: Inside the Law.'

7 E.P. Neufeld, *The Financial System of Canada: Its Growth and Development* (Toronto: Macmillan of Canada 1972), 44

8 The legal opinions submitted to the Governing Committee of the MSE between 1895 and 1933 are contained in three folders (1895–1910, 1911–16, and 1917–33, respectively) at the McGill University Archives in Montreal. References to the opinion letters are identified in the notes as 'Correspondence' and followed by the date of writing.

9 Regrettably, the MSE's archives contain Governing Committee meeting-books from 1922–48 only. See R. Sweeny, *A Guide to the the History and Records of Selected Montreal Businesses before 1947* (Montreal: Montreal Business History Project 1978), 185–6.

10 For a discussion on the often-unappreciated value of legal opinions see generally P. Moore, *Lawyers' Records and the Scholar: Waiving History Goodbye?* (Winnipeg: University of Manitoba Faculty of Law 1992).

11 G.R. Rubin and D. Sugarman, 'Towards a New History of Law and Material Society in England, 1750–1914,' in G.R. Rubin and D. Sugarman, eds., *Law, Economy and Society, 1750–1914: Essays in the History of English Law* (Abingdon, Oxford: Professional Books 1984), 1

12 Ibid.

13 An Act to Incorporate the Montreal Stock Exchange, *Statutes of Quebec* [hereinafter SQ] 1874, c. 54

14 See generally G.B. Baker, 'Law Practice and Statecraft in Mid-Nineteenth-Century Montreal: The Torrance–Morris Firm, 1848 to 1868,' in Wilton, ed., *Beyond the Law*, 45–91.

15 D. Mitchell and J. Slinn, *The History of McMaster Meighen* (Montreal: McMaster Meighen 1989), 21

16 Ibid., 23

17 Ibid., 25

18 Ibid., 38

19 Ibid., 41–2

20 Ibid., 50

21 Ibid., 56

22 Ibid., 48

23 B.J. Young and G. Tulchinsky, 'Sir Hugh Allan,' in *Dictionary of Canadian Biography*, vol. 11 (Toronto: University of Toronto Press 1982), 5–14

24 'CAMMERALL' is still used by McMaster Meighen today for telex identification on firm stationery.

25 Mitchell and Slinn, *McMaster Meighen*, 51

26 Because Shaughnessy had studied law abroad, the legislature had to be petitioned to allow him to practice. See An Act to Authorize the Bar of the Province of Quebec to Admit William James Shaughnessy Amongst Its Members, SQ 1911, c. 140.

27 Mitchell and Slinn, *McMaster Meighen*, 57, 59–60

28 W.K. Hobson, 'Symbol of the New Profession: Emergence of the Large Law Firm, 1870–1915,' in G.W. Gawalt, ed., *The New High Priests: Lawyers in Post–Civil War America* (Westport, CT: Greenwood Press 1984), 5–6

29 Wilton, 'Introduction: Inside the Law,' 14–15

30 Mitchell and Slinn, *McMaster Meighen*, 62–3, 79

31 D.H. Tees, *Chronicles of Ogilvy Renault, 1879–1979* (Montreal: Ogilvy Renault 1979), 31

32 Owing to their frequent visits to the MSE and other clients, the attire of the partners seems to have been more important to the image of the firm than its chambers. F.E. Meredith, for example, was 'always immaculately attired in a morning coat and stock tie with a pearl pin': Mitchell and Slinn, *McMaster Meighen*, 54.

33 D. Mackay, *The Square Mile: Merchant Princes of Montreal* (Vancouver: Douglas and MacIntyre 1987), 143

34 Mitchell and Slinn, *McMaster Meighen*, 20, 32, 38, 42, 52, 54

35 Bliss, *Northern Enterprise*, 278

36 J.S. Johnson, 'History and Organization of the Montreal Stock Exchange and the Montreal Curb Market,' MA thesis, McGill University, 1934, 13–15

37 R.T. Naylor, *The History of Canadian Business, 1867–1914*, vol. 1 (Toronto: Lorimer 1975), 210

38 J.F. Whiteside, 'The Toronto Stock Exchange and the Development of the Share Market to 1885,' *Journal of Canadian Studies* 20/3 (Autumn 1985), 70

39 C. Bergithon, *The Stock Exchange, with Special Reference to the Montreal Stock Exchange and the Montreal Curb Market* (Montreal: privately published 1940), 11

40 Neufeld, *The Financial System of Canada*, 471

41 Bliss, *Northern Enterprise*, 278

42 E.A. Collard, *Chalk to Computers: The Story of the Montreal Stock Exchange* (Montreal: privately published 1974), 13

43 Collard, *Chalk to Computers*, 15

44 Bergithon, *The Stock Exchange*, 12

45 At least one member of the firm profited immensely from investment tips provided by business connections. Campbell was friendly with the executives of the American Gas & Electric Co., and made substantial profits from his investments in that enterprise and the General Electric Co. as Montreal's industries converted to electricity. He died in 1923, leaving an estate valued at more than $2 million. In addition to providing for the upkeep of his prized horse Kodak, the unmarried and civic-minded lawyer left portions of his estate to two hospitals, and established a fund for the creation of parks in less fortunate areas of Montreal: Mitchell and Slinn, *McMaster Meighen*, 52, 56–7.

46 R.C. Michie, 'The Canadian Securities Market, 1850–1914,' *Business History Review* 62/1 (Spring 1988), 56

47 Information from Neufeld, *The Financial System of Canada*, 44, 477, 495; Collard, *Chalk to Computers*, 13–14, 18; and Bergithon, *The Stock Exchange*, 12. The price of membership *circa* 1900 was higher than London but much lower than the fees in New York and Paris. See generally E.V. Morgan and W.A. Thomas, *The London Stock Exchange: Its History and Functions* (New York: St Martin's Press 1962).

48 Bliss, *Northern Enterprise*, 279

49 Collard, *Chalk to Computers*, 18

50 Ibid.

51 See generally B. Young, *In Its Corporate Capacity: The Seminary of Montreal as a Business Institution* (Kingston and Montreal: McGill–Queen's University Press 1986).

52 The MSE was located there until the 1960s, when it moved to the Tour de la Bourse on Victoria Square. The old headquarters is now the home of the Centaur Theatre.

53 Collard, *Chalk to Computers*, 19
54 Michie, 'The Canadian Securities Market,' 47
55 R. Sobel, *The Big Board: The History of the New York Stock Exchange* (New York: The Free Press 1965), 105, 150
56 Michie, 'The Canadian Securities Market,' 43–4
57 Ibid., 47
58 Ibid.
59 Correspondence, 3 November 1903, 3 July 1909
60 Ibid., 16 November 1896
61 Ibid., 14 May 1901
62 Ibid., 17 January 1910
63 Ibid., 20 January 1910
64 Ibid., 2 March 1910
65 Ibid., 14 April 1910
66 Ibid., 27 April 1910
67 Ibid., 14 January 1913
68 Ibid., 6 February 1913. This opinion also suggests that the firm had limited doctrinal resources at its disposal.
69 See generally D.G. Creighton, *The Commercial Empire of the St. Lawrence, 1750–1850* (Toronto: Ryerson 1936). This progression was also reflected in some treatises of the period. For example, the contemporary edition of Theophilus Parsons's *Laws of Business* was intended to cover all jurisdictions in the United States and Canada. The index of this 1911 treatise distinguishes Canadian law from American only four times in more than 800 pages: T. Parsons, *Laws of Business for all the States and Territories of the Union and the Dominion of Canada*, 6th ed. (Hartford, CT: S.S. Scranton 1911).
70 Correspondence, 11 February 1899
71 Ibid., 23 February 1900
72 Montreal Stock Exchange, *By-Laws of the Montreal Stock Exchange* (Montreal: J. Theo. Robinson 1884), 14–15
73 Neufeld, *The Financial System of Canada*, 478
74 *By-Laws*, 14
75 Correspondence, 22 February 1900
76 Neufeld, *The Financial System of Canada*, 497
77 *An Act to Incorporate the Montreal Mining Exchange*, SQ 1900, c. 85, s. 2
78 Correspondence, 22 February 1900
79 See generally J. Lurie, *The Chicago Board of Trade, 1859–1905: The Dynamics of Self-Regulation* (Urbana: The University of Illinois Press 1979).
80 J.W. Markham, *The History of Commodity Futures Trading and Its Regulation* (New York: Praeger 1987), 9

81 Naylor, *The History of Canadian Business*, 214
82 M. Bliss, *A Living Profit: Studies in the Social History of Canadian Business, 1883–1911* (Toronto: McClelland and Stewart 1974), 24–6
83 *By-Laws*, 18
84 Ibid., 20
85 Correspondence, 30 July 1903
86 Ibid., 31 October 1900
87 Ibid., 17 November, 5 December, 10 December 1903
88 Ibid., 21 October 1912
89 Ibid., 17 November, 5 December 1903, 10 December 1903
90 Ibid., 20 July, 21 July, 26 August 1905
91 Ibid., 5 August 1909
92 Ibid., 18 October 1912
93 Whiteside, 'The Toronto Stock Exchange,' 74
94 Ibid.
95 MSE Act, s. 8
96 Ibid., s. 1
97 Ibid., s. 6
98 Ibid., s. 7
99 'Alongside the formal public law practised by the courts there existed the law-like practices of the railway companies, sanctioned by the state, in which considerations of compensation and punishment were as significant as in the courts, but with a different logic and hence different effects': Paul Craven, 'Law and Railway Accidents, 1850–80,' in Canadian Law in History Conference, *Papers Presented at the 1987 Canadian Law in History Conference held at Carleton University, Ottawa, June 8–10, 1987*, vol. 2 (Ottawa, 1987), 69
100 MSE Act, s. 2
101 *By-Laws*, 72
102 H.W. Arthurs, 'Special Courts, Special Law: Legal Pluralism in Nineteenth Century England,' in Rubin and Sugarman, eds., *Law, Economy and Society*, 407
103 Lurie, *The Chicago Board of Trade*, 18, 22
104 R.B. Ferguson, 'The Adjudication of Commercial Disputes and the Legal System in Modern England,' *British Journal of Law and Society* 7 (1980), 141
105 Ibid., 144
106 *By-Laws*, 3
107 Ibid., 4
108 Ibid., 8
109 Ibid., 5
110 Ibid., 7

111 Ibid., 13
112 Ibid., 9–10
113 Ibid., 11
114 Ibid., 12
115 Ibid., 15
116 Ibid., 20
117 Ferguson, 'The Adjudication of Commercial Disputes,' 150–1
118 *By-Laws*, 17
119 Ibid.
120 *Scott* v. *Avery* (1856) 5 HLC 811
121 Ferguson, 'The Adjudication of Commerical Disputes,' 146–8
122 *By-Laws*, 15–16
123 Ibid., 21–2
124 Ferguson, 'The Adjudication of Commercial Disputes,' 155
125 *By-Laws*, 21–2
126 Johnson, 'History and Organization of the Montreal Stock Exchange,' 48
127 Correspondence, 28 November 1910
128 Ibid., 15 April 1913
129 Ibid.
130 Ibid., 16 June 1902
131 Ibid., 7 July 1912
132 Ibid., 28 November 1910
133 *MSE Act*, s. 2
134 Correspondence, 18 April 1912
135 Ibid., 17 April 1912
136 Ibid., 29 May 1912
137 Ibid., 19 April 1912
138 Ibid., 21 May 1912
139 Ibid., 30 May 1912
140 Ibid., 7 June 1912
141 For a study of the work conducted by turn-of-the-century Canadian lawyers
     on behalf for business corporations, see generally Marchildon, 'International
     Corporate Law from a Maritime Base,' in Wilton, ed., *Beyond the Law*, 201–34.
142 C. Wilton, 'Introduction,' in Wilton, ed., *Beyond the Law*, 31
143 D. Sugarman, 'Simple Images and Complex Realities: English Lawyers and
     Their Relationship to Business and Politics, 1750–1950,' *Law and History
     Review* 11/2 (Fall 1993), 257–74

5

The Transformation of an Establishment Firm: From Beatty Blackstock to Faskens, 1902–1915

C. IAN KYER

THE 'REMARKABLE ENTERTAINMENT'

On 13 March 1913, Edward Marion Chadwick, a seventy-three-year-old conveyancing lawyer, wrote to a relative in Ireland about a 'remarkable entertainment' that had recently been held at his house to celebrate the fiftieth anniversary of the Beatty Blackstock firm. He noted that, had William Henry Beatty lived just three months longer, Beatty and Chadwick would have been partners in the firm for fifty years, something that Chadwick believed was 'without parallel in this province.'[1] Chadwick explained:

The fiftieth anniversary was celebrated by the gathering at my house of all of the members of the firm and their wives, and the students, numbering all together about 30, to which we added ourselves and immediate relations to the number of about 20. At the same time the firm entertained the women clerks of the office at McConkey's which you may remember as a swell downtown establishment,[2] where they sat down 18. All of which was quite an expansion from the original two partners and one clerk.

Although this 'remarkable entertainment' was a celebration of fifty years of practice, it could not have been lost on some of the attendees that it was also a wake, marking the passing of one of the great law firms of its time. Chadwick and others noticed that the only former partner of Beatty

Blackstock who attended was Mr Justice William Renwick Riddell. This was not surprising to some. They knew that the Beatty Blackstock firm which Chadwick had help found fifty years earlier was in the process of being completely transformed by two dynamic, entrepreneurial lawyers from Elora – David and Alex Fasken. They also knew that the Faskens' undertaking was not without its casualties and tensions.

It is difficult for us to appreciate the significance of this event. While few people today would even recognize the Beatty Blackstock name, there would have been no such problem in 1913. On W.H. Beatty's death, just months before the Chadwick party, Beatty Blackstock had been said to have done 'more business than any [law firm] in all Canada.'[3] Later it would be referred to as 'Canada's largest law business'[4] and 'the famous Beatty Blackstock firm.'[5]

In looking at the history of any firm, one must look at the key individuals that give it its character. A partnership, unlike a corporation, is not a legal entity with a separate legal existence from its partners. As anyone who has worked in a law partnership knows, this is not a legal fiction. While a law partnership may appear to be a single entity with a common name, office, and perhaps even a distinct character and philosophy, in many respects it is a collection of individuals, each with his or her own practice. These individual practices to a greater or lesser degree overlap and compliment one another. The firm is effectively the aggregation of these individuals, and it draws its character from them, particularly from certain dominant partners – in this case, William Henry Beatty and David Fasken.

Under W.H. Beatty, the firm was extremely large for its day, having fifteen lawyers in 1902. It was in many ways, however, a close-knit group. Most of its members shared a common place in the society of late-nineteenth-century Toronto. They were principally congregants of St James Anglican Cathedral. Politically, they were Conservatives. Most were from prominent Toronto families. It was, in short, an establishment firm. Beatty himself was a pew-holder at St James, a personal friend of Sir John A. Macdonald's, the son-in-law of the late James Gooderham Worts, and the confidant and chief adviser of George Gooderham.

Under Beatty, it was in many respects the Gooderham family firm, serving the legal needs of the Gooderham & Worts businesses and providing employment for the sons and sons-in-law of George Gooderham and their relatives.[6] The Gooderham and the Worts families invested the profits they made from their very lucrative distillery business in financial institutions such as the Bank of Toronto, Manufacturers Life Insurance,

William Henry Beatty, David Fasken, and the Gooderham & Worts distillery, 1896 (courtesy Fasken Campbell Godfrey)

and Canada Permanent Mortgage. The Beatty Blackstock firm, which acted for these 'family businesses,' became pre-eminent among those law firms serving the needs of Canada's burgeoning financial sector.[7]

In the thirteen years from 1902 to 1915, the firm took a sharp turn away from these roots in the Toronto establishment to take on a decidedly different character. David Fasken and his brother, Alex, placed more emphasis on legal skills than on family connections, at least beyond their own strong family bond. The Fasken brothers recruited skilled and experienced lawyers from outside Toronto for their firm.[8] Unlike Beatty, the Faskens were 'self-made' men, Methodists and Liberals. They made immense personal fortunes in insurance and in Ontario's newly developed mining enterprises, and used the law firm to serve the needs of the companies that they themselves directed.

To some extent the changes in the firm reflected changes in the Ontario economy as the province opened its northern lands and as dynamic, hard-working Methodists like Timothy Eaton and Joseph Flavelle came to the fore in Canadian business.[9] But David and Alex Fasken's transformation of Beatty Blackstock was so complete as to be almost unique. They gave the firm a new name and a new office. They brought in new members from outside Toronto, who tended, like themselves, to be Methodists and Liberals. Although they retained key Beatty Blackstock clients, such as the Bank of Toronto and Toronto General Trusts, they acquired many new clients and a new area of expertise.

While much changed, there were some striking similarities between the two firms, principally in their approach to law and business. Both were dominated by a strong managing partner who used the law and the law firm as a stepping-stone into business. In many ways, each was a businessman as much as or even more than he was a business lawyer. Each shaped the firm that he managed in his own image to service his own business interests.

THE EARLY YEARS

Beatty Blackstock, although the largest law firm in the country[10] and one of the largest in North America[11] in 1902, seemingly arose from humble circumstances. As Chadwick recalled in 1913: 'We commenced to practise in one room about half furnished, and when we got along so well so that we were able to have a student we considered we were doing very well, and when we got on so as to be able to take another room and a few more chairs we thought our success was assured.'[12] Chadwick's characterization, however, is somewhat deceiving. The fact is that the firm's success was, if not assured from the beginning, certainly enhanced because of the background of the two partners. Both men were from well-to-do Irish families. Beatty's father, James, had settled in York (as Toronto was then known) in 1830, where he was a prominent merchant, operating the British Woollen and Cotton Warehouse, and a colonel in the militia.[13] The Beatty family lived in a two-storey brick house at 29 William Street,[14] just south of the substantial property owned by the Honourable William Pearce Howland, a prosperous grain merchant, member of the Legislative Assembly, and a future 'Father of Confederation.'[15] Farther up the street was the home of Mr Justice John Hagarty, a Supreme Court judge.[16]

Chadwick's family had formed part of the Irish landed gentry.[17] John Craven Chadwick, Edward Marion's father, had come to Canada in about 1837, settling at Ancaster, in Wentworth County, where Edward Marion, his third son, was born in 1840. When Edward Marion was eleven years old, his family moved to Guelph, where his father served as justice of the peace and was very active in the Anglican Church, serving on the Diocesan Synod of Toronto and the Corporation of Trinity College. The Chadwick family were large landholders and very prominent in the Guelph area.[18] Edward Marion's uncle was a member of the Guelph Board of Trade and would serve as mayor of Guelph. Edward Marion's younger brother, Austin Cooper Chadwick, also went into law, being called to the bar in 1864. Austin was later made a County Court judge for Wellington County in 1873, serving in that capacity until he retired in 1914.

At the time that Beatty and Chadwick studied law, legal education was primarily a matter of apprenticeship to an established practitioner. The period of articles was three years to be admitted as a solicitor (or attorney, as they were then called) and a further one year to be called as a barrister. As the introduction to the 1862 *Law List* stated, 'the professions of Barrister and Attorney may be and usually are followed together.' Students could enter legal studies at age sixteen. Chadwick could not have been much older than this minimum age when he began his studies. Beatty articled with John Leys, a barrister and solicitor who had his office on Church Street in the City Building, just south of King Street and within a very short walk of St James Cathedral.[19] We do not know where Chadwick articled. The hours spent in a law office likely involved assisting in drafting or engrossing legal documents (i.e., writing documents out in long hand), serving and filing materials, doing legal research, and searching land titles. This on-the-job training was supplemented by readings that students were expected to do on their own, as well as, to some extent, by lectures given at Osgoode Hall, the seat of the Law Society of Upper Canada. In 1858 the Law Society had appointed two permanent lecturers, S.H. Strong for equity and J.T. Anderson in law,[20] and it can be assumed that both Beatty and Chadwick attended these lectures. It was likely these lectures that brought Chadwick to Toronto. In 1862, just before Beatty's graduation, the school was expanded further, but it is doubtful that either Beatty or Chadwick benefited from this.

THE GOODERHAM & WORTS CONNECTION

In mid-February 1863, Beatty, who had been admitted as a solicitor on 5 February, entered into partnership with Chadwick, who had been admitted almost a year earlier, on 20 May, 1862.[21] From the very beginning the firm was linked to the milling and distillery partnership of Gooderham & Worts.[22] Beatty and Chadwick's first office, in the Toronto Exchange Building,[23] was between two Gooderham & Worts offices. Beatty was then likely already engaged to marry the daughter of James Gooderham Worts.

In a firm where family relations played a prominent role, it is not surprising that marriages helped cement business relationships for both partners. In 1864, Chadwick married Beatty's sister, Ellen Byrne.[24] Regrettably, in February of the following year, Ellen, only twenty-one years old, died in childbirth.[25] In April 1865, at a time when the newspapers were full of the news of President Lincoln's recent assassination in Washington, Beatty married Charlotte Louisa Worts at Little Trinity Church.[26] The newly-weds made their home at 290 King Street East,[27] not far from the family homes of William Gooderham and James Gooderham Worts, on Front Street.

Chadwick's short-lived marriage to his partner's sister helped bring the two partners together, but the success of the firm was intimately connected with Beatty's marriage. His father-in-law, James Gooderham Worts, was not only one of the two partners in the Gooderham & Worts distillery and milling business but also an important figure in a number of other businesses.

James Gooderham Worts had left England in 1831 at the age of thirteen. Accompanying his father, James Worts, he had come to York to establish a milling business and to make the way easier for other members of his family and the Gooderhams, to whom James was related by marriage, who were to come shortly with William Gooderham, James's brother-in-law. The father and son began to construct a windmill at the mouth of the Don River, to the southeast of the town. The next year, William Gooderham arrived with fifty-four people, including members of both families, servants, and eleven children whose parents had died on the journey. William also brought the combined family fortune, £3,000, to invest in the business. The two brothers-in-law went into partnership as Worts & Gooderham, carrying on a flour-milling business.

Unfortunately, James Gooderham Worts found himself an orphan in 1834, when, following his mother's death in childbirth, his father committed suicide by throwing himself down the family well. William Gooderham assumed control of the milling operation and began to groom his nephew for a role in the family business, which in 1837 was expanded to include a distillery to use surplus grain. The family also operated a cattle business to use by-products of the distillery. In 1845, William Gooderham made his nephew James a full partner and renamed the partnership Gooderham & Worts.

The business proved extremely successful. While William dedicated his energies to the milling and distillery operations, James came to play a prominent role in a number of businesses into which the families invested their profits, including the Bank of Toronto and the Canada Permanent Building and Savings Society.[28]

The families lived on a large estate on Front Street, just north of the distillery and just south of Little Trinity Church. They were devout members of the Anglican congregation of Little Trinity. Both William Gooderham and James Gooderham Worts served as wardens of the church for over thirty years. In his history of Little Trinity, Alan Hayes states that, in this period, 'the parish functioned rather like a proprietary chapel, with

Gooderham, his nephew and partner James Gooderham Worts, and some other captains of industry and commerce of St Lawrence ward as the benevolent proprietors.'[29] In 1850 the Gooderham and Worts families had a gallery of the church constructed and reserved for their use.[30]

This, then, was the family, or, more properly, families that Beatty married into, because, although Beatty married a Worts, he became a member of the Gooderham extended family as well. There were few families in the Toronto of 1865 that could offer a young lawyer so much, and there were few families that were so close-knit.

It is important to note how much the fortunes of the two families were directed by William Gooderham initially, and then later by his son George. Each of these individuals, in turn, played the role of 'paterfamilias,' directing the investments of the family firm and its many enterprises. Through trusts, they owned most of the homes of the various family members. James Gooderham Worts acted as the right-hand man for William Gooderham, his uncle. His son-in-law William Beatty would later assume the same role with George Gooderham.

Although the early success of the Beatty & Chadwick firm was at least in part attributable to Beatty's connections with the Gooderham and the Worts families, Beatty and his law firm had to earn the families' business. This was a pattern that one notes in the Gooderham family: The young men were given small roles in the businesses initially and expected to work their way to the top. Thus, even though Beatty's father-in-law was on the board of directors of the Bank of Toronto and was its vice-president and second-largest shareholder,[31] it was not until 1877 that the firm became the bank's solicitors.[32]

The role that Beatty and his firm were coming to play as company lawyers reflects one of the cardinal principles of William Gooderham and his son George in running the Gooderham & Worts businesses of the day – work was to be kept in the family or given to relatives of family members to the extent possible.[33] These families, in fact, played a key role in all aspects of Beatty's life. In 1875, Beatty's father-in-law, James Gooderham Worts, and Worts's nephew, George Gooderham, helped Beatty build a large brick-and-stone home on Queen's Park Crescent.[34] At about the same time, Joseph Walker Beatty, William's younger brother, is found working as the accountant for Gooderham & Worts.[35]

The relationship between the firm and the bank was cemented when, in 1879, Beatty moved his firm into the Bank of Toronto building at the northwest corner of Church and Wellington streets.[36] This location was across from the site on which the Gooderham Building would be built a decade later. The Bank of Toronto building, constructed by the bank in 1863, was an 'impressive home rivalled by few of the other banks that crowded Toronto. Three storeys high, 64 feet wide on the Wellington Street facade and 100 feet on the Church Street facade, it was impressive in the streetscape for its sheer bulk alone. It was designed in the Italian Renaissance style, faced with Ohio sandstone.'[37]

The firm's link with the bank was solidified in 1881, when, on William Gooderham's death, Beatty's father-in-law became the bank's president, and Beatty its vice-president.[38] Then, in June 1882, Worts died. In a very unusual provision, Worts directed in his will that Beatty be elected to succeed him on the bank's board of directors.[39] This, of course, would not have been binding on the shareholders of the bank, but it did happen, and it does indicate the influence that Worts had and his sense of proprietorship over the bank.

In addition to assuming Worts's seat on the board, Beatty became one of the executors of his father-in-law's estate and, as such, for many years directed the estate's many investments and business interests.[40] This position gave him significant influence and the ability to send much legal work to his firm. It also brought him into direct and bitter confrontation with members of the Worts family. Prior to his father-in-law's death, Beatty and his firm helped James Gooderham Worts establish a trust for his children.[41] The trust empowered the trustees, including Beatty, to continue for a year any business in which Worts had been engaged and to then invest the bulk of the estate in such securities as they thought fit and proper. On 1 August 1882, just a few months after Worts's death, Beatty's firm assisted George Gooderham to incorporate a company known as Gooderham & Worts, Limited. Beatty and the other trustees invested much of the trust funds in the shares of this company. The trustees and George Gooderham entered into a shareholders' agreement that stipulated that up to one-third of the corporate profits were to be retained by the company in a reserve fund and not paid to the shareholders as dividends. Although the investment paid large annual dividends despite this provision, and was sold to George Gooderham in 1889 at a substantial profit, the beneficiaries of the trust brought a series of legal actions against Beatty. Chancellor Boyd of the Ontario court would later find that Beatty and the other trustees had 'technically' breached the terms of the trust, but that no significant harm had been suffered.[42]

Beatty's relations with the Worts family became very strained. In 1882, shortly after his father's death, James Gooderham Worts, Jr, also died. Beatty and the widow, Mary Worts, were appointed co-executors of the estate. In 1887, Mary signed over her rights to Beatty. Then, for whatever reason, there was a falling out. Beatty refused to pay her the annuity due her under her husband's will, and he had her evicted from the home on College Avenue that he rented to her. She brought a legal action, charging him with having procured her agreement in 1887 with fraud and misrepresentation, and with having converted the large estate of her husband to his own purposes. The case was settled, but the rift between Beatty and the Worts family persisted.[43] The rift seems to have been attributable, at least in part, to the fact that Beatty developed a very close relationship with George Gooderham. The Worts family was of the view that Beatty was favouring Gooderham's interests over their own. There can be no doubt that Beatty became Mr Gooderham's principal business and legal adviser, and that Beatty used his position to direct much legal work to his firm.

THE BEATTY BLACKSTOCK LAWYERS IN 1902

By 1902, Beatty's firm[44] had grown to fifteen lawyers, making it the largest in the country.[45] Beatty was the glue that held the firm together. He had gathered lawyers for the firm through the Gooderham family connection, and especially his special relationship with George Gooderham, as well as through wise recruiting. It is very instructive to profile the fifteen men[46] who made up the firm.

For its day, Beatty Blackstock was an exceptionally large and, in many respects, very talented group. What is striking is that family connections played such a key role in the make-up of the firm. There was Beatty, his son, and his son-in-law; two Blackstock brothers; and the two Fasken brothers. Of the fifteen lawyers, two were sons-in-law of the firm's principal client, George Gooderham, and one was Gooderham's son (in 1899 another son-in-law, W.H. Brouse, had left the firm). Almost all were Anglicans and Conservatives and members of prominent Toronto families.

The fact that Anglicans played a key role in the firm was not unusual in Toronto business circles at the end of the last century and the beginning of the twentieth century. There can be no more dramatic proof of the dominant role of Anglicans in the law than to walk through St James Cathedral and read the many plaques commemorating the leaders of Toronto's legal community or to stroll through St James Cemetery, where one finds the remains of many, many 'name partners' in the large Toronto firms, such as the Blakes, the Oslers, and the Beattys. But it is worthy of note that both Beatty and Chadwick were heavily involved in the affairs of the Anglican Church in Toronto[47] and that their firm had a professional involvement in Church matters.

Since 1884, Beatty, Chadwick, and their firm had been key players in a significant, albeit much troubled, project of the Church – the building of St Albans, a magnificent new Anglican cathedral being constructed just north of the then city boundaries in the area which came to be known as the Annex. William Howland, who owned the land, sold it to a syndicate headed by both Beatty and William Howland's son, Oliver, each then managing partner of a different law firm.[48] St Albans Cathedral was to be the centre-piece of the development to be known as Cathedral Park. When the project later failed, Chadwick, who did the real estate and conveyancing work for the syndicate while serving on the building committee for the new cathedral, would be much criticized.[49]

The following profiles of some of the key members of the firm in 1902 take special note of the factors that linked them together as a firm – their religion, their social standing, their politics, and in many cases their ties to the Gooderham family.

The Beattys: Father, Son, and Son-in-Law

William Beatty was the managing partner, overseeing the many details of the firm's operation. He practised as a business lawyer, helping his clients establish and manage their businesses. He oversaw incorporations, helped raise and invest funds, and negotiated on behalf of business clients. But Beatty was more than a business lawyer. He was also a businessman. As the Bank of Toronto board noted: 'His wide experience in commercial affairs and his far-sighted and well balanced judgement made his counsels of the highest value and his deep sense of responsibilities ... made him most scrupulous in the discharge of [his] duties.'[50]

By 1902, Beatty was one of the most prominent members of the developing Canadian financial community. He served as a director of Gooderham & Worts, Limited, and as vice-president of London and Ontario Investment Company, the Toronto General Trusts Corporation (Canada's first trust company), the Bank of Toronto, and the Canada Permanent Mortgage Corporation. He was also president of the Confederation Life Association[51] as well as the Toronto Silver Plate Company, a concern in which he and several of the Gooderhams had a substantial shareholding.[52] He was active in the Toronto Board of Trade, serving as their legal counsel. He also co-authored, with Wallace Nesbitt,[53] a set of arbitration rules for the board and had represented the board in 1896 at the Congress of the Chambers of Commerce of the Empire, in London, England.[54] He also served as president of the Old Boys' Association and as a trustee of Upper Canada College.[55]

Beatty did what he could to direct the legal work from these various enterprises to his law firm. There were instances, however, when he did not do so. Beatty was one of the original 'promoters' of Confederation Life in 1871.[56] He served on its board of directors until shortly before his death and was a member of its Insurance Committee.[57] He became its vice-president in 1893, and its president in 1902. Yet, notwithstanding this close connection, Beatty's firm never seems to have provided legal work to Confederation Life. This was done by James Beatty, QC, who was not related. It may have been thought to have been inappropriate for the firm to represent Confederation Life because it acted for Manufacturers Life, a Gooderham company.

Ironically, it seems to have been the Gooderham family who got Beatty involved in Confederation Life.[58] One of the other promoters was William Gooderham, Jr, the eldest son of William Gooderham, the uncle and partner of Beatty's father-in-law. William, Jr, lacked the business acumen of his father[59] and Beatty was likely asked to assist young William in representing the family interest in Confederation Life. Beatty did, however, invest some of his own money in the enterprise, becoming a holder of fifty shares and the seventh person to be insured by the company.[60] Both Beatty and William Gooderham were elected to the board of the new company, but William Gooderham dropped off the board the next year.

Although, in Beatty's words, he did not take 'any active interest in politics,'[61] he was a 'true blue Conservative'[62] and, when he thought it necessary, he used his political connections and his personal friendship with Sir John A. Macdonald and Sir Charles Tupper to assist his clients. In 1879, for example, he had asked Sir John A. to intercede on behalf of the Bank of Toronto, which was seeking to collect some money owed by the federal government to one of the bank's debtors in connection with the building of the Lachine Canal.[63] In 1888, he had called on Sir John A. to assist the Gooderham & Worts Distillery in preventing the Canadian Pacific Railway from using the former estate of his father-in-law, located just north of the distillery, for a shunting yard.[64] He made it clear that he and George Gooderham had 'a claim not only as citizens' on Macdonald, an obvious reference to financial and other help they had provided to the prime minister.

On Sir John A.'s death, Beatty had been chosen by the local Conservatives to chair the Macdonald Memorial Committee of Toronto.[65] Interestingly he consistently refused appointment as Queen's Counsel, and later King's Counsel, when the honour was offered, first by Macdonald, and later by Tupper,[66] perhaps because he thought it an honour properly bestowed on barristers and he had never acted as one.[67]

By 1902 one of Beatty's sons and one of his sons-in-law were members of the firm. Wallace Nesbitt, Beatty's son-in-law, had left McCarthy Osler Hoskin in 1892, where he had juniored for two of Canada's leading barristers, D'Alton McCarthy and Britton Osler,[68] to join the Beatty Blackstock firm. He was then thirty-three years old. As the 1898 *Men & Woman of the Times* stated, during his days at McCarthy's, he had been 'connected with many important suits, among them the historic legal fight between the firm of Conmee and McLennan, contractors and the Canadian Pacific Railway and the memorable St George's railway disaster.' When Wallace Nesbitt joined the firm, he was a widower, but a few years later he married Amy Gertrude Beatty, Beatty's daughter.[69]

In 1898, three years after being called to the bar, Charles William Beatty, William Henry Beatty's second son, joined the firm. Significantly, C.W. was also George Gooderham's son-in-law, having married Lillian May Gooderham in 1896.

Edward Marion Chadwick

Although E. Marion Chadwick was still with the firm in 1902, by then he was playing a much smaller role. Chadwick's legal practice focused on real estate conveyancing. J.B. Robinson, who would join the firm in 1918 as a conveyancing lawyer, recalled that 'he was an expert in conveyancing and he designed most of the forms used in the office, deeds, powers of attorney, mortgages, etc. and we printed our own forms for many years. He was very strong on not using any excess verbiage and his power of attorney took only one page and was very complete. He also ignored any punctuation in a document[,] claiming that if the words did not speak for themselves without punctuation, the deed was not properly drawn.'[70]

Perhaps it is not surprising that, as a founder of a firm in which family connections were so important, Chadwick was a noted genealogist. As time went on, this work consumed more and more of his energy. In fact, *The Dictionary of Canadian Biography*, prepared by Stewart Wallace, lists Chadwick as a 'genealogist.' From 1898 to 1901 he edited the *Ontario Genealogist and Family Historian*. He also wrote a leading work entitled *Ontarian Families*, which was published in two volumes in 1894–8 and has been republished a number of times since, most recently in 1974. Other books he wrote include *The People of the Long House* (1898)[71] and *The Chadwicks of Guelph and Toronto* (1914).

The Blackstock Brothers

From 1892 the firm had been known as Beatty Blackstock.[72] This reflected the key role played by Thomas Gibbs Blackstock and his brother, George Tate Blackstock, as well as the declining importance of Chadwick.

T.G. Blackstock had joined the law firm in 1879,[73] at a time when he was engaged to Harriet Victoria Gooderham, one of George Gooderham's daughters. They were married early in 1880.[74] Thomas had been called to the bar in 1877 and for a time had practised with Alexander McNabb under the name McNabb & Blackstock. He was the son of the Reverend William S. Blackstock, DD, a Methodist minister who had married a member of the prominent Gibbs family. Reverend Blackstock was pastor of the Berkeley St Methodist Church.[75] Thomas Gibbs Blackstock was named after his grandfather, Senator Thomas Gibbs, who had joined William Beatty as one of the promoters of the Confederation Life Association.

T.G. Blackstock, who was said to be 'one of the best known members of the Ontario Bar,' had a 'corporation law' practice.[76] He assisted Beatty in advising the Gooderham family businesses. He acted as solicitor for the Bank of Toronto (Blackstock was a shareholder and acted as scrutineer for the bank's general meetings in 1888–97 and again in 1901),[77] Manufacturers Life Insurance Company, Gooderham & Worts, Limited, the Central Ontario Railway, and other businesses in which the Gooderhams invested their funds. The fact that he lived immediately north of George Gooderham's mansion in a house that Gooderham had built for him and his wife underlines the close relationship between the two men.[78] He assisted George in many projects, including the building of the King Edward Hotel, in connection with which Blackstock acted as president of the King Edward Hotel Company. He was also involved in some mining ventures, serving as vice-president of the War Eagle, Centre Star, and St Eugene mining companies.[79] In 1901 he had successfully petitioned the federal government to encourage the development of lead mining and smelting in British Columbia. He is said to have 'made an urgent plea for a bounty on lead refining, to be limited in amount, duration and as to tonnage, and claimed that much incidental benefit would accrue to other mining interests from such a policy.'[80]

George Tate Blackstock, Thomas Gibbs's brother, was one of Canada's leading trial lawyers, and as such he was expected to strengthen a weak area in Beatty Blackstock. The firm's shortcomings in this field were laid bare in 1890, when George Gooderham, the firm's foremost client, launched a legal action against the City of Toronto,[81] and the lead counsel was not a member of the firm.[82] Obviously this was not a healthy state of affairs for the practice. Within two years. George Tate Blackstock had joined the firm and, with Wallace Nesbitt, would lay the foundation for the firm's reputation as a top litigation concern.[83]

When G.T. Blackstock died in December 1921, he was referred to as 'one of the foremost members of the Canadian Bar, whose name is associated with many a cause celebre.'[84] Like Beatty and Chadwick, he was politically Conservative. George Tate, however, was much more active politically than his partners. An ardent supporter of the British Empire, calling for a union of the English-speaking races, he often spoke in support of the Conservative party. He ran for office provincially in 1884 in Lennox, and federally in 1887 and 1891 in West Durham, but, each time, was unsuccessful, despite his ability as a gifted speaker.

G.T. Blackstock had been called to the bar in 1879, joining the firm of Rose McDonald Merritt & Blackstock.[85] The senior partner of that firm was John Rose, whose son, Hugh, would later join the Beatty firm. Blackstock was then 'a dark-haired, good looking fellow, with an easy and friendly gift of conversation and an entire freedom from restraint or nervousness on social occasions.'[86] In 1882, Blackstock had left to join Wells Gordon & Sampson, but this was short-lived and soon he was practising as a barrister on his own. He had an active litigation practice, travelling about the province acting in both civil and criminal actions, and as both a defence counsel and a Crown prosecutor. He acted for the Bank of Toronto on occasion, likely work referred to him by his brother. He was for a time counsel to the Canadian Pacific Railway[87] and was involved in the late 1880s in the arbitration between Canadian Pacific and the federal government over the character of the road handed over by the federal government.[88] Then in 1890 he earned much admiration for his skilful, although unsuccessful, defence of Reginald Birchall in a famous Woodstock murder trial.[89]

By 1892, however, Blackstock was beginning to experience serious personal problems. It may well be that he was offered a position in the firm to assist him through a difficult time. He was finding it harder to give his law practice the attention it observed. His friend, Wyly Grier, a noted portrait painter, would later write in his memoirs that 'at times when he was the leading barrister on one or other side of cases of great moment, which called for his undivided absorption in the issues at stake, "domestic worries" made him distraught and preoccupied.'[90] His wife would divorce him in 1896, but it is unclear whether his family problems were the source or the result of his personal difficulties. Wyly Grier states:

A sinister cloud had arisen on the apparently brilliant horizon of this gifted lawyer, nor am I able to say he was entirely blameless when it enveloped him. Battles in court and minor conflicts at home gradually undermined the nervous system which had evoked my father's admiration and bereft Osgoode Hall of one of its most brilliant figures. I remember that a symptom of the approaching breakdown of our friend was confided to me (or more correctly, to my brother, Alex Munro). Blackstock had stated that when waiting for his turn to address the court the perspiration would drop off his finger-ends.

At the suggestion of T.G. Blackstock, his brother-in-law,[90] Melville Ross Gooderham, one of George's sons, joined the firm in 1901. Ross Gooderham, characterized as 'a shy, reserved man, who lived very simply,'[92] was not a force in 1902, but he would be a key figure in the reshaping of the firm.

Lawyers from Other Prominent Families

Thomas Percival (Percy) Galt, then twenty-seven, had joined the firm in 1885. He was another member of a prominent Anglican family who attended St James Cathedral,[93] being the third son of Thomas Galt, who in 1887 became Chief Justice of Ontario. He was also the nephew of Alexander Tilloch Galt, a minister of finance and one of the Fathers of Confederation. Although Galt would remain with Beatty Blackstock for almost thirty years, he never rose to a position of prominence in the firm or the profession. He was competent[94] but lacked the skill and drive of many of the other litigators in the firm.

When George Tate Blackstock joined the firm, he brought with him his junior, Alexander Munro Grier, the brother of Wyly Grier.[95] Munro Grier had been born in England, where his family had travelled from Australia. He had spent some time in Toronto in 1876, when he had first met the Blackstock brothers. He returned with his family to England and was called as a barrister in 1882. He had then returned to Toronto, where he was called in 1884. He had assisted Blackstock in the 1880s in the arbitration between the Canadian Pacific and the federal government, and other similar work. He, too, was an Anglican.

Hugh Rose, another litigator in the firm, was the son of John Edward Rose, a judge of the Ontario High Court of Justice. Born in 1869, he had attended the University of Toronto and graduated with a BA in 1891 and an LLB in 1892. He had articled with Maclaren Macdonald Merritt & Shepley and been called to the bar in 1894.[96] He seems to have joined the Beatty firm about 1900.

The Fasken Brothers

David Fasken was in many ways unlike the other members of the firm. He was not a member of the Toronto establishment, but was one of nine children of a Scottish farmer from Elora. He was a dynamic, entrepreneurial Methodist and a Liberal. Fasken had been born on the family farm on 31 December 1860. After graduating from Elora High School, he had entered the University of Toronto, graduating in 1882 with a BA. He had articled with the Beatty firm, been called to the bar in 1885, and began his practice with the firm then known as Beatty, Chadwick and Blackstock. Why this bright young Methodist joined a staid, Conservative firm is not known. Perhaps it had something to do with the fact that the father of Thomas Gibbs and George Tate Blackstock was a Methodist minister. Perhaps it was related to the fact that William Gooderham, George's older brother, was a Methodist. More likely the answer lies in Marion Chadwick's links to Wellington County, where Chadwick was from and where the Faskens had their family farm.

Whatever the reason for David Fasken's coming to the firm, the reality was that he had administrative abilities, drive, and ambition beyond those of his colleagues – qualities that undoubtedly endeared him to Beatty. As one biographer would later say: 'His outstanding traits were a capacity for sustained and concentrated effort, close attention to detail, and absolutely unprejudiced weighing of facts.'[97] Fasken's role in the development of Excelsior Life Insurance Company is very revealing. Shortly after the incorporation of the company (originally called the Protestant Life Insurance Company) in the late 1880s by the Orange Lodge of Toronto, David Fasken became a shareholder. The company got off to a slow start, and Fasken bought up many of the shares of the struggling, young company. He also encouraged the Gooderhams to invest in it. Their shares, together with his own, gave Fasken control of the company. On 13 February 1900, he was elected president, a position that he was to hold until his death. Although he directed the company's operations on only a part-time basis, he built Excelsior Life into a very successful and profitable business.

By 1902, David Fasken was already well established. That year he moved into his newly constructed, stately home designed by E.J. Lennox, the architect for the new Toronto City Hall, who had also designed an office building for W.H. Beatty and the Gooderham-funded King Edward Hotel.[98] Within the firm, Fasken played a key role. Correspondence from 1896 in the firm's archives casts some light on the nature of that role (as well as on the economics of practice at the time). It seems that the Ocean Accident & Guarantee Corporation of London, England, had heard of the firm. In fact, their general manager would say in a letter of 31 July 1896 that they had 'been mentioned to [them] in the highest possible terms.' As a result, the local agent of the company, George Bennett, wrote to the firm on 29 June, stating:

I am instructed by our General Manager to ask if you will act as our Solicitors for Toronto at an annual retainer of $150 from, say, July 1st next.

We would expect for this all consultations, opinions, the drawing up of documents etc. when required, making collections when necessary and generally all assistance in settling claims as between lawyers. We would expect you to charge fees only when a case goes into court and then only the taxed costs.

Beatty responded on 8 July, apologizing for the delay by saying that both he and 'our Mr. Fasken to whom all matters of this sort are usually referred' had been away from the city. He was happy to 'note a general retainer' for Ocean Accident but went on to negotiate its precise terms.

It seems that Fasken had assumed the role of Beatty's administrative assistant or office manager. In 1902, Beatty was the president of the Confederation Life Association and, given George Gooderham's failing health, he was becoming increasingly involved in such Gooderham ventures as the Bank of Toronto and Canada Permanent. All of this meant that Beatty simply did not have the time necessary for the day-to-day management of the law firm. Increasingly this task fell to 'our Mr. Fasken.'

David seems to have shared some of this responsibility (as well as many client matters) with his younger brother, Alexander Fasken, who had joined the firm in 1899. Alex (referred to by David as 'Dutch')[99] was the youngest of the Fasken children. He had been born on 27 June 1871, on the family farm. After graduating from Elora High School, he had attended the University of Toronto and Osgoode Hall Law School. He had articled with Cassels and Standish and been called to the bar in 1894. Initially, he opened a practice in Fergus, Ontario, but after five years he acceded to David's request and joined him at the firm.

Other Non-Establishment Lawyers

One suspects that it was David Fasken who lured the talented William Renwick Riddell to Toronto in 1895. Like Fasken, Riddell was a supporter of the Liberal party and was from out of town.[100] Riddell, who had been the gold-medallist on his call to the bar in 1883, left his practice in Cobourg to come to Toronto. He had already been a bencher of the Law Society for four years, an office he continued to hold in 1902.

Riddell's Liberal connections brought him some interesting briefs. In 1895 he represented the leaders of the University of Toronto student body before a royal commission inquiry arising out of a student strike. One of the student leaders was William Lyon Mackenzie King, who would later become leader of the Liberal party and prime minister of Canada. In 1903, Riddell would be counsel to the Ontario Liberal government in the Gamie inquiry, and the next year he and Wallace Nesbitt would act for the City of Toronto in an investigation into certain election irregularities.

Another out-of-towner likely recruited by the Faskens was Harper Armstrong, who had joined the firm in 1898. Harper would work with Alex Fasken on many projects. It may well be that Alex was his brother-in-law. In 1896, Alex Fasken had married an Isabelle Armstrong of Fergus.[101]

Thus, in 1902, we find the firm loosely divided into two groups. Beatty led the largest group of Toronto establishment lawyers, but his office administrator, David Fasken, had already started to introduce lawyers into the firm who did not fit the Toronto establishment mould.

THE FASKEN FIRM IN 1915

If we skip ahead to 1915, we note that the firm had only seven lawyers (one of whom was no longer very active) – a dramatic reduction from the fifteen lawyers of just thirteen years earlier. There were no members of the Beatty, Blackstock, or Gooderham families in the 1915 firm. In addition to the two Fasken brothers, the firm had only four active members: Harper Armstrong, who assisted Alex Fasken with the solicitor's work, and Hugh Rose, George H. Sedgewick, and Mahlon K. Cowan, who were litigators. By this time E.M. Chadwick was seventy-five years old. Beyond serving as the principal link to the past, he played little role. J.B. Robinson, who joined the firm in 1918, tells us that Chadwick 'did not do any active work but came in nearly every day. He was not given his own steno and he used to employ a public steno in the building. Unfortunately he was very deaf and any conversation was difficult.'[102]

What had happened? It seems that the transformation of the firm can be attributed to several factors. First, the generation of William Beatty, Thomas Gibbs Blackstock, and George Gooderham, their client, had drawn to its close. Second, the management of the firm had been fully assumed by the Fasken brothers, who had reoriented the firm and taken it into new areas of practice. We will now look at how the Fasken transformation occurred.

The Transformation of Beatty Blackstock

The first indication that the shift from Beatty's management to that of David Fasken troubled at least some members of the firm was the departure in 1903 of Beatty's son-in-law, Wallace Nesbitt. On 16 May 1903, at the very young age of forty-five, Nesbitt was appointed to the Supreme Court of Canada. As Snell and Vaughan say in their history of the Supreme Court, 'though lacking judicial experience, Nesbitt had an outstanding reputation as counsel, and his nomination to the Supreme Court was widely acclaimed.'[103] Snell and Vaughan note that Nesbitt represented a break with the patronage appointments of the day, in part because he was so young. It seems clear in retrospect that Nesbitt wanted out of the Fasken-managed firm. He did not want to offend his father-in-law by going to another Toronto firm, so he accepted an appointment to the bench. Within two years, Nesbitt decided that he had made a mistake in seeking his escape through the Supreme Court, which was then riddled with dissension and was not highly regarded. For 'reasons purely private,' he resigned from the Court.[104] Significantly he did not return to the Beatty Blackstock firm. Instead, he rejoined the McCarthy firm and continued his distinguished career, later becoming treasurer of the Law Society.[105]

In a seemingly unrelated move, Munro Grier also left to take up a position at the Canadian Niagara Power Company, a firm that Beatty would later take over. It may well be that Beatty was behind this departure, moving one of his lawyers to a business in which he and the Gooderhams had invested.

Cobalt and the Mining Industry

In 1903, David Fasken began making moves that would in part change the nature of the law practised by the firm. Under Beatty, the firm's key clients had been financial institutions, such as the Bank of Toronto, Toronto General Trusts, Canada Permanent, and Manufacturers Life.

Although T.G. Blackstock had done some mining work, Fasken was about to direct the firm into mining law in a big way.

At the end of the nineteenth and the beginning of the twentieth century, the Ontario government saw the possibility of encouraging settlement in the 'Clay Belt' west of Lake Temiskaming. This desire to open the region to farming and the timber industry spurred the development of the mineral resources of northern Ontario. The government began to build what is now the Ontario Northland Railway.[106] By 1903 it had reached the north end of Long Lake, where cobalt, nickel, and some silver were discovered. David and Alex Fasken played a key role in the successful development of these finds. As a later observer said, 'David and Alex Fasken, in the late 1890's, were among the first to see the possibilities of mining development in Northern Ontario.'[107] When the Cobalt discovery was made, David acted quickly with Ellis P. Earle and other New York–based investors to form the Nipissing Mining Company Limited and to finance its development. They secured claims covering over 846 acres. As the *Cobalt Daily Nugget* (the local newspaper) said in 1910: 'About 5 times as large as the quarter section of a western farm, Nipissing occupies the very centre of the Cobalt Camp. It is, in fact, the centre.'

The initial agreement drafted by David Fasken on behalf of the newly created Nipissing Mining Company stated that the owners of the original claims were to be paid sixty-five cents for each pound of cobalt mined to date.[108] There was also mention in the agreement of nickel and arsenic. There was no mention of silver, which seems to have been thought to be incidental to the other minerals. However, as one writer has said, 'by the summer of 1904 high-grade silver ore was being shipped out by the carload, and when this news spread there was a rush of prospectors and mining men from all over the world to the wonderful silver camp at Cobalt.'[109] By 1908 the provincial geologist reported that Cobalt was 'not only the world's largest producer of silver, but it absolutely controls the market for cobalt.'

At the time, many bemoaned the fact that Americans, and not Canadians, had come to control the Cobalt mines. The *Monetary Times* noted, however, that, although Canadians had originally held virtually all of the claims, they had sold out prematurely.[110] It pointed out: 'The president of the Nipissing Mines Company is understood to have paid $250,000 for the properties which were chiefly of prospective value. The sellers thought that they had outwitted a Yankee. Now, probably, they are assuring themselves that they were foolish to part with so great a property at so small a price.'

The truth is that Fasken's American investors were willing to put up the large amounts of money that the commercial development of the finds required. David and Alex Fasken proved important in securing both the capital and the sources of power and other utilities necessary to mine in what was then a remote and rugged locale. As E.P. Earle would state in the *Toronto Daily Star* of 24 December 1929 on Fasken's death:

... from the beginning Mr Fasken's guidance and cooperation had much to do with the success of the Company.

In the early days of Cobalt when at times engineers were doubtful of the permanency of the camp, Mr Fasken never lost faith and he showed his courage by investing large sums of money in the development of Hydro Electric for the Camp. Subsequently, Mr Fasken continued his cooperation in the development of power for Porcupine and Kirkland Lake. Probably no one man did as much toward the development of the North country as did Mr Fasken.

David served for a substantial time as Nipissing's president and was one of its directors. He was further involved in Cobalt's development as a director and substantial shareholder of both La Rose Consolidated Mines Limited (which owned Violet Mining Company, Limited) and Trethewey Silver Cobalt Mine Limited, each of which had its mines at Cobalt. In addition, by 1909 Alex Fasken was on the board of two other Cobalt mining companies: the Chambers–Ferland Mining Company, Limited (Harper Armstrong was its vice-president, and George Sedgewick, another firm member, was on the board) and the Temiskaming Mining Company, Limited, for which he also acted as secretary-treasurer.[111] David Fasken did not restrict his interests to mining in Cobalt. He acquired the three power plants which supplied much-needed hydro-electric power to the Cobalt workings and area, and later to discoveries at Porcupine and Kirkland Lake. In 1911 he merged them to form the Northern Ontario Light and Power Company Limited, of which he was president.[112] He also organized the Northern Canada Power Company Limited. As Morris Zaslow has said, 'Cobalt was the opening victory in the long campaign waged by Canadians to wrest mineral wealth from the Precambrian Shield,'[113] and the Faskens were important in achieving that victory.

The success of the Cobalt discovery spurred exploration throughout the region. In summer 1909, the Dome gold discovery was made in the vicinity of Night Hawk Lake, near Timmins. Again, the Faskens were quick to act to develop the claim. This time it was Alex Fasken who led the way. Alex represented the New York syndicate that obtained the option to exploit the claims. He took an active role in the management of the new company, Dome Mines Limited, which the firm incorporated. He was one of the original directors of Dome Mines, and later became a vice-president of that company. When the story of Dome Mines was written, Alex Fasken and Jules Bache, who headed up the investors' syndicate, were said to have been the 'dominant personalities in the company structure.'[114]

Following their successes at Cobalt and Porcupine, the brothers became active supporters of numerous mining-exploration initiatives. David was a part of the group of Canadian and American millionaires who formed the Canadian Mining Exploration Company, a venture that in 1912 was said to have 400 properties under consideration.[115] David and Alex were also key members of the syndicate that grubstaked the prospectors in 1914–15 who filed claims on the Flin Flon mine in northern Manitoba. In 1915 David and Alex actually visited the site in northern Manitoba, travelling at times by oxen and by canoe.[116] They later formed part of the Toronto-based investors' syndicate that optioned these claims. While the others sold their interest before the Flin Flon mine was developed, David hung on. W.F. Currie, one of the original grubstakers, noted in 1927: 'We got out and were quite satisfied to do so. Only David Fasken was left and I hear he's made a very good thing out of sticking to the end.'[117]

Through their hydro-electric interests in northern Ontario, the Faskens became interested in the pulp-and-paper industry. For many years Alex served as a director of Provincial Paper Mills Limited.

The Faskens directed the legal work for the mining and other companies that they were involved with to the firm, helping it become expert in mining law, which in turn attracted other mining clients. J.B. Robinson recalls in his memoirs that, in 1918, when he joined the firm, many of its clients were mining men from the north country. There were long benches in the office for the use of the clients, and at the end of each one was a large brass cuspidor. The miners smoked big cigars and made frequent use of these amenities.

In addition to what one might think of as legal work (such as incorporation, raising capital, negotiating and documenting joint ventures, and dealing with disputed claims, tort actions, and the like), the firm looked after many matters that today would seldom be handled by lawyers. Robinson noted that, for many years, the firm prepared and mailed the dividend cheques for Dome Mines and also undertook the printing and mailing of its annual report. 'Often we would keep a group of the staff down at nights to handle the mailing.' Robinson also recalled that 'considerable correspondence went between our office and the Dome Mines Office at South Porcupine and the Nipissing Mine Office at Cobalt and we were often given urgent letters to be taken not to the Post Office where there might be delay but directly to the Postal Clerk on the Northland train which left the Union Station every night about 6:00 p.m. It was not always easy to work your way through right to the train.'

Gooderham's Death and Beatty's Departure in 1905

If there was a watershed in the transition from the Beatty to the Fasken firm, a point at which the practice began to be shaped more by Fasken than by Beatty, it was in 1905. In that year, George Gooderham, the man who directed the Gooderham businesses, died, and W.H. Beatty and his son left – the former event leading to the latter. Gooderham's death created an even greater need for Beatty to direct the Gooderham family businesses. Beatty became the president of both the Bank of Toronto and Canada Permanent. Although W.H. Beatty's name continued to appear first on the firm's letterhead until his death seven years later, he ceased to practise after Gooderham's death.

With his father no longer active in the firm and David Fasken in charge, Beatty's son, Charles William, also left. He would practise for many years on his own before joining his son, named W.H. Beatty after his grandfather, in a firm known as Beatty & Beatty.[118] C.W. also became one of the founders of the York Club, which was established in 1910 and which moved into his father-in-law's mansion at the corner of Bloor and St George streets.

An incident in 1906 demonstrates the changed relationship between Beatty and the firm. In June, Beatty engineered a take-over of the Canadian Niagara Power Company and became its president. He arranged to have three former members of the firm appointed to the board: Wallace Nesbitt, his son-in-law and now a member of the rival McCarthy firm; A. Munro Grier, who had left the firm in 1903; and William Henry Brouse, a son-in-law of George Gooderham who had left the firm in 1899. Grier acted as the secretary and in-house solicitor to the power company.[119] It is clear that the old family ties were still important to Beatty and that he still commanded loyalty, but these ties and this loyalty were no longer drawing people to the law firm.

One month later, in July 1906, the firm suffered another blow that further accentuated the break with the past – Thomas Gibbs Blackstock died, at the age of fifty-five. The firm now was without its two principal 'name partners.' Beatty Blackstock now had neither Beatty nor Blackstock.

In September, in a written partnership agreement, the remaining partners of the firm gave formal recognition to David Fasken's new status as managing partner. The very fact that the partnership agreement was in writing seems to have been a break with the past.

The agreement, dated 1 September 1906, was between William Henry Beatty, Edward Marion Chadwick, David Fasken, William R. Riddell, Thomas P. Galt, Harper Armstrong, Alexander Fasken, Hugh E. Rose, and Melville Ross Gooderham. The parties were to be co-partners for five years in the practice and profession of barristers, solicitors, and notaries public, under the firm name Beatty Blackstock Fasken & Riddell. The practice was to be carried on 'in the City of Toronto and all parties were to reside there.'

Beatty was not required to perform any 'actual solicitor work' but was to use 'his best endeavours to procure business for the firm.' The agreement went so far as to state that Beatty would not interfere with the operation of the firm. He was to be 'entitled to retain for his own use all emoluments coming to him from any directorship, trusteeship or any other business outside of the firm with which he may be connected.' This is not surprising when one notes that he did not receive any income from the firm. His 'emoluments' and 'the use of a room at the north east end of the building without charge' were all that he got. In return, he agreed to 'give all of the influence he [could] towards the promotion of the interests of the firm.'

The agreement provided that David Fasken 'shall be manager of the business of the firm and shall determine what line of work shall be done by the various partners.' It is quite likely that Fasken's power to determine each partner's work did not sit well with at least some of his partners. David Fasken was also to be entitled to maintain his connection with the Excelsior Life Insurance Company and to receive 'the emoluments therefrom.' If, however, he looked after Excelsior Life business during the day, he was to arrange 'for a proper retainer to cover the time expended by him.'

The agreement also made special provisions for Ross Gooderham, who, on his father's death, had been appointed executor of the estate. He was permitted to retain any commissions to which he was entitled as executor of George Gooderham's estate as well as any director's fees payable to him for serving on any company's board in connection with the estate. He was, however, not to participate in any fees received by the firm from his father's estate.

Although many lawyers of this period combined law and politics, Fasken did not want his partners doing so. No partner was to be a candidate for or contest any public election, municipal or parliamentary. George Tate Blackstock, who had political aspirations, is not listed as a partner in the agreement. It is unclear whether this provision, which must not have sat well with Blackstock, had anything to do with his changed status. A similar provision was inserted in partnership agreements for many years thereafter.

The net profits of the practice were to be divided among the partners as follows:

1 Of the first $30,000 each year, David Fasken and William R. Riddell were to obtain $8,500 each, Alexander Fasken $2,500 and all others either $2,000 or $2,250.
2 Profits over $30,000 were to be divided in varying percentages, depending on the level of profit achieved. For example, if the profits fell between $30,000 and $45,000, David Fasken and William R. Riddell would get 35⅚ per cent, but if the profits were over $60,000 they received only 22½ per cent. In this way Fasken and Riddell would be compensated for the base business that they brought to the firm, but there was some incentive to the younger partners to work hard and bring in new business.

Each partner was entitled to one calendar month's holiday during the year. If absent beyond that, he was to pay to the firm such amount for each day as the majority in interest of the members of the firm should decide upon. Riddell was permitted to take two months without deduction on condition that 'if he shall argue any case in England [before the Privy Council] during the said months he shall not claim any extra vacation on that account.'

David Fasken, himself, commented on the changed relationship between the firm and the Gooderham family interests when he appeared before the Royal Commission on Insurance in 1906.[120] Fasken, as president of Excelsior Life, was questioned about his involvement with the Gooderhams. The shares that George Gooderham's estate had in the company, when combined with Fasken's shares, represented control. In light of the close connection that had existed between George Gooderham and the firm, and the fact that his son and executor, Ross Gooderham, was one of

Fasken's partners, the commission was interested in knowing to what extent these parties acted together. Fasken's answers are very revealing.[121]

Q: I suppose it is fair to say that the Gooderham Estate shares would vote along with your shares?

A: I don't think it is fair. If it suited them they would vote just the opposite. They would do just what was in their interest.

...

Q: You have many interests in common with them do you not?

A: No.

Q: You think not?

A: No.

Q: You think that it is not a fair statement to make?

A: No. I act as their solicitor in a good many matters.

Q: With emphasis upon the good many. But outside of your professional work as a solicitor you say that there are not many financial matters that you are interested in together?

A: No.

Q: You are referring now to the present time?

A: Yes.

Q: Since when?

A: Well, since Mr Gooderham's death.

While the commission counsel may have doubted Fasken's replies, his comments seem to have accurately reflected his relationship with the Gooderhams, and especially Ross Gooderham.

At this time Ross Gooderham was in fact using some of the money he inherited from his father to repurchase Manufacturers Life Insurance (which had been founded by the Gooderhams). His brother-in-law Dr James Frederick William Ross,[122] who was also a director of Excelsior Insurance, assisted in the repurchase. Ross Gooderham assumed the role of second vice-president (a position previously held by his father). Gradually, Gooderham would later say, he 'drifted into insurance'[123] and away from the law.

To add to the woes of the firm, on 10 October 1906 Riddell accepted an appointment to the bench.[124]

A Time of Calm and Rebuilding

In just four years, Beatty, his son, his son-in-law, William Riddell, Munro

Grier, and a young lawyer, R. McKay (who had joined the firm in 1898, likely fresh from his call to the bar), had left the firm, and T.G. Blackstock had died. The firm obviously needed to be rebuilt. David Fasken seems to have set out to do so, and the next five years proved to be a period of relative stability and rebuilding.

In 1906, the firm made one addition, George H. Sedgewick, then twenty-eight years old. He had articled with the firm, reading law with Riddell.[125] J.B. Robinson remembers him as 'one of our Counsel when I joined the firm'. He notes that Sedgewick 'was a fine gentleman at all times' but that 'he found the strain and pressures at the office very hard and it seemed to make him tense.'[126] He would later, in Robinson's words, have 'some difference with [Alex] Fasken' and would leave the firm in 1925. He would act as chairman of the Tariff Board of Canada, and then as a judge of the Ontario Supreme Court.

In 1908, William Gooderham Blackstock, one of the sons of Thomas Gibbs Blackstock, joined the firm. It may well be that he joined at the suggestion of his two uncles, George Tate Blackstock and Ross Gooderham, to assist them. He, however, would remain with the firm only until 1911.

In 1910, the firm added three new members – two juniors, Lionel Davis and G.E. McCann, and one established litigation counsel, Mahlon K. Cowan. Most striking of these additions was young Lionel Davis. Not only was he not Anglican, he was not even a Christian. Davis was a member of one of Toronto's oldest Jewish families.[127] The fact that Davis joined the firm signalled a new openness to religious diversity notably absent from the Beatty firm.

Cowan reflected a different pattern in the Fasken firm. Like Riddell before him, he was an experienced lawyer enticed to Toronto by the Faskens. He was from a farming family in Essex County and had been called to the bar in 1890. He had been elected as a Liberal MP in 1896 but resigned in 1900 to pursue his legal career. He served as counsel to the Grand Trunk Railway from 1904 to 1910. After joining the firm, he acted as counsel to the governments of Saskatchewan and Alberta against the railway companies in rate hearings. Cowan was described 'as a brilliant convincing jury lawyer' with 'a powerful and vibrant voice which he used to good effect. At times he was witty. His tact, courtesy and attractive manner combined to make his presence an exemplar. To his great natural powers, he added from his earliest days, remarkable powers of application.'[128]

The next year the firm added another young lawyer, Austin G. Ross, who had been a medallist at Osgoode Hall Law School in 1907. Like Fasken and Cowan, he was a 'staunch Liberal.'[129]

November 1910 brought two important changes in the personnel of Beatty Blackstock. First, W.H. Beatty, for health reasons, resigned his various positions.[130] Second, Ross Gooderham ceased at this time to be a partner. Gooderham's career change was prompted by Beatty's declining influence at the firm and by the need created by Beatty's resignations for strong management of various Gooderham businesses. Although Gooderham continued to have some small role in Beatty Blackstock, he seems to have dedicated much of his time to the administration of his father's estate and to other business interests, especially Manufacturers Life Insurance.

The 1913 'House-Cleaning'

The key role that Beatty had played in shaping the old Beatty Blackstock firm was emphasized when he died at his home on 20 November 1912.[131] David Fasken seems to have decided that the time was now right to clean house, ridding his firm of those holdovers from the Beatty-dominated firm who Fasken thought were not carrying their weight. Out of a sense of loyalty to Beatty, his former mentor, and to Chadwick, Fasken waited until after Beatty's death and the Chadwick fiftieth-anniversary celebration to do his house-cleaning. In May 1913, George Tate Blackstock, who had just returned from a stay in England, Percy Galt, Ross Gooderham, and young G.E. McCann left the firm to form Blackstock Galt and Gooderham.[132] They packed their possessions and moved across Wellington Street from the Bank of Toronto building to the Gooderham ('Flatiron') Building.

The move does not seem to have hurt Fasken's firm. Certainly Blackstock was not the lawyer he had once been. Galt had never been a 'star,' and Ross Gooderham was only practising part-time. But one would have expected that the Faskens would have wanted to maintain good relations with the Gooderham family, which, although it lacked the drive and leadership of George Gooderham, still had a good deal of money and influence. Perhaps the Faskens were confident in their own ties to the Gooderhams as well as in their new-found mining wealth and their own power and influence in the Toronto and New York business communities. It is important to note that the Bank of Toronto and some of the other Gooderham family business stayed with the eight remaining lawyers of the old firm.

New Premises and a New Name

The dwindling importance of the Gooderham connection to Beatty Blackstock became apparent in 1915, when the firm left the old Bank of Toronto building and moved into the newly completed Excelsior Life Building at 36 Toronto Street. For the first time the firm was not located in a Gooderham-related office.[133] The Excelsior Life Building was tall and had all the modern conveniences. Like David Fasken's own home and the Toronto Western Hospital (of which he was chairman of the board), it had been designed by the leading architect E.J. Lennox, working closely with David Fasken.[134]

In a letter written on 20 September 1915, Chadwick described the new offices as:

quite high toned. Quite a handsome suite of rooms with stylish new furniture in several of the partners' rooms and oriental rugs and everything else to match. We are in a handsome new building just completed from which we have grand views over most of our neighbours' heads. From my room I can see most of the island and bay and have a very good view of the aviators learning to manage their machines. There are two aviation schools on the island. I can see the Niagara steamers coming and going for five miles or more.[135]

The move represented a new viewpoint in more ways than one. It confirmed that the firm was moving further under the control of David Fasken, who was effectively putting his firm in his building. One of the lessons that David seems to have learned from the Gooderhams and W.H. Beatty is that you should always keep your business in the family.

An even more striking indication of Fasken's ascendency is found in the firm's new name. The 1 May 1915 partnership agreement between Chadwick, David Fasken, Mahlon Cowan, Alexander Fasken, and Hugh Rose provided that the firm name was to be Fasken, Cowan, Chadwick & Rose. There was to be no trace of the Beatty Blackstock name under which the firm had become a force in the Toronto legal community. The agreement went further, providing that, on the dissolution of the partnership, none of the partners would use the name 'Beatty and Blackstock, or either of them as a firm name or part of a firm name' without the consent of a majority of the partners, thus effectively ensuring that the former name would never again be used.

David Fasken continued to be 'Manager of the business of the firm' and to 'determine what line of work shall be done by the various partners,' but increasingly David was delegating these duties to his brother Alex. The agreement noted that every partner other than David Fasken was 'entitled to one calendar month's holiday during the year.' David Fasken, by contrast, was 'entitled to such holidays from time to time as he shall desire to take.'

David, and through him Alex, had tremendous power in the partnership. The agreement, provided, for example: 'In case of the death or retirement of any member of the firm or of the dissolution of the said partnership the value of the assets of the firm shall be left to the arbitrament of David Fasken, K.C., and the Accountant of the firm and in the event of the death or inability of either of them to act the same shall be fixed by the other and their or his decision shall be final and binding upon all parties and from which there shall be no appeal ...'

Despite David's dominant role, his compensation from the firm was limited. Net profits up to $18,500 per annum were to be divided so that Cowan and Alex Fasken received $4,700, Mr Chadwick $3,600, David Fasken $3,000, and H.E. Rose $2,500. The profits over $18,500 were to be divided, with 36 per cent going to each of Cowan and Alex Fasken, 15 per cent to H.E. Rose, and only 13 per cent to David Fasken. This reflects the fact that law firm was no longer David's principal source of income.

Notwithstanding David's smaller financial rewards, the agreement gave David Fasken, and to a lesser extent his brother, Alex, very special treatment. All other partners were required to devote all of their time to the partnership, accounting to the partnership for all commissions and revenues which they received in any way connected with the law practice. David Fasken, however, was entitled to have connections with corporations or other businesses in which he was financially interested and to receive commissions and other fees from them, so long as all moneys that he received by way of retainer or other legal services rendered were the property of the firm. Alexander Fasken was entitled to retain all commissions and other fees from his directorship in the Excelsior Life Insurance Company so long as the meetings of directors were held in the evening.

David Fasken indeed had many irons in the fire. In addition to his work at the law firm, his presidency of Excelsior Life, and his mining ventures, he found time to be a governor and president of Toronto Western Hospital (now affiliated with Toronto General) and a member of the Senate of the University of Toronto. He gave freely of his time and money to many charities, donating more than $500,000 to Toronto Western Hospital alone.

David's dealings with Toronto Western Hospital, however, were not entirely altruistic. David created strong links between the hospital, Excelsior Life, and the law firm. The doctors at the hospital provided medical reviews and opinions for the insurance company. The law firm advised both institutions, and even provided legal advice to the patients at the hospital. J.B. Robinson recalls:

As solicitors for Toronto Western Hospital we were often called by the Superintendent to go out there to draw a will for a patient who would not otherwise be known to us. I didn't care much for this because you usually had to do something in long-hand and on one occasion the patient wasn't able to speak and could only make unintelligible sounds. I don't remember any of these wills ever coming into the office to be probated. There certainly was no opportunity for 'Estate Planning.'

The Faskens

By 1915, however, David's interests lay elsewhere. He moved to Texas, likely for health reasons. J.B. Robinson recalled that, by 1918, David was spending most of his time at his ranch near Midland, Texas. He had a large office in the firm's Toronto Street premises, but he came to Toronto only for a few days each year. The Fasken ranch was enormous – 220,000 acres purchased with the thought that he would subdivide the property for farming. In 1917 David founded Fasken, Texas, in east-central Andrew County. He incorporated the Midland Farm Company and built a railway, the Midland and Northwest, to the site. Many lots were sold, but few people moved in, and Fasken, Texas, died in the 1920s. Later oil was found on the Fasken property, and the family became one of the wealthy oil and ranching families in the state.[136]

David Fasken died on 3 December 1929 after a lengthy illness. He left an estate of nearly $2 million (not including the value of the as-yet-untapped oil reserves on the Texas property). The Supreme Court of Canada, in a judgment dealing with the interpretation of his will, would later characterize it as 'very substantial.' His funeral was reported on the front page of the *Toronto Daily Star*, which, ignoring his other interests and achievements, ran the headline: 'David Fasken, Wealthy Mining Magnate, Dies.'[137] Among the honorary pallbearers were E.P. Earle, the New Yorker who had invested in the Cobalt mines; Mr Justice Riddell, one of Fasken's former partners; E.J. Lennox, Fasken's architect; Edward Rogers Wood, the Canadian financier, and, most significantly, Colonel Albert Gooderham, one of the sons of George Gooderham.[138] The presence of Colonel Gooderham was a clear indication that Fasken had not severed all ties with the family that had been so instrumental in the growth of the firm.

On David Fasken's retirement from active practise in 1919, Alex became the managing partner of the firm. As David's right-hand man, Alex had assisted in the management of the firm for years. The partnership agreement makes it clear that Alex, like David before him, was to be free to carry on other pursuits and did not have to dedicate his full time to the law. Alex became the president of Nipissing Mining, and the Northern Ontario Power Company (which later became part of the Power Corporation of Canada). On David's death in 1929, Alex became the president of the Excelsior Life Insurance Company. He continued David's support for the development of the Toronto Western Hospital.

Although David was gone, one sees many similarities with the David Fasken years. Alex continued, for example, David's practice of recruiting leading lawyers from out of town. In 1917, Robert Spelman Robertson was lured from Stratford to join the firm, likely to replace Hugh Rose, who had been appointed to the bench in December 1916, and Mahlon Cowan, KC, who died in 1917. To get Robertson to come, Alex Fasken guaranteed him a minimum of $10,000 a year.

R.S. Robertson, born in Goderich, Ontario, in 1870, was one of seven children. He was called to the bar in 1894 and practised in Stratford with John Idington, who would later be appointed a judge of the Supreme Court of Canada. As the *Globe and Mail* would later state, he was 'slight of build and genial in manner' and 'a family man.' In politics, he was a Liberal. He belonged to the United Church and was an advocate of temperance.[139]

Like his brother, Alex was more a businessman than a lawyer. Bryce Mackenzie noted that Alex 'was more interested in business than in the practise of law. On any legal matter, Mr Fasken relied upon Mr Robertson.'[140] Fasken had chosen his lawyer well. On his retirement, the *Globe* stated that Robertson was 'recognized as one of the finest lawyers Canada has ever produced.' Robertson was dedicated to the law. He was elected a bencher of the Law Society, served as chairman of the Benchers' Discipline Committee, and in 1937 was elected treasurer. In December 1938, Robertson was named Chief Justice of Ontario, an office that he would hold for thirteen years. He finally retired in 1952 at the age of eighty-one.

Alex, even more than his brother had, dominated the firm. Later partnership agreements would state that Alex had 'full authority to engage and discharge employees ... to fix their salary or remuneration and to define their duties.'[141] In fact, those agreements would go so far as to say that 'all office furniture, furnishings, library, typewriters and equipment' were the sole property of Alex Fasken.

Alex oversaw all aspects of the day-to-day operations of the firm in a way that one suspects even his brother had not done. J.B. Robinson recalled that 'Fasken examined all the incoming mail each morning and arranged for its distribution among the partners. All mail was held until his arrival at the office even if he did not appear until noon. He had a good memory for what was going on in the office and would often call in a junior to find out the present status of a particular item ...'[142]

Both J.B. Robinson and Bryce Mackenzie in their memoirs recall that Alex had a board in his office with buttons that rang bells in every office. He would ring when he wanted to speak to any member of the firm or with any secretary. Robinson recalled 'even R.S. Robertson, the senior counsel, would have to leave his client to respond to a summons.' At times, Mackenzie stated, 'he would put his arm across this panel and would ring every bell at once. It created quite a rapid movement of bodies.'[143]

Alex Fasken died in an automobile accident on the Etobicoke Creek bridge on 20 September 1944, leaving an estate in excess of $1 million. There was no fundamental change in the firm following Alex's death, as there had been thirty years before. The firm continues to this day to be known as Faskens. For many years it continued to recruit its lawyers principally from outside Toronto. It continues to act for many of the clients such as Excelsior Life (now Aetna Canada) and Dome Mines (now Placer Dome) that David and his brother help found and operate. It has never again become the sort of establishment firm that Beatty Blackstock had been.

CONCLUSION

The way in which the Faskens transformed the Beatty Blackstock firm provides an interesting case-study of how firms at the turn of the century were organized and developed, and what could motivate fundamental change.

The Beatty firm prospered and grew as a direct result of its strong connection with the Gooderham and Worts families. Those families both provided the legal work for the firm and acted as a source of lawyers. To some extent, the law firm permitted Beatty to consolidate and enhance his social position.

For the Faskens, the law firm provided an opportunity to meet and learn from Toronto's business élite, to make their fortune and achieve a social status they would not otherwise have enjoyed. The Fasken brothers lacked the social connections of Beatty and his partners, but they made up for it with their astute recruiting of skilled practitioners and their entrepreneurial drive, which literally helped create the firm's client base.

Although the Beatty firm had an international clientele, it is clear that it was deeply rooted in the Toronto business community. The Gooderham companies, their principal clients, were based in Toronto. Their lawyers were primarily drawn from prominent Toronto families. Not surprisingly, their principal projects, such as the Cathedral Park real estate development and the building of the King Edward Hotel, were in Toronto.

The Fasken firm was to a much greater extent focused outside Toronto. David and Alex Fasken made their fortunes in northern Ontario. They drew their financing from the New York business community. They recruited their lawyers from outside Toronto. David went so far as to leave the city entirely to live in Texas even before he formally retired.

In the Beatty Blackstock firm, W.H. Beatty was not alone in having significant interests, business and otherwise, outside the firm. Chadwick had his genealogical interests and his church involvement. Thomas Gibbs Blackstock and Ross Gooderham were active in the management of Gooderham family businesses. George Tate Blackstock was heavily involved in politics. One gets the impression that, to some extent, the law firm was the place where the divergent interests of the partners intersected.

The Faskens, by way of contrast, seem to have wanted the lawyers working in their firm to focus their energies on the law. In the partnership agreements, all partners, other than the Fasken brothers themselves, were to dedicate all of their time to the practice of law. In this sense, the Faskens reflected a changing attitude to legal practice. They seem to have stressed talent and commitment rather than family connections. They needed and wanted skilled professional lawyers to serve the legal needs of the companies that they created or attracted as clients. They seem to have put less stock in being the largest firm. They valued, instead, efficiency and profitability.

The dramatic transformation of the Beatty Blackstock firm raises questions about the law firm as an institution. What does it mean when someone says that one firm is the successor of another? How does one measure continuity in a law practice? Is it enough to have a continuing name, a continuity of clients, a continuity of lawyers? For ease of reference, I have talked of the Beatty firm and the Fasken firm, but this is obviously not entirely correct. It is difficult, however, to characterize the firm as it existed during the Beatty Blackstock years and during the Fasken years as the same firm. In one sense, they clearly were. One literally could trace its origin to the other and had the legal right to hold itself out as the successor to the practice of the other. But, as we have seen, in many ways they were very different, and those differences are largely attributable to the key lawyers in each firm.

The period of transition, particularly 1905–6, was a difficult and troublesome one for the lawyers in the firm. It helps us appreciate how important personalities are in keeping a firm together and functioning profitably. Clearly the change in managing partners was not welcomed by all of the firm's members. Until the Faskens peopled the firm with lawyers who accepted their leadership and their management views, many lawyers left or were asked to leave. In the 1890s eleven lawyers had joined Beatty Blackstock and only one had left – a striking contrast with the period 1903–13, when thirteen lawyers (virtually the entire complement of lawyers in 1902) left and only six joined. This illustrates the dramatic change that the Faskens brought about and reminds us that lawyers can and do move their individual practices from one firm to another when the benefits of partnership no longer compensate for the compromises that partnership brings.

Although the firm went through this difficult transition, it did survive and continued to be quite successful. Once established, it attracted and kept good lawyers and served significant clients. Perhaps what it teaches us is that successful firms are ones that can adapt to different times and different personalities.

Appendix: Names by which the Firm Was Known, 1863–1996

Beatty & Chadwick	1863–70
Beatty, Chadwick & Lash	1870–6
Beatty, Chadwick & Lash; Beatty, Millar & Lash	1876–8
Beatty, Chadwick & Biggar; Beatty, Millar & Biggar	1878–9
Beatty, Chadwick, Biggar & Thomson; Beatty, Millar Biggar & Blackstock	1879–82
Beatty, Chadwick, Thomson & Blackstock	1883–5
Beatty, Chadwick, Blackstock & Galt; Beatty, Chadwick, Blackstock & Neville	1885–92
Beatty, Blackstock, Nesbitt & Chadwick	1892–5
Beatty, Blackstock, Nesbitt, Chadwick & Riddell	1895–8
Beatty, Blackstock, Nesbitt, Chadwick & Riddell; Beatty, Blackstock, Galt & Fasken	1898–1903
Beatty, Blackstock, Nesbitt, Fasken & Riddell; Beatty, Blackstock, Chadwick & Galt	1903–4

Beatty, Blackstock, Riddell & Chadwick;	
Beatty, Blackstock, Fasken, Galt & Gooderham	1904–6
Beatty, Blackstock, Fasken & Riddell	1906–7
Beatty, Blackstock, Fasken & Chadwick	1907–10
Beatty, Blackstock, Fasken, Cowan & Chadwick	1910–15
Fasken, Cowan, Chadwick & Rose	1915–17
Fasken, Robertson, Chadwick & Sedgewick	1917–20
Fasken, Robertson, Chadwick, Sedgewick & Aitchison	1920
Fasken, Robertson, Sedgewick & Aitchison	1920–2
Fasken, Robertson, Sedgewick Aitchison & Pickup	1922–5
Fasken, Robertson, Aitchison, Pickup & Calvin	1925–61
Fasken, Calvin, MacKenzie, Williston & Swackhamer	1962–7
Fasken & Calvin	1967–89
Fasken Campbell Godfrey	1989–present

NOTES

I would like to thank Dr Hugh Laurence of Fasken Campbell Godfrey, who has helped with the research for this essay and much more.

1 Letter to Violet Baker, 13 March 1913. Copy in Fasken Campbell Godfrey Archives (hereinafter FCGA), original in archives of Irish Law Society, Dublin
2 See the picture of the Palm Court of McConkey's Restaurant in Marilyn M. Litvak, *Edward James Lennox: "Builder of Toronto"* (Toronto: Dundurn 1995), 64. "Electric lighting arrived in Toronto one evening in 1879 when two arc lamps were turned on at McConkey's Restaurant at 145 Yonge Street ... thus enhancing its reputation as "long the best-known" restaurant in the city': Robert M. Stamp, *Bright Lights Big City: The History of Electricity in Toronto* (Toronto: Market Gallery 1991), 11.
3 *Toronto Mail & Empire*, 21 November 1912. This Beatty obituary is also found in the Metro Toronto Library Scrapbooks, vol. 1, 33
4 *A Standard Dictionary of Canadian Biography, 1875–1933* (Toronto: Trans-Canada Press 1934), vol. 1. See also Henry J. Morgan, *Canadian Men & Women of the Time*, 1st ed. (Toronto: W. Briggs 1898), 173, where the firm is called 'one of the largest and most important in Ontario.'
5 *Toronto Daily Star*, 27 November 1951, in obituary of Melville Ross Gooderham
6 See by way of comparison the essay by Blaine Baker, 'Law Practice and Statecraft in Mid-Nineteenth-Century Montreal: The Torrance–Morris Firm, 1828–1868,' in Carol Wilton, ed., *Essays in the History of Canada Law*, vol. 4: *Beyond the Law: Lawyers and Business in Canada, 1830 to 1930* (Toronto: The Osgoode

Society 1990), 45–91, which looks at the Torrance–Morris firm, which served
the business interests of the Torrance family in Montreal.

7 On the growth of financial institutions, see Michael Bliss, *Northern Enterprise:
Five Centuries of Canadian Business* (Toronto: McClelland and Stewart 1987),
chap. 10: 'Moving Money: The Growth of Financial Services.'

8 When I joined the firm in 1980, the senior partners still thought of it as an 'out
of town' firm, drawing its lawyers from outside of Toronto.

9 On the opening of Ontario's north see Robert J. Surtees, *The Northern Connection: Ontario Northland since 1902* (North York, ON: Captus Press 1992), especially chap. 2: 'The Cobalt Bonanza and Beyond,' and on the Methodist
businessmen see Michael Bliss, *A Canadian Millionaire: The Life and Business
Times of Sir Joseph Flavelle, 1858–1939* (Toronto: Macmillan of Canada 1978).

10 See the chart in the appendices to Curtis Cole, *Osler Hoskin & Harcourt: Portrait
of a Partnership* (Toronto: McGraw-Hill Ryerson 1995).

11 On the development of the U.S. firms, see Wayne Hobson, 'Symbol of the New
Profession: Emergence of the Large Law Firm, 1870–1915,' in Gerald W.
Gawalt, ed., *The New High Priests: Lawyers in Post–Civil War America* (Westport, CT: Greenwood Press 1984), 3–27. He notes in a table on p. 7 that in 1904
there were only two firms in the United States listed in *Hubbell's Legal Directory*
that had between twelve and sixteen members.

12 Letter to Violet Baker, 13 March 1913. Copy in FCGA, original in archives of
Irish Law Society, Dublin

13 *A Standard Dictionary of Canadian Biography, 1875–1933*, vol. 1, 29, and
Edward Marion Chadwick, *Ontarian Families*, 2 vols. (Toronto, 1894–8),
vol. 1, 160. Edith Firth, *The Town of York, 1815–1834* (Toronto: University of
Toronto Press 1966), 76, says that James Beatty came in 1831. The *Toronto
City Directory* for 1866 refers to his widow as 'Mrs. James Beatty (widow of
Col. James).'

14 It was one block west of College Avenue (modern-day University Avenue)
and just north of Queen Street, and was later renamed and numbered as 173
Simcoe, and later still as 197 Simcoe. For a period between 1855 and 1859, the
family moved to 9 Sherbourne Street (just north of Queen Street). At that time
the William Street property is shown as vacant in the *Toronto City Directory*.
See the directories for 1856 and 1859–60.

15 One of Howland's sons was Oliver Aiken Howland. Between 1875 and 1879,
Oliver Howland formed a partnership with Frank Arnoldi under the name
Howland & Arnoldi. This firm eventually became known as Campbell Godfrey & Lewtas. In 1863, when Beatty and Chadwick formed their firm, they
could not have realized that the sixteen-year-old boy next door would found a
rival firm that would eventually merge with theirs 126 years later.

16 Following Confederation he would serve as lieutenant-governor of Ontario (1868–73). See the *Toronto City Directory* for 1861. Hagarty had been a partner of John Willoughby Crawford in the firm that eventually became Fraser & Beatty. See Stanley Edwards, *Fraser & Beatty: The First 150 Years* (Toronto: Fraser & Beatty Desktop Publishing 1989).

17 Chadwick tells us much about himself and his family in his, *The Chadwicks of Guelph and Toronto and Their Cousins* (Toronto: privately printed 1914) and *Ontarian Families* (Toronto: Rolph Smith 1894–8).

18 The *Wellington County Atlas* of 1870 shows large parts of central Guelph and the surrounding area owned by members of the family.

19 *Toronto City Directory*, 1862–3

20 C. Ian Kyer and Jerome B. Bickenbach, *The Fiercest Debate: Cecil A. Wright, the Benchers, and Legal Education in Ontario, 1923–1957* (Toronto: The Osgoode Society 1987), 26

21 At this time one was usually admitted as a solicitor first, and then some time thereafter one was called to the bar. Chadwick was called as a barrister in 1863. Beatty was not called until 1880.

22 The floor plan is reproduced in Eric Arthur, *Toronto: No Mean City*, 3d ed. revised by Stephen A. Otto (Toronto: University of Toronto Press 1986), 119. The plans for the building show a door between offices 11 and 12, suggesting that the partners moved into part of a suite of offices occupied by Gooderham and Worts. The office addresses are found in the *Toronto City Directory* for the years 1862 and 1866.

23 It was a handsome building on Wellington Street East that had been erected in 1855 by a group of millers and grain merchants to house a grain exchange and their offices. See Arthur, *Toronto: No Mean City*, 116–18, for a photograph, plans, etc.

24 Another older sister, Elizabeth, became the third wife of John Craven Chadwick, E.M. Chadwick's father, on 4 May 1876. Elizabeth was then thirty-seven and unmarried. John Chadwick was sixty-one. See the St James Marriage Register, 1807–8, no. 5240.

25 It was three years before Chadwick remarried. He would have five sons and two daughters by his second wife, Maria Martha Fisher.

26 See *The Globe*, 28 April 1865, 3. The Gooderham and Worts families were important members of the congregation of the church. Alex Dixon was instrumental in having the church built in 1843: See Alan L. Hayes, *Holding Forth the Word of Life: Little Trinity Church, 1843–1992* (Toronto: The Corporation of Little Trinity Church 1991).

27 *Toronto City Directory*, 1866

28 Dianne Newell, 'James Gooderham Worts,' *Dictionary of Canadian Biography*

(Toronto: University of Toronto Press 1982), vol. 11, 937–8, and Joseph Schull, *100 Years of Banking in Canada: The Toronto-Dominion Bank* ([Vancouver]: Copp Clark 1958), 39–42

29 Hayes, *Holding Forth the Word of Life*, 11
30 John Ross Robertson, *Landmarks of Toronto* (Toronto: J. Ross Robertson 1894–1914), vol. 1, 2–5. See also Hayes, *Holding Forth the Word of Life*, 12.
31 See various minutes and shareholders lists in the Archives of the Toronto-Dominion Bank.
32 Schull, *100 Years of Banking in Canada*, 71
33 This is seen again and again. In each company you find sons, cousins, and sons-in-law on the board, as officers, or providing professional advice.
34 In December 1875, Beatty assigned the property lease to his father-in-law and George Gooderham as trustees (probably for his wife). The land, part of the University Park development, was leased from the university for $250 a year and gave Beatty an immense corner property with an effective frontage of 400 feet. His property, called 'The Oakes,' had an excellent location, sitting as it did near the garden and fountain that then occupied the south of the present legislative-building site where a statue of Sir John A. Macdonald now stands. A photo in Arthur, *Toronto: No Mean City* (p. 194) shows the site after the erection of the statue of Sir John A. Macdonald. Beatty's home can be seen to the right. See materials in the University of Toronto Archives, and William Dendy, *Lost Toronto*, rev. ed. (Toronto: McClelland and Stewart 1993), 182–3.
35 See the correspondence between Gooderham & Worts and Lanman & Kemp of New York in the Baldwin Room, Metropolitan Toronto Public Library. J.W. Beatty signed the Gooderham & Worts letters starting 15 August 1876. He is termed a clerk in the 1878 *Toronto City Directory* and an accountant in the 1880 edition.
36 Letter to Sir John A. Macdonald, September 1879, PAC, Macdonald Papers, 166547–9, where the letterhead of Beatty Chadwick Biggar Thomson/Beatty Miller Biggar & Blackstock shows the firm as having 'Offices over the Bank of Toronto, Corner Wellington & Church Streets'
37 Dendy, *Lost Toronto*, 54
38 Proceedings of the 26th Annual General Meeting of Shareholders of the Bank of Toronto, 21 June 1882, Archives of the Toronto-Dominion Bank. It is important to note that corporate officers had not yet taken on a significant day-to-day operational role. The Bank of Toronto, for example, was managed by its chief cashier, not its president.
39 Newell, 'James Gooderham Worts,' 938
40 A power of attorney respecting the Worts estate in Beatty's favour, dated 8 May 1900, is in the FCGA.
41 *Worts* v. *Worts* (1889) 18 OR 332

42 Ibid., 340. As trustee he sold J.G. Worts's interest in Gooderham & Worts Limited to George Gooderham for more than $900,000 in June 1892 (agreement in Archives of Toronto-Dominion Bank).

43 This account is based on news clippings from Tuesday, 30 December 1890, in the *Montreal Herald*, provided by Douglas Worts. I wish to thank Stephen Otto for bringing them to my attention.

44 In 1902 there were actually two partnerships – Beatty, Blackstock, Nesbitt, Chadwick & Riddell was one, and Beatty, Blackstock, Galt & Fasken the other. Although in the absence of a written partnership agreement it is difficult to know exactly why this was done, it seems likely that the two firms did different work and shared the profits of that work differently. The use of parallel but separate partnerships as a mechanism to differentiate partnership interests was used intermittently by Beatty from 1876 to 1906. In 1879, for example, one of the partnerships was described as 'Barristers, Attorneys at Law & Solicitors in Insolvency' while the other was referred to as 'Barristers, Solicitors in Chancery & Notaries Public,' suggesting that one had a legal practice, and the other an equity practice.

45 The firm would not be that large again until the 1960s.

46 There were no women in the firm for almost 100 years. The first woman, Georgia Bentley, joined in the mid-1950s.

47 It is revealing to walk through St James Cathedral and note the memorials that are associated with Beatty and Chadwick. There is a beautiful white plaque that Chadwick dedicated to his first wife's memory. It states: 'In memory of Ellen Byrne Chadwick the Beloved Wife of Edward Marion Chadwick Esq. and Daughter of James Beatty Esq. Born 9 November 1843. Married 28 June 1864. Died suddenly 10 February 1865. Him that cometh to me I shall in no wise cast out.' The Beatty family dedicated a set of stained-glass windows to Beatty's wife. Beatty's daughter and her husband, Mr and Mrs W.H. Cawthra, donated St George's chapel.

48 These firms would merge in 1989 to form Fasken Campbell Godfrey. The deed transferring title from William Howland to the syndicate was prepared by the Howland Arnoldi firm, but all other legal work for the syndicate seems to have been prepared by Beatty's firm.

49 The criticism was largely unwarranted. The cathedral was separately represented by Moss Falconbridge & Barwick, and Chadwick does not seem to have participated in the final negotiations. Certainly, Chadwick was hurt by the criticism. Shortly before his death, at a time when the cathedral had been all but officially abandoned, he wrote and published a pamphlet about the cathedral. See the materials in the Archives of the Anglican Diocese, collected by Chadwick.

50 Minutes of the Bank of Toronto board of directors, 27 November 1912, in Archives of Toronto-Dominion Bank. *The Globe* and the *Toronto Telegram* noted that he had 'a great knowledge of commercial law': Henry J. Morgan, *Canadian Men & Women of the Time*, 2nd ed. (Toronto: Briggs 1912), 76, and *The Globe*, 21 November 1912, 9.

51 *A Standard Dictionary of Canadian Biography, 1875–1933*, vol. 1, 29–30. See also *The Canadian Annual Financial Review* for the early years of the twentieth century, which shows the officers and directors of Canada's various financial institutions.

52 The list of shareholders shows several estates. It may well be that Beatty invested these funds as trustee.

53 Nesbitt married Beatty's daughter in 1898. See *A Standard Dictionary of Canadian Biography, 1875–1933*, vol. 1, 380.

54 Ibid., and Morgan, *Canadian Men & Women of the Time*, 2d ed.

55 On Beatty's involvement in Upper Canada College as trustee and 'generous benefactor', see Richard B. Howard, *Upper Canada College, 1829–1979* (Toronto: Macmillan of Canada 1979), 124, 131, 354, 446.

56 See the original petition to the federal government in the archives of Confederation Life, and their published corporate history: I.R. Scott, *Confederation Life Insurance Company, 1871–1971* (Toronto: Confederation Life Insurance Co. 1971).

57 This committee reviewed all requests for insurance received by the company to assess the risk that the company ran in granting a policy. This was no sinecure. The Confederation Life letter-books have a number of letters to Beatty enclosing twenty or more applications. This work brought him into regular contact with John Kay MacDonald, the managing director of the company.

58 Beatty signed the petition to the federal government asking that the life insurance company be chartered as 'Solicitor to the Toronto Grey & Bruce Railway,' which was owned in part by Gooderham & Worts.

59 Leo Johnson, 'William Gooderham,' *Dictionary of Canadian Biography*, vol. 11, 360–1

60 The share-certificate book is in the Confederation Life Archives, as is a special May 1893 supplement of the budget on the opening of the Confederation Life Building. Beatty, a vice-president, was one of the speakers at the opening ceremony, as was an ailing Sir William Pearce Howland. Other directors present included W.S. Gibbs, who was related to Thomas Gibbs Blackstock, and Alfred Gooderham, one of George Gooderham's sons.

61 His father-in-law, James Gooderham Worts, had had a bad experience in his one attempt to win public office when his wealth and prominence in the com-

munity had proved a detriment, and one suspects that this might have swayed Beatty away from politics: See Newell, 'James Gooderham Worts,' 937–8.

62 Letter to Sir John A. Macdonald, 13 July 1883, PAC, Macdonald Papers, 8665–6
63 Letter to Sir John A. Macdonald, September 1879, PAC, Macdonald Papers, 166547–9
64 Letter to Sir John A. Macdonald, 14 April 1888, PAC, Macdonald Papers, 58801–8
65 Morgan, *Canadian Men & Women of the Time*, 2d ed., 76
66 See letter to Sir John A. Macdonald, 22 July 1887, PAC, Macdonald Papers, 8921–4, and Morgan, *Canadian Men & Women of the Time*, 2d ed., 76.
67 He was not called to the bar until 1880, seventeen years after commencing practice. See Archives of the Law Society of Upper Canada.
68 See Cole, *Osler Hoskin & Harcourt*, 61ff., and 'McCarthy, Osler, Hoskin, and Creelman, 1882–1902: Establishing a Reputation, Building a Practice,' in Wilton, ed., *Beyond the Law*, 149–66.
69 Nesbitt married Beatty's daughter in 1898. See *A Standard Dictionary of Canadian Biography*, vol. 1, 380. Beatty's other daughter, Alice Maud Beatty, married William Hubert Cawthra, a member of the wealthy and influential Cawthra family. Cawthra was then a partner in the Howland Arnoldi firm.
70 Memoirs in the FCGA
71 He was made an honorary chief of the Six Nations, of the Anowara or Turtle Clan of the Kanienga, or Mohawks. His Indian name, Shagotyshgivsaks (pronounced Saugo-tyoch-gweesax, meaning 'one who seeks a gathering of the people'), was given to him for his advocacy of the formation of a Six Nations militia regiment. He himself had served as a major in the 2nd Reserve Regiment of the Queen's Own Rifles.
72 See Appendix for the many different names the firm had over the years.
73 T.G. Blackstock was then living with his father, Reverend William Blackstock, and his brother George Tate Blackstock at 444 Parliament. See *Toronto City Directory*, 1880.
74 Ibid., 1881
75 Ibid.
76 *An Encyclopedia of Canadian Biography*, vol. 2 (n.p.: Canadian Press Syndicate 1907), 24
77 See materials in Bank of Toronto Archives.
78 On St George Street, this is now the site of the mainland clubhouse of the Royal Canadian Yacht Club, in which he, Beatty, and Gooderham were very active. A picture of the home is found at the entrance to the clubhouse.
79 *An Encyclopedia of Canadian Biography*, vol. 2, 24
80 *Canadian Annual Review of Public Affairs*, vol. 1, 1901, 55

81 See *Gooderham et al.* v. *The Corporation of the City of Toronto* (1890) 21 OR 120. Gooderham was seeking to prevent the city from extending Saulter, Strange and McGee streets through a 22.5-acre property south of Eastern Avenue that he had acquired for the family's cattle business.

82 One member of the firm, Percy Galt, assisted in the action.

83 They were the first partners who had a barrister's practice.

84 *Toronto Mail and Empire*, 28 December 1921, Metro Toronto Library Scrapbooks, vol. 5, 390

85 *Canadian Law List*, 1879

86 Unpublished autobiography of Wyly Grier, in the Ontario Archives, 46

87 See his obituary in the Metro Toronto Library Scrapbooks, vol. 5, 390.

88 W.H.C. Boyd, 'The Last Chancellor,' 15/4 *Law Society of Upper Canada Gazette* (1981), 363–4

89 See Cole, 'McCarthy, Osler, Hoskin, and Creelman, 1882–1902,' 162, on the role of Britton Bath Osler as prosecutor in the case.

90 Unpublished autobiography of Wyly Grier, in the Ontario Archives, 47

91 Editorial in the *Toronto Daily Star* on the death of Gooderham, 27 November 1951

92 Ibid.

93 Just inside a small room near entrance to St James Cathedral is a plaque to the memory of Sir Thomas Galt and his son Thomas Percival Galt.

94 In the FCGA is a note from David Fasken to 'My Dear Galt,' dated 30 April 1907, in which Galt was given a $1,500 bonus for 'the satisfactory result in the Ritchie litigation.'

95 See Jesse Edgar Middleton, ed., *The Municipality of Toronto: A History*, vol. 2 (Toronto: Dominion Publishers 1923) (chapter on art club in Toronto).

96 Kenneth Jarvis, 'Chief Justice Hugh Rose,' 2 *Law Society of Upper Canada Gazette* 1 (1968), 19, says that he commenced his articles with Maclaren Macdonald Merritt & Shepley, but transfered to the Beatty firm and that, on his call to the bar in 1894, he joined the Beatty firm. Rose, however, does not appear·on the letterhead of the firm until after 1899.

97 *A Standard Dictionary of Canadian Biography*, vol. 2, 149

98 For a description and picture of both the Fasken home and the Beatty Building, see Litvak, *Edward James Lennox*, 7, 18, 54, 67.

99 See, for example, the letter that David Fasken sent to his sister Belle Fasken on 11 July 1912, in the FCGA, where he talks of Dutch spending the day fishing with him at Timagami Island.

100 Hilary Bates Neary, 'William Renwick Riddell: Judge, Ontario Publicist and Man of Letters,' 11 *Law Society of Upper Canada Gazette* 3 (1977), 144–74

101 Belle Armstrong, as she was known, had unsuccessfully sought to marry

Lyman Duff, a story charmingly told by David Ricardo Williams in *Duff: A Life in the Law* (Toronto: The Osgoode Society 1984), 23–7.

102 His notes are in the FCGA.

103 See James G. Snell and Frederick Vaughan, *The Supreme Court of Canada* (Toronto: The Osgoode Society 1985), 86.

104 He resigned on 4 October 1905. See Snell and Vaughan, *The Supreme Court of Canada*, 88, 260.

105 He is buried with William Beatty in the family plot in St James Cemetery in Toronto. The family headstone has a memorial to Beatty on one side, and to Nesbitt on the other.

106 See Surtees *The Northern Connection*, especially chap. 2: 'The Cobalt Bonanza and Beyond.'

107 Obituary notice prepared by the Excelsior Life Insurance Company on the death of Alexander Fasken in September 1944

108 *Cobalt Daily Nugget*, September 1910, 2

109 S.A. Pain, *Three Miles of Gold: The Story of Kirkland Lake* (Toronto: Ryerson Press 1960), 3. The *Cobalt Daily Nugget* of September 1910 reported Nipissing's production from 1905 to halfway through 1910 at a value of $8,375,541.58, with aggregate dividends paid of $5,040,000, plus $400,000 to the syndicate. It also reports, for the period 1904 to 1909, aggregate ore shipments, value of ore shipments, and dividends paid by Cobalt mines as 78,487.58 tons, $32,840,906, and $14,347,969 (or 43.7 per cent of value shipped), respectively.

110 Quoted in H.V. Nelles, *The Politics of Development: Forests, Mines & Hydro-electric Power in Ontario, 1849–1941* (Toronto: Macmillan of Canada 1974), 147–8.

111 *Cobalt Daily Nugget*, September 1910, 10

112 See Morris Zaslow, *The Opening of the Canadian North, 1870–1914* (Toronto: McClelland and Stewart 1971), 184.

113 Ibid., 185

114 Charles Girdwood, Lawrence F. Jones, and George Lonn, *The Big Dome: Over Seventy Years of Gold Mining in Canada* (Toronto: Cybergraphics Co. 1983), 119

115 *The Canadian Annual Review 1912*, 644

116 A review of the history of the Flin Flon mine and David Fasken's role appeared in the *Mail and Empire*, 10 December 1927, 17, complete with pictures of David Fasken with his Indian guides canoeing to the site and riding a large ox.

117 *Mail and Empire*, 10 December 1927, 17

118 See *Canadian Law List*, 1943–52.

119 He would later become counsel to Osler Hoskin & Harcourt. See *Canadian Law List*, 1940.

120 The commission was established because of fears of mismanagement and

irregularities in the insurance industry arising out of a New York State investigation. On the circumstances surrounding the commission and its hearings and findings see *The Canadian Annual Review 1906*, 215ff.

121 *Report of the Royal Commission on Insurance, Minutes of Evidence* (Toronto: Queen's Printer 1907), vol. 1, 1287

122 Dr Ross, who had acted as George Gooderham's personal physician, had married George Gooderham's third daughter, Adelaide Mary. He was head of gynaecology at Toronto General Hospital, an institution to which both George Gooderham and Henry Beatty gave generously.

123 *Toronto Daily Star*, 27 November 1951

124 Neary, 'William Renwick Riddell,' 148

125 *Who's Who in Canada, 1936–7*, 979

126 J.B. Robinson Memoirs, in FCGA

127 See obituary in Metro Toronto Library Scrapbooks, vol. 8, 566.

128 *A Standard Dictionary of Canadian Biography, 1875–1933*, vol. 1, 126–7

129 Obituary in the *Globe and Mail*, 23 April 1963

130 55th Annual Report and List of Shareholders, Bank of Toronto, November 1910, 4 (Archives of the Toronto-Dominion Bank). See also Minutes of Board, Bank of Toronto, 11 January 1911.

131 The Anglican Bishop of Toronto presided at the funeral service.

132 Another young lawyer, Austin G. Ross left as well but he became 'the dean of police court lawyers' (Obituary in the *Globe and Mail*, 23 April 1963).

133 In addition to the office in the Gooderham & Worts suite in the Exchange Building and the office above the Bank of Toronto, the firm was located for a short time at 56 King Street East, next to Rice Lewis and Son Hardware. Rice Lewis had served as a witness at Beatty's wedding, and his daughter married a Gooderham that same year.

134 See Litvak, *Edward James Lennox*, 83–4, 91.

135 Letter to Violet Baker, copy in FCGA

136 Walter Prescott Webb, *Handbook of Texas* (Austin: Texas State Historical Association 1952–76), vol. 3, 293

137 4 December 1929

138 *Toronto Daily Star*, 4 December 1929, 1

139 At one time this would have been unthinkable in the Gooderhams' law firm, but the distillery business was no longer the cornerstone of the firm's clientele, and Gooderham & Worts would soon be sold to Hiram Walker.

140 Memoirs in the FCGA

141 Agreement between Alexander Fasken, Robert S. Robertson, James Aitchison, John Wellington Pickup, and Collamer Chipman Calvin, 1 August 1925, in the FCGA

142 Memoirs, in the FCGA

143 Alex was not remembered with fondness by lawyers in the firm. It is said that, when Alex Fasken died, James Aitchison, his nephew and a partner with a general practice, personally tore out this buzzer system.

6

Élite Relationships, Partnership Arrangements, and Nepotism at Blakes, a Toronto Law Firm, 1858–1942

T.D. REGEHR

Toronto's Blake, Cassels & Graydon, popularly known as Blakes, is one of Canada's oldest, largest, and most influential law firms. Edward Blake, the firm's founder, and those who became senior partners in the first eighty years of the firm's history, all enjoyed excellent family, political, and business connections. These were perpetuated when the senior partners brought their sons and grandsons into the firm, which served primarily the interests and needs of the élite in Canadian society.

A complete history of Blakes must include a great many subjects beyond the scope of a single essay: the clients whose interests lawyers at Blakes defended; the firm's close relations with Osgoode Hall and legal education in Canada; the influence of Blake partners, a number of whom became judges, on the judicial system of Canada; the relations of the partners with political leaders; and many other matters are relevant to the history of a law firm. This study, however, deals mainly with pre–Second World War partnership arrangements, nepotism, and élite relationships at Blakes.

IMAGES OF BLAKES, PAST AND PRESENT

Edward Blake began his law practice in June 1856 while preparing for his bar examinations. He was twenty-three years old, a graduate of Upper Canada College and the University of Toronto, and a student-at-law at Osgoode Hall.[1] In August 1856, after passing his bar exams, he became a junior partner in a law practice established by Stephen Maule Jarvis.[2] That partnership, however, lasted less than a year, and in 1858 Edward Blake established the law firm now known as Blake, Cassels & Graydon, or Blakes. He was joined by his younger brother, Samuel Hume Blake, who began as a clerk but became a partner within two years. The offices of the new firm were briefly located in the Wellington Chambers on the northeast corner of Jordan and Melinda streets, Toronto, but moved in 1859 to the then newly constructed Masonic Hall Building on the west side of Toronto Street. The Blake brothers enjoyed immediate success, and their firm grew quickly to become one of Canada's largest and most prestigious.

In 1995 more than 250 lawyers,[3] with their support staff and modern equipment, worked in the firm's spacious Toronto offices, which occupy the thirteenth through the twenty-eighth floors of Commerce Court West on the corner of Bay and King, at the very centre of Canadian corporate power. The Toronto Stock Exchange, until its recent move, occupied the building directly across Bay, facing Commerce Court West. Huge bank towers occupy all four corners and adjacent lots at Bay and King. Commerce Court houses the head office of the Canadian Imperial Bank of Commerce. Early in his career, Edward Blake had done much of the legal work in the incorporation of the bank, which has remained a Blakes' client and whose board of directors has always included a Blakes' partner.

In addition to their Toronto office, Blakes has branch offices in Calgary, Vancouver, Ottawa, and London, England. In 1995 these offices had thirty-nine, thirty, twelve, and two lawyers, respectively. Blakes also has an affiliation with the Quebec law firm of Lavery, deBilly, which has offices in Montreal and Quebec City.[4]

No members of the founding Blake families are partners in the firm today, but the firm jealously guards and perpetuates the name of its founder. Since 1942 Blakes' partnership agreements have included a clause under which partners who leave the firm relinquish any and all claims to the use of the name of the founder. While the name of the firm has undergone a number of changes, the first place of honour has always gone to the Blake name, even though Edward Blake left it more than one hundred years ago.

Blakes has long been respected for its expertise in equity, corporate, and constitutional law, and for exceptionally thorough, meticulous, and well-informed work. Writing in 1976, Robert Brown, a former manager of the firm, explained:

Masonic Temple Building, Toronto: location of the Blake law firm, 1859–74
(courtesy Blake, Cassels & Graydon)

The two Blakes, Edward and Samuel, who founded the Partnership were without doubt outstanding lawyers. While only some of those who followed them could lay claim to the same great intellectual capacity or legal ability there does not appear to be a single period in the nearly 120 years of the Firm's history – including the present – when there weren't a number of great lawyers in the Partnership. These could not only produce work of the highest quality themselves, but they did – and this is very important to any great law office – exert a strong influence for excellence upon most of those who worked for or with them. The result was that Blakes from its small beginning in 1858 has always enjoyed a reputation for top-quality legal work and service.[5]

Over the years there have been many critics who thought that Blakes, at least until 1942, was a somewhat stuffy, even incestuous, family firm. In its early history, the firm, dominated by the founders and a few exceptionally talented partners, 'had the reputation (whether or not justified) of being a "closed corporation" where entry into partnership, and particularly advancement, depended on one's relationship by birth or marriage with more senior members.'[6] It allegedly consisted of 'a few well-to-do senior Partners and a number of not-too-well-paid junior Partners and associates.'[7]

The dominance of Blake family members in the early history of the firm is indicated by the fact that, in 1896, forty years after Edward Blake began his practice, six of the nine partners in the firm were Blakes.[8] A seventh later married into the Blake family. The other two partners in 1896 were Walter Gibson Pringle Cassels and Zebulon Aiton Lash, who soon brought their sons and grandsons into the partnership. A total of nine members of the two Blake families,[9] six members of the Cassels family covering three generations,[10] and Zebulon A. Lash, two of his sons, and three grandsons[11] became partners or associates in the firm which carried the name of Blake, Lash, Cassels for many years.

Family connections were obviously important in the early history of the firm, but by 1921 direct family connections alone were not essential for success in the firm. Allan Graydon, who joined the firm as a student-at-law in 1921, was not a blood relative of the privileged families. In his 'Reminiscences,' Graydon wrote that his success proved that 'there was not in my time and there certainly is not now any impediment to any person's advancement – everyone who joins as a young barrister and solicitor has an equal chance.'[12] What Graydon did not mention was that, in spite of his family background, he met most of the other professional, social, and cultural expectations, practices, and attitudes of the dominant families. His unimpeded opportunities were really open at Blakes only to White, male Protestants, preferably of Irish background, who were graduates of Upper Canada College or (later) of the Royal Military College, the University of Toronto, and Osgoode Hall. In order to rise to a senior partnership they had to possess outstanding legal talents, a stern work ethic, and the ability to work for and interact closely with the country's most influential business and political leaders.

Politically the firm was strongly identified with the Liberal party, but in their attitude towards the law and its role in Canadian society the partners were conservative. They were an élite firm which served mainly members of Canada's most successful political, business, and social groups. An 'old boys' network' remained strongly entrenched at the firm at least until the outbreak of the Second World War. The original partners were the beneficiaries of the hard fight fought by their parents to dislodge the old Loyalist-dominated Upper Canadian Family Compact. They became the new élites, representing some of the largest transportation (particularly steam and electric railways), financial, and manufacturing interests of a nation experiencing rapid industrialization, and dislodging the older élites who had gained their pre-eminence through huge land grants and control of the water-transport routes of St Lawrence–Great Lakes lowlands. Nevertheless, for Blakes and most of the Canadian industrial élites they represented, pro-British conservative values and loyalties remained as important as they had been for members of the old Family Compact. Those values and loyalties sometimes took precedence over lifelong political affiliations, as was demonstrated when Edward Blake in 1891, and Zebulon Lash twenty years later, broke with the Liberal party in order to oppose trade agreements with the United States, which they feared would weaken British values and institutions in Canada.

The firm also had strong and continuing military connections. Edward Blake, when serving as premier of Ontario and later as leader of the federal Liberal party, took a stern law-and-order approach to the 1869–70 Red River resistance and the 1885 Northwest Rebellion led by Louis Riel. His oldest son, Hume Blake, served as a lieutenant in the Queen's Own Rifles in the 1885 rebellion, and as a member of the Canadian Pension and Claims Board in England, with the rank of lieutenant-colonel, during the First World War. Richard Scougall Cassels, a partner in the firm from 1885 to 1888, also served in the 1885 rebellion, while Edward Blake's youngest son, Sammy, served as a war correspondent in the South African War.[13]

At least eight lawyers who were then, or subsequently became, part-ners in Blakes saw active military service during the First World War, while a ninth tried to enlist but was rejected for health reasons. Two of the men who later became senior partners in the firm were badly gassed.[14] One of them assessed the impact of his military experiences on his subsequent legal career thus:

It may be considered a terrible thing to say, but I enjoyed the First World War despite the bodily damage I incurred and from the consequences of which I am suffering more and more as my age increases. My experience in the Army assisted me greatly in the practice of law due to the fact that when at the age of 19 one has had the responsibility for the lives and well-being of a Section of Artillery consist-ing of about thirty-five drivers and gunners and about thirty horses or mules, one in later years is not troubled by assuming the responsibility for a document, opin-ion or transaction upon which only money is at risk.[15]

The 1943 *Canadian Law List* indicates that seven of the firm's twenty-five partners and associates had enlisted for active service. That list, how-ever, did not include two of Zebulon Lash's grandsons, who had been with the firm until November 1942. Nor did it include George Cassels, who had been a lieutenant in the 58th Canadian Infantry in the First World War, became a senior partner at Blakes, and came out of retire-ment to serve as deputy adjutant-general in the Second World War. Also omitted from this list was Robert E. Anglin, who enlisted late in 1943, and the list obviously does not include Second World War veterans who joined the firm after the war.

In his reminiscences Allan Graydon makes reference to the 'together-ness' which characterized work at the firm in 1921 and in the immedi-ately succeeding years. Office furnishings were spartan. Old-fashioned 'stand-up' desks, similar to those used at the Royal Military College to prevent a cadet from falling asleep, and a unique multiple-user desk for juniors, did service at Blakes even after other firms had adopted more modern furniture. Blakes was, however, one of the first law offices to have its client, the Bell brothers, install telephones in 1878, which pro-vided a direct line to Osgoode Hall.[16] But the newfangled device was not appreciated by the older partners, and junior partners using the tele-phones for a time kept them hidden in a closet. Deference to seniority was a fact of everyday life at Blakes, and those who worked there before the Second World War were members of a professional family firm.

Numerous factors led to significant changes in the firm during and after the war. One of the most traumatic was the severance in 1942 of the long and intimate relations of members of the Lash family with the firm. Over the years the various partners had often disagreed, both over internal partnership arrangements and over interpretations of law and strategies to be followed in particular cases.[17] In 1942 a serious disagreement regarding future partnership arrangements led to the departure of Jack Lash and two of his sons, marking in a symbolic way the end of the old family firm.

The break with members of the Lash family was only one of many changes at Blakes during and after the Second World War. At the time there were twenty-seven lawyers working at Blakes, thirteen of whom were partners. As already indicated, at least seven Blakes' lawyers enlisted for active military service, and several of the senior or recently retired partners became 'dollar-a-year men,' working for the government on various aspects of war work. The professional workforce was thus significantly reduced at a time when the volume of legal work to be done, both during the war and in the prosperous postwar period, increased dramatically. The comfortable family and old boys' network could no longer provide the needed new partners and associates. After 1942 the firm expanded rapidly, and its image and recruitment policies changed in a number of important ways.

One appointment in 1942 is indicative of those changes. Alice Belva Gibson that year became the first female solicitor employed by Blakes. She already had some experience as a solicitor with the Ontario Farm Loan Board and in her father's law firm, but was warned during the hiring interview at Blakes that her employment at the firm should not occasion conceit. 'It was,' Belva was told, 'only because of the critical need for legal staff brought on by the War that the Firm had been reduced to the expedient of hiring a female lawyer.'[18] She was explicitly warned that, while her appointment was a permanent one, she should not expect the same remuneration or advancement opportunities accorded her male counterparts. Harold Walker was the partner delegated to warn her that, 'no matter how hard you worked, there was a ceiling to the amount of salary you could get, and if my memory is correct it was a pretty low ceiling.'[19] She was also warned that she would have to 'fit into the scheme of things,' when the lawyers who were on military or government service returned after the war.

Belva Gibson did not always fit easily into the scheme of things at Blakes. One of the tedious and time-consuming tasks assigned to junior lawyers was to keep the firm's dockets and time-entry system up to date.

Belva was assigned more of this work than she liked and frequently complained: 'If I spend my time on such uninteresting work I simply will not have time to attend to the more urgent and important matters that are assigned to me.'[20] Failure to keep the dockets up to date, however, resulted in condescending memos from the senior partners. On one such occasion a senior partner, after dictating a stiff note to Gibson,[21] complained to a colleague, 'I am getting fed up with the junior people in this office making their entries in the way that they save their time and impose obligations on me or on you.'[22]

Belva Gibson was never reconciled to some of the more tedious work in the firm, but she did her more important work, mainly in the conveyancing department, well enough that she easily broke the glass ceiling she had been warned about in 1942, and in 1952 she had the added distinction of becoming the first woman to be admitted to a partnership in the firm. Her initial salary in 1942 was $1,800. A decade later, just prior to her admission to partnership, it was $5,400.[23]

Gender was not the only presumed qualification for work at Blakes. As late as the 1950s, when the firm wanted to hire additional staff, a junior partner inquired about the firm's attitude with respect to the hiring of a Jewish lawyer. The matter had never come up before, but after R.C.H. Cassels made discreet inquiries at the Toronto Club, he returned with the report that 'it would be the end of the Blake firm.'[24] Apparently the patrons of the Toronto Club had absorbed their war news very selectively.

The Second World War marked a turning-point in the history of the firm. No sons of active partners were brought into the firm after 1942. A strict anti-nepotism policy came into force in the early 1970s, when the partners passed a resolution forbidding the hiring of a lawyer related by blood to an existing associate or partner. Those forming liaisons while both are with the firm can, however, remain. The anti-nepotism policy has opened the partnership to some qualified lawyers previously excluded, but it has also prevented the firm from hiring some excellent offspring, both male and female. Blakes, once regarded as a family firm, has changed. This essay deals with the period during which it was a family firm.[25]

THE FOUNDERS AND EARLY BUILDERS

The history of Blakes really begins long before 1858, when Edward Blake and Samuel Blake joined in the practice of law. Many nineteenth- and early-twentieth-century law firms were established by younger members of families which controlled large corporations. Those law firms sometimes began as little more than another branch of the family business. By contrast, the Blake brothers were not members of families who had prospered in business. The primary loyalties of the Blakes were to the law and the legal profession. They were the sons of Upper Canada's most influential and respected law reformer and jurist, and the work of the father had a profound influence on the sons, and on the way they practised law and structured their law firm.

Edward and Samuel Hume Blake's father, William Hume Blake, was a member of the Irish gentry who had studied medicine and theology at Trinity College, Dublin, before emigrating to Canada in 1832. He turned briefly to farming near present-day London, Ontario, before taking up the study of law in Toronto a year after the birth of his first son, Dominick Edward (Edward) Blake. After completing the required 'term-keeping duties' and legal apprenticeship,[26] William Hume Blake established a successful law practice[27] which served many of the propertied élites of Toronto.[28]

In 1843, while retaining his busy legal practice, William Hume Blake also accepted an appointment as the first professor of law at King's College in the University of Toronto. The professorship afforded 'an opportunity for the successful and busy practitioner to develop as a legal theorist.'[29] He became particularly interested in problems encountered when English jurisprudence was adapted and applied in colonial circumstances.

Politics provided a unique opportunity for William Hume Blake first to examine in depth, and then to restructure and reform, the laws and courts of Canada West. He had articled with a Reform lawyer and was impressed by Reform demands that English law, as applied by the Family Compact, be modified to meet Canadian needs. There were particular problems with the attempted replication of English Courts of Chancery.

Courts of Chancery had been created in England to provide for a Royal prerogative which could mitigate problems and injustices if the precedent and case-bound common law, relying mainly on monetary compensation, was strictly applied in cases involving accidents; mistakes; fraud; the protection of minors, lunatics, and idiots; and the accountability of trustees and executors. In such cases appeals to the monarch, dealt with by his chancellor as the Keeper of the Great Seal, were possible. The chancellor, sometimes called 'the King's conscience,' had greater discretionary powers than those available to judges in the common-law courts to determine equity cases on their merits rather than according to the strict rules of precedent applicable under common-law procedures.

In Upper Canada no parallel Court of Chancery had been created in the 1790s, it being assumed that the lieutenant-governor, as Keeper of the Great Seal of the Province, would also serve as chancellor. Most of the early lieutenant-governors were, however, military men not qualified to administer equity laws, so a separate Court of Chancery was established in Upper Canada in 1837. Its main functions were to be discharged by a vice-chancellor rather than by the lieutenant-governor, but the first appointed vice-chancellor, Robert Sympson Jameson, was an exceedingly cautious and unimaginative jurist. As a result, there were serious delays, some cases allegedly running up to twenty years before a decision was rendered. In the years 1841 to 1844, for example, the court heard 463 suits but settled only 155.[30] Such delay and inefficiency resulted in high legal and court costs, making the administration of equity law cumbersome and expensive.[31] The Reformers demanded a judicial system which retained the best features of English equity law but which was also 'simple, cheap, and accessible to the poorest in the land.'[32]

William Hume Blake, the first law professor in Canada West, served from 1843 to 1845 as the principal member of a commission investigating the operations of the Court of Chancery. Little came immediately of his commission reports, but in 1848 the Baldwin–Lafontaine Reform ministry came to power. William Hume Blake was elected to the Legislative Assembly, and named Solicitor General West. He thus had an opportunity to implement the reforms advocated by the commission he had chaired. The result was passage of the Judicature Acts of 1849, which reformed rather than replaced the Court of Chancery. That legislation reportedly 'laid the groundwork for an indigenous Anglo-Canadian jurisprudence. After 1849, the residents of Canada West enjoyed a fuller judicial system better able to meet their needs, including appeals, and, to do so more cheaply.'[33]

An immediate result of the reforms initiated under the 1849 Judicature Acts was the restructuring of the Court of Chancery and the removal of the unpopular vice-chancellor. There was, however, considerable controversy when William Hume Blake, the politician who had masterminded these reforms, was named to the newly established post of chancellor. He was, however, the foremost legal theoretician in the province, and thus well qualified for the post. A legal historian has summed up Blake's legal reforms thus:

Firmly in the spirit of nineteenth-century liberalism, he advocated an extended popular influence in government, yet never strayed from a devout adherence to constitutional, evolutionary, and orderly development. He was no sympathizer with the techniques of the radical school of reform ... Perhaps in the final analysis Upper Canada's response to its legal dilemmas reflected a lesser need to chart a separate identity and the wisdom to maintain the essentials of a time-proven familiar tradition of jurisprudence rather than a mere aping of the English judicial and legal scheme.[34]

William Hume Blake passed on to his sons an exceptional understanding of the Canadian legal system, particularly of equity law, which was more complex and difficult than the precedent and case-bound common law. That understanding, combined with the diligence with which they prepared their cases, and the eloquence and effectiveness, particularly of Edward Blake, in court, contributed to the firm's reputation for excellence and success.

Edward Blake, like his father, was a complex individual. As a lawyer he naturally defended a great many cases in which neither the issues nor the arguments were always the same. Thus, while he accepted the need for fairly strong government involvement in the economy, he appeared several times in support of Ontario provincial-rights cases which significantly weakened the federal government's ability to take effective economic initiatives. As a politician he believed government should participate in the economy to overcome Canada's geographic problems, but made some of his most impassioned political speeches denouncing the federal government's construction contract with the Canadian Pacific Railway syndicate. Later, however, he served as a solicitor for the CPR when it alleged that the federal government had not met all its obligations under that contract, and as an adjudicator in the bitter disputes about the Onderdonk contracts in British Columbia. It was Edward Blake's lot to serve as leader of the opposition in Parliament and to appear in court on behalf of clients who challenged existing laws and policies. As a result, he seemed to many of his contemporaries, and to his biographer, as 'the man of the other way.' But he was also a person of unusually high principles, and readily accepted political and professional losses to defend cherished ideals. During his long career as an Irish Nationalist member of the British Parliament, he developed a British federalist vision based on his Canadian political experiences.

Edward and Samuel Blake shared the mid-nineteenth-century values which their father had sought to incorporate into Canadian jurisprudence. They were both conservative and reformist: conservative in their high regard for the rule of law in an ordered and civilized society and acceptance of a strong role by governments in the maintenance of peace, order and good government; but reformist in their acceptance of a strong role for private initiative in economic affairs, insistence that the courts be made more accessible to all members of society, and impatience with aristocratic property owners who did not put that property to its best productive use. A legal historian has described those mid-nineteenth-century Canadian legal values thus:

These values were products of English liberalism, qualified by legacies from the Loyalists and the English Tories, and by Canadian geography. They were pragmatic and usually expressed in action and debate about particular issues, rather than extensive statements, but they were strongly held, uniform and consistent. Individual initiative and responsibility were respected and encouraged as moral obligations and as the most efficient foundation of the economy. Material progress was desired and seemed to be continuously available, but it was to be pursued with restraint and not turbulently or aggressively. The government should participate in the economy, to overcome the limitations imposed by a sparse population and the harsh geography.[35]

For the Blakes, individual initiative entailed much hard work and an intense dedication to excellence. Their careers were marked by frequent physical and emotional health problems resulting from overwork, which ultimately limited their success. They had great confidence in their own abilities, and were willing to break with lifelong friends and political associates who disagreed with them on important questions. That streak of independence, coupled with an ethic of hard work and a stern dedication to excellence, often made them seem 'conceited, stern, gruff, rude and unfriendly.'[36] They were men of outstanding ability who tried to reconcile reform ideals and economic liberalism with essentially conservative and Loyalist legal values.

Edward Blake devoted much of his life to politics, where his great ability and high principles resulted in great frustration and disappointment when he failed to gain and hold effective political power. By contrast, the law firm he founded, but from which he gradually withdrew, was a great success. He was described by his political successor, Sir Wilfrid Laurier, as 'the greatest intellectual figure in the history of the nation,' but other writers have called him 'the most tragic figure in Canadian political history.'[37]

Edward Blake left much of the routine work, and particularly the management of the office, to his brother Samuel, who also established a reputation as an excellent lawyer. Samuel seemed quite willing 'to play second fiddle to his illustrious brother,'[38] but in time he came to be regarded as one of Toronto's best legal authorities dealing with property matters and with equity law. When he left the firm in 1872 to accept an appointment as vice-chancellor of the Court of Chancery, his older brother feared the firm would be ruined. And there were some difficult years before the younger Blake returned in 1881 to take over the management of the firm. In assessing Samuel Blake's role in the firm, one former partner said, 'It was Edward who made the headlines but it was Samuel who stayed home and minded the shop.'[39]

Edward and Samuel Blake's involvement with the Ontario Court of Chancery was bizarre. William Hume Blake had, as already indicated, led the drive to reform that court, and became its chancellor. In 1868, Prime Minister John A. Macdonald offered the chancellorship to Edward Blake, apparently with the hope that he would thus remove a dangerous rival from the political stage.[40] Edward Blake declined the appointment, but in 1870 John Alexander Boyd, who had just accepted a partnership in the Blake firm, was appointed Master in Ordinary of the Court of Chancery. Boyd's services were thus lost to the firm, and Edward Blake suspected that the prime minister was trying to destabilize work at the law firm. Two years later the prime minister was at it again, this time offering an appointment to the position of vice-chancellor to Samuel Blake. When the younger Blake accepted, Boyd resigned and returned to the practice of law with Blakes. Then, in 1881, the position of chancellor fell vacant, and the prime minister offered it to John Alexander Boyd. Samuel Blake, as vice-chancellor, had apparently expected the promotion. He regarded Boyd's appointment as a snub, which 'was acknowledged by the younger Blake brother in the usual Blake way.'[41] Samuel Blake resigned the vice-chancellorship and returned to the law firm, 'sore, indignant, irascible, and more than ever needed.'[42]

The younger Blake refused repeated invitations to run for political office. Instead, he devoted much of his time and energy to charitable causes. He was a devout 'low church' Anglican. Concern about 'the Romanizing and unprotestant tendencies and teachings of Trinity College' at the University of Toronto, resulted in the establishment of Wycliffe College, of which Samuel Blake was treasurer and a major financial supporter for many years. He was also an ardent prohibitionist, and some have called him the father of the Toronto Young Men's Christian Association. In his personal relations, he was a man who could resort to strong words. On numerous occasions he 'seems to have been carried away by his great eloquence and to have said or written things which hurt the recipients far beyond what was justified or even intended.'[43]

Neither Edward nor Samuel Blake had athletic interests or abilities, with one important exception. At the family summer home on Murray Bay, Quebec, they had learned sailing – a sport they continued to pursue with great enthusiasm and skill. Later, younger members of the family also became avid golfers. Two, in fact, died on golf courses.

In their law firm, Edward and Samuel Blake drew on the talents of a number of other lawyers. Some stayed for only short periods of time; others served the firm for many years, but the exceptionally high reputation of the firm rested on the work of its most outstanding and successful practitioners. In the first three decades, there were, in addition to the Blake brothers, two other lawyers who were widely regarded as the best in their respective fields. They significantly broadened the base and greatly enhanced the reputation of the firm.

The first of these was Walter Gibson Pringle Cassels. Born in Quebec City, he was educated in Quebec and at the University of Toronto, and began as a student-at-law with Blakes in 1866. In 1870 he became a partner, having developed an expertise in litigation. He attributed his rapid rise in the firm to his bad handwriting. While other students and juniors were kept busy writing out briefs and memoranda, Walter Cassels could pursue more important legal work because his handwriting was so bad no one could read it.[44] He also became one of the most knowledgeable and respected experts in legislation pertaining to patents, trademarks, and intellectual property. Canadian patent law had not kept up with technology and new inventions, particularly in the electrical, automotive, and communications industries. That produced an enormous volume of business for lawyers like Walter Cassels.

In 1908 Cassels was appointed a judge of the Exchequer Court of Canada. Today he is remembered mainly for the work he did in several exceptionally difficult railway arbitration cases. The best-known of these is the arbitration which set the value of the capital stock of the Grand Trunk Railway when it was nationalized after the First World War. With the firm, however, Cassels made his greatest contributions in patent and trademark cases.

The fourth key builder of the firm in its early history was Zebulon Aiton Lash, who joined as a partner in 1882. Lash had been born in Newfoundland, studied law in Toronto, practised briefly in that city, and then accepted an appointment with the federal Justice Department in Ottawa. He was the chief clerk there when Edward Blake became the federal minister of justice in 1875. Blake was so impressed with the abilities of the young lawyer that he made him his deputy minister. In that capacity Lash drafted innovative federal legislation, including provisions for the incorporation and regulation of commercial, financial, transportation, and resource companies. One of his most notable achievements was the drafting of a new section of the Bank Act pertaining to the security to be offered as collateral for bank loans. Known as section 88 of the Bank Act, it laid the foundation of Canadian banking security. That was no small achievement if one considers that the Canadian banking system came to be regarded as one of the most secure anywhere in the world. Lash was the government's most senior legal adviser at a time when the new nation was just setting the legislative framework for its national economic development. He, more than anyone else, drew up the rules for Canadian entrepreneurial development just at the time when Canada became industrialized. 'The entry of Mr. Lash as a member of the firm,' according to one partner, 'made a radical change in the nature of its practice. Previously it had been directed primarily toward Litigation, Real Estate, Wills and Trusts, but with the coming of Mr. Lash corporate law became an increasingly important element until Blakes probably became best known for its practice in the latter branch of law.'[45]

THE FIRST DECADE

Edward Blake achieved immediate success as a lawyer. His biographer reports that, in 1856–7, 'he handled some sixty cases ... and there were five hundred pounds in fees entered on his books. It was a startling sum for those days.'[46] Litigation, land and property conveyances, mortgages, inheritance and estate cases, foreclosures, bankruptcies, corporate reorganizations, and various promotional and investment ventures comprised the bulk of the practice. There always seemed to be more than enough work, and Edward Blake's correspondence is full of complaints about the burden of work awaiting his attention.

One early and highly unusual case brought Edward Blake considerable public and political notoriety in 1858. The case arose out of what Canadian historians have dubbed 'the double shuffle.' On 28 July 1858, the government led by John A. Macdonald and George-Étienne Cartier was defeated in the legislature, and a Reform administration led by George Brown and Antoine-Aimé Dorion took office. Electoral laws at the time required that newly appointed ministers seek confirmation in by-elections. With their appointment to the cabinet, the new Reform ministers ceased to be members of the legislature until re-elected. The Reform party thereby lost its majority and was defeated on a vote in the Assembly.[47] That brought Macdonald, Cartier, and the Tories back into power. They availed themselves of a provision for the waiving of by-elections in routine cabinet shuffles. The provision was never intended to apply to the kind of situation that had arisen in 1858, but Macdonald and Cartier used it to regain office and to avoid by-elections.

George Brown and the Reformers were furious and decided to take the matter to court. Edward Blake was a junior member of an impressive group of Reform lawyers who argued the case. The suit was lost, but George Brown's highly partisan *Globe* newspaper noted that Edward Blake had shown 'great oratorical powers, as well as sterling talent. This gentleman promises to take his father's place at the bar.'[48] The case was the first of many handled by the firm which involved government actions, policies, and disputes.

Careful preparation, an effective courtroom manner, and a keen sensitivity to the nuances of the law and the moods of judges and juries made Edward Blake an unusually effective and successful lawyer who soon had more work than he and his brother could do. In 1859–60 there was a brief association with Henry Cawthra about which almost nothing is known except that Cawthra did not remain long with the firm.[49] A more satisfactory expansion occurred in 1862, when James Kirkpatrick Kerr and Rupert Mears Wells became partners.[50] Wells remained with the firm only until 1872, after which he pursued a career in politics. Kerr, a former civil engineer, developed a particular competence in contract negotiation. In 1864 he married Ann Margaret, sister of Edward and Samuel Blake, but withdrew from the firm in 1885 to set up his own practice. There was speculation that Kerr, an ardent Freemason, withdrew because Edward Blake, who was then in federal politics, had sharply attacked secret societies.[51]

A decision by Edward Blake in 1867 to enter politics, and the withdrawal of Wells in 1870, made the recruitment of new partners necessary. John Alexander Boyd, J.W. Fletcher, and Walter Gibson Pringle Cassels became partners in 1870. Little is known about Fletcher, who left the firm in 1878 because of unexplained personal problems. Boyd's career, as already explained, was interrupted by his appointment as Master in Ordinary of the Court of Chancery. He returned to the firm in 1872, when Samuel Hume Blake was appointed vice-chancellor, but left again in 1881 to become chancellor of the Court of Chancery. The long and distinguished career of Walter Cassels has already been discussed.

The departure of John Alexander Boyd almost immediately after he joined the partnership in 1870 resulted in the addition of James Bethune, but Bethune left within a year. William Redford Mulock, a capable barrister but not one of the firm's great lawyers, became a partner in 1872 and left for Manitoba during the 1882 land boom occasioned by the construction of the Canadian Pacific Railway. C.J. Holman, another capable but not outstanding lawyer, was with the firm from 1876 to 1888. Hamilton and Richard Cassels, the younger brothers of Walter, joined the firm in 1877 and 1883, respectively, but left under less than happy circumstances in 1888.

A measure of the law firm's success during Edward Blake's first ten years of practice is provided by the fact that, when he entered politics in 1867, he had accumulated a fortune of at least $100,000. His annual income allegedly exceeded that of the combined salaries of the entire provincial cabinet.[52] He was the owner of an impressive new home built on the family farm four miles from the city limits, and of an attractive family summer home on Murray Bay. He was also the proud owner and happy captain of a fine yacht – the *Rivet* – which he sailed with great pleasure on Lake Ontario and along the St Lawrence and other Upper Canadian waterways. His legal practice had made him a wealthy man.

POLITICAL DISTRACTIONS

Politics had never been far removed from the Blakes. William Hume Blake, as already noted, had been an influential politician, and it was not long before political calls were also extended to the talented and eloquent sons. Edward responded to that call, which eventually took him to high political office. That route, however, reduced his legal practice and resulted in his effective departure from the firm in 1892, although the official severance did not take place until 1900. His brother Samuel spurned all political entreaties, but in 1872 accepted from the prime minister the judicial appointment which he held for nine years before returning to the practice of law and the management of the firm.

Edward Blake was not an active political participant in the discussions and negotiations leading to Canadian Confederation in 1867. He found the patronage, graft, corruption, and pettiness of politics in the legally united but politically divided Province of Canada distasteful. The political machinations of John A. Macdonald, including his actions in the notorious 'double shuffle,' and of railway promoters and other members of the rising new commercial class, provided particularly odious examples of political evil. Politics in the United Canadas, it seemed to Edward Blake, was not conducted in accordance with high principles.

Until 1867 Edward Blake was preoccupied with his successful and very profitable legal practice, in part because he believed no one should enter politics unless he was financially independent. Entry into public life should be based on a commitment to public service and to high principles, not on selfish motives of personal gain. By 1867 he had achieved the desired level of financial independence to enter politics on his own terms.

In the federal and Ontario provincial elections following Confederation, Edward Blake, after insistent and repeated invitations by Liberal or Reform leaders, agreed to contest the federal constituency of West Durham and the provincial constituency of South Bruce. He was successful in both, and served until 1872 in both the federal and provincial legislatures. His reputation as a courtroom lawyer and his effectiveness as a political speaker quickly marked him as one of the most promising younger members of the still seriously fragmented group of politicians opposed to the governments of Sir John A. Macdonald in Ottawa, and of John Sandfield Macdonald in Ontario.

In the 1860s the legislative sessions in Ottawa and Toronto were relatively short, and Edward Blake's political activities did not immediately require major changes in the legal partnership. Even when Edward Blake became premier of Ontario in 1871, while also serving as a federal member of Parliament, he remained an active partner in the law firm where he held a one-third interest in the assets and profits.[53] Politics nevertheless took up a substantial amount of time, and Blake complained in 1872 that his legal income had fallen to one-third of what it had been.[54]

In 1872 legislation was passed banning dual representation in provincial and federal legislatures, forcing Blake to choose between federal and provincial politics. He chose to remain in the federal arena and resigned the provincial premiership. When the federal Liberals, after a prolonged and bitter fight in which Blake had a leading role, finally defeated the Macdonald government in 1873, there was much talk that Blake would become prime minister. He declined, citing among other things the pressure of work at the law firm. He also refused in 1873 and in 1874 to accept a cabinet post in the Liberal government of Alexander Mackenzie, citing a heavy workload and failing health.

In 1875, after repeated and increasingly insistent requests, Edward Blake entered the cabinet as minister of justice. That made the negotiation of a new partnership agreement necessary. As minister of justice, Blake was the political master and exercised power over the appointment of federal judges, making it inappropriate for him to remain active in any aspect of the practice of law which included court appearances. In a new partnership agreement, dated January 1876, it was stated that Edward Blake would 'retire temporarily from the active practice of his profession,' and that it would not be his duty 'to take any part in the business during the term of the partnership hereby created.'[55] Edward Blake nevertheless retained a 70/350, or one-fifth share, in the assets and in the profits of the firm. That was reduced to 60/350 when the agreement was renegotiated in 1879.

On 27 April 1880, Edward Blake became leader of the Liberal Party of Canada, and Leader of Her Majesty's Loyal Opposition in Parliament. That development, and the appointment of a new chancellor of the Court of Chancery, which removed John Alexander Boyd from the Blake partnership and restored Samuel Hume Blake to the firm, necessitated a major restructuring of the partnership. In several separate agreements dated 16 May 1881,[56] it was agreed that Samuel Hume Blake would take over the shares in the assets and profits of the firm held by John Alexander Boyd and Edward Blake. There was to be a valuation of the assets. Boyd was to be paid $2,000 a year, and Edward Blake $2,500 a year, both in equal monthly payments, until their shares were paid in full. Thus, Edward Blake, the firm's founder, who had been largely inactive in the firm since 1875, ceased to be a participating partner in 1881.

An additional provision was added in a separate indenture, dated 24 March 1882. Zebulon Aiton Lash was admitted to the partnership – with a 77/490 share – and there was a provision under which the firm was to pay Edward Blake $2,500 per year.[57] It was, however, stipulated that none of the funds paid to Edward Blake should 'derive from or on account of business done for the Government of Canada or any of the Provinces of Canada and from or on account of business done before any Committee of the Senate or House of Commons of any of the Legislative Councils or Assemblies of any of the Provinces of Canada.' In addition, it was provided that 'if the said Edward Blake shall at any time during the said partnership choose to devote himself to the practice of his profession he shall be entitled (in addition to the sum of two thousand five hundred dollars) to receive payment to the amount of the work actually done by him not exceeding in any year the sum of two thousand five hundred dollars, it being understood that the total income is not to exceed in any year five thousand dollars.'

Edward Blake's high professional and legal standing was presumably worth $2,500 a year if he did no legal work for the firm, and he was to receive additional compensation if he did any such work. The careful provisions that the compensation should not come from government work was little more than window-dressing. Earnings by the partners were normally pooled, and profits distributed according to the number of shares each partner held. Now two pools would be created, but the net result remained the same. Edward Blake would receive $2,500 a year plus his own earnings, if any, up to a maximum of $5,000 a year, but it would be paid out of the pool which did not include earnings from government work.

This arrangement was modified in 1888 to allow Blake to retain for his own use all retainers, fees, and emoluments he himself earned, but with the firm making up any shortfall to ensure that he received a minimum of $5,000 per year. Those arrangements were altered in 1890, when it was provided that all earnings by Edward Blake were to go to the partnership but that he would be paid an annual sum of $10,000. They were again changed in 1893 after Edward Blake's election as an Irish Nationalist member of Parliament in London, England. The new arrangement provided for a payment of $6,000 in 1893, after which he was to be paid simply what he earned.

The uncertainties and frequent changes in the remuneration paid to Edward Blake were attributable to several considerations. Because his name and reputation alone were worth something to the partnership, it was agreed that he should receive appropriate compensation. The Blake name, of course, had particular value in government and political circles, but Edward Blake wanted no suggestion that he was personally benefiting from government work done by his firm. All the early partnership agreements had a clause which specified that 'none of the partners shall carry on any affair or business as Barrister, Attorney, Solicitor, or Conveyancer separately for their own private and separate advantage but such shall in all cases be carried on for the benefit and advantage of the said copartnership.' In Edward Blake's case it was becoming difficult to apply that clause. After his retirement as Liberal leader, he became increasingly involved in appeals to the Judicial Committee of the Privy Council in London in high-profile cases such as *St Catharines Milling and Lumber Company* v. *the Queen* (colloquially called the 'Indian Titles case'), the Jesuit Estates Act, and Manitoba school legislation. He also played a role in special and contentious political and diplomatic cases such as the dispute over the Alaska boundary. There were very substantial payments for such work, the Alaska boundary case alone holding the promise of a $25,000 fee. The partnership agreements required that such earnings go to the firm, but there was nothing ordinary or predictable about such fees, and it was difficult to arrive at an arrangement that was fair to all concerned.

Edward Blake's involvement in cases appealed to the Judicial Committee of the Privy Council was ironic. In 1875, as minister of justice, he apparently favoured abolition of such appeals. Later, perhaps reflecting his essentially conservative commitment to British legal traditions, he gained a high regard for the work of the Judicial Committee, which he once described thus:

a quiet little room in Downing Street, rather dingy, with no pretence about it, where [there were] sometimes six or seven, sometimes four or five gentlemen, without wigs, without gowns, dressed in morning apparel, not sitting under the names of judges but hearing the prosy arguments ... and dealing with questions arising under the laws of very nearly seventy distinct political communities, each flying the British flag ... in Europe, in Africa, in Asia, in America, in Australia, and including in their systems various laws, law from the ancient custom of France, the old customs of the Monarchy, the Civil Law, the Roman, Dutch law, the Brahminical laws, and the laws of the Mohomedans – all disposed of in this dingy room. I know no greater, no more practical, no more significant proof of the vitality of the British Empire.[58]

The law firm was usually only peripherally involved in the major Privy Council and other high-profile government cases involving Edward Blake. In a few instances other lawyers in the firm were drawn into the preparation of some of the briefs, and until 1892 the remuneration earned by Edward Blake for work of this kind came to the firm. He was then paid according to the provisions already outlined. He effectively ended his professional links with the Toronto law firm when elected, in 1892, as an Irish nationalist to the British House of Commons. The firm retained the name, but Edward Blake no longer worked for it or shared in its profits. He kept whatever he earned and maintained only a nominal relationship with the firm. That arrangement was formally ended in 1900. Politics thus distracted, and eventually removed, Edward Blake entirely from the affairs of his law firm .

FAMILY PROBLEMS

The Blakes were not easy people to get along with. They could get carried away by their own eloquence and sense of importance, and rifts within the families and within the partnership were frequent. The departure of James Kirkpatrick Kerr, brother-in-law of Edward and Samuel Blake, has already been noted. Even more serious difficulties arose when the Blakes brought their sons into the partnership. The first such arrangement occurred in 1885, when William Hume (Will) Blake, son of Samuel Hume Blake, was admitted to the partnership. Will, as he was called, had not yet passed his bar examinations, but the partnership agreements were drawn up for three-year periods and it was expected that he would soon complete his training. A special clause in the 1885 partnership agreement provided that 'William Hume Blake, son of the said the Honourable Samuel Hume Blake, shall upon his being enroled as a solicitor of the Supreme Court of Judicature for Ontario, be admitted into said co-partnership and be interested in and entitled to the assets and profits thereof.' He received 10 of the partnership's 500 shares when he was admitted on 19 November 1885.

Will Blake was a person of diverse interests and enthusiasms. He was a competent but not outstanding lawyer, and his progress in the partnership has been described as 'steady but not spectacular.'[59] He remained with the firm until 1909, when ill health resulted in his retirement, and is better remembered for some of his literary than for his legal accomplishments, including a translation into English of Louis Hémon's *Maria Chapdelaine*, published in 1921, and a book of short stories entitled *Brown Waters and Other Sketches*, which won a prize as the best Canadian book in English published in 1915. He found sailing, golf, and other outdoor activities much more satisfying than legal work and died, perhaps appropriately, while golfing in Vancouver.[60]

Will Blake was also an athlete and outdoor enthusiast who apparently did not inherit 'the vinegary disposition' of his father and grandfather. He made friends easily, and a number of the later partners in the firm joined, in part at least, because of friendships with Will. His admission to the partnership, and subsequent progress in it, were relatively uncontroversial.

Edmund William Hume (Hume) Blake, son of Edward Blake, joined the law firm in 1888, but the arrangements being made for him roused the ire of the other partners. Richard Cassels, one of the junior partners, allegedly made an offhand but critical remark about the preferential treatment accorded the sons of the founders, which deeply offended the fathers. The spat resulted in the departure of Hamilton and Richard Cassels to form their own law firm.[61] It did not, however, prevent the making of similar arrangements for the other two sons of Edward Blake, who became partners in the firm in 1891 as soon as they were admitted to the bar. By that time, however, Edward Blake had largely withdrawn from the ongoing activities of the firm and it was left to Samuel Hume Blake to deal with the problems.

The manner in which Samuel Hume Blake did so created more tension. None of Edward Blake's sons considered the firm their father had founded a happy place to work. The eldest, Hume Blake, reportedly 'had little joy in his employment.'[62] Like other members of the family, he suffered periodically from ill emotional and physical health. Those problems forced him, in 1891, to withdraw from most active work in the firm. However, he retained responsibility for the account of his wealthy father-in-law, Alexander Manning. It was agreed that he should keep whatever was earned on that account, but a year later others in the firm complained that Hume Blake had done nothing and should therefore receive no allowance.[63] They agreed, in 1892, to allow him to keep his office accommodation, but that he would not be required to do any work. If, at some time in the future, he wished to return to active work, the partners agreed to give him 'some suitable professional work,' for which he would receive 'such allowance as may be deemed reasonable.'[64] He never returned,[65] working instead on the legal and financial affairs of his wife's family, particularly after his father-in-law's death.

Edward Blake's younger sons, Edward Francis (Ned) and Samuel Verschoyle (Sammy), became partners in the firm in 1891. In letters to his father, Ned complained about difficulties he was having with his uncle. Samuel Hume Blake, according to Ned, assigned him only junior work and did not give him an adequate allocation in the assets and profits of the firm. But when Ned complained, his uncle

entered at some length into his ideas as to your (Edward Blake's) relation to the firm in a manner which I think was intended to remove from my mind any lingering impression that I was to be treated in any manner differently from the other juniors. He said that you and he were radically opposed on the correct basis of division of profits, that you thought you should get something for your name, that neither he nor Mr Lash had ever drawn what they earned, that you were getting a great deal in receiving your fees net without anything in the way of a tax on income office rent & expenses ... He asked how would Mackenzie, Anglin and Law feel if I were treated in a special way? ... He then went on to say he had given much consideration to my position in the firm; that he did not think I would 'feel at home' in counsel work at any rate for several years (which is quite true since I have not had any).[66]

In the firm his father had founded, Ned seemed 'somehow lost in the shuffle, consigned to the junior work and a junior's share in the profits.'[67] He did not earn enough to become financially independent, but supplemented his professional income by managing his father's business affairs in Canada during the latter's frequent and prolonged absences in England and Ireland. He died of leukaemia at the age of thirty-nine.

Sammy's experiences in the firm were even less satisfactory. He also became a junior partner in 1891 but quickly developed such a distaste for the work assigned him that 'it is all and perhaps more than I am equal to keep from shirking.'[68] He accompanied his father on a trip to New Zealand in 1895 and shortly thereafter withdrew from the Toronto law firm and moved to London, where, somewhat sporadically, he helped his father with Privy Council cases. He died in England at the age of fifty-five while playing golf.

The relations of Alexander Mackenzie, son-in-law of Samuel Hume Blake, with other partners of the firm were more amicable. Mackenzie, who had joined the firm long before he married into the Blake family, spent much of his legal career in South America looking after various electrical and traction companies promoted by Canadian entrepreneurs who were clients of the firm. He rose to the position of president of the Brazilian Traction, Light and Power Company and was closely associated in his business and legal activities with members of the Lash family.

In 1902 the firm had to make special arrangements to retain the services of Zebulon A. Lash who, as already indicated, was legal counsel to some of the country's most ambitious businessmen. He was particularly close to the Canadian Bank of Commerce, the National Trust, and the many Canadian and overseas business ventures of William Mackenzie and Donald Mann, the best-known of which was the Canadian Northern Railway. Mackenzie and Mann, however, were often short of money, preferring to pay for Lash's legal services by issuing shares in one or another of their companies. Lash thus became a shareholder, director, and officer of many of their companies. He also became the major shareholder, on his own, in several moribund companies which he tried to reorganize. All of this made it difficult to enforce the provision of the partnership under which no partner was allowed 'to carry on any affair or business as barrister, attorney, solicitor or conveyancer separately for their own private and separate advantage.' The result was that, in the 1902 partnership agreement, a number of Lash's accounts with Mackenzie and Mann companies were not included.[69] It was understood that he would continue working on these accounts for his own remuneration, and his shares in the partnership were reduced. In 1905 he ceased to participate in the shares and profits of the firm, but was allowed to retain his office.[70] He agreed to 'give as much of his time and attention for purposes of consultation with and advising other members of the firm as he reasonably can,' and to continue the firm's work on the Canadian Bank of Commerce account. It was further agreed that he would receive $333.33 monthly from the firm, decline any work in which the partnership represented an opposite interest, and turn over any work he could not personally handle to the partnership.[71] Lash thus remained a member of the firm, while also becoming active in a large and profitable private legal practice.

Z.A. Lash's son, William Miller Lash, articled with the firm and was called to the bar in 1897, at which time he, on terms similar to those offered the Blake sons, also became a partner in the firm. He took a particular interest in the Latin American business accounts and became a close friend and associate of Alexander Mackenzie, eventually succeeding him as president of Brazilian Traction. Like his father, Miller Lash was elected a director and later served as vice-president of the Canadian Bank of Commerce, having by that time given up his office in the law firm for one with the Brazilian company. His legal work was more closely related to the interests of his father and of Alexander Mackenzie than to the ongoing and often tedious work at the office which the sons of Edward Blake found so frustrating. Miller Lash died in 1941, just before the departure of his brother Jack and Jack's two sons from the Blake law firm.

Z.A. Lash's second son, John Francis (Jack), was admitted to the partnership in 1909, immediately after he was enrolled as a solicitor and called to the bar. Like his father and his older brother, he was interested in corporate law. He had a distinguished military career during the First World War, and in the Canadian Expeditionary Force sent to guard the Trans-Siberian Railway after the Russian revolution. Jack, like his father and brother, was active in corporate law. He was apparently well liked by the junior partners and associates, but his relations with some of the senior partners, particularly Glyn Osler, were sometimes strained.[72] Tensions arising when Jack Lash tried to bring his two sons into the Blake partnership contributed to the departure of all the Lashes in 1942.

The experience of the sons of Walter Cassels when they joined the law firm was more pleasant than that of the Blake sons or of Jack Lash and his sons. The circumstances under which Walter's two younger brothers had left the firm strengthened his resolve that his own sons, when they entered the partnership, would be treated like any other junior partner. Thus, when Walter's oldest son, Robert Cecil Hamilton Cassels, became a partner in 1900, he spent several years doing general legal work before moving to the area of special interest to both him and his father – trademarks and patents. Perhaps his own financial situation as a junior later made Robert Cassels more sympathetic to the financial needs of the junior partners, even suggesting on one occasion that the senior partners should cut their own shares to correct the situation.[73] Robert Cassels's son J. Graham joined the firm in 1930 and became a partner in 1933 but was assigned mainly junior litigation work, which he found tedious. He enlisted for active military service in 1939 and left the partnership after the war to establish and run an insurance agency.

Walter Cassels's second son, George Hamilton, became a partner immediately after his admission to the bar in 1905. He married Vivian Kerr, the daughter of J.K. Kerr, who was a brother-in-law to Edward and Samuel Blake, but in his work at the law firm he worked more closely with Miller Lash in corporate law. In the folklore of the firm, he began a practice later followed by other young and ambitious partners. He took his holidays in the fall, remaining at the office during the summer months, when the senior partners took their holidays. He was thus available to take on varied and interesting work that would normally be handled by the senior partners, and so build up his own client list.

None of the sons and grandsons of the four key founders and builders of the Blake law firm achieved the high standing of their fathers or grandfathers in the legal community. With the exception of Edward Blake's sons, they devoted major portions of their professional lives to the firm, and became competent and highly respected practitioners. Several, most notably the two sons of Z.A. Lash and Robert Cassels, became involved in the same type of legal work as their fathers. It was, however, also necessary for the firm to recruit others to safeguard its reputation as having the best legal talent anywhere in Canada in its chosen fields.

RECRUITING EXCELLENCE

One of the remarkable talents of Edward and Samuel Blake was that they could recognize exceptionally talented young lawyers and bring them into the law firm. Their most notable successes, of course, were the recruitment of Walter Cassels and Zebulon A. Lash. That ability to identify and recruit continued even after the original founders left the firm.

Students-at-law serving their articles at Blakes were the main talent pool from which prospective partners were drawn. That pool, however, was itself very selective. Allan Graydon, who became a student-at-law with Blakes in 1921 and later the senior partner in the firm, described what he called 'the Great Compromise' the firm struck with students-at-law: 'R.C.H. [Cassels] told me that if we were in England I would be required to pay Blakes a fee of 100 guineas a year for the privilege of studying law in their office. He explained the firm's practice was to waive the fee but, on the other hand, not to pay any remuneration to students.'[74] Graydon said that, while he possessed no material assets at the time, he gladly accepted, 'as I regarded the opportunities for the future afforded by being with Blakes as far more valuable than any monetary remuneration.'[75] So he worked for three years without pay. Only exceptionally dedicated young lawyers, or those with rich and influential fathers, could afford such schooling, excellent though it might be.

Those who overcame this initial hurdle had another to clear when invited to become a partner. Graydon described his experiences in that regard thus:

When one was admitted as a partner, he had to pay to the existing partners a sum determined, not only by the book value of the physical assets (such as furniture, library etc.) and of the accounts rendered and receivable, but also by the estimated value of work performed for clients but not rendered – sometimes called 'Work in Progress.' The aggregate sum normally amounted to one's projected income as a partner during one and one-half years, or as one would say in England, one and a half year's 'purchase.' Since one's projected income as a partner rarely exceeded by many dollars the remuneration he was then receiving as an employee, it was difficult to find the required sum without recourse to a father. Certainly when I was admitted as a partner in 1933, in the depths of the 1929 depression, I encountered great obstacles in finding the money within the required time. What few remaining stocks I still owned had to be sold at the bottom of the market (International Nickel for example at what would be the equivalent today of $1.00 per share) and I had to borrow on all my life insurance policies.

One of the present partners elected to have all his income as a partner applied to satisfy the amount payable by him with the result that he had difficulty in buying any bread for himself and his family after the lapse of twelve months.[76]

Invitations to join the firm, and allocations of partnership shares, were often quite informal and idiosyncratic. Many aspiring young lawyers desperately coveted such an invitation, but were never asked. A significant number who did receive such an invitation found the work as juniors too tedious, the remuneration uncompetitive, and the cost of partnership too onerous. The employment and partnership recruitment practices of the firm were obviously highly selective, effectively keeping individuals of undesirable social or economic status at bay, while making entry relatively easy for individuals with the right connections and resources.

The easy entry of Harold C. Walker, son of the president of the Canadian Bank of Commerce, particularly when compared with Allan Graydon's difficulties, is illustrative of the selection process at work at Blakes. Walker, like so many other Blake partners, was an Upper Canada College alumnus. He studied political science at the University of Toronto, but later said, 'my interest in my present wife and in horses took me out of the honours class and into pass arts.' He had completed three years of the four-year course when the First World War broke out, but his father had already made arrangements that he should study law at Cambridge after completing his program at the University of Toronto, and then to do his articles with Miller Lash, director, and later vice-president, of the Canadian Bank of Commerce. Harold Walker never met Miller Lash before enlisting for active military service. Overseas he was assigned to the Canadian School of Gunnery, where 'in spite of the fact that I had absolutely no legal training whatsoever, I took on the job of teaching military law.'[77] Ill health led to his return to Canada in 1917, where he 'got into semi-legal work by joining the Assistant Judge Advocate General in Toronto.' One of the task assigned was to try conscientious objectors by court martial. While Walker was involved, the conscientious objectors were invariably sentenced to death, but the sentence was then commuted in Ottawa. Walker later recalled that 'when I found the routine I made out the papers in advance so that we could speed up the trials enormously. In a good afternoon's work we could sentence six or eight or even a dozen men to death.'[78]

After the war, Walker turned to the study of law and discovered that, 'thanks to the enthusiasm for veterans those days,' he could get one year of credit at the University of Toronto for his war service. With the three years he already had, that was enough for the BA degree. In addition, because he had shown an intention of entering law school, and an arrangement had been made for him to article with Miller Lash, he was given credit for a full year of study at Osgoode Hall.

After the armistice in November 1918, Walker bought a set of notes of the lectures given at Osgoode Hall since the opening of 1918 term and wrote the Christmas exams. He later recalled that 'I had attended no lectures and I don't think read any texts. I am sure I worked on some examination papers. I got through all right.'[79] He completed that year, and then prevailed on Osgoode Hall teachers to offer special classes during the summer which would cover the material for the final year. Once Walker and several of his friends completed those summer classes, they wrote their final law examinations. He later boasted that 'I believe I hold the somewhat unique distinction of being the only student who ever went through Osgoode Hall in 11 months of continuous attendance.' He began work at Blakes in October 1919, remaining with the firm until his death in 1969. He became a partner on the same day as Allan Graydon, 1 June 1933, but, thanks to his father's help, faced few of Graydon's financial problems. These cases, both somewhat extreme, demonstrate that recruitment procedures at Blakes valued both the extraordinary determination of an Allan Graydon and the parental and family influence and prestige enjoyed by Harold Walker.

It is difficult to separate the few truly exceptional lawyers from the firm's many very good and highly respected ones. The partners themselves, however, provided some guidance in that regard when selecting which of them should have their names included in the official name of the firm at various times. In the early days there were a number of changes in the name of the firm, which at various times included lawyers who either remained for only a short time or had legal careers that were not particularly distinguished.[80] Blake, Lash, and Cassels were a part of the firm's official name for many years, but after 1888 the names of only three truly distinguished lawyers who were not founders or early builders were added to or included in the firm's official name.

The first of these was Arthur W. Anglin. He was the son of Timothy Warren Anglin, of Saint John, New Brunswick, a newspaperman and politician. Arthur Anglin studied law at Osgoode Hall, was an articled student at Blakes, and then worked as a salaried lawyer with the firm before becoming a partner in 1897. Admission to partnership reportedly resulted in a drop in his annual income from $1,000 to $700, but he soon gained a reputation as being 'one of the greatest' lawyers in the Blake firm.[81] He was well known for the meticulous care with which he prepared his cases, allegedly never going into court 'unless he felt sure he knew all there was to be known about a case.'[82] His special fields of expertise were banking, and trademark and patent law. He gained a particular reputation for his dry wit in court. Thus, on one occasion, when Anglin was explaining a complicated point, the judge became impatient and said, 'Everything you have said has gone in one ear and out the other.' Anglin responded, 'I'm sorry, My Lord, but I know of nothing to stop it.'[83]

Anglin, like the Blakes, Lashes, and Casselses, brought two of his sons into the firm, in 1923 and 1937, respectively, but neither son found the work entirely satisfactory. Both enlisted for military service in the Second World War and left the partnership shortly after the war.

Glyn Osler, a member of one of Canada's most distinguished families,[84] was the second partner whose name was added to the official designation of the firm after 1888. Unlike most of those who eventually became partners, Glyn Osler was not a student-at-law who articled at Blakes. Nor did he join the firm as a junior partner. He served his articles in the firm in which his uncle Fetherston Britton Osler was a prominent partner. When he graduated and was called to the bar, he sought a position as a solicitor with his uncle's firm, but was allegedly told there was no immediate opening available.[85] He consequently established his own practice, in Ottawa in 1898. Ten years later, he joined Blakes as a 'middle partner,' replacing Walter Cassels, who had done much of the firm's work in Ottawa, but who had accepted an appointment to the Exchequer Court of Canada. According to a colleague, Glyn Osler was 'an all-rounder,' best known for his work in commercial and company law, where he was for years overshadowed by Z.A. and Miller Lash. He allegedly became 'the dominating personality in the firm' after Miller Lash's retirement.[86] He was very much involved in several of the major corporate mergers of the late 1920s, and in the subsequent forced reorganizations in the 1930s. One of the best-known of these was a long-drawn-out battle on behalf of a Bondholders' Committee of the Abitibi Power and Paper Company. In that, and in other cases, Glyn Osler came to rely increasingly on the younger Allan Graydon, who was rapidly rising to a position of pre-eminence in the firm in the 1930s.

Two of Glyn Osler's sons became partners in the Blake firm. Britton Bath Osler served from 1929 until his retirement in the 1980s, while Peter Scarth Osler was with the firm from 1940 until 1988. Both had distinguished legal careers, and Britton Bath Osler eventually occupied a place of eminence in the firm comparable to that of his father.

Allan Graydon was in many ways a transitional figure in the history of the firm. He did not come from a prominent family, and joined the firm as a student-at-law in 1921, following military service during the First World War in which his health was severely affected by a German gas attack. At Osgoode Hall he was a brilliant student in all subjects except real estate. He was, nevertheless, assigned to work in real estate at Blakes and became 'what many claim to be the keenest conveyancer in the history of the Firm.'[87] He assisted in, and gradually took over, much of the commercial and corporate work in which Glyn Osler and the Lashes were involved. In his 1973 obituary, the Abitibi bondholders case, which dragged on for fourteen years, and the equally contentious disputes involving the Barcelona Traction Company with the Spanish government, are mentioned as his best-known cases. In his 'Reminiscences,' Graydon noted that 'the Second World War with its onerous taxation, and the inflation that has taken place particularly in the last few years, have changed the position of lawyers to such an extent that, in my opinion, the "Golden Age" of law has come to an end.'[88] Allan Graydon practised law at Blakes on both sides of the divide of the Second World War. He brought no close relatives into the partnership, but left it his name, which eventually replaced that of Zebulon Lash when that builder's son and grandsons left the firm.

DEPARTURE OF THE LASHES

The salaries paid to junior associates, the terms on which young lawyers were admitted to partnership, the allocation of shares in the assets and profits of the firm, and how new partners paid for their shares in the assets and work in progress were thought, at least by the students and juniors, to be more onerous at Blakes than at most other Toronto law firms of the time. New partners were expected to make substantial payments, but the initial share in the profits of the firm, and hence the income of a junior partner, was often less than 10 per cent of that allocated to the most senior partner.[89] Blakes, as already indicated, reputedly had a few well-to-do senior partners and a number of not-too-well-paid junior partners and associates.

Salary and partnership negotiations could become particularly contentious when sons of the senior partners were involved. When the Blake sons first joined what was then a group of only eight or nine partners, they received approximately 1/50 of the shares, and thus 1/50 of the profits of the firm.[90] That was not sufficient to allow the sons of the founders and early builders to become financially independent while living in the style to which they were accustomed. There are numerous references in the correspondence of Ned Blake with his father to the financial support the sons received from their father, and Ned complained bitterly that he had hoped to become financially independent but that the share allocations and the price to be paid made that impossible[91] – this in spite of the fact that the younger brothers of Walter Cassels still thought the Blake sons were receiving preferential treatment.

There were more serious problems when the grandsons of Z.A. Lash sought entry into the firm. The two sons, Miller and Jack, had become partners on much the same terms as had the Blake sons, but when Ken Lash, son of Miller Lash, joined the firm, he did so as a paid solicitor rather than as a partner. He did not find work in the firm conducive to his interests, and died of tuberculosis at a relatively young age.[92] The sons of Jack Lash, whose mother was a granddaughter of the great Reform lawyer and politician Robert Baldwin, encountered more difficulties. Peter John Baldwin Lash was called to the bar in 1936, after which he was offered and accepted rather onerous conditions to become a junior partner.[93] The depressed economy affected the income of the firm, but its impact was felt most keenly by the associates and junior partners. The overall income of the firm dropped by approximately 15 per cent in the 1930s, but the amount of work done for major corporate clients, handled mainly by the senior partners, actually increased. It was the associates and junior partners who were hardest hit by the reductions in the firm's income in the 1930s, and Peter Lash had great difficulty making ends meet when he became a junior partner.

Peter's brother, Zebulon Robert Baldwin (Bob) Lash, worked briefly as a solicitor at Blakes before enlisting for overseas service in the Second World War.[94] Partners who enlisted retained their partnership shares, and hence their income, while in military service.[95] Bob Lash, however, was not a partner, so his income was not protected when he enlisted.

Jack Lash, the father, naturally wanted adequate provisions made for his sons, particularly since he had health problems and was nearing retirement.[96] The surviving records do not clearly document the precise nature of the resulting dispute. There had been previous clashes, particularly between Jack Lash and Glyn Osler. Osler had long been frustrated because he was overshadowed in the practice of corporate law by Miller Lash, until the latter's death in 1941. After Miller Lash's death, Osler was determined to assert his priority in that field, bringing him into serious conflict with Jack Lash and his sons.

Allan Graydon tells of a discussion he had with Glyn Osler when shares or points were discussed and Graydon had suggested that his (Graydon's) contributions to the firm were as valuable as those of Osler. Osler's response was simple and direct: 'Allan, you are *more* valuable, but I am older.'[97] Graydon also noted that, 'for reasons I never discovered, I could argue with him on a legal point at great length, while disagreement by certain others with his views damned them forever.'[98] By that standard, Jack Lash had been damned forever in Glyn Osler's eyes long before the break-up of 1942. Rivalry and disagreements between Osler, who brought two of his sons into the partnership, and Jack Lash, who also had two sons in the firm, thus had a long history. They came to a head over discussion about the terms and conditions under which Jack Lash's sons would work in the firm in 1942, and resulted in the departure of Jack Lash and his two sons from the partnership.[99] Jack Lash's brother-in-law, R.F.B. Barr, remained with the firm.

The departure was difficult, as the new 1942 Blake partnership agreement showed. That agreement differed in several important respects from the previous partnership agreements. There were new and more explicit provisions for the evaluation of assets, and for the disposition of client accounts. Special provisions were made that allowed the Lashes to retain space in the same building as the remaining Blake partners. The new partnership agreement also included a special provision securing to the surviving partners exclusive use of the Blake name, even though there were no longer any Blakes in the partnership.[100]

The departure of Jack Lash and his sons did not mark the end of attempts by senior partners to bring their sons into the partnership,[101] but the dynamics within the firm had changed. Rapid expansion and increased prosperity after the Second World War brought in new talent and new ideas. No sons or daughters of firm lawyers were hired after 1942. In the early 1970s, there were prospects that several sons of senior partners, and even the talented daughter of one, might be brought into the firm. The partners responded with a stern official anti-nepotism policy. That has made it impossible for Blakes, long regarded as a somewhat stuffy family firm, to hire some excellent lawyers who happened also to be sons or daughters of one of the partners or associates.

CONCLUSION

Five men stand out as founders and early builders of the Blake law firm. William Hume Blake did much to lay the groundwork for an indigenous Anglo-Canadian jurisprudence. Edward and Samuel Blake, Walter Cassels, and Zebulon Lash built a great indigenous Canadian law firm on that groundwork. Each of the four great lawyers in the firm's early history had a comprehensive knowledge of the law, and a particular field of specialization in which he was widely regarded as the best available anywhere in the country. Edward and Samuel Blake had an exceptionally strong grounding in equity law, and over the years Edward Blake also became the country's foremost constitutional lawyer. Walter Cassels was exceptionally knowledgeable about patent and trademark law, while

Zebulon Lash offered an unmatched knowledge and understanding of commercial, banking, and corporate law. These founders and builders, assisted by others of more modest abilities, and succeeded in time by their sons and grandsons, and by some exceptionally talented new partners, achieved and maintained a reputation as 'the leading law firm in Toronto, if not in Canada,' while also retaining, at least until 1942, the image of a 'closed corporation,' where entry and advancement were heavily influenced by élite relationships, and partnership arrangements which favoured the founders, the senior partners, and their sons and grandsons.

Appendix A: The Firm Names, 1856–Present

Edward Blake	1856–7
Edward and S.H. Blake	1858–9
Blake, Cawthra & Blake	1859–60
Blake and Blake	1860–2
Blake, Kerr & Boyd	1862–70
Blake, Kerr & Bethune	1870–2
Blake, Kerr & Boyd	1872–9
Blake, Kerr, Boyd & Cassels	1879–81
Blake, Kerr & Cassels	1881–2
Blake, Kerr, Lash & Cassels	1882–5
Blake, Lash, Cassels & Holman	1885–8
Blake, Lash & Cassels	1888–1909
Blake, Lash, Anglin & Cassels	1909–42
Blake, Anglin, Osler & Cassels	1942–53
Blake, Cassels & Graydon	1953–present

Appendix B: List and Dates of Membership of Partners, 1858–1942

Edward Blake	1858–1900
Samuel H. Blake	1858–72, 1881–1914
Henry Cawthra	1859–60
James K. Kerr	1862–85
Rupert M. Wells	1862–85
John A. Boyd	1870, 1872–81
John W. Fletcher	1870–8
Walter G.P. Cassels	1870–90
James Bethune	1870–2
William R. Muloch	1872–82
Charles Joseph Holman	1879–88
Hamilton Cassels	1879–88
Charles A. Brough	1879–84
Zebulon A. Lash	1881–1920

Kenneth Maclean	1882–5
Richard S. Cassels	1885–8
Alexander Mackenzie	1885–1902
Henry W. Mickle	1885–6
William H. (Will) Blake	1881–1914
William F. Creelman	1888–91
E.W. Hume Blake	1888–92
Edward F. (Ned) Blake	1891–1903
Samuel V. Blake	1892–5
Arthur W. Anglin	1897–1947
Thomas D. Law	1897–1913
W. Archibald H. Kerr	1897–1908
W. Miller Lash	1897–1933
Walter Gow	1900–45
Robert C.H. Cassels	1900–57
George H. Cassels	1905–44
E. Glyn Osler	1908–49
John F. Lash	1909–42
Matthew C. Cameron	1914–24
Samuel G. Crowell	1919–49
Gregory S. Hodgson	1924–32
Gordon R. Munnoch	1924–52
Harold C. Waler	1933–69
Allan R. Graydon	1933–67
Britton B. Osler	1933–
J. Graham Cassels	1933–45
Robert B.F. Barr	1936–74
Peter J.B. Lash	1939–42
James T. Gow	1942–70

Appendix C: Offices of Blakes, 1857–Present

Wellington Chambers, NW corner Melinda & Jordan sts	1857–8
Masonic Temple, West side of Toronto Street	1859–74
Millchamps Bldg, SE corner Adelaide & Victoria sts	1874–80
(Old) Dominion Bank Bldg, SW corner King & Yonge sts	1880–91
(Old) Cdn. Bk of Commerce, SW corner King & Jordan sts	1891–1925
(New) Dominion Bank Bldg, SW corner King & Yonge sts	1925–30
(New) Cdn Bk of Commerce, SW corner King & Jordan sts	1930–72
Commerce Court West, SE corner King & Bay sts	1972–present

NOTES

1 Biographical information on Edward Blake is drawn mainly from Joseph
  Schull, *Edward Blake: The Man of the Other Way (1833–1881)* (Toronto: Mac-

millan of Canada 1975) (hereinafter Schull, *Blake I*); and Joseph Schull, *Edward Blake: Leader and Exile, 1881–1912* (Toronto: Macmillan of Canada 1976) (hereinafter Schull, *Blake II*). Additional information, particularly related to the practices in the law firm, and biographies of the partners, is available in the Blake, Cassels, Graydon Archives (BCGA). These include a manuscript by Robert Brown entitled 'The House That Blake Built' (Toronto, 1978), and another by Allan Graydon, entitled 'Some Reminiscences of Blakes' ('Beauregard,' Paget, Bermuda, 1970)

2 BCGA, Box 34901, Articles of Partnership between Stephen M. Jarvis and Dominick Edward Blake, 27 August 1956. The firm was called 'Jarvis and Blake,' with Jarvis holding a two-thirds interest and Blake one-third.

3 *Canadian Law List, 1995* (Aurora, ON: Canada Law Book 1995), C-177–78 and D-522–53, lists 237 barristers and solicitors, and 18 'Counsel' working for Blake, Cassels, Graydon in Toronto.

4 Ibid., C-10, D-46, C-43, D-176

5 Brown, 'House,' 3

6 Graydon, 'Reminiscences,' 17

7 Brown, 'House,' 8

8 The nine partners in 1896 were Edward Blake (by then inactive), Samuel Hume Blake, William Hume (Will) Blake, Edmund William Hume (Hume) Blake, Edward Francis (Ned) Blake, Samuel Verschoyle (Sammy) Blake, Alexander Mackenzie, Walter G.P. Cassels, and Zebulon Aiton Lash.

9 The nine members of the two Blake families, and the years when they were members of the partnership, are: (1) Edward Blake, 1858–1900; (2) Samuel Hume Blake, 1858–72, 1881–1914; (3) J.K. Kerr (brother-in-law of Edward and Samuel Blake), 1862–85; (4) Alexander Mackenzie (son-in-law of Samuel Hume Blake), 1885–1902; (5) William Hume (Will) Blake (son of Samuel Hume Blake), 1882–1914; (6) Edmund William Hume (Hume) Blake (son of Edward Blake), 1888–92; (7) Edward Francis (Ned) Blake (son of Edward Blake), 1891–1903; (8) Samuel Verschoyle (Sammy) Blake (son of Edward Blake), 1892–5; and (9) T.D. Law (son-in-law of Samuel Hume Blake), 1887–1913. For dates when various partners practised as barristers and solicitors at Blakes, I have relied on Brown, 'House.' It should be noted that these dates indicate when an individual was a member of the partnership. They do not include any time during which the individual was a student-at-law.

The firm has a large picture gallery of all present and former partners in the firm. The dates given in that gallery, however, do not always agree with the dates given by Brown, who has done the most detailed and extensive biographical research on the careers of Blake partners. These dates also differ somewhat from those given in Graydon, 'Reminiscences.' Graydon give the dates when particular individuals practised as barristers and solicitors with Blakes, not necessarily as partners. A comparisons of the dates given by Brown and Graydon, and in the BCG portrait gallery, with the names given in various partnership agreements suggests that Brown's figures are the most reliable available.

10 The six members of the Cassels family, and the dates when they were members of the partnership are: (1) Walter Gibson Pringle Cassels, 1870–1908; (2) Hamilton Cassels (brother of Walter G.P. Cassels), 1879–88; (3) Richard Scougall Cassels (brother of Walter G.P. Cassels), 1885–8; (4) Robert Cecil Hamilton Cassels (son of Walter G.P. Cassels), 1900–57; (5) George Hamilton Cassels (son of Walter G.P. Cassels), 1905–44; and (6) John Graham Cassels (son of Robert C.H. Cassels), 1933–45.

11 Members of the Lash family, and the dates of their partnership in the firm, are: (1) Zebulon Aiton Lash, 1881–1920; (2) William Miller Lash (son of Zebulon Aiton Lash), 1897–1930; (3) John Francis Lash (son of Zebulon Aiton Lash), 1909–42; (4) Peter J.B. Lash (son of John Francis Lash), 1939–42; (5) Ken Lash (son of William Miller Lash) worked as a solicitor but did not become a partner in the firm; (6) Zebulon Robert Barr (Bobs) Lash (son of John Lash) worked as a solicitor but did not become a partner in the firm; and (7) Robert Baldwin Fordyce Barr (brother-in-law of John Francis Lash), 1936–74.

12 Graydon, 'Reminiscences,' 17

13 Information about the military service of various partners is drawn mainly from Brown, 'House.'

14 The two were G.R. Munnoch and Allan R. Graydon.

15 Graydon, 'Reminiscences,' 19

16 I am indebted to Mr John D. Brownlie, QC, who described the 1878 telephone arrangement in a letter to me dated 17 August 1995.

17 Graydon, 'Reminiscences,' 31 and 41–2, describes one such disagreement between Miller Lash and the other partners, pertaining to the use of municipal bonds to finance various undertakings, and of other disputes between Jack Lash and one or several of the other partners.

18 BCGA, Box 10223, file containing biographical information about Belva Gordon Gibson Hammell. Much of this information is drawn from the personal recollections of Harold C. Walker, one of Belva Gibson's colleagues at Blakes. Walker's recollections are also in BCGA, Box 10223. A biographical sketch of Belva Gibson is available in Brown, 'House,' 226–30.

19 BCGA, Box 10223, Belva Gordon Gibson file. Letter from Harold C. Walker to Belva Gibson, written at the time of Gibson's resignation from the firm following her marriage to mining magnate Jack Hammell in 1957.

20 Brown, 'House,' 229

21 BCGA, Box 10223, Belva Gordon Gibson file

22 Ibid.

23 Ibid.

24 Brown, 'House,' 52

25 Ibid., 51–2

26 Detailed information on the training and licensing of lawyers in Upper Canada/Canada West/Ontario in the nineteenth century is given in G. Blaine Baker, 'Legal Education in Upper Canada, 1785–1889,' in David H. Flaherty, ed., *Essays in the History of Canadian Law*, vol. 2 (Toronto: The Osgoode Society 1983), 49–142.

27 John David Blackwell, 'William Hume Blake and Judicial Reform in the United Province of Canada,' MA thesis, Queen's University, 1980, and John David Blackwell, 'William Hume Blake and the Judicature Acts of 1849: The Process of Legal Reform at Mid-Century in Upper Canada,' in David H. Flaherty, ed., *Essays in the History of Canadian Law*, vol. 1 (Toronto: The Osgoode Society 1981), 132–74.

28 BCGA, Box 34901, Articles of Partnership between William Hume Blake and Joseph Curran Morrison, 1 October 1839

29 Blackwell, 'William Hume Blake and the Judicature Acts of 1849,' 141

30 Ibid., 136

31 English equity proceedings were not much quicker or cheaper, until the reforms of the 1850s and 1860s, but the competence of those in charge of such proceedings was not questioned as critically in England as it was in Upper Canada, where there was a growing impatience with the influence of the unpopular 'Family Compact' in both judicial and governmental affairs.

32 Blackwell, 'William Hume Blake and the Judicature Acts of 1849,' 143

33 Blackwell, 'William Hume Blake and Judicial Reform,' 176–7

34 Blackwell, 'William Hume Blake and the Judicature Acts of 1849,' 165, 166. See also R.C.B. Risk, 'The Law and the Economy in Mid-Nineteenth-Century Ontario: A Perspective,' in Flaherty, ed., *Essays in the History of Canadian Law*, vol. 1, 88–131

35 Risk, 'The Law and the Economy,' 106

36 Brown, 'House,' 75. Brown makes specific reference to Samuel Hume Blake here, but it also applies to the other men in the family.

37 As quoted in ibid., 65

38 Ibid., 68

39 Ibid., 76–7

40 Schull, *Blake I*, 62–5

41 Schull, *Blake II*, 9

42 Ibid.

43 All the information and quotes in this paragraph are taken from Brown, 'House,' 67–78.

44 Ibid., 92
45 Graydon, 'Reminiscences,' 16
46 Schull, *Blake I*, 14
47 A good discussion of the 'double shuffle' is provided in J.M.S. Careless, *Brown of the Globe*, Vol. 1: *The Voice of Upper Canada, 1818–1859* (Toronto: The Macmillan Company of Canada Limited 1959), 276–80
48 As cited in Schull, *Blake I*, 14
49 Brown, 'House,' 79–81
50 BCGA, Box 34901, Articles of Partnership between Edward Blake, Samuel Hume Blake, Rupert Mears Wells, and James Kirkpatrick Kerr, 1 October 1862
51 Brown, 'House,' 83
52 Schull, *Blake I*, 34
53 BCGA, Box 34901, has copies of the various partnership agreements. Most agreements were for a three-year period, but interim changes became necessary if one of the partners left or a new one joined the practice.
54 Schull, *Blake I*, 97
55 BCGA, Box 34901, Partnership Agreement, January 1876
56 Ibid., Partnership Agreement, 16 May 1881, and Indenture, 16 May 1881, between Edward Blake and Samuel Hume Blake
57 This payment by the firm was separate from any payment made by Samuel Blake for his brother's shares in the assets and profits of the law firm.
58 As cited in Schull, *Blake II*, 227
59 Brown, 'House,' 132
60 Ibid., 132–4
61 Ibid., 141
62 Schull, *Blake II*, 205
63 BCGA, Box 34901, Correspondence with respect to remuneration of Hume Blake, 24 October 1891–12 October 1892
64 Ibid., Articles of Partnership, 15 December 1892
65 Brown, 'House,' 137
66 BCGA, Box 10223, Edward Francis Blake to Edward Blake, 16 April 1896
67 Schull, *Blake II*, 205
68 Ibid., 202
69 A list of the company accounts not included in the agreement with Lash is attached to BCGA, Box 34901, Partnership Agreement of 14 June 1902.
70 Ibid., Partnership Agreement, 1 June 1905
71 Full details of the arrangement with Z.A. Lash are given in ibid., Partnership Agreement, 21 April 1908.
72 More details on some of the tension between Jack Lash and Glyn Osler are given in Graydon, 'Reminiscences,' 41–2.
73 Brown, 'House,' 174

74 Graydon, 'Reminiscences,' 18

75 Ibid.

76 Ibid., 25

77 BCGA, Box 10223, Personal recollections of Harold C. Walker, youngest son of Sir Edmund Walker, in the Harold C. Walker file

78 Ibid.

79 Ibid.

80 See Appendix A for a listing of the names under which the firm operated at various times.

81 Brown, 'House,' 152

82 Ibid., 153

83 Ibid., 155

84 Anne Wilkinson, *Lions in the Way: A Discursive History of the Oslers* (Toronto: Macmillan of Canada 1956)

85 The firm was then called McCarthy, Osler, Hoskin & Creelman, but later became Osler, Hoskin.

86 Graydon, 'Reminiscences,' 33

87 Brown, 'House,' 207

88 Graydon, 'Reminiscences,' 53

89 In 1885, when Will Blake became a partner, he received 10 of the 500 shares in the assets and profits of the firm. His father, Samuel Blake, had 150 shares. When Miller Lash joined the firm, he received or purchased 10 of the 557½ shares. His father, Zebulon A. Lash, had 150, and Samuel Blake 190 shares.

90 The number of shares varied from one three-year agreement to the next, but junior partners usually received 10 shares when they first entered the partnership. Thus, Will Blake got 10/500 in 1885, Hume Blake 10/500 in 1888, Edward Francis Blake 10/470, Sammy Blake 10/520, Miller Lash 10/557½, Robert Cecil Hamilton Cassels 10/700, when each of these men first joined the partnership in the years before 1900. These figures are all taken from the various partnership agreements in the Blake Archives.

91 See particularly BCGA, Box 10223, Ned Blake to 'the Governor,' 16 April 1896.

92 Brown, 'House,' 166

93 Ibid., 231

94 *Canadian Law List, 1942* (Aurora, ON: Canadian Law List 1942).

95 BCGA, Box 34901, Blake, Anglin, Osler & Cassels, Articles of Partnership dated 1 December 1942. There is no explicit reference in the articles of partnership explaining how partners on active military service were to be remunerated, but they retained their share or interest in the assets and in the profits of the partnership.

96 Graydon, 'Reminiscences,' 41–2; Brown, 'House,' 183–6

97 Graydon, 'Reminiscences,' 36. Graydon does not provide the date on which this conversation took place, but in 1942, seven years before his death, Glyn Osler had 380 of the firm's 1,688 partnership shares, while Allan Graydon had only 113.

98 Ibid.

99 The official announcement appeared in the *Globe and Mail*, 23 November 1942, 26.

100 BCGA, Box 34901, Blake, Anglin, Osler & Cassels, Articles of Partnership dated 1 December 1942

101 Glyn Osler, for example, brought two of his sons into the firm before 1942. He retired in 1949, but the sons remained until their retirement in the 1980s.

7

The George F. Downes Firm in the Development of Edmonton and Its Region, 1903–1930

HENRY C. KLASSEN

A growing number of lawyers organized law firms in the Canadian West of the early twentieth century. These law practices, which ranged from solo businesses to two- or three-member partnerships, to more substantial establishments, became involved in the economic life of the region.

This essay examines the evolution of the George F. Downes law firm from its formation as a small business in Edmonton, Alberta, in 1903 through its development into a regional firm. After operating for almost three decades, mostly as a solo practice but sometimes as a two-member partnership, the firm ceased to exist in 1930. This study analyses the Downes firm's history as a business, but it explores as well the important roles the firm played in the development of Edmonton and its region. From the outset, the firm served clients in the local and regional economies. In the process Downes and his partners participated in the Edmonton area's growth as legal experts, business advisers, and civic leaders.

The Downes firm was one of the small law practices that served as a catalyst for economic expansion in new western settlements. Despite the importance of such small law firms, few have been studied. Historians have focused their energies mainly on attempting to comprehend the development of leading law businesses in large cities. Most recently, the work *Baker & Botts in the Development of Modern Houston* by Kenneth Lipartito and Joseph Pratt, has greatly enhanced our understanding of the growth of the large law firm.[1] Business records of small law practices are not readily available for immediate use. In many cases, there are gaps in the data. Even the information about the Downes firm is incomplete, for some of its files have been lost. Enough primary source materials on the Downes firm are available, however, to add to our comprehension of the nature of small law businesses at Edmonton in the early 1900s.

Downes chose to follow a path of small-firm development in Edmonton, of a small general practitioner who found it rewarding to take responsibility for a number of functions in the law business. In those days, lawyers in some small practices had their specialties, but there is no evidence in the papers of Downes's law firm that he specialized in any activity. Edmonton was capable of producing larger firms of national repute – for example, Woods, Sherry, Collisson, & Field; Short, Cross, MacLean & Macdonald; and Emery, Newell, Ford & Lindsay – but the small firm clearly predominated in the city.[2] Downes did not wish to pursue the aggressive and costly sort of growth that could lead to the emergence of a large law firm, for he was aware that such a strategy entailed the risk of becoming dependent on the money markets and losing control. Rather, Downes was determined to maintain personal control of the firm. Usually cautious, he sought to balance the desire to get ahead in the marketplace with the need for a stable and safe law practice. Stability, however, was often in doubt as he faced a harsh business climate and fierce competition. Lacking a specialty service for a niche market, Downes's law firm had a hard time coexisting with its larger counterparts, such as the firm of Short, Cross, McLean & Macdonald, in the early twentieth century. Still, through personal connections, he was able to attract clients in the city of Edmonton as well as in the surrounding countryside. Gradually, he developed an important country/city law practice. This kind of practice gave the Downes firm an edge over its competitors and allowed the business to break into the regional market and grow.

A COUNTRY/CITY LAW PRACTICE

The Downes law practice had its Edmonton beginning in mid-1903, when its predecessor, the firm of Mills & Downes, was formed in what was then the small town of Strathcona, on the south side of the North Saskatchewan River, a centre with close ties to agriculture in the outlying countryside.[3] Defined especially by its legal work in an intimate, small-town, rural environment, this business was a country practice.[4] There were new opportunities for the Downes firm as the frontier town of Strathcona emerged as a city of several thousand souls in 1907, as the city of Strathcona and the city of Edmonton on the north side of the North

George F. Downes in his Edmonton law office, *c.* 1917 (courtesy Lucy Hawrysz)

Saskatchewan River united under the name Edmonton in 1912, and as Edmonton grew into a regional city of some 94,000 people by 1930.[5] With the emergence of Strathcona as a city, the firm also became a city practice, developing strong, ongoing relationships with urban clients, while maintaining its work with rural clients.

Originally, the firm was a partnership of Nelson D. Mills and George F. Downes. Mills, who had been practising law in Strathcona since 1897 and, before that date, for some years in Toronto, was a native of Essex County, Ontario.[6] Downes and Mills were among the many lawyers who made their appearance in Alberta during the early years of western settlement.

George Francis Downes was born on 6 March 1865 in Vienna, Ontario, near Port Burwell on Lake Erie.[7] He was educated in the local public school and Vienna High School. In 1891, after having gained a Bachelor of Arts degree from the University of Toronto and a law degree from Osgoode Hall, Downes was admitted to the bar of Ontario and began practising law in the prominent Toronto firm of Osler & Osler.[8] A year later, in 1892, Downes was appointed to the Ontario Court of Common

Pleas, in Toronto.[9] In April 1893 he opened a solo practice at Stouffville, a small town north of Toronto. Then, in March 1895, George Downes and John J. Drew, father of George A. Drew, later Ontario Conservative premier, joined in the firm of Drew & Downes, Drew having his office in Guelph, and Downes in Palmerston, a small town north of Stratford.[10] Building up a client base in Palmerston and the outlying area, Downes brought considerable business to the Drew & Downes firm over the next eight years. At the end of 1902, however, the partnership between Drew and Downes dissolved at Downes's request.

Downes's withdrawal occurred because of his desire to practise law in the Northwest Territories, particularly in Alberta, for there he expected to find a milder climate than in Saskatchewan. 'I have the North West fever and if I could get a chance out there I think I would take it at once,' Downes wrote to Drew in September 1902.[11] In Palmerston 'I manage to make a living,' Downes explained to R.G. Macdonald, his old University of Toronto friend and now a lawyer in Brandon, Manitoba, 'but not such a one as I should like.'[12] In his letter to Norman Mackenzie, secretary of the Law Society of the Northwest Territories, Downes said: 'I hear very glowing accounts of the profession out in your country ... I would like to know of some new town with good surroundings which is likely to grow in order that I may locate there as soon as possible.'[13]

Strathcona in north-central Alberta, Downes was informed, was such a town, and in the early months of 1903 he moved to this promising prairie community, where he would remain for the rest of his life. Although the legal profession in Alberta was only loosely organized at this time, the Law Society of the Northwest Territories, as we have seen, had already appeared, and on 11 June 1903 Downes was admitted to this organization.[14] On 16 September 1907, two years after Alberta became a province in Canada, he was admitted to the newly organized Law Society of Alberta.[15] During the early years of his legal career in Ontario and Strathcona, Downes remained a bachelor, but on 1 January 1908, at age forty-two, he married Mary Alice Frost, daughter of W.C. Frost of Hamilton, Ontario.[16] George and Mary had one son, George Frost Downes.

In some respects the demands of law practice at Strathcona in the pre–First World War era were much the same as today. Usually there was more work than could be handled during office hours. The offices of Mills & Downes were open for business at least five days a week, from 9:00 A.M. until 5:00 P.M. on Monday through Friday.[17] Probably the two partners took work home with them or spent evenings and Saturday mornings at the office. Certainly, one of them was normally on hand dur-

TABLE 7.1
Evolution of Firm Name

Name	Period of Use
Mills & Downes	June 1903–Dec. 1905
Geo. F. Downes	Jan. 1906–June 1907
Mills & Downes	July 1907–July 1908
Geo. F. Downes	Aug. 1908–Dec. 1910
Downes & Marks	Jan. 1911–Dec. 1913
Geo. F. Downes	Jan. 1914–Oct. 1914
Downes & Hill-Male	Nov. 1914–Dec. 1914
Geo F. Downes	Jan. 1915–Mar. 1918
Downes, a partner in Rutherford & Jamieson	Apr. 1918–Oct. 1919
Geo. F. Downes	Nov. 1919–1930

Source: George F. Downes Papers

ing office hours to serve clients' needs. From the beginning, Downes prided himself on possessing typewriting skills, and most especially, an office library, to which he added many law books as the years passed.[18] He also had numerous diversions from the office, revelling in the joys of recreational sports such as curling, hockey, tennis, bowling, and hunting.

One way of understanding the history of the Downes firm is through organizational changes. Like many small law firms in Edmonton in the early twentieth century, it possessed little permanence in its formative years.[19] Table 7.1 provides data on the changes in the organization of the business from 1903 through 1930. It was the Mills & Downes firm from spring 1903 to the end of 1905, with Mills its senior and its offices in the Mills Block on Main Street in Strathcona. During this period Downes and Mills were able to work closely together in the firm. After the break-up of the partnership between Mills and Downes in December 1905, owing to Downes's decision to devote part of his time to serving as secretary-treasurer of Strathcona, Downes and Mills each practised alone until June 1907.[20] For one and a half years the Downes firm was thus a solo practice. But in mid-1907 the two men again joined in the firm of Mills & Downes and worked closely together for about a year. Downes's new part-time work as police magistrate of Strathcona, however, interfered so much with the law practice that the firm dissolved in July 1908.[21] From this point until the end of 1910, Downes once more practised alone. During these years he had an office first in the Mills Block, then in the Sheppard's Block on Main Street, and finally at 82 Whyte Avenue East.

In January 1911, George Downes, unable to keep up with all the work that came to his office, took Alfred L. Marks into business as a junior partner and reorganized the firm as Downes & Marks. Downes worked closely with Marks in the succeeding three years. Marks grew up on a farm at Muscoda, in southwestern Wisconsin, and in 1898, at the age of seventeen, he migrated to Strathcona, having become convinced that the surrounding area had great agricultural potential. Rather than developing his new homestead, however, Marks pursued his dream to study law. The absence of a law school in Alberta at this time did not stop him. Following his graduation from the Strathcona High School and the Regina Normal School, Marks studied law at the Detroit College of Law in Detroit, Michigan, and in 1906 obtained his Bachelor of Laws degree and secured his admission to the bar of Michigan. In October 1907, after briefly practising law in Michigan and then teaching for a time in the Alberta public school system, Marks began to article with John R. Lavell, a Strathcona lawyer. Marks was admitted to the Alberta bar in October 1908, at which time he opened his own law business in Leduc, a small town south of Strathcona. As he came into professional contact with George Downes, he learned to respect him. From the time he joined the Downes firm in Strathcona in early 1911 until he withdrew from it at the end of 1913 in search of new opportunities, Marks played an important part in building the practice.[22]

On the break-up of Downes & Marks in December 1913, Downes again became a solo practitioner. However, because of the expanding volume of business, he brought Richard Hill-Male into the practice as a partner in November 1914 and reorganized the firm as Downes & Hill-Male. A native of Wales, a Boer War veteran, and a member of the Law Society of the United Kingdom with thirty years of law practice in Wales behind him, Hill-Male moved to Strathcona sometime in 1910. Aided especially by George Downes and Edmonton lawyer John C.F. Bown, Hill-Male was admitted to the Law Society of Alberta in October 1914. Hill-Male then entered the law office of Downes. What went wrong is unknown, but the partnership between Downes and Hill-Male lasted only about two months, terminating at the end of December 1914.[23]

Downes practised alone between 1915 and 1930, except during the period from spring 1918 to autumn 1919, when he was a partner in the small Edmonton law firm headed by former Alberta premier Alexander C. Rutherford. The First World War created both opportunities and problems for Downes as two law students in Rutherford & Jamieson joined the Canadian Armed Forces for overseas service. As Downes told his

TABLE 7.2
Distribution of Strathcona & Edmonton Law Firms by Size, 1905 and 1930

	1905 Strathcona & Edmonton		1930 Edmonton	
Size Category	Number	Per Cent	Number	Per Cent
Solo firms	9	52.9	40	51.3
2- or 3-member firms	6	35.3	34	43.6
4- or 5-member firms	2	11.8	4	5.1
Total	17	100.0	78	100.0

Source: *Henderson's Manitoba and Northwest Gazetteer and Directory for 1905*, 1284–6; *Henderson's Greater Edmonton Directory for 1930*, 739–40

long-time client Hugh Bain, in Seattle, Washington, 'I joined the Rutherford firm in April 1918 on the understanding that it was to be a permanent thing but soon after the members who had enlisted returned the old man asked me to get out. It was hardly any more polite than that.'[24] After leaving Rutherford & Jamieson, Downes had his office on the second floor of the Canadian Bank of Commerce Building on Whyte Avenue. Thus, as often before, the Downes firm was now a solo practice.

Throughout the period from 1903 to 1930, the Downes practice resembled many other law firms in Edmonton. Such firms were usually solo practices or two- or three-member partnerships. In 1905, Strathcona had four law firms while Edmonton had thirteen. By 1930, there were seventy-eight firms in Edmonton. As table 7.2 shows, in Strathcona and Edmonton in 1905, and in Edmonton in 1930, more than 87 per cent of the lawyers worked either as solo practitioners or in two- or three-member firms. In 1905 firms of this size and organization in Strathcona included J.G. Tipton, D.H. Mackinnon, and Rutherford & Jamieson; in Edmonton they included Lucien Dubuc, MacDonald & Griesbach, and Beck, Emery & Newell. Among the practices of this same size and organization in Edmonton twenty-five years later, there were Joseph A. Clarke; Alfred L. Marks; Lavell & Ross; Tighe & Kerr; Ewing, Harvie & Bury; Rutherford, Rutherford & McCuaig, and Wood, Buchanan & Macdonald. Thus, early-twentieth-century Edmonton had numerous firms similar in style and stature to the Downes firm.

From the beginning, the Downes firm served mainly individual clients who operated in the urban and rural economies. Like other country and small-town lawyers, George Downes was primarily a small businessman, not a partner in a large law firm. Even in the 1920s most of his clients were individuals and small businesspeople – farmers and merchants. Downes, like his country and small-town colleagues, handled a steady stream of small matters. Moreover, like them, he was a general practitioner. But, as was the case with his city colleagues, Downes also received some of his income from serving medium-sized business enterprises in Strathcona during the period in which it evolved from a frontier town into a city, and finally into that part of the city of Edmonton known as South Edmonton. This meant that, within its region, the Downes firm built a strong, ongoing relationship with small and medium-sized businesses in Strathcona, and with farmers and merchants in rural communities in the surrounding countryside such as Rabbit Hill, Clover Bar, Cooking Lake, New Sarepta, Leduc, Wetaskiwin, Tofield, Ranfurly, Innisfree, Bruce, Ponoka, Bawlf, and Stettler.

The small-scale environment in which Downes did most of his legal work in Strathcona, South Edmonton, and the outlying region brought him into intimate relationships with many of his clients. Like his rural and small-town colleagues, he conducted his legal affairs within a network of personal ties. The intimacy of the small-town and rural setting in which Downes operated helped provide him with new business and contributed to his firm's success.

Downes made a name for himself by serving clients inside as well as outside the courtroom. However, he initially preferred office work to courtroom service. 'Prefer office work & as a matter of fact have had very little experience in court work which I do not care for,' Downes wrote to Ford Jones, a Regina lawyer, before moving to Strathcona.[25] Penning a letter to Norman Mackenzie at the same time, Downes emphasized his point: 'Personally I am not fond of litigation.'[26] Nevertheless, upon arriving in Strathcona, Downes soon developed litigation skills. Trial work became an important aspect of his professional life not only during the many years he had a solo practice, but also when he was a member of a partnership, despite the reputation he had for serving his clients, especially in his office, and helping them solve their problems outside the courtroom through face-to-face discussions and correspondence. With Downes's willingness to work both inside and outside the courtroom came public recognition of his rising importance in the legal and business affairs of many of the business enterprises that shaped the economic growth of Edmonton and its region.

FACILITATING ECONOMIC GROWTH

From the outset, the Downes firm worked in its Strathcona office to facilitate economic growth. Reflecting the business thrust of early-twentieth-century Alberta life, Downes and his partners felt that businessmen stood at the heart of progress for Strathcona and the outlying countryside. Businessmen of all kinds – real estate men, bankers, lawyers, newspaper men, farmers – were active in promoting transportation improvements. Strathcona's development started when the town acquired rail links to the East and West. In 1891, Strathcona secured indirect connections through the Canadian Pacific Railway. At the same time, the railway opened farming areas near Strathcona. The rich farming hinterland became a critical element in the town's development. Initially, the town grew as a commercial centre, feeding upon agricultural expansion. Commerce continued to be of central importance for Strathcona's future, but with the passage of time its economy began to diversify as service and industrial businesses developed to serve the rising populations of the town and the surrounding region.

Strathcona benefited from the businesses which the Downes firm helped create and develop. For George Downes, work of this type began in autumn 1903. At this time, Mills & Downes helped the local owners of the old Strathcona Brewery incorporate it as the Strathcona Brewing & Malting Company under Northwest Territories law. Both George Downes and Nelson Mills were active in the creation of this company. Mills & Downes also made arrangements with the Imperial Bank of Canada to fund the new corporation. The company, however, faced difficult financial problems from the start. To solve these problems, Mills & Downes assisted Edmonton and Strathcona businessmen in incorporating the Alberta Brewing Company, and in purchasing the Strathcona Brewing & Malting Company, thereby allowing the business to be refinanced.[27] Both the old and the new breweries, while small businesses by national standards, were medium-sized industrial corporations by Strathcona standards, and they played significant roles in the town's evolution. Moreover, in the creation of the new companies and the arrangement of financing for the corporations, Mills & Downes became involved in the practice of corporate law.

George Downes remained active in such work. In 1904, for example, he helped incorporate the *Strathcona Chronicle*, a weekly newspaper that became an effective town booster.[28] Downes also assisted local businessmen Charles H. Lowther, John R. Mackenzie, and George A. Greene in incorporating the Twin City Manufacturing Company during 1909, a Strathcona enterprise that produced doors, windows, hearses, caskets, and coffins.[29] In participating in the founding of these and other corporations, Downes supplied them with legal and business advice to help them avoid pitfalls and to assist their growth.

Outside the corporate sphere, Downes worked to encourage the development of smaller businesses. For instance, in 1912 he assisted shoemakers Adelard Dumas and Alexis Dumas in organizing a family partnership known as the Great West Shoe Repair Company.[30] The formation of new partnerships such as this one contributed to the expansion of business and enhanced Edmonton's ability to serve local and regional markets.

In an era when homesteaders were streaming into the Strathcona region, the Downes firm also played an important role in developing the homestead economy. After filing for one-quarter section of Dominion land at the local Dominion Lands Office for an administration fee of $10, spending some money to build a house on their free 160-acre homesteads, residing there for at least six months in each of three consecutive years, putting additional funds into breaking at least 10 acres of land a year, and then applying for title to their farms, homesteaders needed more capital to develop them, which often raised legal questions. George Downes not only familiarized himself with the Dominion Lands Act of 1872 and all aspects of the homestead system, but also responded to homesteaders' legal needs, drafting their papers, registering their mortgages, and giving them the attention which their farm businesses required. The homesteaders helped provide the Downes firm with a window on economic life beyond Strathcona.

Typical of Downes's work for homesteaders were his efforts to keep the farm of Clarence H. Stout functioning. Stout, who was also the editor of the *Strathcona Plaindealer*, was constantly developing his homestead, but he was falling behind in the payment of the local improvement and school taxes on his land and in paying off the real estate mortgage on his farm.[31] In March 1910, as he had done several times before, Downes voiced concerns about the unpaid and overdue debts and asked Stout to meet his financial obligations.[32] Downes had a long-term perspective on farming problems in the Strathcona region, and his efforts were clearly aimed at the larger goal of avoiding future difficulties on the Stout homestead and keeping it operating effectively.

In most of his homestead endeavours Downes was concerned with male homesteaders, who represented the overwhelming majority in this class of farmers, but sometimes he also had the opportunity to come to the assistance of women in need of a homestead. In spring 1907, for example, he aided Mrs M.M. Seaman, a widow whom he knew personally, in making a statutory declaration in connection with her decision to file for entry on a free quarter-section homestead in the Strathcona area. At that time, no women except widows, divorcees, and deserted wives had homestead rights. Yet, even widows did not seem to have easy access to homestead privileges at the local Dominion Lands Office. In forwarding the declaration to the Dominion Lands Office in Ottawa, Downes explained that Mrs Seaman was a widow and that she was the head of her family; apparently his intervention helped her secure a free homestead.[33] Homesteaders, whether women or men, frequently needed experienced lawyers like Downes to resolve the complex issues arising from the homestead laws. In assisting homesteaders he promoted the opening up of new farm lands and helped cement Strathcona's ties to the outlying countryside.

At first glance, it might appear that the Downes firm facilitated the growth of Strathcona and its region only through office practice. But a more careful examination of the available evidence shows that the firm also used the courtroom to ensure the development of the town and the surrounding area. Shortly after joining Mills in 1903, Downes became active as a court partner of the firm, though Mills went to court in more cases. At the same time, Downes prepared many cases for trial, taking care of the office business that was required. In some cases both partners made appearances in court, each at different times during the course of the same trial. Such was the situation in 1904, when the firm of Mills & Downes represented John W. Turner, a small harness-maker of Leduc and agent of the Great West Saddlery Company, in the Supreme Court of Alberta at Edmonton in the matter of his claim that Mark Spencer, a Leduc furniture dealer, had made a libellous statement about him in a letter.[34] The final outcome is not clear from the court report. The report, however, reveals that Downes took major responsibility for the argument in the Turner case. In doing so, he built his own reputation, as well as that of Mills & Downes. This helped the firm develop ongoing relationships with small-town businesses and, in carrying out its work for them, it exerted a significant influence on the regional economy.

Litigation concerning small farming businesses also constituted a substantial part of the firm's practice in Strathcona during the years 1903–5. Moreover, in late 1908 and in 1909, when Downes was practising alone, he continued to handle such litigation. During this period he attracted important clients for his business in this line, including Del W. Wilkinson, a small Leduc farmer. Wilkinson required Downes's services for a case that dragged along for more than a year. The case involved a claim by Leduc butcher James S. Johnson against Wilkinson, alleging failure to pay

for goods sold to him. Downes, defending Wilkinson, argued successfully against the claim and eventually Johnson dropped it.[35] Small farmers like Wilkinson provided an underlying dynamic in the growth of the
local and regional economies. Not surprisingly, representing Wilkinson
helped place the Downes firm at the core of the economic life of Strathcona and the outlying countryside.

CIVIC LEADERSHIP

The Downes firm's primary development was through office and provincial court work, but it also grew through civic leadership. George Downes
served Strathcona, later South Edmonton, for more than ten years.[36] He
began as secretary-treasurer of the town of Strathcona in January 1906
and rose to become secretary-treasurer of the new city of Strathcona in
March 1907, a position he held until the beginning of June of that year.
Downes served as Strathcona's police magistrate from November 1907
through January 1912, and as South Edmonton's police magistrate from
February 1912 until 1917.[37]

Of considerable importance for his law firm's future were the personal
friendships and business connections that grew out of George Downes's
work as a town and city officer. Moreover, this activity also helped
increase his income. As secretary-treasurer of the town of Strathcona, he
received a salary of $1,200 a year. 'My reason for taking this position,' he
told his father, George C. Downes, secretary of the Central Ontario School
of Art & Industrial Design in Toronto, 'is that it offers a fair salary and I
think that it will improve. Then I get more or less of a connection which
will be of use to me should I decide to give up the position and go back to
law.'[38] In reality, George F. Downes had never retired from the active
practice of law. Although at this point he expected to 'have to give up law
to a large extent for a time,' he found himself paying a great deal of attention to his law practice, as well as devoting many hours to his civic job.[39]

The situation was the same when Downes became Strathcona's police
magistrate, initially earning a salary of $300 a year. Instinctively seeking
financial security, he used his new position in the city hall to develop the
personal friendships and business ties that would aid his law practice.
Few people understood this better than his father. 'I am glad to hear you
have been appointed Police Magistrate,' wrote his father. 'I suppose it
will help somewhat in your practice.'[40]

Long before George F. Downes became a police magistrate, however,
the opportunity was at hand for him to further his law practice by serving

as secretary-treasurer, first of the town, and then of the city of Strathcona. Once in command of the secretary-treasurer's office, he developed useful business connections by becoming active as a town booster. In the process, Downes's personal fortune became closely interwoven with Strathcona's future. Among his contemporaries, he earned a reputation for being a visionary. Strathcona's competitive atmosphere fired his imagination, moving him to give top priority to trying to forge better transportation links into the rural areas and out to the East and West. To achieve his primary goal, Downes, in February 1906, appealed to Frank W. Morse, general manager of the Grand Trunk Pacific Railway, to push his road west across the prairies through Strathcona and over the North Saskatchewan River into Edmonton.[41] Morse considered building through Strathcona but decided instead to follow a route through the Clover Bar Settlement and over the North Saskatchewan there towards Edmonton, which had already become a transportation centre and contained within its boundaries the yards of the Canadian Northern Railway.

Nevertheless, Downes's desire for improvements for Strathcona persisted. He continued to equate his law firm's growth with civic progress. Along with many other local businessmen and professionals, he helped win approval for improving the town's water supply, sewers, garbage collection, pound facilities, streets and sidewalks, electric lighting, and milk supply.[42] Downes believed that these changes would bring a larger measure of prosperity to Strathcona.

From his efforts at piecemeal town improvements, Downes turned to wider planning. In December 1906 he, together with other leading citizens, proved successful in winning approval for a city charter for Strathcona from the municipal electorate, a step that led to its incorporation as a city in March 1907.[43] Increasing the borrowing powers of the new city for development, the charter strengthened Strathcona's government. With the increase in power, city officials could act more vigorously. Nelson Mills, the newly elected mayor of the city, and George Downes, its first secretary-treasurer, moved quickly to encourage Strathcona's growth, while at the same time using their respective civic positions to build connections that would aid the business of their individual law firms.

Civic achievements in the new city began in spring 1907, when Downes and Mills asked Strathcona to vote on $101,000 in bonds for a city hall, a hospital, and a marketplace.[44] The bonds easily won approval.[45] Clearly, most people shared Mills and Downes's view that Strathcona needed these improvements. Moreover, Downes spoke for many citizens when he said that the city required a new post-office building.[46] Better postal services could aid businessmen, including lawyers. As secretary-treasurer, Downes looked upon civic and personal business progress as being the same, for both could help make Strathcona more prosperous.

Similarly, as police magistrate, Downes mixed business with his desire to improve Strathcona. From 1907 to 1917, he used his police-magistrate powers to create a more favourable urban environment, as well as to help his law firm get ahead. An attractive social environment would, he thought, contribute to his firm's growth and development. Yearning for a society that functioned smoothly without civic disorder and crime, Downes addressed the real problems faced by the Police Magistrate's Court on the main floor of the city hall. For example, in June 1908 he imposed a fine upon J. Gainer, a Strathcona butcher, for burning offal at the abattoir in the open and thereby creating an extremely obnoxious odour in the vicinity, even after a number of citizens had complained about this to the sanitary inspector.[47] More than two years later, in September 1910, Downes fined L.H. Henderson five dollars for assaulting J.T. Hall near the Iroquois Hotel.[48] During the six months ending 12 May 1908, Downes tried more than 90 cases in the Police Magistrate's Court.[49] In 1910, he handled 169 cases, and in 1911 this figure rose to 360. By 1911, the city council had increased Downes's salary to $600 a year.[50]

As the years passed, direct social benefits were seen as coming from Downes's work in the police courtroom by the citizens of Strathcona. The city council supported his efforts as an essential service. Downes wanted the progress of his law business to be replicated in the community around it. Quite naturally, this desire was reflected in his actions in the police court. At the same time, he understood that the business connections that grew out of his leadership in civic affairs in the Police Magistrate's Court represented an important factor in the development of his law firm.

Downes's leadership in other local matters also helped steer business to his firm. A natural joiner and city booster, he blended civic pride and a sense of entrepreneurial purpose. Besides playing a prominent role in the development of the Strathcona Young Men's Club, the Strathcona Tennis Club, the Strathcona Hockey Club, the Strathcona Curling Club, the Edmonton Gun Club, and the Edmonton Lawn Bowling Club, Downes served as secretary of the Strathcona Board of Trade, secretary-treasurer of the Strathcona Public School Board, secretary-treasurer of the Strathcona Conservative Association, secretary of the Strathcona Rink Association, rector's warden in the Holy Trinity Anglican Church in South Edmonton, and president of the Edmonton Horticultural Society.[51] As was often the case among Edmonton lawyers in the early-twentieth-century West, rising to leadership positions within such institutions made Downes well placed to maintain and expand his client base.[52]

Leadership in another institution – Independent Order of Foresters – was of particular significance in helping Downes establish a network of business connections in Strathcona and the outlying region. This Toronto-based institution, which provided fraternal sickness insurance for its members, had made him the financial secretary of its branch at Strathcona by 1908.[53] He remained in that position until the 1930s. As financial secretary of the Strathcona branch of the Independent Order of Foresters, Downes looked after members' sickness insurance needs. He also collected their membership dues. Over the years, many of the members in South Edmonton and the countryside became his clients. At times they combined the payment of their dues and other business in one visit to his office. 'I had a very busy day yesterday,' Downes wrote on 1 June 1927, 'as most of the members left payment till the last day and I had a lot to do for my clients in the way of their regular business.'[54] Thus, in meeting the needs of the South Edmonton branch of the Independent Order of Foresters, one of the city's important social institutions, Downes built his law firm.

FINANCIAL INTERMEDIARY

Amidst this success in civic leadership, Downes also chose to become a financial intermediary. As early as 1903 his law firm enjoyed direct access to Ontario business, the capital of which was significant in the development of Strathcona and its region.[55] Downes's personal connections in Toronto, as well as in Palmerston and other small Ontario towns, were of central importance in securing these funds. Obtaining substantial sums from his father and his sister Cecilia in Toronto, and from his old clients and friends in small-town Ontario, he made decisions in regard to how and when to employ this capital.[56] In making these decisions, Downes was serving as an intermediary between Ontario savings and investments in Strathcona, and especially in the outlying countryside. Downes's choice to provide this financial service was not only a logical outgrowth of his success in law and business, but also a function of the time and place in which he lived. More specifically, his choice was his response to a growing demand in the Strathcona region for outside capital, particularly Ontario capital, in the settlement years.

On 31 August 1908, Downes explained this in his letter to his old friend

Duncan McCallum, the Grand Trunk Railway agent at Wingham, Ontario. 'Having great opportunities here for investing funds at good interest on safe investments, usually farm loans in small amounts, and knowing that you have money drawing probably only 3 or 4 per cent,' wrote Downes, 'it has occurred to me that perhaps you would like to invest it so as to bring you a greater revenue.' Downes added: 'I may say that I have invested considerable for other of my old friends at Palmerston and that they are all pleased with the returns made.' The investments in the Strathcona area were paying interest ranging from 8 to 10 per cent per annum. 'I assure you,' Downes continued, 'that there is not the slightest risk as I never advance more than one half the value of the property and rarely that proportion.' Downes went on to say that 'I secure the loans for which I charge you one per cent of the amount loaned, which on a loan of $500 amounts to $5. Then I look after the collection of the interest and remit same to you less one per cent ... I usually, on receiving the application, and if I consider it a good investment, at once write for the necessary funds and at the same time draw the mortgage and have it registered and see that the title is clear, and, as soon as the money arrives, pay over the amount of the loan' to the borrower.[57] Downes handled a number of loans on city and town properties, but he normally focused on farm finance.

From its portfolio of real estate loans on farm lands and urban property, Downes's law firm generated income for itself. At the same time, it earned a fairly good rate of return for its investors, including George Downes's father. In the process, the firm performed a regional and local role in meeting the credit needs of farmers and urban businessmen. A soundly managed institution, it functioned as a typical frontier law firm that provided the citizens of the Strathcona region with access to broader capital markets.

As an element of a small but active money market in the Strathcona area, the Downes law firm, however, did not always possess the funds to match its investment opportunities. Certainly, this was the case when Downes was a partner in Downes & Marks. 'We have had a number of applications for loans which we have been compelled to turn down owing to the fact that we have no funds available,' wrote Downes in October 1911 to investor William Halfpenny of Kincardine, Ontario, who had, through Downes & Marks, lent more than $500 to A.B. Chapman of the Great West Saddlery Company in Edmonton. 'These are good loans bearing interest at 8 per cent. If you have any friends who have funds to invest the same way our Mr. Downes was looking after the investment of your funds, we wish that you would have them write us as we think we can show them how much better are our investments here than can be obtained in Kincardine and vicinity.'[58] Thus, as one way to attract investment capital to the Strathcona–Edmonton region, the firm of Downes & Marks continued to pay interest at higher rates than could be secured in Ontario.

Few Ontario investors were more aware of this than Downes's father, George C. Downes, whose money had begun flowing through his son's law firm to Strathcona-area farmers and creating profits for him at least as early as 1906. In April of that year, John Wonsch was only one of a number of local farmers using the firm as a means of access to cash and credit from George C. Downes to develop their farms.[59] Four months later, in August 1906, George F. Downes wrote to his father that he was again performing profitable financial services for him: 'I am now putting you out $800 on an improved quarter-section, that is 160 acres. The interest will be 9 per cent and the security is first class and will sell readily at $2,000.'[60] By 1908, John Albert of the Rabbit Hill Settlement had borrowed enough money from George C. Downes through his son's law firm to purchase 320 acres of farm land from the Canadian Pacific Railway, as well as 160 acres from the Hudson's Bay Company.[61] The services of the law firm continued to provide farmers in the Strathcona region with access to funds from George C. Downes during the next decade.[62] Consequently, the business of the firm increased.

Problems nevertheless sometimes arose in connection with the operations of George F. Downes's law firm as a financial intermediary. For instance, in September 1913, Charles G. Broadhead, a New Sarepta farmer, used the firm's services to obtain a $500 loan, carrying an annual interest rate of 10 per cent and secured by his quarter-section farm, from Robert F. Whiteside, of Little Britain, Ontario. Broadhead, however, made no payments. Downes recognized his obligation to try to protect the interests of Whiteside. In 1917, Downes, representing Whiteside, obtained a ruling from the Supreme Court of Alberta that his Little Britain client recover $725.03.[63] Downes's litigation expertise contributed to maintaining public confidence in his financial services, and these services played a significant role in helping his firm grow and mature.

TRANSFERRING WEALTH

An additional important source of growth was Downes's estate-administration practice, which concerned itself with the transfer of wealth from one generation to the next. As in other small, early-twentieth-century Alberta law firms such as the A.J. Arnold practice at High River, in the Downes firm there was a relatively small collection of wills of people whose estates would sooner or later require administration.[64] This collection of wills was a potential asset, for it might bring the firm considerable business.

The role of the Downes firm in the estate-administration process frequently involved the transfer of the family farm from the older to the younger generation. The task was a challenging one, for Downes early discovered that the transition was usually far from smooth. Certainly this was the case with the estate of James Jones, a farmer at Tofield, who died on 15 April 1907. According to Alberta law, the heirs were free to settle Jones's affairs without the assistance of a lawyer.[65] But, like many other heirs in Alberta, they decided that they needed a lawyer's services. The growing recognition of the competence of Downes of Mills & Downes in this area made it natural for them to retain him. The work that Downes faced included the preparation of an inventory of the property owned by Jones, the payment of debts, and the distribution of the residue to the heirs. By his will, James Jones, a widower, left all his possessions to his six children: James, of Rochester, New York; Thomas, of Wetaskiwin; William and Ernest, of Tofield; Ira, of Golden, British Columbia; and Victoria Saunders, of Butte, Montana. James Jones appointed Robert Palmer, a Strathcona foreman, and Albert Stannard, a farmer in the Colchester Settlement near Strathcona, his executors.[66] In helping to settle the affairs of James Jones, Downes had to discuss the question of the family farm with both the executors and the heirs.

During the early years of western settlement, Alberta lawyers like Downes understood that merchants, farmers, and ranchers ruled the economy. In the Alberta economy, businesses often operated as family ventures. Among such ventures, the family farm was most pervasive.

A growing segment of American legal history emphasizes the role of lawyers in facilitating the transfer of wealth in the family farm in the United States.[67] As was the case with many country and small-town lawyers in the United States, the first problem Downes encountered in handling the estate of James Jones was the matter of the family farm. Before his death, James Jones, seeking to preserve family farming operations and to keep land in agricultural production, had transferred the family farm at Tofield to son Ernest. Yet son Thomas was upset, because he did not learn about the transfer until after his father's death. What Thomas did know before his father died was that he had temporarily leased the farm to Henry Lee, a neighbour. This allowed James Jones to maintain the farming operation as a continuing business without interruption into the succeeding generation. Moreover, the rent he collected from the farm enabled him to provide himself with security and a comfortable standard of living during his lifetime. Thomas's views were changed, however, by his willingness to listen to Downes, who persuaded him to accept his father's decision to make over the family farm to Ernest.[68]

Meanwhile, Downes had assisted the executors in preparing an inventory listing the assets owned by James Jones at the time of his death, as well as in drafting a notice advertising for creditors' claims. In the inventory filed by the executors in the District Court of the District of Edmonton, the assets were inventoried at $2,774.55.[69] The main assets consisted of two lots in Strathcona, valued at $1,000, and money secured by two mortgages amounting to $1,017.45. On 5 March 1908, the executors obtained grant of letters of administration of the estate and probate of the will from the Edmonton District Court.[70] Thus, a competent judicial authority had determined the validity of the will.[71]

Yet, a problem with the creditors' claims surfaced. Downes received four claims: J.W. Morton, $205.00; Moffat, McCoppen & Bull Co., $175.00; Henry Lee, $70.39; and David Dunham, $8.50.[72] Downes had to adjust the claims, however; under the trustee ordinance, Henry Lee was forced to withdraw his claim.[73] Lee had put in a claim of $70.39 against the estate to cover the amount he had paid for threshing, but Downes could not accept this claim because it came to his attention that the lease agreement between Lee and James Jones required Lee himself to absorb the threshing costs.[74]

Downes also faced the problem of determining whether or not the children of James Jones owed him any money at the time of his death. Sons Ernest and William claimed that brother Thomas had borrowed $600 from their father but had not repaid him. They did not, however, want to take a public stand on the issue. Yet, Thomas's relationships with his two brothers remained strained. To move forward, Downes advised Thomas to seek the advice and assistance of a solicitor in Strathcona or Edmonton.[75] The Edmonton firm of Mackinnon & Cogswell was willing to look after the interests of Thomas. After extended discussions, it was agreed by all concerned that Thomas had actually paid off his debt prior to the death of his father.[76]

Like James Jones's children, Downes wanted to close the Jones estate and distribute its assets as soon as possible. Closing was delayed by Downes in autumn 1908, however, because of the need to wait until a fair price could be realized for the two lots in Strathcona. The depression of 1907 and its aftermath had significantly reduced the value of this property. The problem was that, although Thomas, James, Ernest, William, and Ira agreed with Downes's cautious approach, Victoria was pressing him to sell the lots.[77] Against the wishes of Victoria, Downes postponed the sale of the lots until the price improved.[78] Even so, the proceeds from the sale would not amount to a great deal of money.

In the interim, Downes supported the executors' plan to wind up the balance of the estate in the very near future. By his will, James Jones left 25 per cent of the residue of his estate and a sewing machine to Victoria; 25 per cent of the residue and a kitchen table to Thomas; 25 per cent of the residue and a bed, bedding, and a chest to William; 25 per cent of the residue and a watch to Ira; the sum of $200 to James; and a clock, an overcoat, and the sum of $5 to Ernest.[79] As was the case with many other Alberta farmers in this period, the net worth of James Jones at death was small. Clearly, he had relatively little wealth to transfer to the next generation. Although the Jones family had become racked with strife during the transition, its lawyer, Downes, had succeeded in helping James Jones keep the family farming operation in the family.

Such activity made it possible for the Downes firm to grow and, at the same time, to help shape the economic development of rural Alberta. The number of farm decedents whose estates the firm administered over the next two decades was relatively small, but in carrying out this responsibility it nevertheless made an important contribution to the growth of the economy. In this endeavour Downes was in close touch with some enterprising farmers in the Edmonton region, and they relied on him to assist them in transferring wealth to the future generation in the countryside.

The Downes firm was also well prepared to take on the job of transferring wealth for its urban clients. In doing so, it provided an essential service for the residents of South Edmonton. One of these was Margaret B. Mathie, who required Downes's legal services. During the post–First World War depression Mathie found herself in unhappy circumstances. In March 1920, she began a suit in the Edmonton District Court for unpaid wages and wrongful dismissal from service against William B. Ferguson, husband of her niece Ethel Margaret Ferguson. Downes acted in the case for Mathie, who had given up her own needlework business to look after the Fergusons' house and take care of their baby girl.[80] William B. Ferguson, the defendant, was represented by Edmonton lawyer George W. Massie.[81] As might be expected, the conflict provoked considerable family bitterness. Mathie claimed $525 for wages over a period of fifteen months and $35 for wrongful dismissal. The suit, tried before Judge John L. Crawford, challenged the determination of William B. Ferguson not to provide Mathie with financial compensation. To all appearances, Downes succeeded in establishing the claims of Margaret Mathie.[82] Downes's knowledge of the law and his effectiveness in handling the case were obvious to all concerned.

With the competency of Downes having been exhibited so clearly, it was not surprising that Mathie asked him to assist her in making her will, which she signed on 5 July 1921.[83] By her will, she appointed Downes her executor and trustee of her estate and left all her possessions to her niece's baby daughter, Ethel Margaret Ferguson. Mathie probably did not have a lot of wealth to transfer to the succeeding generation, but she wanted whatever resources she possessed at death to be used for the care and education of Ethel. Moreover, Mathie trusted Downes enough to leave the entire matter in his hands. Quite naturally, she was impressed by his interest and concern. Even though Mathie–Ferguson family relationships at the adult level had broken down, Margaret Mathie felt that young Ethel was entitled to benefit from the wealth she was able to pass on to her.

Downes likely considered it as a compliment to be named the executor and trustee of Mathie's estate. Without a doubt, such recognition was good for his law firm. In helping South Edmonton residents like Margaret Mathie transfer their possessions to the next generation, Downes was performing an economic function, for his firm as well as for his city and its region.

INTERNAL PROBLEMS AT DOWNES'S LAW FIRM

Long before Downes aided Margaret Mathie, however, there was cause for anxiety about the future of his law practice. As the national and the Alberta business situations began to deteriorate during the depression of 1913, internal problems surfaced at Downes's firm in South Edmonton. The depression and its aftermath cut deeply into the firm's income by crippling many of its clients in South Edmonton and the surrounding countryside. They defaulted on their payments for Downes's services as they ran out of money. The growing stack of uncollected bills at the firm became a serious problem.

Downes could still recall old days of glory, when his professional business had been prospering. Long-run income data are not available, but in the year 1904 the profit-and-loss ledger discloses that his net earnings in the Mills & Downes partnership had risen to $1,653.[84] Despite the good times, Downes, like Mills, watched all expenses very carefully. Expenses at the firm tended to fluctuate, but in 1908 they amounted to $970.[85] This sum covered, among other things, office rent and the cost of stationery, postage, telephone calls, and a stenographer. At this time, the stenographer was Miss Birdie Leard. Her salary was $10 a month, and her work included the typing of the firm's letters. Despite all the assistance she provided, Downes found his own workload extremely heavy and consequently toyed with the idea of adding a law clerk to the one-person support staff, but in the end came to the conclusion that he could not afford one.[86]

Downes helped attract business by observing punctuality. To keep regular office hours for the benefit of his clients was a matter of great personal pride. Downes's professional activity was constantly increasing. Nevertheless, he found time to take short summer holidays. The exception came in 1907, when he had a long vacation – eight weeks – in Ontario. Upon returning in September, Downes discovered a mountain of unanswered letters requiring his attention.[87] After several months' hard work, he left for Hamilton, Ontario, to marry Mary Alice Frost. By mid-January 1908, Downes was back in Strathcona with his wife, once again looking after all the business that had accumulated during his absence.[88]

In 1911, Downes was optimistic enough about the future of his law firm at Strathcona to build a large brick house in the city, at 8721–101st Street. He admired successful lawyers with big homes, and, like many practitioners then and now, consciously tried to emulate them. Reaching for the stars, he showed courtesy and graciousness in much of his social conduct. There was time for relatives and friends at his home, for it was spacious and its grounds covered four city lots. Within a few years, Downes had built an attractive tennis court in his backyard. Even the cost of the splendid home, at almost $12,000, seemed manageable at the time, in part because he could and did borrow $8,000 from his father with the promise to pay interest on the loan at the rate of 10 per cent per annum.[89]

Yet now, in 1913, with the depression threatening to destroy his small law business, Downes's debts, including especially those in connection with his home, were pressing in on him. Things continued to be very tight in his law firm, but he still allowed himself a short vacation in summer 1915.[90] Besides finding his holiday refreshing, Downes continued to benefit from old business connections. For example, through the Wilber Mercantile Agency of Chicago, of which he was a long-time representative at Edmonton, he was able to handle important estate business.[91] Other business in Edmonton that came to Downes through the Wilber Mercantile Agency consisted of a number of debt collections. Yet collections of claims against debtors were often slow and hardly worth the time and energy Downes spent at the task. In 1917, for instance, he found his inability to get one of his own debtors to settle an account of $16.37 with him extremely frustrating.[92] To complicate the situation, Downes came down with the Spanish flu in autumn 1918. Fortunately, he recovered from the blow, but in June 1919 he was still trying to catch up with the work that had been piling up in his office in the Canadian Bank of Commerce Building during his illness.[93]

During the post–First World War period, Downes's law firm faced the problem of having to attend to many small matters that did not provide much remuneration. 'I am too busy but I can not make enough to satisfy my needs and can not afford a stenographer at present prices,' Downes complained in his letter to lawyer J.H. Sissons of Grande Prairie, Alberta, in May 1921.[94] In an effort to hold the business of his existing clients and gain that of new ones, however, Downes, by July of that same year, had hired Miss Effie Brown to serve as his stenographer. Her salary from 8 July to 8 September, as Downes's ledger shows, was $50. For the whole of 1921, Downes's office expenses totaled $977, an amount that was fairly reasonable.[95]

Even more revealing of Downes's costs were the entries in his ledger concerning his house expenses, which for the year 1921 hovered at more than $1,600.[96] The very condition of his law firm would not allow the small business to absorb such high costs, particularly at a time when a great business storm was gathering across the nation. The post–First World War depression highlighted Downes's financial problems, but it was his enormous house debt that was at the root of the difficulty. As might be expected, the situation at his business worsened with the failure of many of his clients to settle their accounts with him. On 11 September 1923, he wrote his old client and friend Valentine Richards, of Santa Monica, California, about the financial storm signals at his South Edmonton law firm: 'I have had to borrow upon my life insurance to get money to pay my living expenses and, to be quite frank with you, I often wonder if I am going to be able to keep my taxes paid on my home and so prevent it from being forfeited to the City ... Perhaps you would suggest that I borrow upon a mortgage of the home. I did this when I built, unfortunately, and have had to borrow further since during the course of the war ... It is impossible to sell the property for more than about $6,000 at the present time and there is more against it than that at the present time. You will realize just how hard up I am.'[97] Three years later, in autumn 1926, Downes penned another worried letter to Valentine Richards: 'I have to put up a considerable sum by Dec. 15th to hold my home and if things do not soon improve I fear the end.'[98]

Still, Downes's law firm survived these difficult times. He had some good days among the many poor ones. Moreover, despite his problems, Downes was able to be analytical about them. The harsh business climate left him with a bewildering issue: the lack of a stenographer, which made it almost impossible for him to be prompt in handling his correspondence. As Downes explained to one of his local clients in February 1927, 'I have never found it so hard to make a living as in the past four years. This is to a large extent owing to the fact that times have been so bad that I can not keep a stenographer to do my typewriting.'[99] A partial solution to this problem nevertheless appeared. Downes fell back on his own experience in typing letters and important legal documents. Each day of good business, like the one he had at the beginning of June 1927, lifted his spirits.[100] But a month and a half later, in mid-July, Downes wrote to the Reverend William Greer of Calgary that 'business is bad and I fear I am going to lose all I have.'[101] Downes did not lose all he possessed, however.

Even at the height of his troubles at his law firm in the years 1927–30, Downes continued to sustain a network of relationships in South Edmonton and the surrounding region, reaching out to them and collecting enough fees for his services to make modest payments in connection with his house debts, thus temporarily satisfying his creditors. Money came in from estate business in the farming community of Bruce, from work related to the incorporation of Sunnyside Hospital Limited in South Edmonton, and from local land-transfer activity.[102]

Downes's failing health, however, did not permit him to continue his law business. Around 1929, he suffered a severe sunstroke, and this deeply affected his practice.[103] Moreover, the strain from sunstroke added to an existing health problem: 'Unfortunately I overworked my brain some five years ago or upwards and as a consequence I have slowed down considerably in my ability to carry on, but I am thankful that my condition is improving,' he told Frank R. Hand in October 1929. 'I feel,' he added, 'that it is impossible for me to continue the law business and regain a clear brain.'[104] After retiring from the active practice of law in 1930, Downes sold fire insurance and life insurance for some time, but he was never able to resume a full business life.[105]

In his waning years Downes waged a long battle with sickness. He died in Edmonton on 25 January 1940 at the age of seventy-four.[106] Though he had left no formal will, there was something equivalent to one in the family records. By the terms of their marriage agreement, dated 31 December 1907, Downes left everything, including his home, to his wife, Mary.[107] The problem was that the Downeses, like many other Edmontonians, had not weathered the Great Depression very well. At the time of his death, Downes was heavily in debt and owed the City of Edmonton a great deal of money for unpaid taxes on the house. With hardly any cash, Mary was faced with the prospect of kissing her home goodbye or coming to an understanding with the city. In an agreement signed by Mary in the early 1940s, the house was deeded to the city for the debt. The city none the less allowed her to live in the home for the rest of her life.

CONCLUSION

The persistence of Downes's small law firm indicates that it was not in its character incapable of facing tough competition in the marketplace. For twenty-seven years, from 1903 to 1930, the firm survived in one form or another and provided a broad range of legal services in Edmonton and the surrounding region. Smallness itself was not a barrier to success in the law business. The evidence presented in this essay shows that solo practitioners and small law partnerships were institutional features of the Edmonton legal landscape in the early twentieth century. Downes moved along a path of small-firm development, of a solo practitioner who derived satisfaction from taking responsibility for numerous functions in the law business. In this period, the typical Edmonton firm was still the small law concern. Edmonton also had its larger firms – Emery, Newell, Ford & Lindsay; Short, Cross, Maclean & Macdonald; and Woods, Sherry, Collisson & Field, to name but a few.[108] These practices had evolved from small beginnings, and if Downes ever considered joining one of them as they expanded, he abandoned the idea.

For Downes, the route to survival did not lie in expensive and spectacular growth, for he knew that such a strategy involved the risk of relying on the money markets and sacrificing control. Instead, Downes was determined to maintain personal control of his business, something he was able to do in his solo practice, as well as in Mill & Downes and Downes & Marks. Like many of his contemporaries in successful small firms, Downes recognized the need to nurture business development through innumerable local and regional friendships and associations. At the same time, one of Downes's high-ranking goals was to adhere to the principle of fostering security over growth in his law practice. Ironically, however, security was frequently transformed into uncertainty as he encountered financial problems relating largely to the cyclical nature of Alberta and Canadian business. Downes's law firm, lacking a specialty service for a niche market, had difficulty in coexisting with its larger counterparts such as Short, Cross, McLean & Macdonald – a firm that was better able to cope with the troubles arising from the 1913–14 and 1919–23 depressions.

Nevertheless, through personal connections and bonds of friendship, Downes succeeded in attracting clients in Edmonton and the surrounding countryside. The country/city practice he built up in the process gave him an edge over his competitors and permitted his firm to break into the regional market, making the business less dependent on a single community. This geographical diversification was healthy for the small Downes law concern and became a significant factor in its survival and development.

The firm was created primarily to serve the needs of Downes, but it served Edmonton and its region as well. This small law practice played an important role in helping the city and the surrounding countryside sustain their commitment to growth and development. During the period 1903–30, Downes's knowledge of law and the local and regional marketplace was a distinct business asset. Besides devoting his attention to meeting the individual requirements of his clients, he kept in personal touch with them. In doing so, Downes developed a law firm that helped make the economies of Edmonton and the outlying area productive and competitive.

NOTES

A number of people have helped me in preparing this essay. Archivists and librarians at the Provincial Archives of Alberta, the City of Edmonton Archives, the Legal Archives Society of Alberta, the Glenbow-Alberta Institute Archives, the University of Calgary, and the Edmonton Police Museum/ Archives deserve my thanks. Thanks are also due to Lucy Hawrysz, in Edmonton; Donald P. McLaws, John Armstrong, Louis A. Knafla, and Neil Watson, in Calgary; Ronald C. Stevenson, in Fredericton; and Howard E. Book, in Toronto. I would especially like to thank Carol Wilton and Peter Oliver for reading and commenting upon earlier drafts of this manuscript.

1 Kenneth Lipartito and Joseph Pratt, *Baker & Botts in the Development of Modern Houston* (Austin: University of Texas Press 1991)
2 *Henderson's Edmonton City Directory for 1919*, 16–17, 542
3 *Edmonton Bulletin*, 26 January 1940
4 Donald D. Landon, 'Clients, Colleagues, and Community: The Shaping of Zealous Advocacy in Country Law Practice,' *American Bar Foundation Research Journal* 1 (1985), 81–111, offers a valuable look at the country law practice in the United States.
5 *Henderson's Edmonton City Directory for 1930*, 55; John Gilpin, 'Failed Metropolis: The City of Strathcona, 1891–1912,' in Alan F.J. Artibise, ed., *Town and City: Aspects of Western Canadian Urban Development* (Regina: Canadian Plains Research Center 1981), 259–88
6 *Strathcona Chronicle*, 6 May 1907
7 The Legal Archives Society of Alberta, Law Society of Alberta, roll for 1907
8 *Edmonton Bulletin*, 26 January 1940. For a useful discussion of the education of a law student in Ontario at the turn of the century see Patrick Boyer, *A Passion for Justice: The Legacy of James Chalmers McRuer* (Toronto: The Osgoode Society 1994), 22–4.
9 Provincial Archives of Alberta, accession no. 76.219, George F. Downes Papers (hereinafter GFDP), box 1, file 1, commission in the Common Pleas Division of the High Court of Justice for Ontario, 9 April 1892
10 *Edmonton Bulletin*, 26 January 1940
11 GFDP, box 4, file 216, letterpress book, Palmerston, 27 September 1902, George F. Downes to John J. Drew
12 Ibid., 19 September 1902, George F. Downes to R.G. Macdonald
13 Ibid., 7 October 1902, George F. Downes to Norman Mackenzie
14 GFDP, box 1, file 3, George F. Downes, diploma of advocate, Law Society of the Northwest Territories 11 June 1903. For a helpful discussion of the Law Society of the Northwest Territories see Louis A. Knafla, 'From Oral to Written Memory: The Common Law Tradition in Western Canada,' in Louis A. Knafla, ed., *Law & Justice in a New Land: Essays in Western Canadian Legal History* (Toronto: Carswell 1986), 53–4.
15 GFDP, box 1, file 3, George F. Downes, advocate certificate, Law Society of Alberta, 16 September 1907
16 Ibid., box 5, file 217, letterpress book, Strathcona, 17 December 1907, George F. Downes to the Mayor and Council of the City of Strathcona
17 Ibid., 27 March 1906, George F. Downes to John Wonsch
18 Ibid., box 4, file 216, letterpress book, Palmerston, 7 October 1902; *Edmonton Journal*, 10 July 1984
19 *Henderson's Edmonton & Strathcona City Directory for 1908*, 219–20, 322; Hender-

son's Twin-City Edmonton and Strathcona Directory for 1910, 452–3; *Henderson's Edmonton City Directory for 1914,* 1019–20; *Henderson's Edmonton City Directory for 1919,* 542; *Henderson's Greater Edmonton Directory for 1930,* 739–40

20 GFDP, box 5, file 217, letterpress book, Strathcona, 13 February 1906, George F. Downes to D.A. McDonald

21 Ibid., box 1, file 32, letterpress book, Strathcona, 19 August 1908, George F. Downes to Del W. Wilkinson

22 The Legal Archives Society of Alberta, Law Society of Alberta members' file, Alfred L. Marks; *Edmonton Journal,* 2 January 1953

23 Ibid., Richard Hill-Male; *Edmonton Bulletin,* 10 December 1929

24 GFDP, box 2, file 135, Edmonton, 20 October 1919, George F. Downes to Hugh Bain

25 Ibid., box 4, file 216, letterpress book, Palmerston, 29 September 1902, George F. Downes to Ford Jones

26 Ibid., 7 October 1902, George F. Downes to Norman Mackenzie

27 Provincial Archives of Alberta, Accession, 69.305, Department of Attorney General, Supreme Court of Alberta Civil Case Files (hereinafter SCACCF), box 38, file 4340, *Ochsner* v. *Powell,* 15 September 1904

28 GFDP, box 1, file 25, papers for the incorporation of the Strathcona Chronicle Publishing Co. Ltd., n.d.

29 Ibid., box 1, file 26, papers for the incorporation of the Twin City Manufacturing Co. Ltd, 11 February 1909

30 Ibid., box 1, file 69, papers for the organization of the Great West Shoe Repair Company, 26 February 1912

31 *Strathcona Plaindealer,* 27 September 1910

32 GFDP, box 1, file 57, Strathcona, 29 March 1910, George F. Downes to Clarence H. Stout; Strathcona, 30 March 1910, same to same

33 Ibid., box 5, file 217, Strathcona, 12 April 1907, George F. Downes to the Ottawa Dominion Lands Office. See also Georgina Binnie-Clark, *Wheat and Woman,* with an Introduction by Susan Jackel (Toronto: University of Toronto Press 1979), xiv–xxxii.

34 SCACCF, box 37, file 4219, *Turner* v. *Spencer,* 7 May 1904

35 GFDP, box 1, file 32, Strathcona, 17 December 1909, George F. Downes to Del W. Wilkinson

36 City of Edmonton Archives, MS 209, file 145, South Edmonton, 18 July 1912, George F. Downes to the mayor and council of the City of Edmonton

37 Edmonton Police Museum/Archives, outgoing correspondence, Edmonton, 12 October 1912, an unidentified City of Edmonton officer to W.J. Bowse

38 GFDP, box 5, file 217, Strathcona, 15 June 1906, George F. Downes to George C. Downes

39 Ibid.
40 Ibid., box 8, file 315, Toronto, 17 November 1907, George C. Downes to George F. Downes
41 City of Edmonton Archives, RG101.1, class 2, Papers of the Secretary-Treasurer of the Town of Strathcona, letterpress book, Strathcona, 8 February 1906, George F. Downes to Frank W. Morse
42 Ibid., letterpress book, Strathcona, 25 January 1906, George F. Downes to the Copeland-Chatterson Co.; Strathcona, 27 March 1906, George F. Downes to the Pettypiece Silex Stone Co.; Strathcona, 9 April 1906, George F. Downes to the Council of the Town of Strathcona; Minute Book, Council of the Town of Strathcona, 379
43 City of Edmonton Archives, Minute Book, Council of the Town of Strathcona, 450
44 *Strathcona Plaindealer*, 10 May 1907; *Strathcona Chronicle*, 15 May 1907
45 *Edmonton Journal*, 30 May 1907
46 City of Edmonton Archives, RG101.1, class 3, Papers of the Secretary-Treasurer of the City of Strathcona, letterpress book, Strathcona, 30 March 1907, George F. Downes to W. McIntyre
47 *Strathcona Plaindealer*, 5 June 1908
48 Ibid., 27 September 1910
49 City of Edmonton Archives, RG100.1, C9/85, Strathcona, 12 May 1908, George F. Downes to the Mayor and Council of the City of Strathcona
50 Ibid., C9/331, Strathcona, 19 December 1911, George F. Downes to the Mayor and Council of the City of Strathcona
51 *Henderson's Edmonton & Strathcona City Directory for 1908*, 269; *Edmonton Bulletin*, 26 January 1940; City of Edmonton Archives, RG101.1, C9/209, Strathcona, 5 February 1910, George F. Downes to Charles E.K. Cox; RG100.1, C9/243, Strathcona, 19 November 1910, George F. Downes to the Mayor and Council of the City of Strathcona; MS 209, file 337, Strathcona, 26 October 1911, George F. Downes to the Mayor and Council of the City of Strathcona
52 *Henderson's Edmonton & Strathcona City Directory for 1908*, 266–7
53 Ibid., 270; *Constitution and General Laws of the Supreme Court of the Independent Order of Foresters* (Toronto: Hunter, Rose, 1898), 18–20. For an account of the importance of a similar institution, see J.C. Herbert Emery, 'The Rise and Fall of Fraternal Methods of Social Insurance: A Case Study of the Independent Order of Oddfellows of British Columbia Sickness Insurance, 1874–1951,' *Business and Economic History* 23 (Fall 1994), 10–15.
54 GFDP, box 8, file 302, Edmonton, 1 June 1927, George F. Downes to the Supreme Secretary of the Independent Order of Foresters

55 SCACCF, box 38, file 4340, *Ochsner* v. *Powell*, 15 September 1904, Mills & Downes letterhead, 26 September 1903

56 GFDP, box 5, file 217, letterpress book, Strathcona, 1 August 1906, George F. Downes to George C. Downes

57 Ibid., box 8, file 328, Strathcona, 31 August 1908, George F. Downes to Duncan McCallum

58 Ibid., box 1, file 70, Strathcona, 3 October 1911, Downes & Marks to William Halfpenny. For further information on lawyers' roles as money lenders in Alberta during this period, see Henry C. Klassen, 'Lawyers, Finance, and Economic Development in Southwestern Alberta, 1884 to 1920,' in Carol Witton, ed., *Essays in the History of Canadian Law*, vol. 4: *Beyond the Law: Lawyers and Business in Canada, 1830 to 1930* (Toronto: The Osgoode Society 1990), 312–13.

59 Ibid., box 5, file 217, letterpress book, Strathcona, 27 March 1906, George F. Downes to John Wonsch

60 Ibid., Strathcona, 1 August 1906, George F. Downes to George C. Downes

61 Ibid., box 1, file 6, Strathcona, 15 January 1908, Mills & Downes to E.T. Griffin; Strathcona, 15 January 1908, Mills & Downes to C.C. Chipman

62 Ibid., box 8, file 324, Toronto, 30 October 1916, George C. Downes to George F. Downes; box 8, file 325, Toronto, 19 March 1917, same to same

63 Ibid., box 3, file 208, *Whiteside* v. *Broadhead* et al., 30 October 1917

64 The Legal Archives Society of Alberta, Arnold & Arnold Papers, box 11, file 242, petition of Mary Emily Gould to Judge A.A. Carpenter of the District Court of the District of Calgary, 25 February 1914

65 *Statutes of the Province of Alberta*, 1907, c. 4

66 GFDP, box 1, file 20, petition of Robert Palmer and Albert Stannard to the District Court of the District of Edmonton, 10 February 1908

67 For American legal literature on estate planning and the family farm in the United States see Neil E. Harl, 'Estate and Business Planning for Farmers,' *The Hastings Law Journal* 19 (January 1968), 271–307. Some writings deal with the transfer of wealth in the Canadian family farm and the American family farm without discussing the role of the lawyer in the transfer. See, for example, Henry C. Klassen, 'Family Business and Inheritance and Succession in Alberta and Montana in the Late Nineteenth and Early Twentieth Centuries,' in Peter A. Baskerville, ed., *Canadian Papers in Business History*, vol. 3 (Victoria, BC: Public History Group, University of Victoria, 1993), 45–69; David Gagan, *Hopeful Travellers: Families, Land and Social Change in Mid-Victorian Peel County, Canada West* (Toronto: University of Toronto Press 1981), 40–60; Mark Friedberger, *Farm Families & Change in Twentieth-Century America* (Lexington: University of Kentucky Press 1988), 74–98.

68 GFDP, box 1, file 20, Strathcona, 16 June 1908, Mills & Downes to Ernest W. Jones

69 Ibid., petition of Robert Palmer and Albert Stannard to the District Court of the District of Edmonton, 10 February 1908

70 Ibid., Strathcona, 5 September 1908, George F. Downes to Short, Cross & Biggar

71 See Edward P. McNeill, 'Grants of Probate and Letters of Administration in Alberta,' *The Alberta Law Quarterly* 1 (December 1934), 96–7

72 GFDP, box 1, file 20, Strathcona, 20 May 1908, Mills & Downes to Robert Palmer and Albert Stannard

73 *Ordinances of the North-West Territories*, 1905, c. 119; GFDP, box 1, file 20, Strathcona, 5 September 1908, George F. Downes to Short, Cross & Biggar

74 GFDP, box 1, file 20, Strathcona, 16 June 1908, George F. Downes to Robert Palmer

75 Ibid., Strathcona, 16 June 1908, Mills & Downes to Thomas H. Jones

76 Ibid., Edmonton, 16 June 1908, MacKinnon & Cogswell to Mills & Downes

77 Ibid., Strathcona, 5 September 1908, George F. Downes to Short, Cross & Biggar

78 Ibid., Strathcona, 29 August 1908, George F. Downes to Mrs Victoria A. Saunders

79 Ibid., petition of Robert Palmer and Albert Stannard to the District Court of the District of Edmonton, 10 February 1908

80 Ibid., box 3, file 187, *Mathie* v. *Ferguson*, statement of claim delivered by George F. Downes, 2 March 1920; Edmonton, 10 January 1920, George F. Downes to William B. Ferguson; Edmonton, sometime in January 1920, Margaret B. Mathie to George F. Downes

81 Ibid., Edmonton, 26 November 1920, George F. Downes to George W. Massie

82 Ibid., Edmonton, 29 September 1920, George F. Downes to Margaret B. Mathie; box 3, file 186, Edmonton, 7 April 1921, Margaret B. Mathie to George F. Downes

83 Ibid., box 3, file 186, will of Margaret Balmain Mathie, 5 July 1921

84 Ibid., box 5, file 222, ledger, 125

85 Ibid., 221–8

86 Lucy Hawrysz collection, Edmonton, Alberta, Strathcona, 8 November 1909, George F. Downes to George C. Downes

87 GFDP, box 5, file 217, letterpress book, Strathcona, 9 October 1907, George F. Downes to Joseph McMillan

88 Ibid., 15 January 1908, George F. Downes to Office Specialty Manufacturing Company

89 Ibid., box 8, file 302, Edmonton, 2 October 1923, George F. Downes to V.T.

Richards; Lucy Hawrysz collection, Pittsburgh, 24 October 1930, Cecil Downes to George F. Downes; certificate of title, 5 May 1916

90 Ibid., box 2, file 142, Edmonton, 2 September 1915, George F. Downes to J.M. Spence

91 Ibid., box 3, file 209, Edmonton, 11 May 1921, George F. Downes to J.H. Sissons

92 Ibid., box 7, file 271, Edmonton, 19 February 1917, George F. Downes to Joseph Murphy

93 Ibid., box 3, file 209, Strathcona, 27 June 1919, George F. Downes to the Wilber Mercantile Agency of Chicago

94 Ibid., 11 May 1921, George F. Downes to J.H. Sissons

95 Ibid., box 6, file 241, ledger, 68–96

96 Ibid.

97 Ibid., box 8, file 302, Edmonton, 11 September 1923, George F. Downes to V.T. Richards

98 Ibid., letter written between 17 August and 25 November 1926, George F. Downes to Valentine Richards

99 Ibid., box 2, file 164, Edmonton, 3 February 1927, George F. Downes to Amelia Harland

100 Ibid., box 8, file 302, Edmonton, 1 June 1927, George F. Downes to the Supreme Secretary of the Independent Order of Foresters

101 Ibid., 19 July 1927, George F. Downes to the Reverend William Greer

102 Ibid., box 3, file 177, Bruce, Alberta, 24 April 1928, A. Willans to George F. Downes; box 2, file 164, Edmonton, 7 May 1929, George F. Downes to Mrs W.M. Charters; box 3, file 194, Edmonton, 17 June 1930, George F. Downes to Donald McBride

103 Ibid., box 8, file 302, Edmonton, 5 February 1932, George F. Downes to the Supreme Secretary of the Independent Order of Foresters

104 Ibid., 16 October 1929, George F. Downes to Frank R. Hand

105 Ibid., 3 June 1930, George F. Downes to Howatt & Howatt

106 *Edmonton Bulletin*, 26 January 1940

107 Lucy Hawrysz collection, memorandum of agreement between George Francis Downes and Mary Alice Frost, 31 December 1907

108 *Henderson's Edmonton City Directory for 1919*, 16–17, 542

8

Corporate Entrepreneurship in Atlantic Canada: The Stewart Law Firm, 1915–1955

GREGORY P. MARCHILDON and BARRY CAHILL

'Laissez-faire is as dead as Jacob Marley.'

– James McGregor Stewart, 1942

'J. McGregor Stewart is ... one of Canada's most interlocking directors.'

– Judith Robinson, 1945

'Mr Stewart told me [in 1952] that in Halifax a man could be a big frog in a small puddle.'

– Frank Covert on James McGregor Stewart, 1980

INTRODUCTION: CORPORATE LAWYERS AS LEGAL, FINANCIAL, AND BUSINESS INSTITUTIONS

With branch offices in St John's, Sydney, Halifax, Moncton, Saint John, and Charlottetown, Stewart McKelvey Stirling Scales is the largest and most conspicuously 'entrepreneurial' law firm east of Montreal. Created in one of the many mergers which transformed the Canadian legal landscape during the late 1980s, the firm has long roots in the Maritime business establishment.[1] The oldest firm in the 1990 merger was Halifax's highest-profile corporate law firm, Stewart, MacKeen and Covert, which in turn had evolved out of the Harris, Henry and Cahan law firm, serving the interests of the finance capitalist John F. Stairs, whose business empire included sugar, cordage, and finance in Halifax; steel and coal in New Glasgow; manufacturing in Amherst; and electrical utilities in the West Indies.[2]

There have been a number of identifiable phases in the evolution of the Halifax firm. From the time of its founding in 1867 by William Alexander Henry, afterwards an original justice of the Supreme Court of Canada, and Malachy Bowes Daly, a son of the colonial administrator, Sir Dominick Daly, until the early 1890s, the firm was a typical law partnership. It provided a range of traditional services to individual clients – wills, estate administration, property transfers, commercial contracts, and courtroom advocacy involving everything from criminal prosecutions to Admiralty litigation.[3]

A new phase was initiated about 1891, when Thomas Ritchie withdrew from the firm while serving as vice-president of the Merchants Bank of Halifax (later the Royal Bank of Canada), and Robert E. Harris left his sole practice in Yarmouth to join Hugh McDonald Henry and his younger brother, William A. Henry, Jr. Through his close association with John F. Stairs, Harris soon became a businessman in his own right; he was a director in numerous Maritime enterprises, such as Royal Securities Corporation, as well as Stairs's successor as president of Nova Scotia Steel and Coal (1904), and Ritchie's as president of Eastern Trust (1909).

When Harris left the firm for a seat on the bench of the Supreme Court of Nova Scotia in 1915, he was replaced by James McGregor Stewart, an accomplished scholar who had been called to the bar and had joined the firm the year before. Thus did W.A. Henry, Jr. become head of the firm, and J. McG. Stewart a partner. Stewart stood to inherit many of Harris's directorships even while carrying on an active and successful practice in high-level appellate advocacy. 'One of the judges told me,' wrote Frank Covert in his memoirs, twenty-five years after Stewart's death, 'that in his early days he was an excellent barrister and that when he appeared before the Nova Scotia Supreme Court *in banco* [court of appeal], the Judges used to fight to sit on the bench to hear him.'[4] As time went by, however, Stewart specialized in corporate law and promotion, participating in the management of many of the companies he helped establish or reorganize. In so doing, he surpassed Harris as a regional business leader, and became nationally recognized as the Maritime linch-pin of the pan-Canadian corporate élite, a position confirmed by his election as vice-president of the Royal Bank of Canada in 1951.

Stewart in turn was succeeded by his former articled clerk Frank Manning Covert, also a recognized leading figure in the Canadian business

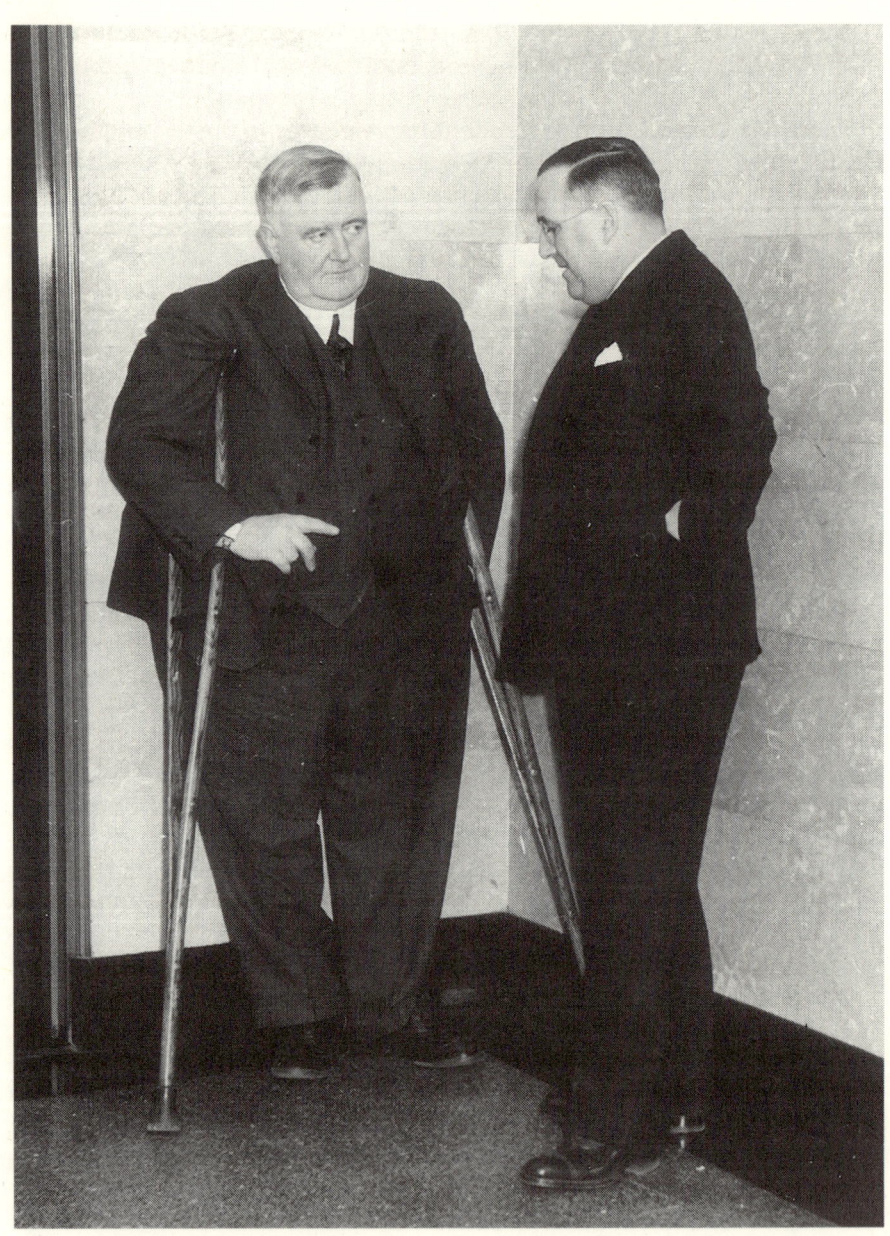

James McGregor Stewart (left), *c.* 1950 (courtesy Vivian S. Morrison)

world of the 1950s through the 1970s, and a far more ubiquitous figure in the literature.[5] Though a regional rather than a national figure, and there-fore less significant historically than Stewart, Covert is far better known than his mentor, whom he succeeded as eastern Canada's 'Mr Lawyer.' Unlike Covert, Stewart never kept a diary or otherwise wrote about him-self, and only a small portion of his scattered personal papers is extant. As a consequence, Stewart is today almost entirely unknown to legal and business history alike. Covert, on the other hand, passed on after his death a treasure trove of documentation, including diaries, memoirs, and a manuscript history of the firm. Covert was succeeded by his protégé, James William Edgar Mingo – the current head of the firm – who has maintained the Harris–Stewart–Covert tradition into the 1990s. Despite sitting on the boards of many of Canada's largest corporations, however, Covert could not reasonably have aspired to the unique hegemony of Stewart. The relative economic decline of the Atlantic region, already evi-dent during the interwar years, undercut his ability to play a leading role in Canadian business and corporate law in the latter half of the twentieth century.

The Harris era has already been dealt with in a previous essay;[6] the subject of this essay is the Stewart era, extending from the First World War to the mid-1950s. During this time, Halifax's third-largest and third-eldest law firm became the dominant one in Atlantic Canada. Stewart himself was largely responsible for the corporate culture which would set the firm apart from others, and which remains evident even today in the portrait gallery of the Halifax head office of Stewart McKelvey Stirling Scales. In particular, the closeness (some would say telescoping) of the solicitor–counsel–client relationship; the independent entrepreneurship, business advocacy, and investment skills of the individual partners; and the unusual nature of the firm's partnership agreement can all be traced to the Stewart era.

THE CORPORATE LAW FIRM AND
ATLANTIC CANADIAN BUSINESS HISTORY

Recent work by Philip Girard has drawn attention to the ideological role of the 'corporate lawyer' as the icon of the legal profession in the early 1900s.[7] The demand for the type of services generally associated with cor-porate law practice – from incorporating, financing, and reorganizing companies, to providing specialized services in income tax, patent, trade-mark, contract, labour–management, and government relations – originally stemmed from the rise of big business during the second Industrial Revolution.[8] In North America, the first 'corporate' law firms emerged in New York City, the financial and legal hub of institutional change, at the very end of the nineteenth century.[9] Here, the early 'law factories' – firms such as Cravath, Swaine & Moore; Sullivan & Cromwell; Shearman & Sterling; and Cadwallader, Wickersham & Taft – serviced the 'robber barons' and their enormous railway and industrial enterprises.[10]

In Canada, the 'giant' law firm did not truly appear until well after the Second World War, owing in part to the much smaller scale of business organization.[11] None the less, from an early date, some 'downtown' firms in the country's largest cities began to provide the specialized corporate legal services increasingly demanded by Canadian big business and high finance, though on a smaller scale than in the large American cities. By 1914 the Blake, Lash & Cassels and the Thomson, Tilley & Johnston firms of Toronto; the Greenshields, the Cahan and the Lovett firms of Montreal; and the Harris, Henry, Rogers & Harris, and the McInnes, Mellish, Fulton & Kenny law firms in Halifax were all servicing the needs of big business.[12]

Wayne Hobson's essay on the emergence of the large law firm in the United States contains two salient facts relevant to this study.[13] First, the corporate law firm grew slowly until well after the Second World War, such that, in 1915, one year after J. McG. Stewart began practising, the average size of the twenty-seven major firms in the five largest American cities was still fewer than nine lawyers. Moreover, the large law firm – defined by Hobson as containing at least five members (i.e., partners and/or associates) – did not begin to dominate the profession until the second half of the twentieth century. Second, as Robert Nelson pointed out in his major study of the transformation of the large American law firm, the 'mega-firms' of today most often originated as corporate law firms during the 'gilded age' – a direct consequence of the intergenerational succession of corporate clients as businesses and law firms developed together in a symbiotic relationship.[14]

As can be seen in table 8-1, the Harris–Henry and later the Henry–Stewart law firm approached, and then equalled, the minimum size of the large law office, as defined by Hobson. More important, from at least 1900, when Robert E. Harris was the senior partner, the firm exhibited the same characteristics as the larger corporate law firms then emerging south of the border as well as in Montreal and Toronto. It was assumed that members of the firm would demonstrate functional specialization – senior partners, such as Harris, remaining 'exclusively office lawyers'

TABLE 8.1
Law-Firm Nomenclature and Size, 1867–1989

Years	Firm name	Number of partners
1867–75	Henry & Daly	2
1876–86	Henry & Weston	2
1887–8	Henry, Ritchie & Weston	3
1889–90	Henry, Ritchie, Weston & Henry	4
1890–1	Henry, Ritchie & Weston	3
1892–3	Henry, Harris & Henry	3
1894–5	Harris & Henry	2
1896–1905	Harris, Henry & Cahan	3–5
1906–8	Harris, Henry, Lovett & Stairs	4–5
1909–10	Harris, Henry, Stairs & Harris	4–5
1911	Harris, Henry, Rogers & Harris	4
1912	Harris, Henry, Rogers, Harris & Stairs	5
1913–15	Harris, Henry, Rogers & Harris	4
1916–26	Henry, Rogers, Harris & Stewart	4
1927–31	Henry Stewart Smith & McCleave	2–4
1932–46	Stewart Smith MacKeen & Rogers	5–7
1947–51	Stewart Smith MacKeen Covert & Rogers	7–8
1952–8	Stewart Smith MacKeen Covert Rogers Sperry & Cowan	9–12
1959–63	Stewart Smith & MacKeen	12–16
1964–89	Stewart MacKeen & Covert	15–46

Sources: Frank M. Covert's manuscript history of Stewart, MacKeen & Covert, January 1980; and legal directories

(counsel–solicitors), rarely if ever appearing in court or chambers, while others, such as Tecumseh Sherman Rogers, handled almost all of the firm's court work. By the turn of the century, moreover, the firm was already making ready use of information and communications technology still comparatively new to law firms, such as the telephone, the telegraph, and the typewriter. Administrative changes included hiring juniors to support the firm's partnership, as well as professional stenographer typists and foot couriers – the latter as numerous as or outnumbering the lawyers themselves. As incredible as it may sound today, such innovations met great resistance even in the large New York firms. When John Foster Dulles, for example, joined Sullivan & Cromwell as a clerk in 1911, he found that the partners insisted on writing other lawyers in longhand rather than using the telephone or resorting to stenographers.[15]

While R.E. Harris had the foresight to introduce these technological and administrative changes very early on, it was the mercurial, physically challenged J. McG. Stewart, promoted to partnership after scarcely a year at the bar and in the firm, who was primarily responsible for establishing the corporate culture which would define the firm for most of the twentieth century. Some of these attributes are similar to the so-called Cravath system in the United States, while others were unique to the Halifax firm: (1) a policy of hiring only the best academically performing graduates from Dalhousie Law School, where at least six partners (including both F.M. Covert and J.W.E. Mingo) have won the University Medal in Law,[16] or from the best law schools in the United States or Canada outside the Maritime region; (2) a policy of internal promotion in place of external recruitment after articling; (3) a bias against promotion based on family connection; (4) a policy of 'nothing in, nothing out' – a system in which lawyers did not pay to become an associate or member, nor did they receive any capital sum upon retiring from the partnership; (5) a policy of encouraging the accrual of outside fees and income through directorships and officerships, the profits from which were retained by individual partners; (6) a strict correspondence between actual billings and the amount which senior partners were allowed to draw as income from the firm; and, most significant of all, (7) an ideology of corporate practice in which lawyers were encouraged to participate directly in the business of clients, or to become entrepreneurs themselves. The late senior counsel to the firm, for example, a distinguished Admiralty lawyer who articled under J. McG. Stewart, operated for many years a successful international marine salvage company.[17]

Though a much smaller city than Montreal or Toronto, Halifax was a major regional centre of business during the first decades of the twentieth century. In straight commercial terms, moreover, Halifax remained Canada's third city, even as it was surpassed in terms of population by cities such as Winnipeg and Vancouver. It was also, in many important respects, better integrated than the western cities into the large central Canadian business and legal community, at least until the postwar years, when the Maritime region declined in economic importance relative to central and western Canada. In other words, while Halifax today may be a third-tier Canadian city, before the Second World War it was a second-tier city with more powerful linkages to the economic metropolises of Montreal and Toronto. During the period in which James McGregor Stewart and the law firm of which he became head in 1927 rose to prominence, therefore, the distinction between the regional economy of the Maritimes and the so-called national economy was much less clear-cut than it was to become in the second half of the twentieth century.

To some degree, this explains the apparently contradictory behaviour of the most prominent members of the firm – one moment protecting local businesses from acquisition by outside interests, the next moment servicing and sitting on the boards of some of the leading central Canadian companies. The anomaly is more apparent than real, however, and not hard to resolve. Benefiting directly from local business as corporate clients, the members of the firm encouraged a vigorous regional economy, but they were not prepared to support or subsidize local business at any cost. Whenever possible, they instead insinuated themselves into the pan-Canadian business establishment, even facilitating the acquisition of local enterprises by the companies with which they were connected. R.E. Harris was more than prepared to allow Nova Scotia Steel and Coal to be taken over by American interests during his final year in the president's chair;[18] Tory J. McG. Stewart would not support the Maritime Rights movement;[19] and Liberal Frank Covert lobbied against the Nova Scotia Conservative government's takeover of the old Dosco steel works in Sydney, Cape Breton, which was about to be closed by its then owner, Hawker–Siddeley.[20]

The decline of Halifax as a regional financial centre, and the consequent magnetic attraction of central Canada, did have one very direct effect on the firm, drawing some of its best and brightest members to Montreal, and later Toronto. Robert E. Harris lost both Charles H. Cahan and H. Almon Lovett to Montreal, where they established their own corporate practices. In 1912 Harris also lost John F. Stairs's lawyer–son, Gilbert Sutherland, a graduate of Harvard Law School and Nova Scotia's first Rhodes Scholar, who joined the Montreal firm of McGibbon, Casgrain, Mitchell & Surveyer (now Kierans Guay), eventually doing extensive work for I.W. Killam's Montreal Engineering Company.[21] Similarly, Stewart ended up losing some of his 'young men' to the bright lights of central Canada, thereby encouraging him to establish the kind of firm which he hoped would provide as many opportunities to juniors as were available to ambitious young corporate lawyers in Montreal and Toronto.

THE EPIPHANY OF JAMES McGREGOR STEWART

In his important article 'The Ideal and the Actual in the Law,' Robert Gordon attempts to explain the ideological sources of the influence and power of the great lawyer–aristocrats during America's gilded age.[22] In practice, they were corporate lawyers, developing skills and a legal technology entirely new to the profession, and incidentally helping to give birth to the second Industrial Revolution. In terms of wealth, prestige, and influence, these men occupied the front rank of the profession, relegating the great appellate advocates down into the second rank.

Despite their daily preoccupation with corporate finance and business and their own great material wealth, these new aristocrats of the intellect were men of very high ideals, often attracted to public service and progressive causes. In Gordon's view, 'their ambition for roles of public virtue was intensified by the fact that, in background, they were not really aristocrats at all, but rather the sons of the Protestant, back-country gentry, the ministers, doctors, and lawyers of small New England and upstate New York towns.' This factor alone might explain their 'high, not to say rigid, personal rectitude' and the fact that their clients, capitalists all – Morgan, Vanderbilt, Fisk, Gould, etc. – entrusted their fortunes completely to them.[23]

Their aristocratic stature related to the fact that these 'lawyer princes' appeared to possess great knowledge and wisdom. Educated at the finest east-coast colleges and universities, they possessed refined tastes and minds honed by exposure to the great works of classical literature. Their legal education, moreover, brought them into intimate contact with the ideal of a unified science of law, then sweeping the 'national' law schools such as Harvard and Columbia. According to this view of legal pedagogy, the study of law had to be regarded, not as a mere artisanal apprenticeship, but as an essay in the theory and practice of jurisprudence. In the eyes of society at large, moreover, corporate lawyers of this vintage were the great and wise counsellors whose integrity and intellectual superiority were beyond question.

In Canada, no barrister better exemplified this type – the lawyer prince – than James McGregor Stewart. Born into a second-generation Scottish immigrant family replete with Presbyterian ministers (uncle, grandfather, and great-uncle), lawyers (father), and doctors (uncle and brother), Stewart's ancestry was the epitome of Protestant, back-country gentry. Heir to the Scottish Free Church Presbyterian tradition of the ethicality of work and the pursuit of knowledge as a good-in-itself, Stewart would all his life emit an air of steely determination and uncompromising moral rectitude. He was trusted and depended upon by some of the country's most influential business figures of the twentieth century, including Izaak Walton Killam, easily the most mistrustful and secretive financier of his generation. In his actions as a corporate legal adviser, Stewart's powers of analysis and judgment became so prized that he was routinely asked to take executive-director positions – including the presidency or vice-presidency – on the boards of industrial companies and financial institutions of national stature. Most important, Stewart relaid the foundation-stone of the Atlantic regional law firm which continues to operate under his banner four decades after his death.

Stewart the Renaissance man spent a lifetime realizing the intellectual ideal of the corporate lawyer as iconic *éminence grise*. Born on 30 June 1889 in the old shire town of Pictou, Nova Scotia, James McGregor Stewart was the son of a prominent local lawyer. His father and namesake, a Dominion QC (1895) who was municipal clerk of Pictou County and a justice of the peace, died suddenly, aged forty-four, a few days before young James's eighth birthday. Winner of the coveted gold medal at Pictou Academy (founded 1816), Stewart *fils* in 1906 joined the queue of clever young Pictonians heading for Halifax in order to matriculate at Dalhousie University – like the Academy itself, a Presbyterian-inspired foundation.

Graduating in Arts in 1909 with First Class Honours in Greek and Latin, and winning the University Medal, Stewart was immediately invited to join the academic staff as tutor (assistant professor) in classics. This helped him finance his law course, which he pursued concurrently with teaching. Though he had been afflicted by polio at about two years of age and afterwards walked only with the aid of crutches, Stewart's extracurricular activities included managing the varsity football (soccer) team; for his herculean efforts, Stewart was named honorary life president of the Dalhousie Amateur Athletic Club.[24] Graduating for the second time in 1914, while serving as president of the students' council, Stewart became a lecturer in the law school, teaching real property, sales, and insurance. He held this post until 1923, when the demands of a busy law practice forced him to abandon teaching; so impressive was his record that two part-time lecturers were needed to fill his shoes. Six years later, however, Stewart was invited to join the board of governors of Dalhousie University, where his uncle, the celebrated Listerian surgeon John Stewart, was dean of medicine.[25] Within three years Stewart had been elected vice-chair of the board, and within eight years chair.[26] Though he prematurely resigned as chair in 1943, Stewart served continuously as an ordinary member of the board to the end of his life. As the university's elder statesman and by far the most powerful and influential board member both during and after his chairmanship, Stewart was sensitive to the perception that the board was overstocked with corporate lawyers. Taking a statesman-like view of the university's situation and long-term prospects, he did not hesitate to warn his hand-picked successor (a non-lawyer) against placing the interests of the law school, which allegedly had 'been a drain on the funds of the university,' ahead of those of the Arts Faculty.[27]

J. McG. STEWART'S FORMATIVE YEARS AT THE BAR, 1914–1925

Stewart began articling in 1911 under Willard Hill Fulton, KC, who was a partner in the 'downtown' Halifax law firm of McInnes, Mellish, Fulton & Kenny (now McInnes Cooper & Robertson).[28] In February 1914, however, two months before graduating from law school, Stewart arranged to transfer his articles to the Harris, Henry, Rogers & Harris law firm.[29] John Erskine Read, a friend, admirer, and former classmate of Stewart's, and the firm's newest junior, acted as midwife at this portentous rebirth of an articled clerk from a rival firm.[30] The senior partner concurred in the reassignment, and Stewart's articles were duly transferred to R.E. Harris's nephew, Reginald V. Harris, to whom Read's articles had also been transferred some four years earlier.[31]

Why Stewart decided to switch firms is unclear, but it is quite possible that he saw more opportunity in R.E. Harris's firm, despite the cachet of the McInnes firm.[32] Harris's clients constituted a 'who's who' of Maritime business – Acadia Sugar Refining, Brandram–Henderson, Eastern Trust, and Nova Scotia Steel and Coal – and Harris himself had recently become a director of the Bank of Nova Scotia. Contemporary remarks about Harris's devoting too much time to business and too little to law missed the point about the integration fundamental to an entrepreneurial corporate law practice.[33] By spending the lion's share of his time 'in business,' Harris was better able to understand and anticipate the needs of his various corporate clients. Preparing the documents – articles of incorporation, memoranda of association, underwriting agreements, contracts, deeds of trust and mortgages – was only the solicitorial part of the job. Advising one's clients as to the most effective, most profitable, and least expensive course of action in any given situation was the heart and soul of the extramural corporate counsel, and this was a much more creative and proactive undertaking than mere draughtsmanship, regardless of the complexity of the legal instruments produced.

Like his contemporary, the famous New York corporate lawyer Paul D. Cravath, Harris had neither an 'instinct for litigation' nor a penchant for abstract legal reasoning, but he did have a 'passion for organization' and a remarkable ability for 'diagnosing practical corporate law problem[s].'[34]

Harris, moreover, actively engaged in business on his own behalf both as an entrepreneur, risking large amounts of money in underwriting new securities issues, and as president of established industrial, financial, and utility enterprises. But he spent even more time in his law office, closely advising various corporate clients, in many of whose businesses he eventually took an investment interest. Many years after his death, Harris's private secretary described with awe his 'mathematical brain' when it came to working with figures. An 'indefatigable worker,' Harris was always the 'first at the office and generally the last to leave.'[35]

By 1914, Harris, aged fifty-four, was planning a graceful retirement from his corporate law practice through pursuing a judicial appointment, and needed to turn over his files to someone in the office. If he did in fact turn them over to his nephew, R.V. Harris, then it seems likely that the younger Harris, a lawyer with neither the appetite nor perhaps the ability to be a top-flight corporate counsel or litigator, simply handed them along to Stewart, his former articled clerk. Active in church, Masonic, and community affairs, as well as in municipal politics, R.V. Harris limited his practice to routine solicitorial work.[36] The year following his elevation to the chief-justiceship, R.E. Harris nepotistically procured for his nephew the sinecure of prothonotary of the Supreme Court.

Whatever the precise links in the chain of events, Stewart was made a partner in the firm when R.E. Harris left for the bench in 1915. He was soon servicing many, if not most, of Harris's corporate clients; indeed, Stewart may have been the only junior able and willing to do the work. William Alexander Henry, senior partner in the firm after Harris's retirement, specialized in Admiralty law, and was to act for the Crown in the official inquiry into the *Imo–Mont Blanc* collision which caused the Halifax Harbour explosion in December 1917.[37] A superb cricketer and footballer in his youth, Henry now spent his time golfing and playing bridge, never allowing the practice of law to interfere with his active social life.[38]

Second to Henry in seniority, Tecumseh Sherman Rogers had left his practice in Amherst to join the Harris firm in 1909. In his Amherst days, Rogers had to run the type of general practice common to industrial towns. Despite this limitation, by the time Rogers came to Halifax he had a well-earned reputation as a superb appellate lawyer. In fact, according to a story which has circulated for generations in the Halifax legal community, Rogers was in England arguing a case before the Judicial Committee of the Privy Council when a telegram from Ottawa arrived at the firm asking for the exact spelling of his given names. Intuiting the reason for the request, R.E. Harris immediately boarded the train for Ottawa, and got himself appointed to the Supreme Court of Nova Scotia in place of Rogers. Rogers, whose promotion to the bench was thus deferred for six years, never forgave Harris for this betrayal.[39]

His own continuing involvement in appellate work notwithstanding, the next ten years would see J. McG. Stewart equal, and then surpass, R.E. Harris as the pre-eminent corporate lawyer in Halifax, and by extension in the Maritime provinces. Following the war, a new generation of partners such as John Erskine Read, who rejoined the firm after his war service ended in 1918,[40] Ingram Oakes (1918),[41] Donald Vaughan White (1922),[42] Robert David McCleave (1922),[43] Henry Poole MacKeen (1923), William Marshall Rogers – son of Tecumseh Sherman – (1923), and Joseph Patrick Connolly (1924) were keen to follow Stewart's leadership in expanding the firm's corporate law practice.[44]

'CANADA'S MYSTERY MAN OF HIGH FINANCE' – AND HIS LAWYER

There was nothing in his academic background of *literae humaniores* to suggest that James McGregor Stewart would become the consummate lawyer–financier of his generation. Lacking any investment capital apart from his own modest income as a university teacher, Stewart nevertheless began promoting companies before he was called to the bar. His involvement in real estate development and commercial shipping ventures as an incorporator/provisional director began as early as 1913, when he was twenty-four.[45] Stewart soon joined forces with his future wife, Elizabeth 'Baptista' (alias Emily) Wilson, a legal secretary who in 1912 had gone to work as a stenographer for the firm then known as Harris, Henry, Rogers & Harris.[46] The future Mrs Stewart was a Roman Catholic from a lower-middle-class background; her father worked for Moirs Limited, chocolate manufacturers, which Stewart reorganized in 1925 and of which he was to become vice-president and majority shareholder. By the time of her 'mixed' marriage to the ultra-Presbyterian Stewart at Richmond Hill, Long Island, in April 1931, Miss Wilson had transformed her position as secretary and confidante to the senior partner into *de facto* 'general manager' of the law firm. Styling herself 'solicitor's clerk,' she frequently appeared with one or more of the firm's partners or the bookkeeper as an incorporator of companies.[47]

Stewart began his career in corporate law innocuously enough by acting as incorporator of new or newly restructured companies and as solicitor for established ones. From solicitor he advanced to counsel, and from

TABLE 8.2
Profile of the Corporate Career of James McGregor Stewart, 1925–1955

Chairman	President	Vice-President	Director
Mersey Paper Maritime Steel and Foundries Maritime National Fish	Maritime Paper Products Acadia Sugar Refining	Royal Bank Nova Scotia Light and Power Moirs Nova Scotia Construction National Sea Products Avon River Power	Markland Shipping United Service Corporation Brandram–Henderson Lovat Steamship Sun Life Assurance Montreal Trust Canada Cement Sobeys Stores Eastern Telephone & Telegraph Industrial Containers Dominion Steel and Coal Ocean Industries Super Service Stations Superline Oils Atlantic Traders MacDonald Construction

Note: This list is neither exhaustive nor sequential, and represents only the highest level known to have been reached by J. McG. Stewart in each company concerned.
Source: Chiefly The Financial Post Directory of [Canadian] Directors, 1931–1955

counsel to director. Many of the companies he served as legal adviser eventually invited him onto their board of directors, from which he was in a position to advance to the executive committee. Stewart's first substantive directorship (1925) was of Acadia Sugar Refining Company Limited, whose original directors had included the former head of the firm, Chief Justice Harris. The successful restructuring and reflotation of Acadia in 1926, which Stewart masterminded, laid the foundation of his enduring reputation as Atlantic Canada's wizard of corporation finance. Acadia, a regional merger promoted by John F. Stairs in 1893, had fallen on hard times both before and after the First World War. Overproduction, regional competition, the loss of one of the company's two remaining refineries in the Halifax Harbour explosion of 1917, and dumping by foreign manufacturers had rendered the English-registered and Scottish-

TABLE 8.3
Large Corporate Clients of the Harris–Henry–Stewart Law Firm, 1909–1955

Acadia Sugar Refining Company*	Famous Players Corporation
Acadia Trust Company	Maritime National Fish*
Avon River Power Company*	Mersey Paper Company*
Bradstreets	Metropolitan Life Insurance
Brandram-Henderson*	Moirs*
Canada Fire Insurance Company	Mutual Life Assurance
Canada Life Assurance Company	National Sea Products*
Canadian Keyes Fibre	Nova Scotia Light and Power*
Canadian Pacific Express Company	Nova Scotia Steel and Coal
Canadian Pacific Railway	Royal Bank of Canada*
Commercial Union Insurance	Royal Securities
Dominion Atlantic Railway	Sun Life Assurance Company*
Dominion Express Company	Union Bank of Halifax
Eastern Trust Company*	United Service Corporation*

Note: Asterisks identify those companies in which James McGregor Stewart is known
to have been an officer or a director.
Sources: *Canadian Law List*, 1909–55; Covert, 'Firm History'

financed company virtually bankrupt. Under a scheme of reorganization
devised by Stewart and adopted by the shareholders in April 1926, the
old company went into voluntary liquidation and transferred its assets to
a new company incorporated under the same name in Nova Scotia and
capitalized at $3 million.[48] Stewart assembled the underwriting syndicate
and drafted the underwriting agreement,[49] while another partner in the
firm acted as incorporator – together with the prospective president and
the continuing secretary–managing director. Two years later the president died and was replaced by Stewart, who remained in the position
until the Second World War, when his appointment as coal administrator
on the Wartime Prices and Trade Board obliged him to relinquish the
post.

Stewart's second executive-directorship emerged from the expatriate
financier Izaak Walton Killam's initial foray back into Nova Scotia – the
Nova Scotia Light & Power Company (now the 'reprivatized' Nova
Scotia Power Inc.) – of which Stewart became a director in 1926, and vice-
president in 1931, while continuing to serve as general counsel. Killam's
minority shareholding in the company, acquired in 1924, was sufficient to
place his cousin, Lawrence Killam (an engineering consultant), in the
presidency and his junior partner from Royal Securities Corporation,
stockbroker Ward Pitfield, in the vice-presidency.[50] Though Killam sold

out of the utility just before the Second World War, Stewart remained vice-president until his death in 1955.[51]

The financial intermediary through which Killam's 'constructive thrust' into the Maritime provinces was engineered was the Royal Securities Corporation, of which Killam acquired majority control in 1919, and sole ownership in 1928. In addition to servicing R.E. Harris's major corporate clients, such as Nova Scotia Steel and Coal and Eastern Trust, Stewart recaptured as a client Royal Securities, which Harris had forfeited during a bitter power struggle with Max Aitken a decade earlier.[52] As a fast-growing investment bank involved in the creation of numerous new enterprises, Royal Securities had formerly generated an enormous volume of business for the Harris law firm. The corporation's head office move from Halifax to Montreal in 1908, and Harris's final rupture with Aitken that year had hurt the firm.[53] Stewart's ability to regain the corporation as a business client, and become the new president–cum–majority shareholder's principal legal adviser, did much to reinvigorate the firm and establish Stewart's national reputation.

Stewart's firm had acted as solicitor for John F. Stairs's investment bank at its creation in 1903, and was to do so again throughout the 1920s as Royal Securities played a major role in financing Killam's electric utility and industrial promotions. Though relocated to Montreal by Aitken in 1908, Royal Securities continued to be registered in Nova Scotia and to maintain regional offices in Halifax, Saint John, Charlottetown, Fredericton, and St John's. By the late 1920s, the Halifax office was under the management of stockbroker J.C. MacKeen, younger brother of one of Stewart's partners in the law firm, H.P. MacKeen. In 1928 Killam instructed Stewart to incorporate a shell company under the slightly variant name Royal Investment Corporation Limited in order to cover Ward Pitfield's minority shareholding – 15 per cent – in Royal Securities while Killam levered the buyout of his former partner. Stewart became secretary of the shell company, Killam acquired sole ownership of Royal Securities, and Royal Investment was liquidated in 1931, its entire property and assets having been transferred to Killam as principal shareholder.[54]

By the early 1920s, Killam and Royal Securities were beginning to make major investments east of Quebec, reclaiming some of the corporation's former importance and lost business opportunities in the Atlantic region. Killam began his program of regional expansion immediately following the First World War by purchasing the Fraser Company in New Brunswick, one of the country's major manufacturers of spruce lumber, cedar shakes, and sulphite pulp.[55] In 1922 Killam sent two of his professional engineers – Denis Stairs (John F. Stairs's nephew) and Geoffrey Gaherty (Stairs's stepson) – to Newfoundland to investigate the St John's Light and Power Company. When Stairs and Gaherty reported favourably, Killam bought the existing properties and set up the consolidated Newfoundland Light and Power Company Limited.[56]

More significant in terms of the evolution of Killam's intercontinental business empire was the role played by the Bolivian Power Company Limited, the flotation of which was Stewart's first major undertaking for Killam.[57] In April 1925 Stewart incorporated the new company, capitalized at $3 million, in order for Killam to acquire the assets of an integrated utility company in La Paz, Bolivia, which was owned by English interests.[58] Bolivian Power was one of the original four Latin American utilities which Killam either owned or had a controlling interest in, and which were afterwards acquired by his holding company, International Power Company Limited.[59] While the origins of Bolivian Power can be traced to the foreign utility promotions of those Halifax finance capitalists – the Scotia group – who had set up Royal Securities in order to generate investment capital and streamline merger promotions, Bolivian Power was unusual in that it was a holding rather than an operating company. Having acquired the electric light, tramway, and telephone operations   in the Bolivian national capital, as well as other electric utilities and hydro-electric concessions, Killam recast the newly integrated utility as a subsidiary of International Power. Incorporated under the Canadian Companies Act in February 1926, International Power immediately took control of Bolivian Power and began to increase its operations and develop its natural-resource concessions in the context of a rapidly expanding Bolivian national economy.

Bolivian Power, moreover, was incorporated in Halifax rather than in Montreal, not only because there was a historic interrelationship among Halifax finance capitalists, those Caribbean and South American electric-utility mergers which they promoted, and the law firm in which Stewart was a partner, but also – and more important – because Stewart was Killam's trusted counsel, and Stewart's firm the solicitor for Killam's companies. Killam, as Stairs's and Aitken's successor in the presidency of Royal Securities Corporation, was perpetuating a tradition of international finance capitalism from a Halifax base – despite the fact that his personal base of operations was the RSC corporate headquarters on St James Street in Montreal. The fundamental similarity between the first of these ventures (Stairs's Trinidad Electric Company, 1901) and the last (Killam's Bolivian Power, 1925) was that both were essentially merger promotions.

Bolivian Power is also a striking example of the intergenerational transfer of active files within a corporate law firm: J. McG. Stewart bequeathed the file to F.M. Covert (partner 1935),[60] who in turn bequeathed it to D.A. Stewart (partner 1968) – no relation to J. McG.[61]

Shortly after the Bolivian Power flotation, Killam asked Stewart to help him select an appropriate Nova Scotian site for a hydro-electric–powered pulp-and-paper manufacturing complex. By 1928, Stewart had convinced Killam that the town of Liverpool, on the South Shore of Nova Scotia, provided the best opportunity available in the country. In March of that year, he exercised his leverage with the Conservative premier, lawyer Edgar Nelson Rhodes, to procure passage of a bill conferring special privileges on Killam's ghost company.[62] Then, in April, Stewart assisted Killam in negotiating the major contract between the Nova Scotia Power Commission and Royal Securities, involving the development of two hydro-electric–generating sites on the Mersey River capable of powering a mill with a production capacity of 200 to 250 tons of paper per day. The Mersey Paper Company Limited was incorporated on 31 July 1928, and Stewart was made a director, becoming vice-president two years later, and in 1949 its first and only chairman. Killam, despite being the majority shareholder, wished to have no formal position on the board; in fact, it was Stewart rather than Killam who presided at the official opening of the paper-mill in December 1929. Together – wrote Frank Covert, who was also present at the creation of Mersey – Stewart and Killam 'ensured the survival of the Company through the Depression. When Killam refused to advance further funds when the Company was in dire straits and told the board they would have to rely on the bank for help, Stewart [by then a director of the bank] persuaded the Royal Bank to carry the Company. On more than one occasion, the bank advanced money to meet the payroll.'[63] The Mersey chronicles reveal that Stewart's ability to act as intermediary, not only between Killam and the Royal Bank, but also between Killam and the ventures he was promoting and financing, was essential to the success of their working relationship.

If Killam was invisible, then Stewart was irreplaceable. When he died, the Mersey board, as a token of respect, declined to fill his vacant chairmanship. The Mersey file, moreover, by contrast with Bolivian Power, did not immediately descend by delegation within Stewart's law firm but temporarily left the firm altogether. Stewart's death, followed within months by that of Killam, and then by the decision of Killam's widow to sell Mersey to Bowaters, caused the file to migrate to another downtown Halifax law firm, Wickwire MacInnes & Wilson. It soon returned, how-

ever, while Covert, who had succeeded to most of Stewart's directorships, in due course became a director of new Mersey and remained one
until the end of his life.[64]

Stewart's most important individual client undoubtedly was I.W. Killam, whose confidential adviser Stewart was for more than thirty years,
until his death in February 1955. Stewart was also one of the few people –
perhaps the only person – from whom the hermetic 'mystery man of high
finance' (per Douglas How) sought both investment counsel and entrepreneurial advice. Not only would Killam visit Halifax purposely to consult with Stewart;[65] but family tradition has it that he would regularly
telephone to Halifax from his offshore residence in the Bahamas after
Stewart had retired for the night and talk at length into the mouthpiece
while Stewart, periodically placing the receiver down on the bed, endeavoured to continue with his leisure reading. The night-owlish Killam even
threatened – half in fun, whole in earnest – to purchase the estate ('Thorn-
vale') adjacent to Stewart's on the Northwest Arm of Halifax Harbour in
order to have the benefit of his sage advice at any hour of the day or
night.[66] In any Nova Scotia company in which Killam was a significant
shareholder, Stewart usually appeared as director or officer or both,[67] and
Stewart's law firm as solicitors. Stewart was not only Killam's trusted
adviser and *alter ego*, moreover, but also his proxy and stand-in. For many
years, Killam would agree to have no one but Stewart personally advise
him, despite the fact that other lawyers from the firm (especially Frank
Covert) were beginning to do significant pieces of solicitorial work for
Killam's companies. Killam also worried about Stewart's indifferent
health, which by 1953–4 had begun to fail.[68] The Stewart–Killam lawyer–
client relationship developed over the years into a close personal friendship and collaboration unique in the annals of Canadian business
history.[69]

THE ROYAL BANK OF CANADA: FROM SOLICITOR TO
VICE-PRESIDENT

If I.W. Killam was Stewart's most important individual client, then the
Royal Bank was both the firm's most important corporate client and
Stewart's most important directorial vice-presidency. 'Particularly influential,' writes Duncan McDowall in his official history of the Royal Bank,
'was J. McGregor Stewart, whose legal erudition and Maritime reputation
would echo through the boardroom from 1931 to 1955.' After twenty
years as a director, Stewart was elected in October 1951 to a non-

executive vice-presidency at a time when 'only four of thirty-three directors were Maritimers.'[70] In order to conserve his health – he was sixty-two
years old and suffering from degenerative heart disease – and devote
more attention to the affairs of the bank, Stewart officially retired from
active law practice and became counsel to the firm of which he had been
the senior partner for twenty years. The firm had not had the luxury of
general counsel since Dean R.C. Weldon, QC (1898–1903), and he had
never been a practising member of it.

While historically the Royal Bank (Merchants Bank of Halifax) was an
important corporate client – it had been so at least since 1886, when
Thomas Ritchie joined the firm – arguing that Stewart as director (1931–
55) and vice-president (1951–5) was able to route all Royal Bank business
in Atlantic Canada to his firm would be an oversimplification. It was
more a matter of Stewart's charting the course of the bank's corporate
investments in Atlantic Canada. Nor did the special relationship between
bank and firm begin with Stewart, or even with the immediately preceding generation of the firm. Stewart is most likely to have received the
Royal Bank file from T.S. Rogers, whose tenure as director of the bank
was foreshortened by his appointment to the bench in 1921, six years after
R.E. Harris's. Rogers is most likely to have received the file from Harris,[71]
and Harris from Thomas Ritchie (1842–1909), the lawyer and finance capitalist who (like Stewart) began as solicitor to the bank and ended up as
vice-president.[72] Unlike Stewart, Rogers, and Harris, however, Ritchie
abandoned his law practice altogether in order to devote himself entirely
to corporate business at the directorial or executive-officer level.[73]

Under Stewart's headship, the firm from 1927 onwards began to provide not only corporate legal services, but also corporate financial services, in the form of intermediation and investment counselling. No
better evocation of Stewart as an *éminence grise* exists than the one given
by supermarket magnate Frank Sobey in an interview with his biographer, Harry Bruce. Stewart, who was instrumental in launching Sobeys
Stores Limited in 1946, *'was* the Royal Bank around here [Nova Scotia],
and there wasn't a single important legal thing it did anywhere in Canada that he wasn't in on. If he said to the Royal Bank, "Do this," the Royal
Bank did it.'[74] In his history of National Sea Products Limited, a complicated postwar merger of regional fish-processing companies which Stewart promoted and of which he became vice-president, Stephen Kimber
has written that Stewart's most important attribute as a lawyer–financier
was 'his role as the key link between the already closely connected members of Nova Scotia's business and financial establishment.'[75] Stewart's

leverage was such that he was apparently able to finesse the appointment not only of his long-time friend, the expatriate Halifax corporate lawyer Lionel Avard ('Laddie') Forsyth, KC, to the presidency of the Dominion Steel and Coal Corporation (Dosco) in 1950, but also of Frank Sobey to the board. Dosco, the board of which 'was part of central Canada's supreme capitalist clique,' was the largest employer in the Maritime provinces and one of the half-dozen largest industrial conglomerates in the country. It was also a major corporate client of the Royal Bank, in which Forsyth – formerly of Montgomery, McMichael, Common & Howard (now Ogilvy, Renault), and by the late 1940s Stewart's only serious rival as the leading corporate lawyer in the country – became a director the same year Stewart became vice-president. Harry Bruce does not exaggerate when he writes: 'Stewart had an Upper Canadian business grapevine like no other Maritimer.'[76] In an age when corporate lawyers as a rule were not corporation financiers, Stewart triumphed at both avocations simultaneously. To lawyers and judges he was the prime sergeant – an intellectually superior 'lawyer's lawyer' whose professional excellence was recognized by his election as president of the Canadian Bar Association in 1941 – while to entrepreneurs he was the venture capitalist *par excellence*.

Perhaps the highest testimonial to Stewart's pre-eminence came from James Muir (1891–1960), chairman and president of the Royal Bank during Stewart's all-too-brief vice-presidency. Muir, who was certainly in a position to recognize and rely on a kindred spirit, and with whom Stewart had much in common, often referred to him as Rudyard Kipling's proverbial 'Thousandth Man.'[77] Muir, like Stewart, 'burned with Presbyterian zeal for advancement,' and Stewart no less than 'Muir epitomized the notion that hard work and Scottish methods lay at the heart of Canadian banking.' Stewart also concurred wholeheartedly with Muir's policy of aggressive expansionism in the corporate sector.[78] Just as Stewart's appointment to the board of directors, aged forty-two, in 1931 reflected the gradual transition from gerontocracy, nepotism, and plutocracy to meritocracy, so a similar transition was to take place at the executive-director level; indeed, it enabled a Scottish immigrant 'bank boy' such as Jimmy Muir to rise from ledger-keeper to president and chairman. On 13 January 1955, Stewart attended the annual general meeting of the bank – only his fourth as vice-president – at which a by-law was enacted doubling the bank's capital stock from $50 million to $100 million. A month later he was dead; Chairman Muir came down from Montreal to act as pallbearer at the funeral of his friend. Though the law firm's connection with the Royal Bank continued through the post-

Stewart era – Stewart arranged that Frank Covert should replace him as director, while J.W.E. Mingo in turn succeeded to Covert's place on the board and remained a director until 1995 – the vice-presidency was not likewise bequeathable.[79] Yet the corporate lawyer who is so often mis-described as the Royal Bank's 'first non-banker vice-president' was destined not even to be its last.[80]

J. McG. Stewart acted as intermediary between entrepreneurs needing venture capital and an aggressively entrepreneurial bank looking for promising corporate investees. In the world of investment banking and corporate finance in Atlantic Canada, Stewart's word was law, and his judgment of the worth of a stock reputedly unerring.[81] Profits from national or regional directorships and executive officerships, however, did not accrue to the firm *qua* partnership; Stewart was in business for himself and his clients – chief among whom was the Royal Bank – and not for the firm, except in the sense that his intimate involvement in the affairs of Canada's largest and fastest-growing bank enhanced the firm's reputation for business acumen and corporate legal wisdom. Stewart, who invested in the companies in which he served as well as in numerous others, died a millionaire.[82]

COUNSEL TO THE ROYAL COMMISSION ON
DOMINION–PROVINCIAL RELATIONS; WARTIME
COAL ADMINISTRATOR/CONTROLLER

James McGregor Stewart was equally at home in both corporate and con-stitutional law. Though after 1930 he rarely practised as a barrister, he was first brought to national attention by the Privy Council's extraterrito-rial revenue-legislation appeal case of July 1932. Appearing before the Judicial Committee as counsel for the appellant, who had won in the Supreme Court of Nova Scotia and in the Supreme Court of Nova Scotia *in banco* (court of appeal) but lost in the Supreme Court of Canada, Stew-art obtained the reversal of a judgment of the Supreme Court of Canada which denied that 'the Canadian federal Parliament ha[d] the power to enact statutes with extraterritorial effect.'[83] In *Croft* v. *Dunphy*, [1933] AC 156, he was instrumental in establishing the legal basis for Canada's twelve-mile offshore limit. Then, in 1938–9, Stewart was senior counsel for the government of Canada in the *Re Eskimos* reference, a leading con-stitutional decision which determined that the term 'Indians' in section 91(24) of the Constitution Act, 1867, included Eskimo (Inuit) inhabitants of Quebec.[84]

Despite the fact that Stewart's services were in demand not only for highest-level appellate advocacy, it was his sense of *noblesse oblige* which induced him to accept the invitation to participate in the most important federal royal commission in Canada's history. In 1937, in response to the dire financial situation faced by the provinces of Saskatchewan and Manitoba caused by their inability to raise sufficient revenue during the Great Depression, Prime Minister W.L. Mackenzie King decided to establish the Royal Commission on Dominion–Provincial Relations. Producing in less than three years more than 10,000 pages of typewritten testimony, dozens of book-length research studies, and a three-volume final report, the so-called Rowell–Sirois Commission was 'the most exhaustive investigation of a working governmental system that has ever been made.'[85]

The original commissioners, Ontario Chief Justice N.W. Rowell, John W. Dafoe (editor of the *Winnipeg Free Press*), and Justice Thibaudeau Rinfret of the Supreme Court of Canada – soon to be replaced, due to ill health, by constitutional-law professor Dr Joseph Sirois, of the Chambre des Notaires du Québec – carefully organized the commission in such a manner as to allay provincial suspicions. In particular, Rowell insisted that the commission rather than the federal government should appoint legal counsel to assist the commission in its public hearings. This was agreed to, and the commissioners chose as senior and junior counsel, respectively, two corporate lawyers then both at the apex of their profession – James McGregor Stewart, of Halifax, and Louis St-Laurent, of Montreal. St-Laurent, having declined to accept appointment as one of the commissioners, was willing to act as assistant counsel to Stewart, who in turn owed his appointment largely to Rowell's intercession. The prime minister, knowing Stewart only by reputation as a powerful back-room Tory lawyer from the Maritimes, disapproved but acquiesced in the choice.[86]

Stewart's role as *de facto* Maritime regional representative on the royal commission was especially significant. As only one counsel was present at each hearing of the commission outside Ottawa, when the commission held its hearings in Halifax, in February 1938, it was Stewart who examined the witnesses, first among whom was his good old Liberal lawyer–friend Premier Angus L. Macdonald: 'Mr Macdonald,' wrote the Menckenian journalist J.B. McGeachy in the *Winnipeg Free Press*, 'was examined by Mr MacGregor Stewart, K.C., Commission counsel and one of the potent lawyers of the Atlantic seaboard. This encounter made a tableau of some interest, since Mr Macdonald is a Grit premier while Mr Stewart is a leading Tory in these parts. Their conversation was polite. The angry passions often supposed to be implicit in any Nova Scotia political argument were not in evidence.'[87] Like St-Laurent, Stewart 'took an active part in the proceedings, questioning witnesses closely and becoming involved in lengthy debates on their briefs.'[88]

The critical role of commission counsel was highlighted during the preparation of the final report in autumn 1938, when a dispute threatened to precipitate Chairman Sirois into writing a dissenting minority report. In contention, among other issues touching the allocation of financial responsibilities and the division of fiscal powers between the two levels of government, was whether or not the federal government could legally assume responsibility for unemployment insurance. Disaster was averted only when St-Laurent and Stewart were summoned to Ottawa for a long meeting with the commissioners and their staff. Quoting an unnamed eyewitness, St-Laurent's biographer writes, '"I was never prouder to see legal minds at work; they were like two tennis players batting the ball back and forth with ease and style."' Sirois, who had grave doubts about the constitutionality of the proposals, was only very reluctantly dissuaded from his opposition to the majority view.[89]

The final report of the Royal Commission on Dominion–Provincial Relations was presented in May 1940, by which time Stewart had been serving as coal administrator for seven months. The outbreak of the Second World War was to create an impasse for Stewart and compel him ultimately to choose between the firm's interests and the unyielding demands of wartime public service. Stewart's appointment as coal administrator responsible to the Wartime Prices and Trade Board (WPTB) in the Department of Labour,[90] though commendably bipartisan, doubtless came through the good offices of the outgoing minister of labour, the ill-fated Norman McLeod Rogers of the Nova Scotia bar, whose uncle (Tecumseh Sherman) and cousin (William Marshall) were quondam partners in the firm. Given the fact that Dosco, of which Stewart had become a director in 1936, controlled some 80 per cent of coal production in eastern Canada, moreover, the appointment was understandable. Serving as a 'dollar-a-year' man obliged Stewart to relinquish his Dosco directorship, because of the conflict of interest between the corporation's operating subsidiary on the board of which Stewart served – Dominion Coal Company – and the coal administration. Initially, Stewart's brief was to

be responsible, in co-operation with the industries and trades concerned and under the direction of the Board, for the conduct of negotiations with United Kingdom authorities for the export of coal and other solid fuels to Canada; in co-operation with the provinces concerned, for maintaining and stimulating where necessary the production of Canadian coal and other solid fuels; for the supervision of the purchase, shipment, distribution and allocation of coal, coke and other solid fuels, whether domestic or imported, and for such other duties as may be assigned to him by the Board.[91]

Stewart's first initiative as coal administrator was to license all dealers and survey them for details of inventory, sales, and prices.[92]

These well-laid plans were soon overtaken by the march of war, however, as the Battle of the Atlantic put an end to coal exports from Great Britain and changed the emphasis to importing coal from the United States and exponentially increasing domestic production. In June 1941 the powers, duties, and functions of the Dominion Fuel Board (DFB) were transferred to the coal administrator, who thus assumed responsibility for administering the Domestic Fuel Act. In August–September 1941, administrative responsibility for the DFB was transferred from the Department of Labour to the Department of Finance, whither the entire WPTB and its various commodity administrations were shifted, lock, stock, and barrel. Despite the realignment, Stewart continued to act under the direction of the WPTB, which supervised the use of domestically mined coal in the manufacture of iron and steel in Canada.

In November 1942, Stewart, as coal administrator, became *ex officio* chair of the newly established Emergency Coal Production Board (ECPB), which had plenary powers of regulation and quasi-judicial powers of coercion.[93] By early 1943, the chief problem facing Stewart was not the coal administration *per se*, but shortfalls in coal production. In March 1943, in direct response to the continuing state of crisis in the coal industry, the 'administration' was upgraded to 'control' and transferred from the WPTB to the Wartime Industries Control Board (WICB) in the Department of Munitions and Supply. The WICB, which had been established in June 1940, consisted of twelve (ultimately seventeen) controllers from outside the civil service acting collectively as supremos over both primary and secondary essential industries. Armed with orders in council issued under the authority of the War Measures Act, accountable to no one but themselves and the director general of the priorities branch of Munitions and Supply, these Orwellian 'controllers' were unpopular with the parliamentary opposition, both Conservative and CCF. The perception that Canada's civilian war effort was in the hands of a very exclusive club of industrialists, corporate lawyers, and financiers, to whom an enlightened despot – C.D. Howe, minister of munitions and supply – had delegated his virtually unlimited authority, created political problems for the government.[94] As coal controller, from March to July 1943, Stewart 'was responsible for the control, maintenance and increase of coal production and coal imports; for the distribution or allocation of coal to domestic consumers, industry and the railways; for the allocation of Canadian coal to export markets and bunker supplies and for the overseeing and allocation of coal supplies to the Armed Services ...'[95]

As early as autumn 1941, the supply 'situation in the Maritimes became acute. Slowdown tactics in the Cape Breton collieries resulted in a shortage of some 800,000 tons of coal.'[96] Production was not increasing fast enough to satisfy the demands of industry and domestic consumers, so in May 1943 the government was obliged to declare a state of national emergency 'in regard to the production of coal in Canada.'[97] Two months later, at the very climax of the crisis, Stewart allegedly asked to be relieved of his critical post, and his 'resignation' was accepted.[98] It seems probable that Stewart was made the scapegoat for the crisis; the line taken by the ministerial press release – Stewart 'had to return to his [law] business in Halifax'[99] – wears the look of a face-saver. Yet the heavy demands of the coal-controllership – the WICB met weekly in Ottawa to consider problems affecting the entire program – had already compelled Stewart not only to resign the presidency of the Canadian Bar Association,[100] but also to give up the chairmanship of the board of governors of Dalhousie University.

Whatever precipitated Stewart's sudden resignation, it must have proved difficult to run the monolithic coal control (which included the former coal administration) from Halifax. Yet Stewart, according to Frank Covert's biographer, Harry Bruce, somehow 'managed Canada's coal industry mostly from Halifax. Beside the telephone in his study, he installed a switch to disconnect other phones in his mansion on the Northwest Arm; in a time when propaganda warned "the walls have ears," he wanted no one to eavesdrop on his discussions about coal shipments.'[101] Nor could Stewart have moved permanently to Ottawa without abandoning the law firm, which officially consisted of nine lawyers but which wartime manpower shortages had more or less reduced to three of the four senior partners whose names appeared on the shingle (Stewart, C.B. Smith, and H.P. MacKeen).[102] For Stewart, perhaps it was Hobson's choice: He could give up either the dual post of coal controller and chair of the Emergency Coal Production Board, or his place as head of the firm.

Stewart did not in any case leave the post of coal controller entirely empty-handed; he was one of forty-six Canadians created a Commander of the Order of the British Empire (CBE), Civil Division in the King's New Year's honours list for 1944 – 'for distinguished wartime service.' The CBE was only the second honour which Stewart received, apart from his KC, a *pro forma* and bipartisan distinction which came to him in the dying days of the provincial Liberal government in June 1925.[103] In August 1939 the University of King's College, an Anglican foundation, held a special sesquicentenary convocation during which the degree of Doctor of Civil Law, *honoris causa*, was conferred on Stewart and twelve other luminaries.[104] Nor was Stewart the only high-flying corporate lawyer honoured on that auspicious occasion. Also receiving his DCL was Lionel A. Forsyth, who was a graduate, former professor of modern languages at the university, and its future chancellor – and, perhaps more significantly, Dosco's general counsel. Ten years later, Forsyth was to do what Stewart would never have done: abandon the active practice of law altogether in order to become executive vice-president, and then president, of Dosco, the industrial conglomerate of which he became a director in 1944 and which he had served as legal adviser since its inception in 1928.

CONCLUSION

James McGregor Stewart was neither compelled nor inclined to make such a choice. The compensation system at his firm encouraged active participation in business; little was lost and much was gained through partners taking on numerous directorships as well as executive-officerships. Stewart was intellectually and emotionally capable of moving from the realm of law – as teacher, appellate litigator, and corporate legal adviser – to business, whether as entrepreneur, manager, or financier, with ease. None the less, Stewart's experience as wartime coal controller demonstrated that even he had to make hard career decisions. The increasing complexity of company law, finance, taxation, and industrial relations during and after the Second World War brought an even greater degree of specialization within the corporate law firm and sounded the death-knell of Olympians such as Stewart.

The entrepreneurial, venture-capitalist culture which Stewart inculcated in his successors would, however, continue to distinguish the firm and to play a major role in its subsequent growth and success. If entry into and promotion within the firm had been based more on family connection than on merit and academic standing, then it is likely that the firm's performance would have been blunted by later generations of practitioners of the relatively low calibre of R.V. Harris and William Alexander Henry, Jr. Indeed, nepotism may very well have retarded the growth of the Stewart firm's chief rival – McInnes, Cooper & Robertson – and prevented it from realizing its full potential.

Even more central to the Stewart firm's ultimate success were its structural attributes, including 'the nothing in, nothing out' system which kept associates and partners on their toes even after years of service. This policy made becoming a partner easier for ambitious and clever but cash-poor outsiders, such as Frank Covert, though even his admission was subject to the unanimous approval of the partnership; pupillage with the senior partner was not enough to put an associate on the fast track for promotion. Finally, since the income of senior partners was strictly proportional to billings, they were less able to live off the prestige of the firm or the labour of juniors, and were effectively barred from superannuation on the capital of the firm. In other words, everyone from the salaried junior or associate to the full partner was expected to pull his weight throughout his career.

This system made everyone within the firm to some extent a free agent. Stewart himself encouraged this behaviour by allowing partners to keep their directors' fees and salaries from executive-officer positions. This, combined with a professional methodology which emphasized the advantages of practical and direct business experience, and which saw no conflict of interest between providing legal advice to corporations while actively participating at a high level in their affairs, produced a culture in which corporate lawyers were eager to roll up their sleeves and get to work solving their clients' business and financial problems, often in innovative ways. In this manner, Stewart's contemporaries as well as his successors were better able to anticipate their clients's needs – even if their advice could, on occasion, suffer from a certain lack of objectivity and width of perspective.

To some extent, this ethos applied also to public service. Stewart, along with other members of his firm, devoted long hours to unpaid or poorly paying jobs in government and academia. This experience redounded to the firm's benefit in the long run, however, since high-level business contacts, not to mention the cultivation of bright young law students at Dalhousie University, brought new clients and fresh blood to the firm. Stewart of course acted from more altruistic and disinterested motives, but the reputation of the man and the firm owes much to these activities. In the Nova Scotia provincial election of 1925, Stewart's contemporary and long-time friend Lionel A. Forsyth ran unsuccessfully for the Liberal party in his home county of Hants. He reacted to his abysmal failure in electoral politics by shaking the dust of Halifax off his feet and moving to Montreal for good; Stewart stayed in Halifax and achieved as much as Forsyth did in Montreal. Stewart's first and abiding loyalty was to the old Halifax law firm which had made him and which he remade in his own Jovian image. It was Laddie Forsyth's tragedy to be migratory and rootless. At Stewart and Co., meanwhile, if the corporate lawyer could not dexterously combine law and business as 'The Boss' himself had done, then he was not altogether firm-fit and was best kicked upstairs to the boardroom or the bench.

NOTES

The authors acknowledge, with grateful thanks, the assistance of the following persons who read and commented upon earlier drafts of the manuscript: Messrs J.W.E. Mingo, QC; David A. Stewart, QC; and George A. Caines, QC, of Stewart McKelvey Stirling Scales (Halifax); Professors Philip Girard and David Ricardo Williams of Dalhousie Law School and the Faculty of Law, University of Victoria, respectively; Dr Carol Wilton and Dr Peter Oliver on behalf of The Osgoode Society for Canadian Legal History; and Mrs Vivian Morrison, who has commissioned the biography of James McGregor Stewart currently in preparation by Barry Cahill.

1 Deborah Watson, 'The 1990s and the Mega-Firms,' *Canadian Lawyer* 13/2 (March 1989), 18–21. Another Atlantic Canadian regional amalgamation has recently taken place: 'Law Firms Merge to Serve Regional Needs of Clients,' *Mail-Star* (Halifax), 22 November 1995. The new mega-firm, known as Patterson Palmer Hunt Murphy, 'will have about 130 lawyers and becomes only the second law firm to operate throughout the Atlantic region.' 'Joining forces in Atlantic Canada' apparently means succumbing to market forces in the shape of irresistible regional, not to mention national business competition.
2 Barry Cahill, 'John Fitzwilliam Stairs,' in *Dictionary of Canadian Biography*, vol. 13 (Toronto: University of Toronto Press 1994), 978–82
3 Phyllis R. Blakeley to H.P. MacKeen (formerly senior partner in firm), 9 February 1967: Stewart McKelvey Stirling Scales (Halifax), corporate archive (hereinafter SMSS). See also Phyllis R. Blakeley, 'William Alexander Henry,' in *Dictionary of Canadian Biography*, vol. 11 (Toronto: University of Toronto Press 1982), 398–400.
4 'From the Diaries of Frank M. Covert: 50 Years in the Practice of Law' (typescript, 1980), 30: courtesy SMSS

5 F.M. Covert (1908–1987), who in 1963 succeeded Stewart's successor, H.P. MacKeen, as head of the firm, was an obsessive self-documenter who abridged and transcribed fifty years' worth of personal diaries and used them as the basis for his unpublished memoirs, completed in 1980. See generally Harry Bruce, *Corporate Navigator: The Life of Frank Manning Covert* (Toronto: McClelland and Stewart 1995); cf. David Ricardo Williams, *Just Lawyers: Seven Portraits* (Toronto: The Osgoode Society 1995), 193–225.

6 Gregory P. Marchildon, 'International Corporate Law from a Maritime Base: The Halifax firm of Harris, Henry and Cahan,' in Carol Wilton, ed., *Essays in the History of Canadian Law*, vol. 4: *Beyond the Law: Lawyers and Business in Canada, 1830 to 1930* (Toronto: The Osgoode Society 1990), 201–34; cf. Christopher Armstrong and H.V. Nelles, 'Getting Your Way in Nova Scotia: "Tweaking" Halifax, 1909–1917,' *Acadiensis* 5/2 (Spring 1976), 105–31

7 Philip Girard, 'The Maritime Provinces, 1850–1939: Lawyers and Legal Institutions,' in 23 *Manitoba Law Journal* 1 & 2 (1995), 379–405; see also *idem*, 'The Supreme Court of Nova Scotia, Responsible Government and the Quest for Legitimacy, 1850–1920,' in 17 *Dalhousie Law Journal* 2 (1994), 430.

8 A contemporaneous illustration of the work constituting this new wave in law practice can be found in the various essays in Francis Lynde Stetson ed., *Some Legal Phases of Corporate Financing, Reorganization, and Regulation* (New York: Macmillan 1927). Of particular interest is Paul D. Cravath's essay, 'The Reorganization of Corporations,' 153–234.

9 See Robert W. Gordon's two articles, 'Legal Thought and Legal Practice in the Age of American Enterprise, 1870–1920,' in G.L. Geison, ed., *Professions and Professional Ideologies in America* (Chapel Hill, NC: University of North Carolina Press 1983), and 'The Ideal and the Actual in the Law,' in G.W. Gawalt, ed., *The New High Priests: Lawyers in Post–Civil War America* (Westport, CT: Greenwood Press 1984), 51–74. Kenneth Lipartito provides a good summary of the literature in 'What Have Lawyers Done for American Business? The Case of Baker & Botts of Houston,' *Business History Review* 64/3 (Autumn 1990), 489–98.

10 Robert T. Swaine, *The Cravath Firm and Its Predecessors, 1819–1947*, 3 vols. (New York: privately printed 1946); Nancy Lisagor and Frank Lipsius, *A Law unto Itself: The Untold Story of the Law Firm of Sullivan & Cromwell* (New York: Morrow 1988); Deborah S. Gardner, *Cadwallader, Wickersham & Taft: A Bicentennial History, 1792–1992* (New York: Cadwallader, Wickersham & Taft 1994).

11 For comparisons of the scale of enterprise, see Graham Taylor and Peter Baskerville, *A Concise History of Canadian Business* (Toronto: Oxford University Press 1994), and Michael Bliss, *Northern Enterprise: Four Centuries of Canadian Business* (Toronto: McClelland and Stewart 1987).

12 See Carol Wilton's editorial Introduction as well as the essays by Gregory P. Marchildon (Harris, Henry & Cahan) and Louis A. Knafla (Lougheed & Bennett). Curtis Cole's essay on McCarthy, Osler, Hoskin & Creelman illustrates the traditional nature of the work of the predecessor firm which would spawn the modern corporate firms of Osler, Hoskin & Harcourt, and McCarthy, Tétrault: Wilton, ed., *Beyond the Law*. See also Declan Brendan Hamill, 'The Campbell, Meredith, Firm of Montreal: A Case-Study of the Role of Canadian Business Lawyers, 1895–1913,' in this volume. On Blake, Lash & Cassels's early corporate work see Christopher Armstrong and H.V. Nelles, *Southern Exposure: Canadian Promoters in Latin America and the Caribbean, 1896–1930* (Toronto: University of Toronto Press 1988), and Duncan McDowall, *The Light: Brazilian Traction, Light and Power Company Limited, 1899–1945* (Toronto: University of Toronto Press 1988). On Cahan and Lovett's activities in Montreal see Gregory P. Marchildon, 'The Role of Lawyers in Corporate Promotion and Management: A Canadian Case Study and Theoretical Speculations,' *Business and Economic History*, 2 ser., 19 (1990), 193–202.

13 Wayne K. Hobson, 'Symbol of the New Profession: Emergence of the Large Law Firm, 1870–1915,' in Gawalt, ed., *The New High Priests*, 3–27

14 Robert L. Nelson, *Partners with Power: The Social Transformation of the Large Law Firm* (Berkeley, CA: University of California Press 1988), 48–55

15 These organizational changes are described by Hobson in 'Symbol of the New Profession,' 10. Cf. Brian D. Bucknall, '"My Dear Osler," "My Dear Boland": Chronicles of an Early Real Estate Flip,' *Law Society of Upper Canada Gazette* 24 (1990), 331–5, cited in the introduction to this volume, at note 97.

16 The prize was not awarded before 1919. Stewart, for his part, graduated with the best academic record that had ever been achieved in the thirty-year history of the law school. The first recipient of the University Medal in Law – Robert David McCleave – practised with Henry, Rogers, Harris & Stewart. At a higher level as well the relationship between law firm and law school has historically been close. The first dean, Richard Chapman Weldon, was counsel to the firm; at least two partners have been full-time faculty (J.E. Read, G.S. Cowan), while one of the two (Read) subsequently became dean. The present dean, Dawn Russell, was formerly an associate with Stewart McKelvey Stirling Scales. Professor Russell is the first woman dean in the 113–year history of Dalhousie Law School.

17 Interview with the late Donald A. Kerr, QC, 26 August 1994

18 R.E. Harris Scrapbook, MG1, vol. 398, Item No. 4, Public Archives of Nova Scotia (hereinafter PANS)

19 It is interesting to note that one of the firm's 'non-corporate' lawyers, Reginald V. Harris, had very early on advocated Maritime union as a vehicle to press

for political reforms which would enhance the region's position in the federa-
tion: See R.V. Harris, 'The Union of the Maritime Provinces,' *Acadiensis* 6
(July–October 1906), 172–84, and 'The Advantages of the Union of the Mari-
time Provinces,' *Acadiensis* 8 (October 1908), 238–49; and E.R. Forbes, *The
Maritime Rights Movement: A Study in Canadian Regionalism* (Kingston and
Montreal: McGill–Queen's University Press 1979), 30–1.

20 Bruce, *Corporate Navigator*, 203

21 B.M. Greene, ed., *Who's Who in Canada, 1928–29* (Toronto: International Press
1929), 959. 'Among the big industrial leaders of Canada he [G.S. Stairs] is
looked upon as the coming corporation lawyer of the Dominion': 'Meet an
Alumnus – Gilbert S. Stairs,' in *(Dalhousie) Alumni News*, January 1931, 3.

22 Gordon, '"The Ideal and the Actual in the Law,"' 51–74

23 Ibid., 56

24 Vivian Morrison, 'James McGregor Stewart,' (typescript). (Mrs Morrison's late
husband, Donald J. Morrison, QC, was a nephew of Mrs James McGregor
Stewart's and a quondam associate in Stewart, MacKeen & Covert.)

25 William March, *Red Line*: The Chronicle–Herald *and* The Mail–Star, *1875–1954*
(Halifax: Chebucto Agencies 1986), 249, 264

26 Stewart was not the first member of his firm to serve as member or chair of the
board of governors of Dalhousie University: Thomas Ritchie replaced John F.
Stairs as chair in 1904, while T.S. (later Judge) Rogers served from 1919 to 1928.
Though the firm has never acted as the university's solicitors, the present
counsel to the firm, Sir Graham Day, who had a distinguished career in British
boardrooms during the Thatcher regime, is chancellor of the university.

27 J. McG. Stewart to K.C. Laurie, 19 March 1945; quoted in John Willis, *A History
of Dalhousie Law School* (Toronto: University of Toronto Press 1979), 119, 129.
See generally Dalhousie University, *President's Report* and Board of Governors'
minutes, 1929–1955: Dalhousie University Archives (hereinafter DUA),
MS-1-1/A-7 to A-13. See also P.B. Waite, *The Lives of Dalhousie University:* Vol.
2: *1925–1980* (Montreal and Kingston: McGill–Queen's University Press, in
press).

28 In 1914 the McInnes firm listed five lawyers, one more than the two other largest downtown firms: Harris, Henry, Rogers & Harris, and MacLean, Paton,
Burchell & Ralston: *McAlpine's Halifax City Directory* (Halifax: McAlpine 1914),
525. For a short anecdotal history of the McInnes firm see Harry Flemming,
McInnes Cooper & Robertson: A Century Plus (Halifax: privately printed 1989).

29 RG 39 'C' (HX), box 582, file B-446, PANS: James McGregor Stewart's bar
admission file (called 4 August 1914)

30 Reminiscences (*ca* 1953) of Susannah W.A. Almon, retired senior secretary in
the Harris–Henry–Stewart law firm: SMSS (Almon had also been R.E. Harris's

private secretary: Susannah W.A. Almon's obituary, *Halifax Mail–Star*,
12 April 1958, 5). So highly regarded was Stewart that, when Read enlisted
and went overseas on active service, Stewart was invited to take his friend's
place as lecturer on Real Property at the law school: Dalhousie University,
President's Report, 1914–1915, 3. Read re-entered the firm after the war but
never became a partner.
31 RG 39 'C' (HX), box 582, file B-446; see also box 573, file A-19720 (John E.
Read's bar admission file), PANS. In Read's case, however, the articles were
being transferred from another partner in the same firm.
32 Flemming, *McInnes Cooper & Robertson.*
33 According to Justice Robert Henry Graham, his contemporary on the Supreme
Court of Nova Scotia (appointed in 1925), Harris 'was a good advocate; but his
business activities forced him to leave Court work to junior members of his
firm.' Moreover, his extensive 'outside business activities' had prevented him
from becoming 'a deep student of the law': Miscellaneous Manuscripts Collection, MG 100 vol. 161 file 52, PANS.
34 Lipartito, 'What Have Lawyers Done for American Business,' 490, citing James
Willard Hurst, *The Growth of American Law: The Law Makers* (Boston: Little,
Brown 1950), 202–5
35 Almon reminiscences, SMSS
36 R.V. Harris joined the firm in 1909, after partners H. Almon Lovett and Henry
B. Stairs removed to Montreal. After his admission to the bar in 1905, Harris
practised briefly in Winnipeg with Aikins, Robson & Co., and in 1910 produced the first Canadian manual of law-office management: Reginald V. Harris, *Hints and Suggestions on the Organization of a Legal Business* (Toronto:
Carswell 1910), 134.
37 Chapter 6 of Frank M. Covert's manuscript chronicle of Stewart, MacKeen &
Covert [January 1980]: SMSS (hereinafter 'Firm History')
38 Almon reminiscences, SMSS
39 Covert, 'Firm History,' Chap. 8. This story was first written down by R.H. Graham: MG 100, vol. 161, file 52, PANS.
40 Read left after only two years to join the faculty of Dalhousie Law School, of
which he became dean in 1924. He was also legal adviser to the Department of
External Affairs and would later be appointed deputy under-secretary of state
for External Affairs in 1944, retiring from that position when elected a judge
of the International Court of Justice two years later: Covert, 'Firm History,'
Chap. 7.
41 Oakes left the firm in 1923 in order to set up his own practice: ibid.
42 Originally from New Brunswick, White retired from the firm when appointed
a County Court judge in his native province in 1929: ibid.

43 Born in 1890 at Stewiacke, Nova Scotia, McCleave died unexpectedly in 1927, the year he became a partner, ending what many considered would have been a brilliant career: ibid.

44 Ibid.

45 The Boulderwood Park Company Limited (2 May 1913), Corunna Shipping Company Limited (12 July 1913), and Nevada Shipping Company Limited (12 July 1913). Each of these Halifax companies was capitalized at $100,000: (*Journal* of the House of Assembly/Legislative Council of Nova Scotia, Appendix 12: Provincial Secretary's Report, 1914, 47, 53.

46 They first appear together as incorporators of the Edgerton Fur Farm Limited in April 1914: Provincial Secretary's Report, 1915, 47. One of their least successful ventures was the Canadian Apartment Company Limited (inc. 21 February 1920), which built the Westminster Apartments, the first structure of its kind in Halifax. Stewart, who was corporate secretary, 'lost heavily, never venturing into real estate again': Morrison, 'James McGregor Stewart,' 6.

47 In his memoirs Frank Covert suggests that the future Mrs Stewart, who was more a paralegal than a legal secretary, originally drafted the memorandum of agreement and articles of association for Izaak Walton Killam's Mersey Paper Company Limited (see below): Covert, '50 Years in the Practice of Law,' 25. It appears that, after Covert became Stewart's articled clerk in 1927, Miss Wilson, who signed Covert's articles of clerkship as a witness and to whom Covert would afterwards refer as 'The G.M.' (general manager), gradually ceased to be Stewart's solicitorial deputy: RG 39 'C' (HX), box 795, file SC1584 (FMC bar admission file), PANS; Bruce, *Corporate Navigator*, 49. The year following Covert's call to the bar and admission to the firm as an associate, the senior partner's marriage to his long-time secretary, confidante, and *belle-amie* was front-page news: *Halifax Herald*, 22 April 1931, 1. It was, of course, *de rigueur* that the former Miss Wilson cease to be an employee of the firm. 'I do not forget,' wrote Covert to Mrs Stewart after her husband's death, 'those early days when you taught me how a law office works!' : Frank Covert to Elizabeth E. Stewart, 13 February 1955, James McGregor Stewart fonds (privately held).

48 *Annual Financial Review* (Toronto), vol. 26 (July 1926), 103

49 This holograph document, written in pencil in a stenographer's notebook, is in SMSS: file 130,830 'FMC/Stewart, J. McG. *Re* Will – Material.'

50 This and what follows is based on Jack Sexton's jubilee history of Montreal Engineering Company Limited, of which Nova Scotia Light & Power was a client and remained so long after Killam had severed his connection with the utility: Jack K. Sexton, *Monenco: The First 75 Years [1907–1982]* (London ON: privately printed 1982), 38–9. See also Gregory P. Marchildon, 'The Montreal Engineering Company and International Power: Overcoming the Limitations

of the Free-Standing Utility,' in G. Schröter and Mira Wilkins, eds., *The Free-Standing Company in International Business History* (Toronto: Oxford University Press, forthcoming).

51 The tradition continues: In February 1996, Joseph Gerald Godsoe, QC, a member of the Stewart firm since 1974, was appointed president and chief executive officer of Nova Scotia Power. Unlike Stewart, however, he resigned his law partnership. Godsoe, who died suddenly less than two months after his appointment, was numbered among Jerry Levitan's '20 Most Powerful Lawyers in Canada,' *Canadian Lawyer* 18/3 (April 1994), 16 – the only Atlantic Canadian lawyer to make the grade. Twenty years earlier the place would have been taken by Frank Covert; forty years earlier, by J. McG. Stewart.

52 On this see Gregory P. Marchildon, *Profits and Politics: Beaverbrook and the Gilded Age of Canadian Finance* (Toronto: University of Toronto Press 1996)

53 Gregory P. Marchildon, 'John F. Stairs, Max Aitken and the Scotia Group: Finance Capitalism and Industrial Decline in the Maritimes, 1890–1914,' in Kris Inwood, ed., *Farm, Factory and Fortune: New Studies in the Economic History of the Maritime Provinces* (Fredericton, NB: Acadiensis Press 1993).

54 The 'new' RSC was incorporated in January 1928 and capitalized at $1 million; for reasons which are unclear, it was reincorporated in January 1947 and continues today on the Nova Scotia registry as Merrill Lynch Canada Inc., which acquired it in 1969: N.S. Department of Justice – Registry of Joint Stock Companies – files 5361, CRA 6088 (microfiche); 'Province of Nova Scotia: No. A: Nova Scotia Companies Act [1900]: 'Ledger,' 96; Registry of Joint Stock Companies fonds, RG 73, vol. 18, PANS; Supreme Court of Nova Scotia, *In re Royal Investment Corporation in liquidation*: RG 39 'C' (HX), box 801, file 2039 (1930), PANS.

55 *Monetary Times*, 3 January 1919, 115; 28 February 1919, 52; 25 January 1925, 25

56 M. Baker, J. Miller Pitt, and R.D.W. Pitt, *The Illustrated History of Newfoundland Light & Power* (St John's, NF: Creative Publishers 1990), chap. 5

57 Bolivian Power continues to be registered in Nova Scotia: Registry of Joint Stock Companies, files 2834, 15477.

58 The original incorporators were Stewart, his partner Henry Poole MacKeen, and the firm's accountant, Henry Charles Winterbourne Powell: Appendix 12, Nova Scotia Provincial Secretary's Report for year ending September 1925. The light, power, tramway, and telephone system served a population of approximately 110,000 by 1925: *Monetary Times*, 7 August 1925, 27; *Annual Financial Review (Canadian)*, 26 (July 1926), 467–8.

59 This and what follows is based on Sexton, *Monenco*, 43–4, 47–50. Killam himself became president of International Power, whose board of directors included a prominent Halifax mercantile associate of Stewart's, George

McGregor Mitchell, who in 1923 had been elected a director of the Royal Bank of Canada.

60 In his memoirs Covert recalled how Stewart had disarmingly 'weaned every one of his clients off' to him: Covert, 'Autobiography,' 200.

61 Note 57, above.

62 Stats. NS, 1928, c. 7: An Act to Confer Certain Powers on a Company to be Incorporated for the Purpose of Owning and Operating a Paper Mill in Nova Scotia. The powers referred to concerned agreements for exemption from or restriction of municipal taxation or assessment, and procedures for expropriating land required for industrial development.

63 F.M. Covert, *Some Mersey Memories 1928–1986 = Some Important Events in the History of Bowater Mersey Paper Company Limited and its Predecessor Mersey Paper Company Limited* [Liverpool, NS, unpublished ms. 1986], 8; cf. Thomas H. Raddall, *The Mersey Story* (Liverpool, NS: Bowater Mersey Paper Co. 1979), 14, 16, 67.

64 Covert, 'Autobiography,' 226; information from J.W.E. Mingo, QC

65 Covert, *Some Mersey Memories*, 1; Covert, 'Autobiography,' 69

66 Information from Vivian Morrison

67 See for example the enumeration given by Douglas How in his biography of Killam and derived from a 1929 newspaper account: Nova Scotia Light and Power, Moirs Limited, Acadia Sugar Refining, Avon River Power (a wholly owned subsidiary of Nova Scotia Light & Power), and Mersey Paper: Douglas How, *Canada's Mystery Man of High Finance: The Story of Izaak Walton Killam and His Glittering Wife Dorothy* (Hantsport, NS: Lancelot Press 1986), 83.

68 Covert, *Some Mersey Memories*, 2

69 Ibid., 1–3, 27–8

70 Duncan McDowall, *Quick to the Frontier: Canada's Royal Bank* (Toronto: McClelland and Stewart 1993), 314; cf. Clifford H. Ince, *The Royal Bank of Canada: A Chronology, 1864–1969* (Montreal: The Royal Bank of Canada 1969), 79.

71 Harris, ironically, went on to become a director of the Bank of Nova Scotia in 1912. Rogers replaced William Robertson, formerly president of the Union Bank of Halifax, which was absorbed by the Royal Bank in 1910: McDowall, *Quick to the Frontier*, 133–5.

72 Thomas Ritchie is to be distinguished from his older relative, with whom he is often confused, Thomas A. Ritchie, the industrial capitalist, who served as director of the bank from 1876 to 1890. The younger Thomas succeeded to the directorship formerly held by his uncle, Joseph Norman Ritchie, QC, who had been the bank's solicitor previous to joining the board. J.N. Ritchie, who served from 1870 to 1886, was the first lawyer–director of the bank; all his predecessors were mercantile or industrial capitalists.

73 Ritchie was a close associate of the merger promoter, John F. Stairs, whom he was to replace as both president of Eastern Trust and chair of the board of governors of Dalhousie University; his retirement from the law firm, in the early 1890s, led to Harris's becoming a member of it.

74 Harry Bruce, *Frank Sobey: The Man and the Empire* (Toronto: Macmillan of Canada 1985), 164. Sobey 'believed that three men – Stewart, industrialist Roy Jodrey, and Horace Enman, president of the Bank of Nova Scotia – did more to develop east-coast industry than "all the government incentives combined."' In April 1929 Stewart incorporated R.A. Jodrey and Company Limited of Hantsport as a holding company for the Minas Basin Pulp and Power Company. As an executive of Mersey Paper, however, Stewart was effectively barred from playing any further role in Jodrey's company, which lay in direct competition with Killam's. On Jodrey see Harry Bruce, *RA: The Story of R.A. Jodrey: Entrepreneur* (Toronto: McClelland and Stewart 1979).

75 Stephen Kimber, *Net Profits: The Story of National Sea* (Halifax: Nimbus Publishing 1989), 73. One of Kimber's interviewees, the lawyer H.P. (Hal) Connor, who eventually became chair of the board of National Sea Products, described Stewart as follows: 'Everyone referred to him as God ... He was the most brilliant lawyer to come out of these parts – one of those people who almost seemed to say nothing, but then when he did say something, you had to listen – and act on what he said': Kimber, *Net Profits*, 73.

76 Bruce, *Frank Sobey*, 179–80. G.W. Bourke, president of the Sun Life Assurance Company of Canada, remarked after Stewart's death that 'no-one from the Maritimes was held in higher esteem': Bourke to A.E. Kerr, 15 February 1955: Dalhousie University. Office of the President, Correspondence, MS-1–3/A-952, DUA.

77 Nineteenth of the twenty-three poems in Rudyard Kipling, *Rewards and Fairies* (1910), which also includes the much-anthologized 'If'; Morrison, '[James McGregor Stewart],' 8

78 McDowall, *Quick to the Frontier*, 94, 317, 338–42, and chap. 9, *passim*. It may be taken as read that Stewart, who became a non-executive vice-president two years after Muir assumed the presidency, was Muir's personal choice to fill the vacancy – perhaps in return for Stewart's exercising his 'particular influence' to help secure Muir's election successively as director in 1947, executive vice-president in 1948, and president in 1949. For a description of the evidence of the 'close tie' between Muir and Stewart the authors are indebted to Duncan McDowall (letter to B. Cahill, 2 December 1995).

79 Royal Bank of Canada, *Annual Report for 1955*, 12; Covert, 'Autobiography,' 208–9

80 Among Stewart's successors were lawyers Wilbert Howard, QC (1957), who
    became a director the same year Stewart became vice-president, and Lazarus
    Phillips, QC (1966), who became a director in 1954.
81 In his memoirs Covert enumerated Stewart's seven-point program for sound
    investment: Covert, 'Autobiography,' 219.
82 In September 1945, Stewart took advantage of a provincial enabling act to
    incorporate a private investment holding company (which still exists) in order
    to administer his own diverse and extensive corporate assets: NS Department
    of Provincial Secretary fonds, RG 7, vol. 284, file 7 ('Braemar Investments Lim-
    ited'), PANS.
83 Peter W. Hogg, *Constitutional Law of Canada*, 3d ed. (Toronto: Carswell 1992),
    316–18. 'This decision,' writes Plaxton, 'is of first rate importance. It finally
    settled any doubt as to the power of the Parliament of Canada to enact laws
    having extra-territorial operation': Charles Percy Plaxton, ed., *Canadian Consti-
    tutional Decisions of the Judicial Committee of the Privy Council, 1930–1939*
    (Ottawa: King's Printer 1939), xlii–xlv, 170–80. See also D.P. O'Connell, 'The
    Doctrine of Colonial Extra-Territorial Legislative Incompetence,' 75 *Law Quar-
    terly Review* (1959), 318.
84 [1939] SCR 104; [1939] 2 DLR 417; both factums, the one on behalf of the attor-
    ney general of Canada, the other the attorney general of Quebec, are among
    Stewart's few surviving legal records. The Supreme Court of Canada unani-
    mously upheld the contention of the government of Quebec that Eskimos
    were indeed aboriginals within the meaning of the Constitution Act.
85 Donald V. Smiley, quoted in *The Rowell–Sirois Report: An Abridgement of
    Book I of the Royal Commission Report on Dominion–Provincial Relations*
    (Toronto: McClelland and Stewart 1963), 1. An abstract of the material pub-
    lished under the authority of the commission can be found in Henderson,
    Royal Commissions, 132–4. See also 'Royal Commission Draws on Dal-
    housie,' *The Alumni News* 1/1 (January 1938), 4, 13. Commissioner MacKay
    held the Eric Dennis Memorial Chair of Government and Political Science,
    and senior counsel Stewart was chair of the university's board of gover-
    nors.
86 W.L. Mackenzie King Diary, 25 August 1937: MG 26 J 13, National Archives
    of Canada (NA). See also Rowell to King, 4 August 1937, King to Rowell,
    14 August 1937, Rowell to King, 13 September 1937 (two letters): King papers,
    MG 26 J 1 box 241 (microfilm), NA. Stewart's only rival for the post of commis-
    sion counsel was the Halifax corporate lawyer James Layton Ralston, whose
    chief claim was that he was a former Liberal MP. Though the evidence is
    equivocal, it appears that Rowell's original intention was to have Stewart
    appointed a commissioner, not counsel. That was too much for King, for

whom Stewart's politics made him *persona non grata* in that more elevated capacity, and the prime minister appears to have vetoed Stewart's appointment as commissioner.

87 'JBM' [J.B. McGeachy], 'Confederation Clinic, 1867–1937,' in *Winnipeg Free Press*, 9 February 1938

88 Dale C. Thomson, *Louis St. Laurent: Canadian* (New York: St Martin's Press 1968), 95–6

89 This eyewitness may have been R.A. MacKay: ibid., 102.

90 Order in Council, PC 3117 (18 October 1939); *Canada Gazette* (Ottawa), 28 October 1939, 1375. This and what follows is derived from the *Labour Gazette* 39/11 (November 1939), 1103–4; *Report of the Royal Commission on Coal: 1946* (Ottawa: King's Printer 1947), 532ff.; J. de N. Kennedy, *History of the Department of Munitions and Supply: Canada in the Second World War* (Ottawa: King's Printer 1950), vol. 2, 52–79; and Robert J. Hayward and Peter Gillis, comp., *Public Archives [of] Canada: Federal Archives Division: General Inventory Series: Records of the Dominion Coal [Fuel] Board (RG 81)* (Ottawa: Public Archives of Canada 1981), 3–4. See also 'James McGregor Stewart, K.C.,' in Corolyn Cox, comp., *Canadian Strength: Biographical Sketches* (Toronto: Ryerson Press 1946), 73–5; based on a wide-ranging personal interview originally published in the *Standard* (Montreal), 11 October 1941.

91 Order in Council, PC 3117 (18 October 1939)

92 James McGregor Stewart, 'The Federal Coal Licensing Plan,' *Ontario Fuel Dealer* 10/5 (June 1940), 32–8

93 Order in Council, PC 10,674 (23 November 1942); see generally *Report of the Royal Commission on Coal: 1946*, 556ff.

94 House of Commons, *Debates*, June 1940–November 1941, *passim*. See also Leslie Roberts, *C.D.: The Life and Times of Clarence Decatur Howe* (Toronto: Clarke, Irwin 1957), 84–9; Robert Bothwell and William Kilbourn, *C.D. Howe: A Biography* (Toronto: McClelland and Stewart 1979), 135–6, 159, 168.

95 Kennedy, *Munitions and Supply*, 54–5

96 Cox, 'James McGregor Stewart,' 75

97 Order in Council, PC 4091 (17 May 1943); *Canada Gazette* (Ottawa), 5 June 1943, 2365. See also House of Commons, *Debates*, 17 May 1943, 2701.

98 Order in Council, PC 5402 (6 July 1943)

99 Cox, *Canadian Strength*, 175

100 E.H. Coleman, 'The Canadian Bar Association,' 26 *Canadian Bar Review* (1948) 18. At the request of the Transport Controller, who was concerned about the impact on the railway system of attendance at large national conventions, Stewart, after consulting with other members of the council, reluctantly agreed to cancel at the last moment the 1942 annual meeting of the CBA in

Windsor, Ontario, which was to have been held in conjunction with the annual meeting of the American Bar Association in Detroit. Stewart's undelivered presidential address was afterwards published in the CBA's journal: James McG. Stewart, 'The Abuse of Freedom,' 20 *Canadian Bar Review* (1942), 649–58.

101 Bruce, *Corporate Navigator*, 102–3

102 Order in Council, PC 1752 (5 March 1943); *Report* of the Wartime Prices and Trade Board, 1 April 1943 to 31 December 1943, 31

103 Province of Nova Scotia: Orders-in-Council: From 18 April 1925 to 30 March 1926: No. 31, p. 34: RG 3, vol. 139, PANS. Also honoured was Stewart's comrade John E. Read, then dean of Dalhousie Law School.

104 Information from Vivian Morrison; Sesquicentenary files, UKC.E.1.1.316–18, University of King's College Archives; *150th Anniversary Celebration and Alumni Reunion of King's College Halifax, N.S.: 1789 – 1939* [Halifax, 1939]

9

Goodall and Cairns: Commercial, Corporate, and Energy Law in Alberta, 1920–1942

LOUIS A. KNAFLA

Goodall and Cairns represented the typical prairie law firm of the inter-war years. Small in size, specialized in clients, and controversial in litigation, the firm was one of several hundred which practised law in Alberta in the interwar years. The typical law firm of the era was one person, as is clear from the *Canada Law List, Alberta* for 1930. Of 386 registered law firms in that year, 277 were one-member firms, 71 were two-member, and the size of the remaining 38 ranged from three to five members (see table 9.1). Thus 51 per cent of lawyers who practised in the province did so on their own, and a further 26 per cent practised in two-member associations.[1] The fluidity of firm composition was another important factor in the era. Not only were law firms largely sole proprietorships, but whenever members joined to form multimember firms, their associations had a shifting composition. For example, of the 59 registered firms with two or more members in 1930, no more than 11 per cent had the same people as members by 1935.[2] This makes the history of law firms, and of the law profession in Alberta specifically, and in the prairies more generally, difficult to research in the interwar years, let alone in previous eras.

BIOGRAPHICAL HISTORY

Goodall and Cairns was, like that of most of its contemporaries, a marriage of convenience. Adam Henry Goodall, known commonly as Harry, was born in Kirkaldy, Scotland, in 1886. Educated at the High School of

TABLE 9.1
Alberta Lawyers, 1930

Firm size	Law Firms			Total Firms	Total lawyers	Per cent
	Calgary	Edmonton	Other areas			
1	57	37	183	277	277	51
2	15	19	37	71	142	26
3	4	15	5	24	72	13
4	7	4	1	12	48	9
5	1	1	0	2	10	2
Total Firms	84	76	226	386		
Total Lawyers	132	141	276		549	

Source: Based on the *Canada Law List, 1929–1938*: *Alberta 1930*

Dunfermline and the University of Edinburgh, he took his legal apprenticeship with James Rose Stevenson, a Dunfermline solicitor. Goodall passed his bar examinations and was enrolled as a Scottish solicitor in April 1909, and he emigrated to Calgary in the following year. He was employed with William Leigh Bernard and his son Michael Charles while he studied for the Alberta law examination that was required for solicitors from other Commonwealth countries. Passing the oral examination in February 1911, and bearing a testimonial from Thomas Gillispie, Goodall paid his $300 enrolment fee, was admitted to the Alberta bar on 18 April 1911, and began practice in that year (see table 9.2).[3]

Goodall returned to Scotland for the First World War, while retaining his membership in the Alberta Law Society. He joined the East Riding Yorkshire Imperial Yeomanry in January 1916. He served in Egypt until spring 1919, then returned briefly to Scotland. The following year he sailed for Canada, and resumed his law career in Calgary with Bernard, Bernard (see table 9.2). In 1921 he married Maude Heap, a native-born Albertan from Fort Macleod and Pincher Creek, in the Proulx Roman Catholic Cathedral. Maude's father, Sam Heap, was an RCMP officer who ran the Garnet Ranch in southern Alberta. Sam was also a neighbour of Justice William Carlos Ives's, and later acted as a land valuator in the region for Ives's son-in-law.

Few files are extant for Goodall's practice with Bernard, Bernard.[4] He left them in 1929 to join his friend Marshall Menzies Porter, known as Marsh, who was partnered with Premier Brownlee and Thomas Charles

TABLE 9.2
Goodall and Cairns:
Predecessor and Sucessor Firms

Bernard and Bernard	1910
Bernard, Bernard and Goodall	1911-13?
Bernard, Bernard and Goodall	1920–29
Brownlee, Porter and Rankine	1929–30
Brownlee, Porter, Goodall and Rankine	1930
Brownlee, Porter and Goodall	1931
Porter and Goodall	1932
Goodall	1932–5
Lougheed, McLaws, Redman and Cairns	1929–30
McLaws, Redman, Lougheed and Cairns	1931–5
Goodall and Cairns	1935–43
McLaws, Cairns and McLaws	1944–5
Cairns	1947
Cairns and Howard	1948–52
Mahaffy and Howard	1953–6
Mahaffy, Howard, Moore and Mackie	1957
Howard, Bessemer, Moore, Dixon and Mackie	1956–60
Howard, Bessemer, Dixon, Mackie and Forsyth	1961–3
Howard, Bessemer, Moore, Dixon, Mackie and Forsyth	1965–8
Howard, Moore, Dixon, Mackie and Forsyth	1969–73
Howard, Dixon, Mackie and Forsyth	1974–8
Howard, Dixon and Mackie	1979–80
Howard Mackie	1981–91

Note: This genealogy is a revised version of that done originally by Anne Lowrey for the Law Society of Alberta Legal Archives Society when the firm's records were transferred from the Glenbow in 1991.

Rankine. The first large group of Goodall's files date from this period. Rankine left the firm in 1930, and it was later dissolved with the famous Brownlee seduction case of 1933–4, which led to the premier's resigning in disgrace.[5] Goodall then left Porter and the others, practising on his own until he was joined by the younger Cairns in 1935. An essentially 'private' man, Goodall lived at the very exclusive Haultain House in southwest Calgary in the 1920s, and was known to have little respect for most of his fellow lawyers.[6] He died prematurely in 1939 at the age of fifty-three.[7]

Conveyancing and collections were the core of Goodall's legal practice, as well as of his legal career. He came to Calgary on the advice of his friend Jack Robertson, whose father, Ernest Victor, had a loan-collections business in the Herald Building. His inaugural law firm – Bernard, Bernard – specialized in lending, and thus most of his early clients were creditors, insurance salesmen, and stockbrokers. The Bernards furnished the deals, while Goodall did the firm's conveyancing and litigating.[8] These clients also enabled Goodall to expand into the areas of real estate, bankruptcy, estates, and securities law in the 1920s. He established a thorough business plan. His stenographers became experts in drafting conveyances, and Louise Anderson (née Charbonneau) followed him throughout his career. Louise, together with her sisters Gertrude, Lucille, and Minnetta, appear throughout his files from 1929 to 1939 as signatories to affidavits and notices of motion.[9] They also did his searches in the city of Calgary's Clerk of Court office.[10]

Goodall retained a number of major clients throughout his career, regardless of the name of the firm or partnership of which he was a member. Unfortunately, the files of Bernard, Bernard disappeared with the death of Mr Bernard in Vancouver in 1936. Thus the files which Goodall brought with him for the establishment of his own practice in 1932 form the majority of those which have survived from 1920. The evidence demonstrates that he acted as solicitor for the Calgary-based business of several corporate clients from 1920 to 1939, including some of the subsidiary companies of the Burns family, the British Traders Insurance Company, the British Dominion Oil and Development Corporation Ltd, Dominion Bridge Company, Farmer's Fire and Hail Insurance Company, the Imperial Life Assurance Company, and (later with Cairns) Irving's Garage.[11]

Once fully established on his own in 1932, Goodall began to act as the Calgary agent for several out-of-town businesses and lawyers for commercial and corporate matters. These included William R. Kinsman, of Regina, and the Zurich General Accident & Liability Insurance Company. Correspondingly, he used several out-of-town lawyers as agents for his clients whose business activities extended beyond Calgary: in particular, W.P. Atton, of Regina; Farris, Farris, McAlpine, Stultz, Bull & Farris, of Vancouver; John A.S. MacDonald, of Fort Macleod; J.R. McClure, of Red Deer; E.H. Read, of Drumheller; and E.A. Rice and C. Patterson, of Lethbridge. Finally, Goodall also served as counsel for the personal legal business of several of his corporate clients, including Guy Armstrong, Louise and Helen Brett, George Farr, J.H. Goodwin, William Henderson, Charles Noble, and Thomas Underwood.

The 1920s was the decade in which Goodall came to specialize in drafting legal documents for oil and gas firms, implementing mortgages and foreclosures for creditors, and administrating estates. His connections in the business world proved enduring, as a few specific clients gave him both their company and their personal legal business. Once he joined

Brownlee, Porter and Rankine in 1929, he became involved in energy and securities law, and was embroiled in the stock-promotion boom of the late 1920s and its crash in the early 1930s. His practice, moreover, did not seem to suffer from his leaving the larger Brownlee firm at the outset of the Great Depression. His case files for Research Securities – Robert Hagerman's specialty brokerage firm for oil and gas securities – brought him into contact with prominent shareholders such as the Gillies family, of the Ottawa Valley lumber industry, and the lieutenant-governor of Ontario, W.D. Ross, even though Hagerman left Goodall with substantial debts in escaping to California.[12]

Perhaps these prominent clients contributed to the connections which Goodall established with the British aristocracy. He was hired, for example, by White and Wasbrough, prominent London barristers, to write a brief for the House of Lords on the validity of the marriage of Frederick George Moore Percival, Earl of Egmont, and Anne G.A. Moodie, who were resident in Priddis, Alberta. The Lords wished to know whether, if the couple had a son born in Priddis, he would be considered born in England in a marriage valid under colonial law, and thus capable of sitting in the House of Lords. Goodall wrote in the affirmative. He added that the earl's ambition was to become a 'Western Canadian,' and that 'he affects most of the eccentricities of dress of a Western cowboy.'[13] Goodall also assisted another British aristocratic settler, Charles, Third Baron Hindlip, in the settlement of his estate.[14]

James Mitchell Cairns was born in Edinburgh, Scotland, on 25 October 1902. The family immigrated to Nelson, British Columbia, in 1910, where his father, Thomas Munro Cairns, operated a fruit farm. James had his primary and secondary schooling in Nelson and Traill, matriculating to the University of British Columbia in 1921, and transferring to the University of Alberta, where he received his BA degree in 1925. He attended the University of Alberta Law School, graduating LLB in 1927, articled under Alexander Macleod Sinclair, KC,[15] and was admitted to the Alberta bar by Chief Justice W.C. Simmons on 28 June 1928.[16]

Cairns joined the Lougheed, McLaws and Redman firm in 1929, becoming a partner in the following year (see table 9.2). He married Florence Macmillan, an aboriginal Albertan, who was a nurse at the Ponoka Mental Hospital. Her father, R.L. Macmillan, owned the Chair Ranch in High River, Alberta. Cairns left that firm in 1935, forming a partnership with Goodall that lasted until the latter's death in 1939. Cairns's legal practice in the early 1930s was typical for a young lawyer of the Depression years. He handled primarily collections and foreclosures. The major clients he acquired prior to joining Goodall included the British Columbia Dental Supply Company, the Canadian Acceptance Corporation, Dominion Life Assurance Company, Freeman Company Ltd, Hazel-Atlax Glass Company, Holt Renfrew Company, and Jeffrey Manufacturing Company.

Cairns expanded this client list when he began his association with Goodall in late March and early April 1935.[17] He moved into Goodall's office in Room 507 of the Lancaster Building on Stephen Avenue, which Goodall had rented since his move from the Lougheed Building down the street after striking out on his own in 1932.[18] However, by the end of 1935, the two associates had made Room 707 their office, which Cairns maintained until the association was wound up several years after Goodall's death. Cairns continued to practise under the former partnership name until 1942, when he rejoined W.H. McLaws to form McLaws, Cairns and McLaws (see table 9.2).

Appointed King's Counsel in 1945, Cairns went on to a prominent judicial career. He became president of the Calgary Bar Association the following year, when the McLaws firm was dissolved, and he joined W.A. Howard. Cairns was a strong proponent of commercial and industrial development in the 1940s, becoming a director of several local companies and serving on the council of the Calgary Chamber of Commerce. He also became involved in politics, working for the local Liberal party and serving as president of the Calgary West Federal Constituency Liberal Association. Considered by observers as a 'snappy dresser,' he was a member of the Glencoe Club, and an active Anglican layman at Christ Church Cathedral, which was located near his home at 3641 Elbow Drive, in southwest Calgary.

Cairns was appointed Justice of the Trial Division of the Supreme Court of Alberta on 4 March 1952, and was appointed to the Appellate Division in 1965, when the Judges Act was amended to increase the number of Justices of Appeal of the Supreme Court from five to six. He was a highly respected justice; most of the judgments he wrote centred on questions of commercial law, and few of his decisions were ever overturned in his lifetime. He retired from the bench in October 1977, five months after his wife, Florence, had died. He passed away himself on 13 December 1978.[19]

CORPORATE HISTORY

The choice of dates for the study of the partnership is as precarious for this firm as it is for any other in the era. For example, only 33 case files are

FIGURE 9.1

Files Opened and Closed, 1920–1942

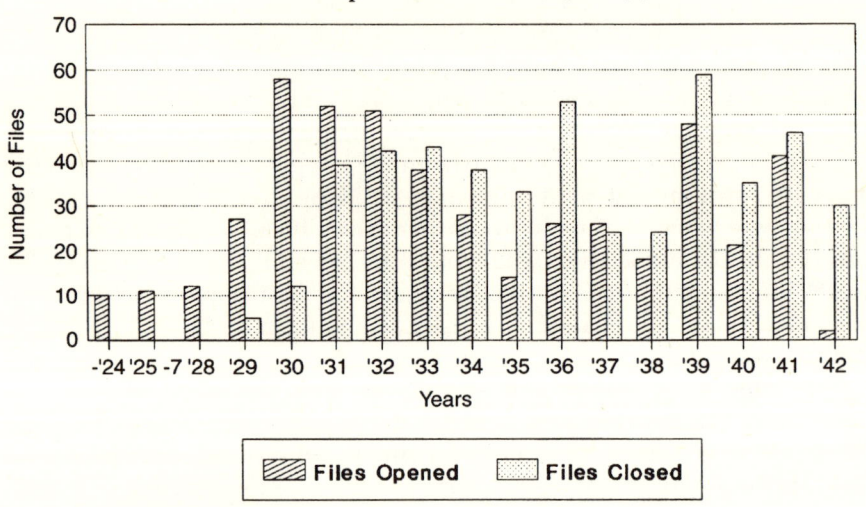

Based on 483 files in LASA fonds 42

extant for the period before Goodall joined Marsh Porter in 1929, while at least 254 files are extant which he opened before being joined by Cairns in 1935 (see figure 9.1). Meanwhile, most of the Cairns files are extant from the advent of his legal practice in 1929 until he wound up Goodall's files in 1942 and joined McLaws in the following year. What we have, therefore, is a fine run of 483 case files which date primarily from 1929 to 1942, and form the Goodall and Cairns deposit as fonds 42 of the Legal Archives Society of Alberta.[20] Since the files extant are those of the individual firm members rather than of the firm generally, the history of 'Goodall and Cairns' is best written as a study of their legal business, which begins with Goodall's (1920–35), Cairns's (1929–35), that of the two associates (1935–9), and that of Cairns back on his own and winding up Goodall's files (1939–42). In this way we can make a general analysis of the rich archival collection of a law firm whose predecessor and successor firms numbered twenty-two over a seventy-two-year period, or an average of 3.72 years per titular firm name (see table 9.2).[21]

As individuals, Goodall and Cairns witnessed significant client growth from 1929 to 1933. Perhaps it was the cumulative 73 per cent drop in new client files from 1932 to 1935 that encouraged them to join as associates in that year (see figure 9.1). While the number of new clients would eventually rise by 1939 to equal the annual newcomers of the early 1930s, the two men would suffer annually more outgoing than incoming clients for 1933–42. Therefore, the value of association may well have been to arrest the large decline of clients that both men had witnessed since 1933, as well as sharing costs in a long Depression that seemed to have no end.

The chronology of the firm's history begins with a partnership that was never formalized, and never put into writing. Adam Henry (Harry) Goodall and James Mitchell Cairns commenced practice as Goodall and Cairns in 1935, although they never signed a partnership agreement.[22] The two men simply made an oral agreement in April 1935 to share an office and put up a joint shared name.[23] Both men had once been members of prominent Calgary partnerships which they had inherited. Therefore, they brought to the new firm not only their files, but also some of the files of their former associates, as well as their own secretaries. The latter comprised for Goodall the Charbonneaus, whom he had known from the early 1920s, and for Cairns, Constance Constable, who had been his legal secretary since 1936. The work of these secretaries is prominent in the files, ranging from stenographic work to witnessing legal documents, delivering legal notices, and being assigned debts owed by clients![24] They would also fill in for one another.[25]

While the main rationale for the two lawyers' association was shared office space and expenses, in later years they shared work on a few accounts, such as Irving's Garage and the Imperial Trust Company. In addition, they also began to experience the underground economy in trading services with their clients. For example, they had a running account with Irving's Garage, balancing purchases of gasoline and mechanical repairs for their vehicles with Irving's legal expenses.[26] In a later episode, Goodall had to accept his client's car and furniture to close out the account.[27] In return, Cairns had some difficulty in resolving the business of his associate at his death.

The legal practices of the two men survived the 1930s on the backs of a number of regular customers. Goodall had lost several major clients by 1935. These included the Alberta Oil Consumers Cooperative Ltd; Anglo-Ecuadorian Oilfields Ltd; Armstrong Funeral Homes; Burns Holding Company; Dominion Bridge; E.P. Ranch; George Farr; Great West Distributors; Great Western Furniture Company; Robert Hagerman; Henderson and Rogers; Jewel Colleries; William Kinsman; and National Fish Foods. His core stable was down to British Dominion Oil; CFCN's 'Voice of the Prairies'; Farmers Fire and Hail Insurance; Farris, Farris, McAlpine and Stultz; and Premier Trust. Cairns had lost the Arrow Suspender &

Garter Company; Chow Don; and the Freeman Company. His core stable, however, was small but viable, including quite frequent and heavy work for the Canadian Acceptance Corporation; Harry Forster Ltd; and Irving's Garage. He would soon gain the accounts of the Canadian Men's Trust Association Ltd; Cummings, Meegan and Company; Edmonton Credit Company; and the Industrial Acceptance Corporation. In addition, both men began to do more estates and family law for clients as their personal affairs seemed to take turns for the worse by the end of the decade.

The final portrait of the firm is one of staying alive in business. While a few large and major clients were added in the mid and late 1930s, the overall situation was bleaker. An examination of the 483 files in the firm's collection has been made with respect to the opening and closing dates of each file (see figure 9.1). The result reveals a very clear pattern of rise and decline for the period from 1925 to 1942. The number of files opened increased dramatically in the years 1929 through 1932, at the peak of the Great Depression. The number of files closed then exceeded the number of files opened every year from 1933 to 1942, except for 1937. Therefore, while Goodall and Cairns prospered in their business association in the mid and late 1930s, the window of future opportunity was closing with each passing year. Perhaps this is why Cairns decided to wind up the firm in 1940–2 after Goodall's death. His associate had failed to add a single major client in his last five years, and his files for current clients were in decline. Cairns, apart from his own efforts, must have been aware of the slow demise in the firm's client base.

The decline in the client base can be seen as a significant one when the frequency of client business is analysed. A compilation of the number of individual files in each client's dossier reveals that 78 per cent of all client dossiers consisted of one file (see figure 9.2).[28] Thus, in numerical terms, this firm conducted the major portion of its business with what we may call 'single-event' clients: persons who came to Goodall and Cairns with a problem and never returned for more business. In fact, the firm had come to rely on four of its clients for half of its legal business. Overall, 61 per cent of the firm's business was derived from eight clients, and 50 per cent from just four.[29] The erosion of the single-event client base was therefore threatening to the long-term viability of the firm, and the loss of any one of its major customers would have a very negative effect on its financial equilibrium. Since Cairns had the collections business of the firm's two major clients – the Industrial Acceptance Company and the Canadian Acceptance Corp. Ltd – he had at least the foundation for a single-proprietor law firm.

FIGURE 9.2

Number of Files per Client

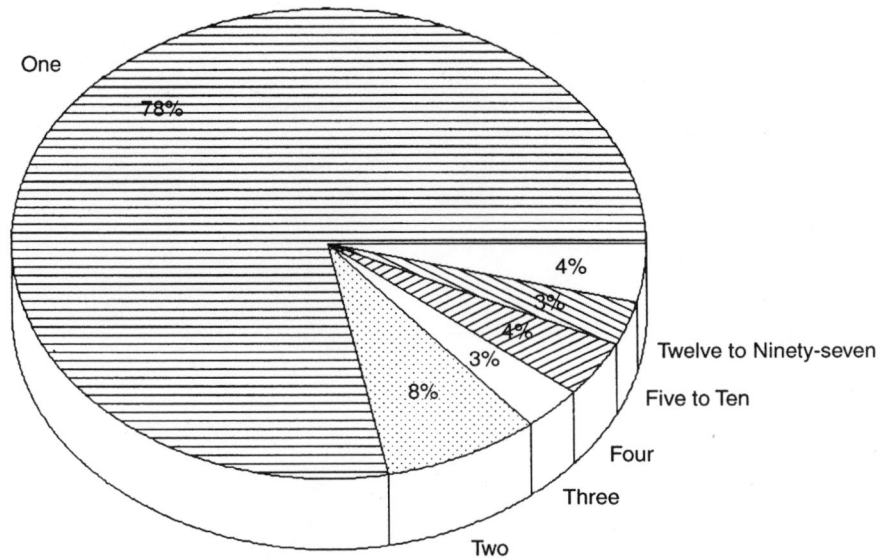

Based on 186 client files: LASA fonds 42

The single-event client phenomenon can also be seen in an analysis of the duration of each individual file (see figure 9.3). In this regard, 172, or 36 per cent, of all files were opened and terminated within the same calendar year. Moreover, 62 per cent of all individual files were opened and closed within a two-year period. This confirms the observation made above that the firm had, by the late 1930s, lost ground in the consistency of its legal marketing by relying increasingly on short, one-off disputes for a significant portion of its legal business. A more speculative, and qualitative analysis of the company's files suggests that both Goodall and Cairns had a larger proportion of their business in repeat customers in the early 1930s than they had in the late 1930s. Whether this phenomenon was attributable to a structural development in the history of the law profession in the 1930s, or to internal developments within the Goodall Cairns firm, precludes speculation at this time.

Finally, the firm's business was firmly entrenched in creditor–debtor relations (see figure 9.4). For example, an examination of the firm's business client by client reveals that the subjects of bankruptcy, real estate, and collections comprised 40 per cent of it. Since a considerable amount

FIGURE 9.3

Length of Case Files

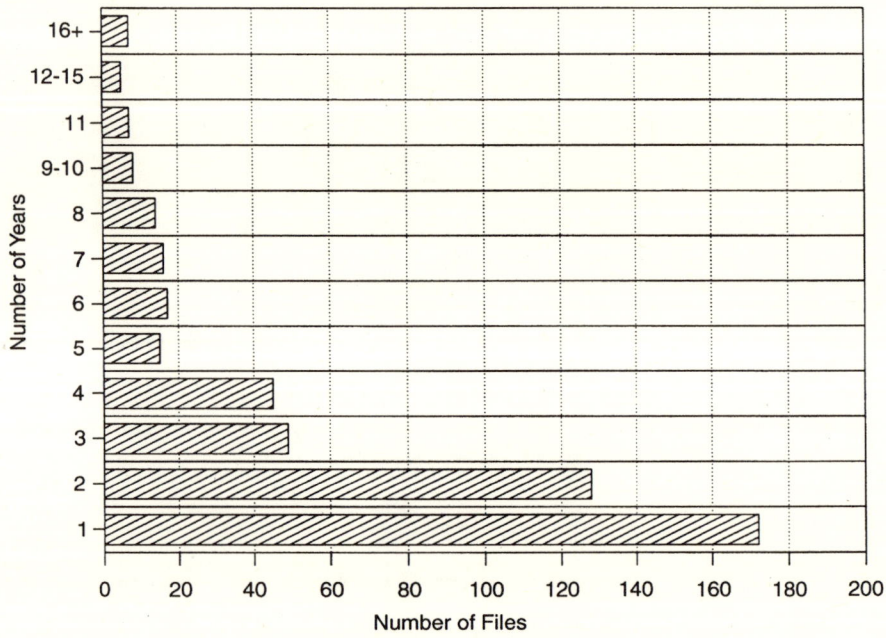

Based on 483 files: LASA fonds 42

of its commercial and corporate business involved creditors as well, one could estimate that clearly more than half of the firm's business stemmed from creditor–debtor relations. Figure 9.4 also shows the subject distribution on a file-by-file basis. Here the distinction is even more paramount, with 70 per cent of the firm's individual files (excluding commercial and corporate) lodged in the creditor–debtor area. The more lucrative (and less continuous) business of litigating oil and gas, securities, and estates law accounted for only 31 per cent and 16 per cent of files, respectively.

What, then, was the firm's quintessential case, day in and day out? The subject would have to be collections, the lawyer would be Cairns, and the issue would be the seizure of a car or truck by a Sheriff's Distress Warrant on the behalf of a local vendor or financial institution. This was also 'law' in its most fundamental sense. A prime example was when Goodall spent more than two years to collect a debt of $8.75 owed by H.L. Jeffries to Beach Foundries Ltd of Ottawa.[30] These were, after all, the Depression

FIGURE 9.4

Subject Areas

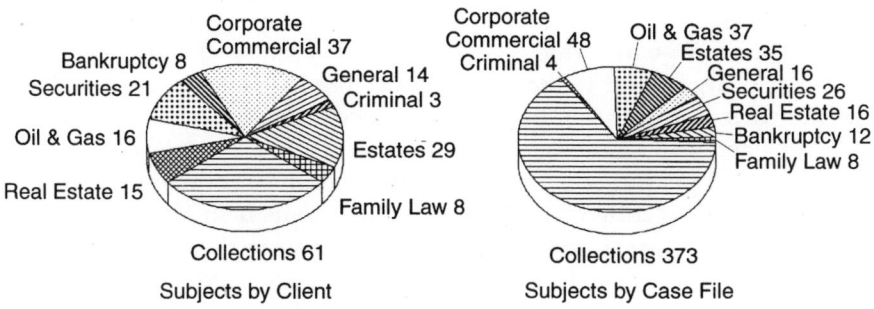

| Corporate Commercial 37 |
| Bankruptcy 8 |
| Securities 21 |
| General 14 |
| Criminal 3 |
| Oil & Gas 16 |
| Estates 29 |
| Real Estate 15 |
| Family Law 8 |
| Collections 61 |

Subjects by Client

| Corporate Commercial 48 |
| Criminal 4 |
| Oil & Gas 37 |
| Estates 35 |
| General 16 |
| Securities 26 |
| Real Estate 16 |
| Bankruptcy 12 |
| Family Law 8 |
| Collections 373 |

Subjects by Case File

Based on 212 clients and 575 case files in LASA fonds 42

years. In the province of Alberta, they were made more perplexing by the legislation of the Social Credit government, including the passage of debt-adjustment acts, in addition to legislation regulating banks, assurance companies, and rents in the years 1936–8. Much of this legislation was ruled unconstitutional by the Supreme Court of Canada in the years 1939–41. This sequence of events not only aided the litigation of property in the 1930s, but also brought the collapse of such litigation in the ensuing war years.[31]

THE LITIGATION: AGENCIES

One can begin an analysis of the functions of Goodall and Cairns with the lawyers from outside Calgary on whom Goodall and Cairns came to rely both for the referral of a fair amount of client business, and as agents who could conduct litigation to implement claims of their clients against debtors who resided outside the city. Given that most manufacturing and trading companies were not located in Alberta, considerable commercial business in the province depended on the maintenance of legal agreements with external companies. For example, the British Traders Insurance Company was one of Goodall's first clients, originating from his days with Bernard, Bernard in 1921. The company often had to sue customers from rural Alberta and Saskatchewan for collections, and preferred to channel its claims for this large region through one firm. Thus, Goodall had several prairie lawyers who would serve as his agents in processing statements of claim and taking collections on the behalf of his client company.

One of these agents was Mr A.O. MacMillen, a barrister of Gravel-bourg, Saskatchewan. After more than a decade of giving him referrals from this eastern company,[32] Goodall made a complaint against him to the Law Society of Saskatchewan. The complaint included the appropriation of funds in trust which MacMillen had used for his own account, excessive charges, and the failure to send monies due to the client from sheriff's seizures. In the penultimate case, MacMillen had acted as Goodall's agent in a suit against Gotlieb Wagner, a local farmer, on the behalf of the insurance company. The insurance company won, but Goodall had great difficulty in collecting the funds held in trust by Mac-Millen. Weekly correspondence developed between the two legal counsel for nearly two months for both an accounting and delivery of the funds. MacMillen eventually paid out the trust fund, but Goodall was so incensed that he launched a complaint against him with the Law Society. The disciplinary committee heard it, but in the end the benchers refused to do anything and eventually convinced Goodall to drop the complaint.[33] This was not unusual for such an independent profession in the interwar years.[34]

Another agency, which worked the other way, was Farris, Farris, McAlpine, Stultz, Vancouver barristers who gave Goodall the business of handling the matters of its clients in Alberta after 1921. These matters ranged from the settlement of estates and mortgages to credit investigations. Sometimes Goodall had to do some snooping. In the Casson family dispute, for example, he reported that Mr Harold Casson, currently in Lethbridge, was in terrible financial difficulty owing to excessive drinking and gambling: 'He seems to be absolutely neglecting his office.'[35] Goodall maintained this long relationship because he continuously met the demands of providing discount rates. Thus, in searching chattel and conditional sales registers for encumbrances against a car, he was asked by cable: 'Also state your fees and keep as low as possible.' Returning the information, he closed: 'as requested by you we kept them as low as possible' ($3.35).[36]

Goodall had a similar relationship with William R. Kinsman, a barrister in Regina, from 1930 to 1935. Here he collected from the southern Alberta debtors of a machinery company and a business college.[37] These early referrals seem to be the foundation on which Goodall began his legal practice. It introduced him to the business of commercial agreements, mortgages, and collections which he later developed into a wider range of commercial law. Eventually, he would build on the unique opportunities provided by the emergence of the oil and gas industry, and the Calgary Stock Exchange, to develop specialities in oil and gas, and securities law, discussed and assessed separately below.

COMMERCIAL AND CORPORATE CASES

Beginning in 1929, the Burns family entrusted Goodall with much of their legal counsel for various companies under their control, particularly those which were engaged in land development, real estate, and oil and gas. In 1926 P. Burns & Company Ltd had sold through its P. Burns Holdings Ltd a tract of land near Olds to a group of Mennonites for $122,435.86, with no money down, interest at 6 per cent, plus taxes and various provisions such as keeping out noxious weeds in compliance with provincial legislation. Then, in 1928, Burns agreed to rewrite the original sale agreement to the twelve Mennonite families individually: Peters, Rempel, Dahl et al. Finally, in autumn 1932, he sued them for non-payment of interest (none had been paid), and the failure to cut down noxious weeds and to perform collateral agreements (for sale of grain and hogs at specified prices) to pay down the principal sum of the loan.[38]

This case was the first one handled for the Burns companies by Goodall. In the examinations for discovery, Superintendent J. Fisher Williams testified that the Mennonites had harvested and sold grain as well as hogs on their own, and had not branded new calves. They claimed, however, that they had nothing to sell at a discount to Burns for the payment of their debts, and Peter Esau threatened that he would mortgage his livestock if the company sued them! Williams also testified that some of them had new cars at their houses. Thus, by 15 September 1932, the total sum due was $128,882.08. In the trial before the Supreme Court of Alberta on 15 October, Justice Tweedie ordered specific performance and injunctions against the farmers on the behalf of Burns, confirming his company's liens on the property and its sole ownership in fee simple. Burns had accepted their division of the properties, but not of the liabilities. Finally, in June 1934, Goodall wound up the case by having each of the Mennonites sign a new agreement for all payments past due, plus all things to perform, which were spelled out in great detail, from the cycle of planting and harvesting to the collection of proceeds from grain and the husbandry farming. The case is interesting because of the major on-site investigative work Goodall had to undertake in order to make his client's suit successful.[39]

In working for the Burns companies, Goodall gained his first experience in corporation law. In 1929 he handled their holding company's purchase of H.A. Benjamin Ltd, insurance brokers, for $30,000.[40] The purchase also included a complex fiscal regime for the avoidance of taxes. Following this takeover, Goodall handled a number of agreements to buy out landowners in British Columbia, from Kamloops and Shuswap down to Fort Steele.[41] It was probably through his connections with Burns that Goodall acquired the business of National Fish Foods Ltd of Edmonton in 1930. It became, unfortunately, a sordid tale. A series of fish shipments from Milwaukee and Chicago went astray; some fish were lost and others arrived unfit for consumption. The debts accrued, the company was sued by the San Juan Fishing & Packing Company, and went bankrupt, costing Goodall most of his fees. He learned here, at the onset of the Depression, just how tough things would get.[42]

Goodall, in addition to working for private companies, also gained some business from public insurance and trust companies in the mid-1920s. Acquiring some files for Alberta and Saskatchewan from the Farmers Fire and Hail Insurance Company, he became involved in settling fire and hail insurance accounts. After 1929, most of these involved foreclosures against farmers whose payments were in arrears, and brought him into battle with provincial debt-adjustment boards. Often he had no recourse after an initial investigation. As a solicitor of Biggar, Saskatchewan, wrote to him later: 'There appears to be no hopes as to any of these with the possible exception of the Judgment against Jacob Yaschuk. To date I have never been able to realize anything from him but he keeps at farming and if he misses the frost one fall something can be recovered.'[43] Having gained some experience in the securities business, Goodall was also able to handle some of the company's bond and stock issues, and call-backs, in the early 1930s.[44]

In 1929, the inauguration of Goodall's long-term relationship with Irving's Garage, Calgary's (and southern Alberta's) distributor of White Trucks, took place. A series of sales contracts, mortgages, judicial sales, repossessions, and the garnishment of wages occupy twenty-nine files, the clients ranging from dealers to truckers throughout the province.[45] When he associated with Cairns in 1935, both of them handled the work of the distributor and continued to do so until the wind-up of the firm in 1942. The attorney's experiences with Farmer's from the mid-1920s, and with Irving from 1929, may have aided him in securing business from several loan and trust companies in the 1930s.

Goodall defended the liquidation of the Colonial Investment & Loan Company against the Imperial Trust Company following the Great Depression. This major case before the superior courts employed him for a decade, and he followed the company to its break-up.[46] His growing expertise in this area caused another Toronto firm, the Premier Trust Company, to retain his services in 1932–7 for the liquidation of debtor companies and properties in southern Alberta. His major case here, which also went to the Supreme Court, was the liquidation of the Busby Estate and Colonial Investment & Loan Company Ltd, which involved foreclosures, judicial sales, debt-adjustment proceedings, insurance, taxes, shareholders' meetings, and dissolution. Eventually settled after his death by Cairns in 1942, the case provided fees which were the largest in the firm's history.[47]

Cairns's major files in commercial and corporate law date significantly from his admittance to legal practice with Lougheed, McLaws, and Redman in 1929. His first large file in this area was from the Jeffrey Manufacturing Company of Montreal. He handled their Alberta contracts for shipping locomotives, and coal-mining, elevator, and crushing machinery.[48] Later in that same year, he landed the collections work of a major firm which would lay the foundation of his law career. The Canadian Acceptance Corporation (CAC) would keep him in fees until the dissolution of the firm, if not until his call to the bench in 1952.

The corporation handled the collections business of some prominent southern Alberta retailers, from car dealers to hardware and grocery stores, meat markets, welders, and repair shops. Cairns took responsibility for at least ninety-seven client files from 1929–1942.[49] He learned very quickly that his client demanded that he be tough. One of his first files concerned defaulting car outlets. The Freeman Company was a distributor of Hudson–Essex motor cars to various dealers in the province. When a dealer defaulted on taking possession of a car for sale, the company's instructions were to force payment. Thus when car dealer I.F. Shacker, of Oyen, wanted to renege on taking possession of a car bought from Freeman, Cairns responded: 'We believe you would be well advised to hammer away at car sales not only moving this car of yours on our premises but securing others and to have this car on your floor for display purposes which we feel sure would be a big factor in creating a desire amongst people in your part of the country for another car.'[50] Cairns also investigated him, and reported: he is 'very weak financially, and was reported slow in retiring his obligations.' Shacker also had begun operating the Oyen Theatre; was sued by the landowner on his mortgage; and had several lien notes, judgment defaults, and judicial seizures against him.[51]

Perhaps the attorney's reputation in collections, together with his new association with Goodall, helped him to land his third-largest client in 1936, the Canadian Credit Men's Trust Association (CCMTA). Like the CAC, this association gave credit to retail firms such as bakers, confectioners, grocers, cafés, and hardware and paint stores for the conduct of their businesses, and Cairns would represent them in the collection of their debts. The failure of the region to escape the ravages of the Depression gave considerable work to the attorney for the CCMTA. Within six years Cairns had accumulated thirty-five files.[52] Most of these files, however, were for very small sums, ranging from $25 to $15. For example, Don's Groceteria of Okotoks gave Cairns a list of thirty unpaid accounts totalling less than $200. The attorney had to write to all the defaulters, several times, including to Mrs Renard for $1.38 and to Mr Hyslop for $0.50. Sometimes he had to supply copies of the sales agreements as well as the accounts. In the end, for this client he collected on only ten of the accounts, for a total of $81.36.[53] Long hours and hard work produced little reward in this file. He must have sometimes wondered about his practice when he had to travel to Field, British Columbia, in September 1939 to collect $60.44 from five customers of Mrs Muzzillo's Economy Store.[54]

Other collection work, however, was more profitable. In 1936 Cairns also landed the business of Harry Forester, who operated a Calgary motor-car dealership. The attorney handled all of the collections, statements of claims, and litigation of the accident files.[55] This prepared him for what became his biggest client, the Industrial Acceptance Company, in 1938. Accumulating seventy-nine files in the following four years, ranging from contracting and electrical supplies to motor-car and motor-supply companies, automobile financiers, and garages,[56] Cairns was in the midst of the growing industrial world of southern Alberta at the outset of the Second World War.

PUBLIC WORKS AND UTILITIES CASES

The firm's first major client in public works was Alberta Trackways Ltd, which planned to construct at public expense a toll highway between Calgary and Banff in 1929. Goodall researched and prepared a private member's bill for the provincial legislature to incorporate the subsidiary company that would own and construct the highway, as well as legislation to purchase the land. He also corresponded with all the local municipalities and district councils for rights of way, and for political support for the project. The letters on file to landowners are interesting in that he emphasizes in them that there will be no commercial value to their land, thereby making the purchase of rights of way inexpensive, but that, down the road, the project will greatly enhance their property values. He also assisted with the advertising campaign in local newspapers, and in the paperwork to raise $3.6 million in share and bond offerings.[57] The project stalled, and was abandoned in 1933.

Cairns, in the same year, represented Brown and Bigelow in their case against the Western Canada Road Route Service 58108. That project failed as well, leaving a line of creditors ranging from Minnesota interests to Revenue Canada.[58] In the following year, Goodall handled a contract negotiation for Dominion Bridge for the construction of an elevated steel watertank for the city of Calgary, which included all the subcontractors. Then, in March 1932, the company asked him to serve as its agent for obtaining contracts from the government of Alberta's $400,000 appropriation for the building of new steel bridges in the province. While nothing came of this, he did act as the company's collection agent, and handled some of its tax disputes with the government, as well as legal disputes with other companies.[59]

Public works and utilities was one of the major areas of litigation in the Canadian West in the late nineteenth and early twentieth centuries. Major national and international securities houses such as the Royal Securities Corporation made fortunes for their investors in the development of these industries in the West.[60] Goodall and Cairns, however, were probably too late to catch this wave,[61] as other prominent Calgary law firms were already established in the area. Goodall, however, was one of the city's first lawyers to get in on the discovery of commercial quantities of oil in the mid-1920s. Combined with his corporate work, this business allowed him to develop a speciality in oil and gas and in securities law that would pay him some useful fees in the 1930s.

OIL AND GAS

The 1930s witnessed the coming of age of the oil and gas industry in Alberta. While petroleum discoveries were made in the province during the First World War, it was not until 1924 that they came on stream commercially, and not until the 1930s that they were produced in significant quantities. The key years for the development of the industry were 1936 to 1940. Production rose geometrically, from 1,312,368 barrels of oil equivalent in 1936 to 8,362,203 in 1940. The annual increases were 110 per cent in 1937, 146 per cent in 1938, and 24 per cent in 1939.[62] Harry Goodall was one of the early lawyers for this aspiring industry, and he used his contacts, with his experience in conveyancing, to enter securities law with the goal of raising share capital and debentures on the behalf of new companies. While he did not become a major player in the area, the business he acquired enabled him to become a wealthy man by the time of his death at age fifty-three.

Goodall's first contact came when he joined Brownlee, Porter, and Rankine in 1929. A.M. Donaldson gave an option to the Canadian Oil & Development Syndicate to purchase two properties for $2,000 to drill for oil on 10 November 1929. The option was later extended for $1,000, and the well was drilled, with a small oil show. Since the purchasers could not complete the purchase price, and failed to pay the bonuses, its members Solloway and Mills were arrested in Toronto. Meanwhile, the company's other holdings were not doing well. Its brokers were initially unable to obtain more money, but eventually funds were raised in London, and Donaldson was paid off. However, problems continued over royalty agreements, and the disputes were eventually resolved in April 1933.[63] The experiences in this file enabled Goodall to learn the whole business, from a drilling option to production.

The attorney's other files in this area began in the following year, springing from his work for the Burns family. The Burns Foundation desired to sell some of its leases in exchange for royalty contracts, and Goodall established for them the London & Western Trust Company, for which he would become the solicitor, to hold the leases. He then arranged for the later famous oilman Thomas A. Weadick, of Faro, Wyoming, to acquire a group of the foundation's former properties, the Bow Valley leases, for $11,701. The agreement included royalty payments for production and pipeline flow-through; drilling a specified number of wells at specified times; and the retention of surface rights, damages, and access for agricultural purposes. Goodall also drew up the legal agreements between London Trust and Weadick with driller Franco Oils in March 1930. Acquiring an immense file, he put his conveyancing skills to good use in drafting complex pooling agreements with companies that had leases on neighbouring land. These companies included Sentinel Oils, Angus Oils, Alberta Federated Oils, and the Consolidated Fruit Company.[64]

Later, Goodall would assist the Burns Foundation in selling other lands in southern Alberta to private buyers, and in drafting contracts with building contractors for construction.[65] Sometimes he would also assist them in a third-party capacity. For example, in August 1933 the foundation successfully offered an option to Sir Francis Caradoc Rose Price, baronet, of Gloucester, England, to purchase some of the interests of the foundation in the Crown leases shared with Raven Oils Ltd in the foothills forest reserve (Dominion lands), north of Pincher Creek. The Hudson's Bay Company was the owner, the Anglo-Ecuadorian Company the lessee, and Goodall the agent. His correspondence included letters from a friend who worked in the oilfields there, suggesting that he also had obtained a source for inside information, independent of his clients.[66]

Goodall's work in this era came from both sides of the energy industry. His next file in the industry concerned the coal-mining companies of Drumheller who petitioned the provincial government to deny permission for the construction of a natural-gas pipeline to Saskatchewan because it would harm severely the Alberta coal industry, and the province, in terms of investment, tax revenues, and employment. He compiled details on the current consumption of coal rates by grade, and the negative impact of gas as opposed to coal exports on capital and employment. Arguing that coal exports would be cut by one-third with the building of the pipeline, he tried to demonstrate what a great catastrophe would occur in Edmonton (the provincial capital) if coal was replaced by natural gas there. He also gathered data on how such a pipeline would affect the railways, and put their annual loss at over $4 million. In the end, he requested on the behalf of the coal operators whom he represented compensation of at least $960,000 yearly to subsidize the loss of capital investment and workers' wages.[67]

Meanwhile, Goodall's legal work for the British Dominion Oil and Development Corporation involved both the provincial and the federal governments. His original suit on the company's behalf, versus the Minister of National Revenue, was filed in the Exchequer Court of Canada on 8 May 1933, appealing assessments for the tax year 1930. The company's balance-sheet for that year had assets of $555,022.72, with virtually no debt. The appeal was for taxes in the sum of $1,371.29. Company policy was to register all expenses, from breaking ground until the sale and marketing of products, as operating costs and not capital, claiming that capital is solely the equipment and chattels used to drill the hole (tangible assets). Since the company could not determine the life of a gas or oil well, all funds from sale of the product were applied to the full recovery costs until they were liquidated, with the remainder going to profit, subject to expenses. Ottawa, however, had set the depreciation allowance at $3/_{12}$ for the year because the well produced only for the last three months of the year. Since the company used the assets for the full year, it claimed that this partial allowance was unacceptable: that depreciation goes on regardless, and that a depletion allowance of 25 per cent of net operating profit (an arbitrary figure) compensates for exhaustion and not for operating expenses, and should be based on gross receipts. The company also appealed its 1931 tax assessments, provincial and federal, to the Supreme Court of Alberta, and the case was sent to the Court of Exchequer in Ottawa. It appears from internal evidence that this company took the government to court on behalf of several others, although it paid Goodall all costs of the suit.[68]

Goodall's experience with the government was not very satisfactory. He objected to filing bonds for the appeal of such small sums, and to Minister E.B. Ryckman's terse denial of their original complaint lodged with the federal government on 20 October 1932. Goodall carefully prepared extensive documentation, including the costs of all wells, current production month by month, and future plans and contingencies. Seldom, however, did he receive a reply. His frustration is evident in a letter to British Dominion, dated 2 May 1934: 'I have received no defence from the Income Tax department but they never are very punctual. I think it is one of those holes the Department would like to crawl out of but so much money is involved by way of tax that eventually no doubt the Department will give me a defence and proceed.'

The trial was set for autumn 1934. In the meantime, a meeting of a number of oil-company people in Calgary was held, as Goodall reported in a private memo to those companies, dated 13 June. The meeting was attended by two prominent lawyers, H.S. Patterson, KC, and L.H. Fenerty, KC, and two prominent chartered accountants, J.H. Williams, FCA, and A.J.J. Fanshaw, CA, 'when the whole matter of liability of Oil Companies to pay income Tax was fully discussed.' According to Goodall, they were told by the Inspector of Income Tax in Calgary that Ottawa, as a result of the appeal, was amending the depletion allowance so that it would be calculated on gross income from production and not the net. The attendees agreed that, if this did not happen very soon, British Dominion should be encouraged to mount its appeal. It was also noted that four other companies had appeals prepared.

Meanwhile, the Calgary tax office was reported to advise that it could work a deal for British Dominion while the change in legislation went forward. The board of directors of the company agreed, and instructed Goodall to prepare and send the necessary correspondence. That the federal government was placed under considerable pressure is revealed in a letter from E.M. Gunderson, Superintendent of Income Tax, dated 1 May 1935: He has recommended the legislative change, and because such an appeal is so expensive, 'I am anxious that this appeal be settled as soon as possible.' A similar letter was sent from W.S. Gray, solicitor for the provincial attorney general's department, dated 17 May. As a result of the appeal, the government changed its terms of taxing the oil and gas industry, which were explained in Goodall's letter to the company's board on 4 June, and the company was allowed to write off the accumulated interest and penalties.[69]

Further work on behalf of the industry's encounters with government involved the jurisdiction of the Soldier Settlement Board of Canada. Goodall acted for several companies to obtain the right of way to drill on Crown land from surface owners and public utility boards. In one instance, surface owner Samuel Scott Thompson, of Hartell Post Office, Alberta, granted the company the right to enter and drill. The government, however, disputed his right to do so, arguing that the land in question was Crown land. Another instance involved the same issue for Hardie Turnbull. These matters were corresponded up through the layers of government to the Department of the Interior. In the end, the federal government agreed that Soldier's lands were not Crown lands, and that the Public Utilities Board had the power to grant surface lease agreements on provincial Crown land. As a result, the government of Alberta also rewrote its terms and procedures for surface rights vested in the Crown of Alberta under the Provincial Lands Act, which was signed into law by Lieutenant-Governor W.L. Walsh on 18 December 1933.[70]

One of the first major lawsuits in which Goodall became involved within the industry was *Northern Oils Ltd* v. *Alberta Oil Consumers Co-Operative Ltd and Great West Distributors Ltd*, which was heard before the Supreme Court of Alberta at Lethbridge, 27 December 1933. Appearing for the plaintiff, Goodall represented the company's statements of claim for gas, tractors, kerosene, and other equipment which had been delivered to the defendant at Morrin & Wetaskiwin. The defendant had assigned its debts to the Maple Leaf Oil & Refining Company, which liquidated under D.E. Hagerman, and Hagerman then assigned them to Great West for a mortgage, which default brought the defendant and its associated companies into liquidation. There was also a claim of fraud. Since Alberta Oil Consumers was the operator of a Montana refinery and drilling concession, its collapse affected a long list of other companies, both Canadian and American, in 1933. The file kept Goodall busy throughout two years.[71] In the end, Alberta Oil Consumers was bought out by Northern Oils for $19,200 in an agreement of 6 June 1935. The bankrupt company had no current assets, accounts payable of $47,393.25, and many creditors. Goodall himself had his bill for dispositions and services unpaid for a year, and called a meeting of the creditors because his account was so long outstanding.[72]

Later, Goodall was able to do some legal work involving the famous early Calgary oil and gas company Royalite. In 1938 he drafted royalty trust agreements between Royalite and the Toronto General Trusts Corporation for British Dominion.[73] In the following year he worked on a subscription of 1,500 Royalite common shares to British Dominion, as well as a natural-gas processing agreement for British Dominion to process any hydrocarbon reserves discovered there, with a royalty override of 20 per cent.[74] Clients such as these also assisted him in developing a small business in securities law, discussed below.

The work in the oil and gas industry, however, was not always profitable. The example of Goodall's activities on the behalf of Baymar Oils, which operated in Ghost River Valley until it became defunct, is a case in point. George H. Webster, president, tried to sell off the company's properties in order to avoid bankruptcy. Since the rest of the company's assets were in creditors' hands, the directors fell out and would not meet. Most shareholders were outside of the province, and the promoters had control of the stock and had flown the coop. Mr H.F. Burne, of Lomond, Alberta, had been assigned some of the company's debt for past services, and had his own debt outstanding to W.G. Burne, of Wimbledon, London, who wrote Goodall to sue H.F. Burne. But since the latter was now a butcher near starvation, Goodall had a long-running correspondence trying to avoid hopeless lawsuits. As he wrote on 14 December: 'if you wish us to sue we will but we hold out no hope of successful recovery in the action.' W.G. then wrote back and asked if Goodall could not help H.F. obtain a loan to pay him off! In the end, $40 was eventually paid, of which Goodall took out $13.25 for expenses and received a nasty letter for the currency charge on the $26.75 remaining. Goodall maintained these files, seldom obtaining compensation for his services.[75]

SECURITIES LITIGATION

Securities law, along with oil and gas, became the predominant practice of Goodall in his later years. Following on the foundation he built with the Burns companies in the mid-1920s, he came to handle the securities work of several small, private companies in the late 1920s. These included Foster & Foster Ltd, a private family holding company for which he did the articles of incorporation in 1927, and maintained the directors' notices and resolutions, minutes, audits, share issues, transfers, legal agreements, and filings with the registrar of companies.[76] He did the same for Henderson & Rogers Ltd, a private company with hotel, land, and iron-works interests;[77] George G. Farr, who had business with the famous Mannix family;[78] and, in the early 1930s, Gray & Farr Ltd, which included some complex takeovers and an eventual bankruptcy.[79]

It was in these years, the early 1930s, that Goodall also began to act on the behalf of companies and individuals in equity-offering, share-registration, and stock-market advice. For example, he acted frequently for Smith, Davidson & Wright, of Vancouver, an American company, as agent and solicitor in Calgary for the Alberta region from 1930 to 1938. Most of his work involved the registration of companies and the preparation and filing of statutory declarations.[80] On the personal side, he had occasional clients such as Phyllis E. Baker, of Calgary, whom he advised on her holdings in the Montreal Investment Trust from 1929 to 1932. In his last letter, he notes the problems she has in receiving dividends in Salisbury, England, and advises her that the stock is virtually worthless with its assets in Beauharnois, Quebec, composed largely of seigneurial rents. She owned twenty-two shares![81] He also fought for British shareholders (including himself) in the Famous Players Corporation.[82]

Some of the securities business, however, was on the shady side in this notorious era of an unregulated-shareholding environment. Cairns was the attorney for William W. Grant, the 'Voice of the Prairies,' and handled the long and tortuous sale of Grant's shares in the radio station. He encountered problems not only with the regulatory authorities, but also with Grant's debts owed to Goodall and himself from work for Grant's Precision Machine & Foundry Ltd. The file also included correspondence with William Aberhart regarding the transfer of the radio licence of CFCN to Voice of the Prairies, and irregularities in the company's unauthorized distribution of common stock.[83]

Perhaps even more disturbing was Cairns's winding-up of the file of his friend Guy Armstrong, for whom he had acted as corporate legal counsel for Tull and Ardern, which had been on the brink of bankruptcy since 1931,[84] and for Armstrong Funeral Homes. Armstrong, with his businesses failing in 1936, had written a stinging letter to Goodall for his deductions and overcharging; for discounting the indebtedness of Mutual Transport Ltd, in which he had to sell his shares; as well as for past tax matters outstanding and the non-return of his collateral. Writing from Los Angeles on 9 December, Armstrong advised Goodall 'to get busy on this at once.' He also threatened to sue Goodall, who 'promised to take care of' the sale of both Armstrong Funeral Homes and Mutual Transport for him, and to release his collateral of $2,500. Goodall, who had arranged the sale of Mutual Transport to the Royal Bank of Canada, which held the liabilities, wrote to Armstrong on 9 November that 'if you think that I relish spending good money to phone or wire you for something so absurd then you are crazy and you know it.' Finally, Cairns and Goodall were able to release Armstrong's collateral by selling his 17,120 shares in Armstrong Funeral Homes to a Mr Shaver for $1.[85]

Goodall, however, was the securities man, and throughout the late 1930s he kept his clients up to date on oil-market stocks. For example, a letter to Reginald Akroyd, of Sutton Court, England, on 17 May 1937, relates the following: 'There was excitement in stocks in companies operating in the Turner Valley oilfields starting about two months and quietening about a month ago. The public simply took one of the crazy spells which the atmosphere here seems to create and most of the dealing was in perfectly worthless stocks, these being carried to many times their value before the boom and which naturally is a great many times beyond their value.' With regard to your 'ex-advisor,' he was 'liberated on parole just before Christmas 1936. Apart from having lost a little weight he appears just as well pleased with himself as ever, but of course he cannot return to the practice of his profession. It probably would have been less of a strain financially on his wife and daughters if the authorities had kept him a little longer where he justly belonged.'[86]

Akroyd had been active himself in the Calgary oil market prior to escaping his creditors in England. He had a safety deposit box for stock certificates at the Royal Bank, in Cranbrook, and paid for his stock by cheques drawn on Lloyd's Bank U.K. He lost his pending fortune on the liquidation of the Champion Stock Raising Company of Lloydminster, Saskatchewan, whose chief executive officer, Ernest G. Pescod, was imprisoned for five years in 1934 for misappropriation of funds. Akroyd was angry that the company's bank accounts had been cleaned out, and Goodall wrote to him on 12 June 1934 that 'the whole affair is a nasty mess and so far as moneys are still owing to you I think your best plan is to forget about them as I do not think anything will ever be recovered.' Pescod, who was a barrister and KC, tried an insanity plea, lost, and pled guilty to embezzlement. He seems to have made a career in raising money for companies from which he then embezzled, and Goodall became his Calgary agent! Some $50,000 in trust funds were never recovered.[87]

A list of Pescod's investments – some of which were made on the advice of Goodall – makes good reading: Wild Horse Gold Mining Syndicate, Stem Winder Mine, Kewatin Mining Syndicate, Enterprise Mine, and Champion Gold Mining Company Ltd. Pescod also received funds in trust for the purchase of oil leases he never paid for or took up. In the end, Goodall advised Akroyd not to go to the Law Society of Alberta because it would be too expensive, and Pescod had no publicly recorded funds remaining. Meanwhile, Goodall kept sending Akroyd invoices for his services, and notices for his mortgages outstanding. Goodall placed perhaps an undue faith in Pescod because he had served as the chancellor of the Anglican Diocese of Calgary, while Akroyd and his wife were considered fine Anglicans. Pescod may also have used his church position and reputation to attract investment funds.[88]

BEHIND DOORS: ESTATE MANAGEMENT AND PERSONAL AFFAIRS

Family law was not a major area of practice for Goodall and Cairns, but they did litigate several separations and divorces, and had a number of estate files. Goodall's earliest estate file is for Shelley J. Gish, of Kentucky, in 1928. Gish possessed land and apartment buildings in Calgary, and a family farm in Three Hills. Goodall handled the land titles, revenues and expenses, income tax, and their eventual sale.[89] He did the same, first for Ella, and then for her husband, Dr Llewellyn Jordan, for their rocky piece of land near Lethbridge, with an overflowing creek, said to be worth $10,474.25.[90] Closer to home, Goodall had prepared the will of Ethel Louisa Boyle, the Edmonton wife of Justice John Robert Boyle. When the sheriff wound up her estate in Calgary, the net proceeds were $153.68. The bailiff had seized and sold her furniture in three rented houses for non-payment. Ethel had problems with her tenants, and her insurance policies could not be found. Her sister, a schoolteacher in Calgary, was the recipient of her slim estate, and there is no record of Goodall's fee.[91]

More challenging, perhaps, was Goodall's search for the disappearing itinerant actor Joseph Burnell Evans, of Ottawa. Having an interest in an estate of property, common stocks, and cash, Evans went to London in the summer of 1934, and by October, Goodall had lost him. Tracing him from Ottawa to Montreal, Hamilton, Winnipeg, Calgary, and Islington, he lost him somewhere in London. Goodall was paid $118.19 for Evans's interest, and had costs of $41.80. Unfortunately, the trustee in Ottawa would not pay Goodall's costs until the $118.19 was returned. Afterwards, the trustee sent the attorney a further $1.48, payable to Evans, and Goodall had to try to find him again. He failed, and therefore had to return the cheque.[92]

His first domestic dispute involved Helen Anderson, the daughter of the late Justice McCarthy, who had married Norman M. Anderson, a Calgary stockbroker who went bankrupt in 1931. After several lawsuits and trials, Anderson eventually went to Drumheller, where he got a job with the Brilliant Coal Company Ltd. Helen wanted to rent the family house in Calgary, and move to Sylvan Lake for peace and good atmosphere. Norman said that he would kill her and her two daughters and/or commit suicide himself, if she did that, and requested a reconciliation in Drumheller. Helen refused to go to meet him, let alone move there. Thus, Goodall corresponded with Norman Anderson's lawyer in Drumheller, W.R. Sandercock, over why neither party would go to the other party's habitat. Helen sued Norman for a judicial separation in 1932, but no outcome exists in the file.[93]

In the same year, Goodall acted for Mrs Elizabeth E. Dingman, of Toronto, whose husband would not take her back and could not afford either alimony or maintenance for their child. Once separated, she would not have anything to do with him, and wanted to go after his father for financial support, while he wanted her to sell the house in Calgary. A suit for alimony and maintenance was adjourned, as Goodall advised that she wait for her husband's circumstances to improve.[94] Later, Cairns acted for Jesse Chandler, an oil driller who had married Mary Jane Mayo, and then contacted venereal disease in Kansas. They separated, and he married an elevator girl there. Mrs Chandler then met a man in Colorado and tried to marry him, but found that she was not legally divorced. In the meantime, Jesse had borrowed $5,000 from Mary Jane and made his fortune in Calgary. She then sued him for the money, which Jesse denied she had given him. The last letter in the file is from her lawyer in Tulsa, who says she is poor and has only a house with two mortgages.[95]

Goodall and Cairns were not infrequently involved in and committed to handling the personal idiosyncrasies of their clients, and often at little or no profit. Cairns, however, had several fee-paying estates to settle in the years 1939–41. These included an estate with a net value of $13,007.68,[96] and a number of estates which he wound up for the Canadian Pacific Railway. The latter was a paying customer, but the work was arduous. Most of the heirs were out of the country, and since the lands of the deceased had been bought and mortgaged from the Canadian Pacific Railway, the documentation was onerous, including copies of the original documents, quit-claim deeds, land evaluations, and judicial sales.[97] In the estate of Catherine Rees, however, the foreclosure resulted in a net deficit, and her Chicago husband was left a disgruntled man.[98]

Perhaps the most fascinating story of a lawyer and the personal affairs of his client concerns Goodall and Louise and Helen M. Brett, the widow and daughter-in-law of Lieutenant-Governor Dr Robert G. Brett, of Alberta, one of the founders of the province. The correspondence files between Goodall and the Bretts comprise one of the largest of the Cairns and Goodall collection. Both women had fascinating personalities and endeared themselves to their friend and legal counsel. Louise involved him in almost every aspect of her life from 1930, as did Helen after her mother-in-law's death in 1935. Thus, when Helen had a fire at her house in Banff, she explained in a letter of 29 April 1937 written from the Grand View Villa Hotel: 'I had a fire dream.' A long correspondence with insurance adjusters who would pay for damage to the house, but not for the furniture, followed. The fire also brought to life a controversy concerning the title of the Banff property, which was not registered with the federal parks, although the lease had been purchased in 1899. This was followed by a correspondence with the Department of the Interior over her wish to build a new bath house there (after the fire) at what was called the Upper Hot Springs. In a peevish mood, writing Goodall from the Queen Charlotte Hotel, she arranged the purchase of the Banff Hospital property, leaving her with $33,703.92 in her bank account at the Imperial Bank of Canada.[99] Louise would have been proud.

Louise Brett was always concerned about money, frequently making lists of her assets and complaining about the administration of the estate of her late husband, George Brett. She felt constantly that rents were being uncollected, properties left untended, and taxes overpaid. At times such as these she wrote Goodall in despair: 'Your poor client is a little sad today, and needs her Lawyer, don't worry, I am doubling up on my Promise to keep out of scrapes, but in reading between the lines in this letter, I see Future trouble for me.'[100] She then gave details on problems concerning land and leases, proposing work for Goodall and intercepting some of his earlier work herself. Whenever she thought of buying a property, she would summon her lawyer to search for title deeds in several towns at once, sending instructions as she changed her mind between them. On one occasion she accused him of being too slow. He responded: 'The real truth of the matter is not that I am too slow as you say but some of your family were too fast for me as I never heard of the ingenious idea of a sub-lease to avoid payment of rentals.'[101]

Louise often litigated her problems, and ran running battles with her lawyer over how the litigation would take place. For example, in suing Royal Trust over their administration of her deceased husband's estate in the Supreme Court of Alberta in 1930, she won an extra $2,000. Nonetheless, she had included items as trust expenses, such as personal bills from bakeries, milk-delivery companies, laundries, and meat markets, most of which ranged in cost from $2 to $15. It also appears from one of Goodall's letters that she excluded some of her properties from her affidavit of assets.[102]

In addition, Louise thought that she was quite capable of proffering legal advice herself. Often she wrote to Goodall, when vacationing with her sister in Pasadena, of the legal schemes and machinations she was hatching. For example, hearing of his pending court appearance in a suit on her behalf, she sends him this advice: 'Be careful of your language.'[103] And in between her professional advice to her lawyer, she writes on subjects ranging from her race horse to the 'Widow's Relief Act.'[104] Louise Brett was quintessentially a lady, and her quixotic personality followed her to the grave.

After Louise's death in March 1935 at the age of eighty-one, her will, the inventory of her goods and possessions, and her death certificate were questioned in court.[105] Letters were filed from the Provincial Mental Hospital, Ponoka, as well as from the Alberta Department of Health. In a final judgment, in *Brett* v. *Brett*, Appellate Division, Supreme Court of Alberta, Chief Justice Harvey upheld the generous bequests to her daughter-in-law by the court in May 1937, accepted the soundness of her mind, and passed over the property claimed by her husband's kin. In this final act of the Brett story, Goodall acted for mother and companion.[106] So he should have done: Helen gave him a one-half interest in Louise Hungerford Brett's estate.[107]

CONCLUSION

The work of the firm reveals several salient features of the socio-economic history of Calgary in the 1920s and 1930s. Both Goodall and Cairns had difficulty in acquiring clients in the 1920s as a result of the failure of the local economy to recover from the economic problems of the First World War era. The return of the soldiers, immigration, extreme climatic conditions, locust plagues, the mechanization of agriculture, and the absence of manufacturing led to a labour glut that was never resolved and to the advent of Social Credit. The population of Calgary increased from approximately 63,000 in 1920 to 84,000 in 1930, while unemployment remained around 11 per cent throughout the decade. In the meantime, registered businesses dropped from 230 to 161, the annual value of building permits from $20 million to $4.7 million, and annual stockyard sales from $20.9 million to $7 million. Meanwhile, annual clearing-house returns, which represent the total amount of commercial transactions, rose only from $438.1 million to $490 million.[108] The sole areas of growth in the economy were in oil and gas – owing to the exploration and development of the Turner Valley oil fields – and milling – owing to world shortages in grain production. Hence the move of Goodall into serving the men who became the new stars of the southern Alberta economy, and of Cairns into the growing chasm of debt collection, provided some opportunity of growth for both lawyers.[109]

The situation did not improve much in the 1930s. The population of the city grew from 84,000 to 89,000. Unemployment rose annually to the 25–30 per cent level. Building permits, stockyard sales, and clearing-house returns declined significantly. Drought and soil erosion contributed to an intense economic depression, which witnessed a price decline in grain exports from $1.24 to $0.64 a bushel. The price did not recover significantly until the Second World War. The financial burden was dramatic, as some 10 to 15 per cent of the city's population was on welfare.[110] Calgary, failing to recover from the Great Depression, became a city where business ventures were perilous, and commerce insecure.

The interwar years were not good ones for the practice of law on the prairies. Goodall and Cairns, however, managed to escape the worst ravages of the era. Unlike Emmett Hall of Saskatoon, they did not have to accept chickens for the payment of their fees.[111] They also fared better than Edmonton lawyer George Downes, whom Henry Klassen has studied in this volume, let alone Stuart Thom, of Regina, who left his practice altogether. They perhaps even did better than Raymond and Honsberger, of Ontario, whom John Honsberger has portrayed as working for peanuts. Nonetheless, they had neither the pedigree of a Lougheed, nor the business and political connections of a Bennett. Shunning the chauffeur-driven motor car, they had no dictation machines, no afternoon tea, and no autocracy.

Their practices, however, had some significant differences. Goodall's mixed menu of debt collection, estates, oil and gas, and securities in the late 1920s had given way to a major decline in the number of his clients by the late 1930s. Of his long-term clients, he had lost eight of the fourteen by his death. Perhaps they aged with him. Cairns, on the other hand, stuck to his knitting. His commercial and corporate clients were anchored by a few major tenants who ensured his success and brought him more as the years passed. By 1939 five of the firm's six largest clients belonged to Cairns. Losing only one major client in the late 1930s, he gained two others and took two of Goodall's (Irving and Premier) in the debt-collection area under his wing into the 1940s.

Their practices also represented, however, a relatively non-litigious

TABLE 9.3
Goodall and Cairns:
Reported Cases, 1920–1942

1920	*McLintock* v. *Lowes*, 15 ALR 229 (SCA App. Div.)	Goodall
	Halpin v. *Grant Smith & Co., and McDonnell Ltd.*,	
	15 ALR 537 (SCA App. Div.)	Goodall
1921	*In Re T., a Solicitor*, 16 ALR 449 (Ch. App. Div.)	Goodall
1922	*McCrindle* v. *London Scottish Canadian Investment*	
	Syndicate Ltd., 18 ALR 645 (SCA App. Div.)	Goodall
1928	*Reid-Welch Furniture Co.* v. *Macdonald*,	
	23 ALR 317 (SCA App. Div.)	Goodall
1929	*Greeman* v. *Minneapolis Threshing Machine Co. &*	
	Christiansen, 24 ALR 274 (SCA App. Div.)	Cairns
	Keay v. *Alberta Co-operative Wheat Producers Ltd.*	
	and Alberta Pool Elevators Ltd.,	
	24 ALR 344 (SCA App. Div.)	Cairns
1930	*Alberta Wheat Pool* v. *Nahajowicz*,	
	24 ALR 400 (SCA App. Div.)	Goodall
	Webster v. *Solloway Mills & Co.*,	
	24 ALR 632 (Ch. App. Div.)	Goodall
	Webster & Kirkness v. *Solloway Mills & Co.*,	
	25 ALR 8 (Ch. App. Div.)	Goodall
	Edmonds v. *Armstrong Funeral Home Ltd. et al.*,	
	25 ALR 173 (SCA App. Div.)	Goodall
1931	*Toronto General Trusts Corp. (Assignee in Bankruptcy*	
	of Gray and Farr Ltd.) v. *Carlisle*,	
	26 ALR 374 (SCA App. Div.)	Goodall
	Pacific Finance Co. Ltd. v. *Freeman Co.*,	
	25 ALR 395 (SCA App. Div.)	Cairns
	Royal Trust Co. v. *Spillers Canadian Milling Co.*,	
	25 ALR 542 (SCA App. Div.)	Cairns
1934	*In re Anderson Estate*, 1 WWR 430 (SCA App. Div.)	Goodall
1935	*In re Allen Estate*, 1 WWR 584 (SCA)	Goodall
1936	*Rex* v. *Constable*, 2 WWR 273 (SCA App. Div.)	Goodall & Cairns
1937	*Brett* v. *Brett*, 2 WWR 593 (SCA)	Goodall & Cairns
1938	*Brett* v. *Brett*, 2 WWR 368 (SCA App. Div.)	Cairns

age. Like most practitioners, seldom did they argue a case before a Supreme Court. Goodall and Cairns do not appear in any prominence in the published law reports of the interwar years. This is not because they were uninvolved in major causes. A search of their client files reveals that they were legal counsel in forty-two cases. A search of the published law reports, however, reveals that only nineteen of those cases were reported (see table 9.3). Nonetheless, an average of eighteen months for a reported case, or a year for one argued before a superior court, does not make them jurists. This is demonstrated by the fact that an examination of the reported cases in which they were involved does not turn up any significant precedents.

In conclusion, the significance of the Goodall and Cairns association lies, not in the law that was made, but in how that law was made, and how legal practice was conducted. Representing the small law firm that still exists in the prairies today, their practice reflected the tensions which were embodied in the law professions and in the lives of the businesses and the people turning the wheels of litigation in an age where the prairie West entered into the commercial and industrial framework of North America.

NOTES

I wish to thank Robert Omura for assisting me in searching the printed law reports for cases involving Goodall and Cairns, 1920–42; Janice Erion, Henry Klassen, Anthony Rasporich, Jonathan Swainger, and Carol Wilton for their comments and suggestions; and the archives and staff at the Glenbow-Alberta Institute, and Rick Klumpenhouwer and the staff at the Legal Archives Society of Alberta for their courteous assistance in my research endeavours there throughout the year.

1 It should be noted that the figures in table 9.1 reveal that Calgary had far more single-member firms than did Edmonton, and fewer two-member firms, while having 10 per cent more practising lawyers.

2 Law Society of Alberta, *Canada Law List, 1929–1938, Alberta*, for the years 1930 and 1935.

3 See the Goodall biographical file in the Glenbow-Alberta Institute Library (hereinafter GAI). Other information has been obtained from his correspondence in the company files. For his admission to the Law Society, see Legal Archives Society of Alberta (hereinafter LASA) fonds, Members Files, vol. 6, fol. 332.

4 See figure 9.1, where the pre-1928 cases are Goodall's; no case files are extant for the prewar years of 1911–13.

5 Thomas Thorner, 'A Study of Seduction: Macmillan vs Brownlee,' *Alberta Law Review* 20 (1981), 447–59. The statement of claim was put in November 1933, the trial began in June 1934, and the premier resigned in July. He lost, and appealed to the Judicial Committee of the Privy Council, where his petition was denied in 1940.

6 LASA, Calgary Bar Association Oral History Project, Accession 90-024, Maude Goodall on the tape of the 'McCaffery Tea' (1982)

7 He died at his home, 3003 Montcalm Crescent, on 15 June 1939, and was buried at Christ Church Cathedral on 17 June.

8 LASA, James Mackie, interviewed by Maude Goodall, 9 February 1991, on tape

9 LASA fonds 42, *passim*

10 Ibid.

11 File references have not been given here or below for lists of clients, and have been reserved for those files which have been noted in particular.

12 LASA fonds 42, box 13, file 109; box 14, file 127

13 Ibid., box 9, file 69, and box 13, file 228, 1932–33. His total fee was $55. The earl had died intestate, leaving his eldest son, aged eighteen.

14 Ibid., box 20, file 360, the Royal Trust Company, 1932

15 Others said that he had articled under McLaws.

16 In general, various newspaper clippings have been collected by the GAI in their Cairns biographical file, together with a short biographical sketch. Other biographical material has been drawn from correspondence in the Goodall–Cairns case files. For his admission to the Law Society, see LASA fonds, Members Files, vol. 36, fol. 536.

17 LASA fonds 42, box 12, file 102

18 The address was rooms 408–410, Lougheed building, Stephen Avenue.

19 'James Mitchell Cairns,' biographical sketch in Louis A. Knafla, ed., *History of the Judges of Alberta* (Calgary: Alberta Legal Archives Society 1996)

20 The files, comprising thirty-one boxes, were acquired by the GAI in 1981 from the Canadian Imperial Bank of Commerce, who had found them abandoned in the attic of the Hollinsworth Building. The GAI inventoried and microfilmed the records, which were then transferred to the LASA in 1991. According to the LASA fond description, most of the files 'were removed before their acquisition' by the GAI, the documents represent 'a very small proportion of the cases handled by the firm,' 'there are no case files corresponding to the letters "L" to "Z,"' and many of their reported cases 'have not survived' in manuscript (Goodall and Cairns fonds, 10). I have found each of these assessments to be only partially accurate, indicating, perhaps, a hasty evaluation of the collection. As a law-firm collection, it is one of the most complete that I have seen in Alberta. Since corporate files are open from fifty years from the

date of the last document, they are all open here, and there are no successor claims.

It should be noted that the collection has two different numbering systems: one for all the documents (which have been microfilmed), and one for those original documents which will be retained. All citations here are to the former reference numbers.

21 The figures on which table 9.1 is based reveal that the average length of time for a firm's partners to remain unchanged was just under five years.

22 LASA fonds 42, box 16, file 153

23 Ibid., letter of 10 April 1935

24 Ibid., box 8, file 57; and vol. 13, file 115

25 Ibid., box 1, file 11

26 Ibid., box 14, file 128

27 Ibid., box 11, file 90

28 The definition of a 'file' has been found to be precarious at best. For example, an individual file could consist of a single statement of claim, or several spread over a number of years. However, since it is not rewarding to attempt a division of each of the 483 files into possible single 'cases,' the firm's individual files have been regarded as independent entities.

29 Namely, the Edmonton Credit Company (10 files), British Dominion Oil and Development Corp. (12), National Fish Foods Ltd (13), William R. Kinsman (18), Irving's Garage Ltd (29), Canadian Credit Men's Trust Association (35), Industrial Acceptance Co. (80), and the Canadian Acceptance Corp. Ltd (97)

30 LASA fonds 42, box 6, file 69

31 Howard Palmer, with Tamara Palmer, *Alberta: A New History* (Edmonton: Hurtig 1990), 270–5

32 LASA fonds 42, box 3, file 33, and box 4, file 39, 1923–9

33 Ibid., vol. 5, file 50, 1921–32; and the letter from J. Kelso Hunter, Secretary of the Society, dated 19 March 1933

34 Peter M. Sibenik, 'The Doorkeepers: The Governance of Territorial and Alberta Lawyers, 1885–1928,' MA thesis, University of Calgary, 1984, 145–92

35 LASA fonds 42, box 14, file 249, 29 December 1928

36 Ibid., 3 December 1936. See also box 15, file 262, and box 16, file 279, 1934–9.

37 LASA fonds 42, box 29, file 529, and box 30, files 522–5 and 528–31, 1930–5

38 The Inter-Continental Land Company, which sold land to the Mennonites, also had its agreements in default: GAI, Canadian Pacific Railway colonization files.

39 LASA fonds 42, box 5, file 53. Cairns later litigated a file for the Industrial Acceptance Corporation against a Mennonite conscientious objector who could not make his car payments and fought its repossession: box 26, file 451, 1941.

40 LASA fonds 42, box 3, file 34, 6 June and 1 August 1929
41 Ibid., box 5, file 45, 1930–2
42 Ibid., box 17, files 298–305, 1930–1
43 Ibid., box 14, file 246, letter of W.J. Gillies, 23 November 1935. See also file 255, and box 15, files 256–7, 1924–36.
44 Ibid., box 14, file 247
45 Ibid., box 23, file 381, through box 26, file 423, *passim*, 1936–42
46 Ibid., box 23, file 386, box 24, files 389 and 397, 1930–9
47 Ibid., box 7, file 87, 1934–42. See also box 23, files 384–5, 1932–6.
48 Ibid., box 29, file 508, 1929–35
49 Ibid., from box 7, file 88, to box 12, file 214, and box 31, files 537–51, *passim*
50 Ibid., box 31, file 537, 1 August 1929
51 Ibid., box 31, file 538, 15 August 1930, and March 1931.
52 Ibid., box 8, file 89, to box 11, file 164, and box 12, file 213
53 Ibid., box 8, file 89, February 1939
54 Ibid., box 8, file 91, 6 September 1939
55 Ibid., box 16, files 269–84, 1936–42
56 Ibid., box 24, file 403 through box 28, file 499, *passim*
57 Ibid., box 1, file 2
58 Ibid., box 6, file 72
59 Ibid., box 13, file 216, 1930–6
60 Louis A. Knafla, 'Richard "Bonfire" Bennett: The Legal Practice of a Prairie Corporate Lawyer, 1898 to 1913,' in Carol Wilton, ed., *Essays in the History of Canadian Law*, vol. 4: *Beyond the Law: Lawyers and Business in Canada, 1830 to 1930* (Toronto: The Osgoode Society 1990), 320–76
61 See briefly, however, one of Goodall's files for Robert Hagerman concerning its financing of some energy properties: LASA fonds 42, box 22, file 379, 1929–30.
62 David Breen, ed., *William Stewart Herron: Father of the Petroleum Industry in Alberta* (Edmonton: Historical Society of Alberta 1984), Appendix 3: Petroleum Production, 1910–1940, 336. See also George de Mille, *Oil in Canada West: The Early Years* (Calgary: Northwest Printing 1969), and David A.A. Finch, 'Turner Valley Oilfield Development 1914–1945,' MA thesis, University of Calgary, 1985.
63 LASA fonds 42, box 13, file 215, A.M. Donaldson, 1929–33
64 Ibid., box 4, box 38, 1930–6
65 Ibid.
66 Ibid., box 2, file 26, letters of C. Barrington Brown, 7 and 12 September 1933
67 Ibid., box 1, file 8, and especially the letter to Premier Brownlee dated 23 January 1931

68 Ibid., box 5, file 58, for this and the quotations below. For the company's early history, see Douglas E. Cass, 'Investment in the Alberta Petroleum Industry, 1912–1930,' MA thesis, University of Calgary, 1985, 36.

69 LASA fonds 42, box 5, file 58. Goodall also worked on a similar problem with the province's Department of Lands and Mines over the calculation of mineral-lease rentals, credits against them for drilling costs, and assignments of the same, with Director of Lands D.H. Boles, October 1933 through February 1934: ibid., box 5, file 59. He also prepared a large dossier on mineral leases, sub-leases, royalty agreements, and indentures, for private investors who wished to participate in drilling projects: ibid., box 5, file 62.

70 Ibid., box 5, file 63

71 Ibid., box 1, file 24; see also the letter of Hagerman for the Laurel Oil & Refining Co., 19 January 1933.

72 Ibid., box 1, file 9

73 Ibid., box 5, file 65. For the company's early history, see de Mille, *Oil in Canada West*, chap. 5.

74 Ibid., box 5, file 64

75 Ibid., box 3, file 32

76 Ibid., box 14, box 248, 1927–37

77 Ibid., box 19, file 337–8, 1928–33

78 Ibid., box 14, files 250 and 252, and box 15, files 259 and 261, 1929–35

79 Ibid., box 17, file 292, and box 19, file 333

80 Ibid., box 4, file 43

81 Ibid., box 5, file 48

82 Ibid., box 17, file 288, George W. Griffith, 1930–5

83 Ibid., box 19, file 328, 1935–9

84 See ibid., box 20, file 352, H. Victor Heaver, 1930–6; and file 355, Sam Heap, 1930–1. These were clients of the stockbrokers Tull and Ardern.

85 Ibid., box 1, files 4 and 9

86 Ibid., box 1, file 15. For stock frauds in the period, see James H. Gray, *The Roar of the Twenties* (Toronto: Macmillan of Canada 1975), 293–309.

87 LASA fonds 42, box 1, file 15

88 Ibid.

89 Ibid., box 16, file 279, 1928–30. See also box 18, file 314, 1932–6.

90 Ibid., box 29, file 510, 1928–39

91 Ibid., box 5, file 49, 1932–6

92 Ibid., box 13, file 227, 1929–34

93 Ibid., box 1, file 14, and box 2, file 19

94 His fee was $5, and the file has no conclusion: ibid., box 13, file 220, 22 July 1932 to 28 June 1933.

95 Ibid., box 10, file 126, Font L. Allen, June–September 1939

96 Ibid., box 7, file 83, J.F. Belcher, 1937–9

97 Ibid., box 1, file 1, box 7, file 86, and box 12, files 189 and 193, 1939–41

98 Ibid., box 12, file 189, 1941

99 Ibid., box 3, file 35

100 Ibid., letter of 7 January 1932

101 Ibid., letter of 27 November 1931

102 Ibid., letter of 29 October 1930

103 Ibid., letter of 24 February 1936

104 Ibid., letter from Vancouver, 30 March 1935, and box 4, file 41

105 Her death certificate cites 'hypostatic pneumonia due to degenerative myocardial failure and arteriosclerosis – senility,' by Dr O.E. Kritzwiser, Banff: ibid., box 6, file 78, 21 October 1935.

106 Ibid., the judgment of 15 June 1938. Goodall's bill of costs was $3,686.75. When the appeal went forward in February 1938, and he wrote for money, Helen responded: 'What the dickens is the matter with you? Dont get the habit of only writing when you need money, like the kids, in school. Im not stingy, but would like a run for my money': ibid., box 6, file 78, 19 February 1938.

107 Ibid., box 5, file 78

108 The sources have been digested most fully by David Bright in 'Class Dismissed? A Social History of the Calgary Labour Movement, 1883–1929,' PhD dissertation, University of Calgary, 1995, Appendices I.3, VI.1, VI.2. See more generally Palmer and Palmer, *Alberta*, 207–9.

109 Palmer and Palmer, Alberta, 209

110 Ibid., 244–7; and more specifically, Peter M. Sibenik, 'Points of Departure: Urban Relief in Alberta, 1930–1937,' in Louis A. Knafla, ed., *Law & Justice in a New Land: Essays in Western Canadian Legal History* (Toronto: Carswell 1986), 313–32

111 Dennis Gruending, *Emmett Hall: Establishment Radical* (Toronto: Macmillan of Canada 1985), 22

10

A Family Firm in Transition: Osler, Hoskin & Harcourt in the 1950s and 1960s

CURTIS COLE

There are only a handful of large, old law firms in Canada. Most of them have offices in the upper reaches of the bank towers clustered around Bay and King streets in Toronto, or the equivalent financial districts of Montreal or Vancouver. They are very influential national institutions. Although few Canadians know much about them, many would recognize the names of these firms. One of the reasons for such recognition is that the firms' names are rooted in Canadian history; names like Blake, McCarthy, Tupper, and Osler were, in many cases, those of some of the great and powerful families of nineteenth-century Canada. However, with very few exceptions, the firms which have survived and grown to become national insitutions are no longer family firms. Somewhere along the way these family proprietorships were transformed into something much different.

Although this transition seems to have taken place in a number of the major firms, it is not the only model of law-firm change. In fact, as Ian C. Kyer and John D. Honsberger demonstrate in their essays in this volume, Canadian law firms have evolved in some very interesting ways at different times and with different results. As Kyer explains, the firm known recently as Fasken Campbell Godfrey underwent a transition in the early twentieth century from one type of family firm – with one set of clients – to an entirely different type of family firm – with an entirely different set of clients. By contrast, as Honsberger tells us, although Raymond & Honsberger began in the late nineteenth century as one of the larger

Toronto law firms, its evolution during the twentieth century has demonstrated that significant growth is not a prerequisite for success for the downtown firm.

One of the downtown Toronto firms which did grow to become a national institution is Osler, Hoskin & Harcourt. Oslers, as the firm is known, dates to 1862.[1] In that year, Britton Bath Osler, whose brothers included Sir Edmund Osler, the financier; Sir William Osler, the physician; and Justice Featherston Osler of the Ontario Court of Appeal, was called to the bar and began practice in Dundas, Ontario. B.B. Osler practised in Dundas, and later in Hamilton, with one or two partners, for some twenty years. During that time he developed a reputation as one of the top litigation counsel in the province.

In 1882 he moved his practice to Toronto and joined forces with one of the other best-known courtroom lawyers in country, D'Alton McCarthy. Together they built a firm, known as McCarthy, Osler, Hoskin & Creelman, into the second-largest in Canada.[2] Like the other major law firms of the day, McCarthy, Osler was a family firm. The heirs-apparent to the firm were the next generation of McCarthys and Oslers. D'Alton McCarthy's son Lally and his nephew Leighton McCarthy, along with B.B. Osler's nephews H.S. and Britton Osler, took over leadership of the firm following the deaths of the senior partners at the end of the century.[3]

In 1902 the firm name was changed to McCarthy, Osler, Hoskin & Harcourt, which remained in use until 1916. In that year, the McCarthys and the Oslers were unable to keep the alliance intact, and the firm split. The McCarthy brothers and cousin left to form the firm of McCarthy & McCarthy, and the Osler brothers remained as Osler, Hoskin & Harcourt. McCarthy & McCarthy grew to become one of the most important firms in the country; and, when it merged with the Montreal firm of Clarkson, Tétrault in 1990 to become McCarthy, Tétrault, it became the largest in Canada.

Osler, Hoskin & Harcourt was, along with the McCarthy and Blake firms, always one of the three or four largest in the country. Although its early years in the late nineteenth century saw the firm's strengths in both litigation and general solicitors' work, for over half a century following the split with the McCarthys, Osler, Hoskin & Harcourt was primarily a corporate firm. Its client base was very strong and included a number of very large mining and commercial/industrial companies, particularly multinationals which expanded into Canada during the interwar years.

During these years the leader of the firm was undoubtedly Britton Osler, who became the dominant partner following his older brother,

H.S. Osler's, semi-retirement in the early 1920s. It was his intention to pass the firm on to the next generation of Oslers, but he married rather late in life, and as a result his three sons would all be too young to be candidates to lead the firm when it came time for Britton Osler to consider retirement. He therefore consciously recruited a nephew to be groomed for this role.

Harold Charles Featherstone Mockridge, known as Hal to his friends, and 'The Prince' to some of the less reverent students, was twenty-two when he graduated from Princeton and accepted his uncle's offer to join Osler, Hoskin & Harcourt as an articling student in 1923.[4] Those who knew and worked with Hal Mockridge during his career with the firm, which spanned six decades, remember him as very business-like, even severe; he was not an easy person to get to know – particularly to students, some of whom found him intimidating – but on closer acquaintance he could be very warm and charming. His one distraction outside of his work was his cottage on Lake Rosseau in Muskoka. He was the son of Britton Osler's sister Beatrice and the Reverend John Mockridge, an Episcopalian minister.[5] During the 1930s Britton Osler increasingly relied on Mockridge to assist him in the legal work for many of the firm's most important clients. When Osler died in late 1943, Mockridge took over not only most of his uncle's files, but also undisputed leadership of the firm.

After the Second World War, although the surname of the firm's senior partner was not Osler, it was still an Osler family firm. However, Osler, Hoskin & Harcourt stood on the verge of a major transformation. With seventeen lawyers it was large by national standards; only two Canadian firms were larger.[6] But of the eleven men who were partners in 1954, five were either members of or directly related to the Osler family, and of the three men who joined the partnership on 31 December 1955, one was the son of a senior Osler partner, and another was the son of the senior Canadian executive of the firm's largest client.[7] Most important, the firm's management was almost exclusively in the hands of one man – a great-nephew of Britton Bath Osler. A generation later the firm had grown to well over fifty lawyers, and it was managed by a partly elected executive committee of the partners, none of whom was an Osler.

In the 1950s Toronto was still very much 'Toronto the Good.' It hadn't been that long since Sunday movies and sporting events were allowed. The mayor of Toronto was Allan Lamport; the premier of Ontario was Leslie Frost, a Conservative; and the prime minister of Canada was a Liberal and former Quebec City corporate lawyer, Louis St Laurent. Although the postwar wave of immigration was beginning to change radically the ethnic and demographic face of the city, it was still dominated by a small white, Anglo-Saxon, Protestant élite.

Osler, Hoskin & Harcourt, like the other large downtown Toronto law firms, was a part of that élite. Every one of the twenty-two lawyers in the firm in 1955 was white and male, and all but two were members of a mainstream Protestant church. Vince Reid, who had been called to the bar a year earlier, in 1954, was the only Roman Catholic in the firm, and Frank Mott-Trille, who was called to the English bar in 1953 and the Ontario bar in 1954, was a Jehovah's Witness.

Things were beginning to change, however; people in Toronto could now hear Elvis Presley and Little Richard on the radio, and, as of 1954, the city had its own subway and a metropolitan municipal government. In 1955 it elected its first Jewish mayor, Nathan Phillips. For the firm, things were also beginning to change, but the change would come slowly. The firm's office was located in the old Dominion Bank Building on the southwest corner of King and Yonge (the building was renamed the Toronto-Dominion Bank Building in 1955, when the Dominion Bank merged with the Bank of Toronto).[8]

The Dominion Bank Building was a brand-new, eleven-storey, state-of-the-art structure equipped with electric elevators manned by white-gloved attendants when McCarthy, Osler, Hoskin & Creelman moved there in 1914. The brochure put out by the bank's leasing agent in 1913 described it as 'the most complete bank and office building in Canada, and one that will not be excelled in America in points of arrangement and equipment.' By the late 1950s, however, it was beginning to show its age. The firm gained a little more space in the mid-1950s, when it moved from the seventh and eighth floors down to the fourth and fifth, but the wide, tiled hallways and dark mahogany trim were still prominent. The lawyers' offices were also dominated by heavy, dark furniture, and globe light fixtures hung from the high ceilings.[9]

If the atmosphere of the firm was old-fashioned, in many ways so was its leadership. In hindsight, of course, there are many good and bad things about being old-fashioned – and this holds true for people as well as furnishings. Although in many ways G.M. 'Mossey' Huycke was his co–senior partner, clearly, Osler, Hoskin & Harcourt's leader during the 1950s was Hal Mockridge.[10] Purdy Crawford, the lawyer who took over many of Mockridge's client responsibilities as the senior man began to move into retirement in the 1960s, remembered it thus: 'He would, in effect, defer to Mossey Huycke in many matters, although he could always call the shot if he wanted to.'[11]

The portrait which accompanies Mockridge's biography in the 1968 edition of *Who's Who in Canada* shows a rather stern and reserved man, but he also seems to have a bit of a twinkle in his eye. This is also how the people who were students and young lawyers at the time remember him. He was a demanding supervisor and meticulous practitioner, but he enjoyed sharing a few drinks with his partners when the work was finished. He was not a tall man, no more than five foot eight or nine, but most remember him as standing very erect and square-shouldered. He also smoked cigarettes; Mockridge's brand was Player's Navy Cut (Imperial Tobacco was an Oslers client).[12]

The most significant aspects of Hal Mockridge's personality involved his leadership and administrative style. Perhaps the most important decisions made in a law firm are those concerning the division of profits. If a firm is to survive, it is essential that the partners feel that the profits are divided fairly – or, perhaps more important, that the process is fair. There are numerous examples of law firms that have split up, but the most common reason seems to be the division of profits among the partners.

Certainly Britton Osler passed on some fundamental values about a partnership to Hal Mockridge. Under both Osler's and Mockridge's leadership, the firm consistently endeavoured to treat clients as the firm's rather than an individual lawyer's. Income distribution among the partners was, therefore, based on overall assessed value to the firm rather than on the amount of fees paid by specific clients. Moreover, the partnership splits were prospectively set; that is, the percentage of profits to be distributed to each partner was agreed upon prior to the start of each partnership term, not after its conclusion. The result was a substantial disincentive for individual partners to covet clients.

One of the practical results of having firm-wide clients was a central filing system. Individual lawyers would keep current files and some files relating to clients for whom they did continuing work in or near their offices, but all clients' files were generally available to all lawyers in the firm. No single partner maintained a proprietary right to a client's files, and therefore its fees.

The fact that the filing procedures in the firm were open does not mean, however, that the firm was run as a democracy; in fact, it was anything but. During the 1950s, Osler, Hoskin & Harcourt was still a dictatorship – a benevolent one – but a dictatorship none the less.

Mockridge's proprietorship of the firm was originally based on his ancestry – according to his widow he always said that 'Uncle Britt left him the firm' – but Britton Osler would not have entrusted him with it, nor would the clients have maintained confidence in him, if he was not obviously competent. Moreover, his partners, including his cousins, would not have bowed to his authority if they did not have confidence in his fairness.

The most tangible evidence of Mockridge's fairness was in the partnership splits which he drafted himself. Under the partnership agreement of 31 December 1955, the profits for the period from 1 January 1956 through 31 December 1958 were to be divided into 380 shares. Of these, Mockridge would receive 57, or 15 per cent. Although the overall profit figures for that time period are not available, this was clearly a great deal of money. Nevertheless it was not inordinate, given his contribution to the firm. In fact, when those who were younger members of the firm at the time look at the partnership splits, they invariably feel that Mockridge's share was substantially below what it would have been if an impartial observer had divided the profits.[13]

This undervaluing of his own contribution was not simply modesty or unselfishness on Mockridge's part. It is true that he was not an overly acquisitive person; unlike some of his contemporaries in corporate law, he did not capitalize on his insider position and play the stock market, but he purposely diminished his own share of the profits in order to maintain the perception of fairness within the firm. Moreover, according to many, he also purposely overvalued the contributions of the junior partners in order to establish their loyalty.

Mockridge was also insistent on a very high standard of ethics within the firm; the best example of this trait was his attitude towards a practice known as tax stripping. Under the Income Tax Act, corporate profits are essentially taxed twice; the corporation's income is taxed, and when the profits are distributed to the shareholders in the form of dividends, the dividends are taxed. During the postwar years it was fairly common practice among tax lawyers to devise schemes by which companies could set up complicated paper chains through which taxable corporate profits would enter one end, and non-taxable profits would end up in the hands of the shareholders at the other. Heward Stikeman, one of the best-known of the early tax specialists, once gave a lecture to the Tax Foundation on the procedure.

Hal Mockridge, although he personally felt that the double-tax provision of the Income Tax Act was an ill-advised policy, made it clear to his clients that he would simply not facilitate tax stripping. Even if the practice was not tax evasion, it was a shady form of tax avoidance, and it was certainly contrary to the intent of the law; if they wanted it done they would have to go to another law firm.[14] Interestingly, Mockridge was vindicated when the Supreme Court of Canada ruled that the practice was contrary to the statute in a case the Department of National Revenue took against Toronto Maple Leafs owner Conn Smythe and his son Stafford in 1969. In the report of the judgment, Heward Stikeman was identified as Conn Smythe's counsel on the case.[15]

All of this makes Hal Mockridge sound a bit like a saint – he was not. He was an excellent lawyer, and generally recognized as a leader of the corporate bar, but he was also a creature of his generation and his class. Among early- to mid-twentieth-century Protestant Canadians of means, genteel religious intolerance was the norm rather than the exception. Although there is no evidence to indicate that Hal Mockridge or any of his partners was a religious bigot, the fact is that there were no Roman Catholic lawyers at Osler, Hoskin & Harcourt until 1954, and the first Jewish lawyer did not join the firm until 1963.[16]

Oslers was not unique in its ethnic and religious homogeneity at the time. In fact virtually all of the élite Toronto law firms were made up of White, male Protestants. As the late Senator David Croll, a Jewish graduate of Osgoode Hall Law School in 1924, remembered it, the largely unspoken religious barrier existed until well after the Second World War. 'There were no Jewish lawyers in any of the large firms. They wouldn't let them in ... A Jewish lawyer couldn't get near a large firm; they didn't want any of us.'[17]

If any of the lawyers at the major Bay Street firms of the 1940s or early 1950s could be asked why this was the case, they would certainly deny that anything as ugly as anti-Semitism was the cause. They would explain that there were Jewish firms, and there were Gentile firms – much like there were Jewish golf courses and Gentile golf courses. In hindsight, we know that this separate-but-equal argument is just as bankrupt as the doctrine which came out of the U.S. Supreme Court's judgment in *Plessy* v. *Ferguson* in 1896, and the Jim Crow segregation laws which it upheld until *Brown* v. *Board of Education* in 1954. It was, however, a view which many people, perhaps most, in 1950s Toronto would have accepted. By the end of the decade, though, things were about to change.[18]

There were two people who were very much a part of the changes which took place at Osler, Hoskin & Harcourt beginning in the late 1950s – Purdy Crawford and Bertha Wilson. Coincidentally, both were graduates of Dalhousie Law School in Halifax, and both were called to the Nova Scotia bar just before moving to Toronto to join Oslers. Significantly, both were outsiders – in more than just a geographic sense.

Madam Justice Bertha Wilson, who many would argue did more than anyone else to breathe life into the Canadian Charter of Rights during her eight years on the Supreme Court of Canada, was born Bertha Wernham in the Scottish port town of Kirkcaldy, across the Firth of Forth from Edinburgh, on 18 September 1923. She graduated from the secondary school ninety miles up the North Sea coast, in Aberdeen, in 1941; in 1944, she received an MA in History and English from the University of Aberdeen, and, in 1945, a teaching parchment from the Aberdeen Training College for Teachers. In December of that year, she married John Wilson, a recently ordained Presbyterian minister who met and courted the young Miss Wernham while he was a theology student at Aberdeen.

Reverend Wilson was posted to Macduff, a rural village overlooking the Moray Firth in the north of Scotland, and at twenty-two, Mrs Wilson found herself the mistress of the parish manse. Whenever she is asked about that time in her life, Justice Wilson says that living and working with the poor people in that fishing village was 'the beginning of my education for living.'[19] As she said in a convocation address to the graduating class at Dalhousie Law School in Halifax in 1980 – after receiving the first of many honorary doctorates – 'It was there that I learned a great deal about people, being privileged to get to know intimately something of the drama of their daily lives and to develop an understanding of their springs of conduct.' In an interview for an article in *Saturday Night* magazine in 1985, she said: 'I became intimately involved with the drama of the daily lives of these people, their joys and their sorrows and, at sea, their terrible tragedies. I discovered how lonely proud people are, how dependent on the rest of us old people are. And how most of us are locked up tight inside ourselves, much of the time, pretending to be something we are not.'[20]

Justice Wilson is a religious person; her motivations in life are essentially moral. Even more important, she is guided by an enormous faith in the dignity of humankind, and in the same speech to the graduating class at Dalhousie she told them that 'God is far more interested in what you *do* when you are behind your desk than He is in what you *say* when you are on your knees.' In that sense, Wilson is a social activist, but she is not radical. Her concern for what is right – in the moral and social sense, as well as in the legal sense – comes through clearly in her judgments, but it is also always placed within the context of her respect for the law – for the rule of law and its institutions. This is not to say that she does not feel that legal institutions should be reformed; on the contrary, that is essential. In

Bertha Wilson (courtesy Osler, Hoskin & Harcourt; photograph by Cavouk)

her mind, Osler, Hoskin and Harcourt was one of those institutions, and in the long run she had a great deal to do with its reform.

The Wilsons stayed in Scotland for four years after their marriage, but in 1949 they emigrated to Canada, and Reverend Wilson became the United Church minister in the Ottawa Valley community of Renfrew, Ontario. When Canada entered the Korean War, however, John enlisted in the Canadian Navy as a seagoing padre. While he was away at sea, Mrs Wilson moved to Ottawa and took a job as a receptionist in a dental office. When John returned from the war in 1954, he stayed in the navy and was posted to Halifax.

When they arrived in Halifax, for the first time in her adult life Mrs Wilson was without a job. In the navy there was no parish for the minister's wife to tend to, and she was not interested in working in another dentist's office. After some thought she telephoned Dalhousie University and made an appointment to see the dean of law. As she put it, she really had no intention of practising law; she felt that law school was simply a way to return to the liberal education she had left off ten years before.

When Wilson explained her reasoning in applying to law school to Dean Horace Read, he responded: 'Madam, we have no room here for dilettantes. Why don't you just go home and take up crocheting?'[21] This was not the first – or last – time Wilson would encounter sexism in her career, but fortunately she did not give up. She convinced Read to give her a chance, and three years later she graduated with an LLB and a number of academic awards.

During her time at Dalhousie, Bertha Wilson fell in love with the law, with its intellectual intricacies and its relevance.[22] And at some point in her time there, she reversed her thinking about practising. When it came time to find an articling position, however, being a woman was once again an obstacle. She enlisted the help of the future Chief Justice of Nova Scotia Lorne Clarke, then a faculty member at Dalhousie, who was also active in Nova Scotia Conservative politics. On Wilson's behalf, Clarke went to see Fred Bissett, a prominent Halifax lawyer and former provincial Conservative party leader, to ask him to, as she put it, 'take this woman in so she can article.'[23]

Bissett's was a one-person practice, centred mostly in criminal law, and Wilson's months there were light-years away from the peaceful hours in the Dalhousie law library. As she described it: 'From the dizzying heights of academia, I was plunged into the stark reality of the police court, with its daily roster of drunks and prostitutes ... And when I became too insufferable in my new-found legal knowledge ..., Fred would say to me, innocent-like, "How would you like to work up a defence on this buggery charge?"'[24]

Although she finished her articles with Bissett and was called to the bar in late 1957, she never practised in Nova Scotia. During the winter of 1957–8, John decided to leave the navy and accept a job with the national office of the United Church of Canada in Toronto. Once again the Wilsons picked up stakes and moved.

Despite being a fully qualified Nova Scotia lawyer, if Wilson wanted to practise in Ontario, the rules of the Law Society of Upper Canada required her to article with an Ontario lawyer for another year in order to qualify for call to the bar of that province. Just as it had been when she finished law school, she knew that finding a firm willing to take in a woman student would be a problem. Fortunately, Fred Bissett had a good friend in Toronto, fellow Nova Scotian Arthur Pattillo, then a senior partner at Blake, Anglin, Osler & Cassels.

When she and her husband arrived in Toronto, Wilson telephoned Blakes and asked for Pattillo. She was told that he was unavailable and was put through to the managing partner. He told her that Pattillo was away from the firm, serving on a commission of inquiry in British Columbia, and would likely be gone for a year or more. She explained that she was a recently called Nova Scotia lawyer and was looking for an articling position to qualify for the Ontario bar. As she remembers it, although he did not sound too enthusiastic, he promised to discuss it with one or two of his partners and call her back.[25]

From the tone of her phone call, however, she didn't hold out too much hope about Blakes, so when she hadn't heard back in a few days she took out the Toronto telephone book and looked up lawyers in the yellow pages. She was particularly interested in the larger firms because, as she put it, 'in a small firm, they could always fob you off with excuses about not having a ladies' washroom.'[26] In truth she was also interested in a large firm because of the range of practice experience it would offer. As she glanced down the list of lawyers and firms in the yellow pages, her finger stopped at one – Osler, Hoskin & Harcourt. The name didn't mean a thing to her, but its list of lawyers was almost as long as Blakes'.

She picked up the phone and called; the receptionist put her through to Ed Huycke, Mossey Huycke's younger son, who was then responsible for students and junior lawyers. Huycke explained that, although the firm did not have a vacancy at the moment, he would arrange an interview for her. When she arrived at the Oslers office in the Dominion Bank Building and took the old elevator up the fifth floor, Ed Huycke spoke to her briefly in his office, and then took her down the hall to meet Gordon D. 'Swatty' Wotherspoon, another of the senior partners in the firm.[27] It was a very happy coincidence – for Wilson, but more significantly for the firm – that Wotherspoon happened to be in that day. Had Huycke taken her to see one of the other senior partners – particularly Hal Mockridge – the story might have been much different.

Wilson had her transcript from Dalhousie with her, and Wotherspoon was suitably impressed with her grades. 'You've done rather well at law school,' he mused.[28] Although she had not won the gold medal, she had finished very high in the class of fifty students and received a couple of the graduating prizes. He was much more impressed, however, with Wilson's military connection. Wotherspoon had been a brigadier-general in the Canadian army during the Second World War and had remained in the reserves after the war, and he was very interested in John Wilson's naval service during the Korean War.

There was more to it than that, however. Despite Wotherspoon's gruff, military manner, he was a very progressive thinker, in many ways in contrast to Hal Mockridge. Wotherspoon knew that the world was changing, and, more particularly, that legal practice was changing, becoming much more competitive. If Osler, Hoskin & Harcourt was to survive and prosper in the new world, it was going to have to be much more forward thinking in a number of ways. One of the most important was in its personnel development. It was going to have to look much more at how good a lawyer might be, rather than at who *his* father was. In addition, Bertha Wilson was – and is – a very charming person. A stranger meeting her for the first time cannot help but warm to her. Wotherspoon ended their chat with, 'Well, I think, my dear, that you deserve a chance; but I will have to speak of course to my colleagues.'[29]

A few days later, Wotherspoon called Wilson in again, this time to meet some of the other lawyers in the firm. At the end of this meeting, he told her that there was one senior partner, a man named Mockridge, who was not particularly enthusiastic about the idea of a woman at Osler, Hoskin & Harcourt. Mockridge was in New York at the time, and nothing further would happen until he returned. Wilson then told him that she had since then had a call from Blakes inviting her to an interview. Wotherspoon asked that she not go for an interview until after he had a chance to change Mockridge's mind, and she agreed.

Mockridge was anything but a reformer. As one of his long-time partners remembered it, 'Certainly Mockridge [and most lawyers of his generation] weren't ground-breakers of that sociological type. To them law was a downtown business for the man, and the lawyer they hired had certain qualities and connections and patterns of behaviour. Women just didn't fit.'[30] When Mockridge returned from New York, however, Wotherspoon was apparently able to convince him that Wilson deserved a chance; they called her in for yet another interview. She had a brief meeting with Mockridge, and then was 'marched down the hall to Mr G.M. Huycke.'[31]

Huycke explained that the firm would offer her a position, and as the future Supreme Court Justice recalls,

but only on the basis that they thought that I deserved a chance to become qualified; they were quite prepared to have me in to article, but as soon as I had completed my articles and got my call to the bar I would be on my own. Their commitment to me was simply that I deserved the opportunity to get qualified. So I said that was fine; I was a little bit irked at that, so I said, 'Well, I think that would be a mutually acceptable arrangement. I might not like it here either.'[32]

Huycke apparently liked her answer and asked her if she could start the following morning.

When she arrived for work the next day, she found her office, a tiny, windowless, converted supply cupboard, and settled in to work. Her first assignment came in a phone call from Swatty Wotherspoon, who opened the conversation with the question 'What is a bond?' Wilson knew perfectly well what a bond was, but was a bit flustered by Wotherspoon's bluntness. She mumbled a little, and he finally said, 'Well, why don't you do a memorandum: "What is a bond?"' She had no idea of the context of the question, if this was related to a client, or why Wotherspoon wanted her to do it, but she went to the firm's library and wrote a detailed memo answering the question.[33]

She remembers getting a number of research assignments like that during the first months at the firm, and slowly realizing that she could learn the context of the research by going to the filing department and pulling the file herself. This was, of course, one of the advantages of working at Oslers, but she was expected to figure it out for herself. In fact, she had almost no face-to-face contact with her superiors at first. She would receive a brief research question and would prepare and send a memorandum back, and that would be the last she heard about it.

On one occasion, however, she got a response from Hal Mockridge, who actually called her down to his office to thank her and discuss a memo she had prepared. She obviously impressed him, because he began to send quite a bit of important corporate work her way. She was originally interested in practising in trust law, a field which she particularly enjoyed at law school, but as Mockridge and Wotherspoon began giving her corporate assignments, there was little time for anything else.[34]

One day the following year, when Wilson had almost completed her articling period, Swatty Wotherspoon came into her office with a research assignment. She recalled the incident with some humour; apparently Wotherspoon began by saying,

'Oh, I've got a really interesting project for you. You're going to enjoy this one.' They all knew, of course, that I loved the law and there was nothing I liked better than to sit down and struggle with some of these problems. So he told me about the project and I said that this is an ongoing problem, this is going to go on for months. He said, 'Oh yes'; and I said, 'I think you'd better get somebody else – you do know that tomorrow is my last day.' He said, 'What do you mean that tomorrow is your last day?' I said, 'I get my call to the bar tomorrow and that's when I leave.' He was just appalled, and he said, 'You mean that no one has spoken to you?' and I said, 'No, no one has,' and he said, 'Don't go anywhere, stay there' and off he went and came back and said, 'We're just all taking it for granted that you're continuing on.' Nobody had ever said anything to me, so of course I did stay on; I stayed on for seventeen years.[35]

Bertha Wilson's tenure with Osler, Hoskin & Harcourt was significant to the history of the firm for many reasons. Obviously the firm was very proud to have one of its alumna serve on the Supreme Court of Canada. But she had an important impact on the firm in many other ways. In part because she was a woman, but also because she loved and was exceptionally good at it, she ended up doing, almost exclusively, research work for the firm. Having her act as a 'super student' doing research kept her from having direct contact with traditional male clients who might not have complete confidence in a woman lawyer.

In the process, however, Wilson became what is now referred to as 'a lawyer's lawyer.' That is, she acted as the adviser to the solicitor on a file. She did not simply research the law; she counselled the lawyer on the advice he should give to the client. In fact, as the firm and its practice continued to grow at a rapid pace, this research function became indispensable to the firm, and Wilson began to attract bright young lawyers from places like the Law Reform Commission to work in her new Research Department. It may have begun as a function of chauvinism, which the firm should not be particularly proud of, but the result was an innovation in which it justifiably takes pride.

The other very significant outsider to join the firm in the late 1950s was a young Nova Scotian named Harold Purdy Crawford. Purdy, as he was known, did not fit the mould of the traditional Oslers lawyer. He had no familial relationship to a senior partner or client; he had not grown up in Rosedale and graduated from a private school; rather, he was the son of a coal miner and had grown up in tiny Five Islands, Nova Scotia. He had attended a two-room rural school up to grade ten, and then travelled fifteen miles up the road and lived in a boarding-house to finish high school in a four-room school.[36]

When he graduated from high school, Crawford made an unusual decision for those from his community and went west to Sackville, New Brunswick, to attend Mount Allison University, which was then, and remains, a very small university with an excellent liberal-arts reputation. When Crawford graduated from Mount Allison with a Bachelor of Arts degree in 1952, he went back to Nova Scotia and enrolled in Dalhousie Law School.[37]

At Dalhousie, Crawford really came into his own. Bertha Wilson, who was two years behind him at Dalhousie, remembers Crawford as being a real leader among the students: 'He was a very giving type of person and very popular.' He would often 'hold court' at the top of the library steps and explain a lecture to a group of students who had not understood it.[38] Towards the end of his final year in law school, Crawford, like many other top Dalhousie students, was urged to go on to Harvard to do a graduate degree. As he remembers it: 'At the time when I decided to apply, I probably was ambivalent in my own mind as to whether my future was in teaching or practice, [but] I very deliberately took courses at Harvard that related to what I would want to do if I was going to practise.'[39]

At Harvard he took courses with, among other professors, Archibald Cox, the long-time faculty member who became famous outside of legal circles as the Watergate Special Prosecutor in 1973; Albert Baker, a utilities-law specialist; and Louis Loss, the securities-law authority.[40]

Although Crawford eventually became a noted securities specialist in his own practice, it was Cox who had the greatest influence on him at Harvard. In fact, when Crawford came back to Canada, his initial intention was to become a labour lawyer. During his first few years at Osler, Hoskin & Harcourt he did quite a bit of labour work.[41]

During his year at Harvard, Crawford made the decision that he would go into practice. He had some offers to go into teaching law, but turned them down. He was interested in law in the fast lane, in the exciting world of corporate law. For most of his classmates at Harvard, this meant Wall Street, but at that time, if he had wanted to practise law in the United States, he would have had to take out U.S. citizenship. Crawford couldn't live with the idea of giving up his Canadian citizenship; if New York was out, it had to be Toronto.

Before going up to Toronto, however, he decided to return to Halifax to complete the short articling period required for a call to the Nova Scotia bar. Unlike Bertha Wilson, Crawford had little difficulty in finding an articling position. As a top Dalhousie student who was also male, he had many more options, and he ended up with Roland Ritchie, who later served on the Supreme Court of Canada. Ritchie, in fact, wrote the majority judgment in the famous 1969 Supreme Court case of *The Queen* v. *Drybones*, the only case to use the 1960 Diefenbaker Bill of Rights to disallow a piece of federal legislation.[42]

Ritchie's practice was a general and wide-ranging one, and a normal docket might include everything from a real estate deal to a manslaughter case, to an admiralty problem. This was the advantage of practising in Halifax; but Ritchie also had the traditional Nova Scotian's distrust of what Maritimers pejoratively call 'Upper Canada.' Ritchie and others in Halifax told Crawford that he should think very carefully before deciding to go up to Toronto to practise. As he remembered it, Ritchie said that Toronto was 'establishment country ... those big law firms will let you work for them, but you'll never break through.'[43]

To some extent Ritchie was right; Toronto was establishment country, but it was about to change. Crawford was certainly not a member of the establishment, but his record at both Dalhousie and Harvard was very impressive, and when he got to Toronto in August 1956, he had interviews with many of the old-line firms. In addition to Oslers, he interviewed at Blakes; Borden & Elliot; Fraser & Beatty; and Wright & McTaggert. He ultimately chose Osler, Hoskin & Harcourt because it had a particularly impressive list of blue-chip clients such as International Nickel, Procter & Gamble, Coca-Cola, General Motors, and Kodak. More important, in looking over the law-list entry for the firm, which indicated the dates of call of the lawyers, he felt – in the brash confidence of youth – that it offered him the best opportunity to advance.[44]

Crawford joined the firm as an articling student in September 1956 and stayed as an associate lawyer after his call to the bar in early 1958. During his time as a student and the first couple of years after his call to the bar, he did primarily labour work, with Tom Delamere, who was Hal Mock-ridge's brother-in-law, and with Britton Osler's oldest son, Brick.[45] Since Delamere joined the firm during the Second World War, Oslers had built up a sizeable practice in labour law. There were three reasons for this: The first was that the demand for legal advice in labour relations was increasing as the scope of federal and provincial industrial-relations regu-lation grew; the second was that the firm had a large group of established corporate employer clients whose workforces were becoming increas-ingly unionized; and the third was that the Osler lawyers, particularly Delamere, Brick Osler, and his brother Campbell, were developing a very good reputation in the field.

While working with Delamere and Brick Osler, doing labour work, however, Purdy Crawford learned a very valuable lesson. Both of these men were lone-wolf practitioners. They were excellent lawyers, but they were not very good at delegating work. Allan Beattie, who joined the firm as an articling student in 1948 and was later a senior partner with Craw-ford, remembers this about Delamere in particular with a story from the early 1950s:

Mr. Delamere as a practitioner ... tended I think to do a lot himself. He was not what I would call a good delegator, so he didn't particularly use the young law-yers a great deal. If he did use a young lawyer, it was usually to do something very specific but you didn't get to work hand in glove with him very often. I can recall an instance of this. We were working on a transaction that involved Ameri-can Standard which was one of Mr. Delamere's principal clients, both labour and outside labour, and this was a corporate transaction of some kind. I was asked to help him do this corporate work. We stayed down one evening to work on this and during the evening I recall there was a particular little agreement that had to be done. So he said to me: 'You do that and we'll discuss it tomorrow sometime.' I went off and I worked away at this and I got a draft of this done. Later the next day we got together and one of the items that we were to talk about was this agreement. So I said: 'Well, I've produced something of a draft.' 'Oh,' he said, 'I've already drafted that!' That's an example of how delegation wasn't one of his great strengths.[46]

The result for Crawford was not a very good learning experience. As he put it: 'Quite frankly ... I could have trained forever and would still only be good enough to go up to Sudbury and sit with them while they argued labour arbitrations [for International Nickel].'[47] The lesson that he learned was that, in order to bring junior lawyers along – and ensure that there is someone within the firm qualified to keep up service to existing clients after you are gone – you have to give them responsibility.

In any event, Crawford found that 'the first couple of years I spent half my time with labour law and the rest of my time wasn't very busy,' so he sought out other work from different senior partners. He began by assisting Stuart Thom, then the firm's senior tax-law specialist, on a number of tax matters, and found that he quite enjoyed it. He also found himself doing quite a bit of securities and other corporate work with Hal Mockridge, and trusts and estates with Mossey Huycke. Before long, Crawford was recognized as a rising star in a number of areas of corporate law – both within the firm and outside of it.

Some observers would describe Crawford as primarily a securities specialist, but during the early years of his practice he was equally involved in tax law. During the 1960s he served on the Ontario Attorney General's Committee on Securities Legislation, and both the Ontario and national taxation sections of the Canadian Bar Association. From 1970 to 1972, he was a member of the board of governors of the Canadian Tax Foundation. He also taught courses on a part-time basis in income tax and securities at Osgoode Hall Law School from 1964 to 1968, the University of Toronto Law School from 1969 to 1971, and the Law Society's bar-admission course from 1969 to 1972.[48]

Crawford apparently had the ability, at a time when the law was becoming more and more complex, to be a multifield specialist and a generalist at the same time. He was able to master the intricacies of a number of areas and still see the big picture.[49] This was particularly important as the trend of the 1960s was towards the large, complex transaction requiring legal advice across a range of specialties; this meant that larger numbers of lawyers would be involved on a single file. To use an analogy common on Bay Street, he was a good quarterback on a deal.

There were obviously a number of aspects to Purdy Crawford's practice and personality which had a very significant impact on the development of Osler, Hoskin & Harcourt. Perhaps the most important of these – and the one which most clearly sets him apart from the previous generation – was his skill as what lawyers call 'a rainmaker'.

Lawyers in Ontario have only recently been allowed to advertise, and the Law Society's rules governing professional advertising are very restrictive compared with those governing other service industries. The rule, which until recently was a complete prohibition on the marketing of legal services through advertising, is rooted in the pre–twentieth-century professionalization of lawyers. One of the things which lawyers, like other professionals, used to distinguish themselves from the non-professional trades was the fact that clients sought them out because they were known to provide skilled service. They did not 'tout their wares.'[50]

Of course, as a number of authors have pointed out, this rule did not hurt élite lawyers and firms as much as those at the lower end of the professional ladder.[51] Firms such as Oslers, who by mid-century had a strong stable of corporate clients and whose lawyers were largely members of the social establishment, had little difficulty in making contact with prospective clients. In addition, the firm's reputation for competent and creative corporate legal advice, particularly in the international business community, meant that client development did not have to be a priority. Men of Hal Mockridge's generation could mildly disapprove of what would later be considered professional entrepreneurship in men like Beverley Matthews at McCarthys and Pete Elliot at Borden & Elliot.

By the beginning of the 1960s, however, the business environment was beginning to change. As the Canadian economy grew and became much more competitive, the old sense of loyalty to a particular law firm began to wane. The result was that the clients were increasingly likely to shop their legal business around, and lawyers had to become much more aggressive marketers. Purdy Crawford saw this and acted on it. During those years the Oslers stable of blue-chip corporate clients grew substantially, and, according to most, Crawford had a lot to do with it.

One of the more significant additions to the Osler client list during the 1960s was Molson, the brewing giant. Molson Breweries maintained its corporate headquarters in Montreal, where the company was founded in 1787, until it moved to Toronto in 1968. Its primary corporate counsel up to that point was the Montreal firm of Chisholm, Smith.[52] Prior to 1953, Molson did not brew beer in Ontario; it had a warehousing and distribution operation in Toronto, and retained Toronto counsel for whatever legal consultation this required.

When Molson began construction of a brewery on Fleet Street in Toronto, it kept the same arrangement, but in the late 1960s the company began a campaign of substantial growth and diversification. It acquired control of a number of companies, most of which were not involved in the brewing industry, and moved the head office of the company to Toronto. On each of these steps, Purdy Crawford acted as legal adviser to the company.

The Osler, Hoskin & Harcourt relationship with Molson actually dated to the early 1960s, when Hal Mockridge went on the board. Unlike some other corporate directorships for lawyers, Mockridge's appointment to the Molson board did not mean that his firm could expect to get legal work from the company. It was not uncommon for a lawyer sitting on the board of a major corporation to serve also as legal counsel to the company, but in this case Hartland Molson made it clear that he was not inviting Mockridge to serve on the board in return for a retainer. In fact, Mockridge would consider it unprofessional to ask that such an understanding be put in place.[53]

Nevertheless, when the company began its diversification program in the late 1960s, it was Purdy Crawford to whom they looked for advice. Crawford – and therefore Osler, Hoskin & Harcourt – became Molson's primary corporate counsel and looked after a number of important transactions for the company in the years which followed.

Oslers' acquisition of Molson Breweries as a client may have represented something of a transition from the old style to the new. Hal Mockridge sat on the company's board of directors, but he did not solicit its legal work.[54] Although Mockridge's directorship probably did not hurt, Purdy Crawford – by making his own name and that of his firm well known – attracted the account. Law-firm client development tends not to involve traditional forms of advertising; although during the 1980s many firms began to retain professional marketing advice, and Oslers even hired a client-development specialist to act as the firm's director of marketing, their methods of making prospective clients aware of their services and expertise are rather more subtle.[55]

In the early days of this trend, Crawford saw the benefits of exposure in venues like part-time law-school lecturing and bar-association activities. As Crawford put it: 'You have to get out from under the bush and make [your firm] known a bit ... That's why I thought it was important to have many people in the firm teaching in law schools, bar courses, going to law schools to talk to students, lecturing, involved in seminars, in programs involving the business community. The more tentacles you can get out there the better.'[56]

Mockridge had some difficulty with this concept. He generally thought of rainmaking as a little unprofessional, and perhaps beneath what he – or his uncle – might have defined as an Oslers' standard. On the other hand, he was very much aware of the changing climate of corporate practice, and he had great confidence in Crawford.

Not surprisingly, Crawford also had great confidence in himself and, more important, in his partners and the other lawyers in the firm. Also, he was able to convey that confidence to clients. This was essential if he was to be able to delegate this new-found client legal work to the rest of the firm. The ability to delegate is an essential prerequisite to rainmaking; if you do not pass work on to others within the firm, you can only take in as much new work as you can do.

A good example of the new clients which Crawford attracted to the firm was OMERS, the retirement fund for Ontario municipal employees. One of Crawford's students at Osgoode Hall Law School in the mid-1960s was very much involved when OMERS was founded some years later, and she sought him out specifically because of their contact at the law school.[57]

The OMERS account represented one type of marketing benefit of Crawford's law teaching, but another, perhaps equally important benefit was marketing the firm to potential lawyers. Just as the client market was becoming much more flexible and less tradition-driven, so too was the market for incoming lawyers – and the law schools were the places to start the recruitment process. Until the arrival of people like Bertha Wilson and Purdy Crawford in the late 1950s, Oslers was a family firm. From that point forward, it was moving towards becoming a meritocracy. The process of change was, however, a slow and, at times, difficult one.

During the 1950s, Crawford and Wilson were the exceptions to the rule. Although the firm recruited some excellent lawyers during the decade, most of them seem to have had some form of familial or other relation to the firm. Fred and Ed Huycke, who joined the firm in 1951 and 1953, respectively, were Mossey Huycke's sons; Allan Beattie was the son of Leslie Beattie, who was the head of Canadian operations for International Nickel, the firm's largest client. The senior Beattie also sat on the Inco board of directors with his close friend Hal Mockridge. And there were others with similar, if not as direct, connections. Jack Ground, who joined the firm as a student in 1957 shortly after his graduation from the University of Toronto Law School, was a fraternity brother of Ed Huycke's.[58]

As Ground, who was a partner in the firm until his appointment to the Ontario Court of Justice in 1992, described the firm in the late 1950s: 'The place was just at the end of the era of being a gentlemen's club. It was very much, I would say, an old Toronto establishment firm and 90 per cent of the people in the firm had gone to one of the Little Big Four schools and it was ... very old Toronto.'[59] The Little Big Four were the most prestigious of the Ontario private boys' high schools: Upper Canada College, Trinity College School, St Andrews, and Ridley College.[60]

Oslers was not unusual in this regard; most law students found articling positions in firms or with lawyers they were related to or knew in some way. Harry Boylan, for instance, who joined the firm as a young lawyer in 1956, articled with the Toronto firm of Armstrong, Young and Burrows because his father-in-law knew Vernon Armstrong.[61]

Family connections were obviously an advantage to some, but those who had them often had a difficult decision to make. Ed Huycke, for instance, thought hard about whether it would be a good idea to join the firm after his call to the bar in 1953. He wondered whether it would be wise to try to practise in his father's shadow, or if he should accept the offer he had from a small firm in Barrie, Ontario.[62] His fears, in fact, were not without foundation; Bertha Wilson remembers Mossey being rather hard on young Ed, probably because they were both in the estates field.[63] Huycke was quick to point out, however, that there were distinct personal benefits as well: 'I am very glad that I made the decision that I did because I think the most rewarding ten or twelve years of my life were my first ... years of practice when I was able to practise with my father. It was a tremendous learning experience because he was an outstanding lawyer; but it was also a very rewarding experience between father and son.'[64]

Ed Huycke obviously credits a good experience with his father with his early training in practice, but there were other advantages to the continuing family nature of the firm. Even as it began to change, the firm was still a close-knit group. Until they moved to the Prudential Building in 1962, most of the younger people ate lunch together almost every day at the same table in Child's Restaurant on King Street, next to the Dominion Bank Building.[65] Many of the lawyers also took part in a series of friendly but very spirited hockey games between teams organized from the two floors of the Dominion Bank Building.[66]

Events like the hockey games showed that, even as the firm was growing, it was maintaining the closeness which sprang from its family roots. And, like an old-style family, the firm was still ruled by a paterfamilias – in this case Hal Mockridge. In this area, however, things were about to change.

The beginning of the changes in the firm's management structure appeared in the 31 December 1958 partnership agreement. That agreement, signed by sixteen partners – including Ed Huycke and Ed Saunders, who were signing for the first time – provided for the appointment of five 'Executive Partners.'[67] The five, who were, not surprisingly, the top five in terms of percentage earnings with the firm, were Hal Mockridge, Mossey Huycke, Swatty Wotherspoon, Tom Delamere, and B.M. Osler.[68]

Although it was not until some years later that this group became officially named the Executive Committee, it was described as such almost from the start. Under the terms of the agreement, the partnership as a whole formally delegated a number of specific management and administrative duties to the Executive Partners. Significantly, the members of this committee were not elected; in theory they were appointed by the partnership as a whole, but in fact they appointed themselves. They were the leaders of the firm, and the more junior partners had neither the inclination nor any reason to challenge their leadership – at least not yet.

In fact, it was still Hal Mockridge and Mossey Huycke who were making most of the important decisions. As Stuart Thom remembers it:

Actually, although I was on the Executive Committee, the Executive Committee during the time I was on it was Mockridge in collaboration with Huycke ... in that order. Not that they were competitors or there was any strain between them, but Mockridge was the senior man and he did what he did or didn't do ... pretty well on his own. People came or dropped out because they displeased him as much as anything, although I don't doubt that ... he acted fairly ... in deciding whether they should come in or not. I can think of a couple of people who left the firm because Mockridge didn't like them and turned out quite well elsewhere. He had certain definite antipathies which were a little hard to discern, to sort of understand, but people would strike him the wrong way and that was the end of that person. It was his show, very much.'[69]

Over the course of the next few years, things began to change, albeit slowly. The Executive Partners held regular meetings, roughly once a month, to deal with matters such as lawyers' charging rates, new personnel, and firm procedures. It is obvious from the minutes of these meetings that the committee was trying to respond to the increasing complexity of practice in the 1960s. An interesting example was the system they established to deal with new legislation.

Complaints from lawyers about the volume of law they keep up to date on are not new. The Canadian law journals would often print letters from lawyers bemoaning the increasing weight of law reports and statute volumes in the late nineteenth century. But, by the mid-twentieth century, they really did have something to complain about. The 1937 *Revised Statutes of Ontario*, a comprehensive set of provincial legislation then in force, totalled four relatively thin volumes. The next edition, published in 1950, was five volumes. The 1960 edition was also five volumes, but each was larger, and the 1970 edition was seven volumes.[70] And the intervening annual volumes of new legislation grew larger every year.

In an effort to divide the workload of keeping up with new legislation in a systematic way, and to make sure that the firm as a whole received the full benefit of each of its member's expertise, in May 1962 the Executive Committee approved a procedure whereby new bills introduced in a provincial legislature or at Ottawa would be distributed to a specific lawyer or lawyers based on the subject-matter of the bill. That person would then prepare a memorandum to the rest of the firm summarizing and commenting on the content of the bill.

The partnership agreement, which was renewed every three years, made no changes to the powers of the Executive Partners in either its 1965 or 1968 versions.[71] During those years, however, Hal Mockridge was slowly relinquishing his decision-making authority to the other members of the committee. The minutes of the committee's meetings during those years show an increasing number of subcommittees and greater bureaucracy in the management process. Until Allan Beattie became the chairman in January 1972, however, Mockridge continued to make the most important decisions.[72]

Mockridge, for instance, still apparently decided on what each partner's share of the firm's profits would be. He would inform the other partners and ask for their opinions, but the final decision was clearly his.[73] The process that he used was to draw up a draft of what he thought would be a fair division and then take it to the next senior partner – during the late 1960s, this would be Mossey Huycke – to ask what he thought. He would then work his way down the letterhead (or, more likely, the existing share-division list) through Delamere, B.M. Osler, etc. In later years, Allan Beattie followed the same procedure, but, as he pointed out, when he did it he was actively trying to build consensus.[74] When Mockridge did it, no consensus-building was necessary; his decision was simply accepted.[75]

One of the most important decisions the firm made during Mockridge's term as chairman of the Executive Committee was to leave the old Toronto-Dominion Bank Building and move across King Street, to the new Prudential Building. At some point during the late 1950s, the partners held a special meeting of the firm in the fifth-floor boardroom in the Toronto-Dominion Bank Building.[76] It was this meeting that began a series of events which necessitated a move to much larger premises.

Hal Mockridge had just made a very important decision, and he wanted to discuss the implications of his decision with his partners. Mockridge had recently been asked to serve on the board of directors of Massey–Ferguson Limited, the giant farm-implements manufacturer, recently taken over by E.P. Taylor's Argus Corporation. It would, naturally, be a personal plum for Mockridge to serve on another prestigious corporate board, but, more important for the firm, and in contrast to the understanding when Mockridge went on the Molson board, the offer also implied that Osler, Hoskin & Harcourt would get a significant portion of Massey's legal work.

As he explained at the meeting, however, Mockridge had reluctantly decided to decline the offer. The firm simply did not have the manpower to serve the client adequately. They had some of the best corporate lawyers in the country; they just did not have enough of them to take on another huge client. But nevertheless he went on to ask the meeting, 'What should we do about this?'[77]

As they began to discuss the question, it became clear that their options were either to keep the firm small, and continue as it had for some years, or make a conscious effort to expand. The latter option had many negative connotations. There was great danger in becoming a 'law factory', the term some critics were using to describe New York firms numbering more than fifty lawyers, of losing the sense of professional intimacy, which was one of the firm's strengths. A small partnership based on trust, and even affection, was something radically different from a large organization with complex rules and bureaucracy. And as they had learned from the W.B. Reid débâcle of only a few years earlier, that it was very important to *know* who your partners were.[78]

Growth would mean a substantial lifestyle change for most of them, but, as Mockridge put it, the status quo was not really an option. If they tried to stay the same size and turn down work because they didn't have the manpower, they would inevitably shrink. The message to clients – potential and existing – would simply be: 'We can't do the work.' Swatty Wotherspoon, in particular, argued that the firm should accept any and all work, and expand whenever necessary to meet the need. In Wotherspoon's view there certainly were dangers which would have to be dealt with, but the alternative was not an option.[79] This was a critical conclusion for the firm. It meant that they would go forward and remain one of the largest firms in Canada. Other firms made the opposite decision during those years, and their fate was what Mockridge and Wotherspoon predicted.

An eventual result of this decision was the firm's move from the old Toronto-Dominion Bank Building across the street to the brand new Prudential Building at the northwest corner of King and Yonge streets. Mockridge and the other Executive Partners began seriously to discuss the possibility of a move in 1960. Space had been a problem in the Toronto-Dominion Bank Building for a number of years; after the 1960 calls to the bar, there were twenty-nine lawyers in the firm, and well in excess of that number in support staff, and the bank building simply had no more room for expansion. The old building was also beginning to show its age, especially in comparison with some of the new buildings in the city. The lack of modern amenities such as air-conditioning – and, most important, sufficient room for expansion of the firm – meant it was time to look elsewhere.

After a survey of available space, the firm decided on the new building owned by the Prudential Insurance Company of America. At twenty storeys, it was one of the tallest of a new wave of buildings in the city, and the firm signed a lease on 1 November 1961 for all of the seventeenth floor and part of the sixteenth.[80]

Swatty Wotherspoon chaired the Accommodations Committee of partners responsible for determining the leasehold improvements the firm would arrange for in its new premises. C.R. Osler, who served on the committee, remembers Wotherspoon asking him to fly down to New York for a tour of Cravath, Swaine & Moore's new offices there. Wotherspoon had done a fair amount of referral work for the Cravath firm since the Interprovincial PipeLine deal some years earlier.[81]

Osler, Hoskin & Harcourt apparently implemented a few of the Cravath designs, but one thing they did not do was establish a stenographic pool. At Cravath, Swaine & Moore, only the very senior lawyers had their own secretaries. The majority of the firm's secretaries worked in a huge typing pool guarded by a matronly supervisor. Lawyers would simply hand dictaphone tapes to the supervisor and she would assign a secretary to do the transcription. The lawyer would then pick up the finished work when it was ready.[82] This was considered far too factory-like and impersonal for Osler, Hoskin & Harcourt.

The firm's relationship with its clients – particularly the Toronto-Dominion Bank as an existing one, and Prudential as potential one – was a consideration in deciding where to move. The Dominion Bank had been a client going back to when B.B. Osler's brother Sir Edmund Osler was still its chairman, but the firm had largely lost the bank's work, even before the merger with the Bank of Toronto in 1955. Harold Shapley had always looked after the bank's file, but, when he died in 1952, it apparently decided to go to Beverley Matthews at McCarthy & McCarthy.[83] The Prudential was not an Oslers client, but significantly, it became one after the move.[84]

The Prudential was a brand-new building, and it offered impressive facilities, but it was not considered the most prestigious address in the city. At least two other new buildings, the Royal Bank Building next door and the Bank of Canada Building at the southwest corner of Queen and University, were more prestigious, but this probably says something about Hal Mockridge and the firm which still reflected his image. He would let Pete Elliot, the senior partner at Borden & Elliot, move his firm into the Bank of Canada Building. The Prudential would do for Oslers.[85]

Borden & Elliot's move to the Bank of Canada Building may have seemed a little pretentious to someone like Mockridge, but it was nothing compared with the move McCarthy & McCarthy made six years later, when the new Toronto-Dominion Centre opened in 1967. The Prudential Building was twenty storeys; the T-D centre was over fifty![86] When McCarthys moved from the Canada Life Building to the new T-D Centre, it raised a few eyebrows by renting very expensive space with a commanding view of Lake Ontario and spending a great deal of money on leasehold improvements, such as a magnificent spiral staircase between floors. According to most observers, this really set the tone for law-firm location and decor. Many other lawyers, including those at Oslers, felt that clients might wonder who was going to pay for all this opulence, but the first-class surroundings certainly did not hurt McCarthys' client list, and other law firms – including Oslers in 1976 – soon followed suit.

The new downtown buildings – particularly the new Toronto City Hall, which was completed in 1965 – were the most tangible evidence of change.[87] During the latter part of the decade, places like Rochdale College and the Yorkville district, where the drug and counter-culture movement blossomed, showed that the old 'Toronto the Good' was gone forever. Osler, Hoskin & Harcourt was changing also, although it was far more than a few blocks from Rochdale College on Bloor Street to the Prudential Building on King Street.

By Canada's Centennial year, 1967, there were forty-seven lawyers in the firm, eighteen of whom were partners. Of the twenty-nine associates, almost all had articled with the firm. Interestingly, although the range of political views within the firm had altered very little, the religious profile of the lawyers was beginning to change. In the view of the man who was then the office manager and knew all of them well, twenty-six of the forty-seven (55 per cent) would be identified either publicly or privately as Conservative party supporters. The remaining twenty-one (45 per cent) were mostly Liberals, but there may have been the odd quiet supporter of the NDP. This contrasts with the group of twenty-three lawyers in the firm in 1957, seventeen of whom (74 per cent) would be described as Conservatives.[88]

Very few of the lawyers in the firm were active in either party, and those who were generally kept their political involvement low-profile. Allan Beattie's friends might describe him as a Liberal, but his political views were very private.[89] He did not list any political affiliation in *Who's Who*, and many of his most prominent clients, including the Bassetts and the Eatons, were Conservatives. Others, such as Bill Bryden, who served for a time as the president of the largely Conservative Albany Club, were more public supporters of a political party. Bryden was listed as a Conservative in *Who's Who*.

After Leighton McCarthy left the firm, along with his brother and cousin in 1916, no one in the firm ran for political office until 1962. In the Ontario general election of that year, Vince Reid ran as Liberal in the Toronto riding of St George, but lost to the Conservative incumbent, Allan Lawrence. Lawrence later served in the Davis cabinet at Queen's Park, and Joe Clark's cabinet in Ottawa.[90]

In other ways, however, the firm was not changing. Nineteen of the twenty-three lawyers with the firm in 1957 were Protestants and, ten years later, thirty-seven of the firm's forty-seven lawyers would be described as members of one of the Protestant denominations. Of the remaining ten, four were Roman Catholics, and six would be described as having no religious affiliation. There were no Jews in the firm.

In addition, as of 1957 there were no women lawyers with the firm, and by 1967 there were only two. Bertha Wilson came to the firm as an articling student in 1958 and was called to the bar in 1959, and Alicia Forgie, who was called to the bar in 1963, joined the firm in 1966. Neither of these women was a partner in 1967. Wilson was invited to join the partnership on 1 January 1968, and Forgie became a partner in 1971.

It is perhaps significant that these women joined the partnership eight and nine years after their calls to the bar, when the average waiting period was much shorter. Similarly, Jack McTague and Vince Reid, the first two Roman Catholic partners in the firm, were made partners fourteen and eleven years, respectively, after their calls to the bar.[91] More significantly, the firm's first Jewish partner was called to the bar in 1973 and offered a partnership in 1977.

At the close of the decade, Hal Mockridge did two things that were particularly symbolic of the transition which had taken place in Osler, Hoskin & Harcourt. One came four months after he turned seventy years old and announced his retirement from the Executive Committee, the second when he purposely left the room to let his partners discuss the decision to invite his son to become an associate lawyer in the firm. Britton Mockridge was Hal Mockridge's second son. He had attended Trinity College School and Princeton (his father's alma mater) and graduated from the University of Toronto law school in 1967. He had articled at Osler, Hoskin & Harcourt and was scheduled to be called to the bar in spring 1969.

A generation earlier there would have been no question about his join-ing Osler, Hoskin & Harcourt – if he had wanted to – and of his father's tak-ing part in the decision. As it turned out, he was offered a place in the firm following his call to the bar and did remain as an associate lawyer for two years. In 1971, however, he decided to leave the firm and go into the petro-leum industry. The details of the partners' discussion regarding his admis-sion to the firm remain confidential to the firm, but the significant fact – in the history of the firm – is that Hal Mockridge took no part in the discus-sion. In fact, he was not in the room. He knew that times had changed, and it was no longer appropriate for him to be present. He knew that, for Osler, Hoskin & Harcourt, the era of the family firm was over.

NOTES

This essay is based on a chapter from the author's monograph *Portrait of a Part-nership: A History of Osler, Hoskin & Harcourt* (Toronto: McGraw-Hill Ryerson 1995).

1 When Canadian lawyers refer to law firms, they often seem to use a short form which adds an 's' to the first surname of the firm name. Thus, Osler, Hoskin & Harcourt becomes 'Oslers,' and McCarthy, Tétrault (formerly McCarthy & McCarthy) becomes 'McCarthys.' The originally proper spelling was probably the possessive 'Osler's,' or even the plural possessive 'Oslers',' because it was a shortened version of 'the Osler brothers' firm.' The apostrophe has appar-ently disappeared in recent years.
2 In 1892 the McCarthy, Osler firm had ten lawyers. Only Blake, Lash & Cassels, with eleven, was larger. It was also a very successful firm, grossing more than $117,000: See generally Curtis Cole, 'McCarthy, Osler, Hoskin & Creelman, 1882–1902: Establishing a Reputation, Building a Practice,' in Carol Wilton ed., *Essays in the History of Canadian Law*, vol. 4: *Beyond the Law: Lawyers and Busi-ness in Canada, 1830 to 1930* (Toronto: The Osgoode Society 1990), 149–166; and Cole, *Profiles of a Partnership*, chap. 2.

3 D'Alton McCarthy died in 1898; B.B. Osler died in 1901. Leighton was the son of D'Alton McCarthy's brother Dr John McCarthy. B.B. Osler had no children; H.S. and Britton were the sons of his brother Featherston. A third McCarthy of this generation, Leighton's younger brother Frank, joined the firm in 1906.

4 Interview by the author with W.M. Bryden, 20 September 1989

5 Although each of Osler's three sons also became a lawyer, and eventually a partner in Osler, Hoskin & Harcourt, they were, respectively, eight, ten, and seventeen years younger than their cousin Hal Mockridge. Mockridge was born on 24 September 1901; Britton M. Osler (generally known as 'Brick') was born on 10 June 1910; John G. Osler was born on 20 May 1912; Campbell R. Osler was born on 21 June 1919.

6 As of 1952, the Montreal firm McMichael, Common, Howard, Ker & Cate had twenty-four lawyers; Toronto's Blake, Anglin, Osler & Cassels had twenty-two. Osler, Hoskin & Harcourt had seventeen, as did McCarthy & McCarthy. The Osler at the Blake firm was Glyn Osler, Britton's and H.S. Osler's younger brother. Glyn Osler's sons, B.B. Osler and Peter Osler, also practised with the Blake firm.

7 The five were Britton Osler's three sons, Britton M., who joined the firm in 1934; John G., who joined in 1937; and Campbell R., who joined in 1948; Hal Mockridge; and Mockridge's brother-in-law Tom Delamere, who had been with the firm since 1942. The three new partners in the 1955 agreement were Fred Huycke, whose father G.M. ('Mossey') Huycke had been with the firm since 1920; Allan Beattie, whose father, Leslie Beattie, was the senior Canadian executive with the firm's most important client, International Nickel; and Bill Bryden.

8 Joseph Schull, *100 Years of Banking in Canada: A History of the Toronto-Dominion Bank* (Toronto: Copp Clark Publishing Co. 1956), 197

9 Interviews by the author with Jim Kennedy, 13 September 1988, and Allan Beattie, 2 February 1989

10 Huycke, known universally as 'Mossey,' was a First World War veteran who was very seriously wounded at the Battle of the Somme in May 1917. He was eventually transferred back to Canada by hospital ship with a piece of shrapnel lodged next to his spine, and had the shrapnel removed at Toronto General Hospital. When he was discharged, he enrolled in the accelerated course for veterans at Osgoode Hall and articled at Osler, Hoskin & Harcourt; he was called to the bar in 1920. By the mid-1950s Mossey Huycke was turning sixty and was well known as a corporate lawyer specializing in mining companies. The origin of his nickname seems to be a mystery. Some think that it was a diminutive of 'Meredith', his middle name, but his son E.J.M. Huycke, a partner with the firm prior to his retirement in 1991, dis-

agrees. He thinks that his father picked it up in the army during the war, or afterwards at the fraternity house he lived in as a law student. 'It no doubt related to some horrendous evening or something. The fact that he never saw fit to even tell my mother leads me to think that it must have been pretty bad!': interview by the author with E.J.M. Huycke, 13 September 1988.

11 Interview by the author with Purdy Crawford, 31 January 1991
12 Interview by the author with John Goodwin, 28 February 1991
13 The other partners' shares under the 1955 agreement were as follows:

G.M. Huycke	57.0 shares (15.0 per cent)
T.D. Delamere	38.5 shares (10.1 per cent)
N.E. Strickland	32.0 shares (8.4 per cent)
B.M. Osler	31.0 shares (8.2 per cent)
G.D. Wotherspoon	31.0 shares (8.2 per cent)
R.G. Ferguson	27.5 shares (7.2 per cent)
S.D. Thom	21.0 shares (5.5 per cent)
H.E. Boston	17.0 shares (4.5 per cent)
J.G. Osler	16.0 shares (4.2 per cent)
C.R. Osler	15 shares (4.0 per cent)
W.M. Bryden	13 shares (3.4 per cent)
F.A.M. Huycke	12 shares (3.15 per cent)
A.L. Beattie	12 shares (3.15 per cent)

14 Interview by the author with Stuart Thom, 11 October 1988
15 Stafford Smythe was represented by John Robinette of McCarthy & McCarthy. Between them, the Smythes owned 82.8 per cent of the stock of C. Smythe Limited and had used the tax-stripping method to avoid paying income tax on almost three-quarters of a million dollars' profit they paid themselves during 1961: *C.S. Smythe et al.* v. *Minister of National Revenue* [1969] *Canada Tax Cases*, 558–65.
16 The first Roman Catholic lawyer with the firm was Vince Reid, who came to the firm as a student in 1952; he was called to the bar in 1954 and became a partner in 1965. The first Jewish lawyer with the firm was Schuyler Sigel, who came as an articling student in 1961. He stayed with the firm for about a year after his call to the bar in 1963, but left to join Stitt & Baker, the firm which eventually became the Toronto office of the giant American firm Baker & Mackenzie. On D'Alton McCarthy's religious bigotry, see Cole, 'McCarthy, Osler, Hoskin & Creelman.'
17 Interview by the author with Senator David A. Croll, 9 November 1987
18 *Plessy* v. *Ferguson* 163 U.S. 537; *Brown* v. *Board of Education* 347 U.S. 483
19 Sandra Gwyn, 'Madame Justice: How Bertha Wilson's Humanity Is Changing

the Last Bastion of Male Power – The Supreme Court of Canada,' *Saturday Night*, July 1985, 13–19

20 Ibid., 16

21 Ibid., 13

22 Bertha Wilson, comments at swearing-in ceremony, Ontario Court of Appeal, 2 January 1976

23 Interview by the author with Madam Justice Bertha Wilson, 18 December 1989

24 Gwyn, 'Madame Justice,' 17

25 Interview by the author with Madam Justice Bertha Wilson, 18 December 1989

26 Gwyn, 'Madame Justice,' 17

27 The origin of Wotherspoon's nickname is unknown. Apparently his brother, his children, and even his nephews are also known as 'Swatty,' but no one seems to know why: interview by the author with E.J.M. Huycke, 13 September 1988.

28 Interview by the author with Madam Justice Bertha Wilson, 18 December 1989

29 Ibid.

30. Interview by the author with Stuart Thom, 11 October 1988

31 Interview by the author with Madam Justice Bertha Wilson, 18 December 1989

32 Ibid.

33 Ibid.

34 Ibid.

35 Ibid.

36 Interview by the author with Purdy Crawford, 31 January 1991

37 Ibid.

38 Interview by the author with Madam Justice Bertha Wilson, 18 December 1989

39 Interview by the author with Purdy Crawford, 31 January 1991

40 Loss has published a number of books on the subject; see, in particular, his *Fundamentals of Securities Regulation* (Boston: Little, Brown 1983).

41 Interview by the author with Purdy Crawford, 31 January 1991

42 The case involved a section of the federal Indian Act, which prohibited intoxication off a reserve, but it was the only instance in which the Supreme Court used the Bill of Rights to protect against racial discrimination. This record contrasts sharply with that of Justice Wilson and her colleagues after the adoption of the Charter in 1982. [1970] *Supreme Court Reports*, 282–307, at 288–300.

43 Interview by the author with Purdy Crawford, 31 January 1991

44 Ibid.

45 Ibid. B.M. Osler, Britton Osler's eldest son, was generally known by the partners as 'Brick.' The nickname apparently dates to his days at the Royal Military College.

46 Interview by the author with Allan Beattie, 2 March 1989

47 Interview by the author with Purdy Crawford, 31 January 1991
48 *Canadian Who's Who* (Toronto: Who's Who Canadian Publishing 1990), s.v. Crawford
49 Interview by the author with John Goodwin, 28 February 1991
50 See this author's '"A Learned and Honorable Body": The Professionalization of the Ontario Bar, 1867–1929,' PhD dissertation, University of Western Ontario, 1987.
51 The best source on this point is Jerrold Auerbach's *Unequal Justice: Lawyers and Social Change in Modern America* (New York: Oxford University Press 1976). See also M.S. Larson, *The Rise of Professionalism: A Sociological Analysis* (Berkeley: CA: University of California Press 1977), and Terence Johnson, *Professions and Power* (London: Macmillan 1972).
52 The full name of this firm in the 1960s was Chisholm, Smith, Davis, Anglin, Laing, Weldon & Courtois. It later became Clarkson, Tétrault, and, when it merged with McCarthy & McCarthy in 1990, McCarthy, Tétrault. Molson also retained Heward Stikeman, of Stikeman, Elliott, Tamaki, Mercier & Turner, on tax and certain corporate matters from time to time: interview by the author with Morgan McCammon, 8 July 1991.
53 Mockridge was invited to sit on the Board at Molson because he was very well respected in the Canadian business community and he was a personal friend of Hartland Molson's: interview by the author with Peter Stewart, 12 June 1991.
54 Ibid.
55 Interview by the author with Paul McKeown, 23 May 1991
56 Interview by the author with Purdy Crawford, 31 January 1991
57 Ibid.
58 Interview by the author with Jack Ground, 27 September 1988
59 Ibid.
60 The Big Four were University of Toronto, McGill University, Queen's University, and the University of Western Ontario. The term comes from the name of the football conference the four played in. Likewise, the Little Big Four was the football conference the private high schools played in.
61 Interview by the author with Harry Boylan, 8 November 1990
62 Interview by the author with E.M. Huycke, 13 September 1988
63 Interview by the author with Madam Justice Bertha Wilson, 18 December 1989
64 Interview by the author with E.M. Huycke, 13 September 1988
65 Hal Mockridge, B.M. Osler, and Bob Ferguson preferred the Toronto Club, and Tom Delamere generally ate lunch just down King Street, at the King Edward Hotel: interview by the author with Allan Beattie, 2 February 1989.
66 Interview by the author with Bill Bryden, 20 September 1988

67 Like many of the other lawyers, Saunders was a private-school graduate, in his case Upper Canada College. He was also a Second World War veteran. He did not, however, article at Oslers. Rather, he articled and practised briefly with the firm of McMaster, Montgomery & Co., a medium-sized firm which had a large real estate practice. A few months after his call to the bar in 1954, he moved to the firm after learning from Fred Huycke, with whom he played bridge, that Oslers might be looking for another young lawyer. Saunders stayed with the firm until 1977, when he was appointed to the Supreme Court of Ontario: interview by the author with Mr Justice Edward Saunders, 13 December 1990.

68 The partnership agreement, which for the first time divided the firm's profits into percentages rather than shares, called for the following division:

H.C.F. Mockridge	12.25 per cent
G.M. Huycke	12.25 per cent
N.E. Strickland	5.25 per cent
R.G. Ferguson	5.25 per cent
T.D. Delamere	10.00 per cent
B.M. Osler	9.50 per cent
G.D. Wotherspoon	10.00 per cent
S.D. Thom	6.00 per cent
J.G. Osler	3.75 per cent
H.E. Boston	3.00 per cent
C.R. Osler	4.25 per cent
W.M. Bryden	4.00 per cent
F.A.M. Huycke	4.00 per cent
A.L. Beattie	4.00 per cent
E.J.M. Huycke	3.25 per cent
E. Saunders	3.25 per cent

In addition, although Boston's share was set at 3 per cent, he was guaranteed a minimum annual share of $12,000: Osler, Hoskin & Harcourt Partnership Agreement, 31 December 1958.

69 Interview by the author with Stuart Thom, 11 October 1988

70 The trend has continued. The 1990 *RSO* is thirteen thick volumes, and is accompanied by the even more voluminous set of statutory regulations, the *Revised Regulations of Ontario.*

71 Osler, Hoskin & Harcourt Articles of Partnership, 1 January 1965 and 1 January 1968

72 Mockridge turned seventy on 24 September 1971, and Beattie was unanimously elected by the Executive Partners as chairman the following January: Osler, Hoskin & Harcourt Executive Committee minutes, 12 January 1972.

73 Interview by the author with Allan Beattie, 16 February 1989
74 Ibid.
75 While Beattie was clearly trying to build a consensus among the partners, it
   was clear that an individual partner's ability to influence the decision was
   directly proportional to his standing on the existing share-division list. In
   effect, under Beattie, the most important decisions were made by a select few.
   Under the partnership agreement of 1 January 1968, Mossey Huycke and
   J.G. Osler became fixed-interest partners. Their fixed shares of the profits were
   $25,000 and $10,000, respectively. The remaining profits were divided as follows:

H.C.F. Mockridge	6.70 per cent
T.D. Delamere	6.25 per cent
B.M. Osler	6.25 per cent
S.D. Thom	6.25 per cent
F.A.M. Huycke	6.25 per cent
A.L Beattie	6.25 per cent
W.M. Bryden	5.80 per cent
C.R. Osler	5.10 per cent
E.J.M. Huycke	5.05 per cent
E. Saunders	5.05 per cent
J.C. McTague	5.05 per cent
Purdy Crawford	4.60 per cent
H.K. Boylan	4.30 per cent
R.G. Ferguson	3.75 per cent
J.D. Ground	3.60 per cent
V.P. Reid	3.25 per cent
D.F. Pattison	2.50 per cent
G.D. Lane	2.50 per cent
J.K. Doran	2.50 per cent
Bertha Wilson	2.40 per cent
J.G. Goodwin	2.20 per cent
J.N. Grieve	2.20 per cent
J.R. Moffatt	2.20 per cent

Vince Reid and Jack Ground became partners on 1 January 1965, and Don Pat-
tison, Dennis Lane, Jim Doran, Bertha Wilson, John Goodwin, John Grieve,
and John Moffatt became partners on 1 January 1968. The 1968 agreement
specified that 'the shares of the net income for subsequent partnership periods
(three years) shall be established by agreement among the partners as they are
at the commencement of each such partnership period. In the event that a new
partner with a percentage interest is taken into the Firm during the course of a

partnership period, the shares of the divisible profits for the remaining portion of the partnership year in which the partner is admitted and for any remaining year or years in the partnership period, shall be established by the Executive Partners subject to the concurrence of the partners.'

76 C.R. Osler remembers the meeting taking place prior to the move to the Prudential Building in 1962, but he is unable to pinpoint the year: interview by the author with C.R. Osler, 7 March 1991.

77 Ibid.

78 W.B. Reid was a junior partner who had embezzled from his clients and the firm. He was disbarred and disappeared in 1953. See Cole, *Portrait of a Partnership*, chap. 5.

79 Interview by the author with C.R. Osler, 7 March 1991

80 Osler, Hoskin & Harcourt Articles of Partnership, 1 January 1962

81 Interview by the author with C.R. Osler, 7 March 1991

82 Ibid.

83 In the merger of the banks, which took place in 1955 (Schull, *100 Years of Banking in Canada*, 197), Beverley Matthews acted for the Dominion Bank, and Fasken, Calvin represented the Bank of Toronto. The latter firm, which had acted for the Bank of Toronto for many years, remained as the Toronto-Dominion Bank's primary counsel after the merger: interviews by the author with Beverley Matthews, 6 November 1989 and C.R. Osler, 7 March 1991.

84 Interview by the author with Allan Beattie, 2 March 1989

85 Borden & Elliot, which Beverley Elliot (known generally as 'Pete') formed during the Depression of the 1930s with former prime minister Robert Borden's nephew Henry Borden, was then known as Borden, Elliot, Kelley & Palmer. They moved into the Bank of Canada Building from their old location in the Bank of Commerce Building at 25 King St West (south side, next to the Dominion Bank Building). C.R. Osler remembers the Bank of Commerce building being built in the late 1920s, on the eve of the Depression. It was then the most prestigious building in the city. One of its other tenants was the Blake firm, which acted as solicitors to the Bank of Commerce: interview by the author with C.R. Osler, 3 November 1989.

86 The Toronto-Dominion Centre was built by the bank in partnership with Cemp Investments of Montreal, the holding company formed by Sam Bronfman for his children Charles, Edgar, Minda, and Phyllis: Michael Bliss, *Northern Enterprise: Five Centuries of Canadian Business* (Toronto: McClelland and Stewart 1987), 491.

87 G.P. deT. Glazebrook, *The Story of Toronto* (Toronto: University of Toronto Press 1971), 249

88 Interview by the author with Frank Clifford, 7 March 1991

89 Speaking at Beattie's retirement dinner in 1987, Harry Boylan affectionately said that, other than his support of the New York Yankees and the Liberal Party of Canada, Allan's judgment was impeccable.

90 One of his colleagues in the short-lived Clark cabinet was another (later) Osler partner, Ron Atkey: See Cole, *Portrait of a Partnership*, chap. 8.

91 However, unlike the practice in later years, during the 1950s and 1960s admissions to the partnership were made only every three years, when a new partnership agreement was signed. Wilson was, therefore, passed over for partnership in 1965, six years following her call to the bar. McTague was called to the bar in 1948, and joined the firm in 1956. He was passed over for partnership in 1959 and became a partner in 1962. Reid, who articled with the firm, was called to the bar in 1954 but did not become a partner until 1965. In McTague's case, the significant time span is probably the six years between his joining the firm and his admission to the partnership. He was also the son of a former judge. His father, Justice Charles P. McTague, sat on the Ontario Supreme Court from 1935 to 1944, and he served as chairman of the Ontario Securities Commission from 1945 to 1948.

11

Dominant Professionals: The Role of Large-Firm Lawyers in Manitoba

DALE BRAWN

Large law firms, virtually unknown in nineteenth-century Canada, now dominate the legal profession. The visible signs of their prestige include superbly appointed offices located in high-rent office towers overlooking Canada's major cities. It is these large-firm lawyers who service the legal needs of Canada's corporate giants. The salaries they receive are the envy of the rest of the profession, not least the law students who compete ferociously for coveted places in such firms. These students know that such a position yields not only wealth, but opportunity for advancement in business, politics, or the profession itself.

Large-firm lawyers are unquestionably influential, but their role remains mysterious; they are proverbially secretive. Neither the media coverage of their activities, nor the histories that chronicle their headlong expansion, truly reflect the role of large law firms in Canadian society. This essay uses the Winnipeg bar from 1899 to 1959 as a case-study to examine systematically the extent of that role. Over that period, there was an increasing tendency for those entering professional practice to do so as either members of multilawyer associations or solo practitioners. Those starting their career at either end of the legal spectrum were destined to remain there. This produced two results: It ensured that Winnipeg lawyers did not share a common professional experience, and it created a highly differentiated and stratified bar dominated by members of large firms. By controlling both the Law Society and the Manitoba Law School, members of large firms marginalized women, Jews, and small-firm prac-

TABLE 11.1
The Bar of the Province of Manitoba

Location	Number of Lawyers						
	1899	1909	1919	1929	1939	1949	1959
Winnipeg	72	193	325	389	359	331	443
Rest of Manitoba	72	104	109	157	150	133	141

titioners. In so doing they perpetuated their control of the profession and guaranteed its continued stratification. Lawyers in the city's largest and smallest firms practised a different kind of law for a different kind of client, for reasons this essay explains.

To get behind the façade of large firms, this essay combines a critical examination of existing studies of the profession with a quantitative analysis of litigation, lawyer mobility, law-firm growth, specialization, and Law Society elections. It explores the client base of varying sizes of firms and the impact client type had on how law was practised. This essay suggests that not only is the relationship between large-firm lawyers and their clients dominated by clients, but that clients' values are adopted by those at the top of the legal hierarchy.

This essay also reveals startling new information about how lawyers in large Winnipeg law firms have come to dominate a profession composed largely of small-firm practitioners. It indicates that large firms essentially put their undoubted talents at the service of corporate clients, leaving the 'little guy' to the generalists of the profession. Moreover, the significant presence of large-firm alumni on the bench ensured that the interests of former clients continued to be represented for years after their appointment. In addition to virtually monopolizing the most lucrative forms of legal work, as well as judicial posts, members of large law firms influenced the development of both the Law Society and the Manitoba Law School during their formative stages. Further, their presence in politics guaranteed that corporate interests would be protected in the public as well as the private arena.

Table 11.1 describes the composition of Manitoba's legal profession between 1899 and 1959. It suggests that, by the start of the second half of the twentieth century, 70 per cent of lawyers who practised law in the province did so in Winnipeg. What is important in understanding the evolution of Winnipeg law firms, however, is less the number of lawyers who practised in the city than the size of the firms with which they practised.

TABLE 11.2
Manitoba's Largest Law Firms

Firm name	Rank in Terms of Size						
	1899	1909	1919	1929	1939	1949	1959
Pitblado, Hoskin	4	2	5	3	2	1	1
Aikins, MacAulay	1	5	5	1	3	2	2
MacInnes, Burbidge	–	1	1	3	1	3	4
Thorvaldson, Eggertson	–	–	3	–	5	3	–
Hudson, Ormand	–	2	-	2	4	–	–
Thompson, Dorfman	–	–	–	–	–	5	2
Walsh, McMurray	–	–	–	–	–	5	4
Parker, Tallin	4	–	5	–	–	–	–
Hughes, Inkster	–	–	–	3	5	–	–
Tupper, Tupper	2	4	–	–	–	–	–
Filmore, Riley	–	–	1	–	–	–	–
Fisher, Wilson	2	5	3	–	–	–	–

Tables 11.2 and 11.3 divide Manitoba and Winnipeg law firms, respectively, according to the number of associates or partners employed. Large firms are defined as those containing six or more lawyers; and medium firms, those with between three and five lawyers. When the term 'small firm' is used, it refers to both solo and two-lawyer practices. Prior to 1959, only fourteen Manitoba law firms employed more than five lawyers in any given year, and all were located in Winnipeg. Of these, table 11.2 describes the twelve which at one time or another were ranked among the largest five.

A comparison of the growth patterns of just the Pitblado and Aikins firms suggests that, in the first half of this century, large-firm growth was both planned and incremental. Such differences as exist between the firms can probably be attributed to the personalities of their founders. Between 1909 and 1959, for example, both Pitblado, Hoskin and Aikins, MacAulay grew by approximately two lawyers per decade, but 20 per cent of Pitblado lawyers came from small or medium-sized firms compared with just 2 per cent for Aikins (whose recruits came primarily from the government or corporations). Moreover, lawyers who started out with Pitblado were twice as likely to remain with that firm for their entire career as were those who started out with Aikins. Both findings reflect the fact that Pitblado grew up in a much less affluent and privileged environment than Aikins and made a greater effort to get along with his associates.[1] And although both were well respected, Aikins was not much liked: 'Sir

TABLE 11.3
Winnipeg Law Firms

Size of Firm	Number of Firms					
	1904	1914	1924	1934	1944	1954
Large	1	5	10	6	4	8
Medium	10	31	42	27	30	35
Two lawyers	17	45	45	46	30	33
Solo practitioners	20	60	92	155	128	137

TABLE 11.4
Law-Firm Profile

Year	Small				Medium		Large	
	1 Lawyer		2 Lawyers		3–5 Lawyers		6+ Lawyers	
	Actual	%	Actual	%	Actual	%	Actual	%
1899	27	38	26	36	19	26	0	0
1909	31	16	52	29	82	41	28	14
1919	71	22	72	22	115	35	67	21
1929	112	29	86	22	118	30	73	19
1939	135	38	84	23	90	25	50	14
1949	118	36	76	23	82	25	55	16
1959	135	30	82	19	143	32	83	19

James had not been a popular person. A humourless man of Methodist persuasion and consuming ambition, he almost invariable put business before pleasure, and found little time to develop close personal relationships. And although capable of impulsive generosity, [he] had a reputation of niggardliness.'[2]

LAW-FIRM SIZE AND STATUS

The size of the law firm with which lawyers practise has a profound impact on their career and the type of clients they attract. This section examines the significance of size in the context of law-firm growth, and lawyer mobility and status.

Table 11.3 suggests that, notwithstanding the modest growth enjoyed by medium-sized firms after 1914, lawyers entering the legal profession increasingly did so either as members of large firms or as solo practitioners.

Table 11.4 illustrates the extent of this trend more clearly. It indicates that, between 1909 and 1959, the number of practitioners working in two-lawyer and medium-size firms declined by 37 and 24 per cent, respectively (from 30 to 19 per cent and from 42 to 32 per cent), while those employed in large firms increased by 36 per cent (from 14 to 19 per cent).

The most dramatic change, however, involved solo practitioners. In 1909 they made up just 16 per cent of the legal profession. By 1959 that figure had virtually doubled (from 16 to 30 per cent). This pattern likely had much to do with the growth of specialization. Economies of scale dictated that lawyers could maximize their income potential by working either alone or in a firm sufficiently large to permit them to focus their practice in a single area of law or on a particular type of client. Over time the effect of this trend was to produce a bifurcation of the Winnipeg bar.

The patterns of growth described in Table 11.4 were neither haphazard nor insignificant. In his study of the ethics of New York lawyers, Jerome Carlin made a similar discovery. He determined that lawyers tend to remain in the same stratum of the bar in which they begin their careers. Any movement that occurs typically involves just one step, either up or down.[3] Carlin categorized firms as large, medium, small, or individual practitioner. He concluded that, if a lawyer did not start out with a large firm, very rarely would he or she move into one later, although a considerable number of large-firm lawyers moved down into medium-sized firms. He also found that a majority of lawyers who begin practising in small firms eventually end up as solo practitioners.

According to Carlin, the net effect of this stratification was that lawyers in the upper and lower strata did not share a common professional experience. Only 10 per cent of large-firm lawyers ever practised on their own, and only 7 per cent of solo practitioners became members of large firms. As dramatic as Carlin's findings were, those described in table 11.5 are even more so. This table details the movement between firms for lawyers who commenced practice in Winnipeg every fifth year between 1900 and 1950.

The data described in table 11.5 suggest that the stratification of the Winnipeg bar was even greater than that found by Carlin in New York. Only five of eighty-three lawyers who began their practice in a large firm became single practitioners and just 3 per cent of Manitoba lawyers who started out practising on their own eventually joined a large firm (compared with 7 per cent in New York). With the exception of members of large firms, when a Winnipeg lawyer changed firms it was almost always to practise alone.

The subject of law-firm size is particularly deserving of study for at

TABLE 11.5
Lawyer Mobility

Size of first firm	Numbers of Lawyers				
	1900s	1910s	1920s	1930s	1940s
Solo practitioner					
– no change	7	18	36	15	9
– to a two-lawyer firm	15	14	6	6	5
– to a medium firm	2	4	2	10	5
– to a large firm	2	0	1	1	1
Two-lawyer firm					
– no change/same size	17	21	17	8	12
– to practise alone	18	20	25	10	3
– to a medium firm	5	5	3	1	3
– to a large firm	3	2	0	0	0
Medium firm					
– no change/same size	34	31	15	18	17
– to practise alone	11	20	19	3	5
– to a two-lawyer firm	3	4	9	2	2
– to a large firm	2	0	1	1	1
Large firm					
– no change/same size	8	17	14	10	12
– to practise alone	0	0	1	3	1
– to a two-lawyer firm	1	3	3	0	0
– to a medium firm	3	2	5	0	0

least one significant reason. The perception the public and other members of the legal profession have of a practitioner is based largely on the size of firm with which he or she practises. Status is a product of a social stratification, which places those employed by large firms at the top of the professional hierarchy and those employed by small firms at the bottom. According to Jerome Carlin, the characteristic common to those at the top is not talent, but, rather race, religion, and social background.[4] As LoPucki points out, clients attracted to large firms typically share a background similar to that of their lawyer. Moreover, they are inclined to retain practitioners who are at least their social equal.[5] Richard Abel examines lawyers at the other end of the legal spectrum. He concludes that the clients of small-firm lawyers are typically lower- or middle-class business proprietors. The services they receive are routine and non-specialized. According to Abel, lawyers practising at the bottom of the professional hierarchy are usually from more modest backgrounds than lawyers in large firms, and are seldom able to attract corporate clients or individuals requiring ongoing legal services. Carlin and Howard argue that these lawyers are the least competent members of the bar.[6]

Regardless of whether practitioners work alone or in large firms, if they specialize according to client type, such specialization is usually class-specific. Some serve a working- or middle-class clientele. Others serve business concerns and the affluent. Few serve both.[7] Abel suggests that this fact has had a direct impact on how lawyers practise and whose value systems they espouse. Small-firm practitioners are usually the social superiors of their clients and seldom have an ongoing relationship with them. This gives them a degree of independence not permitted lawyers in large firms. They often refuse to represent clients whose beliefs clash with their own. The relationship between members of large firms and their clients, on the other hand, is very much dominated by the clients, in part because corporations and the financially advantaged can bring to bear a great deal of political, economic, and professional muscle to ensure that they get their way. In addition, as repeat customers, large-firm clients are a valuable commercial commodity. Finally, as the social equals or superiors of their lawyer, they are not intimidated by the legal process. Conflict between large-firm practitioners and their clients is almost non-existent, probably because these lawyers typically have no reluctance in carrying out the wishes of their clients. Paid well, they follow orders implicitly.[8]

In the first half of the twentieth century, large Winnipeg firms represented the kinds of clients most small-firm lawyers would meet only as customers. Aikins, MacAulay, for example, represented the Canadian Pacific Railway, the Great West Life Assurance Company, the Dominion Express Company, both the Imperial Bank and the Bank of Ottawa, the Canadian Fire Insurance Company, the Canadian Indemnity Company, and the Northern Trust Company.[9] Pitblado, Hoskin was solicitor of record for the Bank of Hamilton, Mutual Life of Canada, the Landed Banking and Loan Company, the Toronto General Trust Corporation, the Home Investment Association of Manitoba, the Reliance Loan and Savings Customer, the City of Winnipeg, the Winnipeg Board of Trade, the Winnipeg Grain Exchange, both the federal and provincial governments, and virtually all of the nation's rail interests.[10] By the 1920s, satisfying the needs of corporate clients of this sort permitted large Winnipeg firms to grow and to specialize. It was a process, however, which did not occur until transportation and communication facilities had greatly improved, and society had become concentrated.

SPECIALIZATION

In their study of legal specialization in America, Glenn Greenwood and Robert Frederickson suggest that, as the economy in North America became more complex, the services performed by lawyers became more specialized.[11] Law-firm growth permitted an in-house compartmentalization of work. Over time, the relationship between growth and specialization grew symbiotically. A 1983 study of legal specialization commissioned by the Canadian Bar Association concluded that it was 'common knowledge in the [legal] profession that the growth of large firms is often based on teamwork within the context of a high degree of individual specialization.'[12] Barlow Christensen notes that the issue of why legal specialists are mostly concentrated in large firms has spawned little academic interest because the reasons are so self-evident.[13] Equally self-evident, according to Christensen, is the fact that specialists provide legal services superior in quality to those offered by generalists: 'Other things being equal, any given service, legal or otherwise, can be better performed by one who devotes his entire time and attention to that kind of service than by one who spreads his talents and attentions over a broad field.'[14] Certainly this was the perception in Manitoba by the second-last decade of the nineteenth century.

In 1882, pioneer Winnipeg lawyer Colin Campbell cited two reasons for leaving his partner and joining two other practitioners in a medium-sized firm. Such a move, he felt, could not help but enhance his professional status, since 'a small firm cannot command the same standing & reputation' as a larger firm. Equally important, it would allow him to specialize: 'I will take Common Law or Civil and Commercial Department, Crawford the chancery and Robertson insolvency and general work. We each get what we like and what each is best up in.'[15] Twenty years later, John Ewart became a specialist of a different sort. He moved to Ottawa and restricted his practice to cases in which he could appear before either the Supreme Court of Canada or the Privy Council. That law firms should specialize was perhaps inevitable. By virtue of their training and need first to recognize and then to solve problems, lawyers have always specialized. It was only when the legal problems of clients began to require more complex solutions, however, that practitioners were presented with the opportunity truly to focus their practice. Doing so enabled them to acquire more specialized knowledge and skills. To an extent, law-firm growth and increased specialization became the natural consequences of the growing complexity of legal regulation. Large firms increasingly became the instruments by which corporations attempted to come to grips with the demands of a new and more regulated business environment.[16]

According to Robert Nelson, legal firms typically grow in one of two ways – by developing a core of clients for whom the firm provides a full range of general services, or by offering specialized services to a wide range of clients on an *ad hoc* basis. He refers to the first method as 'general service growth' and to the second as 'growth by special representation.'[17] General-service clients are usually banks, corporations, and utilities. Special-representation clients are typically individuals, municipalities, and real estate concerns. The older the firm, the greater the likelihood it grew through general-service relationships. The newer the firm, the greater the likelihood it lacked an institutional base and was hired by clients on a one-shot basis. An examination of the client lists of both the Aikins and Pitblado firms suggests the two grew by providing a wide range of generalized services.

The structure of large firms is inherently more facilitative of specialization than that of small firms for a number of reasons. Traditionally these firms have large and stable clients with multiple legal problems. They are less dependent on walk-in traffic than are small firms. Their clientele typically recognize the need for specialized services and can afford to pay for them. There is evidence which suggests that all large firms, regardless of whether their practices are general-service or specialized, provide clients with a better quality of legal service than do small firms. In 1952 G.W. Saunders, secretary of the province's first legal-aid scheme, complained that the advice given by small-firm practitioners was 'on the most part hurried, casual and matter-of-fact.' There is, he said, 'a need for a new step forward to be taken toward the goal of justice for the poor.'[18] Twenty years later, a lay bencher of the Manitoba Law Society echoed the same sentiment. Muriel Smith, an Oxford graduate and holder of three university degrees, suggested that Winnipeg's needy were often poorly served by the legal service they received: 'The fact that there are greater financial benefits accruing to lawyers who specialize in cases involving conflicts over property and money, as distinct from cases involving interpersonal conflicts, has led to a concentration of lawyers in these more lucrative areas, with a consequent down-playing of concern for the problems of the already disadvantaged. Put bluntly, under the current system, more legal service goes to the rich rather than to the poor.'[19]

The reason large-firm Winnipeg lawyers could provide a better quality of legal service than could small-firm practitioners was the ongoing nature of their involvement with repeat clients. This provided them with financial security and the opportunity to recognize the difference between a client's short-term needs and long-term objectives. With recognition came the ability to analyse legal problems objectively. There are two reasons why large-firm specialists were able to develop this facility, whereas small-firm lawyers were not. First, they benefited from experience gained doing similar work for the same client. Second, the daily interaction of same-firm lawyers with expertise in different areas sensitized each to changes in both law and tactics. This explains why experienced large-firm lawyers with no particular expertise in a given area are able to achieve similar or better results than lawyers with more specific but less general knowledge. The effectiveness of a lawyer, and particularly a large-firm lawyer, thus has less to do with the small and more to do with the large picture. Dietrich Rueschemeyer put it another way: A 'good deal of the lawyer's competence is connected with his legal knowledge only indirectly or not at all. Since the law is a generalized mechanism of social control, its application covers a great variety of social institutions. Different applications require a grasp of these social contexts as well as of the law. From the good lawyer we may therefore expect a generalized capacity for defining situations and a great variety of "worldly knowledge."'[20]

A lawyer in the Aikins firm was referring to this capacity when he noted that the strength of senior partner John MacAulay did not come from his knowledge of the law. Instead, it came from his unique ability to size up both the quality of an opponent's case and the quality of an opponent's lawyer. He used as an example the outcome of a trial with which MacAulay had insisted on proceeding, despite the weakness of his client's legal position. 'What won the day was not his [MacAulay's] perception of the law, but the weakness of his opponent's knees.'[21]

Regardless of to whom legal services were supplied, if they came from a member of a large Winnipeg firm in the first half of the twentieth century, they were not provided by either a woman or a Jew. Although women had practised law in Ontario since 1893, it was not until shortly before Manitoba became the first province in Canada to adopt a policy of female suffrage that its Law Society admitted a woman to the bar. In 1915, Melrose Sissons and Winnifred Wilton shared the distinction of becoming Manitoba's first women lawyers. Two years later, Isabel MacLean also received her call. She promptly became the first woman to establish her own practice and, in 1953, the first to be named a Queen's Counsel. Four years later, another Manitoba woman made history. When Nellie McNichol Sanders was appointed to the Winnipeg Juvenile and Family Court in 1957, she became the first female member of the province's judiciary. But, by 1969, although thirty-nine women had entered the legal profession, a female practising in a large firm remained a rarity. Between 1915 and 1972, for example, the Aikins firm hired just one woman (Elizabeth Morrison), and she remained for only two years before resigning in 1947 to become Dean of Women at United College. Mildred McMurray was another rarity. She worked briefly for Macdonald, Craig, Tarr and Armstrong between receiving her call in 1922 and setting up her own practice a few years later.

Large Winnipeg law firms were just as unlikely to hire Jews as they were women. In 1906, E.A.Cohen became the first Jewish lawyer to practise in Manitoba. He was almost immediately followed into the profession by Max Steinkopf, S. Hart Green, Marcus Hyman, and M.J. Finkelstein. With few exceptions, these men, and most of the Jewish lawyers who followed them, practised alone or with one associate. By 1931, forty-seven Jews were members of Winnipeg's bar. Ten years later, that number had risen to sixty-two, not including the province's first two Jewish police magistrates, who, in 1941, were both appointed to a bench outside the city. But the lack of professional recognition afforded Jewish lawyers was not unique to Winnipeg. When Samuel Freedman was elevated to Manitoba's Court of Queen's Bench in 1952, he became only the second Jew in Canadian history to be appointed to a provincial superior court.

While Jewish lawyers may have been denied membership in a large firm, there is no evidence that they were systematically denied admission to the legal profession itself. Nor were the sexist and racist attitudes held by many senior barristers unique to lawyers. In fact, the kind of quota system adopted by the Manitoba Medical College in the 1920s to keep Slavs and Jews out of medicine was rejected by the Law Society. Statistics alone can neither prove nor refute the reality of discrimination, but in the case of Winnipeg lawyers they suggest that, as a percentage of the total population, the number of Jews practising law was actually higher than for non-Jews. In 1931, for example, there was one non-Jewish lawyer for every 589 non-Jewish residents, compared with one Jewish lawyer for every 366 Jewish residents. Ten years later, those figures were 690 and 274, respectively.

The personal and professional belief systems possessed by many of the founders of Winnipeg's oldest and largest law firms were one reason that women, Jews, and members of other minorities were successfully isolated from the legal mainstream. These men almost all shared a common set of values. United by their Protestant religion and British heritage, they were practical, material-oriented individuals who saw themselves as carriers of tradition and agents of improvement. Men like James Albert Manning Aikins, Colin Campbell, and Alfred Andrews arrived in Winnipeg during the last years of the nineteenth century just as that city was undergoing a tremendous transformation. Immigrants were entering the West in previously unheard-of numbers. Almost overnight, fortunes were made in real estate speculation. These expatriate eastern lawyers joined a Winnipeg élite made up of merchants and businessmen who believed that rapid, sustained growth was to be achieved at the expense of all other considerations, including social justice.[22] The handful of lawyers who came West before the dawn of the twentieth century believed absolutely in their right to use political power and personal connections to become a linch-pin between a rapidly industrializing East and the untapped potential of a resource-laden prairie West. The size and economic might of their clients positioned men like Aikins to acquire private wealth and professional power, and to use both in the pursuit of their own agendas.

JAMES ALBERT MANNING AIKINS

When Aikins arrived in Winnipeg, he immediately made use of an eastern connection he was to nurture for years to come – a father who had already been a member of one John A. Macdonald cabinet and was about to become a member of another. But he also possessed something which was to have a profound effect on the evolution of the Winnipeg bar and the provincial Law Society – an unwavering desire to mould both in his own likeness. He was absolutely convinced that the values and beliefs he had acquired while studying in Toronto reflected the best in the British legal tradition. On his arrival in Winnipeg, he parlayed his father's social capital and his own ambition into positions as a Law Society bencher and counsel to the Canadian Pacific Railway, the federal Department of Justice, and the Province of Manitoba. He thereby laid the basis for one of Manitoba's oldest and most influential law firms.

While Aikins was taking advantage of a boom in Winnipeg real estate to establish a personal fortune, he was simultaneously entering the political arena. First, he became a leading member of a number of federal and provincial commissions, and then, in 1911, Member of Parliament for Brandon. After being denied entry into the federal cabinet (probably the only time in his adult life he was not able to control his own destiny), he returned to Manitoba in 1915 to take over the reins of the provincial Conservative party. The Manitoba Tories had been left in a shambles following the forced resignation of party leader and provincial premier Rodmond Roblin. Although Aikins was unable to slow his party's dramatic decline, his efforts were ultimately rewarded with the provincial lieutenant-governorship. But Aikins did not restrict his activities to politics. He was a leader in the Methodist Church, first president of the Winnipeg YMCA, and lead organizer of the local Boy Scout movement. In 1914 he resurrected the Canadian Bar Association and remained as that body's president until two years before his death in 1929. He also founded the Commission on Uniformity of Legislation and, not surprisingly, became its first president. By the end of the 1920s, Aikins had been honoured with a knighthood and honorary doctorates of law from the universities of Manitoba, Toronto, Alberta, and Queen's and McMaster.

ISAAC PITBLADO

Isaac Pitblado was born in Nova Scotia and attended Dalhousie University until his minister–father was transferred to a Winnipeg pulpit. Like Aikins, he had a bent for learning, eventually earning three university degrees. Pitblado received his call to the Manitoba bar in 1890. He remained with the Aikins, Culver firm for a year before joining Alfred Andrews in a partnership which was to last until he rejoined Aikins in 1899. In 1903, he and Colin Campbell, Henry Grundy, and Alfred Hoskin formed a law firm which, from its inception, has been among the province's largest.

Pitblado's area of specialization was freight rates. It was a speciality he dominated on a national level from the 1890s until the 1950s. His abilities produced for his firm retainers from local, provincial, and federal interests. But it was his eloquence and reputation for integrity rather than his knowledge of the railway industry which prompted Manitoba premiers Norris and Bracken to retain him when they were, at different times, charged with wrongdoing. Pitblado was elected a bencher in 1901 and remained one for sixty-three years. By the time he died, at ninety-seven years of age, he had been practising law for seventy-four years and had received honorary doctorates from Dalhousie University and the University of Manitoba.

While the careers of Aikins and Pitblado were unique, they illustrate how large-firm lawyers used personal connections and professional status to further their own ambitions. In the case of Aikins, altruism was tempered by a driving ambition to control, not only his own destiny, but that of the Winnipeg bar. His personal standards became those of every member of his firm. Since a sizeable portion of Manitoba's judiciary were alumni of the Aikins firm, the influence he exerted by association was considerable. Pitblado was quite different from his former mentor. He was less irascible and arguably possessed a different set of personal priorities. Yet he too used his position at the top of Winnipeg's legal hierarchy to attract the kind of corporate and government clients which enabled his associates to specialize in a number of different areas of law.

One reason men like Aikins and Pitblado could so easily play such a significant role in the affairs of their adopted home was that their firms grew with the city. As Winnipeg developed, so too did their influence. When the first bar of the newly created Province of Manitoba met in 1871, the population of Winnipeg was 271. Ten years later, it stood at 7,985, and in 1891 at 25,639. Between 1901 and 1911, the population increased by more than 220 per cent. This pattern of sustained growth brought to Manitoba an influx of lawyers. The number practising in Winnipeg grew by 68 per cent between 1899 and 1909, and by a further 64 per cent in the following decade.

LEGAL ACTIVITY

In their study of litigation filed in America's federal courts between 1900 and 1970, Joel Grossman and Austin Sarat adopt a formula capable of measuring the extent of legal activity occurring in a community at any given time. They suggest that economic and population growth is usually accompanied by an increase in the number of lawyers. While lawyers are not involved in all aspects of the legal process, Grossman and Sarat argue that an increase or decrease in their number relative to changes in population is an accurate indicator of all resort to law.[23] According to their formula, legal activity is determined by dividing the number of lawyers practising in a community into the community's population. They suggest that the use of a lawyer/population ratio should produce two results: It should increase over time, and there should be a relationship between that increase and economic activity. Contrary to their expectations, however, Grossman and Sarat found that, in the United States, legal activity actually declined as both economic activity and litigation rates

TABLE 11.6
Legal-Activity Indicator 1901–1951

Year	City of Winnipeg			The rest of Manitoba		
	Population	Lawyers	Index	Population	Lawyers	Index
1901	42,340	72	1.7	212,871	72	0.3
1911	136,035	193	1.4	325,359	104	0.3
1921	179,087	325	1.8	431,031	109	0.25
1931	218,785	389	1.8	481,354	157	0.3
1941	221,960	359	1.6	507,784	150	0.3
1951	235,710	331	1.4	540,831	133	0.24

rose. The situation in Winnipeg was exactly the opposite. Just as Grossman and Sarat predicted, legal activity increased as economic activity did. And those increases were accompanied by a corresponding decrease in the number of lawsuits filed.

Table 11.6 shows legal activity for Winnipeg and the rest of Manitoba. Table 11.7 compares the activity for Winnipeg with that city's litigation rate. Legal-activity indices (lawyer/population ratios) are determined by dividing the population of Winnipeg and the rest of Manitoba, in thousands, into the number of lawyers practising in each area. The resulting indices are then compared with each other and with changes in the provincial economy. According to Grossman and Sarat, an increase in a legal-activity index indicates that informal and formal resort to law has increased. When it falls, legal activity has declined. They suggest that both changes should reflect a corresponding increase or decrease in economic activity. The data in table 11.6 suggest two things: first, that legal activity in Winnipeg was between five and six times as great as that in the rest of the province, and, second, that it did indeed increase or decrease according to the level of economic activity occurring in the city.

History suggests that changes in the indices shown in table 11.6 did reflect the changing circumstances of the time. The period 1901 to 1911, for example, was a boom time in the West. As land in Ontario suitable for settlement grew increasingly scarce, the movement of new settlers into Manitoba accelerated. Between 1901 and 1903, land values doubled. Wheat output rose from 14 million to 60 million bushels. Industry laboured long and hard to provide the railways, elevators, stockyards, and other facilities demanded by an economy still largely agrarian in nature. At the centre of all this activity stood Winnipeg, gateway to the West. In 1907 alone, over $12 million in new construction was carried out

TABLE 11.7
Legal Activity and Litigation Rates

	1909	1919	1929	1939
Legal activity	1.4	1.8	1.8	1.6
Litigation rate	8.7	6.1	2.5	1.5

in the city. Entire streets sprang up almost overnight. Between 1900 and 1910, the industrial output of Manitoba increased from $13 million to $15 million, and its labour force from 5,000 to 17,000. The level of prosperity experienced by the province, and in particular Winnipeg, is reflected in the legal-activity indicator for 1901. Changes in the way Winnipeg's economy was structured in the second decade of the century is reflected in the index for 1911. Table 11.6 suggests that, between 1901 and 1911, resort to law, and by implication economic activity, declined by 18 per cent. History indicates that indeed was the case. By 1912 boom times in Manitoba were over. Settlers increasingly passed through the province on their way to Saskatchewan and Alberta. War in the Balkans produced a reversal of the flood of money which had traditionally flowed from Britain into the West, and with the opening of the Panama Canal it suddenly became cheaper to ship goods by water through Vancouver than by rail through Winnipeg.

The index for 1921 suggests that the short-lived boom experienced by Winnipeg in the late 1920s produced an increase in legal activity. Although the city's economy still lagged behind that of Montreal, Toronto, and Vancouver, by 1927 it was once again on the upswing. For the first time in the history of Manitoba, industrial production exceeded that of the agricultural sector. The dominant role played by industry is reflected in the fact that, between 1911 and 1921, legal activity increased by 29 per cent in Winnipeg, while it declined by 17 per cent in the rest of the province. When the worldwide Depression of the 1930s struck, however, circumstances changed again. Winnipeg struggled to keep its economy afloat. It was only the industrial expansion generated by an impending war that kept legal activity at the same level it had been at ten years earlier. During this period, rural Manitoba experienced less of an economic slowdown than Winnipeg. This was so because it had far fewer industries and, as a consequence, fewer unemployed. Its indicator of legal activity actually rose 20 per cent in the Depression decade. Both Manitoba indices declined by 1951, although the decline was 7 per cent less in Winnipeg than in the rest of the province as industrial growth continued to outpace agricultural production.

In table 11.7 litigation rates are calculated by dividing the population of Winnipeg in thousands into the number of claims filed in the city's Court of King's Bench every tenth year between 1909 and 1939. The results are then compared with Winnipeg's legal-activity indicator. According to Grossman and Sarat, an increase in overall legal activity should be accompanied by a corresponding decrease in the rate of litigation. They suggest that formal resort to law typically declines when economic activity increases because filing law suits is disruptive of ongoing business relations.

The data presented in table 11.7 suggest that the amount of litigation filed in Winnipeg's highest trial court declined by 83 per cent between 1909 and 1939 (from 8.7 to 1.5), while the index which measured all legal activity increased by 14 per cent (1.4 to 1.6). These findings indicate two things: First, since an increase in litigation rates usually reflects a disruption in the ordering of society, a decline suggests that the dispute-resolution mechanisms of a community are working to keep disagreements within structured bounds; second, as Winnipeg underwent an industrial expansion during the first half of this century, law firms kept pace by shifting the focus of their activity away from litigation to law practised outside courtrooms.

LITIGATION AND SOCIAL CHANGE

Willard Hurst suggests that an examination of what lawyers do, and for whom, can reveal much about the changing nature of our society.[24] An analysis of litigation filed in Winnipeg's Court of King's Bench in 1909, 1919, 1929, and 1939 illustrates one aspect of this. Not only did Winnipeg's litigation rate decline as its pace of industrialization increased, but also, as the number of claims filed and defended by large firms went down, the number filed by small firms went up. Both changes occurred during a period in which the amount of overall legal activity increased. This finding provides support for the suggestion that, between 1909 and 1939, the focus of large firms shifted away from the courtroom. It also indicates that the vacuum created by that change was filled by those at the bottom of the legal hierarchy.

Table 11.8 describes the results produced by grouping claims and defences according to the size of the law firm which filed them. The five

TABLE 11.8
Law Firms Involved in Litigation

Year	Firms filing a Claim	Filings	Claims per firm	Firms filing a defence	Filings	Defences per firm
Non-specialist litigators						
1909	83	703	8	73	261	4
1919	97	692	7	95	285	3
1929	101	353	3	72	154	2
1939	85	168	2	49	62	1
Specialist litigators						
1909	15	474	31	15	205	14
1919	15	394	26	15	206	14
1929	15	196	13	15	93	6
1939	15	168	11	15	143	10

most active litigators among each of large, medium, and small firms were identified. The extent of their involvement in the court process was determined by dividing their number (fifteen) into the number of filings with which each was involved. The fifteen are referred to in the table as 'specialist litigators.' The remaining firms which filed at least one statement of claim or defence are referred to as 'non-specialist litigators.' Their involvement in litigation was determined by dividing their number into the number of claims and defences they filed.

Table 11.8 indicates that, by 1939, specialist litigators filed one out of every two statements of claim filed in Winnipeg, and seven of every ten statements of defence. To appreciate the extent of the role they played, however, these findings must be analysed in the context of those described in Table 11.7. The data in table 11.8 suggest that, between 1909 and 1939, the degree to which specialist litigators dominated the court process increased at the same time as their involvement in litigation generally declined. That this occurred while the totality of legal activity was increasing suggests that specialists had shifted the focus of their practice away from courtrooms. The findings described in table 11.7 suggest when this change began. Between 1909 and 1919, for example, the legal activity index rose by 29 per cent (from 1.4 to 1.8) while King's Bench filings fell by 30 per cent. In the period 1919 to 1929, resort to law remained unchanged, yet litigation rates fell by a further 59 per cent. Over the next decade, they fell another 40 per cent. The data indicate that, between the

TABLE 11.9
Litigation Trends According to Firm Size

Firm size	Percentages of all filings			
	1909	1919	1929	1939
Large	27	22	21	24
Medium	42	39	37	33
Small	25	32	36	37
Other	6	7	5	5

end of the First World War and the start of the Second World War, the focus of specialist practice had moved quite dramatically away from courts.

Table 11.9 suggests that this refocusing affected the practices of all specialists except those practising at the bottom of the legal hierarchy. As medium- and large-firm lawyers left courtrooms to practise law in areas outside the public glare, small-firm practioners took their place. By 1939 just under 40 per cent of litigation filed in Winnipeg's Court of King's Bench was filed by one- and two-person firms.

The data shown in table 11.9 are suggestive of the impact client type has on the law practised by firms of various size. For instance, as corporations grew in sophistication, they found it disrupted business relationships to resort to courts. They began litigating less, and the involvement their lawyers had with courts declined. Individuals, on the other hand, began resorting to law more often. Injuries in the workplace and on the province's roadways increasingly brought them into contact with small-firm lawyers. The next effect was that, as lawyers at one end of the professional spectrum shifted the focus of their practice in one direction, those at the other end shifted theirs in another. By 1939 approximately one in four lawsuits involved corporations. Two in three involved men, and one in ten, women. Large firms were 70 per cent more likely to represent a corporation than were small firms. Small firms, on the other hand, were 48 per cent more likely to act for women and 17 per cent more likely to act for men. In 1972 Marc Galanter offered an explanation for these findings.[25]

GALANTER'S REPEAT-PLAYER THEORY

Galanter's theory is based on the premise that, in North America, both wealth and power are widely but unevenly distributed, and that some members of society, those with the greatest amount of both, utilize the courts to make or defend claims more often than do those with little of either. The former he refers to as 'repeat players,' or 'haves,' and the latter as 'one-shotters,' or 'have not's.' The stakes in any particular case are smaller for repeat players, relative to their total worth, than for one-shotters. Repeat players are usually the larger of the two units. They anticipate litigation, have low stakes in the outcome of any one case, and have the resources to pursue long-term interests. A one-shotter, on the other hand, pursues claims that are either too large, relative to its size, or too small, relative to the cost of a likely outcome. As a result they cannot manage litigation easily or rationally. Because repeat players litigate often and for long-term goals, they develop the ability to recognize a weak position and are able to minimize likely losses. And because of the pressure to settle lawsuits inherent in the court system, 'haves' will almost always settle cases where they expect unfavourable outcomes and pursue only those most likely to yield a positive result. They are the type of litigant most likely to recognize the advantages to be gained from dealing with a legal specialist.

Individuals, on the other hand, are less likely than corporations to require the services of a lawyer. When they do so, their involvement is more likely to be on a one-shot basis. Even when this is not the case, their needs are likely to be episodic rather than ongoing. Individuals typically lack one or more of resources, experience, and an awareness of the advantages to be gained from dealing with a specialist. The legal services they receive are usually provided by a lawyer whose practice is located relatively near their place of residence and who is typically a member of a small firm. Not only are these litigators unlikely to be retained on an ongoing basis, but they are not likely to receive a sizeable fee or gain other clients as a result of their efforts. In short, corporations seek out lawyers in large firms because of the specialized services those professionals can provide.

Individuals seek out small-firm practitioners because they perceive their legal needs to be immediate, pressing, and best met by someone with whom they can relate and for whose services they can afford to pay. The problem for small-firm clients, however, is that these things mean that there is a good chance the legal advice they receive will be *ad hoc*, poorly researched, and of inferior quality to the advice rendered to the clientele of large firms.

It is possible to determine if repeat players in Winnipeg used the court system in a different way than individuals by examining the causes they

TABLE 11.10
Specialization According to Cause of Action

Causes of action	Percentage of all claims and defences			
	1909	1919	1929	1939
Contract	30	33	24	18
Goods & services	19	9	6	3
Negotiable instruments	17	10	11	5
Negligence	5	8	19	43

litigated over a long-enough period to discern patterns of change. In table 11.10, claims and defences filed in the city's Court of King's Bench in 1909, 1919, 1929, and 1939 are divided according to the cause of action they represent. Table 11.10 describes the four most litigated.

As has already been noted, throughout the period 1909–39, large firms typically represented corporate clients. Changes in what large firms litigate therefore arguably reflect changes in the way their clients conducted their affairs. In 1909 and 1919, for example, most disputes involved negotiable instruments, the provision of goods and services, and contract disagreements. Large firms almost always acted for plaintiffs. Over time, however, as the number of these suits declined and negligence actions increased, the involvement of large firms in litigation changed. They continued to act for the same parties, but their clients were no longer plaintiffs. Insurance companies and industrial concerns began defending actions rather than pursuing them, and their lawyers increasingly became defence specialists. One reason for this change was the increased use of automobiles. By 1939 large-firm litigators in Winnipeg were acting for defendants nearly 80 per cent of the time, almost always in negligence suits. Small firms typically represented plaintiffs, usually in the same actions.

The litigation with which Winnipeg lawyers became involved in the years spanning the two world wars reveals much about the changing nature of Manitoba society. The way individuals and corporations managed their businesses between 1909 and 1939 became more sophisticated. That is reflected in a 72 per cent decline in commercial claims. The 600 per cent rise in negligence suits over the same period clearly resulted from changes in modes of transportation. Such an increase arguably also represented a heightened belief that, in a more ordered society, individuals who had been harmed had a right to expect compensation. Changes in the way corporations litigated no doubt paralleled their involvement in society generally. Railways and merchants were usually plaintiffs in 1909. By 1939, they were almost always defendants. A complete absence of actions either for or against them marked the passage from Manitoba's history of land-settlement companies. And litigation started to reflect the new role women had begun to play in society. In the period 1909–39, their involvement in the court process increased by 271 per cent (7 to 26 per cent) and their participation in their own capacity rather than as co-litigant rose by 260 per cent.

These findings provide support for the suggestion that small-firm Winnipeg lawyers represented those for whom an involvement with formal law was a one-shot occurrence. The men and women who typically filed negligence suits could not anticipate their need for a lawyer's services, nor was it likely that the event which created that need would recur. In terms of their relationship with each other, small-firm litigators and small-firm clients were one-shotters. Insurance companies, on the other hand, anticipated that claims would be made against them and retained the ongoing services of a specialist in the expectation that their advice would be required.

THE LAW SOCIETY OF MANITOBA

In 1871 the statute which anticipated by six years the passage of Manitoba's Law Society Act admitted to the legal profession its first ten members and empowered them to form a bar society. By the end of the year, its membership stood at fifteen. When the Law Society Act was ultimately passed by the provincial legislature, it transferred from the courts to the new organization the power to admit and discipline lawyers. From that time onwards, the right to practise in the province was restricted to its members. All had to agree to be bound by the rules passed by the Law Society's governing body, the Convocation of Benchers. In 1877 the government appointed the province's first nine benchers and directed them to draw up a set of rules governing admission and practice. In 1886 these rules were amended to increase the number of benchers to twelve. Ten were to represent the Eastern Judicial District (Winnipeg and immediate environs), and two the rest of the province. Between 1886 and 1916, the Central, Southern, Northern, and Dauphin districts were created, and the number of benchers increased to twenty. Fourteen were to come from the Eastern District, two from the Western (Brandon and immediate environs), and one each from the remaining four. Except for a brief experiment with a formal nomination procedure, until 1956 an open ballot was

TABLE 11.11
Profile of Winnipeg Benchers

| | 1904–33 | | 1934–59 | |
Size of firm	% of all lawyers	Number of benchers	% of all lawyers	Number of benchers
Large	15	63	15	37
Medium	36	35	28	38
Two–lawyer firms	26	2	21	24
Solo practitioners	22	2	36	1

used for all elections. Over time, the Law Society Act was further amended to bestow life-bencherships on retiring presidents and those who had served at least five terms as benchers.

Open-ballot elections and life-bencherships were examples of how senior barristers attempted to perpetuate their control of the Law Society. The policies produced two results. First, they enabled some lawyers to serve as benchers for virtually their entire career. Second, it put control of Manitoba's legal profession into the hands of members of Winnipeg's largest law firms. Isaac Pitblado, for example, was a bencher for sixty-three years, Aikins for forty-nine, Alfred Hoskin for forty-four, and Alfred Andrews for forty-two. The influence exercised by those rewarded with a life-benchership was not significantly diminished when they no longer had to be elected. Robert Blackwood Graham was a bencher for twenty-six years; when he died in 1951, he was still chair of the Society's Discipline Committee and member of three others. Charles Stuart Anderson Rogers had a similar, though longer, involvement with the Law Society. He sat on its Discipline Committee for twenty-nine years, on Finance for twenty-eight, and on the Examining Committee for twelve. Of the forty years that Rogers was a bencher, he was elected in only fifteen. Even elevation to the bench did not lessen the influence some senior barristers exerted over their profession. One of the first things Justice-elect E.K.Williams did on being advised of this appointment was to inform the Law Society of his intention to remain active in its affairs. With the exception of Graham, all these men were member of large and prestigious firms.

Table 11.11 describes Winnipeg lawyers who sat as Law Society benchers between 1904 and 1959. They are categorized according to the size of firm with which they were associated at the time of their election. It is immediately apparent that large-firm lawyers were overrepresented on the Law Society, and solo practitioners underrepresented.

TABLE 11.12
Bencher Longevity

Size of firm	Number of law firms, 1904–59	Firms electing 1 or more benchers	Average terms as bencher
Large	14	13	7.0
Medium	134	15	2.0
Two–lawyer firms	–	7	3.0
Solo practitioners	–	2	1.5

In the period 1904–33, sixty-eight Winnipeg lawyers served as benchers. Of these, one practised in a two-lawyer firm and another worked alone. This means that, in the first three decades of the twentieth century, two benchers represented 48 per cent of the bar. Forty-three represented just 15 per cent. The contrast between the electoral success of large- and small-firm lawyers was slightly less sharp between 1934 and 1959, but solo practitioners were, if anything, even more marginalized than they had been before 1934. Over the period 1934 to 1959, eighty-two benchers were elected in the Eastern Judicial District, only one of whom practised alone.

The control over the Law Society exercised by large-firm lawyers was even greater than the data in table 11.11 suggest. Between 1904 and 1959, the average number of terms served by large-firm benchers was 7. The average served by all other practitioners was between 1.5 and 3 (see table 11.12). When the Law Society set at 5 the number of terms benchers had to serve before they were awarded a life-benchership, only one segment of the bar benefited.

The findings described in table 11.11 suggest that the Law Society's life-bencher policy produced three results. First, since no solo practitioner was ever elected president of the Society, none became a life bencher that way. Second, since the average number of terms served by all but large-firm benchers was less than the number required to qualify for a life-benchership, few became benchers that way. Finally, because its presidents and most of its benchers were usually large-firm lawyers, the Law Society ensured that control over its affairs remained in the hands of a minority of its members.

Another way this control was perpetuated was through open-ballot elections. Lawyers qualified to vote simply wrote the name of the person they were going to vote for on a ballot and deposited it with the Law Society. Since campaigning was considered unethical, the effect of large-firm members voting for one of their own arguably ensured that solo practitioners had little chance of being elected.

There is reason to believe, however, that the marginalizatiion of such a large portion of the bar was systemic rather than the result of a deliberate policy. Small-firm lawyers were unlikely either to have wanted or to have been able to take part in Law Society activities for a number of reasons. They could ill afford the time or cost associated with being away from their office for extended periods. They lacked the kind of office support which permitted large-firm lawyers to attend meetings and other professional functions. And, finally, participating in Law Society activities was unlikely to earn them either the respect of their peers or new clients.

An even more persuasive explanation for why small-firm practitioners seldom became members of the Law Society's executive is offered by Richard Abel.[26] He argues that the involvement of lawyers in bar associations varies according to their professional status. Participation in such activities by members of firms with a large institutional base of clients (like Aikins, MacAulay and Pitblado, Hoskin) is part of an overall external orientation towards the practice of law. Taking part in Law Society functions is merely part of a general tendency to use political, social, civic, and professional forums as a means of attracting new clients and building a reputation. The problem for the legal profession, however, is that, when it comes to actually taking part in the work of bar committees, many large-firm lawyers use their positions to further the agenda of clients rather than that of the profession: 'The lawyers of elite (large) firms may well take progressive stands on certain issues within the profession, may lead efforts at legal rationalization, and may exhibit a liberal orientation on general political questions, but both the direction of their reform activities and their approach to the issues that arise in ordinary practice ultimately are determined by the positions of their clients.'[27]

The reform activities of large-firm lawyers are usually directed towards producing a result which will benefit either themselves or their clients. In seeking to bring about reform, they actively exploit the advantages of time and money, which they possess in far greater abundance than do solo practitioners. Absent a direct and overriding interest of a client, these lawyers share a single common interest – preserving the system in which they are the élite.[28] Winnipeg lay bencher Muriel Smith suggests that her involvement with the Law Society of Manitoba caused her to become disillusioned with the reform efforts of some members of the Winnipeg bar. Senior lawyers, she notes, are more concerned with preserving the status quo, and their position within the profession, than with changing it.[29] Smith, however, ignores the fact that often it is those who have the least who most oppose reform. While there is little doubt that large-firm lawyers are not reluctant to advance the position of clients, that fact alone is not suggestive that all either are or were anti-reform. The contrasting position taken by two prominent Manitoba judges illustrates this point.

Prior to the appointment of E.K.Williams to the Court of King's Bench in 1946, there was a growing sentiment among Winnipeg lawyers that many of the anachronistic customs associated with the practice of law should be done away with. Court of Appeal justice R.M. Dennistoun shared those sentiments. He argued that superior court judges should no longer be addressed by the deferential 'My Lord' or 'Your Lordship': 'We judges have no legal right to be so addressed. We are not Lordships, and in a country where real titles have been discarded, it seems inconsistent to perpetuate fictitious ones. They savour of old colonial days when official snobbery was in evidence. We have in Canada no Lord Justices of Appeal, nor Lords of Appeal in Ordinary, nor are we members of the House of Lords. English judges so created are rightly addressed as Your Lordships. We have no such right.'[30]

These sentiments were not shared by Williams. Like Dennistoun, he was an alumnus of a large firm. Unlike him, Williams possessed a nearly overwhelming reverence for legal traditions, even those which had not previously existed in Manitoba. During his tenure as Chief Justice, for example, the black robes customarily worn by justices of the Court of King's Bench were replaced by violet, mauve, and scarlet gowns similar to those of English trial judges. The beliefs of men like Williams, and their attitudes towards women, Jewish lawyers, and tradition, deserve special attention. They were part of a relatively small group of Winnipeg lawyers who, until the 1930s, exercised nearly absolute control over both the Law Society of Manitoba and the province's system of legal education.

THE MANITOBA LAW SCHOOL

By setting the agenda of Manitoba's only law school, influential large-firm lawyers attempted to guarantee that their firms would be provided with a supply of practitioners who possessed the belief systems and expertise they valued.

Although the University of Manitoba established a reading course in law in 1885, the first systematic attempt made by the Law Society to provide articling students with a formal education did not occur until a series of lectures was organized in 1911. Three years later, the Law Society and the university entered into an agreement jointly to establish and operate the Manitoba Law School. Students were to take three years of lectures, receive a law degree, and be admitted to the bar. The new institution was initially located in premises leased from the YMCA. Its affairs were managed by a board of five trustees, and its faculty consisted of a full-time recorder and seven part-time lecturers. In 1918 the school's first full-time employee resigned over a wage dispute. Administration of academic matters was placed in the hands of a board of supervisors consisting of lawyers D.H. Laird, J.B. Hugg, and A.T. Hawley. That situation continued until 1921, when J.T. Thorson, a local practitioner, became the first official dean. He remained as such until 1926. In that year he resigned to sit as Member of Parliament for Winnipeg South.

In 1925, future superior court judge C. Rhodes Smith was appointed law professor, but to make ends meet both he and lecturer Henry Streight continued to practise part-time. A year after Smith's tenure began, one of the institution's founders, Hugh Robson, became its acting dean. He continued in that capacity until 1929, when Winnipeg bencher E.H. Coleman became the school's second dean. Coleman carried on as full-time academic and part-time lawyer for four years. He then resigned to become Canada's under-secretary of state. In 1934, T.W. Laidlaw replaced him at the law school, where he remained for ten years. When he returned to private practice, he was succeeded by Rhodes Scholar and well-known lawyer G.P.R. Tallin. In 1958, the board of trustees announced it intended to improve the quality of education provided by the Manitoba Law School. To that end it hired Clifford Edwards as lecturer, and it made the deanship a full-time position. In 1963 Tallin retired and was replaced by Edwards.

The Manitoba Law School was the creation of a handful of Winnipeg lawyers, virtually all of whom were members of large firms. Hugh Robson and E.K. Williams, however, have been credited with playing the most instrumental role in the school's founding. Both were considerably more than just lawyers. Each was an alumnus of Aikins, MacAulay, each maintained an association with the law school throughout his career, and each became an influential member of the province's judiciary. In effect, for most of the first half of this century, the values of two men became the values of an entire bar.

By the 1940s, however, lecturers from medium-sized firms had replaced large-firm lawyers on the school's faculty (see table 11.13). This

TABLE 11.13
Law-School Lecturers, 1941–1959

Size of firm	Number of lectures	Per cent
Large firms	11	21
Medium firms	21	39
Two–lawyer firms	4	8
Solo practitioners	1	2
Municipal/corporate lawyers	8	15
Retired and non-lawyers	8	15

shift in influence took place at the same time as a similar change was occurring within the Law Society. While both likely reflected the emergence of a more polyglot bar, table 11.13 suggests that small-firm lawyers continued to be isolated from the professional mainstream. Of fifty-three men who lectured at the Manitoba Law School between 1941 and 1959, only one practised alone and just four worked in two-lawyer firms.

The reasons those practising alone did not participate in the activities of the Manitoba Law School are largely the same as those which explain a similar lack of involvement in the affairs of the Law Society. An examination of the school's history therefore reinforces the extent to which those at the bottom of the legal hierarchy were isolated from the professional mainstream. It also helps explain why control of the school gradually shifted away from large-firm lawyers to members of medium-sized firms. As the men who founded the law school aged, their priorities shifted and their involvement in its affairs decreased. Younger associates, caught up in the process of building specialized practices, arguably did not share the same commitment to formal legal education as did their senior partners. Their place on the school's faculty was taken by members of medium-sized firms. Their involvement was part of a growing external orientation towards the practice of law. They likely recognized that participation in the law school's teaching program not only would increase their status at the bar, but would also attract the attention of clients who had historically retained only lawyers who practised in large firms. Finally, the reform measures referred to earlier confirm that, by the 1940s, the school had acquired a poor reputation in both the academic and the legal community. Members of Winnipeg's élite firms may well have become reluctant to continue an association which no longer increased their profile, either inside or outside the profession.

LAWYERS AND POLITICS

Regardless of the many changes which occurred in the legal history of Manitoba, between 1900 and 1960 one thing remained constant. The one forum in which lawyers from small and medium-sized firms could achieve the same kind of prominence as members of large firms was politics. When large-firm lawyers like Colin Campbell, Hugh Robson, Hugh John Macdonald, C. Rhodes Smith, and James Aikins entered politics, they enjoyed advantages not shared by members of small practices. These ranged from the support of office staffs to sharing the power and prestige of influential clients. Campbell, for example, dominated the Winnipeg bar in the first decade of the twentieth century as Premier Rodmond Roblin's attorney general. Robson was deputy attorney general for the Northwest Territories before becoming a twice-appointed member of the judiciary, first chairman of the province's Public Utilities Commission, and co-founder of the Manitoba Law School. Hugh John Macdonald was one of three sons of Fathers of Confederation to practise law in Winnipeg. By the time he died in 1929, Macdonald had been a member of Parliament, premier of the province, and city police magistrate. Smith served as attorney general of Manitoba, justice of the Court of King's Bench, and dean of the provincial law school. And when James Aikins completed the second of his two terms as Manitoba's lieutenant-governor, his office was filled a few years later by two other large-firm lawyers, W.J. Tupper and R.F. McWilliams.

But not all lawyers who became prominent in politics were associated with large-firms. An early example is Joseph Dubuc. He arrived in Manitoba in the 1870s and throughout his career enjoyed none of the advantages associated with large-firm practice. By the time he retired as Chief Justice of Manitoba, however, he had been Speaker of the provincial legislature, attorney general, member of Parliament, and a thirty-one-year veteran of the Court of King's Bench. Dubuc was not unique. Neither of the two lawyers appointed to the bench after the 1922 federal election were members of large firms. Both were, however, defeated Liberal candidates. John Adamson was one of them. He became the first Manitoba-born lawyer ever appointed to a provincial superior court. The other was Lewis St George Stubbs. He was perhaps the most controversial lawyer to practise in Winnipeg, both before and after he became the first Manitoba judicial appointment made by the newly elected Liberal government of Mackenzie King. A prominent lawyer–politician who was neither appointed to the bench nor a member of a large firm was Stuart Garson. After spending five years as premier of Manitoba, he left the province in 1948 to become federal minister of justice.

Not only did the prominence of small- and medium-firm lawyer–politicians rival that of members of large firms, but many of the former did not even get their start in Winnipeg. Thomas Mayne Daly, for example, was Brandon's first mayor and a member of Parliament before he gained a reputation as well-regarded Winnipeg Police Court magistrate. He subsequently became judge of the country's first juvenile court. Portage la Prairie's Arthur Meighen gained considerably greater fame when he became Canada's prime minister in 1921.

Regardless of the size of the law firm with which they practised, lawyers who entered politics benefited their firms in at least one way: They acquired recognition. Public platforms were the means by which many exposed themselves, and their firms, to potential clients. For those at the top of the professional ladder, becoming active in politics was just part of an overall external orientation to the practice of law. For small-firm lawyers, however, membership in a political party provided a level playing field and many of the advantages denied them professionally. It gave even the most marginalized an opportunity to be both seen and heard.

THE JUDICIARY

Involvement in the Law Society and the Manitoba Law School were only two ways in which large firms attempted to exert control over the legal profession. Equally important was the influence they exercised in determining who was elevated to the Bench. For that reason alone it is important to examine the role the judiciary played in the legal process. There is, however, an even more compelling reason to do so. Robert Nelson and Richard Abel suggest that the values of large-firm lawyers accurately reflect those of their clients. And R.C.B. Risk argues that, in Canada, the common law is made by judges whose values are those of society's most powerful groups.[31] These factors, together with the expectations and institutional pressures associated with meting out justice, mean that law is usually applied in a like manner by all members of a provincial judiciary. With one exception, that in fact proved to be the case in Manitoba. When large-firm lawyers are elevated to the bench, they do not automatically discard the attitudes of the social group of which they form a part. Winnipeg barrister John Ewart alluded to this in a speech he made in 1903:

TABLE 11.14
Background of Manitoba's Judiciary

Background	Number	Percentage
Politician	7	14
Rural practitioners	5	10
Two-lawyer firm	8	17
Medium-sized firm	9	19
Large firm	19	40

If I be asked whether I think that government jobs and railway passes influence judges, I reply that human nature is weak; that motive and mental influences work subtly, and their operations are much more easily discerned by onlookers than by the one affected; that such things usually do produce a frame of mind favourable to the donors, and ... that elevation to the Bench is not equivalent to inoculation against the feelings of gratitude for past favours or pleasing anticipation of those to come.[32]

Hurst suggests that judges have their widest influence through the pressure they exert simply remaining in the background.[33] Rosenthal argues that judicial preferences and prejudices hang like a hammer over the heads of lawyers because of the power judges have to influence the outcome of future applications.[34] In this context an examination of the role the judiciary played in Manitoba in the first half of the twentieth century is revealing. It confirms that a significant number of those appointed to one or the other of the province's two superior courts had practised with a larger firm prior to their appointment. And it suggests that the inclination for members of the judiciary to award judgments to defendants increased with the length of time a judge sat.

As table 11.14 indicates, between 1900 and 1959, forty-eight men were appointed to one or other of the province's two superior courts. Of these, seven received their appointment as an obvious political reward. Each was, at the time of his appointment, a sitting member of a legislative body or had been defeated in an attempt to join one. Five judges practised outside Winnipeg prior to their elevation to the bench, eight worked in association with other lawyers, and twenty-eight were members of large or medium-sized firms. Of these last, nineteen were alumni of a large firm and, of that number, nine had been associated with Aikins, MacAulay.

With one exception, between 1909 and 1939 every member of Manitoba's Court of King's Bench became more inclined to decide trials in

TABLE 11.15
Trial Judgments, 1909–1939

Decisions in favour of	Percentage			
	1909	1919	1929	1939
Plaintiff	87	62	61	53
Defendant	13	38	39	47

favour of defendants the longer he sat on the bench. Table 11.15 illustrates this tendency. One explanation is the inclination of the judiciary to identify with those who were, by 1939, increasingly being brought into the court process as defendants – wealthy individuals and corporations. American studies suggest that the value system of those who act for this type of client is that of the client, and that conflict between the two is virtually non-existent.[35] Since lawyers from the highest stratum of the bar make up just under one-half of the judiciary, there is reason to believe that most judges possess similar values. Their collective values are arguably those inherited from former clients. Table 11.15 suggests that it may not be coincidence that the number of decisions favouring those clients increased as corporations began defending more actions than they filed.

A second explanation for the results described above is the selection effect inherent in cases which proceed to trial and the effect produced when corporations withdrew from the court process.[36] The selection effect holds that when both a plaintiff and a defendant share the same opinion of the likely outcome of litigation, chances of settlement increase. The greater the disagreement over the likely outcome, the greater the chances that a dispute will be litigated. The critical determinant of litigation and of the rate of success of plaintiffs or defendants is the error of the parties in predicting the likely outcome of the dispute. Where the error variance is small and approximately equal for both parties, the likelihood that the plaintiff will win is close to 50 per cent. As the error of the parties diminishes, the proportion of disputes litigated declines and the settlement rate increases. As the litigation rate declines, the proportion of plaintiff victories will more closely approach 50 per cent.

Three factors loom large in the selection effect – litigation costs, settlement costs, and the size of the judgment. When litigation costs are lower than settlement costs or where judgments are exceptionally large, most disputes will be litigated, and the proportion of plaintiff victories will likely be less than 50 per cent. In short, where the gains or losses from litigation are equal for both plaintiff and defendant, the individual maximizing decisions of the parties creates a bias towards a 50 per cent rate of success, regardless of the substantive standard of law.

In the context of litigation filed in Winnipeg's Court of King's Bench, however, it is the exception to the selection effect which perhaps best explains the tendency of members of the Manitoba judiciary increasingly to render decisions in favour of defendants. As corporations grew in size and sophistication, they gradually withdrew from the court process. This occurred primarily because resort to law was both expensive and disruptive of business relationships. Over time, large-firm clients were drawn into a courtroom only when not to do so would damage their reputation and a victory would restore it, or in circumstances where losing a dispute would affect future business or require them to change an existing practice at an increase in cost. In such cases, when the stakes are greater for a defendant than for a plaintiff, fewer disputes will be litigated, but the outcome of those which are will usually favour a defendant.[37] The effect produced when corporations began entering the courtroom as defendants rather than plaintiffs was to narrow considerably the gap between plaintiff wins and defendant losses.

A third explanation for a shift in the decision-making propensity of the Manitoba judiciary is related to growth of quasi-judicial bodies. Many disputes in which the liability of a defendant was readily apparent were suddenly removed from the formal adjudication process.[38] This left the judiciary only those cases where a defendant had either a valid or a strongly perceived defence. The net effect was to lessen the number of cases filed with courts and to increase the number of trial decisions favouring defendants.

CONCLUSION

In the first ninety years of Winnipeg's history, only fourteen law firms employed more than five lawyers at any given time. As the city grew, so too did the influence of these few large firms. Over time law-firm size came to have a significant impact on the professional lives of lawyers. It not only determined their status at the bar, but dictated the type of client they attracted. The larger the firm, the greater the likelihood that clients were wealthy individuals or corporations. Servicing the needs of those with power and influence permitted large-firm lawyers not only to specialize, but to play a dominant role in the affairs of the Law Society and the Manitoba Law School.

The influence of senior members of Manitoba's oldest and largest firms was exaggerated primarily because these individuals shared a common set of values. As a result, women, Jews, and small-firm practitioners were excluded from large-firm practice and isolated from the legal mainstream. One route to prominence for those marginalized by the professional establishment was politics. For many, joining a political party was like becoming a member of a large law firm: It brought acceptance and the opportunity to distinguish themselves in the eyes of other lawyers and potential clients.

As large firms grew and became more specialized, their focus shifted away from the courtroom. The needs of corporate clients were increasingly satisfied outside the glare of public scrutiny. Filling the void left by large-firm litigators were those who occupied the lowest rungs of the professional ladder. Their clients were lower- and middle-class individuals. As the number of commercial actions typically filed by corporations declined, negligence suits filed by individuals increased. With that change small-firm practitioners began to play a more significant role in the court process. They continued, however, to be shut out from both the Law Society and from teaching positions at the province's law school.

An examination of the legal history of Manitoba suggests that the founders of Winnipeg's largest firms share a lasting legacy – a highly differentiated and stratified bar. There is no reason, however, to believe that such a circumstance is unique to Manitoba. Recent bencher elections in Ontario suggest that the legal profession in that province is also stratified, albeit along different lines. Further research will no doubt also show that the influence of wealthy individuals and corporations pervades metropolitan bars both inside and outside Canada. By adopting the kind of methodology described in this essay, researchers should be able to measure both the extent and the effect of that influence. It should also be possible to identify groups marginalized by inequities inherent in the structure of modern law firms and in other law societies and professional organizations. Only in this way can the legal profession truly embrace the notion of reform.

NOTES

I would like to thank Harry Arthurs, Douglas Hay, and Fred Zemans for their comments on an earlier draft of this essay. My greatest debt is to Carol Wilton for her guidance at every stage in the writing of this article.

1 Anna Tillenius, *Learned Friends, Reminiscences: Pitblado, Hoskin, 1882 – 1974* (Winnipeg: Pitblado, Hoskin 1975)

2 Dale Gibson and Lee Gibson, *Substantial Justice: Law and Lawyers in Manitoba, 1670 – 1970* (Winnipeg: Peguis 1967)

3 Jerome E. Carlin, *Lawyer's Ethics: a Survey of the New York City Bar* (New York: Russell Sage Foundation 1966)

4 Ibid.

5 Lynn M. LoPucki, *The De Facto Pattern of Lawyer Specialization* (Madison: Institute of Legal Studies, University of Wisconsin–Madison Law School 1990), 19

6 Jerome E. Carlin and Jan Howard, 'Legal Representation and Class Justice,' in Vilhelm Aubert, ed., *Sociology of Law* (Middlesex: Penguin 1969), 336

7 Richard L. Abel, *American Lawyers* (New York: Oxford University Press 1989)

8 Robert L. Nelson, *Partners with Power: The Social Transformation of the Large Law Firm* (Berkeley: University of California Press 1968) and John P. Heinz and Edward O. Laumann, *Chicago Lawyers: The Social Structure of the Bar* (Evanston: Russell Sage Foundation 1982)

9 Lee Gibson, *A Proud Heritage* (Winnipeg: Aikins, MacAulay 1993)

10 Richard W. Willie, '"It Is Every Man for Himself": Winnipeg Lawyers and the Law Business, 1870 to 1903,' in Carol Wilton, ed., *Essays in the History of Canadian Law*, vol. 4: *Beyond the Law: Lawyers and Business in Canada, 1830 to 1930* (Toronto: The Osgoode Society 1990), 283

11 Glenn Greenwood and Robert F. Frederickson, *Specialization in the Medical and Legal Professions* (Mundelein: Callalghan 1964)

12 Canadian Bar Association (Special Committee), *The Unknown Experts: Legal Specialists in Canada Today* (Ottawa: Canadian Bar Association 1983)

13 Barlow F. Christensen, *Specialization* (Chicago: American Bar Foundation 1967)

14 Ibid., 3

15 Willie, '"It Is Every Man for Himself,"' 275

16 Nelson, *Partners with Power*, 17

17 Ibid., 40

18 Quoted in Norman Larsen, 'Legal Aid in Manitoba,' in Cameron Harvey, ed., *The Law Society of Manitoba, 1877–1977* (Winnipeg: Peguis 1977), 167

19 Muriel Smith, 'The Legal Profession – A Lay View' in Harvey, ed., *The Law Society of Manitoba*, 182

20 Dietrich Rueschemeyer, 'Lawyers and Doctors: A Comparison of Two Professions,' in Aubert, ed., *Sociology of Law*, 271

21 Gibson, *A Proud Heritage*, 138

22 Alan F. Artibise, Winnipeg: *A Social History of Urban Growth, 1874–1914* (Montreal: McGill-Queen's University Press 1975).

23 Joel B. Grossman and Austin Sarat, 'Litigation in the Federal Courts: A Comparative Study,' in 9 *Law and Society Review* 2 (1975), 332

24 James Willard Hurst, *The Growth of American Law: 'The Law Makers'* (Boston: Little, Brown 1950), 295

25 Marc Galanter, *Why the 'Have's' Come Out Ahead: Speculations on the Setting and Limits of Legal Change* (New Haven, CT: Yale Law School 1972)

26 Richard L. Abel, *American Lawyer* (New York: Oxford University Press 1989)

27 Nelson, *Partners with Power*, 232

28 Ibid., 262

29 Smith, 'The Legal Profession,' 177

30 Quoted in Gibson and Gibson, *Substantial Justice*, 287

31 R.C.B. Risk, 'The Law and the Economy in Mid-Nineteenth-Century Ontario: A Perspective,' in David Flaherty, ed., *Essays in the History of Canadian Law*, vol. 1 (Toronto: The Osgoode Society 1981) 106

32 Gibson and Gibson, *Substantial Justice*, 172

33 Hurst, *Growth of American Law*, 172

34 Douglas E. Rosenthal, *Lawyer and Client: Who's in Charge?* (New York: Russell Sage Foundation 1974) 86

35 Nelson, *Partners with Power*, and Heinz and Laumann, *Chicago Lawyers*

36 George L. Priest and Benjamin Klein, *The Selection of Disputes for Litigation* (Toronto: University of Toronto Press 1982)

37 Ibid., 38

38 Jamie Benidickson, 'Private Rights and Public Purposes in the Lakes, Rivers, and Streams of Ontario, 1870–1930,' in David Flaherty, ed., *Essays in the History of Canadian Law*, vol. 2 (Toronto: The Osgoode Society 1983), 365

12

Raymond and Honsberger: A Small Firm That Stayed Small, 1889–1989

JOHN D. HONSBERGER

Raymond and Honsberger is and always has been a small Toronto law firm. Established in 1889, it had five members or fewer for most of its history. However, it slowly expanded, and had twelve members when it celebrated its centenary in 1989. By Toronto standards, it is a large small firm.

There were about four hundred lawyers in Toronto when the firm was founded. They practised, for the most part, by themselves or in small partnerships. This was the traditional way to practise law in the Anglo-American world for the previous two centuries or more, and it still is for large numbers in the profession.

The rise of the 'mega-firm' is a fairly recent phenomenon. The number of such firms keeps increasing rapidly. Perhaps, not unnaturally, most literature on law-firm histories has concentrated on them.[1] Small firms, however, continue to attract a large number of practitioners. At present, more than a hundred years after Raymond and Honsberger was established, some 49 per cent of lawyers in Ontario work in firms of three members or fewer, and approximately 30 per cent of lawyers in the province are sole practitioners. They constitute 71 per cent of the total number of firms for the province. The numbers in Toronto are somewhat lower: There, about 15 per cent are practising by themselves. The numbers for both the province and Toronto would be greater if they were to include the large small firms such as Raymond and Honsberger.[2]

The story of the smaller firms, however, remains largely untold. When it is told, it will reflect, to a considerable extent, an interplay between professionalism and independence. It may also show that small firms have demonstrated a greater flexibility in the face of economic change than their larger counterparts, and a greater capacity to accommodate the diverse interests and capabilities of their members.

FOUNDATION, EXPANSION, AND DIVERSIFICATION, 1889–1915

DuVernet, Macdonnell and Hanning, the first of the predecessor firms to Raymond and Honsberger, was established in 1889. DuVernet and Macdonnell had just been called to the bar and admitted as solicitors. Hanning had been admitted to be a solicitor a year earlier but had not been called to the bar.[3]

It was a good time in Toronto to enter law. The population was 130,000 or so, having increased by more than two-thirds in less than a decade through immigration, natural growth, and amalgamation. The growth in population was prompted in part by increased industrial, commercial, and financial activity. This produced a surge of legal business, including that in criminal law. It also introduced opportunities for occupational diversity and specialization, particularly in corporate and commercial law.

There were clouds on the horizon, however, which would affect the new firm. The prosperous 1880s would give way to the hard times of the 1890s. The demand for professional services would decline, forcing lawyers to adapt to economic change.

Change with implications for the firm would also be seen in the political, racial, and ethnic composition of the city over the years. Toronto was British and predominantly Protestant in 1889. More than 92 per cent of the population at the time had come from the United Kingdom.[4] Politically, Toronto was solidly Conservative, although there were prominent and influential Liberals among the members of the mercantile community.

Race, religion, politics, and gender determined one's place in society and within the profession, as well as one's ability to get ahead and succeed. Thus, there was an advantage for a Toronto lawyer in 1889 to be of British descent; Protestant, preferably Anglican; and Conservative in politics. It is not insignificant that DuVernet, who was the driving force in the new firm, was of Anglo-Huguenot stock, an Anglican, and a Conservative. His father was an Anglican clergyman who became the Anglican Bishop of Sherbrooke. His brother later would become the Anglican

Bishop of Prince Rupert. The gender of the Canadian profession was male. This was the case until Clara Brett Martin, the first woman to practise law in the British Empire, was called to the bar and admitted to practice as a solicitor in Ontario eight years after the firm was established.[5] As John Hagan has shown, however, Clara Martin's example was not widely followed, and the Canadian legal profession remained overwhelmingly male-dominated well into the twentieth century.[6]

DuVernet and his new firm did not have to wait for business. Most of it came to DuVernet. This was not unnatural, as he really was the firm, for all intents and purposes. He was, first and foremost, a barrister, for which he was well suited in temperament. His career before the courts was meteoric. Much of his early work was in the Police Magistrate's Court and the County Court Judges' Criminal Court. These were the 'bread and butter' cases that paid the rent. The small criminal cases soon were followed by many cases under the new liquor licence act.[7] Many of these cases went on to appeal. DuVernet very quickly made a name for himself in this new area of law, with the result that much work was referred to him from around the province.

The criminal and liquor-related offences cushioned the firm from the impact of the recession of the 1890s. The firm thereby largely escaped the zenith of discontent among professional men at the time caused by the decreasing demand for professional services, attributable to falling personal incomes, unemployment, and business failures.[8]

The ability of DuVernet soon came to the attention of the attorney general, who began to retain him to prosecute cases. At this time, because there were no full-time Crown attorneys, appointments were made from the private bar for each assize. Among DuVernet's early prosecutions while acting for the Crown were a number of election cases. He soon was appearing in many of the celebrated cases of the day.

One must wonder how DuVernet physically could handle the volume of business he did, and run the office, when much of the time he was in court. Alexander Macdonell left the firm after only a year to form his own firm. This no doubt involved a dispute over the distribution of profits, and a clash in personalities. DuVernet essentially was a 'loner' and always felt that he had to be in charge. Hanning, the third partner, a year or two later moved to Preston, where he carried on practice as a solicitor only. He, however, entered into a new partnership with DuVernet. This seems to have involved DuVernet's carrying on a barrister's practice in Toronto, and Hanning's referring business to him from Preston. The arrangement shows the adaptability and flexibility of DuVernet to change direction and reach out for new business. This is often an essential attribute for small firms if they are to survive.

DuVernet, hard-pressed to keep up with his expanding practice, enlisted the help of James Edmund Jones in 1892. They formed the new partnership of DuVernet and Jones. Jones was of Welsh descent. His father was Cannon Septimus Jones, who for many years was the rector of the Church of the Redeemer at Avenue Road and Bloor Street in Toronto. Jimmy Jones, as he was usually known, had been educated at Upper Canada College, at which he became Head Boy. He received a Prince of Wales scholarship and obtained his BA from the University of Toronto in 1888. He then attended Osgoode Hall Law School, and was called to the bar of Ontario and admitted as a solicitor in the Easter term of 1891.

Jones, like DuVernet, needed a small firm in which to practice. However, in most matters Jones was the antithesis of DuVernet. DuVernet was the single-minded, aggressive barrister and legal entrepreneur whose complete life was the law. Jones had a good mind and was a good lawyer, but he had strong interests outside the practice of law, to which he directed much of his energies. For this, the independence of working at a small firm that did not need all of his time was attractive. While DuVernet was driven to prove himself constantly, Jones was not: He knew who he was, and he was happy with himself.

Jones was an authority on work with young men and boys. He was a founder of the Aura Lee Boys Club, and its president from 1887 to 1925. A principal recreation, as one would expect of a man of Welsh descent, was singing. He also was a naturalist and outdoorsman. He camped and canoed, particularly through Algonquin Park in the summer. He snowshoed in the winter.

Jones compiled a number of song books, including the *University of Toronto Song Book*. He was a prime mover for securing action for the Revised Book of Common Praise for the Church of England. He was also a member of the Hymnal Revision Committee of the Canadian Methodist Church. As a result, he was widely known as 'Hymny Jimmy.'[9] With his boys' work background and his concern throughout his life with the underprivileged, he became one of the earliest proponents for a system of legal aid.[10] The *Toronto News* once referred to him as 'a man who spends one-half of his day working for himself and the other half working for his fellows.'[11] DuVernet and Jones were unusual and talented men. Each was very different from the other, but they worked well together.

The fact that both DuVernet and Jones came from clerical families and that both entered the legal profession, as did B.B. Osler a generation before, might be a minor indication of secularization. It is more likely, as all three were members of the Anglican Church, an example of the relationship between religious affiliation and professional membership. It is probable that the close link between the social élite of English-speaking Canada with Great Britain made Anglicanism the appropriate religion for them. The sects were the important frontier religion. Gradually, with the growth of industry and urbanism, they acquired within the cities a membership as respectable as the Anglican Church's.[12] This pattern would be seen within the firm over the years.

The firm thrived. DuVernet spent all of his time in the courts. Jones also did considerable counsel work. He had his own briefs and handled the work that DuVernet could not or did not want to take. He largely managed the office and did most of the solicitor's work.

DuVernet and Jones soon too found that they could not handle all of the business that came their way. Two new lawyers were brought into the firm in 1904. D.C. Ross was to do considerable conveyancing and general solicitor's work but increasingly devoted most of his time to reading law and preparing briefs for DuVernet. Holford Ardagh was the opposite to the bookish, shy, and retiring Ross. He became the 'sporty' member of the firm. He did mostly counsel work and handled much of the employers' liability work that DuVernet attracted after becoming general counsel to a large insurer.

It was a high point for the firm. It had doubled in size in twelve months. It had, with its four members, become in the fifteen years of its existence one of the most prominent medium-sized firms in the city.

DuVernet was a clever, highly independent legal entrepreneur. He would have been a good general. Like Wellington he used string to tie his plans together[13] ('Bonaparte's were made in wire') so that they could easily be broken to change direction after 'guessing what was on the other side of the hill.'[14] DuVernet saw that the profession was going through a period of restructuring. This was caused in part by more wealth in the country and a growing population, which resulted in the need for new and expanded legal services. This in turn encouraged both specialization and expansion to meet the needs of corporate clients resulting from changes in economic circumstances and government regulations.

DuVernet chose specialization. He had formed a chamber of barristers, of which he was the leader with Jones, Ross, and Ardagh, who gave him support. This permitted DuVernet to concentrate his skills and energies in a way that would enhance his prestige and status. It also permitted him to retain his independence, which he greatly valued. The small firm was the ideal arrangement. In today's terms, he had organized a boutique.

DuVernet, however, was soon to find that the prestige based upon his high profile as a leading barrister was being undermined by the growth of a new Toronto business élite. This consisted of the merchant princes, banking magnates, railway entrepreneurs, industrialists, and financiers. They, through bank investments, church connections, and intermarriages, were in the process of producing a new social order or family compact, which also held staunch British ties.[15] The new corporate and commercial lawyers who provided the legal services for the new business élite, such as Zebulon Lash, provided new leaders for the profession. There were still leading counsel, but they had to share leadership, status, power, and wealth with the leading solicitors.

DuVernet swiftly changed direction.[16] He made a series of bold moves in 1906 that were deemed quite remarkable at the time and more so in hindsight. One after the other, in quick succession, he acquired a small bank, a controlling interest in a large trust company, and a new partner skilled in banking and commerce. His ambition was daunting. He was not content to join the new élite in the profession. He would leap over that élite and became himself a member of the larger élite of business leaders and financiers, such as Joseph Flavelle (later Sir Joseph Flavelle), Senator George Cox, Edmund Byron Walker, Edmund Boyd Osler, and Henry Pellatt (later Sir Henry Pellatt). It was Wellington all over again. It was also a variation on the theme of entrepreneurialism among lawyers that was becoming increasingly frequent.[17]

DuVernet acquired the Pacific Bank of Canada, which had been incorporated in 1903 by four Toronto businessmen and a country lawyer. He changed its name to the United Empire Bank of Canada, moved its chief office to Toronto, and increased the capital to $5 million.

Almost simultaneously DuVernet, with the support of some friends, acquired the controlling interest in the Union Trust Company. By an agreement dated 3 May 1906, he arranged through an option to purchase 6,000 shares of the total of 16,000 shares for $763,530. It was a large sum even in those days.[18]

The third move made by DuVernet in 1906 was to persuade W.B. Raymond to join the firm. He was a senior member and the managing partner of one of the largest and oldest firms in the city.[19] He had considerable experience in banking, corporate, and commercial law, and was thus superbly well qualified to service the needs of the bank and the trust company. Raymond, who was the senior of DuVernet in years and in the pro-

W.B. Raymond, KC (photo in possession of John D. Honsberger)

fession, became second in seniority in the DuVernet firm. The association between the two men worked reasonably well. DuVernet brought in much business, which Raymond largely handled.

The chief interest and responsibility of Raymond was to organize and administer the firm to best provide the legal work for DuVernet's bank and trust company and for the increasing number of commercial clients they attracted.

Raymond, who was an Anglican, like DuVernet and Jones, soon found that Jones, for whom he had a high personal regard, was spending too much time in the revision of the Anglican Book of Common Praise. Jones left the firm as a result in 1910. This ended an eighteen-year association. He moved to a smaller firm. A few years later, he became a Toronto police magistrate and as such was highly respected.

Outside the law, Jones and Raymond had many common interests. Jones was to write a book in 1930 titled *Mushrooms, Ferns and Grasses.* Raymond also was an expert on mushrooms. H. Stanley Honsberger, his long-time partner, would recall the Monday mornings when weekend mushroom gatherers would bring in their collections to Mr Raymond to be told which were edible and which were not. As a young man, Raymond was also an outdoorsman and did much canoeing in the Georgian Bay area. He was patron of the Riverside Boxing Club, as was Sir Edward Beatty, and used to watch most of the fights. In addition, Raymond was a serious scholar who read widely, and even learned ancient Greek when he was in his sixties so that he could read Homer in the original.

Both Jones and Raymond had many interests outside the law. Neither could be happy with the law alone. They both benefited by the fewer restraints a smaller firm had on their outside interests. It was, however, a matter of degree. Raymond recognized that times had changed. A firm still could be small, but it had to be run on a business basis. It was acceptable to take some time from a business day for other interests, but Jones took too much time. He pushed the limits of small-firm flexibility too far, particularly during busy times when there was work to be done. It was a turning-point from a period when dilettantism was acceptable to one where business considerations were increasingly impinging upon or constraining outside activities. It was difficult, however, for most lawyers to completely reject all outside interests. As members of the profession they were looked up to as leaders of the community and were expected to be involved in its affairs.

The United Empire Bank eventually opened five branches, in addition to an office in London, England. There were, however, three failures of banks based in Toronto shortly after the bank opened, the most serious of which was the Farmers Bank of Canada, which failed in 1910. This had a serious effect on the United Empire Bank. DuVernet wrote in a letter, dated 27 January 1911, to his brother-in-law in New York that 'if we had a run on the bank we could not make it ... It looks as if the day of the small bank has gone.'[20] This prompted a merger later in the year of the United Empire Bank with the Union Bank of Canada, making it the fifth-largest bank in the country.

DuVernet became a director of the Union Bank of Canada. He was an active director of it, as he continued to be of the trust company. He worked at a frenetic pace. He travelled extensively, doing business for both the bank and trust company, and was in England once or twice each year, sometimes in respect of his financial interests and at other times on appeals to the Privy Council. He was in England in 1914 when war was declared.

At home, as Crown attorney he became involved in a number of treason trials. The most sensational was that of Emil Nerlick, a German citizen living in Toronto. He had built up a substantial importing business of dry goods, china, and toys, mostly from Germany and Austria. He was acquainted with the twenty-three-year-old Arthur Zirzow, who was also a German citizen living in Toronto and a German reserve officer. When war came, Nerlick advanced money to Zirzow to help him to get to New York and, from there, to Germany to rejoin his regiment. Nerlick was charged with treason. The trial opened in February 1915 and ended with an acquittal in June, with an interruption for the Court of Appeal to answer a number of questions.

Mr and Mrs Raymond had a dinner party in their home on the evening of 31 May 1915. Mr and Mrs DuVernet were two of the guests. Afterwards, as the DuVernets entered their front door on their return from the party, DuVernet slumped to the floor dead. The cause of his death was an 'acute attack of apoplexy.' He was forty-nine years old. Perhaps the real cause of his death was his lifestyle, in which he combined two full-time careers, a wife, and at least casual interests outside the home. At the same time, he knew that he must soon acknowledge that he was insolvent. It was more than a case of burning two ends of the candle. He lived towards the end as if he almost wished to die. 'Better now than later,' he was heard to say.

His death could not have come at a worse time for the firm. It was found that he was hopelessly insolvent. He had a number of creditors, principal among them the investment bankers Lazard Bros & Co., to whom he owed $375,000. This debt arose out of a personal guarantee he had given to facilitate a sale to it of some debentures which afterwards proved to be of no value. He also owed considerable amounts to members of his family, friends, and the trustee of the marriage settlement for his wife. He was in debt to the partners of his firm as well. Union Trust shares owned by them, and held by DuVernet for voting purposes, had been sold or pledged by him to meet pressing needs. It was distressing to the firm that he had betrayed the trust they had in him.

DuVernet remains an example of a case in which the ability to be flexible in one's practice had not proved to be an asset for a small firm where, the failure of one member could pull down the entire practice.

The late teens and early twenties was a period of major readjustment for the firm following the loss of its senior partner and the chaos he left behind. The returning servicemen who contributed to severe personnel problems and economic dislocation complicated the efforts of the firm to re-establish itself.

CATASTROPHE, REBIRTH, AND HARD TIMES, 1915–1945

The firm survived DuVernet's death, but it was not easy. The short-term reaction was the distancing of the firm from DuVernet's name. It changed its name a few months after his death to Raymond, Ross and Ardagh. The cable address was changed from 'DuVernet' to 'Raroar,' an acronym created by combining the first two letters of the names of the three partners. At age fifty-five, Raymond became the head of the firm.

In the longer term, DuVernet's professional disgrace became an enduring element in the culture of the firm. H.S. Honsberger, who had come to the firm as a student a few months before DuVernet's death, would afterwards say that, having seen what happened when the firm was based upon a few large clients, he had learned a lesson. He saw the risk of following Mark Twain's advice 'to put all of your eggs in one basket and watch the basket.' Honsberger would say that he favoured the advice of Cervantes: ''Tis the part of a wise man to keep himself to-day for to-morrow, and not venture all his eggs in one basket.' For the rest of his life, Honsberger favoured having many smaller clients over having a few larger ones. Once bitten, twice shy.

Another beneficial effect that DuVernet's death had on the firm was the adaption and growth of a more collegial atmosphere and structure. There would be no longer a leader for whom the primary responsibility of the rest of the firm was to give logistic support, and where so much depended upon a single member. Instead, each member would have more or less an equal share of the entire practice of the firm, and each member would look out for and after every other member.

The first order of business for the firm after DuVernet's death was damage control. Raymond realized that the firm as it was constituted could not work together. He persuaded both Ross and Ardagh to stay on for three years in order to hold together the business it had. Ross was given responsibility for untangling the DuVernet connection with the firm and for responding to the claims made against it. Ardagh, however, soon left to go to war.

The European war, as it was known at the time, left its mark upon the profession as well as on the firm. Almost all of the members of the profession eligible for service had enlisted by the end of the war. The County of York Law Association, whose members were almost all from the city of Toronto, saw 10 per cent of its membership enlist by January 1916.[21] This increased to 20 per cent by 1918. One-half of those who went to war did not come back.[22]

It was much the same with the firm. First, the students enlisted, beginning with Michael Chitty.[23] Then Ardagh enlisted in the 124th Overseas Battalion of the Canadian Expeditionary Force and went to France with it in 1917. The firm was now reduced to Raymond and Ross. They had one student, H. Stanley Honsberger, who had been rejected for military service. The clerks, the office boys, the other students, and most of the secretaries were gone. It had become a very small firm in a matter of months. However, the great majority of all lawyers in Toronto were practising at the time in one- or two-person firms. There were only a few firms with a half-dozen or more members.

Business dropped substantially with DuVernet gone. There was not the counsel work that it did when it had both DuVernet and Ardagh. Moreover, Ross was spending much of his time on sorting out the mess DuVernet had left and in handling claims of and against the firm. Much business, too, had been lost by the enactment of the Workmen's Compensation Act. There were no new employer-liability cases, which constituted much of DuVernet's and Ardagh's practice. There were still, however, old cases that had commenced before the statute was enacted which took some time to be concluded.

There were larger problems as well. Both the Union Bank and the Union Trust Company got into difficulties. The bank had too many non-performing loans incurred in the buoyant pre-war days. (Many years later, in the 1980s, other Canadian banks found themselves in a similar situation.) The bank was to be hurt still more by the Depression of the early 1920s. It eventually merged with the Royal Bank of Canada in 1925 with the result the firm at that time lost all of its remaining bank business.

When DuVernet died, Henry F. Gooderham became the president of the Union Trust Company in his place. He was a Toronto solicitor and a member of the firm of Gregory and Gooderham. He had shown an interest in the trust company as an investment. He purchased his original shares from DuVernet. A year or so before DuVernet's death, Gooderham become a member of the board of directors on DuVernet's recommendation.

Gooderham rewarded DuVernet's sponsorship by taking over an increasingly large share of the trust-company business after DuVernet's death. The Gooderham firm, however, had almost no corporate or commercial experience, its practice being almost entirely conveyancing. Gooderham's tried at one point to persuade Raymond to merge the firm with Gregory and Gooderham to give it the capacity to do the work and the prestige of having Raymond as corporate counsel. If it had been a firm other than Gregory and Gooderham, Raymond might have considered the proposal. He did not, however, have any respect for W.D. Gregory, who was loud and abrasive[24] and an altogether different type of man from Raymond. Moreover, Gregory indicated that he hoped to bring into the firm his son Goldwyn, who was a drunkard. Raymond would have nothing to do with them. A merger with the Gooderham firm would undoubtedly have produced a greater income, but at the cost of his style of practice, which was the opposite of that of Gregory and Gooderham. Raymond decided against the merger on the grounds that the gap between the cultures of the two firms was too great to bridge.[25] The ability to choose or refuse to take a decision that goes against one's grain in order to keep the business of large clients, or indeed to promote one's own interest, is an example of the independence often associated with a small firm.

Raymond's decision was astute for other reasons than the incompatibility of firm cultures, since the client whose business would have provided the occasion of the merger slowly self-destructed. The Union Trust Company was torn apart by Gooderham's fighting with James K. Pickett, the general manager. Pickett, who was bringing in much bond business, moved to the Dominion Trust Company in Waterloo and took his business with him. The new general manager did not have the standing to get new business. The company declined, and it was eventually taken over by the Trust and Guaranty Company, which in turn, several years later, was taken over by the Crown Trust Company.

The Union Bank and the Union Trust Company are examples of how a firm can rely on a few very large clients for a large part of its income. This can seriously hurt the firm, and indeed can often destroy it by the loss of the business of those clients, which can result from no fault of the firm.

The Armistice eventually came and masqueraded as Peace. The country and the firm were no longer the same. Neither could return to its former stability in an unstable world. That would be the future of the firm for several years. How could it achieve stability in an unstable society in an unstable world?[26] This problem was not unique to the firm: All firms, big and small, had it in common.

At the war's end, lawyers like other returned soldiers, sought to pick up their former lives. Holford Ardagh was discharged from the army with the rank of major. He returned to the firm and tried to pick up his practice where he had left it. This was difficult. The employer-liability work had all but disappeared with the enactment of the Workmen's Compensation Act. Solicitors who had previously forwarded work to him had been referring their work to others during the war and were not always ready to give it back to Ardagh. New and younger barristers were competing for the work. While Ardagh was quite a good counsel, he was not aggressive in bringing in new work. He worked better as a junior and later an associate, with senior counsel such as DuVernet.

Ross was much the same. He was still at loose ends, as he had been since the death of DuVernet. They had worked well together, but Ross did not work well on his own. His principal skill and primary interest was reading and researching law. He worked best with direction.

Ross had done a little of the court work that Ardagh would have done when he was away during the war. He also did almost all of the conveyancing for the firm, with Honsberger as a senior law student doing most the leg work. There was and is always a certain amount of conveyancing. During and after the war, the firm looked to it as a source of work, as it had not done before. One took what work there was.

Ross, however, was happiest in reading his reports and entering up his common placebooks. He was always ready to help other lawyers, who would came into the office almost weekly seeking his assistance.[27] A frequent visitor was Clara Brett Martin, whose office was only a short block away. He was glad to help her, even though most members of the profession were at best indifferent to her situation as the only woman member. He almost never sent in a bill to those who sought his advice. Ross, in a way, was something like Jones. Each had considerable knowledge of law. Ross had tied for fifth in his class and had graduated with honours. How-

ever, both Jones and Ross had trouble making the transition from a relatively non-demanding, almost casual, approach to practice, to the
pressure and demands of the more strenuous and aggressive practice of
the 1920s required by increasing overheads, changing times, and an
unstable world.

The last straw for the firm was when Ross took on an important case
for the Public Trustee. It was tried in Whitby, and had taken much preparation. Ross won, but, although he had paid all of his expenses, he
rendered an all-inclusive bill for only $70 when $400 to $500 might have
been more appropriate. Ardagh particularly was incensed. The firm
decided reluctantly that enough was enough and asked Ross to leave. He
did, severing an association with the firm that extended from 1904 to
1920. Although practice in a small firm is, as a rule, not so demanding day
in and day out as that in a large firm, there is less room in a small firm for
someone who does not carry his weight.

A year or two earlier, the firm had invited their student, H. Stanley
Honsberger, to become a member. It was somewhat a gamble for the firm
as it meant doubling its members, from Raymond and Ross, as it had
been for most of the war years, to include the return of Ardagh and the
admission of Honsberger.

Honsberger came to the firm first in 1914 as an articling student. This
began an association that was to last sixty-five years, until his death in
1979. He had graduated in honours from law school in 1917. However,
owing to some problem with his articles, he was not called to the bar and
admitted to be a solicitor until 1918. Honsberger, like Raymond, came
from an United Empire Loyalist family that had settled in the Niagara
District. They were a farming family until Honsberger's father left the
farm and came to the city, where he became a grocer. Honsberger was the
first of the family both to receive an education beyond secondary school
and to become a member of a profession. This was a great satisfaction to
him, but he never forgot where he came from. His practice was marked
by a measure of unselfishness and freedom from purely personal considerations or advantage. He practised for his clients and viewed them as
would a priest or minister his parishioners or congregation. This is the
touchstone of a true professional.

The interaction between Raymond and Honsberger was to mean much
to the firm. The example Raymond offered to the young Honsberger, and
Honsberger's background and ideals, ensured that he would not only fit
into this aspect of the culture of the firm but also carry it on in his own
way in the future.

When Ross left the firm in 1920, a partnership agreement provided that profits were to be divided into eighty-eight shares, with forty-two going to Raymond, thirty to Ardagh, and sixteen to Honsberger.[23] It further provided for the admission a year later of Norman Munnoch, a third-year law student. At that time Munnoch would receive twelve shares and an additional share for the following two years. 'not out of H.S.H's shares, but to be arranged by W.B.R and B.H.A.' It also provided 'if there should possibly be less than sufficient funds collected in the early period of the entrance of Honsberger and Munnoch to keep them going, we will favour them in distribution cheques in advance of available collections.' This was a new concept within the firm, but it was vintage Raymond. He was always considerate and understanding. He suppressed personal interests to overriding interests of the firm. He was a partner in the highest sense of the term. He felt a responsibility to the younger members in paying them more than they earned when they needed more.

The new firm of Raymond, Ardagh and Honsberger, which came into existence on 2 June 1920, did not get off to a good start. Soon, Raymond's health, which had never been robust, began to fail. He had pneumonia during the winter of 1920–1. He was advised by his doctor that he should spend the following winter in a warm climate. He took this advice and spent the winter in Sicily.

Almost at the moment Raymond sailed for Sicily, Edwin Bell, who had been the secretary of the Law Society since 1912, retired. The position of secretary was advertised, and Ardagh applied for it, as did twenty others. At a convocation held on 19 January 1922, Ardagh received a majority of votes on the first ballot. He thereupon was appointed secretary, at a salary of $3,600 payable at $300 per month, which was at least $1,000 more per year than he had received the previous year from the firm. His appointment too occurred only a few months before Norman Munnoch was to join the firm, which would have further reduced Ardagh's income. With Raymond in Sicily, Ardagh in the secretary's office, and Munnoch not yet admitted to the firm, Honsberger, who had been practising only for some four years, was the only one in the office for several months.

The early 1920s were not good times for the firm. There was a severe roller-coaster of price changes, which had started during the war. The cost-of-living index had almost doubled between 1915 and 1920. Prices broke in what merchants called a 'buyers' strike' in the summer of 1920 and then collapsed dramatically.[30] This resulted in high unemployment and many business failures. 'The twenties roared in the United States'; 'the Canadian economy was much more troubled' and did not return to normalcy until 1926 or later. This was a result of greater wartime strains caused by a longer war for Canada than for the United States, and in part by the excesses of the pre-war boom in Canada.[31]

The firm was badly hurt. Nut Crust Bakeries had provided the firm with considerable corporate work. It had a chain of stores throughout the city and across the province. Each store was operated by a separate corporation incorporated by the firm. Raymond did most of its work, with the help of Honsberger. It unfortunately was one of the casualties of the recession and failed. Similarly, Reliable Furniture Co., one of the first companies to make a specialty of credit sales, sent considerable collection work to the firm, which was handled mostly by Norman Munnoch. It, too, failed. There was also United Artists, the film company, for which the firm did its Canadian legal work. The company rented films in Canada to theatres across the country. There were never fewer than thirty or forty collections going on at any one time. Occasionally the firm also acted for the principals of the company and the early 'stars,' such as Charlie Chaplin and Mary Pickford in respect to their personal business in the country. Again, it was unfortunate for the firm that, in the early 1920s, several film companies doing business in Canada joined to form an industry collection agency which took away most of the business of the film-company client.

In a very short time, a substantial part of the practice of the firm was lost through no fault of its own. It was almost a repetition of the blow the firm received when it lost the business of the Union Trust Company and the Union Bank. It was disaster on top of disaster.

Munnoch joined the firm, as expected, in 1922 on his call and admission. The name of the firm was changed to Raymond, Honsberger and Munnoch. However, when business continued to decline, Munnoch told his partners in 1925 that, as the income of the firm was not enough to support all of them, he, as the junior, would drop out. He went shortly thereafter to another Toronto firm, and then joined the legal department of the Bell Telephone Company in Montreal. He became its general counsel and was a vice-president at the time of his retirement in the 1950s. Munnoch was a very good lawyer, and one can speculate about the effect he might have had on the firm if he could have stayed on.

In 1925, on the resignation of Munnoch, the firm was reduced to Raymond and Honsberger. The name was changed to Raymond & Honsberger, which continues in use more than seventy years later. There is only one other firm in the city with an older name.[32] W.B. Raymond and H. Stanley Honsberger would be the only partners of the firm for the next twenty-five years. Raymond was sixty-five at the time, and Honsberger thirty-six.

The principal effort of the firm during the 1920s was to reorganize and down-scale to a size that could provide a living to its partners. A decade later, all of its efforts would be devoted to merely surviving.

The firm worked its way slowly out of the recession of the 1920s. It had experience in this, having gone through the economic crises of the 1890s, 1900, 1907, and 1913–14 and the downward turn each time in the business cycle. Sometimes there was a rosy side to these recessions. The Bankruptcy Act, for example, was legislated in 1919 and, as a result, the firm attracted some insolvency work in the recession of 1920.

The practice of the firm was slowly rebuilt. Raymond maintained his reputation in corporate and commercial work. During this time he continued to do some Union Bank work, including litigation. He also did some arbitration and opinion work. Moving into his late sixties, he began to receive more estate work on the death of friends and acquaintances. Although all was not rosy with the practice, Raymond probably enjoyed his work at this time more than at any other time in his career. He had time to enjoy a number of activities within and without the profession. He wrote a few articles and case comments which were published in the *Canadian Law Times* and the *Journal of the Canadian Bankers Association*. He had a poem published in the *Canadian Bar Review*. His studies in ancient Greek proved personally rewarding. He enjoyed the English *fin de siècle* and later literary magazines such as the *Yellow Book*, *The Chap Book*, and the *Philistine*,[33] to all of which he subscribed.

Honsberger was handling most of the conveyancing for the firm. This was work that he was beginning to attract as his friends and acquaintances married, established themselves, and bought homes. He also began to take over from Raymond the agency business of the firm. Notwithstanding that the firm was open for business for five and a half days a week, he found time to be with his wife and family to the extent that a heavier work schedule would not have permitted.

By the end of the 1920s, the firm's practice was predominantly general, and its clients mainly individuals and small corporations. The practice consisted of conveyancing; estates and wills; mortgages; landlord and tenant; some general corporate and commercial, including collections; agency work; and most of the litigation needed by its clients. The economy had largely recovered by 1926, and the firm was doing reasonably well. However, it did not have long to enjoy the new prosperity before the Depression.

The Depression of the 1930s was 'great' in terms not just of its severity but also of its duration.[34] Almost one-third of Canada's labour force was unemployed in 1932–3, gross national income was little more than one-half of the 1929 level, and one in five Canadians became dependent upon government relief.[35] Recovery was slow and incomplete until the war began in 1939.[36]

Fees plummeted in 1930 and continued downward for some years afterwards. It has been said that 1932 and 1933 were the worst years of the Depression.[37] However, the depth of the Depression as far as the firm was concerned was 1936. In that year the income of the firm for the year had declined to $2,372.90. The expenses were $780.00 rent, $825.00 salary for a single secretary, $142.00 telephone, and $349.07 for sundries, leaving $290.00 for distribution between Raymond and Honsberger, who each received $145.00 for the year. The two together took home less than one-half of what their only secretary received. The distribution was almost doubled in 1937, to $275.00 to each of the partners, and almost doubled again in 1938 to $525.00. In 1940 each partner received $925.00. For a decade each member of the firm received less than $1,000.00 per annum.

The Raymond period might be said to have ended in 1935. At that time Raymond was seventy-five, and his health was not good. He had less energy and was working fewer hours. Honsberger had taken over the effective management of the firm. He was forty-six at the time and had been practising for seventeen years. In addition to the constant worry over making ends meet in the office, he had much to worry about in his personal life. His wife, after giving birth to their third child in 1926, contracted an infection and was hospitalized for five years. He had his hands more than full looking after three small children and making weekly visits to a sick wife some distance away.

Practising in the 1930s was hard and heartbreaking. Honsberger would later recall that

income practically disappeared. At the end of the month you were fortunate if you had enough to pay the rent, the telephone and the salary of the one stenographer. For three consecutive years I drew less than $400.00 on which to keep a family. I don't know how we lived. Somehow a few years before I had purchased a $1,000.00 bond. I sold this. Then I borrowed all I could on my life insurance and finally borrowed $800.00 to $1,200.00 from father.

It was pretty discouraging working hard every day and doing little more than paying the overhead and I was busy. Because of the Depression our clients always seemed to be in trouble, and yet I knew all the time that they would not be able to pay my bills. I was not paid for 75% of the work I did during this period.

I considered giving up the office and trying to practice at my home without a secretary or giving up law and trying to get a job with a trust or insurance company.

My three standbys were Mr. Bustard, Louis Bruno and Hochman.[38] They seemed to be continually in my office and quite often met there. Louis Bruno referred to them as 'The Three Musketeers.' They provided a lot of work, but practically no money.

However, I was not prepared to admit that I was a failure at my chosen profession. I hung on and ultimately conditions improved. But, it was a long haul ...

A letter from Raymond to his broker in January 1934 gives another description of what it was like to practise in the depth of the Depression. His broker had written him to say:

We have not had a payment against your account for some considerable time. The debit balance is $2,060.95.

It was very fortunate the Union Trust was sold when it was.

We would be very glad to hear from you what the situation is and if we may expect a payment in the near future.

Raymond replied in a letter dated 10 January 1934:

Dear Sirs:–
I this morning have received your letter of yesterday (not dated) asking as to the situation and expectation of payment. You are quite entitled to the courtesy of a full answer. I have no property or means at present. My total earnings for 1931 were $296.67; for 1932 $772.00; and 1933 may show something like the latter. What 1934 may bring forth no one knows. How have I lived since 1929 when I lost every cent of savings as well as paper profits in the account of which you are aware? The answer is my wife has borrowed on a small policy she holds on my life; she sold one or two odds and ends of stuff she had under marriage settlement, and a relative has lent the rest without security. We have had no servant in our apartment for three years.

Having, fortunately, good health, I am at my office from 9 a.m. every day. We are busy, but at what is small business, in keeping with the experience of many during late years, and what we earn goes in what business houses call overhead, except what I have stated as distributed. Any increase in exports and imports, textile and other business (I hope also Brokerage business) has not yet had any effect on smaller law firms. Real estate transactions, sales, mortgage loans, building operations, corporation formations, are still at a standstill as you probably know, and loan and trust companies, insurance companies and other monied sources have not 'loosened up.' The Moratorium Act is partly responsible because lenders are restricted in ordinary rights of recovery of their loans.

I trust this will be intelligible to you, and I should like it to be treated as confidential because it does not do any good with the public to put on a 'poor face.'
Obliging

Yours faithfully,

Raymond, the good lawyer that he was, is seen by the following handwritten endorsement he wrote to his copy of the above letter:

Note on the above. As is apparent there is no acknowledgment in the above of the debt claimed.
W.B.R.

He well knew that, if he was careless enough to acknowledge the debt, the limitation period for suing on the debt would recommence from the date of the acknowledgment, and the time that had already passed would not apply to the time needed to bar the enforcement of the debt.

The firm, like most other tenants in the office building, fell behind in its rent. The landlord was very good, however. It took no action to enforce its rent, but, for several years, until the early years of the Second World War, the firm paid $10 to $15 extra each month with its rent to be applied against the arrears. Merely to stay in business was in itself an achievement. The cellar of the office building was full of furniture abandoned by tenants who could no longer hold out.

Much ingenuity was required to survive. On one occasion Honsberger brought home several live chickens in his car from a visit to a client in the country who gave them to him on account of his bill. On another occasion a client of Honsberger's who owned a little block of stores and walk-up apartments on north Yonge Street offered to have a tenant of his who was a tailor make Honsberger a suit which Honsberger would apply against his bill to the client, who in turn would deduct the value of the suit from the arrears of rent the tenant owed the client. Honsberger refused the offer unless Raymond also received a suit. This was arranged, and double the amount was deducted from the amount owed by the client to the firm and by the tenant of the client to the client. Most important, however, both Honsberger and Raymond received much better suits than either could have hoped to have bought at the time. Both incidents indicate the extent to which people resorted to barter during the Depression when so little money was available. It was like much of Continental Europe at the end of the Second World War.

All lawyers at the time were more or less in the same position. Honsberger once said that, little as he got from the firm, at least he did not have to pay anything into the office to make up the overhead, as the partners of some firms were obliged to do. A friend and fellow lawyer, Joseph Hilley, was forced to give up wearing underwear and was working at night as a supervisor of city playgrounds to get by. Still another lawyer, Keiller Mackay, who had offices in the same building and who went on to a distinguished career on the bench and as lieutenant-governor of the province, was able to ignore a hole in his trousers painfully visible to everyone else.

It helped to have a strong faith, a measure of humour, and infinite fortitude. At least some consolation could be obtained by the knowledge that one had company in misery. Thirty per cent of the labour force was unemployed. More than 15 per cent of the population was on relief.[39]

Business began to improve, but very slowly. It was a 'long haul,' as Honsberger said. By the beginning of the Second World War, Raymond, who was eighty years old, started to go home at noon, and then stopped coming down entirely. A short time earlier, Honsberger had been told that he could have a County Court judgeship. He refused. He did not like the thought of winding-up the firm, as Raymond could not carry it on alone. Moreover, Raymond needed the income, small as it was. There was no question about it. One looked after one's own.

THE FAMILY FIRM, 1945–1965

During the war, Honsberger's two sons, John and Hugh, indicated that they intended to go into law. John was in the army with the anti-tank artillery. Hugh was in the navy in the fleet air arm. Although Honsberger was essentially alone in the office during the war, with Raymond for the most part retired, and the firm was becoming busier, he held off taking on a junior to help him. The result was that, for him, the 1940s were perhaps his busiest years, when he was carrying the firm by himself and keeping space for his two sons, assuming they returned from the war and followed through with their intention to go into law.

Raymond saw the end of the war but died that fall, in November 1945 at age eighty-five. John and Hugh Honsberger returned, took their discharges and accelerated arts degrees, and then attended law school. They were called to the bar and admitted as solicitors, and joined the firm in 1950. It had become a family firm after sixty years, and was to remain one for more than a generation. It could have been a different family firm if either DuVernet or Raymond had had children. DuVernet had none, to his regret; Raymond had one, a son, who died in infancy. However, once the firm did become a family operation, it was a powerful source for the transmission of the firm culture. It also had the effect of stabilizing the firm's need for new lawyers for some years.

The decision to triple the size of the firm in one step was a venture in faith. Would the practice support three members? Surprisingly, it did. The firm billed in 1950 almost 50 per cent more than it had in 1949, not-withstanding the fact that the Honsberger boys brought no business to the firm during that year. Times, however, were prosperous. The country was still in the midst of catching-up in the supply of needs and services suspended during wartime. The demand for housing was particularly acute. Subdivision after subdivision was opened up in the fields of Etobi-coke, North York, and Scarborough. The construction industry boomed. This brought considerable conveyancing and small-company and com-mercial work to the office. There was a significant increase in the demand for all legal services during the 1950s, and it was a good time to enter the profession.

Profits of the new firm were, from the beginning, distributed equally among the three partners. Honsberger, Sr, with his experience during the Depression, knew that there could be a considerable fluctuation in the firm's income. As he used to say, 'You can always live on less, but it takes a little time to make the downward adjustment and it helps to have a reg-ular income, no matter how small.' It was for this reason that he proposed in 1950 not to distribute all profits and to build up a reserve account. It could ensure regular distribution of profits to members and cushion any necessary reduction in distributions. The reserve account and its method of capitalizing the firm were to continue for thirty-five years or more.

The monthly distribution to the partners of the firm for the last six months of 1950, the period immediately after John and Hugh joined, was $150. The going rate for first-year lawyers at the time was between $125 and $200 per month. This was, accordingly, quite a reasonable arrange-ment for the two junior partners. It was, on the surface, not so reasonable for the senior partner. He, however, had a large measure of unselfishness and, in his personal and professional life, was governed by consider-ations other than those of personal advantage. He recognized, too, that both in the profession and in a partnership in law, as has been said, one looked after one's own. His role model had been W.B. Raymond. That of the Honsberger boys was their father.

When Honsberger, Sr, was a junior member of the firm with a young family, Raymond would insist on his taking a greater share of the firm's profits than that to which he was strictly entitled. In the last few years of Raymond's life, when he could not work full-time, Honsberger insisted that Raymond receive more than he earned because he needed it, having used most of his savings during the Depression. It was only natural that Honsberger should insist that he and his two sons share equally the income of the new firm. He was acting as much from parental concern as from professional responsibility. Both Honsberger and Raymond were professionals of the old school. Both were gentlemen.

One-third or more of the practice of the firm in 1950 was conveyancing, as a result of a construction boom to meet the postwar demand for housing. Several of Honsberger's tradesmen clients, such as bricklayers and carpenters, who were mostly post–First World War immigrants from such places as Italy, Poland, and Ukraine, made the leap and became builders overnight. Some of them became quite large and built seventy-five to a hundred houses a year. A few of them became land developers. They bought farm land in the suburbs, subdivided and serviced it, and then built upon it. There was, too, all the work of a general practice. Rent-control regulations enacted during the war still existed, but they were becoming less stringent. They were complex and difficult to interpret and contained many traps for the unwary. They were, however, a source of some business for the firm, and this was an area in which it developed some competence. A few solicitors who were not prepared to take the time to understand these regulations referred their work to the firm. The regulations and controls were soon phased out and became another example of the depreciation of knowledge and expertise and the need to find new sources of work as former sources disappeared or when excess competition in some areas made the work uneconomical.

The non-British first-generation European immigrant clients had first come into the office in the 1930s and 1940s. Many of them became valued clients in the 1950s and 1960s. They changed the almost-exclusively British background of the clients up to that time. As time went on, the clients became increasingly multiracial, reflecting the changing population of the city. A number of Japanese who had lived in British Columbia and were interned during the war before being moved into central Canada by the government became clients during and shortly after the war. They were followed by a number of German, Dutch, and Central Europeans, who were a part of the postwar immigration to the country. The 1980s and 1990s brought many new clients, who more often than not were refugees rather than immigrants, from Bangladesh, Pakistan, China, and several African countries.

The 1960s was the time that Honsberger, Senior, as he became known in the firm (along with 'Mr John' and 'Mr Hugh') most enjoyed his practice. For the first time in years, he had no financial pressures. His children were educated. He had a nice home and a large garden. He was persuaded by his neighbours to stand for election to the municipal council for the Township of North York. He was elected, and thereafter received acclamations for several elections. When he retired he was a member of the Committee of Adjustment for many years. He received the same satisfaction in representing his neighbours as he did his clients.

His clients were both his practice and his pride. He always had time for all of them. They sought his advice and counsel in both legal and personal matters. His clients were his friends. He and they respected each other. He attended the weddings of their children. He attended many of their funerals and was the executor of their wills. Honsberger enjoyed the practice that a small firm permitted. It provided him with independence, and ultimately financial security. His practice provided what his clients wanted and he continued and reinforced the tradition of the small firm.

The years during which Honsberger Senior managed the firm were from the early 1930s, when he largely took over from Raymond, until the early 1960s when the Honsberger boys largely took over from him. In 1960, Honsberger, Senior, was seventy-one, John was thirty-seven, and Hugh thirty-five.

The Honsberger boys, by temperament, fitted into a small firm. Neither one considered joining another firm. They, like their father before them, came to appreciate the advantages of the independence such a firm offered. It gave them a much-valued control over their working life, which meant much to them. A diverse client base, made up primarily of small clients, was an advantage in this regard. The independence it permitted gave time for other activities not strictly related to the practice.

John and Hugh Honsberger started off in practice doing much as they had done as students. Both of them had taken on the work of different clients. Gradually, as the clients became accustomed to one or another doing their work, new business began to go to each of them directly. It was a slow and gradual division of clients, which they largely accepted, as the elder Honsberger was always in the background and available if needed.

In the early 1950s approximately 30 to 40 per cent of the fees of the firm related in some way to conveyancing. In time, however, each of the younger Honsbergers began to develop areas of specialization prompted by his interests and by economic changes.

Hugh Honsberger became interested in criminal law and began to build a practice in this branch. By the end of his first decade with the firm, perhaps 15 to 20 per cent of his practice was devoted to criminal work, and the proportion was to increase. And this was a time before there was legal aid. For several years he acted as a special federal Crown attorney in prosecuting drug offences. This type of practice fitted well into a small firm.

John Honsberger was more interested in civil litigation. In time he built a modest practice in this area, handling most of the civil litigation for the firm and referrals from other firms. For a few years he was a reporter to the editor of the *Ontario Reports*. This required his attendance a few hours a day for a couple of weeks a month in the Court of Appeal, taking notes of the argument of counsel. The experience was valuable and interesting. But it was the type of work that one would not expect a large firm to permit, for the remuneration was fixed at $30 a day or $15 for a half-day.

The professional interests of John Honsberger would take him on several 'frolics of his own' along the less-trodden paths of the profession. He did considerable writing. He completed a book on real property started by Mr Justice Anger, who died while writing the first part of the book. He contributed a number of small columns for *Chitty's Law Journal* and a few case comments and book reviews for the *Canadian Bar Review* and other journals. This ultimately led to his appointment as the editor, and thus far the only editor, of the *Law Society of Upper Canada Gazette*, which is personally satisfying, takes a reasonable amount of time, and brings very little money into the office. It is again an example of an interest that seems to be accommodated better in a small firm.

The incident that had the greatest effect on John Honsberger's professional life was when Lewis Duncan, whose office was in the same building in which the firm had its offices, asked him to write a third edition of his book, *Bankruptcy in Canada*. Shortly after it was published, Honsberger was appointed to a federal Study Committee on Bankruptcy and Insolvency. Thereafter his principal interest in law was bankruptcy and insolvency.

John Honsberger became a school trustee for a number of years, as well as a trustee of the County of York Law Association, and eventually its president. He and his brother became involved in the early informal legal-aid scheme, where a panel of lawyers met Monday nights in Sheriff Conover's office to give advice to those in need. When the new Ontario Legal Aid Plan came into existence in 1966, John Honsberger was appointed to be an original member of the York County Legal Aid Plan Area Committee, and still is a member. The firm had had a long involvement in legal aid before the term was coined.[40] Jones, with his interest in boys' work, had run his own legal-aid program for them. When he became a police magistrate, he was one of the earliest proponents of an organized system of legal aid.[41] Raymond had a long connection with the Toronto Children's Aid Society, serving for a time as a director. Whenever any of its wards got into trouble with the criminal side of the law, they were referred to him or the firm, and their cases were handled without cost. This continued until the legal-aid plan was established. There was, however, some compensation to the firm: Whenever someone left a bequest to the Children's Aid Society, the Society would ask the firm to attend at the passing of the accounts of the testator's estate, which usually resulted in a small fee being awarded to the firm.

John Honsberger's interests have been diverse and as wide or wider than those of any other member of the firm. They, however, have been more focused on the law than other interests or activities. The law has been his hobby. While many of his interests were after-hours activities, many were not. Even the time devoted to them outside of the office restricted the amount of after-hours office work. The extramural work often could represent, over an extended period of time, at least 10 to 15 per cent of John Honsberger's time; during his work on the Bankruptcy and Insolvency Study Committee, he was in Ottawa for two days a week for almost four years, at a very nominal *per diem* fee. It demonstrates, however, one aspect of practising in a small firm, where this type of activity was possible if not encouraged, provided one carried a reasonable share of the work of the firm. There was, of course, a financial price to pay. 'Time is money,' said Benjamin Franklin. One's earnings were not comparable to those achievable by working exclusively on firm business in order to bill the 1,500 or more hours per annum that are often required in larger firms.

The practice of the firm grew steadily during the 1950s. This was encouraged by the booming economy that produced not only new wealth, but new legal business. In a matter of only a few years, a one-man practice had grown into a busy three-man practice with almost more work than it could do.

It continued to be a general practice. The increasing strength of the firm was the number of small clients that Honsberger, Senior, had attracted and nursed along in the 1930s and 1940s. They represented the changing racial origin of the citizens of the city: Poles, Ukrainians, Japanese, Italians, and some from the Middle East. There was a similar cross-section of religions, from Roman Catholics to Jews, to Buddhists. It seems strange now to describe the clients this way, as one would not think of doing so today, but it does show the contrast between them and the primarily British clientele of the firm until after the First World War. These changes would be reflected later in the composition of the firm itself.

As so often had happened, by the end of the 1950s the firm had too much work for its three members. Honsberger, Senior, turned seventy in 1959. He had not slackened in the amount of work he did, but clearly the firm needed to prepare for his eventual retirement.

Commencing in 1958, the firm took on three young solicitors, one after the other; after staying on for only a year or two, all of them moved out of the city or to other offices, where they thought that they would get the business that they would like to do. Interestingly, none of them joined larger firms. Siegfrid Quickert changed the pattern. He came to the firm in 1965 and remained with it for several years. He had been born in East Germany, and, as a young boy, after the war had emigrated with his family to Canada, where he received most of his education. Quickert's coming to the firm indicated the extent of the change in the ethnic origin of the population of the city at the time and its acceptance as a fact. It also indicated the change in the composition of Toronto law firms that was beginning to appear. They were no longer based upon race, religion, and politics, or a combination thereof. Quickert was the first non-British member of the firm,[42] and the first of its members who had not been born in Canada. The firm at that point had been in existence for a little over seventy-five years.

THE LARGE SMALL FIRM, 1965–1989

Quickert's joining the firm was also indicative of an awareness that, if the firm was to continue to thrive, it had to reach out for clients to the increasing number of new Canadians in the city. This, too, was one response to economic change which a small firm is sometimes able to do quicker, if not better, than is a large firm. The admission of Siegfrid Quickert to the firm made its membership automatically one-quarter new Canadian and it was able to do business in another language. Significantly, too, in hiring

Quickert, the firm was making a decisive shift away from its character as a family firm, laying the groundwork for future expansion.

The trend away from the family-based firm accelerated when Hugh Honsberger was appointed to the bench of the County Court of the County of York in summer 1970. He replaced His Honour Judge Ian Macdonnel, who was a son of A. McLean Macdonnel, a founding partner of the firm. The departure of Hugh Honsberger caused some disruption. Fully one-half his practice was litigation, and most of that was criminal work. The firm lost all of his criminal work as there was no one to take it over. It lost, too, much of the larger civil-litigation practice he was handling at the time of his appointment.

The firm was in little doubt but that it should replace Honsberger immediately. R. Browning Watt, just out of law school, was invited to join the firm. In time he showed a special interest in estate work. Increasingly, his practice was confined to this area of law, creating for the firm what in effect was a small department or area of specialization. It is an example that was to repeat itself in the future; often lawyers joined the firm at an early stage of their careers, when they had no strong feelings concerning the area of law that interested them the most. For the most part, the firm, to the extent that there was business available, generally has been flexible enough to accommodate a range of diverse interests, depending upon the inclinations and capabilities of its members.

It is an indication of the prosperity of the 1970s that it was not long after Roly Watt joined to replace Hugh Honsberger that the firm again found that it had more work than it could handle comfortably while simultaneously providing good service to the clients. It began to look for a new member.

Aline C. Grenon joined the firm in 1974. She had just been called to the bar and admitted as a solicitor. She was from an old Quebec family, although her parents had moved to northern Ontario on their marriage. Mme Grenon was the first, and thus far the only French-Canadian member of the firm, as well as being the first woman member. Her coming to the firm indicated in a small way the increasing number of women in the profession. The firm had not, however, decided that it should hire a woman and then looked for one. The short list of five applicants contained three women. This would not have been the case even a few years before. The firm was drawn to admit Aline Grenon, not because she was a woman, but because she was the best-qualified and most suitable of the applicants.

The first warning signs that the firm might have to be prepared to respond to a changing business climate came in the mid-1970s. The office overhead began to increase faster than fees billed and collected. Salaries increased annually. Manual typewriters were replaced by electric typewriters, and then memory typewriters. Computers followed. There were a series of photocopy machines, progressing from 'wet' to 'dry' methods, and adding-machines were replaced by calculators. There were then 'one-write' systems of bookkeeping, later to be replaced by computers. 'Cash flow' became a new and important term in reference to the business of the firm. During the postwar years, one did one's work and sent out bills, which were paid more or less on receipt. There were few bad debts and little was written off, usually not more than 1 per cent of fees rendered. Occasionally, there was a shortage of cash. This required a cessation in one's normal work for a day or two to get up to date in sending out accounts for work done but not billed. It was a satisfying way to practise. The office more or less ran by itself. There was no great time needed for the business side. All of that was to change.

Rampant double-digit inflation led to the federal government enacting the Anti-Inflation Act in fall 1975, which introduced wage and price controls. One effect of the controls was to force the firm to be more businesslike and productive. However, one had to work harder to stand still. An office day from 9:00 A.M. to 5:30 P.M. with only two or three billable hours was not enough. The Anti-Inflation Act did not restrict the work one took on, only the amount one charged. The need to be more productive could erode and depersonalize the traditional solicitor–client relationship, even in small firms.

Change remained constant. Siegfrid Quickert left the firm after some years to work in a family business. Aline Grenon left shortly afterwards to take a doctoral course in international commercial law in France. And, a little later, Stanley Honsberger died in 1979, in his ninety-first year.

There was no hesitancy on the part of the firm about replacing Quickert and Grenon. It was not a coincidence that Quickert was replaced by Philipp Straub, who, like Quickert, had been born in Germany and had emigrated to Canada with his parents as a young child. Aline Grenon was replaced by Harriet Lewis.[43] She had been in practice for a couple of years in a larger firm. She chose to leave it as she felt that she would be more comfortable in a small firm. She was the second woman lawyer to be made a member, and the first who was of the Jewish faith. When the firm invited Harriet Lewis to join, it was not to replace one woman member with another. She was the best of those who had applied.

The recession of the early 1980s had an impact upon the firm which resulted in part in another change of direction. There was a significant falling-off in the demand for discretionary legal services. Houses were not being built or sold. There was little lending activity. Commercial work in general declined substantially.

The one area of law that thrived was insolvency work. Here, the firm was well positioned. John Honsberger had continued his interest in the area since working on the Bankruptcy and Insolvency Committee. He had also worked on another study committee, examining the possibility of a federal securities commission. He had participated in the negotiation of a bankruptcy treaty between Canada and the United States, and had done considerable writing on the subject. This resulted, at the time, in little return to the firm. The *per diem* fees for the government work were low; the writing brought in nothing; and there had been very little bankruptcy work in the prosperous 1970s. The important benefit for the firm, however, was that it brought the firm, and particularly Honsberger, recognition as an authority in the area, notably in the United States.

The insolvency work of the firm in the early 1980s flourished, and indeed was a life-saver. Almost 70 per cent of its total fees rendered for a couple of years came from this comparatively new area of its practice. The work, for the most part, was confined to some of the larger insolvencies of the time, which frequently involved subsidiaries of American corporations and often were a part of larger proceedings involving subsidiaries in several countries. There were, in addition to the insolvency proceedings that were actually commenced, other insolvencies that were resolved through successful and often last-minute work-outs with lenders. They, however, required extensive and secret contingency plans and preparations on an international scale, which were to be used only as a last resort if negotiations with lenders failed.

The early 1980s, notwithstanding the insolvency work, were critical times for the firm. Cash flow was uneven, and the overhead did not go down, as it takes some time for this to happen. In the meantime, 'those who do not remember their past are condemned to repeat it.'[44] The firm, however, did have advantage of its history. Stories of experiences of the Great Depression had been handed down, and they gave some feeling as to what should be avoided and what should be done. Essentially, the decision the firm took was to bunker down, avoid all non-essential expenditures, and keep out of debt.

However, after some time, the firm came to the conclusion that it could not continue to survive for any appreciable length of time as it was then constituted. There was increasing evidence that the time was passing for a too-small downtown law firm. Firm after firm of this type was disappearing. In some cases, firms dissolved when their leases came to an end. Many more small firms merged with large firms. It was a time when large firms became larger and many small firms vanished.

There were two acceptable choices for the firm: to merge or to grow larger. In the end the decision was made to rebuild by expanding to a large small firm of ten to fifteen members. In a period of the five years, from 1983 to 1989, the firm grew from four to twelve members. This growth created a new chemistry and a different distribution of the firm's practice.

The new members brought new capabilities and new interests and, in some cases, brought with them their own practices, which were merged with that of the firm. It was a far cry from the male, White, British earlier members, who were all Anglican in religion and Conservative in politics. A new woman member and recruits born in England, Ireland, Germany, and Romania joined the firm. Their religion and politics were their own affair. The firm represented the multiracial background of the city, and its proportion of women members was not far from that in the entire profession.

As the firm grew to a large small firm, it functioned and had to be administered differently. Size brought new concerns, but, for the most part, expansion simply increased the size of the organizational needs and requirements that always existed. There was, however, some benefit derived from the economy of size, but it became increasingly necessary to be more efficient and cost conscious. A large small firm is and has to be different from a small firm. They are not the same. There remained, however, the same emphasis and interplay between professionalism and independence and a capacity to accommodate the different interests and capabilities of its members.

In 1989 the firm celebrated its centennial by holding a dinner in Osgoode Hall at which members of the firm, former members, older clients, and friends attended. It had entered its second century.

CONCLUSION

The firm, as has been seen, has had a long history of change. It constantly has had to reinvent itself.[45] It has had to adjust its practice to reflect economic changes, the needs of its clients, and the changing interests of its members. Throughout, it remained small, although not what might be called the classic small firm of the solo practitioner or a partnership of two or three who find an advantage in working together. Very often, however, it was found that, 'given a certain critical mass of business, the work of the barrister and the ... solicitor could be split between partners and, by their combined activities, each generating work for the other, profits could be attained which equalled more than the sum of their individual contributions.'[46] That was close to the original organization of the firm. DuVernet wanted the support he needed as a barrister and for someone to run the office. Jones was happy to do this. They worked well together.

The organization of the firm changed towards a system that could better handle the increased solicitors' work that came with DuVernet's business ventures. If he had lived longer, he and Raymond might have set the firm on a course that would have led it to expansion, like other firms at the time. However, with the crash of DuVernet's business empire and with the impact it had on the firm, the DuVernet legacy, whereby the firm relied excessively on a few large clients for business, was repudiated. The firm sought, instead, a more diversified clientele. For many years afterwards, the firm was built around the individual practices of its members, where accommodations were made based upon needs, age, health, and interests inside and outside the office. By the 1960s the organization of the firm again began to reflect a degree of specialization on the part of some of its members. In the mid-1980s, the firm was specializing to some extent in a variety of areas, such as insolvency, litigation, corporate and commercial work, wills and estates, and conveyancing. It began to expand at this time and, by its centennial, had twelve members. It had become a large small firm.

The stimuli that prompted the firm over the years to change direction, to grow or not to grow, were many. In the 1890s, the firm was primarily oriented to litigation arising out of such legislation as the Liquor Licence Act and Canada Temperance Act. The expanding economy of the country between 1906 and 1915 prompted the firm to become more business-oriented. The Depression in the early 1920s found the firm doing collection work and handling smaller business matters, and relying more on supplying the needs of individuals for personal legal services. The firm was severely tested during the Great Depression. The Wartime Price Regulations and rent controls brought some work to the firm during the Second World War and shortly afterwards. This was followed by the housing boom in the 1950s, when builders became important clients, and mortgage and conveyancing work represented a significant source of income. Organized legal aid had its impact upon the firm, starting in the

1960s, but this was not so great as upon other firms. Changing social attitudes towards marriage and divorce brought to the firm an increasing amount of family-law work, starting in the 1960s and 1970s. The recession in the early 1980s found the firm well placed to handle insolvencies affecting large businesses. Litigation once more became important as it was affected less by the recession. As the recession continued into the end of the 1980s, insolvency work became less important to the firm owing to increased competition caused by almost every firm of any size developing an insolvency group. It was at this time that the firm began to do considerable refugee and immigration work. It became a new area of specialization and, within a year or two, produced more fees than those from its insolvency work.

The firm has changed direction so often primarily to find new business and to respond to new needs in the community. The practice of law provides a service. Needs for service constantly must be identified, and firms must be prepared to respond quickly to the changing needs.

The nature of the practice of the firm, its culture, and its reputation have been influenced by its size. Size, however, is something like the 'chicken and the egg' riddle. Which came first? It could be said that the firm was small because it chose to be small. It could also be said that, because of the nature of its practice and the interests of its members, it has had to be small. Firms that supply legal services to individual clients are generally small, as there is not the same need to become large in order to better provide those services and there are not the same benefits to be gained by a larger size. Most clients for legal services are individuals, and they generally seek the small firm to supply them, in part because larger firms are not well equipped nor do they want to meet their needs. The great majority of all firms are small.[47] Firms that supply legal services to corporations are larger by the necessity of providing more complex and wider-ranging services. The needs of task specialization, with the resulting diversification of investment in human capital needed to supply the necessary services, coupled with the economic benefit of spreading such fixed costs as those of large libraries, word-processing, and support personnel, require the base that only a larger firm can supply.[48] Thus, the size of the firm has been largely dictated by the fact the great majority of its clients are individuals and its practice is designed to meet their needs.

The culture of the firm is, too, largely what it is by reason of its size. A firm's culture is created generally through the personalities of its members, how they believe law should be practised, and years of shared professional and personal successes and disappointments of lawyers working closely together in condition of intimacy and collegiality. This can be seen particularly in the relationship between W.B. Raymond and H. Stanley Honsberger. Their association began when Honsberger joined the firm as an articling student in 1914 and ended when Raymond died in 1945. The culture they created was largely maintained by, and was transmitted as a result of, its slow growth. Others have taken the place of Raymond and of Honsberger in the firm, but their mantles have been taken too. New members bear the same impressed stamp of office personality. The advice they give is more often than not the advice that W.B. Raymond and H. Stanley Honsberger would have given,[49] although the writer is the only present member of the firm who knew either one of them. Large firms, particularly rapidly expanding ones, have more difficulty in establishing a unique culture and, when established, preventing it from eroding because of a loss of intimacy and collegiality.[50] There is the added difficulty when two firms with different cultures merge. The culture of the firm, however, is not a static condition. Every new member creates a new chemistry. The culture of the firm in 1989 is both the same as and different from what it was twenty-five or fifty years ago or longer. The present culture represents a slow, continuous evolution that has been possible by reason of its small size and members who have been with it for some time.

The reputation and good name of any firm consists, in part, in the reputation of the firm itself, and in the reputations of the members that constitute it. The reputation of a firm, to a large extent, is its identity. A good reputation is a special type of capital possessed by a firm. The reputation of a small firm or one that expands slowly is better maintained and more easily transmitted than that of a large firm.

The firm's bias against legal entrepreneurialism over the years encouraged its members to direct their interests and energies in part elsewhere. The result has been that members of the firm have had many outside professional and personal activities. Although professional life today is not so carefree[51] as it was when the firm was organized, the outside interests of members can give a richer life and a satisfaction to the practice of law that cannot be obtained by devoting the whole of a day to practice. Those outside interests, moreover, help to fashion the reputation of the member and of the firm.

The nature of the firm, and its culture and reputation, may be seen by what members of the firm have done or become in the century of its existence. Three members of the firm, for example, became judges; one became a secretary of the Law Society; others have contributed in many ways to the work of the Law Society, Canadian Bar Association, the County of York Law Association, and other professional organizations. Several members have participated in and continue to be involved in the bar-admission course and in lecturing in law schools, in continuing-education courses, and in seminars both within and without the country. Two members left the firm to become full-time law teachers. A member has participated in the work of the Ontario Law Reform Commission, and the revision of bankruptcy and insolvency and other legislation for the federal government. Textbooks have been written by members on constitutional law, real property, bankruptcy, and debt restructuring. Outside of law, members have been involved in the work of municipal councils, school boards, churches, and synagogues; in coaching hockey teams; in choral groups; and work with boys and in the community more generally. Hymnbooks have been revised, books of poetry and songbooks written, as well as a variety of pamphlets on such subjects as wild flowers, mushrooms, ferns, and grasses. One feature of the firm, unusual for its size, is that it has acquired a reputation that extends beyond the city, and indeed the country. In recent years this perhaps has been primarily attributable to its insolvency work, which has led it as far as central European countries which have needed assistance in drafting bankruptcy legislation required after rejecting communism and adopting market economies.

The firm started off with a short lease on life. However, several options for renewal have been exercised. The fact that it has survived is significant in itself. A careful examination may indicate that its past may have revealed the future.[52]

NOTES

The author is grateful to Carol Wilton for encouraging him to write this essay and for the insightful suggestions she made both before and after reading an early draft. From the author's point of view, it was a valuable collaboration between a professional and an amateur historian. Neither one alone could have written this essay.

1 Examples from Britain include J. Slinn. *A History of Freshfields* (London: Freshfields 1984) and, J. Slinn, *Linklaters & Paines: The First One Hundred and Fifty Years* (London: Longman 1987). Contributions from the United States include R.T. Swaine, *The Cravath Firm and Its Predecessors*, 2 vols. (New York: Ad Press

1946 and 1948); Lincoln Caplan, *Scaddon: Power, Money and the Rise of a Legal Empire* (New York: Farrar Straus Geroux 1993); J. Kenneth Lipartito and Joseph A. Pratt, *Baker & Botts in the Development of Modern Houston* (Austin: University of Texas Press 1991). Examples from Canada include Douglas H. Tees, *Chronicles of Ogilvy, Renault 1879–1979* (Montreal: Ogilvy, Renault 1979), and Doug Mitchell, and Judy Slinn, *The History of McMaster Meighen*, (McMaster Meighen, 1989).

2 *L.P.I.C.* (Lawyer Professional Indemnity Co.) *News*, June 1995, and see John Hagan, 'Transitions in the Legal Profession,' *Law Society of Upper Canada Gazette* 27 (1993), at 96, 101, and 102; Elizabeth Bloomfield, 'Lawyers as Members of Urban Business Elites in Southern Ontario' in Carol Wilton, ed., *Essays in the History of Canadian Law*, vol. 4: *Beyond the Law: Lawyers and Business in Canada, 1830 to 1930* (Toronto: The Osgoode Society 1990), 122.

3 See John D. Honsberger, 'E.E.A. DuVernet, K.C.: Lawyer, Capitalist 1866 to 1915,' in Wilton, ed., *Beyond the Law*, 167–200, where DuVernet's career is more fully described.

4 J.M.S. Careless, *Toronto to 1918* (Toronto: Lorimer and National Museums of Canada 1984), table VIII, 262: 'Ethnic Origins of Toronto's Population, 1851–1921'

5 Constance Backhouse, *Petticoats and Prejudice: Women and Law in Nineteenth-Century Canada* (Toronto: The Osgoode Society 1991) 293

6 Hagan, 'Transitions in the Legal Profession,' 94

7 See for example *Regina v. Clarke* (1891), 20 OR 642; *Regina v. Scott* (1891), 20 OR 646; *Regina v. Southwaite* (1892), 21 OR 670; *McGill v. The Licence Com. of Brantford* (1892), 21 OR 665; *Regina v. Davis* (1893), 22 OR 652; *Regina v. Flarman* (1893), 22 OR 445; *Re Dunlop* (1893), 22 OR 22; *Brunker v. Corp of Two of Mariposa* (1893), 22 OR 120 (Local Option Act – DuVernet and Jones were co-counsel); *Huson v. Twp of South Norwich* (1893), 24 SCR 145 (Local Option Act).

8 R.D. Gidney, and W.P.J. Millar, *Professional Gentlemen: The Professions Nineteenth-Century Ontario* (Toronto: University of Toronto Press 1994), 347

9 Philip Carrington, *The Anglican Church in Canada* (Toronto: Collins 1963), 230

10 See John D. Honsberger, *The County of York Law Association: A History of the First Hundred Years, 1885–1985* (County of York Law Association, 1989), 68; James Edmond Jones, 'Legal Aid for the Poor' 9 *Canadian Bar Review* (1934), 271–6.

11 This citation from the *Toronto News* concluded the biography of James Edmond Jones contained in Henry J. Morgan, *Canadian Men & Women of the Time*, 2d ed. (Toronto: Briggs 1912) 592.

12 John Porter, *The Vertical Mosaic* (Toronto: University of Toronto Press 1965), 288

13 An anecdote of George Bernard Shaw, who was always interested in the exploits and conversations of the Duke of Wellington, a fellow countryman, quoted by Osbert Sitwell in *Laughter in the Next Room* (Boston: Little, Brown 1948), 123.

14 John Wilson Croker, *The Croker Papers*, 2d. rev. ed. (London: Murray 1885), vol. 3, 276

15 See Careless, *Toronto to 1918*, 128. See also Michael Bliss, *A Canadian Millionaire: The Life and Business Times of Sir Joseph Flavelle, Bart. 1859–1939* (Toronto: Macmillan of Canada 1979), and Christopher Armstrong and H.V. Nelles, *Monopoly's Moment: The Organization and Regulation of Canadian Utilities, 1830–1930* (Philadelphia: Temple University Press 1986).

16 See Honsberger, 'E.E.A. DuVernet,' 181 ff., where these matters are described in greater detail.

17 Ibid.

18 E.E.A. DuVernet Papers, Public Archives of Ontario (hereinafter PAO)

19 W.B. Raymond came to the firm from McCarthy, Osler, Hoskin and Harcourt, in which he had been the third partner in seniority.

20 E.E.A. DuVernet Papers, PAO, letter to C.C. Marling

21 County of York Law Association, 30th Annual Meeting, 7 February 1916, *Minutes*, vol. 3, 118

22 The membership of the County of York Law Association was 422 at the end of 1918 (33d Annual Meeting, 27 January 1919, ibid., 205). The war-memorial tablet of the association was unveiled in November 1924. It contained the names of forty-one members and law students killed or died on active service. A separate handwritten honour roll in the possession of the association names another forty-seven members who had been in active service and returned (meeting of trustees, 30 September 1921, ibid., 301).

23 John D. Honsberger, 'Robert Michael Willes Chitty,' 28 *Law Society of Upper Canada Gazette* (1994), 79

24 H. Stanley Honsberger was articled to W.D. Gregory for one year before he moved to the DuVernet firm. Honsberger recalls overhearing Gregory one day on the telephone. He was having trouble making himself understood. However, everyone in Gregory's office could hear him shouting, 'W.D. Gregory; W.D., W.D.; D., D., D., Dan, Daniel and the Devil.'

25 On law-firm expansion generally, see Ronald J. Daniels, 'Growing Pains: The Why and How of Law Firm Expansion,' 43 *University of Toronto Law Journal* (1993), 147–206.

26 Léon Blum, in *L'Échelle humaine*, said: 'no government can remain stable in an unstable society and an unstable world.'

27 'And gladly woide he lerne, and gladly teche,' Geoffrey Chaucer (1340?–1400), *Canterbury Tales*, Prologue, 1, 308

28 Peter Wright, 'What Is a "Profession"?' 29 *Canadian Bar Review* (1951), 756
29 W.B. Raymond Papers, PAO
30 Michael Bliss, *Northern Enterprise: Five Centuries of Canadian Business* (Toronto: McClelland and Stewart 1987), 382–4
31 Ibid., 384
32 Osler, Hoskin and Harcourt, which has had the same name since 1923.
33 The *Philistine* was edited by Elbert Hubbard and published by his Roycraft Press, of East Aurora, New York; he unsuccessfully tried to ape the Kelmscott Press of William Morris. Hubbard died in the sinking of the *Lusitania*, as did the *Philistine*.
34 Graham D. Taylor and Peter A. Baskerville, *A Concise History of Business in Canada* (Toronto: Oxford University Press 1994), 371
35 *The Canadian Encyclopedia* (Edmonton: Hurtig 1985), vol. 2, 770
36 Taylor and Baskerville, *A Concise History of Business in Canada*, 371–2
37 Bliss, *Northern Enterprise*, 418
38 R.C. Bustard was of Northern Irish stock. He had been a builder of upscale houses until the Depression came. After that he did a number of things but never recovered his former financial comfort. Louis Bruno was an Italian bricklayer who became a builder of large houses after the war. Nathan Hochman was a Russian Jew who usually had a number of irons in the fire at the same time and ultimately did quite well by becoming a large scrap-metal dealer during the war, when the price for scrap metal was high.
39 *The Canadian Encyclopedia*, Vol. 2, 770
40 'Legal aid,' when legal services are rendered to those who need them but cannot pay, is generally referred to 'pro bono' or 'pro bono publico' in the United States. The term 'pro bono' work has only recently been introduced into Canada.
41 See Jones, 'Legal Aid for the Poor,' 272.
42 The Honsbergers were early Mennonites who often were forced to leave their homes as a result of religious persecution. Thus, it is difficult to know with certainty their original homeland. It is probably The Netherlands, Switzerland, or The Palatinate in Germany, but more likely Switzerland or Germany. A branch of the family emigrated to Pennsylvania in the mid-eighteenth century and then moved to Canada as United Empire Loyalists. Eight generations later, they are more Anglo-Celtic than Pennsylvania 'Dutch' (Deutch).
43 None of the new members of the firm from this point on is mentioned by name in order to maintain a historical emphasis and to avoid any appearance of being promotional.
44 George Santayana, *The Life of Reason*, vol 1, chap. 12
45 See Daniels, 'Growing Pains,' 206, where Sartre is paraphrased saying: 'The Organization, like persons, is constantly in the process of becoming.'

46 Gidney and Millar, *Professional Gentlemen*, 148

47 Hagan, 'Transitions in the Legal Profession'

48 See Daniels, 'Growing Pains,' 152–3.

49 See similar comments of Reginald L. Hine respecting Hawkins & Co. of Hitchin, England, which was established in 1591, making it one of the oldest firms in the country: *Confessions of an Uncommon Attorney* (London: J.M. Dent & Son, 1946) 112.

50 See Daniels, 'Growing Pains,' 177–80.

51 Hine, *Confession of An Uncommon Attorney*, 5: 'Gone are the care-free days when country attorneys, tossing aside all weightier matters of the law would forgather in provincial societies or in private dinner parties, and make merry over the foibles of their clients, or the last howlers of so called learned counsel, e.g. that of Bartte Frere who in a defence-to an action for seduction, seriously set up a plea of "contributory negligence", or the diabolical ingenuity of articled clerks who were wont to propound such posers as this: Sir, does the phrase *en ventre sa mere* mean the same thing as *in loco parentis?* Gone are the days of the market ordinaries, when for two solid hours, one could feed and fraternize with the farmers. Gone are the days when solicitors like Armigel Wade of Hitchen, could post up champagne in their book of petty expenses.'

52 Pierre Teilhard de Chardin (1881–1955), 'Letters from a Traveller': 'The past has revealed to me the structure of the Future.'

13

'A Small United Nations': The Hamilton Firm of Millar, Alexander, Tokiwa, and Isaacs, 1962–1993

PHILIP J. SWORDEN

The legal profession may be headed by the recent emergence of the mega-firm, but the history of the former Hamilton firm of Millar, Alexander, Tokiwa, and Isaacs shows that small law firms can still offer significant leadership to other lawyers. Specifically, this small firm was a leader in addressing the issue of race and the practice of law. It earned itself the title of Hamilton's 'United Nations' law firm, and was one of the first firms to challenge the traditional practice of hiring mostly well-connected, White males. As such, it was an inspiration to other visible minority lawyers who have experienced many difficulties gaining access to Ontario's legal profession.

These difficulties existed for a long time. Perhaps the most notorious early episode involved Delos Rogest Davis, the first Black lawyer to practise in the province.[1] Because of prejudices against his colour, Davis could not obtain articles with another lawyer for many years, and a special act of the legislature was needed to admit him to the Ontario bar in 1886.[2] Women were another early 'visible minority' to the profession, and they too needed a special legislative act to provide for their later admission to the study and practice of law.[3] Chinese Canadians in British Columbia initially were also barred from the legal profession.[4] However, prejudice against visible minorities alone was not their only handicap in becoming lawyers. Many lacked the crucial financial support necessary for university, and then law school. Even after qualifying as lawyers, many were initially excluded from élite Anglo-Celtic law firms in the province by entrenched hiring conventions which in the main favoured White male lawyers with family connections to these firms' partners and clients.[5] Their opportunities to become lawyers have improved with the advent of government multiculturalism policies and affirmative-action hiring programs,[6] but Black law students are still concerned about their difficulties in obtaining articling positions.[7] The same is also true for other visible minorities.[8] As a result, the Law Society of Upper Canada has at last begun to study this problem, recognizing that it might be out of touch with multiracism in contemporary Canadian society.[9] In addition, the Osgoode Society for Canadian Legal History has conducted many oral interviews with older visible-minority lawyers to document their personal recollections in this respect.[10] Further insight about this problem can also be gained from the history of Millar, Alexander, Tokiwa, and Isaacs, a firm that provided leadership in hiring visible-minority lawyers at a time when multiracial law firms were rare. This small Hamilton firm, which existed from 1962 to 1993, comprised four partners who were of Irish, Black, Japanese, and aboriginal Canadian descent, making it a remarkable case-study of lawyers working together successfully regardless of race or colour.

This essay examines the early background of each of the four lawyers who practised in this small multiracial law firm to reveal how it began in 1962, to explain its success in Hamilton, and to assess its general significance to the legal profession. Its beginning and success were strongly linked to the character of its founder, John Millar, but also to important political, social, and economic forces reshaping Canadian society in the post–Second World War era, which together began to change how law was practised in this country. Small law firms, too, have generally been neglected in the literature on law firms, yet they reveal much about the profession – and in this particular instance much about multiracism and practising law. The firm's unique history reveals that small law firms with favourable conditions could exercise a degree of flexibility in relation to race that was then mostly unknown to the larger corporate law firms in Ontario. Its history also provides an example of a law firm that was flexible in terms of the work that it did, taking advantage of the real estate boom in Hamilton in the 1960s. To a great extent, the firm was able to transform what would have been a disadvantage in earlier circumstances – its multiracial character – into an advantage in the context of changing ideas of race in postwar Canadian society.

Lawyers like John Millar, who began this firm in 1962, were in the vanguard of postwar forces that marked a broad transition from a predominantly male and Anglo-Celtic Ontario bar to one that was slowly changing to include more visible minorities and women.[11] Indeed, ever since the first lawyers began practising law in Hamilton, its bar was dominated by older, Anglo-Celtic White males. Such notable Hamilton lawyers as Sir Allan MacNab (1798–1862), Sir Aemilius Irving (1823–1913), Britton Bath Osler (1839–1901), and Sir John Morison Gibson (1842–1929)[12] were at the top of the city's legal profession in talent, prestige, and positions. Along with other Hamilton lawyers such as George Mills (1827–1901), Robert Gage (1840–1918), and Thomas Stinson (1860–1892), and established city firms like Martin & Martin and Lazier & Lazier,[13] these lawyers as a class formed what Michael Katz called, in his study of Hamilton in the mid-nineteenth century, an 'overlapping elite, governing all the major activities within the city.'[14] Hamilton lawyers, for example, held influential positions such as city clerk, member of Parliament, senator, Crown attorney, police magistrate, mayor, and city solicitor. Others were prominent landlords and corporate counsel to city businesses. Most had their offices around downtown Hamilton's Gore Park, close to the city's magnificent Victorian court-house. Many, too, lived comfortably in fine homes in the prime southwest part of the city under Hamilton's 'mountain,' that part of the Niagara Escarpment which stretches along the city's southern side.[15] The Hamilton Thistle Club, Royal Hamilton Yacht Club, Tamahaac Club, Hamilton Club, Armouries, and Hamilton Golf and Country Club were main preserves for these Hamilton lawyers to socialize and conduct business. Some, like city lawyer James Chisholm (1858–1944), for example, centred their lives on their practices and regiments – in Chisholm's case, Hamilton's own 91st Highlanders.[16] In essence the city's legal culture was gentlemanly and patrician, and for a long time a Hamilton lawyer had to be part of this social environment to have any chance of great success practising law in the city.

But this close-knit, Anglo-Celtic Hamilton bar began to change in the decades after the Second World War, when many new lawyers who were neither male nor Anglo-Celtic began to practise there. Many of these new lawyers began 'ethnic' law firms to service the thousands of Eastern European immigrants then coming to Hamilton to work at the city's expanding steel mills.[17] Such immigrants helped convert Hamilton from a predominantly British city before 1900 to one in which, by 1961, only about 59 per cent claimed British origins.[18] These recent immigrants first lived and worked away from the downtown core, also prompting many of these new lawyers to establish law practices in storefront offices and in plazas, where most had a general practice doing legal-aid and real estate work.[19] It was in this transition era that John Millar, as mentioned, began his own practice. However, it is significant that Millar had some key advantages over other new lawyers then beginning to practise law in the city.

The son of a Hamilton policeman, John Sydney Millar was born in the city on 14 August 1928. He attended primary school there, and determined early in his life to receive a good education. In 1941 he enrolled in Hamilton's prestigious Central Collegiate, an old Romanesque-style school building opened in 1897 in the central part of the city.[20] The school attracted many returning war veterans and, among them, Millar encountered his future law partner, Lincoln Alexander. Alexander was an Air Force veteran also hoping to acquire the necessary qualifications to be admitted to university. Although born in Toronto, Alexander had come to Hamilton after the war primarily because his future wife lived in this city, and at Central the two men began a friendship that was to span almost fifty years. Like most other Central graduates in 1946, their first choice for university was McMaster, situated in the city's west end.

McMaster University in 1946 was another scholastic institution then experiencing the effects of returning war veterans. Most of them were extremely conscientious and, because of their recent war experience, were attuned to political and world events in ways that most 'regular' students were not. Campus societies and organizations like the Politics Club and International Relations Club focused on issues that were important to the postwar world.[21] Millar and Alexander both studied history and political economy while at McMaster, which provided them with a formative perspective on postwar problems and concerns that seemed to underlie their respective later careers.

Both men graduated in 1949. The McMaster *Marmor* yearbook noted that Millar had entered McMaster 'with the intention of future study in the field of law.'[22] He accomplished this goal and entered Osgoode Hall Law School that same year.[23] At that time articling was required in a student's third year at Osgoode. Millar undertook his articling with the prominent Hamilton law firm of Gibson, Levy and Inch.[24] This firm was located in the Bank of Commerce building, at the corner of King and James streets in downtown Hamilton. Here Millar worked, doing mainly real estate law, with Donald Cannon, who later became land registrar for the Registry Division of Wentworth. Millar's habit of hard work attracted the attention of noted Hamilton real estate lawyer James Gage, a partner in the nearby firm of Christilaw & Gage. Gage came from an old Hamilton family that had extensive real estate holdings in the city,[25] and Gage recruited Millar to work for him when he graduated from Osgoode in 1953. Faced with the pleasant prospect of being offered a job with the federal government in Ottawa after graduation, a position at $65 a week at Gibson, Levy and Inch, or one at $100 a week with Christilaw & Gage, Millar chose the last.[26]

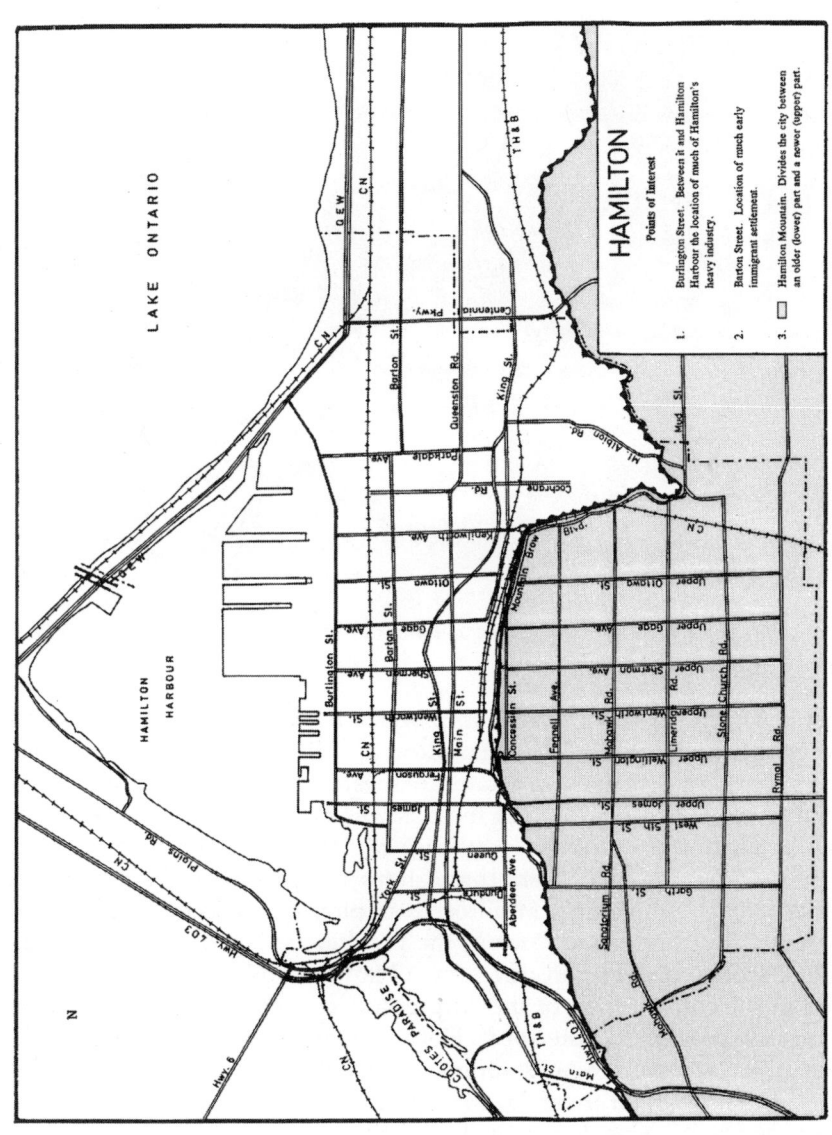

HAMILTON

Points of Interest

1. Burlington Street. Between it and Hamilton Harbour the location of much of Hamilton's heavy industry.

2. Barton Street. Location of much early immigrant settlement.

3. Hamilton Mountain. Divides the city between an older (lower) part and a newer (upper) part.

Courtesy Mills Library, McMaster University. Modified by the author.

Partners (left to right): Peter Isaacs, Paul Tokiwa, Lincoln Alexander, John Millar (courtesy Millar, Alexander)

   This law firm was an impressive place to begin a legal career. One of those established Anglo-Celtic Hamilton law firms, it comprised senior lawyers working primarily in estates, real estate, and corporate and commercial law. At the beginning of the postwar housing boom, it had a tremendous real estate practice, servicing builders, developers, mortgage lenders, and new homeowners throughout Hamilton and its vicinity. It was one of the first firms in Hamilton to employ title searchers.[27] The firm was located on the second floor of the prestigious Victorian-era Canada Life (later Birks) building in downtown Hamilton. No expense had been spared in the construction of this impressive edifice, and imported stone and marble graced its interior.[28] Here, Millar started out as a junior, working for James Gage, and soon developed his own expertise in real estate law. He worked there for nine years, eventually becoming a partner. By 1962 Millar was doing much of the firm's real estate work as Gage was frequently away. Confident that he could do this work on his own, Millar left that year and moved back to the Bank of Commerce building to establish his own practice.

Many lawyers are apprehensive about establishing their own firms. Millar, however, had some important initial advantages over other new Hamilton lawyers. Most important, when he began his new venture as a sole practitioner, he had a secure client base to provide a steady source of work. When he left Christilaw & Gage, many of the builders, mortgage lenders, developers, and clients for whom he had previously done legal work continued to use him as their lawyer.,[29] which was a comment on his competence in this area. Around this same time, Hamilton was continuing to experience a boom in real estate development, primarily as a result of new housing sales on the city's mountain. Millar acquired a substantial part of this market and quickly became deluged with real estate work. As a busy sole practitioner, he had the flexibility to chose and hire a junior lawyer to help him service this clientele. This flexibility, combined with his character and abilities, allowed him to make an auspicious break with past Hamilton law-firm hiring practices, which had long favoured White males. Instead he hired a Japanese-Canadian lawyer newly called to the bar and newly arrived in Hamilton: Paul Yoshiharu Tokiwa.

Paul Tokiwa's background contrasted vividly with Millar's. Tokiwa was born in Ocean Falls, British Columbia, on 24 October 1927. His family was part of the small and segregated Japanese-Canadian community that had settled along the BC coast at the turn of the century. Tokiwa attended school in Ocean Falls until Grade 5, when his parents sent him to Japan in 1939 for a Japanese education. When the Second World War began, Tokiwa was stranded there for the duration, and completed his primary and secondary education in Japan, attending college there for three years, and university for one.[30] He returned to Canada in 1951, not to his home in British Columbia, but to a new one in Toronto, where his family had finally settled after being forced by the Canadian government to leave British Columbia during the war.[31]

Though Tokiwa was out of Canada from 1939 to 1951, the sufferings of Asians in British Columbia before and during the Second World War had a lasting impact on him. In the nineteenth century, the Chinese there had suffered discriminatory legislation such as a head tax on immigration and restrictive legislation on their employment. Both they and the Japanese there were initially disenfranchised by an 1895 provincial act preventing them from voting in provincial elections.[32] This led to the two famous early civil-rights cases: *Union Colliery* v. *Bryden*,[33] challenging provincial legislation forbidding 'Chinamen' working underground in BC coal mines, and *Cunningham* v. *Tomey Homma*,[34] challenging the provincial Elections Act that denied the franchise to Japanese. In both cases the Judicial Committee of the Privy Council refused to consider whether the provincial legislation against Chinese working underground was exercised 'wisely,' and held in determining the franchise issue and naturalization that 'the policy or impolicy of such an enactment as that which excludes a particular race from the franchise is not a topic which their Lordships are entitled to consider.'[35] As a result of these decisions, noted W.S. Tarnopolsky, the Judicial Committee made it 'quite clear from both cases that as long as provincial legislation was not beyond the jurisdiction of the province, it was valid, even though it discriminated on racial or any other grounds.'[36] Even as a child, Tokiwa was well aware of increasing racial intolerance against Japanese Canadians in British Columbia, especially after the Japanese invasion of Manchuria in 1937. Such racial intolerance increased dramatically after Pearl Harbor in 1941.[37] The federal government, acting under the War Measures Act, evacuated most Japanese Canadians then living within one hundred miles of the Pacific coast, relocating them in the interior of British Columbia and elsewhere in Canada under government supervision. More than 21,000 of them (about 90 per cent of the entire Japanese population then living in Canada) were interned in detention camps, their homes and property were confiscated, and their civil rights were violated.[38]

Toronto, the city which became the Tokiwa family's new home, lacked the tradition of virulent anti-oriental racism prevalent in British Columbia, but even there Japanese Canadians experienced racial prejudice. One Japanese Canadian, George Tanaka, recalled later that, when he arrived in Toronto in 1942 to look for a place to live, many times 'the door would be slammed in our face.'[39] The city was, however, the focal point of resettlement and the home of considerable Japanese-Canadian activism.[40] It was headquarters for the Japanese-Canadian Citizens' Association, formed to assist Japanese Canadians with their relocation difficulties. It was also the centre for other Japanese committees, which in time had as their long-range project obtaining compensation from the federal government for war losses, later achieved in 1988 under the Mulroney government.[41] Tokiwa himself was deeply impressed by the value of these ethnic organizations; when he moved from Toronto to Hamilton, he was instrumental in organizing a number of activities there to address the interests of Japanese Canadians, including a major conference in 1977 at McMaster University on the War Measures Act.[42]

After Tokiwa graduated from the University of Toronto in 1954, he obtained a job with the newly opened Japanese consulate in Toronto, mainly on the strength of having both a Japanese and a Canadian education. He worked there for three years, becoming increasingly well known to the growing Japanese-Canadian community in that city. Yet he never forgot the wartime discrimination against his people, and his desire to help remedy this and prevent future civil-rights injustices led him to study law.[43] He attended Osgoode Hall Law School in 1957 as one of its first Japanese-Canadian students, and graduated in 1960.

After graduation, Tokiwa married a Hamilton woman and commuted to Toronto, where he articled with Donald Lamont, QC, the prominent author of a major textbook on real estate law used by many law students and lawyers. Tokiwa intended to practise law in Toronto when he finished articling, but changed his mind when his wife's family was unable to move there. He then had his articles transferred to the Hamilton law firm of O'Leary and Dubeck. Called to the bar in 1962, and still living in Hamilton, he heard that John Millar had recently opened his own law office and was looking for a junior to assist him with his real estate practice. Millar hired him, and Tokiwa became the first Japanese-Canadian lawyer to practise in the city.[44]

Millar was also aware that it would be prudent to have another lawyer at his small firm to practise family, criminal, and motor-vehicle law and do other legal work which neither he nor Tokiwa was inclined to do. As the principal of this small firm, he still had the flexibility to hire anyone. A chance meeting with Lincoln Alexander held the solution to the firm's labour shortage.

Lincoln Alexander was born in Toronto on 21 January 1922. His father came there from St Vincent and the Grenadines, and his mother from Jamaica. During the 1920s, many other West Indians came to Toronto specifically to work on the railways. 'The only job you could get that was set aside primarily for Blacks,' recalled Harry Gairey, who also came to Toronto from the Caribbean in this early period, 'was porter on the railroad.'[45] 'You couldn't go to Eaton's and ask for a job, or to the Bell Telephone,' continued Gairey, and 'it was unheard of to go to a restaurant or a public dance. You wouldn't go there because you knew you weren't welcome.'[46] Blacks too were then often refused service in many restaurants and hotels and received little help in seeking redress over discrimination from the courts.[47] Alexander's father also became a railway porter, and his mother a domestic maid.

When he was sixteen, Alexander's parents separated, and his mother took him to New York City's Harlem district to live. Soon after the Second World War began, Alexander returned alone to Canada and served with the Royal Canadian Air Force as a corporal from 1942 to 1945. After his discharge, he, like Tokiwa, married a woman from Hamilton in 1948. Encouraged by his mother to seek a higher education, Alexander attended Hamilton's Central Collegiate and McMaster University, hoping this would 'open doors' and help him get ahead in life.[48]

After graduating from McMaster in 1949, Alexander faced racial prejudice in the workplace. Like many other McMaster graduates, and as a war veteran too, he applied for a job at one of Hamilton's large steel mills. 'The other graduates were getting jobs left, right and centre,' recalled Alexander later. 'They were willing to give me a job in production, but I wanted a job in sales.'[49] Alexander did not like the inference that, as a Black in sales, he would create problems for the company's image. Partly as a result of this experience, he too decided to become a lawyer.[50] Like Paul Tokiwa's, Alexander's experience with prejudice led him to study law.

Alexander began Osgoode Hall Law School in 1949, commuting from his home in Hamilton. The financial support he received as a war veteran enabled him to undertake this prolonged course of study. In contrast to his classmate, Millar, one difficulty he soon faced was obtaining an articling position. Articling jobs for minorities were scarce. Most big-city corporate firms (and many smaller ones too) then hired neither members of visible minorities nor women,[51] and Alexander was able to article with Sam Gotfrid, QC. Lawyers who then apparently hired visible-minority law students for articling positions were the few other Black or Jewish lawyers already in practice in Toronto,[52] who were themselves often victims of hiring discrimination.[53] They were a kind of legal subculture of non-élite ethnic groups whose values differed substantially from those of the élite corporate firms in Toronto and elsewhere, and who were willing to extend a helping hand to members of other ethnic or racial minorities.

When Alexander graduated from Osgoode in 1953, he experienced another hiring difficulty when he applied for a position as a junior with an established Anglo-Celtic Hamilton law firm. His written application as an excellent law student and war veteran were well received by the firm. But when Alexander inquired over the telephone if the firm would have a problem with his being Black, negotiations about the job offer quickly ceased. While this firm offered him goodwill and some financial assistance to get started, it would not offer him the position. Alexander had no doubt at all that the sole reason was because he was Black.[54]

Alexander's postwar difficulty in finding a legal position paralleled that of James Watson, another Black who later became the city solicitor in Windsor, Ontario. Watson, too, was a returning war veteran looking for legal employment after the war who found the experience of prejudice against hiring him troubling. 'Notwithstanding the fact that I was still in uniform and would wear my uniform when I made the rounds of these various legal offices,' recalled Watson of his job search. 'The end result was that I was unsuccessful in getting any definite prospect of employment.'[55] In fact, getting established in law was so difficult for Watson when he was called to the bar earlier in 1937 that, on weekends, he still worked at his old porter's job on the Canadian Pacific Railway. It was this railway work, he later recalled, which made it possible for him to survive financially at that time.[56] Both their difficulties contrasted vividly with Millar's own employment experience, with three excellent job offers at the same time as Alexander. Racism was prevalent in Canada's postwar legal culture, as it was in Canada generally in this period.

The first Hamilton law firm to hire Alexander was the Polish brother-and-sister firm of Okuloski and Okuloski, one of those newer types of 'ethnic' law firms described earlier. It was located in Hamilton's east end, close to the steel factories, where many recent Poles and other Eastern European immigrants to Hamilton worked and lived. In this and in other ways, it was far removed from the élite Hamilton law firm where Millar was then practising law. It was, for example, one of the few Hamilton law firms with a woman partner. 'Helen [Okuloski] didn't hire me out of sympathy because I was Black,' said Alexander; 'all she wanted to know was whether I had the ability, aggressiveness, and mental capacity to do the job.'[57] Woman lawyers were then still a small minority,[58] and Helen Okuloski was an example of a minority lawyer helping another minority lawyer. When she hired Alexander, he became only the second Black lawyer (Oliver Holland was the first) to practise in Hamilton.

Alexander was a pioneer in another respect. When he went into partnership in 1954 with fellow Hamilton lawyer David Duncan, it, according to the *Hamilton Spectator*, was 'Canada's first black–white law partnership.'[59] One lasting legacy of his association with Duncan was Alexander's increasing involvement in politics, with Hamilton's local Conservative party. Duncan, a prominent Hamilton Tory, had helped Ellen Fairclough become Hamilton's first woman member of Parliament in a 1950 federal by-election. [60] Duncan himself was a city alderman from 1954 to 1958. Politics is a common way for lawyers to draw attention to themselves, but for Alexander, as a Black, it had greater significance than for many others. His increasing involvement with Hamilton's Conservative party helped raise his profile in the later 1960s. Blacks were beginning to find greater acceptance as political parties sought their support in a growing, multicultural Canada, and Alexander even received some national attention.

Alexander's partnership with Duncan lasted until 1962, when Duncan accepted a position as senior solicitor for the Ontario Department of Transport. Left on his own, Alexander was finding it financially problematic to maintain a secure practice. Among the main reasons was the fact that he was having difficulties (unlike Millar) establishing a crucial real estate practice, the traditional 'bread and butter' of any successful Hamilton law firm. Then, 'as it is today,' noted Lance Talbot, 'the most lucrative form of practice was that dealing with real estate transactions and commercial or corporate representation. Since Blacks did not have ready access to such clients the ability to earn a prosperous living was greatly diminished.'[61] In 1961 there were only about 470 Blacks in Hamilton, and they were mostly renters living downtown, [62] so there was relatively little real estate and commercial or corporate business there.

Moreover, Alexander had difficulties in attracting business from Hamilton's Blacks. This was a surprisingly common experience shared by other first-generation visible-minority lawyers in those days. For example, Kew Dock Yip, the first Chinese lawyer in Canada, claimed that, when he first began to practise law in Toronto after the Second World War, 'even my own people discriminated against me.' The Chinese there, recalled Yip, 'had no confidence' in him and he had to 'fight my way up.'[63] He attributed this, in part, to the fact that Chinese had been suppressed for so long in Canada, and noted that it was mainly after he began to win cases and became successful as a lawyer that their business came to him.[64] David Nahwegahbow, an aboriginal Ojibwa lawyer, also observed that 'it is hard to convince your own people that you are capable of doing the job ... so it took some time ... for Native people to believe that we could do an adequate job.'[65] As well, legal aid in Ontario was not then developed enough to sustain lawyers practising criminal and family law before the courts, whatever their ethnic background.[66]

Thus, Alexander had reason to be worried about his practice. Then, one evening in 1962, when visiting his son in a city hospital, fate intervened. John Millar was visiting his father in the same hospital. The two men started to chat, and 'out of the blue,' recalled Alexander, Millar said, 'I would like you to join me in the practice of law as a partner.'[67] The meeting was indeed fortunate. Alexander knew that 'even then Jack [Millar] was a very successful lawyer and I had little to offer him, but many Hamiltonians, including some of his clients and even colleagues in the profession, did not believe Black was beautiful as Jack did and told him so, which disturbed [Millar] very much.'[68] Millar empathized with his situation, as he did earlier with Tokiwa's. He insisted Alexander join him – not because Alexander was Black but because he knew that Alexander was a good lawyer. These two former classmates had kept in touch professionally, and Millar assured Alexander that he could assist him in his burgeoning real estate practice as well as developing criminal and family-law, litigation, and other related work at his firm.[69] Alexander then became Millar's first law partner in 1962, before Tokiwa. By chance more than by design, it was the first law firm in Hamilton, and perhaps in Canada, with both a Black and a Japanese lawyer.

But the firm was not yet complete. When Alexander became further involved in federal politics and won a Hamilton seat in 1968, an opening developed for someone to replace him and continue this other type of legal work. This time, however, Millar's choice for a new lawyer was made after careful thought as regards race and the practice of law. So entered Peter Isaacs.

A Canadian Mohawk, Peter Isaacs was born in 1938. Though raised in Hamilton, he was born at nearby Ohsweken, on what was then called the Six Nations Reserve just southwest of the city. His father, Bill Isaacs, was a celebrated lacrosse player in the 1930s and 1940s. When he retired from the game, he worked for Dofasco, a Hamilton steelmaker. Isaacs lived in Hamilton's east end, not far from the steel mill where his father worked. Although the city had a small number of aboriginal Canadians (and was the original site of the Neutrals),[70] Isaacs grew up without much contact with other aboriginals there. Like members of other visible minorities, Hamilton's aboriginal Canadians also faced prejudice in many areas. Some citizens had preconceived ideas of the Six Nations Reserve as a place of poor housing, unemployment, drinking, and crime.[71] Aboriginals were also disturbed by anti-aboriginal stereotypes in city newspaper advertisements, political cartoons, or radio commercials, and were affronted when a new housing development on the city's mountain uncovered earlier Neutral burial-grounds.[72] Indeed, an excellent perspective on what it was then like to be an aboriginal Canadian from the Six Nations was provided by Howard Staats, a Six Nations Mohawk who attended Osgoode Hall Law School and who began practising law around the same time as Isaacs, in nearby Brantford.[73] When Isaacs graduated from high school, and then the University of Western Ontario, he tried for a permanent job at the steel company. Like Alexander, he discovered that a job in production there seemed to be his destiny; and, when faced with the same realization as Alexander, he also decided to go into law.[74]

Isaacs began Osgoode Hall Law School in 1963, graduating in 1966. Returning to Hamilton, he articled with the large firm of Agro, Cooper, Zaffiro, Parente, and Orzel, located in the same downtown office building as Millar, Alexander, and Tokiwa. He often met these three lawyers in this building and attended social functions with them. When he completed his articles and bar-admission course in 1968, Isaacs returned to

Agro, Cooper as a junior. He was working there for several months when fate favoured his career as well. That same year Alexander won the federal riding of Hamilton West for the Conservatives, and Millar had an opening in his firm for someone to take over Alexander's practice. Millar's choice was Isaacs; but more was involved this time than simply hiring someone he knew.

By 1968 the firm had been in existence for six years. Millar and the other lawyers there were increasingly proud of the fact that their small law firm was a leader in addressing the issue of race and the practice of law. Other members of the Hamilton bar were also impressed both with what Millar called his 'United Nations'[75] law firm, and with the excellent legal work being done by Alexander and Tokiwa. 'Every lawyer in town,' recalled fellow Hamilton lawyer John Reesor, QC, 'was proud of John's leadership in this respect at a time when such relationships were rare.'[76] Many Hamilton articling students and junior lawyers wanted to join this firm because of this leadership, and Millar could have chosen any one of them to work at his firm. But, for several reasons, his choice was Isaacs. First, Millar recognized Isaacs as a promising young lawyer. More important, Millar felt that Isaacs, being an aboriginal Canadian (and the first one also to practise in Hamilton) would continue his precedent for maintaining a multiracial law firm.[77] A tradition had been established, and now it would be strengthened and extended. Interestingly, Millar's wife, Marjorie, who had lived on the Six Nations Reserve for eleven years when her father, an RCMP officer, was stationed there, encouraged Millar to hire Isaacs over all other candidates.[78] Millar did so, and soon this small Hamilton law firm had three visible-minority partners.

While this firm's formation owed much to Millar's liberal values and character, he was not alone in being responsible for the firm's rapid success. Other factors were involved, including portentous political, social, and demographic changes occurring in postwar Canada. But one essential element in building up the firm's success was establishing its good reputation. 'There are, of course, a great many factors involved in attracting and maintaining a client base,' noted Curtis Cole in his article on a predecessor firm to Toronto's McCarthy, Tétrault, 'but most lawyers would agree that a good reputation is paramount.'[79] Initially, Millar faced some risk in hiring these three visible-minority lawyers. As Alexander stated, he endured criticism from some of his colleagues and some of his own clients for doing so. But, as Canada became more of a multicultural and multiracial mosaic after the Second World War, this new society redeemed Millar's sense of vision and commitment to multiracism. His firm proved uniquely able to transform what would have been a disadvantage in earlier circumstances – its multiracial character – into an advantage which gave it a distinctive character and contributed immeasurably to establishing its reputation. Here the most important person who helped establish this firm's outstanding reputation and success relative to these changing attitudes to multiculturalism and race was Lincoln Alexander.

Blacks lived in Hamilton almost from its beginning. In the 1820s, many Blacks who escaped slavery in America came to the city, and many settled on Hamilton's mountain brow. Given land there by the Green and Burkholder families, who were both pioneer Loyalists, this early Black settlement became known as 'Little Africa.'[80] This settlement gradually declined by the late 1800s, and Hamilton's main Black settlement moved to the downtown core. Centred close to Stewart Memorial Church on John Street north, Hamilton's earliest Blacks, like most others then in Canada, first worked as railway porters, bellhops, domestic maids, and in other low-paying service jobs. In time they started to secure a better life, and accomplished this in Hamilton, especially after the Second World War. Probably the most revealing example of their changing civic fortunes was Reverend John Holland, of Stewart Memorial Church, chosen Hamilton's distinguished citizen of the year in 1953. The son of a fugitive slave, Holland worked his way up from being a porter and chef on Hamilton's Toronto, Hamilton & Buffalo Railway to become a leader of Hamilton's Black community and proud minister of their beloved church.[81] Something of the city's changing attitude towards Blacks was displayed at his award presentation speech from then mayor Lloyd Jackson. 'There will be repercussions outside this city because of this selection,' said Jackson, but 'these reactions will make it known to all that we in this city do not stand for anything in the nature of racial intolerance. Whenever that sort of thing rears its ugly head, I hope every citizen will rise to denounce it.'[82] Not everyone did, but some people in the city were then trying to overcome racial prejudice.

Holland's life and civic recognition inspired Hamilton's Blacks and helped promote greater tolerance for them, which helped Alexander as a Black lawyer. More specifically, Alexander received further recognition through his continued involvement with Hamilton's Conservative party. Edward Okuloski, with whom Alexander first worked, was active for many years in this party.[83] So was Alexander's first law partner, David Duncan. Here, too, Hamilton's political scene in the 1950s was changing to reflect new postwar political realities, and the city's Conservative party was in its vanguard. Ellen Fairclough, a Conservative, became the city's first woman member of Parliament. In 1957, in Hamilton East, Quinto Martini was elected for the Conservatives, becoming the first Italo-Canadian elected to Parliament – both for Hamilton and for all of Canada.[84] At the provincial level, Hamilton's Ada Pritchard was elected as the first woman Conservative in the Ontario Legislature. Both Fairclough and Pritchard were first elected city aldermen and were among the first women in the city to articulate women's concerns, such as equal pay for equal work, at City Council.[85] In 1962 Victor Copps, a dynamic and flamboyant individual (and a Liberal), who was very much in touch with the 'new generation,' became the city's first Roman Catholic mayor.[86] The city's postwar political landscape was in transition, as all these electoral breakthroughs revealed, so that the further possibility of a city Black being elected was growing more conceivable.

At the same time, other postwar changes at the provincial level helped Blacks (and other visible minorities) overcome prejudice. In 1944 the Ontario Legislature passed what was probably the first Canadian human-rights statute. This Racial Discrimination Act prohibited the publication or display of signs, symbols, or other representations expressing racial or religious discrimination.[87] It also passed a Fair Employment Practices Act and a Fair Accommodation Practices Act, reflecting again a new awareness of these problems, as well as underlying pressure to do something about them from more vocal Blacks in labour unions.[88] In 1962 the legislature consolidated this human-rights legislation into the Ontario Human Rights Code, to be administered by the Ontario Human Rights Commission, headed by Daniel Hill, a Black.[89] As well, a changing judicial attitude towards racial discrimination was revealed in the seminal postwar Ontario case of *Re Drummond Wren*.[90] In that case the purchaser of land in York sought to have a restrictive covenant declared invalid, which said that the land was 'not to be sold to Jews or persons of objectionable nationality.' Mackay, J, examined the then recent San Francisco U.N. Charter and Ontario's Racial Discrimination Act, among other documents, for guidance in determining public policy on this issue. 'If the sale of one piece of land can be so prohibited, the sale of other pieces of land can likewise be prohibited,' said Mackay, J, in his judgment, and 'nothing could be more calculated to create or deepen divisions between existing religious and ethnic groups in this province.'[91] He then held the covenant void, as against public policy. As a result, slowly but surely in these post-war years, a civil-rights infrastructure was being built in Ontario from which visible minorities could seek assistance. As well, many other Canadians viewing sweeping civil-rights changes being advocated by Martin Luther King and other Blacks in America were becoming sensitized to the debilitating effects of prejudice.

The federal government, too, was moving into the area of civil rights in these postwar years. In 1948 it signed the United Nations Universal Declaration of Human Rights.[92] In the 1950s and 1960s Canadians also saw their new prime minister, John Diefenbaker, become a strong critic of ethnic and racial discrimination, both in Canada itself and in the Commonwealth. In 1960 his famous Bill of Rights passed into law. Then, at a Commonwealth Prime Ministers' meeting the next year, Diefenbaker spoke out strongly and openly against apartheid in South Africa.[93] More significantly for Hamilton, and for Millar's firm, in particular, Diefenbaker demonstrated his commitment to change when he personally asked Alexander to run for Parliament.[94] Diefenbaker had already appointed Hamilton's Ellen Fairclough as the first woman cabinet minister in Canada, and knew about this other remarkable Hamiltonian, especially since Alexander was a strong Conservative and had taken, along with seventeen others from the Hamilton region, a fact-finding 'goodwill safari' to Africa in 1960 under the auspices of the United Church of Canada to visit Church missions there and report on the role of missionaries.[95] Flattered by the call, Alexander accepted.

As a result of these postwar changes in attitudes about racial prejudice, Hamiltonians were becoming increasingly aware of the momentous fact that, if Alexander won his seat in Hamilton West in the 1968 federal election (he had run previously in 1965 and narrowly lost), Hamilton voters would be making further electoral history by electing Parliament's first Black. Alexander did win this seat after a hard-fought campaign, helping defeat prejudice by encouraging many members of other visible minorities and young people in the riding to work for him during his campaign,[96] and also defeating 'Trudeaumania,' which swept the city's other ridings for the Liberals.

Alexander's victory greatly enhanced his law firm's public profile. During the election campaign, many Hamiltonians had a personal opportunity to experience Alexander's gracious personality, see his accomplishments overcoming prejudice, and note the unique law firm where he practised. Working on political campaigns is not, of course, uncommon for lawyers, and is a recognized way to develop a firm's reputation. But this particular candidate was very different, and so were his law partners who assisted him in his campaign in every conceivable way. These lawyers were well aware what their efforts in electing Alexander might mean for furthering multiculturalism and for other minorities in Canada.[97] Many people liked what they saw. Furthermore, the media made all of Canada aware of Alexander's victory, so that the firm also received national, and even international, recognition. *Ebony*, America's Black magazine, followed Alexander's campaign win closely, noting 'Canada's Black Member of Parliament' who was 'in partnership with three other lawyers – one British, one Japanese and one Canadian Indian.'[98] Few other Canadian law firms have ever benefited as much from election coverage in helping them establish a reputation. Such benefit continued with Alexander's subsequent electoral campaigns. In ways he could not at first probably have imagined, Millar reaped the benefits of his earlier efforts to create such a firm.

However, the success of Millar's law firm was not just related to the publicity and business that Alexander's political involvement attracted. The firm was also well positioned to enhance its legal reputation and further increase its legal business as a result of other important demographic changes occurring in Hamilton, and especially in housing trends there in the late 1950s and 1960s. Around the time this firm began in 1962, hundreds, then thousands, of Hamiltonians were moving from the lower city up onto Hamilton's mountain. At the same time, new Canadian immigrants from Eastern Europe and Asia were changing the character of the city's population. A law firm with a mountain connection, with lawyers recognized as highly competent in real estate law practising in a multiracial firm reflecting these new demographic changes, had great potential to succeed. Once again Millar's firm was ideally positioned to capitalize on such new demographic opportunities.

The transition away from the British population in the city began around the turn of the century with the establishment of heavy industrial plants in Hamilton. City lawyers like Sir John Morison Gibson anticipated the potential of Hamilton's proximity to water, rail lines, and markets for such industry to locate in the east end of Hamilton and began to buy land there. In addition, 'those owning land in the east-end of Hamilton were aware,' noted Carolyn Gray in her study of Gibson, 'that establishment of new industries in that area would intensify the demand for real estate, both for industrial and residential use and would boost land values.'[99] Gibson joined forces with John Patterson and other Hamilton investors to form a syndicate to develop this area for industry.[100] As a result of their efforts, soon after the turn of the century Hamilton's east end attracted companies like Westinghouse, International Harvester, Otis

Elevator, and Canada's two largest steel companies – Stelco and Dofasco. Textile factories also came here, as well as canning factories, to utilize Hamilton's location close by rich Niagara Peninsula farmland. In short order this part of Hamilton became one of the most industrialized areas of Canada.

Industry needs workers, and Hamilton then began to attract many immigrants from Europe anxious to find work in the city's developing industries. Most of these immigrants first settled in Hamilton's north end and in new subdivisions built for them in the city's east end, both close to the factories. As a result, noted John Weaver in his excellent study on this transition, Hamilton's housing stock nearly tripled between 1901 and 1921.[101] There were never enough houses, however, and many immigrants boarded. As a result, this part of Hamilton became increasingly crowded and dirty from the fumes, noise, smoke, traffic, and pollution from the nearby industries. Thus it was no wonder that many of these new immigrants felt their first home in Hamilton would only be temporary until they could earn enough money to relocate elsewhere in the city. Some moved to the city's west end,[102] but most preferred Hamilton's mountain.

Hamilton's mountain was at last attracting new homeowners for many reasons. Earlier, its isolated higher elevation and steep access routes discouraged widespread settlement. This continued for many years, as immigrants first settled in the lower part of the city in search of work. But, in time, many Hamiltonians who were unable to buy a home during the Great Depression or else could not find a suitable one for their family's needs during the Second World War, were at long last able to do so when prosperity and jobs returned after the war. Many immigrants who had spent their first years living close to the steel mills could finally leave this area and move to the mountain, the last great area of available land that could be annexed to the city.[103] As well, most of Hamilton's postwar 'baby boom' generation perceived the mountain as an area free of pollution, with safe streets, where their children could play and where new houses had all the modern conveniences, such as gas heat.[104] In more general terms, they were part of the great postwar phenomenon of Canadians moving to the suburbs.[105] Moreover, many of these new mountain homeowners could now afford to purchase their first home because of the postwar creation by the federal government of Central Mortgage and Housing Corporation (CMHC), which offered affordable mortgages for the first time. As a result of these changes, 'growth on the Mountain was spectacular,' noted Doucet and Weaver, and population there increased from an estimated 10,000–12,000 in 1945 to 25,000 by 1952, and to 50,000 by 1960.[106] Many recent residents of the mountain were the city's Italians, who started to have higher levels of new homeownership than Hamilton's older British population. They were joined by Eastern European immigrants, such as Ukrainians and Poles, who all possessed a fierce desire to own their own land.[107] In addition, in these postwar decades, most of the city's Japanese population relocated from the lower city up to the mountain.[108] All these mountain home-buyers needed lawyers for their new home purchase.

Millar's firm was not only able to service the legal needs of such a clientele, but also had features which distinguished it from other Hamilton law firms also riding the crest of consumer demand for new housing after the war. Millar himself was a lifelong mountain resident. His connections to many service clubs and other organizations located on the mountain secured many new clients for the firm. He had long fostered crucial contacts with prominent city builders, real estate developers, and institutional mortgage lenders who were actively servicing these new mountain homeowners, and was able to obtain more clients from them.[109] Paul Tokiwa was also a mountain resident, and, with his background, was slowly able to secure an increasing amount of legal work from the new Japanese community resettling on the mountain. Like other first-generation visible-minority lawyers, Tokiwa had few Japanese clients at first, but in time they comprised approximately 60 to 70 per cent of his clientele,[110] and the firm was able to do business in another language. When these clients and others needed legal work in such areas as family, motor-vehicle litigation, or criminal law, Peter Isaacs was on hand to service their needs. Lastly, the firm's multiracial composition had a subtle appeal to many newly affluent racial- and ethnic-minority clients who were not Anglo-Celtic. 'We were a visual example of tolerance,' noted Isaacs, 'where these people felt comfortable.'[111] As a small law firm, it also had the advantage of being able to deal with these clients on a one-to-one basis.

The firm also attracted more real estate clients on the mountain and elsewhere because of its complementary reputation as one of the best real estate firms in Hamilton. Over the years Millar specialized in real estate law and in this field, said Alexander, was a 'lawyer's lawyer,'[112] achieving the ultimate legal compliment when other lawyers called him for real estate advice. The practice of real estate law was becoming increasingly complicated in these postwar decades, after, for example, the province passed the complex Planning Act. In addition, the city made new plans of subdivision harder and more time-consuming for builders and developers to obtain. Millar was a member of the Hamilton Property Standards Committee and a member of the city's Planning Board in 1964, and served as its chairman from 1967 to 1972.[113] This brought him and his firm further recognition and business from real estate builders, institutional mortgage lenders such as the Mutual Life Assurance Company of Canada, and many other new clients seeking a good real estate firm for their home purchase or sale. Above all, recalled Alexander, the firm 'pursued excellence' and clients knew their interests would be well looked after.[114] Their reputation as good lawyers, then, was just as important for the firm's success.

The firm enjoyed this success for many years, but began to dissolve as a partnership when Alexander was appointed federal minister of labour in 1979, and conflict-of-interest guidelines forced him to resign from the firm. Subsequently he became chairman of Ontario's Workers' Compensation Board (1980–5), the province's twenty-fourth lieutenant-governor (1985–91), and chancellor of the University of Guelph in 1991. Tokiwa left in 1983 to practise on his own, and died in 1994. John Millar died in 1992. The partnership finally dissolved when Isaacs left in 1993. He is currently an Ontario Provincial Court judge. However, the firm's name continues with Millar's two sons, who practise under the proud firm name of 'Millar, Alexander.'

Millar, Alexander, Tokiwa, and Isaacs was one of the most prominent law firms in Hamilton. Millar never consciously began his practice wanting a multiracial firm, but as the firm became successful, he saw no reason to change it. This was a result of many factors: his willingness to be among the first Anglo-Celtic lawyers to hire visible-minority lawyers; his unwitting ability to anticipate changing times in postwar Canada; and his decision to remain within the structure of a classic small law firm of four partners in a smaller city.[115] As the firm succeeded, Millar had many subsequent opportunities to enlarge it or merge it with other firms, but resisted, mainly to keep personal control over its business and multicultural direction.[116] It also appears that the flexible structure of a small law firm allowed Millar the opportunity to build such a multiracial firm when perhaps the bureaucratic and autocratic administration of larger élite corporate firms then in the province hindered them moving sooner in this multiracial direction. As a result, Millar's firm was significant to the profession for establishing the value of a now widely copied convention of practice – that visible-minority lawyers in a law firm could be successful in attracting new ethnic and multiracial clients to the firm without losing established ones. Indeed, as Canada has become more multicultural and multiracial, and business has become more international, a law firm that does not currently service this market may now perhaps be at a disadvantage.

As well, this firm also provided empowerment to its visible-minority lawyers. Practising together within a small-law-firm structure instilled confidence in each of them, and gave these lawyers a singular opportunity for financial success very different from what they might have first encountered as sole practitioners. Moreover, their great success had symbolic meaning to others in the community. Alexander, Tokiwa, and Isaacs were given the unique opportunity to be perceived as leading role models for members of other visible minorities aspiring to better themselves in law and elsewhere. Millar may not have suspected these visible–minority lawyers would go so far, but the law firm he created gave them an opening to do so. Tokiwa became a recognized leader for Japanese Canadians living in Hamilton. Isaacs, too, became a leader for aboriginal Canadians and was lauded by *Toronto Star* columnist Gary Lautens, who in 1990 wrote that Canada's 'Natives' future hinges on people like Pete Isaacs.'[117] Perhaps the ultimate significance of the firm and its accomplishment was expressed by Alexander. When Alexander won his seat in 1968, he remarked: 'I hope my victory will give other people faith that in Canada anyone can win, no matter what [their] race, creed, color or religion.'[118] This firm had a large part in making this happen.

NOTES

I would like to thank the Honourable Lincoln Alexander, Peter Isaacs, Paul Tokiwa, and John Millar Jr for their comments on, and assistance with, previous drafts of this essay. The responsibility for any errors remains my own.

1 However, there may have been a Black lawyer before Davis. See I. Malcolm, 'Robert Sutherland: The First Black Lawyer in Canada?,' *Law Society of Upper Canada Gazette* (hereinafter *LSUCG*) 26 (1992), 183; J. Isaac, 'Delos Rogest Davis, K.C.,' *LSUCG* 24 (1990), 293.

2 Isaac, 'Delos Rogest Davis, K.C.,' 296

3 'An Act to Provide for the Admission of Women to the Study of Law,' *Ontario Statutes*, (1892) c. 32, quoted in Isaac, 'Delos Rogest Davis, K.C.,' 301. See also C.B. Backhouse, '"To Open the Way for Others of My Sex": Clara Brett Martin's Career as Canada's First Woman Lawyer,' *Canadian Journal of Women and the*

Law 1(1985), 1; J. Hagan, 'Transitions in the Legal Profession,' *LSUCG* 27 (1993), 91.

4 B.S. Bolaria and P.S. Li, eds., *Racial Oppression in Canada* (Toronto: Garamond 1985), 87. This related to not being on the Voters' List.

5 See generally J. Hagan, M. Huxter, and P. Parker, 'Class Structure and Legal Practice: Inequality and Mobility among Toronto Lawyers,' *Law and Society Review* 22 (1988), 9.

6 See M. Weinfeld, 'The Development of Affirmative Action in Canada,' *Canadian Ethnic Studies* 13 (1981), 23; *Report of the Special Committee on Visible Minorities in Canadian Society* (Ottawa, 1984).

7 *Law Times*, 27 June–3 July 1994. See also L.C. Talbot, 'The Formation of the Black Law Students' Association (Canada),' *LSUCG* 26 (1992), 187.

8 B. McDougall, 'Law's Changing Face,' *Canadian Lawyer* (November 1991), 14

9 Law Society of Upper Canada, *Report of the Special Committee on Equity in Legal Education and Practice* (1991); *Report of the Special Committee on Minority Groups Assistance Programs* (circa 1990)

10 Available at the Osgoode Society, Osgoode Hall Toronto, and at the Archives of Ontario, Osgoode Society Oral History Collection, C-81. Some access restrictions apply.

11 For general overviews of the profession in Ontario see C.P. McTague, 'Survey of the Legal Profession in Canada,' *Canadian Bar Review* 27 (1949), 951; H.W. Arthurs, J. Willms, and L. Taman, 'The Toronto Legal Profession: An Exploratory Survey,' *University of Toronto Law Journal* 21 (1971), 498, and B.D. Adam and D.E Baer, 'The Social Mobility of Women and Men in the Ontario Legal Profession,' *Canadian Review of Sociology and Anthropology* (hereinafter *CRSA*) 21 (1984), 21.

12 Entries for these lawyers found in T.M. Bailey, ed., *Dictionary of Hamilton Biography*, 3 vols. (Hamilton: W.L. Griffin 1981, 1991, 1992). See also D.R. Beer, *Sir Allan Napier MacNab* (Hamilton: Dictionary of Hamilton Biography 1984), and P.J. Sworden, 'Sir Aemilius Irving: The Law Society's Longest Serving Treasurer,' *LSUCG* 28 (1994), 45.

13 Entries in *Dictionary of Hamilton Biography*. See also Hamilton Public Library Special Collections (hereinafter HPLSC), *H.F. Gardiner Scrapbook*, vol. 253, 151–2.

14 M.B. Katz, *The People of Hamilton, Canada West: Family and Class in a Mid-Nineteenth-Century City* (Cambridge, MA: Harvard University Press 1975), 184

15 See map of Hamilton with this essay.

16 J.C. Best and R.L. Fraser, 'James Chisholm,' *Dictionary of Hamilton Biography* vol.3, 28

17 See generally J.C. Weaver, *Hamilton: An Illustrated History* (Toronto: Lorimer

1982); B.D. Palmer, *A Culture in Conflict: Skilled Workers and Industrial Capitalism in Hamilton, Ontario, 1860–1914* (Montreal and Kingston: McGill–Queen's University Press 1979).

18 M.J. Foster, 'Ethnic Settlement in the Barton Street Region of Hamilton, 1921 to 1961,' MA thesis, McMaster University, 1965, 10–11; P.C. Pineo, *Ethnicity in Hamilton: Demographic and Socioeconomic Features* (McMaster University, Hamilton Ethnicity Project Working Paper no.1, June 1967)

19 See N. Rahman, 'An Ecological Study of Ethnic Groups of Hamilton,' MA thesis, McMaster University, 1977.

20 Interview with Marjorie Millar, John Millar's widow, 8 June 1994

21 C.M. Johnston, *McMaster University: The Early Years in Hamilton, 1930–1957*, vol. 2 (Toronto: University of Toronto Press 1981), 144–6

22 McMaster *Marmor*, 1949, 31

23 See G.A. Johnston, 'Osgoode Hall as It Was in 1949,' *LSUCG* 19 (1985), 254

24 Marjorie Millar, interview, 8 June 1994

25 'J. Walter Gage,' *Dictionary of Hamilton Biography*, vol. 3, 65

26 Marjorie Millar, interview, 8 June 1994

27 Interview with Marilyn Pryor, title searcher for Millar at this firm, 2 June 1994

28 E.S. Vickers, 'The Victorian Buildings of Hamilton,' *Wentworth Bygones* 7 (1967), 55

29 Interview with John Millar Jr, Millar's son and lawyer continuing the practice, 2 June 1994

30 Interview with Paul Tokiwa, 14 June 1994

31 Ibid.

32 Bolaria and Li, *Racial Oppression in Canada*, 81–115. See also W. Peter Ward, *The Japanese in Canada* (Ottawa: Canadian Historical Association 1982).

33 *Union Colliery* v. *Bryden* [1899] AC 580

34 *Cunningham* v. *Tomey Homma* [1903] AC 151

35 Ibid., 155–6, the Lord Chancellor. A later Supreme Court of Canada case, *Quong-Wing* v. *The King* [1914] 49 SCR 440, continued this same type of reasoning in upholding the validity of a Saskatchewan act prohibiting White women working in places of business managed by Chinese. 'Once I find its subject-matter is not within the power of the Dominion Parliament and is within that of the provincial legislature, I cannot inquire into its policy or justice or into the motives which prompted its passage': Davies J, at 448.

36 W.S. Tarnopolsky, 'The Control of Racial Discrimination,' in O. McKague, ed., *Racism in Canada* (Saskatoon: Fifth House 1991), 181

37 P.E. Roy, 'The Illusion of Toleration: White Opinions of Asians in British Columbia, 1929–37,' in K.V. Ojimoto and G. Hirabayashi, eds., *Visible Minorities and Multiculturalism: Asians in Canada* (Toronto: Butterworths 1980), 81–7

38 K. Adachi, *The Enemy That Never Was: A History of the Japanese Canadians* (Toronto: McClelland and Stewart 1976); A.G. Sunahara, *The Politics of Racism: The Uprooting of Japanese Canadians during the Second World War* (Toronto: Lorimer 1981); B. Broadfoot, *Years of Sorrow, Years of Shame: The Story of the Japanese Canadians in World War II* (Toronto: Doubleday 1977)

39 G. Tanaka, 'Wartime Toronto and Japanese Canadians,' *Polyphony* 6 (1984), 240–1

40 Ibid. M.A. Sunahara, 'Historical Leadership Trends among Japanese Canadians, 1940–1950,' *Canadian Ethnic Studies* 11 (1979), 1

41 R. Miki and C. Kobayashi, *Justice in Our Time: The Japanese Canadian Redress Settlement* (Vancouver: Talon Books 1991)

42 Japanese Canadian Centennial Society Hamilton Chapter, *Proceedings of the War Measures Act Conference, Hamilton Canada April 23,1977* (London, ON: Anas 1978)

43 Paul Tokiwa, interview, 14 June 1994. See M. Kendrick, 'Canadians at Risk? The Japanese Experience Stands as a Warning to Everyone,' *Hamilton Cue*, September 1985, 6

44 Paul Tokiwa, interview, 14 June 1994

45 H. Gairey, 'A Black Man's Toronto,' *Polyphony* 6 (1984), 237. See A. Calliste, 'Blacks on Canadian Railways,' *Canadian Ethnic Studies* 20 (1988), 36.

46 Quoted in Donna Hill, ed., *A Black Man's Toronto, 1914–1980: The Reminiscences of Harry Gairey* (Toronto: Multicultural History Society of Ontario 1981), 9.

47 In *Franklin* v. *Evans* (1924) 55 OLR 349, a Black was refused service in a restaurant. Lennox J, at 350, noted that 'I could not but be touched by the pathetic eloquence of his appeal for recognition as a human being, of common origin with ourselves,' but dismissed the action, holding that a restaurant owner was not bound to supply food to every person who demanded it. Similarly, in *Christie* v. *York Corporation* [1940] SCR 139, a Black was refused service in a Quebec tavern. Rinfret J, for the majority of the Court, held at 142 that the tavern could refuse him service on the ground that 'the general principle of the law of Quebec is that of complete freedom of commerce. Any merchant is free to deal as he may chose with any individual member of the public.'

48 Interview with Lincoln Alexander, 12 August 1994

49 *Hamilton Spectator*, 31 July 1979; HPLSC, *Lincoln Alexander: Scrapbook of Clippings 1954– *, vol. 1, 54

50 Interview with Lincoln Alexander, 20 May 1994

51 See V. Schatzker, *Borden & Elliot: The First Fifty Years, 1936–1986* (Toronto: Borden & Elliot 1986), 49; S.E. Edwards, *Fraser & Beatty: The First 150 Years* (Toronto: Fraser & Beatty 1989), 31.

52 See L.C. Talbot, 'History of Blacks in the Law Society of Upper Canada,'

LSUCG 24 (1990), 65. Talbot notes at 68 that 'at this time, and well into the 1950's the only people with whom Blacks or visible minorities could article, though admittedly their numbers were sparse, were under the direction of other Blacks or Jews. The traditional members of the bar, despite their good will and interest, were reluctant to be of assistance.'

53 See B.D. Adam and K.A. Lahey, 'Professional Opportunities: A Survey of the Ontario Legal Profession,' *Canadian Bar Review* 59 (1981), 684–5; Adam and Baer, 'The Social Mobility of Women and Men in the Ontario Legal Profession,' 40. For a different study see B.D. Adam, 'Stigma and Employability: Discrimination by Sex and Sexual Orientation in the Ontario Legal Profession,' *CRSA* 18 (1981), 216.

54 Lincoln Alexander, interview, 20 May 1994

55 James Watson, Oral History Interview [transcript], The Osgoode Society, Toronto, 36

56 Ibid., 18–20

57 Quoted in J. Foley, 'Lincoln Alexander: Hamilton's Tough Guy in Ottawa,' *Hamilton*, October 1979, 56. See M.Cappuccitti, 'Women in Law,' *Hamilton Cue Magazine*, May 1983, 23.

58 See J. Brockman, D. Evans, and K. Reid, 'Feminist Perspectives for the Study of Gender Bias in the Legal Profession,' *Canadian Journal of Women and the Law* 5 (1992), 37; J. Brockman, '"Resistance by the Club" to the Feminization of the Legal Profession,' *Canadian Journal of Law and Society* 7 (1992), 47.

59 *Hamilton Spectator*, 15 January 1991; HPLSC, David Duncan Clipping File

60 *Hamilton Spectator*, 16 May 1950; HPLSC, *Ellen Fairclough: A Scrapbook of Clippings*. Vol.1: 1945–1983, 49

61 Talbot, 'History of Blacks in the Law Society of Upper Canada,' 66

62 F.J. Henry, *The Experience of Discrimination: A Case Study Approach* (San Francisco: R and E Research Associates 1974), 9, 42. Henry's study was on discrimination experienced by Blacks and Japanese living in Hamilton in the 1960s.

63 Kew Dock Yip, Oral History Interview [transcript], The Osgoode Society, Toronto, 54–5

64 Ibid., 58, 116. Said Yip (117): 'I have to make myself seem to have a lot of money, before people trust me.'

65 David Nahwegahbow, Oral History Interview [transcript], Archives of Ontario C-81, 62

66 One notable early Black lawyer who did practise mainly criminal law was B.J. Spencer Pitt. Pitt was a mentor for other Black law students, and many articled for him. See L.C. Talbot, 'History of Blacks in the Law Society of Upper Canada,' 67–8.

67 Lincoln Alexander, 'Eulogy on the Occasion of the Funeral Service for John
    Sydney Millar,' Hamilton, 13 July 1992, 4
68 Ibid.
69 Lincoln Alexander, interview, 20 May 1994
70 When the city's aboriginal cultural centre opened in 1972, the *Hamilton Specta-
    tor* estimated it would serve the needs of the city's 1,500–2,000 natives: *Hamil-
    ton Spectator*, 2 February, 1972. HPLSC, Hamilton – Indians of North America
    Clippings File. See also Frank Ridley, *Archaeology of the Neutral Indian* (Port
    Credit: Etobicoke Historical Society 1961).
71 See L. Murdoch, 'Home and Native Land,' *Hamilton This Month*, October 1992,
    17–19.
72 *Hamilton Spectator*, 10 June 1972, 13 June 1981, 11 August 1986; 4 March 1987,
    4 February 1992; HPLSC, Hamilton – Indians of North America Clipping File
73 Howard Staats, Oral History Interview [transcript], The Osgoode Society,
    Toronto
74 Interview with Peter Isaacs, 14 June 1994
75 Paul Tokiwa, interview, 14 June 1994
76 J.F. Reesor, QC, 'In Memoriam, John Sydney Millar, QC,' *Hamilton Lawyer*,
    July 1992, 5
77 John Millar, Jr, interview, 2 June 1994
78 Marjorie Millar, interview, 8 June 1994
79 C. Cole, 'McCarthy, Osler, Hoskin, and Creelman, 1882 to 1902: Establishing a
    Reputation, Building a Practice,' in C. Wilton, ed., *Essays in the History of Cana-
    dian Law*, vol. 4: *Beyond the Law: Lawyers and Business in Canada, 1830 to 1930*
    (Toronto: The Osgoode Society 1990), 149.
80 Daniel G. Hill, *The Freedom-Seekers: Blacks in Early Canada* (Agincourt: Book
    Society of Canada 1981), 48–58; see also HPLSC, Hamilton – Blacks Clipping
    File.
81 HPLSC, *Hamilton News – Obituaries*, vol. 1, 30–1
82 HPLSC, *Hamilton News – Biographies*, vol. B3, 31
83 HPLSC, Edward Okuloski Clipping File
84 *Hamilton Spectator*, 12 June 1957; HPLSC, Quinto Martini Clipping File
85 *Hamilton Spectator*, 31 December 1963; 30 January 1952. HPLSC, *Hamilton –
    Women Scrapbook*, vol. 1, 1925–83, 47, 10–13. See also D. McCubbin, 'Women
    of Hamilton,' *Chatelaine* (August 1955).
86 M.F. Campbell, *A Mountain and a City: The Story of Hamilton* (Toronto: McClel-
    land and Stewart 1966), 279
87 R.W. Winks, *The Blacks in Canada: A History* (New Haven, CT: Yale University
    Press 1971), 427
88 Ibid., 423, 427

89 See J. Keene, *Human Rights in Ontario*, 2d ed. (Toronto: Carswell 1992).

90 *Re Drummond Wren*, [1945] OR 778

91 Ibid., 782–3. See also the later Supreme Court of Canada case *Noble and Wolf v. Alley*, [1951] SCR 64.

92 C.S. Ungerleider, 'Immigration, Multiculturalism, and Citizenship: The Development of the Canadian Social Justice Infrastructure,' *Canadian Ethnic Studies* 24 (1992), 7

93 Winks, *The Blacks in Canada*, 428

94 *One Canada: Memoirs of the Right Honourable John G. Diefenbaker*, vol. 2 (Toronto: Macmillan of Canada 1976), 249–50

95 Lincoln Alexander, interview, 12 August 1994. Alexander noted that the trip 'inspired him' to realize Blacks had the power and competence to be leaders.

96 Lincoln Alexander, interview, 20 May 1994. For another perspective on campaigning and 'ethnic politics' see P. Oliver, *Unlikely Tory: The Life and Politics of Allan Grossman* (Toronto: Lester & Orpen Dennys 1985).

97 Paul Tokiwa, interview, 14 June 1994

98 *Ebony*, April 1969, 140

99 C. Gray, 'Sir John Morison Gibson,' *Dictionary of Hamilton Biography*, vol. 3, 71

100 W.M. Cody, 'Who Were the Five Johns?' *Wentworth Bygones* 5 (1964), 14

101 Weaver, *Hamilton: An Illustrated History*, 97

102 See J.C. Weaver, 'From Land Assembly to Social Maturity. The Suburban Life of Westdale (Hamilton), Ontario, 1911–1951,' *Social History* 11 (1978), 411.

103 See Weaver, *Hamilton: An Illustrated History*, 159–79.

104 *Hamilton Spectator*, 22 April, 1989; HPLSC, *Hamilton Real Estate Scrapbook*, vol. 2, 1980–9, 137

105 J.M. Bumsted, 'Home Sweet Suburb,' *The Beaver*, October/November 1992, 26

106 M. Doucet and J. Weaver, *Housing the North American City* (Montreal and Kingston: McGill–Queen's University Press 1991), 135

107 Ibid., 335–49. See also E. Perri, 'The Italian-Canadian Experience in a Changing Hamilton,' MA thesis, McMaster University, 1990, 44

108 Henry, *The Experience of Discrimination*, 42

109 John Millar, Jr, interview, 2 June 1994

110 Paul Tokiwa, interview, 14 June 1994

111 Peter Isaacs, interview, 14 June 1994. See generally, J.R. Burnet and H. Palmer, *'Coming Canadians': An Introduction to a History of Canada's Peoples* (Toronto: McClelland and Stewart 1988).

112 Lincoln Alexander, interview, 20 May 1994

113 John Millar, Jr, interview, 2 June 1994

114 Lincoln Alexander, interview, 12 August 1994

115 For a perspective on immigrant lawyers beginning their practice in a city, see

T.L. Shaffer and M.M. Shaffer, *American Lawyers and Their Communities: Ethics in the Legal Profession* (Notre Dame: University of Notre Dame Press 1991). I am grateful to professor Alvin Esau for this reference. For a Canadian perspective on practising law in a small town, see F.X. Ribordy, 'The Small Town Lawyers,' *LSUCG* 16 (1982), 118.

116 Marjorie Millar, interview, 8 June 1994
117 *Toronto Star*, 28 September 1990. See also 'New Job a Triumph for Native Judge,' *Hamilton Spectator*, 10 April 1995, and R.L. Jamieson, 'The Aboriginal Fact: A New Opportunity For Canada,' *LSUCG* 25 (1991), 81.
118 *Niagara Falls Review*, 27 June 1968, in HPLSC, *Lincoln Alexander Scrapbook*, 10

14

Law on the Pacific Coast:
Bull, Housser and Tupper, 1945–1990

REGINALD H. ROY

A little over two hundred years ago, Alexander Mackenzie became the first European to cross Canada by land to reach the Pacific Coast. For about another century anyone wishing to attempt a similar journey used the same method of travel as he did – foot and canoe. A sea passage became the easiest, and thus the normal, route to reach the colonies of Vancouver Island and British Columbia when they were established in the middle of the nineteenth century. Of all of the realms and territories which came under the British Crown, few were more remote from the centre of Empire. This feeling of isolation had a direct impact on the growth and development of British Columbia and its institutions. Up until the gold rush of 1858, for example, law and order was a rough-and-ready affair, usually administered by senior officials of the Hudson's Bay Company. When the gold rush brought in thousands of prospectors from the United States and elsewhere, the British government quickly sent out the first lawyer ever to arrive in British Columbia. Matthew Baillie Begbie was to be appointed the first judge in the colony and soon established a reputation as a staunch upholder of British law.

The legal profession expanded slowly after his arrival, even after British Columbia entered Confederation in 1871. At that time the new province had a White population of only 12,000 people. The majority voted in favour of joining Confederation because the government in Ottawa had promised them a railway which would connect them with eastern Canada. For years the economy had been based on the export of furs, and then gold, items which were high in value but low in volume and weight. Later the forestry industry started in areas where the logs could be floated to the sea. A modest but growing export of fish products helped the economy, but even by 1881 the province could boast of a population of only 24,000.[1]

People in eastern Canada probably find it difficult to appreciate the impact on British Columbia of the completion of the Canadian Pacific Railway. It was like water flowing into a desert. When the main line reached Tidewater, there followed a period of building branch lines which could transport produce from the farms, ranches, mines, orchards, and huge interior forests, either westward for ocean shipment or eastward to consumer markets on the prairies or in central Canada. The CPR reached Port Moody in 1885. When it was extended a year later to Burrard Inlet, Vancouver had a population of 8,000 people. Sixteen years later it had become a small city of 30,000 and, before the Great War, it had grown to 134,000.[2] The surge of population growth and increase in business enterprises brought about by the spreading railway network throughout the province meant there was a growing need for legal services. The growth of Bull, Housser and Tupper, the firm that is the topic of this essay, was closely connected with the economic well-being of the province. As a legal firm it had a somewhat later beginning than many of the larger firms east of the mountains. For the most part, however, the founders of the firm came from eastern Canada or the prairies. The talent and skill they brought with them provided a solid foundation for later growth, and the burgeoning economic expansion of both the city and the province led the partners to seize the opportunity to become one of Vancouver's largest and best-known legal firms.

The growth of Bull, Housser after the Second World War was based on two factors: the tremendous expansion of British Columbia's economic growth and the legal talent and skill of the firm's partners. It was the partners who guided the development of the firm and, as such, considerable attention has been given in this account to some of the lawyers who played a significant role in opening up new areas of practice and guiding the firm into its present pre-eminence in Vancouver.

Bull, Housser and Tupper had its origin in the years shortly after the completion of the Canadian Pacific Railway. All of the original partners came from eastern Canada and all came west by rail. The earliest partnership, McPhillips and Williams, was open for business in 1890. At about the same time, another partnership was starting. Its leading personality was Sir Charles Hibbert Tupper, a former federal cabinet minister whose father was for a brief period the prime minister of Canada. Tupper had come west in 1897 and formed a partnership with another Maritimer, Frederick Peters. Both men were in practice in Vancouver in 1900.

There was still much of the 'frontier society' about Vancouver at the turn of the century, but this would change fairly rapidly. However, it should be kept in mind that, as young men, the early partners could remember a time when there were no automobiles, no electric lights, no telephones, and no streetcars. Wireless telegraphy was just beginning when the early partnership was formed, a young man named Henry Ford started to build his first car two years later, and two years after that the first motion-picture camera was invented. The oldest of the partners, Adolphus Williams, was born only twenty-five years after the death of Napoleon. It would not be stretching a point to say that, in 1890, the partners of the two firms would have been more at home in a law firm in the 1790s than they would be in the 1990s.

Both firms grew slowly after the turn of the century. By 1911 the older firm had become Walsh, McKim, Housser and Molson. The younger, in 1917, had become Tupper and Bull. In 1927 the two partnerships decided to merge to form the firm called Walsh, Bull, Housser, Tupper, McKim and Molson. The reasons for the amalgamation are not known, but one can speculate about some of them. Sir Charles had died earlier in the year. His son, Reginald, had joined his father's firm after service in the Great War. Reginald Tupper was a good friend of Molson's. Moreover, all partners were on friendly terms with one another, and each had special interests which, when pooled, would strengthen the new group as a whole. There was also a benefit to be derived from size in that one could save on staff, rent, telephone bills, and the like. The new firm became one of the largest legal partnerships in the city. This was a time when the national economy was booming, the city was growing, and the proliferation of the automobile gave people the opportunity to travel farther and more frequently than ever before.

In 1930 the firm moved to its new quarters in the Royal Bank building on West Hastings Street. It was to remain there for the next four decades. The move took place about a year after the Great Depression started, an economic disaster which had its impact on everyone. As one of the articled students reported: 'The firm did consent to hiring movers for the heavy furniture, but the voluminous files, the library and all the small equipment was moved by the junior lawyers and students led by Mr. Baguley, the accountant. He was provided with two dozen beer (one at each office) and seventy-five cents each for a magnificent dinner at the Cafe Parisienne on Pender Street. It is unlikely the whole move cost the firm as much as $100.'[3]

During the 'Dirty Thirties,' and indeed on into the Second World War years, the firm did not expand. It had a small staff, a few articling students, and a professional group consisting of six partners and two juniors. Since the partners shaped the fortunes of the firm during the 1930s and, in large measure, determined its method of operation through the war years, a brief description of their interests gives some idea of the way the firm developed.

The oldest partner was Walter W. Walsh. Born in 1875, he had been an articled student to Adolphus Williams. Walsh was one of Vancouver's leading practitioners in real property law, with a large clientele of corporations in the field. George E. Housser had become prominent in litigation over insurance law. He was born a year before Karl Benz built the first one-cylinder motor car in 1885. He became an automobile enthusiast early in life and, as a lawyer, was an expert in automobile insurance and accidents. Alfred Bull was a year younger. He had been brought into the firm by Sir Charles Tupper. He was emerging as a leading counsel, which he soon became. Reginald Tupper, Sir Charles's son, was gaining recognition as one of the province's leading corporate practitioners. Active, energetic, and interested in a wide variety of fields, he was to emerge as the dominant partner, managing the firm in the 1940s. Harold McKim had joined Williams and Walsh in 1911. A good and experienced general practitioner, he died shortly after the firm moved into the Royal Bank building. Harold Molson, at that time, was a junior counsel, an understudy to Alfred Bull, and undertaking most of the less important litigation. Arthur Hugo Ray, born in 1904, was then a junior lawyer. He was a graduate of the University of British Columbia who understudied Housser and Molson. He was interested in litigation and was to be compared to 'Rumpole of the Bailey' in later life. The newest junior was Arthur Carroll, who had been called to the bar in 1926 and was an understudy to Walsh and Tupper.

During the Depression years, the firm maintained its strength. As one young lawyer put it: 'there was little business expansion but many business foreclosures.'[4] Whether one is buying a house or selling it, the normal prudent thing to do would be to engage legal advice. If the house had fallen in value from $10,000 to $5,000 owing to a decline in market value, it still was advisable to hire a lawyer. Financially, therefore, the firm did not suffer to the extent that other business enterprises did. Indeed, considering the high degree of unemployment in the country, a young man thought himself fortunate to be earning a living.

There was little hiring done by the firm during the Depression, and therefore there were only a few articled students accepted. Typical, perhaps, was Jordan Guy. He received his degree in economics from the University of British Columbia in 1931. As he said later: 'I sold haberdashery in the Hudson's Bay Company. I remember I spent a summer with Pemberton Holmes at the desk trying to explain securities to an unsuspecting public when the market was really on its way down. I canned corn in Chilliwack for a while. I did all sorts of odd jobs and finally my father said, "Why don't you study law?"'[5] Guy accepted the idea and took his articles with two different legal firms in Vancouver. With special permission from the Law Society, he worked four months each summer as a purser on the SS *Princess Marguerite* in order to maintain himself. As a result, he was not called and admitted until July 1938, the ceremony taking place in the old court-house in Victoria. Only five students were in the graduating class. It was Reginald Tupper who invited him to come to the firm. Two of his young lawyers had joined the army, and trained lawyers were becoming scarce. Guy was welcomed into the firm in 1942 and became a partner following the death of Walter Walsh in 1947.

When Guy joined the firm, he was thirty-three years old; Walsh, the senior partner, was sixty-seven; and the firm itself had celebrated its fiftieth anniversary, just as the Second World War was under way. In a sense, the wartime years were to be a watershed in the firm's history. For a number of years the partnership would continue to be guided by senior members whose views and attitudes were shaped by men whose values and outlook were those common to the Victorian era.

An example of this can be seen in the document signed by Walsh in 1896, when he became an articled student to Williams. In the agreement Walsh promised he 'will well, faithfully and diligently serve [Williams] as his Clerk in the practice or profession of a solicitor of the Supreme Court ...' He also promised he would not 'cancel, obliterate, injure, spoil, destroy, waste, embezzle, spend or make away with any of the books, paper, documents [et cetera].' Should anything go amiss and Williams sustain loss or damage, Walsh had to be prepared to pay for it.[6] In many respects the agreement, at least in intent, was not too dissimilar to an 1850 agreement used by the Hudson's Bay Company when hiring an employee to work in North America. He had to 'perform all such work and service by night and by day' and 'with courage and fidelity ... defend the property of the said Company ...'[7] Articling students were never asked to defend the fort, but the concept of the role of the students and the position of the partners continued to have a Victorian-age aura about it until after the Second World War. All this, and indeed the method of carrying out a legal business, was on the verge of a rapid change with the coming of peace in 1945.

By the end of the 1940s, Vancouver was booming. The pent-up wartime demand for everything from houses to automobiles gave a tremendous surge to business and stimulated the mining, forestry, construction, and other enterprises throughout the province. The student population in the university and colleges trebled as veterans swarmed into the classrooms to start or complete their post-secondary education. For the first time, the University of British Columbia established a faculty of law.[8] As the volume of production for national consumption rose steadily, the demand for British Columbia's products in Europe provided another stimulus to the economy. The increasing birthrate, coupled with a tremendous surge in immigration, fuelled the demand even further. It was a time for growth, optimism, and expansion in all fields, including the law. It is at this point that we should return to what was then known as Bull, Housser, Tupper, Ray, Carroll and Guy, still located in their former offices at the old Royal Bank building in the downtown core of Vancouver.

If there was one man who best represented the link between the prewar and postwar eras, it was Reginald Hibbert Tupper. A veteran of the Great War, he had joined his father's firm in 1917. His ability, dynamism, and administrative talents resulted in his becoming the 'managing partner' almost before the term was invented. A good description of him is given by a lawyer who joined the firm in 1955:

[He] was a real gentleman. He was the kind of lawyer who went to the heart of the matter right away and believed in spending as little time as possible to do what he considered to be an adequate job for a client. As a result, he was highly productive.

Mr. Tupper was the first lawyer to come to the office in the morning, usually by 7:30 a.m. at the latest. When the staff and other lawyers came in, he had usually been through all the mail and he would be standing by waiting for his own secretary so he could dictate to her. He did not use the dictating machine and I do not think he ever learned how to use it. He was a non-mechanical person. I remember going into his office one day and he was having trouble putting a refill in a pencil and he asked me if I would do it.[9]

Tupper was the senior corporate lawyer in the office. He had made his own reputation through sheer ability. When dealing with clients he could produce results in an incredibly short time. 'When he incorporated companies,' a colleague recalled, 'he did it in just no time and charged $100 whereas very young lawyers would charge $150 to $200. One problem was to get Reggie Tupper to charge $200 for what he thought was so easy to do.'[10] Tupper was one of those fortunate people who had an almost photographic memory. He could sort through a mass of material, analyse it, and quickly see the essential points of it. He was not the most patient individual, and not the easiest person to work with in harness, in part because of his speed.

New lawyers coming to the firm in the postwar era held Tupper and the senior partners in awe. 'As far as I was concerned,' one of them said, 'they had been practising law since Christ was a corporal.' The firm, he continued, 'still had the "sole practitioner mentality" which was to remain for many years until the firm underwent a rapid expansion phase in the late 1970s and 1980s. The partners of the 1950s and 1960s wanted to use the model of the barristers' system where the junior "devilled" but didn't participate in advising the client, formulating the strategy or preparing the documents.'[11]

There were many veterans who went into law at the end of the war, and it was only natural that Bull, Housser and Tupper[12] should accept a number of them as the volume of work increased. One was Ivan Quinn, who was hired in the early 1950s at $225 a month. At that time, he recalled,

they never expected our group to bring in business. They had all kinds of business. All they wanted was workers, and we were the workers. They had the Royal Bank as the principal client, they had mortgage companies ..., insurance business and so on. We had various corporate clients that always had work to be done ... Bread and butter is the routine work like land title work, mortgages, conveyancing and steady corporate work like doing debentures ... We were always big enough and efficient enough to draw the business ... As Reggie [Tupper] said, 'if you're good, they will come to you. And if you're not good, they shouldn't come to you anyway.'[13]

For years Tupper had the determining voice in how the firm was run. His fellow partners relied on him for business guidance and deferred to his decisions in everything except major affairs, when, of course, he would consult with them. There appear to have been no regular formal meetings of the partners when minutes were kept. Rather, the partners would meet informally, a consensus would be reached, and Tupper would be left to carry on the administration of the firm while the other partners pursued their legal business. Tupper was what one would call a 'workaholic.' He had the energy, not only to manage the firm, but to look after his own clients and bring in business as well.

Tupper's approach to running the firm could be termed 'paternalistic.' He did not have a title, and there was no formal partnership agreement until 1958. 'Policy,' a junior partner recalled, 'came from Mr Tupper's office and that was it.'[14] Another junior remembers that when the partners met, they just sat around and decided things. If Tupper called a meeting for a specific time and nobody turned up within three minutes, he left the room. There would be no meeting. When all went well and Tupper decided the meeting was over, he stood up and left, and the meeting ended. As a boy, Tupper had had a strict Scottish governess who had him read the Bible from one end to the other four times. He frequently reached into it and used proverbs to clinch his decisions. On one occasion raises for young lawyers came up for discussion and Tupper remarked: 'Shall we muzzle the ox that treads out the corn?' The young lawyers got their raises and that was that.[15]

There was a somewhat old-fashioned attitude towards billing as well, one that lasted well into the postwar period. On one occasion in the mid-1950s, three of the firm's lawyers were attending a lawyers' conference in eastern Canada. There they sat in on a discussion on an automated system of recording the time lawyers actually spent working on a client's case. 'We brought back the idea,' one of them reported, 'and we were able to convince the [senior partners] that this was a good idea. They weren't too keen on it because in the old days they used to take a file when the job was finished and say "Well, how much is that worth? How much does it weigh? We'll charge them $500"... What a hell of a way to run a railroad. But it was very pleasant and they all made a good living. But it was a wasteful system.'[16]

An organized billing system in the firm was in operation by 1957. Prior to that time, the charge for service rendered depended largely on the individual lawyer, who would fix the amount of the fee and send it out. When the new system came in, each partner was assigned an hourly fee scale. At that time, for example, R.H. Tupper's fee was $50 an hour. Built into the fee was the overhead factor. At least 50 per cent of the fee was used to pay for such things as rent, light, heat, telephone, staff wages, bar fees and insurance, leasing machines, furniture, stationery, and many other expenses incurred in running the firm. Expenses incurred in pursuing a case – travel, hiring experts, and so forth – would be added to the fee. The system brought in a measure of efficiency to an expanding firm.

Every law firm has its 'characters' and in Bull, Housser there was one lawyer who will long be remembered. Arthur Hugo le Plastriere Ray, after being graduated at UBC, articled with Walsh, Housser for three years before being called and admitted to the bar in 1927. A childhood injury had left him with a limp but at maturity he was bulky and strong as the proverbial ox. His, a colleague said, 'was the face of some jovial teutonic robber-baron or jolly and benevolent Santa Claus. His twinkling blue eyes surveyed the world from that rubicund and cherubic countenance with constant merriment and boundless enthusiasm for every day of his life. His mind was sharp, his wit was ready, at repartee he was unsurpassed, his memory was photographic.'[17]

Ray became a partner in the firm and during the 1930s, and in the postwar years his reputation grew steadily. 'He was one of our greatest characters, the Pickwickian part of the firm,' one of his colleagues said. 'He was very effective before a jury. He would roll into the courtroom like a sailor and was very brash. He really couldn't be put down by anybody.' Another added: 'Everyone liked him. He liked jokes. I remember once when Arthur Carroll had a client who tried to climb out the window of his office. [After the incident] Arthur was nervous and just shaking after this terrible experience when Hugo came bustling in and said: "For God's sake, Arthur, you've got to be more careful about presenting your bills!"'[18]

Another barrister who enhanced the firm's reputation in court was Alfred Bull. Like Ray, he had a sharp mind and quick wit, and he, too, was able to absorb a great deal of information before walking into the courtroom. One story told about him is worth repeating. There had been a major fire in a sawmill. Bull, Housser acted for the insurance company, and there was evidence that it might have been arson. 'It was a jury trial,' a colleague recalled, 'and whoever was acting for the claimant had a beautiful picture of the mill in its working days – trucks moving, horses hauling waggons, smoke pouring from the mill's chimneys and so forth. Then they had a picture of it after the fire and it was just a bloody mess. The judge said: "Mr Bull, haven't you any pictures to help the jury in making their decision?" Bull replied: "I'm sorry, my lord, we didn't know it was going to burn down!" "The jury will ignore that remark," the judge said – but that was the end of the case right there. How can the jury ignore the remark?'[19]

Lawyers such as Ray, Bull, Tupper, and others in the firm enhanced its reputation, attracted more clients, and brought more law students to its door. It was during the postwar period when the firm began to improve its relationship with articling students. For decades legal firms looked upon such students as being privileged to be accepted and taught the legal profession. Indeed, the first such student in the firm, Walter Walsh, contributed a token one dollar to Adolphus William as 'payment' for the instruction he was about to receive. During the years he remained under instruction, the student was expected to work as well as learn and, as time progressed, he became a valuable asset to the firm.

Before the war, the firm normally accepted two types of articling students, those with a university degree and those who had completed their high-school education. The latter could anticipate five years' service as an articling student, the former three. When a faculty of law was established at the University of British Columbia, its graduates required only one year's articling. Bull, Housser and Tupper began to accept more students with an LLB degree than ever before. Such a person was easier to train and could be more useful to the firm. Since many of these students were veterans, they brought with them a maturity of outlook and experience which would bring about certain changes in the way they were treated.

When Cecil Merritt, Tupper's nephew, was an articling student in the early 1930s, he was paid $30 a month in his third year with the firm. In his time, there were usually two or three students. On a typical day, he recalled,

you had to go up to the Court House around ten o'clock in the morning to do the various filings in the Registry Office or serve documents on other firms or parties. You might be sent to the Law Library to study some point of law; you might be sent to the Land Registry office to search a lot of titles and you might occasionally go to the City Hall. You could be sent down to the Police Court. The great practicing part of the student's life was in the Small Debts Court.

There was always a certain amount of devilling – researching and also assisting the lawyer almost as junior counsel.[20]

In the postwar years, the students were given similar tasks but, at the same time, were expected to carry out any other instruction which might be assigned to them. One such student was Ivan Quinn, a friend of John Walsh's and David Tupper's, both of whom were sons of partners. Quinn came in 1950, when the firm still occupied only one floor of the Royal Bank building. 'In those days,' he said, 'it was still semi "horse and buggy"... They always stopped for tea around 3:30–4:00 o'clock. Everybody would come in if they weren't terribly busy ... and have tea. It was really good because you stopped work. It was small enough to do that ...'[21]

A decade later, the volume of work had increased. In 1963, when Barry Dryvynsyde telephoned David Tupper from England to enquire about the possibility of becoming a student with the firm, Tupper phoned back to enquire: 'When can you come?' At that time, Dryvynsyde recalled, 'It was a student's market. There was a shortage of students, the firms were busy and they were looking for students.'[22] Control of the students within the firm was not as structured, as it became later. Among other tasks, they were expected to look after the firm's library, which entailed everything from shelving and sorting books to polishing the furniture. As for instruction, another student reported: 'We each had a principal, but we weren't particularly under that principal's tutelage. I think he was responsible for our general well-being ... and at that stage we would be doing work for different lawyers on different matters.'[23]

By the early 1960s, other steps were being undertaken to improve the firm's relationship with its students. In 1960, for example, the partners agreed that all commencing students should be paid a salary of $175 per month.[24] Another decision was taken to improve the method of accepting students. For decades the normal practice had been to bring in young men who were known to the partners. Some were sons or nephews, others were friends of relatives, and there were those who were graduates from the better-known Canadian or British universities. In almost all cases, the student came knocking at the door of the firm. This was a comfortable situation as long as the firm was small and could manage with three or four students, but as it grew it needed more. In 1961 it was decided to raise the number to six. It was also appreciated that there was increasing competition for good students from other legal firms in the city. As one partner put it: 'Law firms grow through the good people they attract, and you have to have good people to get good clients. So the articling process and attracting good articling students is a critical part of the firm's business.'[25]

With that in mind, the partners agreed that one of them be appointed 'to act in liaison with the U.B.C. Law School on a continuing basis, and to take positive action to arrange for additional students to be articled with the firm.'[26] As a result, arrangements were made to meet law students close to their time of graduation. The interviewer would put to them the advantages of serving with Bull, Housser, he would answer their enquiries and, at the same time, he would get some idea of their background, character, intelligence, and attitude, which would reveal their potential as a future lawyer. Getting the 'right' students was not always easy, but it never had been. The student's academic record was always available, but the personal interviews revealed a great deal as well. Moreover, the firm instituted monthly meetings with the students, during which one of the partners would talk on his particular area of expertise. By the 1970s, the firm established a student committee and it brought in a rotation system whereby students were given the opportunity to serve, for specific periods, with the various specialized departments established as the firm expanded. The committee was also able to monitor the students better as to both capability and potential suitability within the firm.

The new system and its more structured format seemed to work. As time went on and the firm kept expanding, the number of students increased until there were twelve by the early 1980s. By that time they included women as well as men. Moreover, there was no longer a shortage of students. Another faculty of law had been established in 1975, at the University of Victoria, and, as the supply became larger, the firm could be more selective and the interviewing system more sophisticated. In 1903 a student, articling with L.G. McPhillips, signed a note promising to abstain from all intoxicants and not to go into a bar room or gambling-house until he became a barrister and solicitor. By the 1970s, the potential articling student could be invited to a lunch or dinner with some of the partners, where drinking was quite accepted. No eyebrows would be raised or glances exchanged, unless, perhaps, he or she put mustard on the salad.

Even before the firm began to send out a 'head-hunter' for the best and brightest students, it was fortunate to attract many who had excellent qualifications and who decided to remain with the firm. In the postwar period, a number of these were veterans who, in time, were responsible for guiding the firm's growth. One, for example, was Wilfred J. Wallace, who had a Bachelor's degree in Applied Science. After service in the navy he obtained his LLB from Osgoode Hall, came to Vancouver, joined Bull, Housser, and found Hugo Ray needed help in litigation. With his engineering and law degrees, he began to specialize in engineering and construction litigation, creating the firm's reputation in that field. In 1979 he was appointed to the Supreme Court of British Columbia. Another veteran who came to the firm was David Brander-Smith. He, too, was a navy veteran and he became interested in the Admiralty side of the firm's business. It already had good connections with several British shipping firms, and Brander-Smith worked successfully to bring in local towboat and maritime insurance as well. Eventually the firm was to have four lawyers and two paralegals involved in maritime and Admiralty law.[27]

Most of the student veterans who came to the firm did so in the 1950s. In the following decade, the background of new entrants varied widely. Jurgen T. Lau, for example, was in Germany when the war broke out. After studying geology at the University of Hamburg, he came to Canada, worked for a geophysical contractor in northern Canada, got a degree as a geological engineer, and later decided to obtain a law degree from UBC. He came to Bull, Housser in 1965 and was soon helping lawyers in mining and construction cases. He had a lot of friends and acquaintances in the mining business whom he used to meet in the North. Working on this, he began to build up that area of the firm's business, until there were two or three lawyers, together with legal assistants, helping him. When Lau became an associate partner, the value of mineral production in the province was about $300 million annually. Five years later, it was close to half a billion dollars, and ten years later, it was well over a billion. The firm was to feel the financial benefit of this expansion.

One final example of a student coming to the firm who was able to combine his interests with his legal profession might be mentioned. This was J.D.L. Morrison. As a boy he had been in the Sea Cadets and later joined the Royal Canadian Naval Reserve. He received his upper-deck watchkeeping and command certification and eventually was promoted to the rank of lieutenant-commander. Since Bull, Housser was one of two large legal firms in Vancouver specializing in maritime law, when he completed his articling, he was asked to stay with the firm. His own naval experience made it much easier for him to deal with clients in the field. Also, the volume of shipping in Vancouver was growing year by year and, with it, the request for legal services grew proportionately. By the 1980s, there were four lawyers and a legal assistant involved in the field of maritime law, and all were kept busy.

When Morrison entered the firm in the 1960s, the total number of partners had almost quadrupled since the wartime years. With the addition of new partners and more staff came the demand for more space. By 1962 the firm was occupying space on three floors of the Royal Bank building and was still feeling cramped. An additional 2,100 square feet was leased in 1967, by which time the firm was paying an annual rent of $33,580, or $3.50 per square foot.[28] Even before it moved in to its new offices, the firm had decided to appoint a long-range planning committee to look into its future accommodation and equipment needs.

As early as 1960, Harry Housser had distributed a memorandum to his partners pointing out the need for better, more efficient, and decently furnished offices. Three years later, he circulated another memo, this time to the Partnership Planning Committee. He mentioned the talk he had heard about a 'population explosion' in Vancouver and added: 'Since my last discussion with the City Planning Department, I understood that they were considering a city of three quarters of a million by 1975 and were laying out zoning, traffic and building plans accordingly. Since then I have heard revised estimates ... that anticipate considerably in excess of three quarters of a million by 1975.'[29] Housser suggested that if it were accepted that the city would grow, and if the firm wished to remain among the top three or four legal firms in the city, then it must grow. Planning should begin for office space based on requirements ten or fifteen years hence. He pointed out that, by 1970, the firm would consist of about thirty-five lawyers (exclusive of students) and that, between 1970 and 1980, the number of lawyers would double.

It was obvious from Housser's report that the firm would have to move. Its current lease terminated in 1971. Fortunately, at this time Vancouver was experiencing a building boom in its downtown core. Large twenty- and thirty-storey office towers were under construction, and others were being planned. The Royal Bank of Canada decided to build its own office tower, the 'Royal Centre.' Bull, Housser decided to stay with the bank, which was also one of its oldest clients, and moved into the new building when it was completed in the summer of 1973. At first the firm occupied two complete floors of the building, which, among other things, allowed more space for a better library. It had hired a permanent law librarian just before the move. By the mid-1970s it held about 10,000 books, not including the various journals, which took up more shelf space. By the late 1980s, the number of books had doubled, as had the library budget.

The growth of the firm in the 1950s and 1960s brought with it changes in management and administration. As we have seen, an organized billing system was started in 1957. When the partners began to meet regularly under the chairmanship of Reginald Tupper, one of the first committees it formed was the Management Committee in 1958. The partners also decided to hire a chartered accountant as an office manager. With a staff of about forty people, even Tupper was finding it impossible to manage the firm. Indeed, by the early 1960s Tupper was beginning to shift some of his responsibilities to younger partners, and these, in turn, formed committees to resolve the problems faced by the firm.

One of the interesting proposals put forth by the Management Committee was 'that every effort should be made to obtain new clients.'[30] Significantly, it was felt as a first step that a list should be made of the clubs to which all the partners and associates belonged, what community and service organizations they actively supported, and whether or not they were involved in political activities. If business, political, sports, and a variety of other associations could help to increase the breadth of contacts of the lawyers, it should reflect favourably on the firm's business. A lawyer might excel in aviation law, for example, but unless he or she became friendly with people in the aviation business, his or her talents might not be sought out.

A question which emerged periodically at the partners' meetings at this time was just how large the firm should become. To resolve it, a partnership planning committee was formed in 1963. Two of its members were given the particular task of proposing a better organization of the firm. Shortly afterward, a partner was in Seattle attending the Pacific Northwest Regional Meeting of the American Bar Association. He was there 'to obtain the benefit of the seminars on Law Office Administration, Fees and Billing Procedures and Lawyer–Client Relationship.'[31] He brought back all the papers and brochures available at the seminar and also spoke on the number of firms which had a managing partner, i.e., one who devoted most of his time to managing the law firm on behalf of the partners rather than on the law and his own clients.

The idea was a good one, but it was two years before it was acted upon. Further enquiries were made about the administrative arrangements of other law firms in Seattle and Vancouver. In 1968 the partners agreed to invite Mr Stanley Long to talk to them. He was the managing partner of Bogle, Gates, Dobvin, Wakefield and Long, a firm a bit larger than Bull, Housser and Tupper, but close enough in size to make comparisons. Long spoke for two hours to the partners and a lengthy question period followed. He covered a great variety of topics – the pay scale of associates, his firm's profit-sharing methods, staff benefits, retirement, insurance for lawyers, committee work, partners' meetings, filing systems, billing systems, time recording, office equipment, charity work, and more. He described his own work as managing partner, which, he stated, took up 53 per cent of his time on the job. The partners were impressed. It was Long's speech, really, which decided them in the following month to institute a system somewhat similar to the one he had outlined. Ivan Quinn, who had come to the firm as an articling student in 1946, was appointed the Managing Partner, to be assisted by an Executive Committee.

The trend towards more structure and specialization within the firm as it grew larger was a necessity, but it took time to get accustomed to it. As one partner put it:

He [Quinn] had a very difficult task because it is difficult for some partners ... to change from their daily diet of giving their opinion on every subject that touched or concerned the operation and management of the firm, to only being able to give an opinion on certain prescribed subjects ... only at a regular monthly meeting is quite a shock. All of a sudden you move from being quite an active participant in the ongoing enterprise to being almost an employee. Although you are a partner, all of a sudden the world is silent around you ... It was that process that Ivan had to put the firm through. It was done by consensus. Certainly ... there was nothing autocratic in what he was doing. He was making decisions, but he would have to make sure that he discussed matters.[32]

One of the advantages of the new system was that, instead of having monthly meetings, the partners met only once a quarter. In time, as the firm grew, the Management Committee (the Executive Committee was dropped) met with the managing partner weekly. It also marked the beginning of other committees formed to look after special areas of concern such as the Students' Committee, Partnership Committee, and the Firm Development Committee. This trend towards more structure and specialization within the firm as it grew larger was a necessity but, as Dryvynsyde said, it took time to get used to it and some of the old intimacy was lost.

Quinn's term of office ended in 1972 when Hamish Cameron took over from him. One of the things Cameron did during his first year was to draw up a partnership agreement. It was no easy task. In the old days the professional core of the firm consisted of partners, one or two qualified lawyers waiting to be invited into the partnership, and a couple of articling students. By the late 1950s this had changed to admit more categories such as junior partners and associates. Surprisingly, for decades there had been no formal agreement. The partnership had been operating on the basis of mutual trust and respect. Occasionally a document would be accepted, such as the recommendations proposed in 1968 by the Committee on Partnership, to clarify certain points of understanding. After three-quarters of a century, however, it was time to define the partnership more formally. It was Cameron and his small committee who deserve most of the credit for getting everyone's agreement to the document.

It was in Cameron's term that the firm moved to its new offices in the

Royal Centre. The last time it had moved, he noted in the firm's internal newsletter *The Weekly Bull*, was two years before he was born.[33] The firm was there only for a few years, however, when the new managing partner, Harvey Bowering, began to send out signals that more space in the building would have to be acquired. At the February 1977 Meeting of Partners, Bowering pointed out that in May there would be forty-five lawyers in the firm. Investigation revealed that, during the previous twenty-six years, the total number of staff had grown at an average rate of 6 per cent annually. At the time, the firm had a staff of 132 persons, occupying 27,500 square feet of office space. By 1982, estimating a rate of growth of only 3 per cent, there would be 152 people, occupying almost 30,000 square feet. If the rate of growth continued at a full 6 per cent, there would be 176 employees, which would require about half a floor more than the firm presently occupied.[34]

Part of the reason for the growth of the firm, of course, was the growth of Vancouver and its surrounding municipalities. In 1951, for example, Greater Vancouver had a population of 586,200. Two decades later it had almost doubled, to 1,082,352. By 1977, some were predicting the next census would show more than 1.25 million in the metropolitan area, and it was anyone's guess what it might be in the decade after that.[35] Not only did the firm grow with the city, it grew with the country as well. Canada's immigration policy was liberal, and the nation's population had doubled since the end of the war. There were more business firms with coast-to-coast interests and, as they increased in size, so, too, did their need for legal advice and consultation. In addition to this natural increase, there was more attention paid to the active pursuit of legal business by the partners themselves.

The expansion of the firm brought with it an increase in the number of support staff to the extent that in 1980 the firm appointed a personnel manager to assist the director of administration, as the former manager was now called. This was Frances Tessier. She had been with the firm a number of years, long enough to remember when some of the older partners would not use dictaphones, a few still hung on to the old wire-recording dictaphones, and others used the 'newer,' smaller cylinder types. She had seen the change-over to electric typewriters and, by 1978, she was learning how to operate the new word-processors coming into vogue. Her new job gave her the task of looking after all the non-professional staff in the firm. That put her in charge of paralegals, secretaries, accounting staff, library staff, receptionists, switchboard operators, mail-room staff, supply and services staff, and others. Within a decade, there would be close to 200 staff members, and while her workload increased, a considerable burden was taken off the shoulders of the office administrator.

In 1980, Barry Dryvynsyde succeeded David Tupper as managing partner. David was the grandson of Sir Charles Tupper. His father, Reginald, whose hand had held the helm of the firm for so many years, had died in 1972. Six years later, another Tupper, David, guided the firm during a period of steady growth until Dryvynsyde took over. Dryvynsyde was to remain as managing partner for four years, a period of slow but steady expansion as well as a time when office equipment grew more complex while providing greater productivity.

It was during his tenure that Dryvynsyde had to lease more space in the Royal Centre, both in 1980 and in 1983. It was all a costly business involving over a million dollars. All of the new offices, boardrooms, reception areas, et cetera had to be carpeted, furnished, decorated, and fitted out with new telephones and equipment. Added to that were architects' fees and renovations made to existing office space on the floor. It would not be an understatement to say that the firm paid more in one year of expansion and moving costs during Dryvynsyde's tenure than it did in the first sixty years of its existence. On the other hand, clients were no longer being charged fifty dollars for an hour's time of a senior partner, as they had in 1945.

When Jurgen Lau stepped into Dryvynsyde's shoes in 1984, Bull, Housser was ranked by *British Columbia Business* magazine as one of the largest legal firms in the province. It listed Bull, Housser as having eighty-two partners, associates, barristers, and solicitors, but excluding students, office managers, and staff. Close competitors were Russell & Du Moulin, with eighty; Ladner Downs, with seventy-five; Campney and Murphy, with sixty-one; and Clark Wilson and Co., with fifty-six.[36] Some idea of the diversity within the firm was reported the following year. In answer to a questionnaire, the *Weekly Bull* found that there were lawyers in the firm who spoke French, German, Spanish, Danish, Afrikaans, Japanese, Chinese, and one of the Indian dialects. Among the staff were those who spoke French, Spanish, Tamil, Portuguese, and Chinese. In many ways, the firm now reflected the cultural mosaic which was becoming more obvious in Vancouver with each passing year.

By the mid-1980s, Bull, Housser had expanded to roughly ten times the size it had been at the end of the Second World War. The postwar growth had brought both advantages and disadvantages. The old intimacy was lost as more partners and staff arrived. Instead of issuing an interoffice memo, it was found to be easier and much less costly to insert a notice in the *Weekly Bull*. If growth slowly undermined the former cosiness of the firm, there was a positive side to it. The increasing numbers of partners created a pool of talent and expertise. Thus if one partner had a case to deal with involving estate, insurance, and corporate law, he knew that, if he ran into difficulties, he could nip down the hall and consult a colleague who was an expert in the field.

In some ways, too, a larger firm could reduce expenses in running an office. A small firm of a dozen lawyers would require a receptionist; the same person could look after double or triple that number. The same would hold true of a telephone switchboard operator or a librarian. Similarly, some of the office equipment was becoming very expensive and would pay for itself only if it had a high volume of use, which a large firm would ensure.

Another point sometimes mentioned favouring large firms – a point frequently debated, one might add – is the prestige factor. Large firms in large cities are often regarded as the best. It is an assumption hard to prove, but many articling students seek them out to work with first-rate lawyers. Moreover, as one partner reflected,

... the large firms are much more likely to get the best work. If you want to do the really challenging work, most likely you will find it in large firms. There are, obviously, many small firms that do very challenging work, but the odds are the best work is going to be in the big firms. If you want to do the best work, you need the resources to throw at it, ... large library, large number of students to draw on, a large number of disciplines under one roof that you can draw on, et cetera. And when you have a large deal, you may need ten lawyers to work on it. You can't do that in a small firm. You couldn't do the deal justice.[37]

The increase in the size of the firm brought with it departmentalization, a natural result of specialization and increasing business. A partner with special interests or expertise, especially one who brought in more clients, would need more assistance. Additional lawyers might be hired, until there might be half a dozen or a dozen working in the same field. In the 1960s and 1970s, these groups were constituted into departments, with the senior partner in the group acting as the department head. Frequently he was the person who represented his department at the meetings of the Management Committee. It would be the committee, however, or even a full meeting of the partners, which would decide on any conflicting demand for resources between departments, should the issue arise.

Increasing size and departmentalization brought with them a fear that the firm might develop into a conglomerate of special interests and that the unity of the whole group might suffer. In 1976 the then managing partner, David Tupper, suggested 'that there should be a meeting of associates and partners at some congenial spot where issues relating to the long-term aspects of our firm may be discussed.'[38] He thought 'think tanks' should be adopted 'to facilitate communication between the different ages and stages of lawyers ... [to] assist the Managing Partner and his Committee to manage by consensus.'[39] Potential topics suggested ranged from the means of measuring the individual performance of a partner to the potential expansion of the firm and the direction it should take. The idea of the 'think tank' was accepted and, in the years that followed, the partners would select a location where they could hold a 'retreat' among pleasant surroundings to thrash out company policies and plans.

One of the policies which was approved by most was that the firm should grow. Moreover, it was agreed that a Firm Development Committee should draw up guidelines for the partners seeking to enhance the firm's business. It was recognized that 'the growth and development of the firm requires enlarged social connections to include persons who may become clients of the firm.' This might require the expenditure of reasonable amounts on appropriate forms of entertainment.[40] All agreed that this was acceptable. In the old days, there was a term sometimes used to describe the difference between those partners who actively sought new clients and those who were more content to labour at the work that came in. They were referred to as 'the finders and grinders.' Now everyone was to consider herself or himself as a 'rainmaker.'

There were numerous suggestions made respecting how best to accomplish this. One was as old as the profession itself, that is, to get out and meet more people. Partners were encouraged to become more involved in a wide variety of activities at all levels. They were urged to attend seminars on legal matters to keep themselves up to scratch and to offer to give lectures to interested groups on topics related to their special field. Membership in clubs were suggested as a means of meeting business, commercial, and professional men in the city whom lawyers might not otherwise encounter. Since the firm received a considerable amount of work from eastern Canada, the United States, Great Britain, and elsewhere, partners travelling to Toronto or New York on business were encouraged to stay over a few extra days, visit other clients, and talk with them about new areas of expertise within the firm.

The 'think tanks' would also analyse various potential markets. In the postwar era, there were many new businesses moving to British Columbia, and new areas where legal advice was needed. For example, cablevision companies began to spin their web of wires across Canada in the 1950s and 1960s. This was also the period when there emerged a greater concern about pollution and the environment. New laws were coming into effect respecting these and other matters, and the firm had to consider whether or not it should become involved. In the 1970s the flood of immigrants into Canada, many of them from Pacific Rim countries, resulted in the demand for more lawyers specializing in immigration law.

There was one potential for expansion which the firm had decided to avoid many years earlier. Some firms had become closely associated with political parties over the years. If 'Boggs and Boggs,' for example, had supported the Liberal party, either financially or otherwise, it could anticipate a certain amount of legal work coming its way when the Liberals were in power. If it was a large firm, it could anticipate a large amount. Since one of the founding fathers of Bull, Housser was a former Conservative cabinet minister, and another partner became a Conservative member of Parliament, it might be expected that Bull, Housser would be a strong supporter of the Progressive Conservative party. Such, however, was not the case. The consensus among the partners was that work coming in from a federal or provincial government was welcome, but it was transitory and, in the long run, disruptive. Governments change and the impact of the sudden loss of business if a favoured political party lost at the polls was something the firm felt it could do without.

One of the firm's committees that was a topic for discussion at the 'think tanks' was the Long-Range Planning Committee. In a memorandum prepared early in 1984, a chart showed that in 1973 there were thirty-seven lawyers in the firm. Ten years later that number had doubled, and the firm had taken over four floors of the Royal Centre. A growth projection for the period 1984–94 indicated that, at maximum estimated growth, a fifth floor would be needed in 1988, and yet another five years later. These potential accommodation needs of the firm had to be planned for years ahead and, as has been mentioned, could be expensive.

During this period, the Long-Range Planning Committee circulated a number of questionnaires to the partners to obtain their opinion on how and in what direction the firm should expand. One question asked, for example, was whether Bull, Housser should consider opening offices in other cities. Almost two-thirds of those who replied were against the idea. Of those who favoured it, most felt that an additional office should be opened, not in Canada, but in the Far East. It is interesting to note that at this time, Canada's volume of trade with the Far East was beginning to equal, and then surpass, its export trade to Europe.

Another question the partners were asked was whether consideration should be given to a merger and/or acquisition with other legal firms in Vancouver or other cities. The reaction was mixed. Those for it favoured absorbing a small firm of specialty lawyers in Vancouver. This did occur in 1987, when the principals at Carver and Co. brought their practice to join Bull, Housser's technology group. Carver and Co., founded in 1916, was a patent agent firm with whom Bull, Housser had had cordial contact for many years.

Although the partners accepted internal growth and the need for departmentalization, it was realized that there must be a balance. Excessive growth by any one or two departments could create tension and lead to 'firms within the firm – potentially the most serious threat to the firm as a whole.'[41] All agreed that it was better to have a full-service firm rather than 'a related group of boutique practices' and that every care must be taken to avoid departmental isolation.

One feature of the firm's growth which might be emphasized at this point was the increasing number of female lawyers at Bull, Housser. There had never been any reluctance to accept them into the firm. In 1916 Sir Charles H. Tupper had hired Edith L. Patterson to work for his partnership. She worked for Tupper and Bull for three years before opening her own office, the first female lawyer in Vancouver to do so. There were only a few female lawyers in the entire province before the Second World War, however, and it was only when the faculty of law was opened at UBC after the war that more began to appear on the scene. At that, their numbers were still small. In 1951, for example, only about 7 per cent of the graduating class were women. Margaret Fairweather, who articled with Bull, Housser in 1971 and later became an associate, remembers there were only 6 women in classes of about 200 students. Fairweather became a junior partner in 1977 and, two years later, a full partner.

Another female lawyer who joined the firm as an articling student in the 1970s was Mary Ellen Boyd. She recalled: 'When I joined the firm, Beverly McLachlin practised there. She is now the Chief Justice of the Supreme Court of BC. Rose Mok was a lovely woman who worked in Wills and Estates. Margaret Fairweather ... was in Real Estate and doing a lot of municipal law. I think the firm was proud, in fact made a point of the fact, that women had steadily, over the years, practised and found a place at Bull, Housser. This was very different from many, many other firms, as I felt quite comfortable there.'[42] Boyd was to be appointed to the bench of the County Court of Vancouver in 1985. Four years earlier, her colleague Beverley McLachlin had been elevated to the same bench. Later, McLachlin was to be the first woman to serve on the province's Court of Appeal; the first to be appointed Chief Justice of the Supreme Court of British Columbia; and, in 1989, the third woman to be appointed to sit on the Supreme Court of Canada. These were but two of a number of partners who had been elevated to the bench, but it is a measure of the talent to be found at Bull, Housser during the years under review.

With the advent of better business machines, the increasing volume of work at Bull, Housser continued to be done efficiently. When Peter Grove, a chartered accountant, took over as the firm's director of administration in the mid-1970s, the 'computer age' was well under way and the move to acquire more 'high tech' equipment was suddenly no longer a luxury but a necessity. The firm had rented its first photocopying machine in 1961. Four years later it paid about $7,000 to purchase enough dictation machines to supply everyone who wanted one. These saved the time of secretaries and, when computers and word-processors began to be available in the late 1960s and early 1970s, they had the capabilities to perform functions in minutes which previously involved long hours of dull, grinding work. In the late 1970s, when Daniel Webster was reporting to the partners on the proposed new word-processing centre for the firm, and talking about the AES and Micom System and Optical Character Reader, he was using words and terms which former partners would not have understood.[43] They would also have been very surprised that, today, the centre, although smaller, operates twenty-four hours a day, seven days a week. As the administrator put it, 'We have people there working throughout the night on work the lawyers left from the evening before.'[44]

The steady improvement in transmitting the written word spilled over to the spoken word in the 1980s. The firm's switchboard operators were good, but the equipment became overburdened as more lawyers joined the firm. In 1980, when Bull, Housser was preparing to take over the twenty-sixth floor at the Royal Centre, it called in independent telephone consultants to advise them. The problem was solved by installing a $300,000 Focus II switchboard early in 1982. It was an expensive conversion, but the money would be recoverable in six or seven years from savings on rental payments to the local telephone company. Later improvements included individual telephone-answering recorders for lawyers and secretaries alike. In a firm where Benjamin Franklin's old saying 'Time is money' is accepted as a truism, these instruments would pay for themselves as well.

The advent of the fax machine has sped up the pace of communication enormously and has put increasing pressure on law offices to have work completed in less time. The ability to send copies of letters, graphs, photographs, charts, drawings, and other documents across the country or over the oceans in a matter of minutes has been a major breakthrough in communication. It has made air-mail service look more like the old Pony Express. Moreover, since faxed material could be used in court, it helped both lawyers and judges to avoid delays in the legal process.

While communication satellites were now able to transmit radio, telephone, and television pictures and messages around the world with increasing sophistication and efficiency, the world was coming closer to the concept of 'the global village,' a term used to indicate the growing interdependence among nations and regions as the means of communication and transportation overcame former isolationism and distance. One of the features of this era was the growth of international business and the amalgamation of firms which found size would increase their profit margin. As the interests of institutions ranging from banks to accounting firms began to spread farther afield, it was only natural that, in turn, they would seek legal advice from lawyers who were familiar with the international as well as the national scene or who, at the very least, had good overseas connections with foreign legal firms. This development was not lost on Bull, Housser. In the 1980s it decided to branch out in areas the firm had previously avoided.

The first suggestion that the firm should establish an office in the Far East appeared in the 1975 Minutes of Partners' Meeting. It was made by Frank Low-Beer, who felt an effort should be made to open a branch in Hong Kong. Trade between Canada and the Pacific Rim countries had been expanding steadily. Moreover, there was a large amount of investment money flowing into British Columbia, especially into Greater Vancouver. It was not until after the death of Mao Tse-Tung and, later, the reestablishment of normal diplomatic relations with China in 1983 that the topic was raised again. In that year, the Seventh Commonwealth Law Conference was due to be held in Hong Kong. Three partners felt this might be a good opportunity to examine 'the potential for legal work generated from the Pacific Rim/East Asia [area]' and to find out if it 'appears to be sufficiently great that it warrants further study.'[45] The Firm Development Committee agreed with the proposal, especially if the venture could be made in connection with a large law firm in Hong Kong. Later that year, Low-Beer and Hamish Cameron went to Hong Kong with the former going to Manila and Singapore as well.

When the two travellers returned, they reported favourably on Hong Kong, which, at that time, was the third-largest financial centre in the world. It was also one of the focal points for world trade with the People's Republic of China. There were only two Canadian firms which had branch offices in the colony and they also noted some restrictions by the Hong Kong bar on foreign lawyers. They reported, too, that Hong Kong was an expensive location and that a branch would probably not break even, much less make a profit, until its third year in operation. It was decided to postpone decisive action until 1985, but meanwhile the firm agreed it should try to hire Clive Ansley, a Canadian lawyer well steeped in Chinese history and culture then teaching at UBC. Both he and his wife were fluent in Chinese, and he had recently been invited to teach at the Sun Yat-sen University for a year. While there he could assess the potential for the firm in the Far East. Some months later, Bull, Housser brought another Chinese-speaking lawyer into the firm – Mason Loh. He was born in Hong Kong, spoke Cantonese and Mandarin, and had numerous Chinese connections. Loh joined as an associate in 1984.

When Ansley reported on his observation in China, a special meeting of the partners was held, and the focus began to change from Hong Kong to the mainland. China was opening up politically and was 'expected to have great economic potential in the future.'[46] Competition would be less. There were only four or five foreign law firms in Beijing and none in Shanghai. The latter soon gained favour. It was the largest city in China, with a population of about 12 million people. It was the old commercial centre of the country, it was in one of the new economic zones which the central government was establishing, and it would be cheaper there to establish an office as international consultants. There were other positive points as well. If the plan succeeded, Bull, Housser would be the first Canadian law firm to establish a base on mainland China. This, as one partner put it, 'would raise the firm's profile with major Canadian corporations both here and in the East. It would also put us in a position to participate in any work generated by Chinese government agencies intending to do business in Canada.'[47] The prospects looked good, and after a considerable amount of negotiation, including arrangements to share office space with an accounting firm, Bull, Housser was open for business in Shanghai in 1985.

For a short time the firm had representation in Beijing. Its representative there was Perry Keller, a commercial lawyer who had studied in

China and who was fluent in Mandarin. His marriage to a British diplomat and her posting to Beijing had been a major factor in the firm's decision for him to be its representative in spring 1987. The arrangement lasted only a year, however, because the Chinese government passed a law restricting the employment of the husbands or wives of diplomats in China.

During 1987, the firm brought in more people who had the legal and linguistic ability both to support those serving overseas and to provide a base for expansion. Mark Sachs, for example, transferred his articles from Davis and Co. to Bull, Housser. He spoke Mandarin, wanted to do Asia–Pacific Rim work, and felt there was greater opportunity at Bull, Housser. He was to go to Shanghai as an associate. Later that year, Peter Scarrow came to the firm. He had lived in Taiwan for several years, working for a few trading companies there. Later he went into the legal profession. He spoke Mandarin and already had clients in Taipei in Taiwan. By the end of 1988, the firm had ten lawyers who could write and speak Chinese, and one lawyer and student who could speak Korean. By February 1989, Bull, Housser had established offices in Shanghai, Taipei, and Hong Kong and was looking farther afield.

The decision to open an office in Hong Kong deserves some explanation. In 1984 the decision to open a branch there had been turned down in favour of Shanghai. A Hong Kong office needed the right people, since it represented an expensive and risky venture. In the same year, Mason Loh was engaged by the firm. He spoke both Mandarin and Cantonese, and he was bright and interested in working overseas. In 1985 he visited China to survey the situation in part for the firm and in part on his own behalf. With an additional two years' experience with the firm, he felt competent to represent Bull, Housser in Hong Kong.

Late in 1987, the firm's Pacific Rim Committee convinced the Management Committee that the time was ripe to open a Hong Kong office, provided this could be done in association with a Hong Kong firm, which would ease the financial burden associated with a venture in one of the most expensive cities in the world. It happened that, about this time, one of the partners had occasion to visit the Haight Gardner law firm in New York. It had a Hong Kong office and suggested an office-sharing arrangement. Further talks were held, and an agreement was made to cooperate with the American firm, with the result that Bull, Housser was able to open an office there by spring 1988.

The 1970s and 1980s will be remembered by many as a time of mergers, takeovers, acquisitions, and amalgamations. The trend had not gone unnoticed at Bull, Housser. It had happened to some of its client firms. On a fellow-professional basis, accounting firms had been going through a process of forming national, and even international, relationships. The possibility of law firms attempting to establish branch offices in other provinces had been forbidden by law. In the 1980s, this interprovincial prohibition was challenged by a Toronto law firm which claimed it was unconstitutional. Ultimately the Supreme Court of Canada was to find that there was no legal impediment to law firms merging, and this, in turn, set in train a series of events which was to have a major impact on Bull, Housser.

Even before the Supreme Court decision, the partners in the firm felt the Court would rule in favour of it. Law firms in the United States and in Australia had been expanding through mergers and associations, so why not in Canada? In autumn 1986, Bull, Housser struck a future-association committee, chaired by E.F. Horsey, to consider and report on the matter of interprovincial law firms. As the managing partner related later:

A great deal of very useful work was done by that committee, particularly under the guidance of Ted Horsey ... We analysed in a very pragmatic way this whole notion of interprovincial connections. We [examined] what kind of business were we getting from law firms in the East ...; what was the danger to us of Eastern law firms coming out to Vancouver and forming their own offices here ... We addressed issues, such as could we compete with Toronto law firms because of their larger size, their capital bases ... Our initial conclusions were that we liked life very much the way it was ... and we were attracted to the idea of remaining a British Columbia law firm, but we realized there were changes afoot and we had to be ready for them.[48]

While the committee's work went on, partners visiting Toronto and Montreal on business took the opportunity to meet with members of some of the larger firms in those cities but found they had not given serious thought to interprovincial expansion. However, this changed early in 1989, when the Supreme Court ruled it quite legal for law firms to establish offices anywhere they wished. As a result, Stikeman, Elliott, an eastern Canadian law firm, decided to establish an office in Vancouver. One of its Hong Kong clients had decided to invest heavily on the former site of Expo. He would be spending tens of millions in development in Vancouver, and their legal services would be needed. At about the same time Blake, Cassels, a very large law firm in Toronto, also moved into the city through the established offices of Jordan and Gall.

Another factor pushing Bull, Housser into some sort of association was coming from the Far East. If it wished to represent Canadian interests in the Orient, and Oriental interests in Canada, it was obvious that overseas clients were interested in doing business in eastern as well as western Canada. As Daniel Webster put it: 'We realized that to the extent Bull, Housser and Tupper was becoming international, particularly in the Pacific Rim perspective, it was necessary for us to have a national perspective in order to service the needs of those international clients. So there was tremendous pressure on the firm, both from the people in our Hong Kong office and our lawyers here charged with Pacific Rim marketing, to do something in Toronto.'[49]

This, in turn, led to a more vigorous approach by Bull, Housser. It retained Price Waterhouse to provide a short list of five legal firms in eastern Canada which would be compatible for consideration. One was McMillan Binch, a firm with 120 lawyers which had been established in Toronto in 1905. In April 1989, two senior partners visited the firm in Toronto and reported back on the warmth of the greeting extended to them. This was followed by other meetings in both Toronto and Vancouver. The partners of both firms found they shared a tremendous area of similar interests. Added to that was a high degree of interpersonal compatibility, an essential element when planning an association of this nature. The partners at Bull, Housser gave the managing partner their full endorsement to 'proceed to detailed discussions with McMillan Binch to map out specifics of an association with that firm.'[50]

When Bull, Housser was exchanging a mass of business information with McMillan Binch, the latter had an enquiry from a Montreal firm, Byers Casgrain, which was looking for some sort of association with the Toronto firm. Byers Casgrain had started in 1905 and was a well-known commercial law firm in Montreal. Like Bull, Housser, it had grown rapidly in the 1970s and 1980s and had diversified its practice during the last quarter of a century. Although smaller than the Toronto and Vancouver firms, it had a similar outlook. Like the others, it was interested in widening its scope to a national and international level. For Bull, Housser, it was also a happy coincidence that Byers Casgrain was one of the firms in Montreal it was planning to approach in due course. As it turned out also, meetings with the partners in Byers Casgrain produced the same warm feelings as had those with the McMillan Binch firm.

During summer 1989 a series of meetings was held among the senior partners of three firms. Earlier discussions with McMillan Binch revealed they had interests in both China and Japan, although they had no offices there. Looking into the future, if the three firms were intending to form a truly national and international association, should not some thought be given to filling the gaps between Toronto, Montreal, and Vancouver? Perhaps there should be offices in Calgary, Winnipeg, and somewhere in Atlantic Canada as well. And what about expansion into Europe and the United States? The European Common Market was scheduled to take another major stride towards integration in 1992 and, since all firms had some European clients, would it not be advisable to establish some sort of relationship with a European law firm, or perhaps establish an office in Europe which could stand on its own?

Aside from the overseas interests, the negotiating partners had to consider the implications which the Free Trade Agreement between the United States and Canada might have. The United States represented a tremendous market, and obviously the geographic location of the three firms presupposed special areas of interest which each might cultivate in due course.

For Bull, Housser, the crunch came in mid-October. The thirteenth and fourteenth days of that month were devoted to meetings and discussion of the draft protocol which had been drawn up. The form the relationship should take concerned everyone, and it was realized this was one of the most important steps the partners had taken in the firm's history. Essentially it was a decision of whether the firm would remain in the front ranks of the leading law firms in Vancouver, and indeed in Canada, or face the possibility of gradual diminution as the more aggressive and internationally minded firms surged ahead. It called for a bold decision, but, at the same time, no one wished to see the firm submerged in a national organization where the firm's hard-won reputation would be lost to public view. Having agreed to the union in principle, it was felt, as the managing partner at the time, put it,

that what we should do is have a protocol in which each of the firms continued to maintain its own independence, its own name within its own jurisdiction, but that we would form a national association called McMillan, Bull and Casgrain. It would be managed by an association committee comprised of the three managing partners and it would coordinate marketing activities common to the three firms ... It was also decided to form an international partnership in which each of the three firms would be a partner. That international partnership would also be known as McMillan, Bull and Casgrain. The three firms would contribute to the costs of operating foreign offices and to the expenses involved in marketing offshore.[51]

The announcement that the three firms formed a national association and an international partnership, effective 1 December 1989, was published in various major newspapers throughout Canada. It may not have been the beginning of a new era for Bull, Housser, but it certainly was a new stage in the firm's development.

The new association came on the eve of Bull, Housser's centennial. The changes during the last hundred years have been tremendous. The two earliest partners, McPhillips and Williams, had both been born well before Confederation. When they started to practise in Vancouver, the speed law for automobiles in the city was nine miles an hour, and a city by-law stated that residents were not permitted to keep more than two cows on their property. The partnership had grown with the city. By the time the firm announced its association with the eastern Canadian law firms, Greater Vancouver contained more people (approximately 1.5 million) than there were in all of British Columbia at the end of the war.

It was, of course, more than the growth of Vancouver that led to the increased size of Bull, Housser in the postwar era. R.H. Tupper had been right when he had said, years earlier, that the prime requisite to attract clients was to do quality work at a reasonable charge and in good time. He and his colleagues were fortunate that the lawyers they attracted into the firm were both intelligent and hard-working. The decision to seek out systematically the best graduates from the universities' law schools helped to maintain the high quality of work within the firm which Tupper deemed so essential.

Other reasons for the firm's growth, of course, were the increase in business activity throughout the province, the creation of business empires, and the continued spread of government rules and regulations affecting the daily life of Canadian citizens, of which the prime example is probably the Charter of Rights. Business transactions, too, have become far more complex. A hundred years ago, it was not uncommon for two men to complete and confirm a business deal with a handshake. Today the same deal would be confirmed by a document of twenty pages or more which had been scrutinized by lawyers representing both parties. The advances in technology have opened up new fields in the law. The first partners had been practising for almost twenty years before the first airplane flight took place in Canada, and twenty-two years before the first radio station went on the air in Vancouver. Technological advances of every sort have affected Canadian life, and thus Canadian law. All contributed to the growth of the firm, as did the decision of the partners themselves to enlarge their horizons and expand to meet the needs of their clients, both old and new.

By the 1990s, Bull, Housser and Tupper had expanded into a firm with almost 100 lawyers. Of this number, approximately 25 per cent are women. The range of interests and expertise within the firm covers a wide spectrum of the law, wider than the original partners would have thought possible in their wildest dreams. The firm has come through a century of change and expansion, of peace and war, of depression and prosperity. It has been a century of challenge but, throughout the decades, for the firm it has been a century of service.

NOTES

1 The best source of the early history of the province is Margaret A. Ormsby, *British Columbia: A History* (Toronto: Macmillan of Canada 1950).
2 See Anne Kloppenborg, *Vancouver's First Century* (Vancouver: J.J. Douglas 1977).
3 Bull, Housser and Tupper Archives, statement by C.C.I. Merritt on the history of Bull, Housser. Merritt was the nephew of R.H. Tupper.
4 Ibid., 6
5 Interview with Jordan Guy, 22 September 1988, 2. Typed copies of interviews of the firm's partners with the author are held in the Bull, Housser, Tupper Archives.
6 The Articles of Agreement between Williams and Walsh are located in the Law Society of BC files in the Provincial Archives of BC.
7 Document in possession of the author
8 Reginald Tupper had been a strong advocate of a faculty of law for years.
9 Interview with H.C. Murray, September 1987
10 Interview with David Brander-Smith, 18 January 1988, 19
11 Interview with Hamish Cameron, 20 May 1988, 7
12 The shortened name was formally adopted in 1962.
13 Interview with Ivan B. Quinn, 23 October 1987, 53
14 Interview with Jordan Guy, 22 September 1988, 28
15 Interview with Hamish Cameron, 20 May 1988, 27
16 Interview with Ivan B. Quinn, 23 October 1987, 39
17 Bull, Housser and Tupper Archives, John Walsh, 'Biographical Sketch of Arthur Hugo Le Plestiere Ray, Q.C.'
18 Interview with the Honourable W.I. Wallace, Ivan B. Quinn, and David W.H. Tupper, 19 May 1988, 23–4
19 Interview with Robert Orr, 22 October 1987, 27
20 Interview with C.C.I. Merritt, 12 November 1987, 12–36

21 Interview with Ivan B. Quinn, 23 October 1987, 36
22 Interview with B. O'N. Dryvynsyde, 12 July 1988, 12
23 Interview with William C. Bice, 8 April 1988, 16
24 Bull, Housser and Tupper Archives, Minutes of Meeting of Partners, 7 June 1960
25 Interview with R.J. Bauman, 16 May 1989, 15
26 Bull, Housser and Tupper Archives, Minutes of Meeting of Partners, October 1961
27 Interview with David Brander-Smith, 28 January 1988, 25
28 Bull, Housser and Tupper Archives, Minutes of the Meeting of Partners, 17 April and 17 May 1966
29 Ibid., 18 April 1967, Appendix 1
30 Ibid., 20 November 1961
31 Ibid., 21 September 1964
32 Interview with B. O'N. Dryvynsyde, 12 July 1988
33 Quoted in the ninth-anniversary edition of, *The Weekly Bull*, 17 September 1982. Cameron's memo was dated 17 September 1973.
34 Bull, Housser and Tupper Archives, 'Management Committee Minutes File,' 1977, paper entitled 'Future Expansion'
35 The 1991 census showed there were 1,603,000 people living in Greater Vancouver.
36 Quoted in *The Weekly Bull*, August 1984
37 Interview with R.J. Bauman, 16 May 1989
38 Bull, Housser and Tupper Archives, Minutes of the Meeting of Partners, 16 November 1976
39 Ibid., Appendix, Memorandum: 'Further Notes on the "Think Tank"'
40 Bull, Housser and Tupper Archives, Memorandum by Hugh Murray, 29 March 1977 re Committee on Business Development, Seminars and Conventions
41 Bull, Housser and Tupper Archives, 'Strategic Planning – Outline of Remarks by R.J. Bauman,' 3
42 Interview with the Honourable Judge Mary Ellen Boyd, 22 September 1988
43 Bull, Housser and Tupper Archives, Minutes of the Annual Meeting, 19 February 1979
44 Interview with Peter Grove, 17 October 1989, 11
45 Bull, Housser and Tupper Archives, Memorandum, E.F. Horsey to B.O. Dryvynsyde, 29 June 1983
46 Minutes of a Special Meeting of the Partners, 8 March 1985
47 Ibid.
48 Interview with D.A. Webster, 12 December 1989, 5
49 Ibid., 7. See also Minutes of Meeting of Partners, 1 December 1988
50 Minutes of Meeting of Partners, 16 May 1989
51 Interview with D.A. Webster, 12 December 1989, 17–18

15

Hierarchy in Practice: The Significance of Gender in Ontario Law Firms

JOHN HAGAN and FIONA KAY

It is common to note how dramatically the legal profession has changed in this century, with particular concern about the growth of the profession, and especially its large firms. Many worry about the future of this changing profession. To some it has seemed that the forces of change are out of control,[1] leading to excessive litigation,[2] and competition among lawyers who are increasingly organized in firms that aggressively compete for access to an uncertain income base.[3] Many worry not only that the pocketbooks and bank accounts of lawyers are threatened, but also that the very heart and soul of the profession are in jeopardy.[4]

Yet, for minorities, the economically disadvantaged, and women, the pace and scope of change seem much more limited. Among these groups there is growing concern that law firms themselves are barriers to real reform in the profession.[5] This is no less true in Ontario than in many other advanced Western industrial settings.[6]

This essay considers some of the demographic dimensions along which these changes have occurred in Ontario, and in comparison with other North American settings. We begin by focusing on the changing membership of the profession, with special attention to the growing representation of women in its ranks and their recruitment into law firms. We do so to make the point that the history of the profession and its firms looks very different from the viewpoints of women and of men. We will suggest that, especially for women, as well as for members of minority groups who have struggled with related problems, the profession and its firms have proven resistant to meaningful change.

In particular, and in spite of some fundamental evidence of change, we will suggest that the overall hierarchical structure of law firms and the profession has remained intact, or has even intensified, and that this can be recognized by a careful consideration of the place of women in the legal profession at large, and more recently and specifically in firm practice. We will suggest that the hierarchy of the profession and its firms has not so much changed in its fundamental character as it has adapted structurally to its new political and societal environment. Like many other institutions in modern society,[7] the practice of law in Ontario, especially in law firms, has demonstrated a remarkable ability to modify its structure in ways that have preserved its fundamental hierarchical character, both as a source and as a reflection of the stratified society in which it is set. This structural modification has involved the increasing centralization and concentration of incoming lawyers in large hierarchically structured law firms.

We make these points through a consideration of materials drawn from several sources, including census data from Canadian and U.S. government sources and our own contemporary surveys of Ontario lawyers in firms and other settings. The census data allow us to analyse comparative patterns of change that stretch back to the beginning of this century. The survey data provide information on lawyers who entered the profession at the middle of this century and through the following decades. We will focus, first, on the broad outlines of change during this century in the Ontario legal profession, and then turn to the more specific role of law firms in restructuring the changing environment of legal practice in Ontario. It is impossible to understand the place of women in contemporary law-firm practice in Ontario without first examining how women broke into the profession. Before the structure and functions of law firms would become significant issues, women first had to gain entrance to the legal profession and to find acceptance as practising lawyers.

PRIVILEGE AND PRACTICE IN ONTARIO AND OTHER SETTINGS

There is good reason to believe that lawyers and law firms have been influential and privileged groups in Canadian society, and this is an important part of why women have wanted to join both the profession and its firms, and have experienced difficulty in doing so. It has long been argued that Canada is a more élite-based society than the United States,

FIGURE 15.1

Lawyers per 1,000 Population in Canada,
Ontario, Quebec, and the United States, 1911–1986

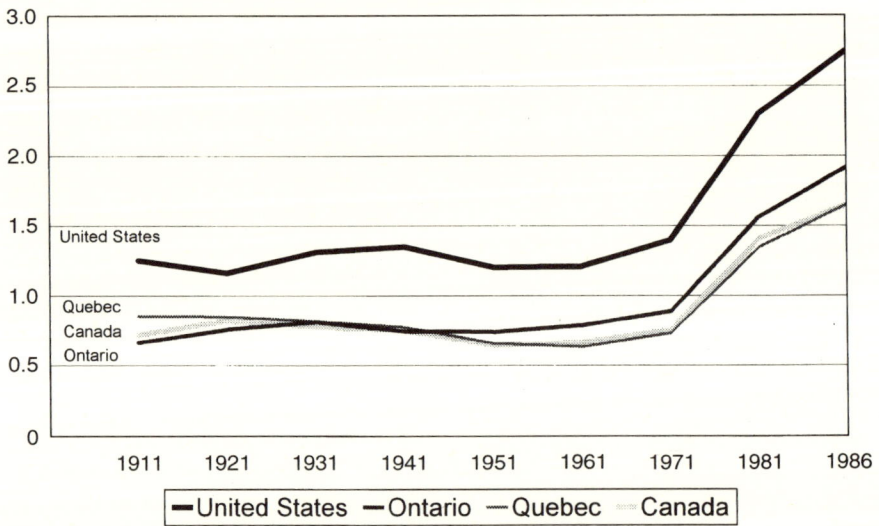

Note: Calculations for Quebec include *avocats* and *notaires*.

and that lawyers in Canada are more highly represented among economic and political élites than are lawyers in other Western nations.[8] At
the same time, there are relatively few lawyers in Canada, at least in comparison with the United States, and this has meant that entry into law in
Canada has been more difficult. We will show that this is so despite a
common perception that the interpenetration of the economies of the
United States and Canada is producing a convergence of national trends,[9]
with the prospect that Canada is becoming more like the United States in
the growth of its lawyer population. More specifically, while it is the case
that large law firms have become the dominant settings for legal practice
in both countries, this has not altered a fundamental difference in the
scale of legal practice in these national settings.

Census data on the per-capita growth of the legal profession shown in
figure 15.1 reveal that, throughout the first half of this century, the ratio of
lawyers to population was substantially higher in the United States than
in English or French Canada. This national difference occurred in the context of dramatic growth in both the numbers of lawyers and the general
populations of these countries: in the first half of this century there was

an approximate doubling of lawyers and the general population in both settings. Because lawyers and the general population grew in tandem over this period, the ratio of lawyers to population remained until 1961 at about 0.7 per 1,000 persons in Canada, and about 1.25 per 1,000 in the United States. With only one minor deviation in 1921, in every decade from 1911 to 1961 the number of lawyers per 1,000 population was more than one and one half times larger in the United States than in Canada.

ENTER WOMEN

However, other changes also occurred in the legal professions of both of these countries. For example, while the ratio of lawyers to population remained nearly constant during the first half of this century, the ratio of men to women lawyers began to decline. Although law historically has been a male-dominated profession, small but steady gains occurred for women in both the United States and Canada through most of this century, with the most pronounced gains occurring in the past two decades. Women lawyers account for a large part of the growth in the profession of both countries since 1971, especially through their entry into firm practices. However, this represents a major departure from the history of the profession, and some of the effects of this history endure. Our discussion will draw on experiences beyond Ontario, especially in the United States, to make the point that developments in Ontario paralleled those in other settings.

Initially, of course, there was great resistance to the entry of women into the profession. This resistance was signalled, for example, by Lord Buckmaster when he moved second reading of a bill in the English House of Lords in 1917 to lift the barriers against women being admitted to the Roll of Solicitors in England. On this occasion he appealed for belated support, urging that 'I would beg of your Lordships not to delay consent until time will have robbed it of all its graciousness, and what today might be a free and dignified act of justice will become tainted with the meanness and the cowardice of expediency.'[10] Law was notably more grudging in its acceptance of women than were other occupations and professions.

For example, medicine opened its doors to women before law did, although, through the first half of this century, both professions were primarily concerned with establishing their professional identities by restricting their memberships, both to women and to others.[11] Medicine probably opened its doors to women earlier than law because this occupational role was closer to stereotyped conceptions of women as maternal and nurturing, while legal work was regarded as more adversarial. At the core of these conceptions was the notion that women and men naturally occupied separate spheres, so that even before the legal profession became more restrictive in allowing individuals into its membership, women were joined with convicted felons as two groups generally excluded from legal practice.[12] Women found earlier acceptance in education, nursing, and clerical jobs.

The reluctance to accept women into the legal profession was apparent from its beginnings in the United States and Canada, both in the solo practices and in the small family firms that then dominated the profession. Prior to this century, Dixon and Pestrong[13] observe, lawyers in the United States practiced in a profession characterized by few formal education requirements for entry, uniformity in the social characteristics of its members, homogeneity in practice settings, and a lack of specialization in the type of law practised. The result was that recruitment was limited to upper-class White Protestant males whose status and rewards were relatively similar. These lawyers typically performed a similar range of tasks in solo practices or in small family firms. The early practice of law was a prestigious occupation with relatively little of the internal differentiation or stratification that was to emerge later with the growth of firms. Those few women who first entered the profession often did so by joining their fathers or husbands in small family practices. Larger 'law factories' were only in the process of becoming institutionalized during this period, as Wayne Hobson has observed in regard to the United States.[14]

The first American female attorney was addressed in person and in early court records as 'Gentleman Margaret Brent.'[15] Myra Bradwell, of Chicago, who had studied law under her husband, applied to the Illinois bar in 1869 and was refused admission because, as a married woman, her contracts would not be binding.[16] The court proclaimed that 'God designed the sexes to occupy different spheres of action, and that it belonged to men to make, apply, and execute the laws.'[17] In 1894 the Supreme Court confirmed that Belva Lockwood could not practise law in Virginia because she was not a 'male person.'[18] Women were barred from many U.S. law schools until well into the twentieth century. Harvard University did not accept women until 1950, and the last U.S. law school to admit women was, in 1972, Washington and Lee in Virginia.[19]

In Ontario, it took Clara Brett Martin six years to overcome opposition to her admission to the Law Society of Upper Canada, the first such admission to the bar in the British Commonwealth.[20] Martin had begun her fight in 1891, when she was denied admission to study law by the Law Society of Upper Canada on the grounds that the authorizing statute applied exclusively to males. She persuaded the Ontario legislature to pass an Act to Provide for the Admission of Women to the Study and Practice of Law in 1892, but still the Law Society denied her admission. The attorney general of the province intervened, and after she had finally been admitted for study and completed her articling period and required examinations, it was necessary for the legislature to pass another Act to Amend the Act to Provide for the Admission of Women to the Study and Practice of Law in 1895. It was only after still further intervention by the attorney general that Martin was finally admitted as a barrister in 1897.[21] In *Petticoats and Prejudice*, Constance Backhouse recaptures the context of the late nineteenth century and the circumstances of women's involvement with the law. Women could not be voters, legislators, coroners, magistrates, judges, or jurors.[22]

So the entry of women into the legal profession of Ontario obviously did not come easily, and, when it did come, it was not in a form that allowed women to assume prominent places in the profession. As Mary Jane Mossman notes,[23] the Law Society of Upper Canada hardly opened the floodgates when it grudgingly admitted Clara Brett Martin to membership in 1897: Only one woman was admitted as a lawyer by the Law Society in each of the years 1902, 1907, and 1908. By 1911, as indicated in table 15.1, there were still only four women lawyers in the Province of Ontario. By 1923, 27 of the 35 women who had entered the profession had been admitted after 1918. Of the 100 admitted by 1939, more than half had entered the profession in the 1920s and 1930s. The pace was at last beginning to quicken slightly.

New Brunswick, Quebec, and British Columbia continued to litigate women's admissibility to the legal profession for twenty years following Clara Brett Martin's admission in Ontario. Mossman's analysis of the legal reasoning underlying three cases in the years after Clara Brett Martin was admitted to law practice in Ontario (Mabel Penery French in New Brunswick, and later in British Columbia, and Annie Macdonald Langstaff in Quebec) reveals that, in each case, the courts denied the claim that women could be lawyers until legislative action permitted women to become lawyers.[24] In the case of Langstaff's application for admission to the Quebec bar, Mr Justice Saint-Pierre emphasized that his role was not to determine whether women should reasonably be permitted to become lawyers, but only whether the legislature had intended to include women in the use of the male pronoun in the statute.[25] Mr Justice Saint-Pierre stated: 'I would put within the range of possibilities though by no means a commendable one, the admission of a woman to the profession of solic-

TABLE 15.1

Gender Ratios in the Legal Professions of Canada and the United States

Year	Canada			Ontario			Quebec			Year	United States		
	Women	Men	Ratio	Women	Men	Ratio	Women	Men	Ratio		Women	Men	Ratio
1911	7	5,197	742.43	4	1,604	401.00	1	1,715	1,715.00	1910	558	114,146	204.56
1921	64	7,145	111.64	23	2,208	96.00	9	1,995	221.67	1920	1,738	120,781	69.49
1931	54	8,004	148.22	32	2,760	86.25	4	2,347	586.75	1930	3,385	157,220	46.45
1941	129	8,492	65.83	73	2,744	37.59	5	2,582	516.40	1940	4,187	173,456	41.43
1951	197	8,841	44.88	107	3,281	30.66	30	2,639	87.97	1950	6,256	174,205	27.85
1961	311	11,777	37.87	162	4,740	29.26	59	3,263	55.30	1960	7,434	210,089	28.26
1971	785	15,585	19.85	345	6,500	18.84	225	4,175	18.55	1970	13,964	273,044	19.53
1981	5,175	29,030	5.61	1,705	11,740	6.89	1,590	7,075	4.45	1980	72,312	452,494	6.26
1991	15,610	37,965	2.43	5,945	15,615	2.63	4,765	9,235	1.94	1990	182,745	564,332	3.09

Notes:
1 Canadian data are taken from J. Hagan. 'Gender and the Structural Transformation of the Legal Profession in the U.S. and Canada,' in M.T. Hallinan, D.M. Klein, and J. Glass, eds., *Changes in Societal Institutions*. (New York: Plenum Press 1990), 49–70 (Table 2). Reprinted by permission of Plenum Publishing Corporation.
2 U.S. data for the years 1911–81 are taken from T. Halliday, 'Six Score Years and Ten: Demographic Transitions in the American Legal Profession, 1850–1980,' *Law and Society Review* 20 (1986), 53–78 (Table 2, p. 62).
3 U.S. data for the year 1990 are taken from United States, *Census of Population: Supplementary Reports. Detailed Occupation and Other Characteristics from the EEO File for the United States*, October 1992.
4 1991 Canadian data are taken from Statistics Canada, *Occupation: The Nation* (1991 Census), Catalogue 93-327 (Ottawa: Statistics Canada 1993), Table 1, 28, 107, 127. This category includes *avocats* and *notaires* in Quebec.

itor or to that of *avoué*, but I hold that to admit a woman and more particularly a married woman as a *barrister*, that is to say, as a *person who pleads
cases at the bar before judges or juries in open court and in the presence of the
public*, would be nothing short of a direct infringement upon public order
and a manifest violation of the law of good morals and public decency.'[26]

In the early twentieth century of Canadian legal history, the male standard of what constituted a 'lawyer' was used as the basis for the amending statutes enacted in both British Columbia and New Brunswick, both
of which provided for the admission of women 'on the same terms as
men.' As Mossman points out, 'the legislative amendments confirmed the
idea of lawyers as male at the same time that they permitted women who
conformed to the "male lawyer" standard to be admitted to the legal profession.'[27] This basis for exclusion and subsequent standard for admission
to the profession was also applied to cases in other Canadian provinces.
This is the conceptual backdrop against which women struggled not only
in gaining entry to the profession, but also in finding a meaningful place
in practice once they got there. It is a backdrop that is still today recognized in the observation of the Canadian Bar Association *Touchstones*
report that the legal profession and its most prominent large firms continue to be dominated by a 'male culture.'[28]

In May 1911, Melrose Sissons applied to the Law Society of Manitoba to
be admitted as a student. Sissons was following the examples set in
Ontario by Clara Brett Martin and in New Brunswick by Mabel French.
The Manitoba Law Society refused permission, citing the precedent used
in the other two provinces that 'the word person interpreted in this connection meant male person.'[29] At the next session an amendment was
introduced to the Law Society Act by which women would be enabled to
practise as barristers on the same terms as men.[30] Between 1915, when
Sissons was admitted to the practice of law, and 1971, fifty women were
admitted to the Manitoba bar. As Kinnear points out in her study of Manitoba lawyers, these were the successful ones. Many more women
intended to be lawyers, but quit before qualifying. Thirteen women were
admitted to the Law Society as students-at-law but did not complete their
training. A further thirteen earned LLB degrees from the University of
Manitoba but were not subsequently admitted to the bar. Of the LLB
graduates who did not proceed to the bar, none worked in a legal capacity.[31] Kinnear's research shows that the fifty women called to the Manitoba bar between 1911 and 1971 shared distinctive career characteristics.

For example, government provided employment for nearly as many of
the women lawyers as went into private practice. Women lawyers also

tended to work only briefly in a practice unless they were married to a lawyer in a partnership of two. Non–family-based and larger law firms were still hostile to the idea of having women, especially married women and mothers, among their ranks. Kinnear observes: 'It was usual for the woman to retire from professional work on marriage, and it was a commonplace that the women put their families first when family responsibilities conflicted with work demands.'[32] So the small numbers of women lawyers, combined with the attitudes of male lawyers, meant that even those women who gained entrance into the profession during the early part of this century found the nature of their participation in practice very limited.

In a study of women lawyers called to the British Columbia bar between 1912 and 1931, Joan Brockman finds that those who continued to practise law took one of three paths: They remained unmarried; they left the practice of law during the period when their children were young; or they married, remained childless, and practised law. None of the women achieved what Brockman terms 'full integration,' that is, the combination of legal career, child, and husband.[33] The patterns of work and family adopted by women lawyers in the early part of the century demonstrate that they encountered few real choices. For such women, the 'choice' available was a career in law or family life, but seldom both.[34] Brockman comments that women who practised law in the 1920s and 1930s largely accepted that women lawyers played a different role in firms than men. 'Most were prepared to play supportive roles, work in the office, and limit their practice to that which "women [were] particularly fitted."'[35]

Yet, brief descriptions of some of the notable women who entered the profession in Ontario in the 1920s and 1930s give a sense of the slowly changing times.[36]

- Helen Kinnear was called to the bar in 1920 and became the first woman to appear before the supreme courts of Ontario and Canada. She was also the first woman appointed as king's counsel in the British Empire and as a judge of the county bench in Ontario.
- Margaret Hyndman was called to the Ontario bar six years later, in 1926, and became the second woman named king's counsel. She actively campaigned for women's rights and helped establish Women's College Hospital in Toronto.
- Vera Parsons graduated in 1924 and became the first woman criminal lawyer in Ontario, and the third woman king's counsel. Vera Parsons

was among the first woman lawyers to visibly confront challenges of multiple discrimination, having been physically disabled as a child by polio. She was the first Ontario woman to appear before a judge and jury.

• Edra Sanders graduated in 1930 and joined her father in the family firm that became Sanders & Sanders. She assumed many leadership positions in the community of St Thomas, Ontario, and was the first woman appointed to the senate of the University of Western Ontario.

These women are representative of the 1920s and 1930s and the challenges women confronted and overcame in joining the legal profession and public life. Even after legal barriers were dismantled, more informal structural, cultural, and social barriers remained.[37]

The deeply entrenched and lingering views that law was an exclusively male profession, and that women's appropriate domain was the home, are apparent in an interview conducted in 1978 with the Honourable Walter Stewart Owen, QC, LLD. Owen was a leading British Columbian lawyer and former lieutenant-governor of the province:[38]

JUDGE WATTS [interviewer]: I believe you were quoted again some years ago as being against women generally working. I take it that's not your view now.

MR OWEN: No, it's not ... I said that if they could do equal work, they might get paid for it but I didn't want to encourage women to leave the home and go out into the business world. I felt they had to be staying at home and raising a family. Now that sort of Victorian view I don't have now, but I had it then, very definitely.

JUDGE WATTS: Do you differentiate between the desirability of lady solicitors and lady barristers?

MR OWEN: No. I think that ... for instance, I think it's too bad when women go into the practice of law, because I am thinking of *them* more than anything else. I think it tends to make them harder and more like a man, and that would be a dreadful thing if women came to be like men.

JUDGE WATTS: And do you think that that applies equally to women doing a solicitor's job as doing the counsel work?

MR OWEN: No, I don't. I think there's a hardness that develops when they do court work which isn't misplaced in a man, but it is misplaced in a woman. It makes her less attractive, I think; I don't know whether I'm treading on dangerous ground now or not.

The numbers of women entering the profession continued to increase slowly in the 1940s and 1950s. As indicated in table 15.1, there were 73 women lawyers in Ontario in 1941, and 107 in 1951. The Second World War took men away from law schools and firms, and women were encouraged to fill office needs, although they rarely played a prominent role with clients or appeared in court. Women were at last beginning to enter larger firm practices, but their activities were primarily within firm-office settings, with little visibility beyond. Similarly, women were still excluded from most professional organizations and clubs in Ontario, and they formed their own Kappa Beta Pi sorority and the Women's Law Association of Ontario. In 1969 there were still only 162 women lawyers in Ontario. The experiences of Sandra Day O'Connor and Bertha Wilson, later to become the first women Supreme Court Justices in the United States and Canada, respectively, were representative of women entering law at mid-century: Both were obliged to accept background office positions in firms, where they were assigned research and writing roles that removed them from client and courtroom exposure. Wilson's role in the Toronto firm of Osler, Hoskin and Harcourt is discussed by Curtis Cole in his essay in this volume.

These real-life experiences are a striking contrast to the portrayal, in the 1949 film *Adam's Rib*, of a spirited courtroom battle between a wife and husband who were also lawyers, played by Katharine Hepburn and Spencer Tracy. As late as the 1960s, Smigel concluded from his interviews in New York law firms that 'they ... want lawyers who are Nordic, have pleasing personalities and clean-cut appearances, are graduates of the right schools, have the right social background and experience in the affairs of the world and are endowed with tremendous stamina.'[39] Smigel should have added that these lawyers also were almost always expected to be men.

BIGGER CHANGES TO COME

The 1960s and 1970s brought the beginning of major changes for both women and men lawyers and for the organization of legal practice in firms in Canada and the United States. This was signalled by a spike upwards in numbers of Canadian and American lawyers per capita in the 1970s, as reflected in the growth curves for both countries shown in figure 15.1. Although there are signs that this upturn began slightly earlier in the United States,[40] the number of lawyers in both countries more than tripled over the following quarter-century. Between 1971 and 1981 in Canada, the number of lawyers per 1,000 population nearly doubled,[41] from 0.76 to 1.41, and continued to increase to 1.69 in 1986. The figures adjusted to population in Ontario and Quebec are similar to those for Canada. By 1986 there were 2.76 lawyers per 1,000 population in the United States. So, in spite of the growth in the ratio of lawyers to population during this period in both countries, there remained more than one and a half times more lawyers per 1,000 population in the United States than in Canada.

Women accounted for a large part of the growth in the legal profession of both countries between the early 1960s and the mid-1980s, and this could not have occurred without the eventual opening up of firms to women. The number of women increased from 3 to 14 per cent of U.S. lawyers,[42] and from about 3 to over 15 per cent of Canadian lawyers.[43] This mirrored more general changes in the labour forces of both countries. Nearly 40 per cent of women were in the labour force by the early 1960s, and their involvement increased steadily over the next quarter-century. This increase was in part a response to the growth of post-secondary education generally, and legal education specifically.

Through the early decades of the twentieth century, Osgoode Hall Law School, under the auspices of the Law Society of Upper Canada, operated as the gatekeeper to the profession in Ontario. Legal education in Ontario shifted towards university training following the Second World War. This dramatic transformation was largely the result of the return of large numbers of veterans to universities and radical changes in U.S. legal education, including a strong emphasis on law schools for legal training.[44] The Law Society ended its primary role in legal education in Ontario in the 1950s.[45] The proportion of women students entering law schools increased from about 4 per cent in the 1950s to about 50 per cent by the early 1990s, with the largest significant increase starting in the 1970s.

Many reasons can be given for this change, including demographic, social, and ideological forces. Life expectancies were increasing, and women were therefore living greater parts of their lives without children in the home. Changes occurred in birth control, marriages were becoming less permanent, and women became more independent. The increasing availability of higher education and the feminist movement encouraged new attitudes and ambitions. The influx of women in the legal profession has also been attributed to the variations in availability of traditional women's jobs such as nursing, teaching, and librarianships.[46] Ontario and North America more generally were experiencing rapid social change. The legal profession and its firms were more clearly a part of the changing social landscape than a leading force in this change.

One way this can be seen is through the changing characteristics of the composition of the profession across a number of dimensions in the latter half of this century, and especially since 1960. This is reflected in the cohorts entering the profession in each decade of the last half of this century. We have re-created a picture of this period of change in table 15.2 by separating our sample of Toronto lawyers of various ages, whom we surveyed in 1985,[47] into a series of cohorts who entered the profession in the 1950s, 1960s, 1970s, and in the first half of the 1980s.

The results of dividing the survey of Toronto lawyers in this way is first to show again how dramatically its gender composition had changed by the 1980s. While in the 1950s and 1960s more than 95 per cent of the cohorts entering the profession were male, in the 1970s this figure dropped to about 84 per cent, and in the first half of the 1980s the proportion of men entering the profession declined to about two-thirds. However, this shift was accompanied and also preceded by a number of other alterations in the Ontario legal community.

For example, while White, Anglo-Saxon Protestants made up more than one-half of Toronto lawyers in the 1950s, this proportion dropped in every decade following, so that by the early 1980s only about one-fifth of the profession was of White, Anglo-Saxon, Protestant background. Further, while more than 90 per cent of Toronto lawyers attended Osgoode Hall or the University of Toronto law schools in the 1950s and 1960s, this number dropped to two-thirds in the 1970s, and to just over one-half in the 1980s. Meanwhile, while as many as 17 per cent of Toronto lawyers had parents (almost always fathers) who were lawyers in the 1950s, this number declined to less than 9 per cent in the 1980s. This coincides with the decline in the significance of family firms during this period. More dramatically, while about 80 per cent of the entering lawyers of the 1950s and 1960s considered themselves supporters of the Progressive Conservative Party of Ontario, and almost none supported the Co-operative Commonwealth Federation (CCF), reorganized in 1961 as the New Democratic Party (NDP), by the 1980s less than one-half identified with the Progressive Conservative party and nearly a quarter were New Democrats.[49] Membership in the Liberal party also increased over this period.

There are also signs of change in table 15.2 that reflect the further emergence of non–family-based law firms as a newly dominant form of legal practice. While only about one-fifth of entering lawyers in Toronto in the 1950s took jobs in large firms (with more than twenty members), more than one-third of entering lawyers did so in the 1980s. Similarly, while

TABLE 15.2

Characteristics of Lawyers Cohorts Admitted to the Bar, *circa* 1950, 1960, 1970, and 1980 (N = 1,052)

Cohort	Male (%)	WASP (%)	Lawyer– parent (%)	Osgoode & Toronto graduates (%)	Provincial Conserva- tives (%)	Provincial NDP (%)	Helped to find articles (%)	Working- class parent (%)	Started in large firm (%)	Started in general practice (%)
1950	98.2	56.1	17.7	91.6	80.8	1.0	34.2	24.8	19.5	43.5
1960	96.8	26.3	15.5	91.5	80.0	0.7	25.8	18.3	36.4	20.9
1970	83.6	18.2	5.3	62.0	56.3	12.7	26.9	20.0	27.7	14.1
1980	67.3	20.4	8.8	51.8	46.6	24.8	21.8	22.5	37.7	10.8

Note: The period covered by the survey is to 1984.

more than 40 per cent of these lawyers began in general practices in the 1950s, this figure decreased in each following decade, so that, by the 1980s, only about 10 per cent of lawyers did so. Professional specialization was a key part of the organization of lawyers in firms. Meanwhile, the one telling sign that some things remained unchanged involved the proportion of new lawyers entering the Toronto legal profession in each decade whose head of household was of working-class background. About one-quarter of Toronto lawyers (24.8 per cent) were of this background in the 1950s, and this remained essentially unchanged in the 1980s (22.5 per cent). So, while the gender composition of the legal profession has altered dramatically in recent years, the same cannot be said with regard to social class. The majority of women and men entering law are still from middle- to upper-class backgrounds,[50] and racial minorities remain vastly underrepresented in the profession.[51]

Despite the slowness of the profession to change in racial and class terms, it can be said that the legal profession was otherwise showing signs of substantially broadening the diversity of its membership in the latter half of this decade. The entry of women into the profession was a part of this change, rarely leading and often lagging behind other changes that were occurring in Canada, and initially lagging as well behind changes that were occurring to the south, in the United States. Still, the profession was changing, and this coincides with the change in the size and organizational structure of law firms.

So that, while in 1911 there were only seven women lawyers in all of Canada, by 1986 there were nearly 10,000. However, the rate of change was initially faster in the United States. This can be seen by comparing the ratios of men to women lawyers in each country, presented in table 15.2. At the four-decade intervals beginning in 1941, the ratios of men to women lawyers in Canada were respectively 66:1; 45:1; 38:1; and 20:1. In the United States they were 41:1; 28:1; 28:1; and 20:1. In 1981 in both countries the ratio was about 6:1, and in 1986 these ratios were below 4:1. The latest figures from the 1991 census put the ratio in the United States at about 3:1, and in Canada at about 2.4:1. This means that, while the change in the Canadian ratios lagged in relation to the American for a number of decades, Canada has more recently outpaced the United States in increasing the relative representation of women in the profession. At the current rate of change, women in both countries should constitute more than a third of practising lawyers, and may approach one-half of the legal profession by the turn of the century.[52] Women currently form about half of the younger and larger cohorts of the profession. At prevailing rates of change, women in Canada should reach parity representation with men before their U.S. counterparts do.[53]

While there continue to be fewer lawyers relative to population in Canada than in the United States generally, and in Ontario specifically, the lawyer populations of both countries are growing, and this increase includes a very notable one in the representation of women. This growth is surpassed by the recent experience in Quebec, where the representation of women is increasing faster; and there remains perhaps the more telling issue of not only the entry, but also the advancement of women in the legal profession. We turn next to the use of our Toronto surveys to assess, in a more recent context, the question of just how the profession of law is changing, and with what consequences, specifically for women, and in the expanding law firms that were a newly dominant feature of the profession.

THE CHANGING STRUCTURE OF LEGAL PRACTICE

To this point we have focused primarily on the changing size and composition of the legal profession. However, this profession, in Ontario and elsewhere, is also experiencing structural change. The most notable reflection of this change has involved the concentration and centralization of large numbers of lawyers in firms, or in what Marc Galanter has more evocatively referred to as 'mega-firms.'[54] These firms are notable, not only for their large size, but also for their highly differentiated, hierarchical structures.[55] Historically, this has involved the profession changing from a model of legal organization built largely around solo practitioners to a model of legal bureaucracy organized around law firms of increasing size, with partners and tiered levels of lawyer employees. This has made law more than a business; it has made law into a bureaucratic enterprise with its own internally differentiated hierarchical structure.

Our knowledge of the transition from self-employment and small-firm organization to larger firms is limited by the uncertain quality of historical data on the decline of solo practice and the growth of firms. However, Curran estimates that, in the United States, the proportion of lawyers who practised law alone fell from 64 per cent in 1960, to 52 per cent in 1970, to 49 per cent in 1980.[56] Similarly, Abel estimates that, while 64 per cent of all lawyers practised by themselves in 1948, only 37 per cent did so by 1970, and 33 per cent by 1980.[57] Only 16 per cent of Chicago lawyers practised by themselves in 1975, [58] while about 12 per cent did so in Toronto in 1985.[59]

Seen another way, there were only 38 U.S. law firms with more than 50 lawyers in the 1950s,[60] while there were more than 500 firms of this size by the mid-1980s.[61] Canadian law-firm growth patterns seem to parallel American trends. Daniels's study of 48 law firms across Canada reveals that these firms grew by constant or increasing rates from 1960 to 1990.[62] As of the late 1980s, more than 2,000 of the approximately 8,000 lawyers in Toronto were in firms of 20 lawyers or more,[63] and by 1990 there were 19 Toronto firms with 100 or more lawyers.[64] Since the 1980s, the largest law firms have continued to expand by absorbing or merging with other law firms.[65] One of the largest mergers occurred in the late 1980s, when McCarthy and McCarthy of Toronto joined with law firms in Vancouver (75 lawyers) and Calgary (33 lawyers), and then added 110 more lawyers when it joined with a Montreal firm.[66]

Another distinctive feature of law-firm growth in the last ten years involves its globalization. Galanter comments on the propensity of large U.S. corporate firms to grow by opening offices in cities beyond where the firm originated.[67] The trend towards geographic dispersion occurred somewhat later in Canada, but is particularly dramatic for the period 1985–90. During this five-year period, fourteen Canadian firms opened eighteen foreign offices. This is in sharp contrast to only six openings in the twenty years prior to 1985.[68] As Galanter observes, 'the attraction of this style of lawyering is not confined to the United States. In recent years, the American big firm became a model for firms in Canada, Australia, and England.'[69]

Galanter and Palay contend that, at the centre of this style of large-firm lawyering, is an ongoing competition that they call the 'promotion-to-partner tournament.'[70] Even though it is uncertain to what extent the tournament model has spread beyond large U.S. cities such as New York, this model is much discussed, and its implications are important to our understanding of debates about modern law firms. The tournament metaphor refers to the process by which the new associates hired into firms compete for a limited number of partnership positions. The essence of this tournament is its pyramid-like structure, in which there must always be many associates relative to partners in order to produce the profit base that supports the latter group's elevated earnings. Galanter and Palay suggest that, as associates are promoted, new associates must be hired to fill their positions so that the surplus capital of senior lawyers continues to be fully leveraged. So long as the ratio of partners to associates is kept constant, Galanter and Palay argue, the promotion of associates to partnership rank will dictate an exponential increase in the size of the firm.[71]

In good times this pyramid can develop through growth at all levels of the firm except the very top, while in bad times the pyramid effect may be achieved by selective attrition.

However, Galanter and Palay's depiction of the promotion-to-partner tournament is perhaps more typical of large-city U.S. mega-law firms, and the theory itself is limited. Sander and Williams argue that empirical tests offered by Galanter and Palay do not conclusively show a relationship between the tournament for partnership and law-firm growth. Rather, they find that the growth is more irregular than the tournament theory predicts, and that partnership promotion rates are often less consistent than the theory implies.[72] In addition, Daniels argues that Galanter and Palay's work focuses principally on supply-side factors and thus neglects the central role of demand factors in stimulating and constraining law-firm growth.[73] Firms are not able to leverage fully their human capital in ways that are impervious to market constraints. As Daniels notes of the tournament model: 'Should a firm's client base be affected by a cyclical downturn in the economy or by an unanticipated adverse shift in consumer preferences, the demand for that firm's services will, not surprisingly, contract. In this scenario, irrespective of the leveraging objectives of the firm's partners, only egregious folly would cause the firm to undertake expansion in an environment of enervated demand.'[74] A further difficulty with the promotion-to-partner analysis is its inability to explain recent merger activity that occurred among law firms in the United States and Canada. If partnership ratios are consistent across law firms of similar size, growth through merger activity would not confer significant leveraging gains.[75]

The promotion tournament is also not a unique explanation of constant percentage growth. As Nelson points out, it is 'equally plausible to think of constant percentage growth as a limit on the rate at which firms can respond to dramatically increased demand, rather than the other way around.'[76] For Nelson the key to law-firm growth is twofold: The demand for corporate legal services has increased dramatically, and existing big firms have managed to capture this growth.[77] Nelson argues that greater weight should be accorded to the professional ideologies of lawyers as a force of change. The 'economistic turn' in law-firm management represents an ideological shift that not only is the result of internal pressures, but also derives from professional-cultural changes in the corporate sector of the profession.[78] Thus, Nelson argues that a 'new set of managerial ideologies appeared inside law firms that emphasized strategic planning and the economic rationalization of the internal operations of firms.'[79]

Moreover, even if Galanter and Palay's theory of law-firm growth is accurate, Canadian law firms may not use leverage in the same way that some large U.S. law firms do. The ability of New York, Chicago, and Washington law firms to engage in the 'promotion-to-partner tournament' may be dependent on a structuring of firm practice that is different in the United States than in Canada. While many lawyers in the United States may not succeed in making partner at a particular firm, there may be greater opportunity for the movement of associates between law firms, across metropolitan centres of corporate legal practice, and across states, than is the case in Canadian legal practice.

None the less, there remains little doubt that Canadian law practice, particularly in Toronto law firms, has undergone a transformation in recent years. Galanter and Palay's 'promotion-to-partner tournament' may not offer the fullest explanation of the sources of change nor describe differences in the contours of change between Canada and the United States; however, their analysis does highlight the growth in law firms and the expansion of the associate base of firms prevalent in both countries. As firms grew in size and hired lawyers as associates, the percentage of self-employed lawyers declined steadily. In Canada the figure for men dropped from 92 per cent in 1931 to 70 per cent in 1986. For women, the change was even more pronounced: from 76 per cent in 1931 and 1941 to 45 per cent in 1986.[80] The total effect is that the ratio of partners to salaried lawyers declined from 3:1 in 1971 to 2:1 in 1986.[81] Stager and Arthurs indicate that one source of this change is financial, involving economies of scale associated with the sharing of overhead expenses among lawyers who no longer practise alone.[82] The number of lawyers practising as partners in small firms seems also to have declined, while the number of lawyers working as associates in larger firms has increased. The consequence of these changes has been a broadening of the organizational base of law firms.

IMPLICATIONS OF THE BROADENING BASE

By now it is apparent that the broadening of the base of law practice could not have occurred without a growth in the number of new lawyers admitted to practice and hired into firms. And as we have noted, many of these new lawyers have been women. While both men and women entering the profession have likely been affected by the changes in law-firm structure, it may be women that are uniquely affected. This effect may include the emergence of a ceiling on the advancement of women in firm practices, an 'invisible bar'[83] that is the legal analogue to the 'glass ceiling' that is so often discussed in other professional and business settings.

It may often be difficult to discern this bar or ceiling because of the large absolute numbers of women and men involved in the growth of the profession and its firms. In absolute terms the numbers of the women and men who are partners in firms has increased, but this may only be because the numbers involved in the expansion of the profession have been so large. In relative terms, the proportion of all lawyers who are partners has likely declined, while the proportions as well as absolute numbers of lawyers at lower levels of the profession have increased. We consider this possibility with recent Ontario data on practising lawyers below. First, we consider some of the background to these apparent changes.

Finding Positions in Firms

The primary avenue to a position practising law in Ontario is through the apprenticeship of articling, which involves an interviewing process that leaves room for personal and proactive contacts, as well as more formally structured methods of placement. Large firms in particular use articling as a mechanism to 'try out' students whom they might want to 'hire back' as new associates following their completion of a bar-admission course and final bar-admission examination given by the Law Society of Upper Canada. Smaller firms are more likely to use articling students as a means of easing their workload, with students less frequently hired back into more permanent positions.[84] Students more eagerly seek large-firm placements, then, not only for their prestige and professional quality, but also for the prospects of continuing employment they provide. These placements are therefore a potential source of disparity in the entry of women into privileged positions in firm practice.

The first Canadian study of women in legal practice was published by Harvey in 1970, and therefore predates the large-scale entry of women into the profession.[85] Although 106 respondents in this study reported they felt the existence of discrimination, 166 respondents either did not respond or stated that discrimination did not occur, indicating that it existed 'only in the minds of women who were going to inordinate lengths to find or imagine it.'[86] A second study by Dranoff from about the same period focused on women lawyers in Toronto. Dranoff found that 74 per cent of the respondents perceived discrimination while searching for articling positions, compared with 60 per cent who perceived discrimination in seeking positions after the bar-admission exam.[87] In the same year, Smith, Stephenson, and Quijano reported on the difficulties women were having finding articling positions in British Columbia.[88] They observed that 'it is a matter of more men having more to choose from, and sooner, than most women ... more men are able to place in firms of their first choice.'[89]

Marie Huxter undertook a large and systematic study of articling and the job search in Canada during the late 1970s in Ontario.[90] Nearly 3,000 graduates of six Ontario law schools took part in a survey focused on the search for articling positions and first jobs. With specific reference to preferred jobs in firms, Huxter found that 71 per cent of the men compared with 62 per cent of the women were successful in finding articling positions with the size or kind of firm desired. Men ranked lack of contacts as their biggest hindrance in finding positions, while women ranked gender first, marital status second, and contacts third. The women in Huxter's Ontario study were particularly shocked at the kinds of questions they were asked, frequently in firms, in the course of their interviews. These questions often focused on plans for marriage and children, and about their 'feminist' attitudes towards issues of gender in the profession.

In our own research in Ontario, we gave particular attention to the role of personal contacts in finding entry positions into practice.[91] We found that contacts in preferred firm settings were advantageous, with a quarter to a third of all articling positions resulting from personal contacts and help in finding jobs. Private-school connections were especially helpful to men. We found that male lawyers were more likely to have attended private school and were better able to sustain and capitalize on these contacts in finding first jobs in large firms, which were preferred placements for both men and women entering practice. However, we also found that law-school grades were more consistent and stronger than personal contacts or other background factors in predicting articling and first-job placements. This last finding hints at the possibility that entry into the profession may be a more meritocratic and less particularistic process than is the case at later career stages.

Indeed, the early stages of lawyers' careers, from articling through first-job placement, may have come to represent a caricature of what sociologists who study work and occupations call 'contest mobility,' a process in which firms may often be content to see entrants to the profession engage in relatively unfettered competition. One respondent in our research summarized this orientation in hiring articling students during the recessionary period of the early 1980s when she was hired: 'I was called [to the bar] in 1981, at a very bad time for new lawyers. There were few jobs in Toronto with lots of competition. The policy at that time was to hire as many new articling students as the firm could afford and let them fight it out.'

Of course, the existence of the above kinds of practices would not mean that the profession is without prejudice or bias that is linked to gender, as we note in much greater empirical detail later in this essay. Furthermore, the kinds of questions that are still reportedly asked in articling interviews are testimony to the strength of such biases, and to the occurrence of gender harassment, if not discrimination. There is also the serious problem noted in the Canadian Bar Association *Touchstones* report, that women in articling positions often feel unable to complain about discrimination during articling for fear that doing so will severely impair their chances of being hired back.[92] However, at the point of entry into practice, firms in particular may also be well served to receive the best new lawyers they can find, regardless of background or orientation. This may have been true during the competitively expansionary 1980s, and probably remains true during the competitive retrenchment of the 1990s. If this is the case, problems of gender discrimination may be more likely to become apparent as women and men move towards decisions about partnership.

Partners in Practice

The partnership decision is an especially important barrier at a crucial fork in the professional lives of many women lawyers, with one path leading to the continued development of a legal career in firm practice, and alternative paths leading to other occupational settings or away from remunerative work altogether. Since partnership decisions are also regarded as fateful to the future success of law firms, it is not surprising that much attention is focused on these decisions, and that some litigation of partnership decisions has resulted.

In the widely noted American case of *Hishon* v. *King and Spalding*,[93] Elizabeth Hishon filed suit against the Atlanta firm of King and Spalding, claiming a violation of Title VII of the 1969 U.S. Civil Rights Act.[94] The district court dismissed the claim, finding that Title VII did not apply to partnership decisions. Subsequently, a divided panel of the Eleventh Circuit affirmed the dismissal. However, the U.S. Supreme Court ultimately reversed the decision, holding that Title VII does apply to partnership decisions, in that becoming partner is a condition of employment. This decision established that denying a woman partnership based on sex is unacceptable.[95] This case brought widespread attention to the issue of partnership, and to the disparate treatment of male and female lawyers.

The Canadian Bar Association *Touchstones* report indicates that, while there are no reported cases on the issue of partnership in Canada, it seems highly likely that discrimination in admissions to partnership would be prohibited by our human-rights legislation. This legislation covers all employment-related decisions. The *Touchstones* report notes that a promise to be considered for partnership is a benefit or privilege of employment that must be made without discrimination and is not protected from scrutiny, as other partnership decisions might be.[96]

Our own research on partnership decisions in Ontario, the first empirical analysis of this kind we can find in Canada, and one of only a few such studies in North America, was stimulated by a widely based perception among women lawyers that discrimination persists in various forms in relation to promotion to partnership.[97] Younger women we interviewed in our research consistently noted the pervasiveness of gender bias and discrimination in the profession. The issue of quality of life is clearly tied for many women to the problems of combining parenting with the demands of partnership and the lack of accommodation that women feel firms are willing to provide for women with families.

One respondent in our Toronto research offered the following view of the problems posed by firm attitudes: 'The reason women are not becoming senior partners in law firms is that the "old boy" attitude in private practice does not allow a female lawyer with a small child any chance for advancement unless she basically has full-time child care or works eight to five and then does the "mommy shift" (after the child goes to bed) from nine to midnight. This is no way to live – for the parent or the child – and this is why I am no longer in practice.' Again and again, this issue was raised by women in our research. One woman lawyer remarked: 'As a woman who is planning to have a family, I am concerned about my relationship with my child if I continue to work full-time. At this time, I am somewhat apprehensive how my employers will address my maternity leave and whether it will affect my consideration for partnership. We have only one woman partner, who had children about twelve years ago. There are no other women in our firm with children.'

A young woman associate included in our research from a large firm effectively summarized the prevalence of concerns about mixing partnership with parenthood when she reported that 'the associates in our firm have just had a retreat ... during which we discussed many of these issues ... We are concerned that the demands for hours and billings are ever-increasing. Many feel that the only choice is the "fast-track" for partnership or "no track" at all.' The basis for such fears is reinforced by harrowing reports like the following from our research:

Upon learning of my pregnancy ... the partners of the law firm I worked for were not willing to assist me in managing my practice during my short maternity leave – they would not even consider hiring an articling student, which seemed to me the ideal option, as we would have to make only a short term commitment at a low cost, and the student would have assisted with my practice while I had my child and cared for him in the first few months ... I knew that I would not be able to continue a busy practice, the responsibilities of motherhood to my first child (who was three years at the time), and the physical strains of pregnancy and birth. I therefore decided to leave the firm ... When I advised the senior partner of this decision, he suggested that a termination of the pregnancy was a better solution than terminating my employment, and told me that if I wanted to be a mother that I had no business being a lawyer and taking up valuable space in law school. Although I gave ample notice (three months) of my departure, the partners insisted that I continue working until the due date and beyond ... When I refused and left the office ..., they continuously harassed me by telephone and letter. One partner even telephoned me at the hospital, the day after my child was born by Caesarean section and I was heavily sedated, to inform me that there was a problem on one of my files that needed my immediate attention, and he insisted that I have it resolved in three days. They also had delivered to the hospital a non-competition agreement that I was forced to sign.

The empirical data we analysed from our studies of lawyers across Ontario and in Toronto provided statistical support for the concerns expressed by the interviews quoted above. Even when a range of variables was included in multivariate statistical analyses of all lawyers who began practice, men were shown to be more likely than women to become partners in firms. More specifically, when we simulated statistically the effects of women and men having the same experience and background characteristics, we found that nearly half of the men, compared with about a third of the women, in the Toronto sample were successful in becoming partners.[98] Our analyses also confirmed the expectation that taking parental leaves is a source of the reduced prospects of women for partnership.[99]

Several scholars have argued that, as long as partnership decisions coincide in time with the years of optimal childbearing for women, the number of women able to succeed will not equal that of men.[100] Even when firms permit maternity leaves or allow part-time work, some who avail themselves of such 'innovations' find that they are considered less committed to their work as lawyers. These women often seem to be perceived as 'opting out,' without considering how presumably 'neutral' rules of existing work structures have a 'disparate impact' on women.[101] The effects of childbearing and child care may result for women in denial or delay of partnership, or departure from firm settings or the practice of law entirely. These potential consequences were perceived and commented upon by many women practitioners in our study. The Canadian Bar Association *Touchstone* report predicts that 'it is likely only a matter of time before the courts and tribunals will consider these issues in the context of the legal profession.'[102] Meanwhile, there is further evidence that recruitment and promotion practices in firms are playing a major role in changing the more general structure of the profession.

The Changing Hierarchy of Legal Practice

If law firms are both hiring larger numbers of associates and proportionately reducing the prospects of achieving partnerships, as we have suggested in the preceding sections of this essay, this should be reflected in a changing structure of the legal profession in which employed lawyers at the lower levels of the professional hierarchy increasingly outnumber employed lawyers at the higher levels of the profession. This is the process through which, as we suggested earlier in this essay, the base of the legal profession has been broadened, with a corresponding centralization and concentration of partnerships at the top of the profession, and therefore an intensification of the hierarchical structure of the profession.

To explore whether this process has actually occurred in the Ontario legal profession, we undertook an analysis based on a linkage of two surveys of Toronto lawyers we conducted in 1985 and 1991, respectively, together with records of the Law Society of Upper Canada.[103] The 1985 mail-back survey of Toronto lawyers was stratified by gender and type of practice to include approximately equal numbers of men and women across different sizes of law firms and non-firm settings. With two follow-up reminders, 1,051 survey instruments were returned (i.e., a 65.3 per cent response rate). The second survey was conducted five years later, in 1991. Of the 1,051 Toronto lawyers surveyed in the first wave of the study in 1985, 815 were resurveyed in the second wave of the study. If retired and deceased lawyers are excluded, the response rate to the second survey was nearly 80 per cent (79.3 per cent). This high rate of retention in our longitudinal study allows a good representation of the continuing lawyer population of Toronto.[104]

The Toronto surveys were then combined with data gathered for 1977 and 1988 from the records of the Law Society of Upper Canada. These data enabled us to chart changes in the structure of law practice for men and women in Toronto over a recent decade-long period. The linkage of information from the different data sources involves imputing the lawyer categories from the Toronto survey results into the 1977 and 1988 Law Society records, based on simplified types of employment and experience groupings that can be identified in all three sources. We have described elsewhere in greater detail the application of a strategy to combine data sets to analyse changes in occupational structure.[105] We now summarize this work to give a general picture of the changing structure of the place of women and men in the Toronto legal profession over a ten-year period; we then supplement this with a shorter, five-year assessment based on a comparison of the primary data from our surveys of Toronto lawyers. Although restricted to a half rather than a full decade, the latter comparison should be more precise than our initial analysis, and it includes the beginning of the recession of the 1980s and early 1990s. To the extent the two accounts converge, we can be especially confident of our conclusions.

The results of these analyses are presented in table 15.3. The first column of this table separates Toronto lawyers into an array of categories that differ markedly in their levels of influence and power in legal practice. We emphasize in this summary discussion the upper and lower categories of practice. This typology borrows from one employed in research on the changing structure of social classes.[106] The emphasis of this typology is on resources of power, authority, and decision making. The measurement of power relations in this model is based on self-reported features of work experiences that allow for analyses within and across occupations. As such, the categories used in this typology bear similarities to common terminology in law firms, but are not purely specific to law-firm practice.

For example, managing partners in our typology are in an ownership or employer relationship (i.e., they are partners), in a medium to large firm (i.e., ten or more lawyer–employees), where they exercise sanctioning (e.g., deciding on promotions, raises, etc.) or task authority (e.g., giving directions), participate directly in decision making, and have two or more levels of subordinates other than secretaries below them. In contrast, the term 'managing partner' is more specifically understood in

TABLE 15.3
Changes in the Structure of the Legal Profession for Women and Men, Toronto, 1977–1988, 1985–1990

Positions	1977–88 Estimates				1985–90 Estimates			
	Men Lawyers		Women Lawyers		Men Lawyers		Women Lawyers	
	1977 (N = 3,796)	1988 (N = 6,537)	1977 (N = 251)	1988 (N = 1,842)	1985 (N = 583)	1990 (N = 574)	1985 (N = 185)	1990 (N = 265)
Managing partners [a]	20.5	16.9	6.4	5.5	14.1 (3.6)	8.3 (7.1)	6.0 (2.5)	3.3 (2.8)
Supervising partners	15.5	12.2	6.0	4.9	11.3	11.2	5.0	5.2
Partners in small firms	18.2	15.2	13.9	5.6	13.2	3.4	7.2	1.9
Solo practitioners	14.5	10.1	13.9	8.1	8.6	18.7	7.9	8.1
Managing/supervising lawyers	8.9	13.0	12.8	17.6	12.5	10.2	11.9	9.7
Semi-autonomous lawyers	17.7	24.9	31.5	39.9	29.3	32.2	34.9	42.7
Non-autonomous lawyers	5.7	7.7	15.5	18.3	9.1	14.8	17.2	19.0
Part-time or unemployed lawyers					1.8	1.1	9.9	10.1

[a] Figures for managing partners in large, élite firms in parentheses.

large law firms in Toronto to mean a 'chief executive officer' or 'chief operating officer' of a law firm.[107] Our usage of the term managing partner is intended to refer to a somewhat larger grouping that likely includes all those lawyers traditionally known by this label in law firms, as well as other lawyers not commonly known in this way in their firms but who none the less engage in management functions and who are located in a larger but still high stratum of the profession. Supervising partners, partners in small firms, and solo practitioners are also identified at somewhat lower but still high levels of our typology.

At the other end of the professional hierarchy are what we have called 'semi-autonomous' and 'non-autonomous' lawyers, who in addition to not being partners in firms also have relatively little autonomy in their work. Semi-autonomous lawyers are typically associates in law firms where they have no managerial or supervisory responsibilities and no one below them organizationally other than secretaries; however, they do independently design some important aspects of their work. In contrast, non-autonomous lawyers are likely to be more junior associates, or even articling students, who design only a few or no important aspects of their work.[108] This last grouping may correspond to what some have called a 'deprofessionalized working class,' 'mental workers,' or a 'professional proletariat.'[109]

The results presented in table 15.3 generally support our speculation about the growing centralization and concentration of positions of power in firms. For example, in the left-hand part of this table that focuses on the period from 1977 to 1988, we see that the proportion of male lawyers in the lower semi-autonomous and non-autonomous groupings increased from about 23 to 33 per cent, while the proportion of female lawyers in these groupings increased from about 47 to over 58 per cent. At the higher end of the hierarchy, in 1988 nearly 17 per cent of the men, compared with less than 6 per cent of women, were managing partners, and altogether about 54 per cent of the men were partners, compared with about 24 per cent of the women. In 1977, the respective figures were about 69 per cent for men and 40 per cent for women. Both genders lost in terms of partnership shares over the decade, but in relative terms women lost more.

It might reasonably be argued that these aggregate changes within genders in partnership shares reflect changes in the experience composition of men and women lawyers in the profession, for we have seen that many young lawyers entered legal practice over this period. However, our attempts to assess the effects of this change soon revealed a flaw in this argument. The flaw is that, as we have seen, by 1977 women had already begun to enter the profession in large numbers, and with few predecessors, so that by 1988 their aggregate age actually increased. So women should actually have increased their partnership shares between 1977 and 1988. Apparently both men and women encountered a ceiling on mobility during this period, and women were affected more by this ceiling than were men.

Finally, we can confirm and extend the preceding analysis by combining results from our 1985 Toronto survey with results from a subsequent survey in 1990. These results, on the right-hand side of table 15.3, indicate again that the proportion of men and women who are managing partners declined between 1985 and 1990, from about 14 to 8 per cent for men, and from about 6 to 3 per cent for women. Both men and women again increased their representation in semi-autonomous and non-autonomous positions. By 1990 in Toronto, about 47 per cent of men lawyers were in these positions, compared with about 62 per cent of women. Again, men and women were affected by these changes, but women were affected more.

Issues of Earnings

Closely related to the problems of partnership and the hierarchical concentration of power at the top of the legal profession are connected issues of lawyers' earnings, the final aspect of law-firm life we address. In many ways, issues of earnings crystallize the consequences of the kinds of structural changes we have considered in this essay.

The last several decades have revolutionized the procedures by which law firms allocate earnings. Firms that once were largely governed by principles of seniority, with older partners expecting and receiving a highly disproportionate share of practice earnings, today are increasingly concerned with productivity, with partners of all ages staking claims to practice earnings based on credit expected and received for the accumulation of billings. This credit is usually grounded in accounting regimes whose currency consists of billable hours, the units in which everyday lawyering activities in firms often are calibrated.

For many years law firms were somewhat casual about monitoring the hourly work of lawyers and their methods of charging clients. Large firms seem not to have kept accurate time records prior to the end of the Second World War,[110] and although diary and time sheets were used to keep track of time in some firms in the 1950s,[111] it was not until the mid-1960s that billing for lawyer hours became a standard method of calculating fees.[112]

As the billable-hours method of calculating fees took hold, its use as a device to simultaneously track productivity became increasingly pervasive. By the mid-1970s firms began to set targets for partners and associates that ranged from 1,500 to 2,000 billable hours per year.[113] These targets were used in latent, and then more manifest, ways to stimulate and monitor productivity in firms. Epstein succinctly notes that 'time diaries and the billing system are watchdogs.'[114]

Observers of law firms note that this record-keeping can be precise, to the point that 'hours may appear as quarters or as six-minute bits,' with lawyers keeping accurate timed accounts of 'telephone calls, letters dictated, cases looked up in the library, as well as meetings, [and] court appearances.'[115] When lawyers are dilatory about this responsibility, 'they become diary delinquents, and firms devise various penalties to enforce record keeping.'[116] All of this can be quite crucial for women, because, as the Canadian Bar Association *Touchstones* report notes: 'In effect, if billable hours are used as the sole or even primary standard of performance evaluation, they have an adverse impact on women and constitute an unlawful form of sex discrimination. The problem ... is not with billable hours per se but with the unrealistic targets that are set and the fact that they are beyond the reach of women with child rearing responsibilities. They discriminate against these women as a group and some accommodation must be made to take account of this social reality.'[117]

Behind this important assertion lies a crucial assumption regarding differences between men and women in the hours they bill. As with many other areas of law-firm practice, the reality of gender patterns in billing is not extensively researched, and this situation is further complicated by the fact that the existing empirical literature is entirely U.S.–based and also uncertain in its assessment of the time investment that women lawyers actually make in their work. Consider the following record of research.

Epstein reports that 'most women interviewed in New York firms said that they devoted the same amount of time to work as their male colleagues and some even claim to work harder in order to prove themselves.'[118] Similarly, Rhode reports that 'folklore abounds with examples of the dedicated professional who bills 2,000 hours while pregnant or is back "faster than a speeding bullet" after childbirth.'[119] Yet, when Epstein turned to census measures from 1970, she found that women lawyers worked an average of 38.7 hours a week, while male lawyers worked an average of 45.8 hours a week. Menkel-Meadow similarly reports that the 1980 U.S. census data indicate that 'women ... work for fewer hours ... and women's hours drop when children are born.'[120] Epstein also reveals that, in her own interviewing, 'it was difficult to learn the precise hours worked ... because the women themselves did not always have a clear idea what they were.'[121]

Some of this confusion follows from uncertainty about what is meant by 'hours worked.' Not all hours spent at work are billable hours. Indeed, women lawyers often complained in our Ontario research that men lawyers spend many useless office hours 'showing the flag' and wastefully engaging in what Goffman calls 'interaction rituals.'[122] In any case, many hours spent at work are distinct from hours more specifically *docketed* for firm-committee assignments, *pro bono* obligations, community activities, and firm promotional efforts, as well as for clients. Hours *billed* to clients are a crucial subset of both hours worked overall and docketed hours. One of our Toronto respondents noted that 'almost everyone works a ten-hour day to bill seven hours.' Another of our respondents remarked that 'though I bill about forty hours a week, I routinely work over seventy.' Spangler reports that, in the Boston firms she studied, there was an understanding that time billable to clients constitutes about two-thirds of the total hours worked,[123] a figure very close to that we found for Toronto firms.

However, this is only part of the problem, for we cannot assume that hours are billed in a one-to-one fashion with hours spent on a case or file, or that these counts are in any sense perfectly accurate. As Galanter and Palay note, '"billable hours" are a product not only of actual time spent but of recording and billing practices, which may change independently of the former.'[124] More generally, Granovetter notes that productivity is rarely measured well, except in certain well-defined and individualized jobs, and, more important, that the difficulties are more than merely technical.[125] 'Rather,' Granovetter notes, 'the productivity of individual workers is inextricably intermeshed in a network of relations with other workers,'[126] which he calls the 'social context of production.'[127] The potential importance of this context is well illustrated by considering social aspects of the production of billable hours in legal practice.

First, there is likely an important element of hierarchy (a factor we have emphasized throughout this essay) in who obtains credit for the difference between actual time spent and time recorded and billed. To begin, lawyers in our Toronto research spoke of the need to exercise discretion in 'writing up' or 'writing down' hours. Spangler notes that, 'once a cli-

ent, or a particular case or matter, has been accepted, the partner managing the work is also free to staff the project as he or she sees fit ... the
partner in charge is free to bill for the firm's time at exactly the number
of hours logged; at a discount if a young associate was trained on the
project or if an error was made; or at a premium if the client concluded
a very lucrative transaction or if extraordinary efforts ("all night at the
printer's") were required.'[128] Lawyers in our Toronto research sometimes
spoke of 'power billing' to refer to situations in which they felt free to
increase the numbers of hours they charged clients for services that they
felt able to perform with unusual efficiency.

These are likely not small or idle points, for women can be greatly
affected in the credit they take and receive in billing for hours they work.
The problem partly derives from power relationships between men and
women in firms. We have documented a changing hierarchical structure
in firms earlier in this essay that is affecting women more than men lawyers. Meanwhile, Bielby and Bielby cite experimental evidence that
women in general undervalue and underreward their own efforts relative
to men.[129] A male respondent in our Toronto research remarked of
women that 'they seem less aggressive on their own behalf.' This may
make it less likely that women will use the hierarchical positions that they
attain in firms to reward their work in the same way that men do. And if
they do not take their fair share of credit, it is less likely that it will be
received, for, as Martin notes, 'power relationships become apparent
when the important and often unspoken question of given, allowed and
permitted by whom is asked.'[130]

A number of women lawyers in our Toronto research commented on
the related problems of obtaining access to good files and promising
cases. One woman lawyer observed that 'senior male partners prefer to
work with male associates. As a result the quality of work that a female
associate receives is well below the quality of work that a male associate
receives.' There are further problems that go along with women being
underrepresented, such as their work being more heavily scrutinized and
assessed against especially rigorous standards, while at the same time
they are to take on special burdens, such as increased committee work
that decreases time available for more instrumental tasks – namely,
developing promising files and billing clients.[131] Women may also be
channelled into specializations that demand fewer hours and away from
cases and files that offer greater opportunities for extended, profitable
billing,[132] and they may be excluded from informal networks that can
enhance the flow of billable work and the opportunity to assume credit

for it. A Toronto respondent noted that 'from an early stage men are groomed and promoted and are seen as more able because of their exposure to files ... Women often do not get major responsibility on files.'

On several occasions in our research lawyers referred to 'pink and blue files' in response to questions about channelling productive cases to men and away from women lawyers. The Canadian Bar Association *Touchstones* report similarly concludes that 'women are allocated more "pink" files which involve less high-profile matters, less client contact and correspondence, and reduced opportunities to develop legal skills and a client base.'[133] Although this problem may more often be mentioned in relation to large firms, it actually can be more severe for women in smaller firms. Epstein makes this point when she observes that women in small practices must depend more exclusively on relationships with men, and that obviously 'women who do not have such relationships are at a distinct disadvantage.'[134] Having wider access, albeit through weaker ties, to a larger firm's referral base, and therefore also to more women as sources of referrals, may increase opportunities for productive work.

When we turned to the quantitative results from our Toronto analysis of lawyers' earnings, we found support for many of the above expectations. For example, we found that, although women and men reported working about the same number of hours overall, men reported docketing and billing larger numbers of hours than did women. This was so despite the fact that women who continued to work full-time in firms after having children increased their commitment to work (for example, as indicated by reports of importance attached to their careers), while women outside this sector also resumed and increased their commitment to work as their children progressed into and through school. We also found evidence that men gained billable hours through the use of their positions of power and influence in firms. Finally, our analysis revealed that men gained nearly twice the return in earnings compared with women for the hours that they worked. In sum, we found a large income gap in the earnings of men and women lawyers that was tightly linked to hourly billing practices. Perhaps the real surprise in this analysis of earnings was that so many women remained so highly committed to their careers in the absence of equity in their resulting earnings.[135]

HIERARCHY IN PRACTICE

The practice of law in Ontario has changed dramatically over the last century, but in doing so it has retained a pronounced if not intensified hierarchical form. There are a number of reasons why the legal profession has changed. At first the profession simply grew along with the population and the economy. This meant an increase not only in the size of the profession, but also in the diversity of its membership. The opening of educational and occupational opportunities and the changing roles of women more generally provided a context in which the legal profession at first reluctantly, and then more willingly, accepted women into its ranks. This occurred during the first half of this century through family practices and government work,[136] while in more recent decades it has involved the larger firms that increasingly dominate the profession. This more recent phase is crucial, not only because it has changed so markedly the involvement of women in the profession, but also because it is changing the shape of the profession itself.

The practice of law became much more highly centralized and concentrated in large firms during the 1970s and 1980s. After nearly a half a century in which the population of lawyers grew at about the same rate as the population, through the 1970s and 1980s the growth rate of lawyers was several times that of the general population. This growth occurred in government and business, but it was led by the expansion of large firms that could not have developed as they did without admitting large numbers of women as well as men. This period of growth involved, in relative terms, a shrinking pool of centralized and concentrated partnerships in large firms, with increasing numbers of lawyers in intermediate and lower positions. In short, this was a period of growth, but with a ceiling on upward outcomes that is not likely to have improved in the early recessionary period of the 1990s.

One of the most notable consequences of this changing structure of the legal profession has involved the emergence of a ceiling on the mobility prospects for women. This ceiling became an increasing reality in the Toronto legal profession during the 1980s, especially for women, but also for men. Although the actual numbers of women and men lawyers at partnership levels in firms increased in absolute terms during this period, their relative shares of partnership positions declined, and this ceiling effect was more pronounced for women than for men. During this period, men and women were developing careers in a legal profession whose parameters were changing in ways that traditional conceptions of professional autonomy would not have predicted.

In sum, the base of law-firm practice has broadened and become more diverse through a process of expansion that has perhaps most notably involved the increased admission of women to practice in many areas and settings, including the increasingly prominent large firms. However, the hierarchical structure of the profession has endured, if not intensified, and many women, and to a lesser extent men, find themselves competing for firm partnerships that are declining in relative proportion to the growth of the profession.[137] Furthermore, a large gap continues to exist between the incomes of women and of men in the profession, which is linked to hierarchically influenced patterns of granting credit for billings in firms. These findings raise fundamental questions about ways in which the profession is changing.

These questions involve issues of both access to and advancement in the profession. For example, while women currently are focused on breaking through the glass ceiling that we have emphasized, other ethnic- and minority-group members are still confronted with the more basic problem of getting through the front door and onto the ground floor of legal practice.[138] The Canadian Bar Association *Touchstones* report refers to this as the problem of 'the Glass Ceiling and the Steel Door.'[139] So few minorities are yet represented in the data sources we have considered in this essay that we have had little or nothing to say about their unique experiences. However, we did make note of the fact that the class background of members of the profession has changed little over the same period in which other compositional characteristics of the profession have changed dramatically.

It is likely that in coming years the ethnic and minority composition of the profession will begin to change, as admissions policies to law schools and hiring practices are modified. However, neither women nor minorities will benefit from law-school admission and employment practices that offer poor prospects, once admitted and employed, for retention and advancement. The structural changes that are continuing to occur in the legal profession ensure that these will be pressing issues as we enter the next century of legal practice in Ontario.

NOTES

1 For a review and critique of such concerns see Richard Abel, 'The Transformation of the American Legal Profession,' *Law & Society Review* 20 (1986), 7–17.
2 For a review and refutation of such claims see Marc Galanter and Thomas Palay, *Tournament of Lawyers: The Transformation of the Big Law Firm* (Chicago: University of Chicago Press 1991).
3 For example see David Stager and David Foot, 'Changes in Lawyers' Earnings:

The Impact of Differentiation and Growth in the Canadian Legal Profession,' *Law & Social Inquiry* 13 (1988), 71–85.

4 See Anthony Kronman, *The Lost Lawyer: Failing Ideals of the Legal Profession* (Cambridge, MA: The Belknap Press of Harvard University Press 1993).

5 This point is developed at length in *Touchstones for Change: Equality, Diversity and Accountability*, The Report on Gender Equality in the Legal Profession (Ottawa: Canadian Bar Association 1993), and in our own recent work: John Hagan and Fiona Kay, *Gender in Practice: A Study of Lawyers' Lives* (New York: Oxford University Press 1995).

6 Marc Galanter, 'Mega-Law and Mega-Lawyering in the Contemporary United States,' in R. Dingwall and P. Lewis, eds., *The Sociology of the Professions: Lawyers, Doctors and Others* (London: Macmillan 1983), 152–76

7 John Meyer and Brian Rowan, 'Institutionalized Organizations: Formal Structure as Myth and Ceremony,' *American Journal of Sociology* 83 (1977), 340–63

8 See John Porter, *The Vertical Mosaic* (Toronto: University of Toronto Press 1965); Wallace Clement, *The Canadian Corporate Elite: An Analysis of Economic Power* (Toronto: McClelland and Stewart 1975); S.M. Lipset, 'Historical Traditions and National Characteristics: A Comparative Analysis of Canada and the U.S.,' *Canadian Journal of Sociology* 11 (1986), 113–55; Robert Presthus, *Elite Accommodation in Canadian Politics* (Toronto: Macmillan of Canada 1973).

9 See, for example, Arthur K. Davis, 'Canadian Society as Hinterland Versus Metropolis,' in Richard Ossenberg, ed., *Canadian Society: Pluralism, Change and Conflict* (Scarborough, ON: Prentice-Hall 1971); Irving Horowitz, 'The Hemispheric Connection: A Critique and Corrective to the Entrepreneurial Thesis of Development with Special Emphasis on the Canadian Case,' *Queen's Quarterly* 80 (1973), 327–59; but see also John Hagan, 'Gender and the Structural Transformation of the Legal Profession in the United States and Canada,' in M. Hallinan, D.M. Klein, and J. Glass, eds., *Change in Societal Institutions* (New York: Plenum Press 1990), 49–70.

10 Cited in *Touchstones*, 5. The Honourable Justice Bertha Wilson chaired the Task Force on Gender Equality in the Legal Profession for the Canadian Bar Association. Justice Wilson followed her 1917 quote from Lord Buckmaster with the following closing statement in the introduction to the 1993 *Touchstones* report: 'That was 1917 and this is 1993. Will the reforms the Task Force advocates in this Report be implemented as a free and dignified act of Justice? Is the profession ready for equality of opportunity for all women – white women, Women of Colour, Aboriginal women, women with disabilities, lesbian women? Or will their male colleagues make them wait another fifty years until time will have robbed their consent of its graciousness and tainted it with the meanness and cowardice of expediency?'

11 Magali Larson, *The Rise of Professionalism* (Berkeley: University of California Press 1977)

12 Deborah Rhode, 'Moral Character as a Professional Credential,' *Yale Law Journal* 94 (1984), 491–603

13 Jo Dixon and Jordana Pestrong, 'The Changing Terrain of Sex Stratification in the Legal Profession,' Helena Lopata and Anne Figert, eds., *Current Research on Occupations and Professions*, vol. 9, (Greenwich, CT: JAI Press 1996), 233–47

14 Wayne Hobson, 'Symbol of the New Profession: Emergence of the Large Law Firm, 1870–1915,' in Gerard Gawalt, ed., *The New High Priests: Lawyers in Post-Civil War America* (Westport, CT: Greenwood Press 1984)

15 Karen Morello, *The Invisible Bar: The Woman Lawyer in America: 1638 to the Present* (New York: Random House 1986), 3

16 For a discussion of the case, see Sandra Day O'Connor, 'Portia's Progress,' *New York Law Review* 66 (1991), 1547.

17 *In re Bradwell*, 55 Ill. (1869), 539

18 See Deborah Rhode, 'Perspectives on Professional Women,' *Stanford Law Review* 40 (1988), 1163–1207.

19 Carrie Menkel-Meadow, 'The Comparative Sociology of Women Lawyers: The "Feminization" of the Legal Profession,' *Osgoode Hall Law Journal* 24 (1986), 902

20 C. Backhouse, 'To Open the Way for Others of My Sex: Clara Brett Martin's Career as Canada's First Woman Lawyer,' *Canadian Journal of Women and the Law* 1 (1985), 1–41

21 Ibid., 30

22 Constance Backhouse, *Petticoats and Prejudice: Women and Law in Nineteenth Century Canada* (Toronto: The Osgoode Society 1991)

23 Mary Jane Mossman, 'The Past as Prologue: Women and the Law,' in A. Esau and J. Penner, eds., *Lawyering and Legal Education into the 21st Century* (Winnipeg: Legal Research Institute 1990), 27–33

24 Mary Jane Mossman, '"Invisible" Constraints on Lawyering and Leadership: The Case of Women Lawyers,' *Ottawa Law Review* 20 (1988), 567–600

25 *Langstaff* v. *Bar of Quebec* (1915), 47 RJQ 131 (CS), 137–8. For an in-depth analysis of the nature of the legal claims in each of these cases and the legal reasoning denying the claims, see Mossman, '"Invisible Constraints,"' 567–600.

26 *Langstaff* v. *Bar of Quebec* (1915), 47 RJQ 131 (CS) 139; emphasis in original

27 Mossman, '"Invisible Constraints,"' 583–4

28 *Touchstones*, 82

29 *Winnipeg Free Press*, 1 December 1911, cited in Mary Kinnear, '"That There Woman Lawyer": Women Lawyers in Manitoba, 1915–1970,' *Canadian Journal of Women and the Law* 5 (1992), 412.

30 Kinnear, '"That There Woman Lawyer,"' 412

31 Ibid., 413–14
32 Ibid., 418
33 Joan Brockman, 'Exclusionary Tactics: The History of Women and Visible Minorities in the Legal Profession in British Columbia,' in Hamar Foster and John McLaren, eds., *Essays in the History of Canadian Law*, Vol. 6, *British Columbia and the Yukon* (Toronto: The Osgoode Society 1995), 530
34 Mary Jane Mossman, 'Lawyers and Family Life: New Directions for the 1990s (Part One),' *Feminist Legal Studies* 2 (1994), 64–5; Ronald Chester, *Unequal Access: Women Lawyers in a Changing America* (South Hadley, MA: Bergin and Garvey 1985)
35 Brockman, 'Exclusionary Tactics,' 533
36 These descriptions are developed from *Crossing the Bar: A Century of Women's Experience Upon the Rough and Troubled Seas of Legal Practice in Ontario* (Law Society of Upper Canada Archives 1993).
37 For a discussion of visible and invisible barriers to women's success in law practice see Joan Brockman, '"Resistance by the Club" to the Feminization of the Legal Profession,' *Canadian Journal of Law and Society* 7 (1992), 48–51; see also Brockman, 'Exclusionary Tactics,' 535.
38 British Columbia Aural History Archives of the Law Society of British Columbia, the interview with Walter Stewart Owen by Judge Watts, 64–5.
39 Erwin Smigel, *The Wall Street Lawyer: Professional Organization Man?* (Bloomington: Indiana University Press 1969)
40 Terrence Halliday, 'Six Score Years and Ten: Demographic Transitions in the American Legal Profession, 1850–1980,' *Law & Society Review* 20 (1986), 53–78
41 See also David A.A. Stager and Harry W. Arthurs, *Lawyers in Canada* (Toronto: University of Toronto Press 1990), 6.
42 Rhode, 'Perspectives on Professional Women,' 1178
43 Hagan, 'Gender and the Structural Transformation of the Legal Profession'; see also Stager and Arthurs, *Lawyers in Canada*, 148.
44 Stager and Arthurs, *Lawyers in Canada*, 88
45 Law Society of Upper Canada, Special Committee on Legal Education, *Report* (Toronto: The Law Society of Upper Canada 1957), 9; Stager and Arthurs, *Lawyers in Canada*, 88–92
46 Carrie Menkel-Meadow, 'Exploring a Research Agenda for the Feminization of the Legal Profession: Theories of Gender and Social Change,' *Law and Social Inquiry* 14 (1989), 305
47 A more detailed description of this survey of Toronto lawyers is provided later in this essay.
48 This survey was undertaken as part of our larger study of the Toronto legal profession reported in our book, *Gender in Practice*.

49 The Progressive Conservative party represents a more right-wing 'Tory' position in Canada, while the New Democratic Party (formerly the Co-operative Commonwealth Federation) occupies a more left-wing or socialist stance in the forum of Canadian politics.
50 Abel, 'Comparative Sociology,' 83
51 Shelina Neallani, 'Women of Color in the Legal Profession: Facing the Familiar Barriers of Race and Sex,' *Canadian Journal of Women and the Law* 5 (1992), 148–65; Steven Greer and Colin Samson, 'Ethnic Minorities in the Legal Profession: A Case Study of the San Francisco Bar,' *Anglo-American Law Review* 22 (1993), 321–36; Mona Harrington, *Women Lawyers: Rewriting the Rules* (New York: Knopf 1994)
52 See Morello, *The Invisible Bar*, 248.
53 However, while it might be satisfying to think that the faster rate of entry for women in Canada was the product of changes occurring in Ontario, the data presented in table 15.2 suggest otherwise. The greater change in the Canadian legal profession's gender profile came from Quebec rather than from Ontario. The ratios of men to women lawyers in Ontario and Quebec indicate that, although historically the legal profession was much more male-dominated in Quebec than in English Canada or in the United States, the ratios converged and crossed in 1971, when the ratios in Ontario and Quebec were nearly identical. Expressed as a ratio of men to women, in 1971 these ratios were about 19:1. However, in 1981 and 1986 the ratios were smaller in Quebec: 4.45:1 and 2.93:1, compared with 6.89:1 and 4.01:1 in Ontario. In 1991 the ratio of men to women lawyers in Quebec was 1.94, and in Ontario 2.63.
54 Galanter, 'Mega-Law and Mega-Lawyering'
55 Robert Nelson, 'The Changing Structure of Opportunity: Recruitment and Careers in Large Law Firms,' *American Bar Foundation Research Journal* 1983, 109–42; Robert Nelson, *Partners with Power: The Social Transformation of the Large Law Firm* (Berkeley: University of California Press 1988)
56 Barbara Curran, Katherine J. Roskh, Clara N. Carson, and Mark C. Puccetti, *The Lawyer Statistical Report: A Statistical Profile of the U.S. Legal Profession in the 1980s* (Chicago: American Bar Foundation 1985)
57 Richard Abel, 'Comparative Sociology of Legal Professions,' in R. Abel and P. Lewis, eds., *Lawyers in Society*, vol. 3: *Comparative Theories* (Berkeley: University of California Press 1989), 80–153
58 John Heinz and Edward Laumann, *Chicago Lawyers: The Social Structure of the Bar* (New York: Russell Sage Foundation; Chicago: American Bar Foundation 1982)
59 John Hagan, Marie Huxter, and Patricia Parker, 'Class Structure and Legal

Practice: Inequality and Mobility among Toronto Lawyers,' *Law & Society Review* 22 (1988), 9

60 Smigel, *The Wall Street Lawyer*

61 Barbara A. Curran, *The Lawyer Statistical Report: A Statistical Profile of the U.S. Legal Profession in 1985* (Chicago: American Bar Foundation 1986)

62 Ronald J. Daniels, 'Growing Pains: The Why and How of Law Firm Expansion,' *University of Toronto Law Journal* 43 (1993), 157

63 John Hagan, Marjorie Zatz, Bruce Arnold, and Fiona Kay, 'Cultural Capital, Gender and the Structural Transformation of Legal Practice,' *Law & Society Review* 25 (1991), 239–62

64 Daniels, 'Growing Pains,' 147–206

65 Stager and Arthurs, *Lawyers in Canada*, 174

66 Robert Collison, 'The National Dream of McCarthy and McCarthy,' *Report on Business Magazine* (Toronto: The Globe and Mail 1989), 42–9; Stager and Arthurs, *Lawyers in Canada*, 174

67 Galanter, 'Mega-Law and Mega-Lawyering,' 155

68 Daniels, 'Growing Pains,' 157

69 Galanter, 'Mega-Law and Mega-Lawyering,' 155

70 Galanter and Palay, *Tournament of Lawyers*, 100

71 Galanter and Palay, *Tournament of Lawyers*; Marc Galanter and Thomas M. Palay, 'Why the Big Get Bigger: The Promotion-to-Partner Tournament and the Growth of Large Law Firms,' *Virginia Law Review* 76 (1990), 747–811; Marc Galanter and Thomas Palay, 'The Many Futures of the Big Law Firm,' *South Carolina Law Review* 45 (1994), 905–36

72 Richard H. Sander and E. Douglass Williams, 'A Little Theorizing about the Big Law Firm: Galanter, Palay, and the Economics of Growth,' *Law and Social Inquiry* 17 (1992), 410

73 Daniels, 'Growing Pains,' 160

74 Ibid.

75 Ibid.

76 Robert L. Nelson, 'Of Tournaments and Transformations: Explaining the Growth of Large Law Firms,' *Wisconsin Law Review* (1992), 743

77 Nelson, *Partners with Power* 121

78 Nelson, 'Of Tournaments and Transformations,' 745

79 Ibid., 746

80 Stager and Arthurs, *Lawyers in Canada*

81 Complete data on the restructuring of law firms in Canada have not as of yet been compiled; however, comparisons of annual listings in legal directories indicate that most activity in formation and modification of partnerships occurred in the smaller firms. As Stager and Arthurs point out, 'Even the very

recent spate of mergers of large law firms is numerically less significant that the growth and change in small firms'; see ibid., 166.

82 Ibid., 170–1

83 Morello, *The Invisible Bar*

84 H.W. Arthurs, R. Weisman, and F.H. Zemans, 'The Canadian Legal Profession,' *American Bar Foundation Research Journal*, 1986, 447–532

85 C. Harvey, 'Women in Law in Canada,' *Manitoba Law Journal* 4 (1970), 9–38

86 Ibid.

87 Linda Silver Dranoff, 'Women as Lawyers in Toronto,' *Osgoode Hall Law Journal* 10 (1972), 177–90

88 Lynn Smith, Marylee Stephenson, and Gina Quijano, 'The Legal Profession and Women: Finding Articles in British Columbia,' *University of British Columbia Law Review* 8 (1973), 137–75

89 Ibid., 162

90 Marie Huxter, 'Survey of Employment Opportunities for Articling Students and Graduates of the Bar Admission Course in Ontario,' *Law Society of Upper Canada Gazette* 15 (1981), 169–213

91 Hagan and Kay, *Gender in Practise*, chap. 3

92 *Touchstones*, 58

93 467 U.S. 69 (1984)

94 28 USC 1447 (1982)

95 For a discussion of the case, see K. Donovan, 'Women Associates' Advancement to Partner Status in Private Law Firms,' *Georgetown Journal of Legal Ethics* 4 (1990), 135–52

96 *Touchstones*, 64

97 Our analyses of partnership decisions are reported in Hagan and Kay, *Gender in Practice*, chap. 4, and in Fiona Kay and John Hagan, 'Changing Opportunities for Partnership for Men and Women Lawyers during the Transformation of the Modern Law Firm,' *Osgoode Hall Law Journal* 32 (1994), 413–56.

98 See Hagan and Kay, *Gender in Practice*, 92; also Kay and Hagan, 'Changing Opportunities,' 447–8.

99 See Hagan and Kay, *Gender in Practice*, 92; and Kay and Hagan, 'Changing Opportunities,' 447–8.

100 Stanford Law Project, 'Gender, Legal Education, and the Legal Profession: An Empirical Study of Stanford Law Students and Graduates,' *Stanford Law Review* 40 (1988), 1209; J. Abramson and B. Franklin, *Where Are They Now? The Story of the Women of Harvard Law 1974* (New York: Doubleday 1986); Lisa Hill Fenning, 'Report from the Front: Progress in the Battle Against Gender Bias in the Legal Profession,' paper presented at the Conference on Women in the Legal Profession (Madison, Wisconsin, 1987)

101 Carrie Menkel-Meadow, 'Feminization of the Legal Profession: The Comparative Sociology of Women Lawyers,' in R.L. Abel and P.S.C. Lewis, eds., *Lawyers in Society*, vol. 3: *Comparative Theories* (Berkeley: University of California Press 1989), 196–255

102 *Touchstones*, 65

103 Hagan et al., 'Cultural Capital,' 239–55

104 For a detailed discussion of the two survey designs see Hagan and Kay, *Gender in Practice*, 17–21.

105 Hagan et al., 'Cultural Capital,' 247–50

106 Eric O. Wright, Cynthia Costello, David Hachen, and Joey Sprague, 'The American Class Structure,' *American Sociological Review* 47 (1982), 709

107 Managing partners are sometimes the most senior and important practitioners in the firm. More commonly, managing partners are of mid-range seniority and are appointed for short periods to add administrative obligations to their client-service work.

108 For a more detailed discussion of the full typology of law-practice hierarchy see Hagan et al., 'Cultural Capital,' 247–50.

109 See Charles Derber, ed., *Professionals as Workers: Mental Labor in Advanced Capitalism* (Boston: G.K. Hall 1982); Eve Spangler, *Lawyers for Hire: Salaried Professionals at Work* (New Haven, CT: Yale University Press 1986); Stager and Arthurs refer to these two lower categories when they discuss the 'grinders' of large corporate firms. Junior lawyer–employees, including associates, are the 'grinders' who do much of the legal research and drafting. Well-established senior lawyers operate as the 'finders' of clients through business and social connections, while other relatively mid-level lawyers in the firm perform as 'minders' who maintain regular contact with clients. See Stager and Arthurs, *Lawyers in Canada*, 167.

110 Walter Earle and Charles Perlin, *Shearman & Sterling, 1873–1973*, 2d ed. (New York: privately printed 1973); cited in Galanter and Palay, *Tournament of Lawyers*, 34

111 Spencer Klaw, 'The Wall Street Lawyers,' *Fortune* 98 (1958), 112–20

112 Smigel, *The Wall Street Lawyer*

113 Peter Bernstein, 'The Wall Street Lawyers are Thriving on Change,' *Fortune* 97 (1978), 104–12; Paul Hoffman, *Lions in the Street: The Inside Story of the Great Wall Street Law Firms* (New York: Saturday Review Press 1973)

114 Cynthia Fuchs Epstein, *Women in Law* (New York: Basic Books 1981)

115 Martin Mayer, *The Lawyers* (New York: Harper & Row 1967)

116 Spangler, *Lawyers for Hire*

117 *Touchstones*, 98

118 Epstein, *Women in Law*, 210

119 Rhode, 'Perspectives on Professional Women,' 1185–6

120 Menkel-Meadow, ' Feminization of the Legal Profession,' 218

121 Epstein, *Women in Law*, 315

122 Erving Goffman, *Relations in Public* (New York: Basic Books 1971)

123 Spangler, *Lawyers for Hire*, 53

124 Galanter and Palay, *Tournament of Lawyers*, 35

125 Mark Granovetter, 'The Strength of Weak Ties: A Network Theory Revisited,' *Sociological Theory* 1 (1983), 201–33

126 Ibid., 251

127 Ibid., 252

128 Spangler, *Lawyers for Hire*, 40

129 Denise Bielby and William Bielby, 'She Works Hard for the Money: Household Responsibilities and the Allocation of Effort,' *American Journal of Sociology* 93 (1988), 1031–59

130 Sheilah Martin, 'The Dynamics of Exclusion: Women in the Legal Profession,' paper presented at the Conference on Gender Equality for the Legal Profession (Toronto, Ontario, 29 October 1992), 9

131 Rhode, 'Perspectives on Professional Women,' 1191

132 Epstein, *Women in Law*, 318

133 *Touchstones*, 87

134 Epstein, *Women in Law*, 166

135 Our research on billing practices and earnings is reported in Hagan and Kay, *Gender in Practice*, chap. 6

136 For an insightful account of this period in the United States, see Ronald Chester, *Unequal Access: Women Lawyers in a Changing America* (South Hadley, MA: Bergin & Garvey 1985).

137 These inequities are even more extreme for women of colour. Neallani points out that there are virtually no women of colour who are partners in the large prestigious firms in Canada, very few are in partnership-track positions, or even in articling positions at these firms: See Neallani, 'Women of Color,' 148–65

138 For discussions of the barriers confronting ethnic and racial minorities in the legal profession see Neallani, 'Women of Color,' 148–65; Steven Greer and Colin Samson, 'Ethnic Minorities in the Legal Profession: A Case Study of the San Francisco Bar,' *Anglo-American Law Review* 22 (1993), 321–36; Harrington, *Women Lawyers*.

139 *Touchstones*, 60

Index

Note: The names of law firms frequently change. Space considerations made it impossible to cite in this index cross-references for all the names by which firms were known. However, many of the essays on individual firms include a historical catalogue of a particular firm's name changes.

Brian Young, *The Politics of Codification: The Lower Canadian Civil Code of 1866*

1995 David Williams, *Just Lawyers: Seven Portraits*

Hamar Foster and John McLaren, eds., *Essays in the History of Canadian Law: Volume VI – British Columbia and the Yukon*

W.H. Morrow, ed., *Northern Justice: The Memoirs of Mr Justice William G. Morrow*

Beverley Boissery, *A Deep Sense of Wrong: The Treason, Trials and Transportation to New South Wales of Lower Canadian Rebels after the 1838 Rebellion*

1996 Carol Wilton, ed., *Essays in the History of Canadian Law: Volume VII – Inside the Law: Canadian Law Firms in Historical Perspective*

William Kaplan, *Bad Judgment: The Case of Mr Justice Leo A. Landreville*

F. Murray Greenwood and Barry Wright, eds., *Canadian State Trials Series: Volume I – Law, Politics, and Security Measures, 1608–1837*